Visual Basic .NET and SQL Server 2000:
Building an Effective Data Layer

Tony Bain

Denise Gosnell

Jonathon A. Walsh

Wrox Press Ltd. ®

Visual Basic .NET and SQL Server 2000: Building an Effective Data Layer

Published by Wrox Press Ltd,
Arden House, 1102 Warwick Road, Acocks Green,
Birmingham, B27 6BH, UK
Printed in the United States
ISBN 1861007051

Trademark Acknowledgements

Wrox has endeavored to provide trademark information about all the companies and products mentioned in this book by the appropriate use of capitals. However, Wrox cannot guarantee the accuracy of this information.

Credits

Authors
Tony Bain
Denise Gosnell
Jonathon A. Walsh

Additional Material
Robin Dewson

Managing Editors
Viv Emery
Louay Fatoohi
Fiona McParland

Comissioning Editors
Ian Blackham
Kate Hall

Technical Editors
Gareth Oakley
Sarah Larder

Indexers
Bill Johncocks
Andrew Criddle

Project Managers
Fiona McParland
Beth Sacks

Author Agent
Cilmara Lion

Technical Reviewers
Michael Benkovich
Michael Erickson
Damien Foggon
Paul Morris
Gary Nicholson
J. Boyd Nolan, PE
Sreekanth Gongalareddy
Thearon Willis

Cover
Natalie O'Donnell

Production Manager
Liz Toy

Production Coordinator
Pip Wonson

Illustrations
Rachel Taylor

Proofreader
Agnes Wiggers

About the Authors

Tony Bain

Tony Bain (MCSE, MCSD, MCDBA) is a senior database consultant for SQL Services in New Zealand, and has over 5 years experience with SQL Server. During this time he has been responsible for the design, development, and administration of numerous SQL Server based solutions for clients in such industries as utilities, property, government, technology, and insurance.

Tony is passionate about all database technologies especially when they relate to enterprise availability and scalability. Tony spends a lot of his time presenting and writing about various database topics, and in the few moments he has spare Tony hosts a SQL Server resource site (www.sqlserver.co.nz).

Thanks to Linda for her continued support and thanks also to our beautiful girls, Laura and Stephanie, who remain my motivation. And to "Bob", I look forward to meeting you soon!

Denise Gosnell

Denise Gosnell is software attorney with Woodard, Emhardt, Naughton, Moriarty, & McNett, a worldwide intellectual property law firm based in Indianapolis, Indiana. Denise has a unique background in both technology and law, and presently uses her deep technical and legal expertise to help hi-tech clients protect their intellectual property interests.

Denise has 8 years of experience in computer software development. Prior to joining the Woodard firm in 2002, she worked for Microsoft in the Microsoft Consulting Services organization, helping government clients implement hi-tech solutions. She received a bachelor's degree in Computer Science – Business (summa cum laude) from Anderson University, and a Doctor of Jurisprudence from Indiana University School of Law in Indianapolis. Denise is also a Microsoft Certified Solution Developer.

Denise has co-authored four software development books to date: *MSDE Bible* (IDG Books, ISBN: 0764546813), *Professional SQL Server 2000 Programming* (Wrox Press, ISBN: 1861004486), *Professional .NET Framework* (Wrox Press, ISBN 1861005563), and *Beginning Visual Basic .NET Databases* (Wrox Press, ISBN: 1861005555). She was a featured technology speaker at the Microsoft European Professional Developer's Conference in December 2001 representing Microsoft Corporation and Wrox Press. She also has assisted Microsoft's Training and Certification group in creating new .NET exams for their Microsoft Certified Solution Developer (MCSD) certification that measures developer skills on Microsoft technologies.

Denise can be reached at: dgosnell@uspatent.com.

To my husband Jake for your continued encouragement of all my writing and career efforts. I love you! To the great editors at Wrox Press for your patience and help and for making this book a reality.

Jonathon A. Walsh

Jonathon is an MCP, and a graduate from Alfred University with a Bachelor of Science in Business Administration. He majored in Information Systems with minors in Computer Science and Economics. He currently works as a Senior Consultant in the Mid-West specializing in rapid development of enterprise-class Microsoft solutions. Jonathon has worked on some of the largest Visual Basic applications in the world and now helps organizations to build .NET solutions, ranging from supply-chain web sites to physical access control systems. He can be reached at jonathon_walsh@hotmail.com.

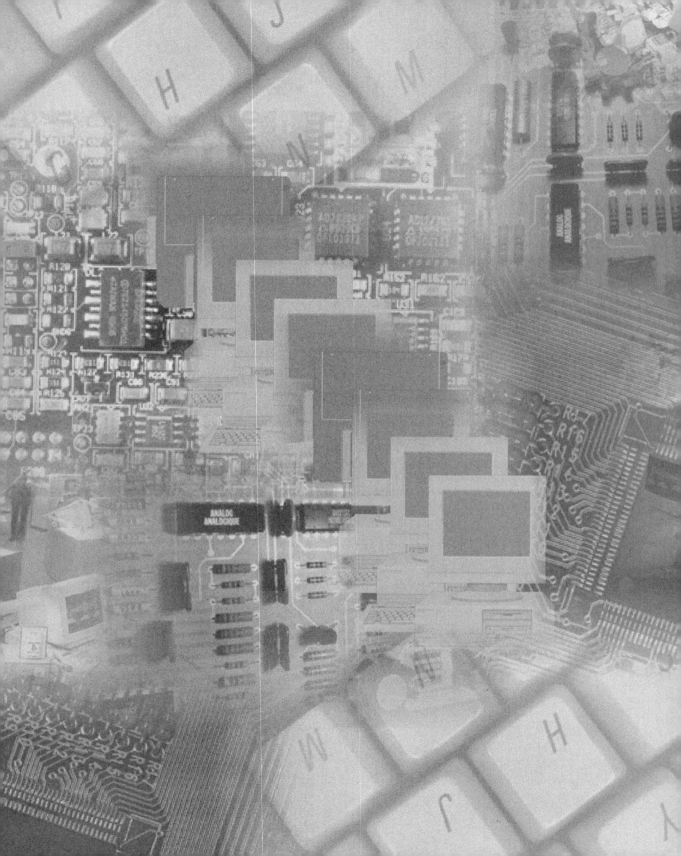

Table of Contents

Table of Contents

Table of Contents

Table of Contents

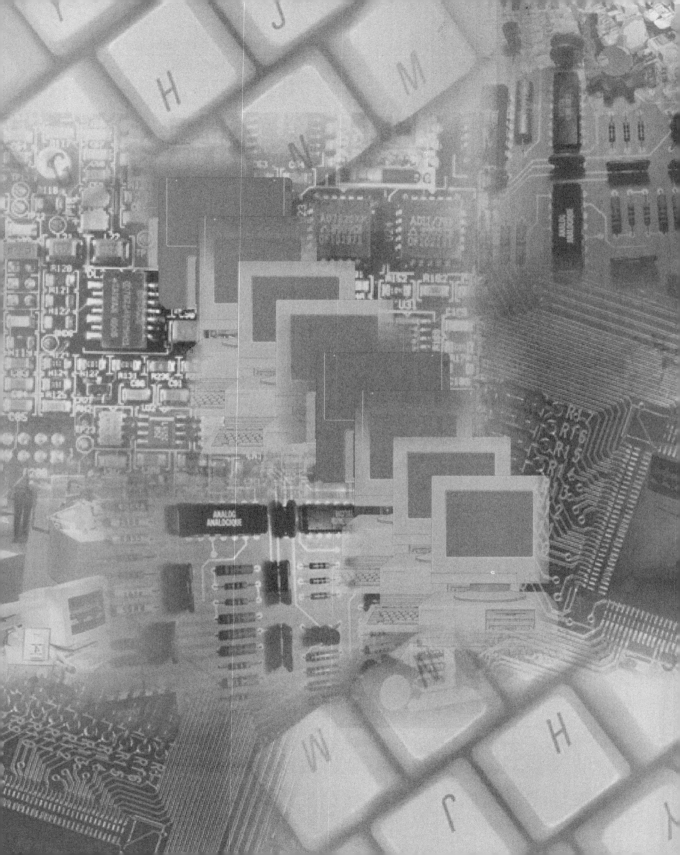

Introduction

With the release of Microsoft's .NET Framework has come a whole new raft of coding for the Visual Basic developer to get to grips with. Not only have there been significant changes made to Visual Basic 6 in order to ensure compatibility with the .NET Framework, but also enhancement of ADO by way of the new ADO.NET data access methodology. ADO.NET provides a whole set of classes that enable us to retrieve and manipulate data, and as such is far more than a simple upgrade of ADO for compatibility with the .NET Framework. Utilizing ADO.NET classes in fully realizing .NET data support will become essential in developing data-driven applications. The aim of this book is to give you, as a developer getting to grips with the new world of VB.NET, the information you need to write applications which utilize data from database instances. While we focus on connection to SQL Server 2000 in this book, it is important to note that the information given here is also pertinent to classes that deal with connection to other data sources (such as Access 2000 or Oracle 8*i* for example). This will allow you to fully utilize the data access capabilities of the .NET Framework in both Windows Forms and Web Forms applications. In that regard the book breaks down as follows:

Chapter 1 – Our introductory chapter discusses the new world of ADO.NET, giving you an overview of the class structures and capabilities, which are now pertinent to the development of applications. Specifically we introduce the System.Data namespace, and the major objects contained within it. This chapter gives you a roadmap to the areas that we will discuss in the rest of the book.

Chapter 2 – Here is where we begin to get our teeth into the world of ADO.NET with a look at the SqlClient namespace. This namespace contains all the classes necessary in order to connect to data sources from your business object code. All the new objects, such as DataReader, Connection, Command, and DataAdapter are introduced, as well as DataSet and DataTable objects. We describe how to use Command objects to connect to the database, and how DataAdapters link Command objects with the data retrieved. The use of DataSet and DataTable objects are discussed, as well as the underlying structures of these, namely DataRow and DataColumn objects.

We also look at how to maintain referential integrity within the data you retrieve using `DataRelations`. By the end of the chapter you will understand how to use these objects and classes in connecting to a database, and manipulating data.

Chapter 3 – In this chapter we discuss the sample application that we will use throughout the rest of the book. The sample `HumanResources` database provides an illustration of a typical HR resource, containing details regarding Employees, payments made to employees, salary details, and personal development courses that they have attended. In the course of creating and populating the database, we also create a sample VB.NET Windows Application, in order to illustrate the use of ADO.NET classes in connecting to, and manipulating data in, the database. This application provides an interface that allows us not only to verify that our connection to the database is working, but also to update records within the database.

Chapter 4 – This chapter takes a closer look at the `DataReader` object, and some of the methods associated with it. Returning data through the use of a simple `SELECT` statement, as well as by utilizing a stored procedure is discussed. We also look at how to return multiple resultsets, update data, and populate controls through the use of `DataReader` objects.

Chapter 5 – In this chapter we consider the benefits of stored procedures in creating efficiently managed code. The discussion centres around writing efficient stored procedures with an extensive look at the means to read, write, and update data in an efficient manner. In particular we take a look at joining data from multiple tables, through the use of the `INNER JOIN`, `OUTER JOIN`, and `CROSS JOIN` commands, and the use of global and local tables in storing data required for manipulation. We also take a look at conditional logic, and how to isolate the problems that may occur when retrieving data via stored procedures. In addition, we look at how to extend the power of stored procedures by writing user-defined functions. The performance impact of poorly written code cannot be underestimated, particularly as systems continue to increase in size, and this chapter aims to help in ensuring that, as a developer, you have done all you can to maximize the efficiency of your data transfer and manipulation of data from various data sources.

Chapter 6 – Having discussed how to write efficiently performing stored procedures, this chapter looks at how to execute them from within VB.NET code. It builds on the knowledge accumulated in the previous chapter, and illustrates the use of stored procedures in applications, which use the sample `HumanResources` database. In particular we look at examples of executing stored procedures through the use of a `DataReader`, returning multiple resultsets, passing parameters in and out of stored procedures, and retrieving and passing XML data. By the end of this chapter you will be fully equipped to write efficient stored procedures capable of manipulating data in a wide variety of ways.

Chapter 7 – Having previously looked at the `SqlClient` namespace, and the key objects used in ADO.NET to manipulate data within SQL Server 2000, in this chapter we consider the nature of data binding. In the world of .NET VB developers have enhanced data binding capabilities, in comparison to those available in previous versions of Visual Basic, and we illustrate them here. We consider the nature of simple and complex data binding, and look specifically at using controls such as textboxes and datagrids to bind data. Binding of data to controls, both in Windows Forms applications and Web Forms applications, is covered here.

Chapter 8 – This chapter looks at another important concept in database application development, namely transactions and locks. Concurrent access to data held in any system is of paramount importance in today's age of distributed database systems, and high intensity user access. With the increased number of users comes the problem of data maintenance.

In this chapter we consider the atomicity of transactions, what requirements there are in conducting transactions, and how we can implement systems that deal with multiple users efficiently. The problems that can occur in updating records within the database, and ensuring the referential integrity of all the data presented to users, are considered in some detail in this chapter.

Chapter 9 – In this chapter we consider the nature of Component Services in the world of .NET. The System.EnterpriseServices namespace uses COM+ behind the scenes in working with components, making the process of dealing with DLL files much cleaner than previously with ADO. We discuss the nature of serviced components and their use in distributed transactions. We go on to illustrate the creation of a simple assembly, and how to register this through the use of the Sn and RegSvcs tools. Finally we create a client component, which can utilize the registered assembly and return values illustrating our use of components.

Chapter 10 – This chapter discusses the nature of XML support in SQL Server 2000 in some depth. We look in detail at the FOR XML EXPLICIT clause, and the data structure we require to return XML resultsets suitable for further manipulation within our data applications. The plus points ands drawbacks of this clause are outlined, before we look at an alternative method of formatting data through the use of XSL stylesheets to transform data retrieved from SQL Server. Finally we run through an example of how to create a stored procedure as a web service by using the SQLXML capabilities available for use with SQL Server 2000 and the .NET Framework.

Chapter 11 – This chapter is a form of checklist, considering a number of topics traditionally associated with the role of the DBA. In this regard we will discuss how to restrict access to SQL Server by the granting of privileges to user logins. The nature of SQL Server logins, as well as Windows Groups and Windows Users is discussed, both in terms of manipulating these within SQL Server Enterprise Manager, and automatically using the SQL-DMO (Distributed Management Objects) objects. We also consider database users and roles. The chapter then moves on to consider the performance of SQL Server, and how to monitor this through the use of the Profiler tool. Indexes are a key contributor to database performance, and a discussion of the Index Tuning Wizard is also provided here. We round off by looking at how to move and restore databases, and the means to generate scripts, which can be used to create databases, and the objects contained within them.

Chapter 12 – We finish off with a Case Study, which aims to illustrate many of the concepts discussed throughout the book. It discusses a banking application, which allows the user to log banking transactions in various accounts. It will also sum the credit and debits carried out to provide a balance for the accounts in question. The application breaks down as a traditional three-tier application, with a database in the data layer, a number of code modules (business objects) in the middle tier, and a presentation tier with a Web Form user interface.

Who Is This Book For?

This book will appeal to those Visual Basic programmers who are confident in writing VB middle-tier code, but want to learn more about writing data-centric code. This book provides the reader with the means to quickly get to grips with the new ADO.NET classes and objects. By the end of the book the reader will be familiar with all aspects of retrieving data from SQL Server, and manipulating it in order to output desired results. Not only will the reader be comfortable in developing applications which use data in a variety of formats, but they will also be happy with the security and integrity of that data. In summary, this book provides a blueprint for high-performance, secure data applications written in Visual Basic .NET.

The reader should be an intermediate level VB.NET developer, with a sound basic knowledge of the whole .NET Framework, and some experience of ADO or ADO.NET (and possibly both). It is also assumed that they are familiar with simple T-SQL statements, and will have used stored procedures in SQL Server (version 7.0 and above).

What You Need To Use This Book

To make full use of this book you will need the full product release of the Enterprise or Professional Edition of Visual Studio .NET, along with access to an instance of SQL Server 2000 (Standard, Development, or Enterprise Edition).

Conventions

To help you understand what's going on, and in order to maintain consistency, we've used a number of conventions throughout the book:

When we introduce new terms, we **highlight** them.

> **These boxes hold important information.**

Advice, hints, and background information are presented like this.

Bulleted lists will appear indented as follows:

❑ Object 1

❑ Object 2

❑ Object 3

Words that appear on the screen in menus like the File or Window menu are in a similar font to what you see on screen. URLs are also displayed in this font. Keys that you press on the keyboard, like *Ctrl* and *Enter*, are in italics.

In the book text, we use a fixed-width font when we talk about code. For example, if you see `Object`, then you'll know that we are talking about a filename, namespace, object name or function name.

If you've not seen a block of code before, then we show it as a gray box:

```
if condition then
   my_proc( value1 );
end if;
```

Sometimes you'll see code in a mixture of styles, like this:

```
if condition then
   my_proc( value1 );
else
   my_proc( value2 );
end if;
```

In this case, we want you to focus on the code with the gray background. The code with a white background is code we've already looked at and that we don't wish to examine further.

Customer Support

We always value hearing from our readers, and we want to know what you think about this book: what you liked, what you didn't like, and what you think we can do better next time. You can send us your comments, either by returning the reply card in the back of the book, or by e-mail to feedback@wrox.com. Please be sure to mention the book title in your message.

How To Download the Sample Code for the Book

When you visit the Wrox site, http://www.wrox.com/, locate the title through our Search facility or by using one of the title lists. Click on Download in the Code column or on Download Code on the book's detail page.

The files that are available for download from our site have been archived using WinZip. When you have saved the file to a folder on your hard-drive, you need to extract the files using a de-compression program such as WinZip or PKUnzip. When you extract the files, the code is usually extracted into chapter folders. When you start the extraction process, ensure your software is set to use folder names.

Errata

We've made every effort to make sure that there are no errors in the text or in the code in this book. However, no one is perfect and mistakes do occur. If you find an error in one of our books, like a spelling mistake or a faulty piece of code, we would be very grateful for feedback. By sending in errata you may save a future reader hours of frustration, and of course, you will be helping us provide even higher quality information. Simply e-mail the information to support@wrox.com, your information will be checked and if correct, posted to the errata page for that title and used in subsequent editions of the book.

To see if there are any errata for this book on the web site, go to http://www.wrox.com/, and locate the title through our Search facility or title list. Click on the Book Errata link, which is below the cover graphic on the book's detail page.

E-mail Support

If you wish to directly query a problem in the book with an expert who knows the book in detail then e-mail support@wrox.com. A typical e-mail should include the following things:

- ❑ The **title of the book, last four digits of the ISBN,** and **page number** of the problem in the Subject field.

- ❑ Your **name, contact information,** and the **problem** in the body of the message.

We *won't* send you junk mail. We need the details to save your time and ours. When you send an e-mail message, it will go through the following chain of support:

- ❑ Customer Support – Your message is delivered to our customer support staff, who are the first people to read it. They have files on most frequently asked questions and will answer anything general about the book or the web site immediately.

- ❑ Editorial – Deeper queries are forwarded to the technical editor responsible for that book. They have experience with the programming language or particular product, and are able to answer detailed technical questions on the subject.

- ❑ The Authors – Finally, in the unlikely event that the editor cannot answer your problem, he or she will forward the request to the author. We do try to protect the author from any distractions to their work; however, we are quite happy to forward specific requests to them. All Wrox authors help with the support on their books. They will e-mail the customer and the editor with their response, and again all readers should benefit.

The Wrox Support process can only offer support to issues that are directly pertinent to the content of our published title. Support for questions that fall outside the scope of normal book support is provided via the community lists of our http://p2p.wrox.com/ forum.

p2p.wrox.com

For author and peer discussion, join the programmer to programmer (P2P) mailing lists. At p2p.wrox.com you will find a number of different lists that will help you, not only while you read this book, but also as you develop your own applications. Particularly appropriate to this book are the Oracle lists.

To subscribe to a mailing list just follow these steps:

- ❑ Go to http://p2p.wrox.com/

- ❑ Choose the appropriate category from the left menu bar (in this case, Databases)

- ❑ Click on the mailing list you wish to join

- ❑ Follow the instructions to subscribe and fill in your e-mail address and password

- ❑ Reply to the confirmation e-mail you receive

- ❑ Use the subscription manager to join more lists and set your e-mail preferences

You can choose to join the mailing lists or you can receive them as a weekly digest. If you don't have the time, or facility, to receive the mailing list, then you can search our online archives. Queries about joining or leaving lists, and any other general queries about lists, should be sent to listsupport@p2p.wrox.com.

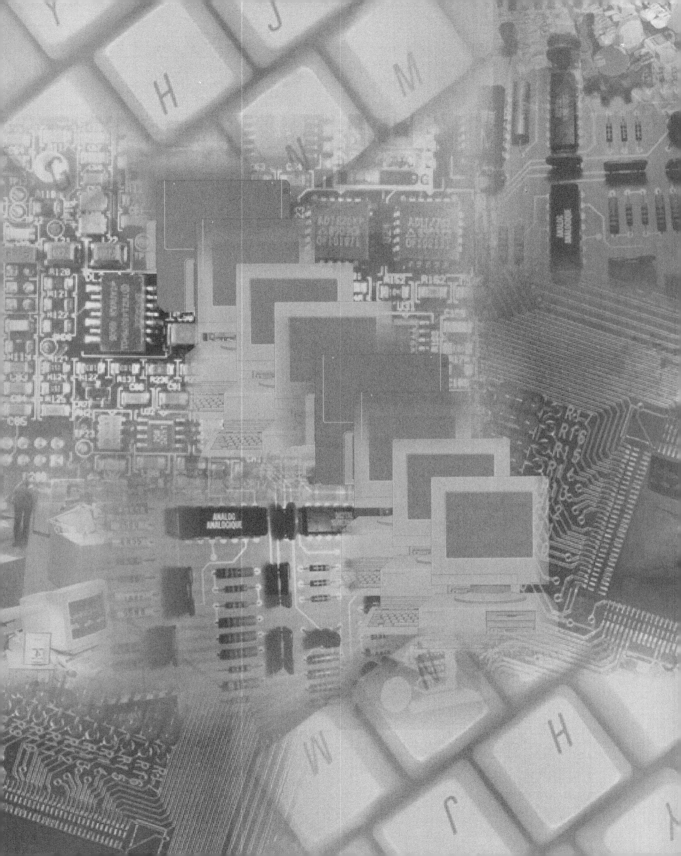

1

ADO.NET

We begin our journey into the world of Visual Basic .NET database application development by presenting an overview of the past and present of data access methodologies: ADO and ADO.NET. The rest of the book will delve into the details of designing VB.NET database applications, with numerous source code examples demonstrating the practical implementation of the concepts we introduce. However, it is important to begin by outlining the role that ADO.NET plays in giving access to the data we require in our applications. To this end, we will look at the following in the course of the chapter:

❑   A brief history of ADO

❑   Introduction to the world of ADO.NET

❑   Introduction to `DataSets` and `DataReaders`

❑   Retrieving data from a data store through a Managed Provider

❑   Overview of the `System.Data` namespace

❑   Overview of the `System.Data.SqlClient` and `System.Data.OleDb` namespaces

Let's begin then, with a review of ADO.

History of Universal Data Access and ADO

Before jumping into the details of ADO.NET, it is important that we take a moment to briefly recap the history of universal data access and **ActiveX Data Objects (ADO)**. ADO is the predecessor to ADO.NET. ADO replaced the **Data Access Objects (DAO)** and **Remote Data Objects (RDO)** data access methodologies, and provided a more powerful means of retrieving and managing data. DAO and RDO were designed for client server applications and were very good for that purpose.

However, as distributed computing with multiple-tiered applications and diverse data stores became more common, a more sophisticated means of data access was needed to communicate across platforms and with a variety of data sources. OLE DB was designed to solve that problem and ADO was the means for accessing OLE DB through your applications. OLE DB is Microsoft's data access methodology for universal access to data, regardless of whether that data resides in a relational database, file system, e mail server, and so on. OLE DB takes the world of **Open Database Connectivity (ODBC)** to the next level by allowing data from both relational and non relational databases to be quickly gathered together in meaningful ways. ODBC was a very powerful database API and allowed you to access nearly any relational database. ODBC also provided support for non relational databases, but it was typically very slow because a relational structure had to be created on top of the non relational structure. ADO, on the other hand, can deal with text files, relational databases, and a variety of relational and non relational data sources quickly and efficiently. In addition to allowing access to OLE DB data stores, ADO also provided support for ODBC, since ODBC was very widely used in systems.

The ADO object model contains the following objects:

- ❏ `Connection`
- ❏ `Command`
- ❏ `Parameter`
- ❏ `Recordset`
- ❏ `Field`
- ❏ `Property`
- ❏ `Error`

The ADO object model contains the following collections:

- ❏ `Fields`
- ❏ `Properties`
- ❏ `Parameters`
- ❏ `Errors`

The `Recordset` is at the heart of the ADO object model, and allows for retrieving and storing data in a manner that looks like a single table. The `Field` and `Property` objects relate to storing `Recordset` information, as do the `Fields` and `Properties` collections. For example, a `Recordset` will contain `Field` objects, which consist of the data elements it is populated with. Since there can be one or more fields in a given `Recordset`, there is a `Fields` collection to allow for storing multiple records. The `Property` object contains information describing the `Recordset`, and has a `Properties` collection to allow for storing multiple values. The same is true for the `Error` object and `Errors` collection. The `Connection` object allows you to establish a connection with a data source and the `Command` object allows you to send that data source commands to act upon. You can use the `Parameter` object and the `Parameters` collection to pass parameters to commands (such as stored procedure parameters) that are performed on the underlying data store.

ADO is very reliable and has become the default standard methodology for data access from Visual Studio applications. While it was an excellent step in the right direction over the other data access methodologies of the past, ADO still has several weaknesses:

- ❑ The ADO `Recordset` object looks like a single table

- ❑ The `Recordset` has no support for relationships between tables. When you need to retrieve data from multiple data sources, the `Recordset` requires you to assemble them into a single result table by specifying the source of the recordset to be a single SQL statement. This statement joins multiple tables together to form the single result.

- ❑ The `Recordset` operates primarily in a connected mode (although it can be used in a disconnected mode with extra work). This can cause more database locks and active connections and thus impact the performance and scalability of your application.

- ❑ COM marshaling is used to transmit a disconnected `Recordset` across the wire. With only COM data types inherently supported, this consumes system resources because type conversions must take place.

- ❑ Communicating across firewalls is hard to do, since most firewalls are configured to prevent system level requests such as COM marshaling.

- ❑ XML is very valuable when communicating across firewalls, but the `Recordset` has no inherent support for XML. The limited XML support available with ADO meant that, for example, arbitrary XML documents could not be loaded into a `Recordset`.

Now that we have a basic idea of the features and limitations of ADO, let's look at ADO.NET and see how it is an improvement over ADO.

ADO.NET   The New World of Data Access

ADO.NET is the new data access strategy that is much more than an improved version of ADO. In many ways it involves a new way of thinking, in moving to a realm where you commonly work with data that is disconnected from its source. The idea is that in a highly interconnected world, data in your application might come from multiple sources (an e-mail server in Indiana, a database in Florida, or a file server in London for example) and in several formats. This means that you want to get the data back quickly so you can work with it locally, without maintaining the connection to that data store. Any modifications can be propagated to the base data store later, at the time desired (again, by making a quick connection to make the changes). The essence of the world of disconnected data is somewhat different from the world of ADO where the majority of `Recordsets` maintained connections to the underlying data store while it was in use. The inherent support for XML that ADO.NET provides, also makes the process of transmitting data across firewalls easier than ever before. And in the event that you need to make use of ADO for legacy reasons, you can still access the ADO libraries.

ADO.NET provides two primary means of accessing data: through `DataReaders` and `DataSets`. A `DataReader` is a forward only read, only stream of data that is designed for fast and efficient access to data. The `DataSet` is what people often think of when they hear the term ADO.NET, since the `DataSet` replaces the concept of a `Recordset` with several new features. Let's look at each of these means of accessing data in more detail, beginning with the `DataReader`.

DataReader

The DataReader operates in connected mode and retrieves a forward only, read only copy of data in the data store. The connection to the database remains open while you are accessing the DataReader and must be closed when you are finished with it. It is designed for fast data access where you connect, retrieve information (that is then displayed via a web browser or Windows Form, for example), and then close the database connection. The DataReader doesn't support scrolling back and forward, or modifications. It bears the closest resemblance to the ADO forward only Recordset.

Let's look at how the DataSet differs and then we'll discuss when to use one over the other.

DataSet

The DataSet is the heart of ADO.NET and is an in memory copy of the data. Unlike the ADO Recordset, it can contain multiple tables, each of which could come from a different data store. The tables in the DataSet can be related to each other with relationships. In essence, the DataSet is just an in memory database, disconnected from the underlying data store(s) it was populated from.

Let's look at a diagram to see how the DataSet works:

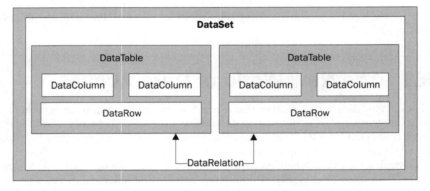

As shown in the above diagram, the DataSet can contain one or more DataTables, which are populated with information from a data store. Each DataTable in the DataSet will have one or more DataColumns that define which columns of data it is holding. It will also have one or more DataRows that are the actual values for each record being stored. DataRelations are used in order to describe relationships between tables in the DataSet. It is also important to note, as illustrated in the diagram, that you can create a DataView of data in the DataSet, which creates a filter of a single DataTable. The concept of a DataView is similar to the database concept of a View. The DataView feature is most commonly used for binding controls to values in a DataSet; for binding to work you must specify which DataTable (or DataView of a DataTable) the control should get its data from (in other words be bound to). Another common use for a DataView is to filter a larger DataSet down into a smaller subset based on some criteria.

The DataSet uses XML to transfer data across platforms and tiers. XML allows you to describe hierarchical data in a text based format, which is ideal for communicating across systems and organizations in a standardized way that they each can understand. Standards for XML were developed by the World Wide Web Consortium (W3C), which is an independent body, established for the purpose of developing standard communication protocols. In order for systems to exchange data, they have to be 'marked up' in some way to allow the system receiving the data to understand and use it. Suppose you pass a piece of data to a system that looks like this:

```
John Doe
```

You could guess that this is probably a name, but what is it supposed to be used for? Who is this person, and why does the other system care about them? Let's now consider the case where this data is passed as follows:

```
<Order>
    <CustomerName>John Doe</CustomerName>
</Order>
```

Now we have some additional information that is meaningful. The 'markup' tags that have been added, tell us that John Doe placed an order and that he is a customer. Perhaps we are sending this information and other details about his order to a supplier who is going to fulfill the order. See how much of a difference it makes to have a standard way of 'marking up' text data to pass it to a variety of platforms? This is where the power of XML lies.

Unlike with ADO `Recordsets` (which typically required add ons to support XML), the ADO.NET `DataSet` supports XML natively. With XML at the core of the ADO.NET, data can be transmitted across the wire much more easily than ever before:

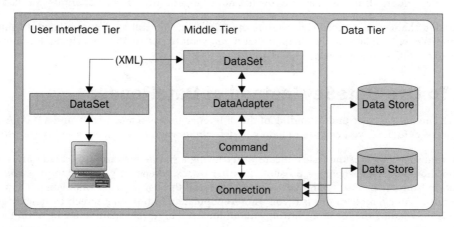

The diagram above shows how the user interface tier communicates with the middle tier to retrieve some data. The middle tier is responsible for communicating with the underlying data stores and then building the `DataSet`. The `DataSet` is passed back to the user interface tier as XML. Since the `DataSet` is an in memory copy of data, it is also in the memory of the client it gets passed back to.

> Note that the `DataSet` has several methods for allowing manipulation of data in an XML format. We already learned that a `DataSet` is transmitted as XML automatically. But you also have a lot of flexibility in making specific use of XML in your code as well. Here is a short list of some of the methods available as part of the `DataSet` object: `GetXml`, `GetXmlSchema`, `InferXmlSchema`, `ReadXmlSchema`, `WriteXml`, and `WriteXmlSchema`. ADO.NET was built from the ground up with XML in mind and provides a number of other XML libraries in addition to those that are part of the `DataSet` object.

A `DataSet` provides numerous features that allow you to control the changes that get made to your local copy. Let's take a quick look at how that works. You can think of a `DataSet` as a mini database that happens to be in memory. It has tables with columns and rows, and one or more of the tables may be related to each other. Before the change being made gets permanently committed to your local in memory copy of the `DataSet`, you must call the `AcceptChanges` method. For further flexibility, you can also call the `AcceptChanges` method at the `DataTable` or `DataRow` level. These are called automatically if you call the `AcceptChanges` method on the `DataSet`. The `RejectChanges` method allows you to reject any changes so they are not made permanent in the `DataSet`. The `RejectChanges` method can also be applied on the `DataTable` and `DataRow` objects individually. You need some manner of deciding what got changed or whether to accept the change that was made, so the `RowState` property is provided to allow you to do so. The `RowState` property allows you to look at a particular row in the `DataSet` and determine its state, such as whether it has been modified, added, and so on. The `RowState` property can contain the following values:

❑ `Added` Indicates that a new row has been added and `AcceptChanges` has not been called yet.

❑ `Modified` Indicates that the row has been changed and `AcceptChanges` has not been called yet.

❑ `Deleted` Indicates that the row has been deleted and `AcceptChanges` has not been called yet.

❑ `Unchanged` Indicates that the row has not changed since `AcceptChanges` was last called.

By accepting changes that have been made in the `DataSet`, you still have not updated the underlying data store. We will see later in this chapter that if you want to update the underlying data store, you need to take a different approach.

When To Use DataSet Instead of DataReader

Now that you have a basic understanding of the difference between a `DataSet` and a `DataReader`, let's look at some guidelines you can use to help you determine when to use one instead of the other.

The `DataReader` object is the fastest means of retrieving a simple forward only, read only stream of data, and should be used whenever possible. In other words, whenever you need to get some information from the data store and you can quickly scroll through it to get what you need, just use a `DataReader`. An example of this is if you want to populate a listbox on a screen by quickly getting the data back and loading the list box control, without the need to further manipulate or scroll back and forth among the records. Another example might be if you want to get some information from the database and display it on a web page. You will want to move information in and out of the database quickly, streaming the results to your page.

Reasons to use a `DataSet` instead might be:

❑ If you need an in memory copy of data for further manipulation, analysis, or scrolling.

❑ If you need the ability to handle sophisticated updates and want to take advantage of the `DataSet`'s change tracking and update features.

❑ When you need to pass data across processes (and in some cases across systems), or from an XML web service. (You don't want to pass a `DataReader` around in such an instance because it keeps an open connection to the data store until you close it. Passing around a `DataSet`, which is transmitted as XML and is disconnected from any data store, is the most efficient means of achieving this.)

   ❑   If you need to interact with data dynamically, such as binding data to a `DataGrid` for interactive analysis.

   ❑   If you need to provide a hierarchical XML view of relational data and use a XML Path Language (XPath) Query or XSL Transformation.

> **Note that the** `DataSet` **isn't as fast as the** `DataReader` **because it is actually using a** `DataReader` **behind the scenes to populate the** `DataSet`**. Also keep in mind that you want to limit the size of your** `DataSet` **and** `DataReader` **as much as possible since it will consume valuable local system memory.**

Managed Providers

In the .NET world of database applications, there are data providers and data consumers. **Data providers** will connect to the database to execute commands and return results. Those commands can then either be processed directly (such as to update data), be returned in a `DataReader` forward only stream, or populate a `DataSet`. In ADO.NET, data providers are called **managed providers** simply because they are managed by ADO.NET. **Data consumers** are those applications that use the services of a data provider for the purpose of manipulating or retrieving data.

In general, a data provider consists of the following objects: `Connection`, `Command`, `DataAdapter`, and `DataReader`. The diagram below and the sections that follow explain these in greater detail.

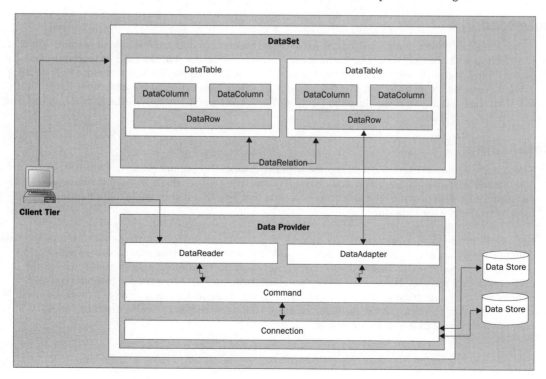

In the diagram overleaf, notice how there are two different paths that the client can follow to access data from the data store: either through a `DataSet` or a `DataReader`. In the case of a `DataSet`, a database connection is opened and the `DataAdapter` sends `Commands` over the `Connection` to retrieve results from the underlying data store. The `DataAdapter` then populates the `DataSet` with the values and returns it to the client. Remember that behind the scenes, ADO.NET uses a `DataReader` to load the data into the `DataSet`.

When using a `DataReader`, a database connection is opened and the `DataReader` sends `Commands` over the `Connection` to retrieve a forward only stream of results. Note that the double headed arrow shown in the diagram between the `DataReader` and `Command` objects, simply indicates that the `DataReader` executes a `Command` to retrieve the data. In both `DataSet` and `DataReader` paths, the data provider facilitates the retrieval and communication with the data store. Let's now look at each of the four data provider objects in a bit more detail.

Connection

The `Connection` object establishes a connection to a specific data store. It can be opened by using the `Open` method on the `Connection` object or implicitly when using a `DataAdapter`.

Command

The `Command` object works over a `Connection` object to pass parameters and execute a command on the data store. It then returns data to a `DataReader` or `DataSet`, as described in the following paragraphs. Examples of parameters include SQL statements, stored procedure parameters, and return values.

DataReader

A `DataReader` object reads a read only, forward only stream of data from the database and works in conjunction with the `Command` and `Connection` objects. Since the `DataReader` is read only and forward only, it can provide for fast access to data. As you learned earlier, it is therefore faster than using a `DataSet`. Note however, that it maintains an active connection to the data store while it is in use. This means that you must close the `DataReader` object when you are finished with it, in order to free up the connection.

DataAdapter

The `DataAdapter` is used to communicate with the database to populate a `DataSet`. It works in conjunction with the `Connection` and `Command` objects to retrieve the data from the data store. The `DataAdapter` also provides the ability to save data that was changed in the local in memory `DataSet` back to its underlying data store.

Let's delve deeper into how you can use a `DataAdapter` in conjunction with the `DataSet` to work with data and save the changes back to the data store. We learned earlier that a `DataSet` operates in disconnected mode, which means that, once populated, it no longer maintains a connection to the underlying data store(s). This makes it very different from the ADO `Recordset`, which typically maintained the connection to the data store for the entire time that the `Recordset` was being used. We also learned that you can call the `AcceptChanges` method of the `DataSet` in order to make the changes permanent in the in memory copy.

OK, so it is great that you have flexibility in controlling how records are modified in your local `DataSet`, and that you can tell which ones were affected, but you are still probably wondering how you are going to get the changes back in the data store. That is where the `DataAdapter` comes in. Let's look at how this works. If you have already called the `AcceptChanges` method of the local `Dataset`, then the values will not be updated in the data source, since at that point the `DataSet` no longer tracks the changes made prior to the `AcceptChanges`. Thus, for the following steps to work, the `AcceptChanges` method must *not* have been called. Here is the basic flow of how you can use a `DataSet` and `DataAdapter` to update data in the underlying database:

❑ Specify the `SelectCommand`, `InsertCommand`, `UpdateCommand`, and `DeleteCommand` of the `DataAdapter`.

❑ Use the `DataAdapter` to retrieve the data from the database and fill the `DataSet`.

❑ Allow the users or system to make the changes to the `DataSet`.

❑ Call the `GetChanges` method to populate a new `DataSet` with only the changed values you want to have updated in the underlying data store (in other words the method accepts `RowState` as an optional parameter and if none specified, will return all modified rows).

❑ Call the `DataAdapter`'s `Update` method and pass that `DataSet` containing the changes as the parameter. For any inserts being made, the `InsertCommand` property value will be used. For any updates to existing rows being made, the `UpdateCommand` property value will be used. For any records to delete, the `DeleteCommand` property value will be used. The beauty is that ADO.NET will automatically call the proper command based on the type of modification (insert, update, or delete) that needs to be made on the underlying data store.

Now that we have the big-picture definition of the new ADO.NET concepts, let's look at some code samples showing how to put these to use.

The Namespaces for Accessing Data

Namespaces are logical groupings of class libraries that make it easier for the developer to find the code features that are related to each other. When you add a reference to a namespace into your Visual Basic .NET project, you then have access to all of the code packaged in that namespace. You can then add an `Imports` statement at the top of your declaration, in order to avoid having to write out the full name of every namespace you want to use. The `System.Data` namespace is where all of the ADO.NET functionality resides. Simply stated: `System.Data` = ADO.NET.

Thus, in any class module where you want to make use of data access features, you should add an `Imports` statement to the top of your class declaration, as shown below:

```
Imports System.Data
```

After adding the main namespace, you should then add an `Imports` statement for the managed provider you want to use to retrieve data, so as to shorten the code you need to type. ADO.NET inherently provides two managed providers for dealing with data stores: `SqlClient` and `OleDb`.

❑ **The SQL Server Data Provider** (`System.Data.SqlClient`) should be used for SQL Server 7.0 databases and higher. It is faster than the OLE DB provider because it works directly with SQL Server without going through an OLE DB layer.

❑ **The OLE DB Data Provider** (`System.Data.OleDb`) should be used to access any OLE DB provider such as Oracle, Microsoft Access, SQL Server versions prior to 7.0, and others. It can also be used when you need to access data from SQL Server and other databases together (such as both SQL Server and Oracle), since it supports multiple databases.

If you will be working with SQL Server database version 7.0 or higher, then the SQL Server data provider is your best choice for optimum performance. Otherwise, you will have to use the OLE DB provider. Your application's performance and functional requirements will determine which provider is best, but this is a helpful guideline.

> **An ODBC .NET Data Provider was added to Visual Studio .NET after release and is available as a separate download at http://msdn.microsoft.com/downloads/.**

The namespaces in .NET where these two managed providers can be found are shown in the diagram below:

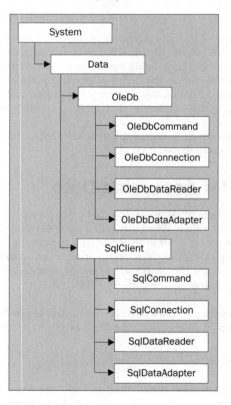

Earlier in this chapter we learned that a data provider generally provides four features in the form of `Command`, `Connection`, `DataReader`, and `DataAdapter` functionality. Notice how both the `OleDb` and `SqlClient` managed providers implement this functionality, only with their respective names as the prefix. For example: `OleDbCommand` for the OLE DB implementation of the `Command` object, `SqlCommand` for the SQL Server implementation of the `Command` object, and so on.

Let's now look at some code samples showing how you can actually use these namespaces to get data from data stores.

Using the System.Data.SQLClient Namespace To Retrieve Data

If you plan to work with the SQL Server Managed Provider then, in addition to importing the `System.Data` namespace at the top of your class, you should also import the `System.Data.SqlClient` namespace:

```
Imports System.Data.SqlClient
```

To connect to a SQL Server database using the `SqlClient` namespace, you add code similar to the following:

```
Dim strConnection As String = "Server=MyServer;" _
        & "Database=Northwind;" _
        & "User Id=sa;Password=;"

Dim cnSqlServer As New SqlConnection(strConnection)

'open the connection
cnSqlServer.Open()

'work with the connection to retrieve data, etc.

'close the connection
cnSQLServer.Close()
```

Notice how the connection string above contains the `Data Source` and `Initial Catalog` to look for data in, as well as the `User Id` and `Password` to connect with. The next line declares a new `SqlConnection` object and the lines that follow then open and close the connection.

Populating a DataSet

Now, let's look at how to use a `SqlConnection` and a `SqlDataAdapter` to populate a `DataSet`. The `DataSet` and all its related objects are in the `System.Data` main ADO.NET namespace, as shown in the diagram below:

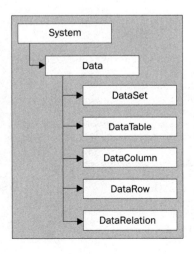

To populate a DataSet, we would open a connection to the database, and then use a SqlDataAdapter to communicate with the database and fill the DataSet. Here is an example:

```
Dim strConnection As String = "Server=MyServer;" _
    & "Database=Northwind;" _
    & "User Id=sa;Password=;"

Dim cnSqlServer As New SqlConnection(strConnection)

'open the connection
cnSqlServer.Open()

'work with the connection to retrieve data, etc.

Dim dsResults As New DataSet()
Dim strSQL As String = "SELECT * FROM Products"
Dim dtAdapter As New SqlDataAdapter(strSQL, cnSQLServer)

dtAdapter.Fill(dsResults)

'close the connection
cnSqlServer.Close()
```

Notice how the SqlConnection is first opened, then a new DataSet declared, followed by a SQL string that defines what to populate the DataSet with. Then, using a newly declared SqlDataAdapter, the DataSet is filled and the connection closed.

This first example shows how to use just the SqlConnection and SqlDataAdapter objects to fill a DataSet. Let's look at how to use a SqlCommand object to pass a command, such as a stored procedure name, to the database to fill the DataSet.

```
Dim strConnection As String = "Server=MyServer;" _
    & "Database=Northwind;" _
    & "User Id=sa;Password=;"

Dim cnSqlServer As New SqlConnection(strConnection)

'open the connection
cnSqlServer.Open()

'work with the connection to retrieve data, etc.

Dim dsResults As New DataSet()
Dim strSPName As String = "[Ten Most Expensive Products]"

Dim cmd As New SqlCommand(strSPName, cnSqlServer)
cmd.CommandType = CommandType.StoredProcedure

Dim dtAdapter As New SqlDataAdapter()
dtAdapter.SelectCommand = cmd
dtAdapter.Fill(dsResults)

'close the connection
cnSqlServer.Close()
```

Notice how the stored procedure name to be called is declared in a string variable called strSPName. Then, when the new SqlCommand object is created, the stored procedure and open connection are passed as parameters. The CommandType of the SqlCommand object is set to StoredProcedure so that we know what type of command we're using. The SelectCommand of the SqlDataAdapter is assigned to the SqlCommand object so that it will know which stored procedure to execute. We could have also listed this as one of the parameters where we declared the new SqlDataAdapter object, since there is a constructor for the SqlDataAdapter object that will accept that as another parameter too. Then, the Fill method of the SqlDataAdapter is called to fill the DataSet with results from running the stored procedure.

This is a simple example of calling a stored procedure that doesn't require any parameters. However, it is more likely that you would want to call a stored procedure, which has required parameters. The next example shows how to call a stored procedure and pass it parameters.

```
Dim strConnection As String = "Server=MyServer;" _
    & "Database=Northwind;" _
    & "User Id=sa;Password=;"

Dim cnSqlServer As New SqlConnection(strConnection)

'open the connection
cnSqlServer.Open()

'work with the connection to retrieve data, etc.

Dim dsResults As New DataSet()
Dim strSPName As String = "[Sales By Year]"

Dim dtBeginDate As Date = "01-01-1998"
Dim dtEndDate As Date = "01-01-2000"

Dim cmd As New SqlCommand(strSPName, cnSqlServer)
cmd.CommandType = CommandType.StoredProcedure

' Add @Beginning_Date Parameter
Dim parameterBeginDate As New SqlParameter("@Beginning_Date", _
                                       SqlDbType.DateTime, 4)
parameterBeginDate.Value = dtBeginDate
cmd.Parameters.Add(parameterBeginDate)

' Add @Ending_Date Parameter
Dim parameterEndDate As New SqlParameter("@Ending_Date", _
                                     SqlDbType.DateTime, 4)
parameterEndDate.Value = dtEndDate
cmd.Parameters.Add(parameterEndDate)

Dim dtAdapter As New SqlDataAdapter()
dtAdapter.SelectCommand = cmd
dtAdapter.Fill(dsResults)

'close the connection
cnSqlServer.Close()
```

In the example overleaf, we want to populate a `DataSet` with the results of a stored procedure that requires two parameters: `@Beginning_Date` and `@Ending_Date`. We assign some local variables (`dtBeginDate` and `dtEndDate`) to date values that we want to pass to the stored procedure when it runs. After declaring the new `SqlCommand` object and setting its `CommandType` to `StoredProcedure`, we then declare the two parameter objects. The `SqlParameter` object allows you to specify the parameter name as it is called in the SQL Server stored procedure, as well as its data type and size. Next, you specify the value that you want to assign to that parameter. Finally, you add that parameter to the `SqlCommand` object so that it will be passed to the stored procedure when it is called.

Just as in the prior example, we then use a `SqlDataAdapter` to fill the `DataSet` after specifying the commands it should use. Now that we have looked at several examples of how to populate a `DataSet` using the `SqlClient` namespace, let's look at an example of how to get data using a `DataReader`.

Using a DataReader

Recall that a `DataReader` is a read only, forward only stream of data that maintains an active connection to the database until it is closed. In using a `DataReader`, you open it, get one record at a time and take some action on it (such as load it onto the screen), and then close it.

Here is an example:

```
Dim strConnection As String = "Server=MyServer;" _
    & "Database=Northwind;" _
    & "User Id=sa;Password=;"

Dim cnSqlServer As New SqlConnection(strConnection)

'open the connection
cnSqlServer.Open()

'work with the connection to retrieve data, etc.

Dim strSQL As String = "SELECT * FROM Products"
Dim drReader As SqlDataReader
Dim cmd As New SqlCommand(strSQL, cnSqlServer)

    drReader = cmd.ExecuteReader

    Do While drReader.Read
        'do something with the results
        Console.WriteLine(drReader("ProductName"))
    Loop

'close the data reader
    drReader.Close()

'close the connection
    cnSqlServer.Close()
```

Notice how we are using the same SELECT statement as in a prior example to return all products in the Northwind database. A SqlDataReader object is declared, before a new SqlCommand object is declared and assigned to use both the strSQL SQL statement and SqlConnection object. To open the DataReader, you call the ExecuteReader method of the SqlCommand object. Once you open the DataReader, you can then read from it one record at a time and take some action on that record. The example above simply writes the ProductName value in the DataReader to the console. It is very important to note that the DataReader should then be closed immediately after you are finished with it, as shown above.

Using the System.Data.OleDb Namespace To Retrieve Data

Now that you have a reasonable idea of how to work with the SqlClient namespace to retrieve data from SQL Server databases, let's look at how similar the OleDb namespace is.

Recall that the System.Data.OleDb namespace contains the following objects: OleDbConnection, OleDbCommand, OleDbDataAdapter, and OleDbDataReader. The only modifications you have to make to take advantage of the OleDb managed provider functionality are to use these objects instead of the SqlClient objects (in other words change the object references) and to specify the proper connection string.

Before you can use the OleDb objects, you should first import the System.Data.OleDb namespace into your project, as shown below:

```
Imports System.Data.OleDb
```

Now, you can make use of the OleDbConnection, OleDbCommand, OleDbDataAdapter, and OleDbDataReader objects. Below is the sample syntax for opening a connection using the OleDb namespace:

```
Dim strConnection As String = _
    "Provider=Microsoft.Jet.OLEDB.4.0;" _
    & "Data Source=" _
    & "C:\Program Files\Microsoft Office\Office10\Samples\Northwind.mdb"

Dim cnOleDb As New OleDbConnection(strConnection)

'open the connection
cnOleDb.Open()

'work with the connection to retrieve data, etc.

'close the connection
cnOleDb.Close()
```

This code should look very familiar. It is identical to the code you saw in the SqlClient connection samples except for the connection string itself. The only other difference is that you just need to declare your variables using the OleDb object names, such as shown overleaf:

```
Dim strConnection As String = _
    "Provider=Microsoft.Jet.OLEDB.4.0;" _
    & "Data Source=" _
    & "C:\Program Files\Microsoft Office\Office10\Samples\Northwind.mdb"

Dim cnOleDb As New OleDbConnection(strConnection)

'open the connection
cnOleDb.Open()

'work with the connection to retrieve data, etc.

Dim dsResults As New DataSet()
Dim strSQL As String = "SELECT * FROM Products"
Dim dtAdapter As New OleDbDataAdapter(strSQL, cnOleDb)

    dtAdapter.Fill(dsResults)

'close the connection
cnOleDb.Close()
```

The reason you are able to switch between the two managed providers with little effort is because they are both based on common classes and interfaces. The interfaces such as ICommand, IConnection, IDataAdapter, and IDataReader are part of the System.Data namespace. Furthermore, the System.Data.Common namespace has base classes such as Command, Connection, DataAdapter, and DataReader, which provide a base implementation for those interfaces. These interfaces and classes can be used by any data provider, and therefore allow you to create your own data providers if you so desire.

Summary

In this chapter, we've explored the basics of ADO.NET and learned how it differs from ADO. At this point, you should have a good understanding of:

❑   How ADO.NET differs from ADO

❑   What a DataReader is and how to use it

❑   What a DataSet is and how to use it

❑   What a DataAdapter is and how to use it

❑   What a Data Provider is and what role it plays

❑   When to use the SqlClient data provider rather than the OleDb data provider

❑   How to retrieve data from a data store using the System.Data namespace

The concepts described in this chapter will be discussed later in this book in much more detail, and were introduced here in order to give you an overview of ADO.NET. We'll begin our more detailed exploration in the next chapter where we delve into the SqlClient namespace and related topics.

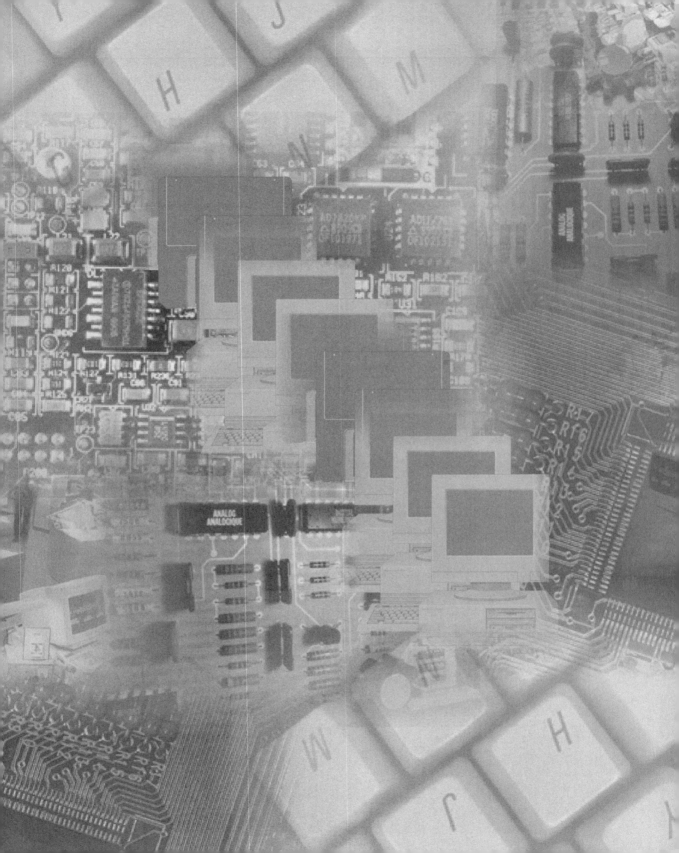

2

The SqlClient Namespace

Now that ADO.NET has been covered in Chapter 1, we can move on and use .NET objects, which capitalize on the power contained within ADO.NET.

In this chapter we will discuss the `SqlClient` namespace and how to utilize its classes in connecting to SQL Server, extracting data, and then manipulating it, through the use of T-SQL or stored procedures. Whilst doing this we will take a look at:

❑ Establishing a connection to a SQL Server instance using the `SqlConnection` class

❑ Executing T-SQL statements via the `SqlCommand` object

❑ The `SqlDataAdapter` object, and how it links together your SQL Server connection and the data you retrieve

❑ The `DataSet` object containing your data, and how this relates to the `DataTable`, `DataRow`, and `DataColumn` objects

❑ How to maintain referential integrity constraints on the data you return from your database, through the use of `DataRelation` objects

Let's begin with `SqlClient`'s `SqlConnection` object.

SqlConnection Object

The `SqlConnection` class, along with the commands and classes contained within the `System.Data.SqlClient` namespace, has been created by Microsoft to be used specifically for SQL Server databases, and has been optimized as such.

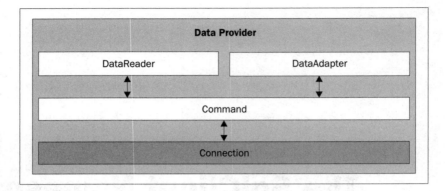

A new instance of a `SqlConnection` has to be created for every separate connection to a SQL Server database that you require. It is advisable to keep the number of connections to a minimum and in most cases a single connection will suffice. Only when working in a cross-server scenario will you find situations where you require more than one connection.

We'll begin by taking a look at the properties associated with the `SqlConnection` class:

Properties

There are a number of properties within the `SqlConnection` class, which are split between those that are setting and those that are getting. We will identify these differences as we look at each property in turn. If you have used ADO before, most of these properties will be familiar. Having said that however, the way they react when the action of setting takes place differs quite considerably in some cases:

Property	Description
ConnectionString	The connection string contains all the attributes required to make a connection to a particular SQL Server. This includes such attributes as the server name, authentication information, database to be used, and so on. The values of attributes in the connection string are specified using the = operator (for example `Database=master`), and attributes are separated using a semicolon. We look at the attributes that can be used within a connection string in the following section.
ConnectionTimeout	This property returns the timeout period for establishing the connection that was supplied as part of the connection string. This is specified in seconds.
Database	When the connection is open this property will return the current database for the connection. If a database name was specified with the `Database` attribute in the connection string, then this property will return that database name when the connection is closed. If no database was specified in the connection string, this property returns an empty string when the connection is closed.

Property	Description
DataSource	Returns the name of the SQL Server instance that the connection is, or will be, established with. If you do not specify the data source as part of the connection string, this will return an empty string when the connection is closed.
PacketSize	Returns the size of the network packet that the client uses to communicate with the SQL Server instance. This is measured in bytes and can be set as an attribute of the connection string.
ServerVersion	This property will return the version of SQL Server that you are connected to. This property can only be read once the connection is established. If you try and use it while the connection is closed, a System.InvalidOperationException will be thrown.
State	Returns the current connection state. Will either return 0 for closed or 1 for open. If you use the ToString method, this will return Closed and Open.
WorkstationID	Returns the value of the WorkstationID attribute specified in the connection string. If the WorkstationID attribute isn't included as part of the connection string, this will default to the local machine name.

ConnectionString

The ConnectionString property passes all the details of the connection you wish to make to the SqlConnection class. If you have worked with ADO in previous versions of Visual Basic, or with the OleDbConnection object, then the format of the connection string will be very familiar to you. There are a number of possible attributes that you can set within this property, as we will see shortly. The main difference from the SqlConnection object is that there is no Provider attribute for the connection string, because it can only make a connection to SQL Server using the native .NET SQL Server data provider.

It should be noted here that the connection information is processed and validated as soon as the property receives it. This is in contrast to what happens in ADO where it takes place when the connection to the server is attempted. A number of different validation actions occur:

❑ When the ConnectionString property is set, the SqlConnection class checks whether or not you are trying to modify the details of an open connection. If you need to do this, you must close the connection, modify the details, and then re-open your access to the database. If you try to alter an open connection inadvertently, a System.InvalidOperationException will be thrown.

❑ Once the SqlConnection class has established that it is working with a closed or a non-initialized SqlConnection object, the connection string is then parsed for valid syntax and known attributes. Once again, an error is thrown if there are problems with the string; however a different type of exception occurs, a System.ArgumentException, which also has to be handled.

In the case of a connection string to a SQL Server instance, the following attributes may be included:

Some of the attributes have more than one name, which allows you to choose the name you are most familiar with. The various names for each attribute have no effect on the function of the attribute however. The attribute names in bold are what I would recommend you use for clarity, if you have no current preference.

Attribute Name	Default value	Description
Application Name	.NET SqlClient data provider	The name of the application that is requesting the log in. Optional. Mainly used if you are auditing to find which applications are connecting.
AttachDBFilename / Extended Properties / Initial File Name		Used to attach to a database that is currently detached. The database can be attached for use by using this property and giving the full path name of where the primary .mdf file for the database resides. The name of the database being attached must also be specified in the connection string with the Database attribute.
		If the database is already attached, then this attribute is ignored and the database will remain attached when the connection is closed.
Connect Timeout / **Connection Timeout**	15	The time your SqlConnection class will wait for a response (in seconds) before it decides that a connection hasn't taken place and throws an exception.
Connection Lifetime	0	Used to determine the length of time a connection exists within a connection pool. 0 is default and means infinity.
Connection Reset	True	Used in connection pooling and, when set to True, will reset the connection so that a new connection will have to be made. See the *Pooling Connections* section next.
Current Language	Default language for the user	Used to set the language environment for the connection.
Data Source / **Server** / Address / Addr / Network Address		The name of the SQL Server, or the address on the network of the SQL Server.
		This can be omitted, set to (local) or set to "." to create a connection to the default instance of SQL Server on the local machine.

Attribute Name	Default value	Description
Enlist	True	When `True`, the connection pooling service automatically enlists the connection in the creation thread's current transaction context.
Initial Catalog / **Database**	Default database for the user	The name of the database the connection will be made to. Can be changed after the connection is opened using the `ChangeDatabase` method.
Integrated Security / Trusted Connection	False	A setting of `True` or `SSPI` indicates you are using Trusted Connection/Windows Authentication.
Max Pool Size	100	The maximum number of concurrent connections held within the connection pool (Pooling is discussed next).
Min Pool Size	0	The minimum number of connections within the connection pool.
Net / Network Library	dbmssocn	The library used to connect to SQL Server. A value of dbmssocn indicates TCP/IP (further possible values are discussed below in the *Network Library* section).
Packet Size	8192	The size of each packet of data to send over the network.
Password / Pwd		The password for the user ID logging in. Not required when using Integrated Security but it is mandatory for login requests when using SQL Server authentication.
Persist Security Info	False	A setting of `False` indicates that the password used to authenticate the connection is removed from the connection string once the connection has been opened.
Pooling	True	Enables or disables connection pooling. See the section later on for more information.
User ID / UID		Ignored when using Integrated Security to authenticate; however, when using SQL Server authentication this is required. This attribute specifies the SQL Server Login ID for authenticating with the SQL Server instance.
Workstation ID	Local computer name	The machine ID requesting the login. This defaults to the local machine name but can be set to any value.

> When specifying the attributes for a connection string, the order of specification does not matter.

The following example shows a basic connection string that could be used to establish a connection to SQL Server located on the same machine as the code is being run:

```
Dim Conn As New SqlConnection _
  ("Server=(local); Database=Northwind; Integrated Security=SSPI;")
```

The next example shows a connection string that could be used to connect to a remote server using SQL Server authentication. Here we also specify an `Application Name` attribute and a `Connection Timeout` of 20 seconds:

```
Dim Conn As New SqlConnection("Server=MyServer;" _
                    & "User ID=MyUser;" _
                    & "Password = MyPassword;" _
                    & "Database=Northwind;" _
                    & "Application Name=MyClient App;" _
                    & "Connection Timeout=20;")
```

Network Library

The `Network Library` property specifies the protocol the client will use to communicate with a SQL Server. The Network Library used by the client initiating the connection must be configured as a protocol that the SQL Server is listening for on the connection to be successful.

The following is a list of network libraries available for use using SQL Server 2000:

Network Library	Short Name	Description
Named Pipes	dbnmpntw	Supports use with multiple network protocols, such as TCP/IP or IPX. Connects using a pipe between the client and server. This requires authentication at the OS level before the connection can be established.
TCP/IP	dbmssocn	The default SQL Server network protocol for SQL Server 2000. Provides the best connection speed and most reliable connections when connecting to a remote server across a WAN.
Multiprotocol	dbmsrpcn	Supports integrated security and basic encryption. Usage of this network library is decreasing, because it does not support named instances and it also requires the use of numerous RPC ports.
NWLink	dbmsspxn	Allows for communication over IPX. While most corporate networks now support TCP/IP, this network protocol is supported if you only have an IPX network.

Network Library	Short Name	Description
AppleTalk	dbmsadsn	Supported to allow connections from Apple clients.
Shared Memory	dbmsipcn	Supported for improved connection performance on Windows 98 and Windows 2000 Professional systems when connecting to a local install of SQL Server 2000. Using the Shared Memory protocol bypasses the network stack resulting in efficient database connections.

Unless you have a particular reason to use another network library, TCP/IP will usually provide the best performance when used with SQL Server 2000. Conveniently it is also the default library available after installation of SQL Server. Additional third-party network libraries may be available that provide highly efficient connections using specialized hardware, if you have it.

The selection of the network library is an environmental issue in that it depends on the particular network environment where the application is running. If you are creating applications that will be used in a network environment that you don't control, it is recommended that you do **not** specify the network library as part of the connection string. If you omit the network library attribute from the connection string, the connection will attempt to use the default network library for the client machine, as configured using the SQL Server Client Network Utility. For more information on this utility see SQL Server Books Online.

ConnectionTimeout

This is a read-only attribute that is exposed from the SqlConnection class. The value is set within your ConnectionString above and is used to determine how long the class waits for the connection to the server to succeed, or fail.

It is not a mandatory setting, and if no value is set then the default value of 15 seconds kicks in. This is long enough even for slow networks with high volumes of traffic, or for looking at Internet connections. However if you do find connection timeouts happening, then you can increase the limit.

If you set a value of less than zero for the ConnectionTimeout attribute within your ConnectionString an ArgumentException error will be thrown.

> Note that this property is only required for connections being opened, and is not used whilst waiting on stored procedures running or queries executing. Once connected to SQL Server the **CommandTimeout** property of the **SqlCommand** object is used to control the waiting time of executing code.

The most common reason for a connection to time out is because the server name is incorrect or the server is not currently available on the network. The former is particularly common if you have applications that require users to enter the server name as part of the application login process. It is important that you strike a balance between allowing enough time to ensure successful connection when the network bandwidth is low, and the amount of time the user must wait for the connection to time-out. There is little that is more frustrating to a user than being forced to wait an excessively long time for the connection to time-out because they have entered a typo in their server name.

> Never set the `ConnectionTimeout` property to 0 since this means that your program waits indefinitely. It is better to raise an error than have a user wait an indeterminate amount of time. A setting of 15 seconds will allow most networks to return a response and the only time the setting needs to be longer would be either over a very slow remote network, or perhaps when using a network connection over a modem.

ServerVersion

As we saw above, the `ServerVersion` property will return the version of SQL Server that you are currently connected to. This can be useful if your application requires functionality delivered by a specified version of SQL Server, or if your application has alternative methods of achieving a task based on which version of SQL Server is in use.

The SQL Server version number uses the format `XX.XX.XXX`. The first part of the version number represents the server version, 7 for SQL Server 7 and 8 for SQL Server 2000. The middle `XX` represents a major re-release of the same version. There haven't been any major version releases for either SQL Server 7 or 2000 but SQL Server 6.5 was a major version release of SQL Server 6.0. The last `XXX` is the minor release version number. This is what changes when you apply a service pack, or when you apply some hot fixes.

Here is a list of valid SQL Server versions that can be used with the .NET SQL Server Data Provider, at the time of writing:

Version Number	Server Version
7.00.623	SQL Server 7.0 RTM
7.00.699	SQL Server 7.0 with Service Pack 1 applied
7.00.842	SQL Server 7.0 with Service Pack 2 applied
7.00.961	SQL Server 7.0 with Service Pack 3 applied
7.00.1062	SQL Server 7.0 with Service Pack 4 Beta applied
8.00.194	SQL Server 2000 RTM
8.00.384	SQL Server 2000 with Service Pack 1 applied
8.00.532	SQL Server 2000 with Service Pack 2 applied

Your server may return a different version number if you have applied any subsequent service packs, or if you have been provided with a hot fix from Microsoft product support. Generally you will only want to check the major component of the version number, either 7 or 8, but some service packs do introduce new functionality. If you are using this new functionality, you may need to check the entire version number and act appropriately if you are connected to a server version that doesn't support your requirements.

`SqlConnection` also has methods, which we look at next.

Methods

Method	Description
ChangeDatabase	Changes the database currently used for the connection. This method can only be used when the connection is open. An exception will be thrown if ChangeDatabase is called and the connection is currently closed.
Close	This method closes a currently open connection.
Open	This method opens the connection using the connection details specified in the connection string.

The following example uses all three of the SqlConnection object methods. First it opens a connection to a SQL Server instance, changes the database once connected and finally closes the connection:

```
Dim Conn As New SqlConnection("Server=MyServer; Database=Northwind;" _
                    & "User ID=sa;Password=;")
Conn.Open()
Conn.ChangeDatabase("Pubs")
Conn.Close()
```

Pooling Connections

In more traditional three-tier applications there may be more than one connection made per application. For example, you may have components embedded in your application which make their own connections, or perhaps you need to keep more than one connection open for different data accesses. When initiating a connection, two or three trips over the network may be made each time to authenticate and establish the connection to the database. If you are on a busy or slow network, then this can lead to several seconds delay. If you are writing an application that only requires a connection to a database for a short period of time, but will constantly be opening and closing connections within the lifetime of the application, then you need to take a look at **connection pooling**.

Pooling is a simple concept. Every time a connection is made to a database, the connection details, including the authentication details, are held and stored in a **resource pool**. When a subsequent connection request is made, the resource pool is first checked to see if there are existing connections available where the authentication details are the same, and you are connecting to the same server and database. If there is an existing connection that matches our connection criteria, this is used instead of creating a new one. However if no suitable connection is available in the pool then a new one will be established.

While connection pooling is enabled by default in ADO.NET, it is possible to use the connection string properties and methods of the connection object to customize its behavior. To prevent a database connection from being held within a connection pool, you can set the Pooling attribute within the connection string to False. You may wish to do this to minimize resource utilization if you know this is a one-off connection that will not be used again during the execution of your application, for example:

```
Dim Conn As New SqlConnection("Server=MyServer; Database=Pubs; _
                        & "User ID=sa;Password=; Pooling=False")
```

Physical database connections are not shared concurrently by multiple objects, so you can think of a connection pool as a holding facility for currently unused database connections. A call to the Open method of a SqlConnection object causes the connection pool to release an existing database connection from the pool to the requesting connection object. That database connection is not admitted back into the connection pool until the Close method of the SqlConnection object is explicitly called. When returned to the pool the database connection is once again available for use by other SqlConnection objects.

> Make sure you always call the **Close** method when you have finished using your **SqlConnection** object so the connection returns to the connection pool. Letting the **SqlConnection** object go out of scope will not return the connection back into the pool.

Min and Max Pool Sizes

The Min Pool Size and Max Pool Size attributes of a connection string allow you to customize the number of connections that will be held within the pool. The Min Pool Size dictates how many connections are opened in total when the request to open the first connection in the pool is made. This defaults to 0 but you may wish to increase this if you use multiple simultaneous connections to a particular data source often. This is not common for standard client-server applications, but it may be appropriate if you are developing components to be used within a web-based environment.

The Max Pool Size attribute, on the other hand, specifies the maximum number of connections that can exist within the pool. This allows you to restrict the number of connections that can be open from your application. By preventing an excessive number of database connections from being opened, you can avoid performance degradation of the database server for other users. If a connection object using pooling requests a connection from an existing pool that has reached its Max Pool Size limit, it will wait for the ConnectionTimeout period for a connection to become available. If no connection becomes available in this time an InvalidOperationException will be thrown.

For example, in the following code the first two connections will be created within the connection pool. The third connection request will wait for the timeout period and, as no connection in the pool will become available, this connection request will eventually time out raising an exception.

```
Dim Conn As New SqlConnection("Server=MyServer; User ID=sa; Password=;" _
                        & "Pooling=true; Max Pool Size=2;")

Conn.Open() 'Connection succeeds

Dim Conn1 As New SqlConnection("Server=MyServer; User ID=sa; Password=;" _
                        & "Pooling=true; Max Pool Size=2;")

Conn1.Open() 'Connection succeeds

Dim Conn2 As New SqlConnection("Server=MyServer; User ID=sa; Password=;" _
                        & "Pooling=true; Max Pool Size=2;")

Conn2.Open() ' Timeout occurs as no connection available in the pool
```

It is important to note the connection string must be exactly the same for all connections using the pool and this includes the setting of the Min and Max Pool Sizes. If these are different, or specified for some connections and not others, multiple connection pools will be created.

Connection Reset

The Connection Reset attribute of the connection string dictates whether the connection is reset when it is removed from the pool by a SqlCommand object that is opening a database connection.

If the connection is not reset, previous connection properties that the new user of the connection doesn't expect may still be in place. The following example shows the establishment of two database connections. Both have the ConnectionReset set to False and specify the master database should be the current database for the connection:

```
Dim sqlConn As New SqlConnection("Server=MyServer; User ID=sa;" _
                                 & "Password =; Database=master;" _
                                 & "Connection Reset=False;")
sqlConn.Open()
```

At this point we output the current database to the Console window, and indeed it is the master database. Next we change the current database to Northwind before closing our connection:

```
Console.WriteLine(sqlConn.Database)
sqlConn.ChangeDatabase("Northwind")
sqlConn.Close()
```

As our next connection has the same connection string as the previous one, the existing connection is retrieved from the connection pool to be used for this connection request. As we have specified that we don't wish the connection to be reset it is used "as is".

```
Dim sqlConn2 As New SqlConnection("Server=MyServer; User ID=sa;" _
                                  & "Password =; Database=master;" _
                                  & "Connection Reset=False;")
sqlConn2.Open()
```

Now we output the current database we discover that it is still Northwind, even though we explicitly specified the master database in the connection string.

```
Console.WriteLine(sqlConn2.Database)
sqlConn2.Close()
```

Since setting Connection Reset to False can lead to very hard-to-diagnose problems within your application, the connection should always be reset unless you have a special situation that requires it to be disabled.

Now that we know how to create a connection object, we need to do something with it, so let's take a look at the SqlCommand object.

SqlCommand Object

SqlCommand gives us access to properties and methods to execute any T-SQL command we wish, and to verify what has happened with those commands. It also allows us, in conjunction with the SqlConnection class, to perform transactional processing, as we will see in Chapter 8.

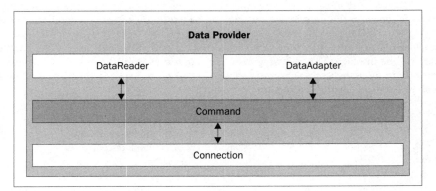

The SqlCommand object can be used with a DataReader object or a SqlDataAdapter. We will concentrate on the SqlDataAdapter usage in this chapter, while giving an overview of the four Execute statements that are also linked with this object through DataReaders, which will be discussed in Chapter 4.

We'll begin by taking a look at the properties and methods associated with a SqlCommand object.

Properties

Property	Description
CommandText	Gets or sets the table name, T-SQL code, or stored procedure to execute at the data source.
CommandTimeout	Determines the length of time the SqlCommand class waits before declaring the commands being executed have timed out. If a timeout occurs, the command is terminated, and an exception thrown.
CommandType	Set to one of three potential values for a SqlConnection. These are: ❑ Text, which is the default and defines that the value in CommandText is straight T-SQL. ❑ StoredProcedure, which specifies the name of a stored procedure to be executed. ❑ TableDirect, which allows a table name to be specified in CommandText where that table is to have its entire contents returned.

Property	Description
Connection	Gets or sets the `SqlConnection` object to be used to execute the command over. The connection to SQL Server must be open before one of the `SqlCommand` execute methods are called, otherwise an exception will be thrown.
Parameters	Retrieves the collection of parameters that have been set when executing a stored procedure, or parameterized T-SQL statements. The collection comes from the `SqlParameterCollection` class.
	The parameters associated with a `SqlCommand` object can be `Input` parameters, `Output` parameters or both in the form of `Input/Output` parameters. We will see examples of using parameters later in Chapter 6.
Transaction	Sets or gets the `SqlTransaction` object that this command will execute within. If a transaction object already exists on the connection being used by this command, this property will default to the currently open transaction. Lots of examples of using transaction objects are shown in Chapter 8.
UpdatedRowSource	For use with the `Update` method on a `SqlDataAdapter`. Determines how the results of the command are applied to the `DataRow`.

Let's now take a look at one of these properties in greater detail.

CommandText

This is the most used property within the `SqlCommand` class, and can consist of any valid T-SQL command, or group of T-SQL commands. Examples include SELECT, INSERT, UPDATE, and DELETE statements as well as stored procedures. If you are using the `TableDirect` command type this could also simply be a table name, or a list of table names separated by commas.

When executing a stored procedure you should prefix the procedure name with the owner of the object in the database, which really ought to be dbo. Although not a major problem, there is a performance gain by prefixing all objects from stored procedures through to tables, with their owner prefix. If the object (such as table or stored procedure) is referred to in an unqualified manner (such as sp_productlist), SQL Server first checks to see if there's an object named product owned by the current user. If there isn't, then SQL Server checks to see if there's an object of this name owned by the database owner (dbo). Finally, for stored procedures, if the procedure name is prefixed with sp_ then SQL Server checks the master database to see if there is a procedure of this name located there. This is an unnecessary (and sometimes confusing) overhead that can be avoided simply by specifying the object owner along with the object name.

Our first example shows using a command type of Text and specifies a T-SQL command as the text for the `SqlCommand` object:

```
Dim MySQLCmd As New SqlCommand()
MySQLCmd.CommandType = CommandType.Text
MySQLCmd.CommandText = "SELECT * FROM dbo.authors"
```

Next, we use the `TableDirect` command type to instruct our `SqlCommand` object to retrieve all the columns and rows directly from the table name that we specified in the `CommandText` property:

```
Dim MySQLCmd As New SqlCommand()
MySQLCmd.CommandType = CommandType.TableDirect
MySQLCmd.CommandText = "dbo.authors"
```

Finally, using the `StoredProcedure` command type we instruct our `SqlCommand` object to execute the stored procedure specified in the `CommandText` property:

```
Dim MySQLCmd As New SqlCommand()
MySQLCmd.CommandType = CommandType.StoredProcedure
MySQLCmd.CommandText = "dbo.sp_get_authors"
```

Methods

There are a number of methods also associated with this class, which we'll list here. We will see some of them in more detail when we look at the coding for our sample application in the next chapter.

Method	Description
Cancel	If any execution is in progress, this will send a `Cancel Execution` request to the server. Only when the server can deal with the `Cancel` method, will the execution actually halt. While the execution of the `SqlCommand` object itself runs synchronously, this could be useful if you have a multi-threaded application and you are executing the `SqlCommand` object asynchronously to other threads.
CreateParameter	Creates an object of `SqlParameter`, which will be used to pass any parameters in and out of stored procedures or parameterized T-SQL.
ExecuteNonQuery	Designed for commands that will not return any rows of data, for example `CREATE`, or `INSERT`.
ExecuteReader	Used when executing T-SQL that will be returning rows of data in non-XML format. Returns a `SqlDataReader` object containing the rows and columns returned from the execution of the specified T-SQL.
ExecuteScalar	Returns the first column of the first row only from the data. Ideal for statements such as `COUNT(*)` that return single-column, single-row values.
ExecuteXmlReader	If you desire your data back in XML format, use this execution method along with `FOR XML` in your `SELECT` statement.
Prepare	Causes the execution plan to be prepared and retained for subsequent executions of the same SQL command. Can offer performance increases when executing a command on multiple occasions.
ResetCommandTimeout	Resets the `CommandTimeout` to the default of 30 seconds.

Execute Methods

There are four different routes that can be taken when executing T-SQL against any SQL Server source, which we touched on earlier when listing the methods of the `SqlCommand` class. It is not the intention of this chapter to look at the `Execute` methods in detail, but we do need to know a bit about the four methods before we can look at retrieving data at this point in the book.

All of these methods work in a very similar way under the hood. Each of them passes the command details that have been built up within the `SqlCommand` object to the connection object that you have created. The T-SQL is then executed on your SQL Server through the `SqlConnection` object, which will then produce a set of data for the `SqlCommand` object to be placed in a `SqlDataReader`.

ExecuteNonQuery

This method will execute the specified T-SQL on the SQL Server but will only return an integer that indicates the number of rows affected by the T-SQL. It is therefore suitable for use with T-SQL commands that do not return resultsets. These include **Data Definition Language** (**DDL**) commands such as CREATE TABLE, CREATE VIEW, DROP TABLE, and **Data Manipulation Language** (**DML**) commands such as INSERT, UPDATE, and DELETE. This can also be used for executing stored procedures that do not return a resultset.

The following code establishes a connection to SQL Server and uses the `ExecuteNonQuery` to run three T-SQL commands. The first creates a new temporary table, the second inserts a row into this temporary table and also writes the returned row's affected parameter to the console, and the third `ExecuteNonQuery` command drops this temporary table.

```
Dim MySQLConn As New SqlClient.SqlConnection _
                    ("Server=MyServer;User ID=sa;Password=;Database=pubs")
Dim MySQLCmd As New SqlCommand()
Dim RowsAffected As Integer

MySQLConn.Open()
MySQLCmd.CommandType = CommandType.Text
MySQLCmd.Connection = MySQLConn

MySQLCmd.CommandText = "CREATE TABLE #MyTempTable(IDCol Int)"
MySQLCmd.ExecuteNonQuery()

MySQLCmd.CommandText = "INSERT #MyTempTable(IDCol) VALUES(1)"
RowsAffected = MySQLCmd.ExecuteNonQuery()
Console.WriteLine(RowsAffected)

MySQLCmd.CommandText = "DROP TABLE #MyTempTable"
MySQLCmd.ExecuteNonQuery()

MySQLConn.Close()
```

If the `ExecuteNonQuery` method is used to execute a T-SQL command that does return a resultset, then this is ignored and not made accessible from the client application.

ExecuteReader

The `ExecuteReader` method is used to return a `DataReader` object that contains the rows returned from the command executed by SQL Server. As we discussed in Chapter 1, the `DataReader` object is a high-speed, read-only method of retrieving single resultsets from SQL Server.

The following code executes the specified T-SQL command and iterates through the resultset, outputting the values contained within a few of the resultset columns to the console window:

```
Dim MySQLConn As New SqlClient.SqlConnection _
                 ("Server=MyServer;User ID=sa;Password=;Database=pubs")

Dim MySQLCmd As New SqlCommand()
MySQLCmd.Connection = MySQLConn
MySQLCmd.CommandType = CommandType.Text
MySQLCmd.CommandText = "SELECT * FROM dbo.authors"

Dim mySQLDataReader As SqlDataReader

MySQLConn.Open()

mySQLDataReader = MySQLCmd.ExecuteReader

While mySQLDataReader.Read
   Console.Write(mySQLDataReader.Item("au_id"))
   Console.Write(mySQLDataReader.Item("au_lname"))
   Console.WriteLine(mySQLDataReader.Item("au_fname"))
End While

mySQLDataReader.Close()
MySQLConn.Close()
```

ExecuteScalar

The `ExecuteScalar` method is used to run queries that return a single column within a single row. This is especially useful, and efficient, when running aggregations such as `COUNT(*)` to find out the number of rows in a particular table. For example, the following code executes a `COUNT(*)` on a table using the `ExecuteScalar` method. The result of the `COUNT(*)` is returned and outputted to the console window:

```
Dim MySQLConn As New SqlClient.SqlConnection _
                 ("Server=MyServer;User ID=sa;Password=;Database=pubs")

Dim MySQLCmd As New SqlCommand()
MySQLCmd.Connection = MySQLConn
MySQLCmd.CommandType = CommandType.Text

MySQLCmd.CommandText = "SELECT Count(*) FROM authors"
Dim mySQLDataReader As SqlDataReader
Dim AuthorsCount As Integer

MySQLConn.Open()
AuthorsCount = MySQLCmd.ExecuteScalar
Console.WriteLine("There are " & AuthorsCount & " authors.")
MySQLConn.Close()
```

ExecuteXmlReader

This can be used to execute T-SQL commands that output XML, such as a SELECT statement using the FOR XML option. This command creates an XmlReader object that we can use to navigate the XML tree. More information on the ExecuteXmlReader method and examples of its use, can be found in Chapter 10.

Prepare

The Prepare method specifies that on the first execution of the SqlCommand object, the execution plan for this command be retained for subsequent use on this connection.

> *Whenever a command is submitted to SQL Server an execution plan is generated by SQL Server that details how the command is to be carried out.*

This takes up resource. Often this is very minimal resource for simple commands but it is increased when submitting complex queries with large numbers of joins.

To improve efficiency when submitting the same command a number of times to SQL Server, the execution plan can be cached on the first execution of the command. SQL Server then uses this previously prepared execution plan for subsequent execution requests of this command made by the client application. However, if any changes are made to the command text between executions, a new query plan will be generated. Parameter values, on the other hand, can change between execution requests of a particular command without a new execution plan being generated.

In the following example we use the Prepare method to prepare a simple SELECT statement. Subsequent executions of the same command use the cached, prepared command rather than resubmitting the command itself to SQL Server:

```
Dim MySQLConn As New SqlClient.SqlConnection _
                  ("Server=MyServer;User ID=sa;Password=;Database=pubs")
Dim MySQLCmd As New SqlCommand()
Dim MySQLDR As SqlDataReader
MySQLCmd.Connection = MySQLConn
MySQLCmd.CommandType = CommandType.Text

MySQLCmd.CommandText = "SELECT * FROM dbo.authors"

MySQLConn.Open()
MySQLCmd.Prepare()

MySQLDR = MySQLCmd.ExecuteReader() 'Initial execution
MySQLDR.Close()

MySQLDR = MySQLCmd.ExecuteReader()
MySQLDR.Close()

MySQLDR = MySQLCmd.ExecuteReader()
MySQLDR.Close()

MySQLConn.Close()
```

As all this happens in the background, it's hard for us to tell what is going on just by looking at the code. If we use SQL Server Profiler to trace the actual commands that have been sent to SQL Server, we get the following result:

```
declare @P1 int
set @P1=1
exec sp_prepexec @P1 output, N'', N'SELECT * FROM dbo.authors'
select @P1
go
```

This is the command sent to SQL Server after the first ExecuteReader method is called. The subsequent executions of this same command are handled quite differently; the SqlCommand object now just passes a pointer to the prepared command:

```
exec sp_execute 1
go
exec sp_execute 1
go
```

And when the connection is closed, any prepared commands are unprepared to free that resource:

```
exec sp_unprepare 1
go
```

If you execute the Prepare method on a SqlCommand object, and a prepared execution plan already exists from a previous call to the Prepare method, the existing prepared plan is first unprepared before the new execution plan is cached.

Next, let's take a look at the SqlDataReader.

SqlDataReader Object

In Chapter 1 we learned that a DataReader provides is a forward-only, read-only stream of data. We also discussed how the DataReader operates in connected mode, which means the connection to the database must be open when retrieving rows from the DataReader for use in your application. In this section we look at the various properties and methods of the SQL Server-specific implementation of this, the SqlDataReader.

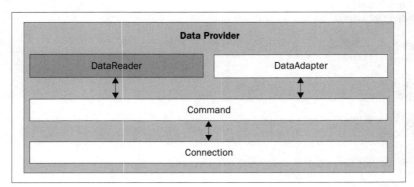

As the `SqlDataReader` provides the fastest method of retrieving data from a SQL Server database, you should check to see if it offers the functionality you require when you need to query data within your application. While you cannot modify the data that is returned from a SqlDataReader, there are usually many operations in most applications that only require retrieval of the data. Web-based applications are particularly good examples as a typical web application has a high number of data retrieval operations, used for populating pages and so on, in comparison with operations that make changes to that data.

The `SqlDataReader` does not interact with a SQL Server connection directly, because it is passed to a `DataReader` object from a call to the `SqlCommand.ExecuteReader` method. This `DataReader` object can then be worked through iteratively to access the values contained in each row.

It is worth clarifying the read-only issue here. This does not mean you cannot use the `SqlDataReader` with a `SqlCommand` object containing T-SQL that modifies rows within a database. The read only restriction applies to the resultset returned to the `SqlDataReader` object from the `SqlCommand` object. There is no direct ability to modify this resultset and have the changes propagated back to SQL Server.

Properties

Property	Description
FieldCount	Returns the number of columns within the current row.
Item	Returns the value of a particular column for the current row.
RecordsAffected	The number of records affected by an INSERT, UPDATE, or DELETE command. If a SELECT command is issued then this will return −1.
Depth	Indicates how deeply nested the current row is. The outermost table has a depth of zero. Note that nesting is not supported by the SqlDataReader (only by the OleDbDataReader) so will always return zero for this property.
IsClosed	Indicates whether the DataReader is closed

To see examples of the usage of these properties please review the example code shown in Chapter 4.

Methods

Method	Description
Close	Closes the SqlDataReader. You must always call the Close method once you have finished using the SqlDataReader.
GetBoolean, GetByte, GetChar, GetDecimal, GetDouble, GetFloat, GetGuid, GetInt16, GetInt32, GetInt64	Returns the column value as the specified System data type. This does not convert the column value so it must already be of the requested type.

Table continued on following page

Method	Description
GetBytes, GetChars	Get a stream of bytes or a stream of characters from a specified offset within a column.
GetDataTypeName	Returns the SQL Server data type name of the specified column.
GetFieldType	Returns the object type of the specified column. Could also be determined by calling the `item(ordinal).GetType` method of the `SqlDataReader` object.
GetName	Returns the column name of the column specified by ordinal reference.
GetSchemaTable	Returns a `DataTable` object that contains the column meta data from the resultset.
GetSqlBinary, GetSqlBoolean, GetSqlByte, GetSqlDateTime, GetSqlDecimal, GetSqlDouble, GetSqlGuid, GetSqlInt16, GetSqlInt32, GetSqlInt64, GetSqlMoney, GetSqlSingle, GetSqlString	Returns the column value as the specified SQL data type. This does not convert the column value so it must already be of the requested type, or of a compatible base type such as `System.Int16` and `SQLInt16`.
GetSqlValue / GetValue	Returns the column value in its native SQL Server or .NET data type respectively.
GetSqlValues / GetValues	Populates an array with the column values in their native SQL Server or .NET data types respectively.
IsDBNull	Used to check if a column contains a `NULL` value. You should use this to check the column before calling one of the typed gets, as a typed get on a `NULL` column will result in an exception being thrown.
NextResult	Moves to the next resultset in the `SqlDataReader`, if one is available. If no further resultsets are available then this returns `False`, otherwise it returns `True`.
Read	Moves to the next row in the current resultset, if available. If no further rows are available then this returns `False`, otherwise it returns `True`.

The Read method is used to get the next row from the DataReader. Notice that there are no Back or First methods, which is why we refer to the SqlDataReader as being forward only. If no further rows are available then the Read method will return False.

While this completes our discussion of the `SqlDataReader` object here, there are many code examples showing how to use the various properties and methods available, in Chapter 4.

To complete our picture, we now need to examine the role of the `SqlDataAdapter`, which provides the link between the data connection to the SQL Server database, and the `DataSet` object that will hold the physical data returned from your query. We will look at the `DataSet` itself, in some detail, in the section after next.

SqlDataAdapter Object

As we discussed in Chapter 1, when using the `SqlDataAdapter` with data within .NET, it is held as a disconnected `recordset` that is memory resident within an object defined as a `DataSet`.

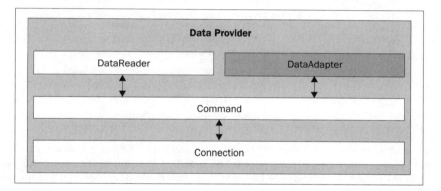

While it was possible to work with disconnected `recordsets` in previous versions of ADO, they were difficult to code. When you connected to a SQL Server, the connection remained open by default. It then had to be serviced by the server and the network whilst the connection remained open. Imagine you had a system built for a branch office, which performed well with just a handful of users. Licensing requirements covered the number of connections, and the server built for the SQL Server solution could cope with such low stress levels. If the application was then expanded to several branches running over the company intranet, the number of licenses would increase along with the number of open and concurrent connections. The server would have to continue to ensure that all the connections remained valid, and the application performance would suffer as a result of the increased processing overhead. For this reason we are much better placed with ADO.NET because we do not have to maintain concurrent, open connections in this way.

When creating an instance of a `SqlDataAdapter` in an object, it is possible to specify the connection details and command text for the data adapter's `SelectCommand` property. The connection can either be specified as a `ConnectionString` or as a `Connection` object itself, however populating the `SelectCommand` during creation of the `SqlDataAdapter` is not mandatory.

Once a connection is made, and the T-SQL commands are in place, you then move to populating the `DataSet`. This is performed using the `Fill` method called from the `DataAdapter` object. Any errors that occur in populating the `DataSet`, such as a loss of connection, will result in a `FillError` event being passed to the `DataAdapter`.

DataAdapters, and this includes the OleDb flavor of adapter, are mainly used for data retrieval from a SQL Server table or number of tables directly, without the use of stored procedures. A SqlDataAdapter will normally be associated with a single DataSet, which will be used to return data directly from a T-SQL command. Once the DataSet has been filled with the data, you can then inspect the table and the rows of information that have been returned. The flow diagram below shows a simplified representation of the actions that are involved in retrieving data from a SQL Server:

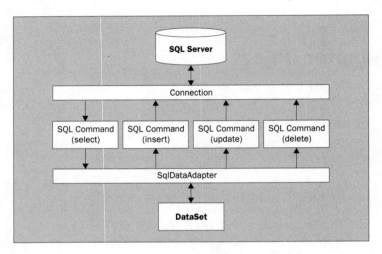

As we mentioned when discussing creating the SqlDataAdapter object, it is not compulsory to create a connection prior to initializing it, since it could be specified as a ConnectionString passed during the creation of the object. The difference between these two methods relates to when the connection is closed. In the first scenario, where the connection already exists, it is down to the program to close and dispose of the connection as it sees fit. Taking the second method, the connection will be closed automatically as soon as the T-SQL command has completed. To give an example of this second method, take a look at the code below:

```
Dim Adapter As SqlDataAdapter = New SqlDataAdapter _
        ("SELECT Description FROM Categories", _
        "Data Source=MyServer;" + _
        "User ID=sa; Password=;Database=Northwind")
```

Here we create a SqlDataAdpater object. When it is created, it will open a server connection using Windows Authentication, select the Northwind database, then execute the T-SQL code. Now the data is held within the SqlDataAdapter and can be moved to a DataSet using further commands. However, once the command has been executed the connection has already been closed and the data is disconnected at this point from the data source.

As you will see in Chapter 4, DataReaders can also deal with data and are much faster than using DataSets, so why does the SqlDataAdapter exist? Simply it comes down to what functionality you require. If you need a simple read-only representation of the data returned from your command, then it is likely a DataReader is the best option. However, if you plan on making changes to the data and intend to synchronize those changes with your data sources, then a DataSet is required.

Let's take a look at the properties and methods that you can use with a SqlDataAdapter.

Properties

Property	Description
AcceptChangesDuringFill	Specifies if AcceptChanges is called on a DataRow when it is added to a DataTable during the Fill operation.
	When used in conjunction with MissingSchemaAction, it determines if existing rows within a DataSet are updated or appended during a Fill operation. The default value is True.
ContinueUpdateOnError	If this is set to True an exception is not thrown when an error occurs during an update. Instead the row that caused the error is skipped and the update continues. The error information can be retrieved from the RowError collection of the DataRow that caused the error. If this is set to False, an exception will be thrown when the update row error is encountered. The default value is False.
DeleteCommand	The SqlCommand to be used when you delete records from a DataSet and wish to have the changes reflected in the data source.
InsertCommand	The SqlCommand object to be used for inserting rows in the data source, when the changes made in the DataSet are being propagated to it.
MissingMappingAction	If you are retrieving data and there is a problem mapping from the sent data to the stored data from a structural viewpoint, this will determine what action to take. The default is PassThrough.
MissingSchemaAction	Similar to MissingMappingAction but simply concerned with the structure. The default is Add. See below for a further discussion of this property and its possible values.
SelectCommand	The SqlCommand used to populate a DataSet with records from a database.
TableMappings	Used to define the mappings of tables between the DataSet and the DataAdapter.
UpdateCommand	Any data updates to be performed use this SqlCommand object.

MissingSchemaAction

When the Fill method is executed, the SqlDataAdapter checks the DataSet to see if it has the schema information from the data source. If the schema information isn't present, the value of the MissingSchemaAction property determines how the DataAdapter will react. The possible values for this property are:

❑ Error – The Fill will not complete and an exception will be thrown.

❑   `Ignore` – The `Fill` will only populate the schema that is present and ignore the rest of the columns.

❑   `Add` – When the `Fill` occurs, the schema will be added based on the data source. This is the default value. The primary key information from the data source is not included in the schema that is created within the `DataSet`.

❑   `AddWithKey` – The schema is added based on the data source, as with the `Add` method. However `AddWithKey` also creates the schema with the primary keys that are present on the underlying tables at the data source. Having this primary key information allows subsequent fills to update the data source with any changes that have been made in the `DataSet`.

Methods

Method	Description
Fill	Populates or refreshes the rows within the specified `DataSet` object to be the same as the data source.
FillSchema	Populates the `DataSet` with the schema from `SelectCommand` but doesn't actually populate the schema with any data.
GetFillParameters	Gets the returned parameters from the `SelectCommand` used for the `Fill` method. The parameters may be output parameters of a stored procedure or a parameterized T-SQL command.
Update	Calls the appropriate INSERT, UPDATE, and DELETE command objects to update the data source to reflect the changes that have been made in the `DataSet`. This will re-establish the connection to the data sources as necessary.

Fill & AcceptChangesDuringFill

When you wish to retrieve data from a SQL Server table, once you have set up the `SelectCommand` for the `SqlDataAdapter`, it is necessary to pull the data across into the `DataSet` object that has been set up. By executing the `Fill` method of the `SqlDataAdapter`, this will populate the `DataSet` and therefore the underlying `DataTable` with the necessary rows from the SQL Server data source.

If you are filling an existing `DataSet`, then any existing rows within the `DataTables` are retained and the rows from the data source from the subsequent `Fill` are appended to the table. This happens unless there is a primary key constraint defined for the `DataTable` with a corresponding primary key at the data source. If this is true, then the rows that match the primary key will be refreshed from the data source so long as `AcceptChanges` had been called after the previous `Fill` of the `DataSet`, either automatically by setting `AccepChangesDuringFill` to `True` or by calling the `AcceptChanges` method of the `DataSet`. Any pending row changes on these rows will be overwritten and lost.

Our first example populates the `DataSet` with a `DataTable` that has a primary key, and accepts the changes after the `Fill`. The subsequent population of the `DataSet` updates the existing rows, and the row changes we had made that were not to the primary key are lost.

```
Dim mySQLConn As New SqlConnection _
                    ("Server=MyServer;Database=pubs;User ID=sa;Password=;")
Dim myDataSet As New DataSet()
Dim iLoop As Integer

Dim mySQLDA As New SqlDataAdapter("SELECT * FROM dbo.employee", mySQLConn)
Dim mySQLDA2 As New SqlDataAdapter("SELECT * FROM dbo.employee", mySQLConn)

mySQLDA.MissingSchemaAction = MissingSchemaAction.AddWithKey
mySQLDA.AcceptChangesDuringFill = True
mySQLDA.Fill(myDataSet)
```

The `Fill` method of the `DataSet` populates a new data table that has primary key information, and accepts the changes once done. Next we modify two rows, in the first row we change the value of the `emp_id` column, the primary key for this table. In the second modification we change the `lname` column:

```
'Make changes to a row
myDataSet.Tables("table").Rows(0).Item("emp_id") = "BBBBB"
myDataSet.Tables("table").Rows(1).Item("lname") = "Glucina"
myDataSet.AcceptChanges()
```

A subsequent population of the `DataSet` updates the rows to reflect the data source based on the primary key. As we have modified one of the rows (row 0) to have a new primary key, this isn't updated. Instead the row from the data source that matched this row before it was changed, is appended to the table as a new row. Our second row change is overwritten as this is updated from the data source based on the primary key:

```
mySQLDA2.MissingSchemaAction = MissingSchemaAction.AddWithKey
mySQLDA2.AcceptChangesDuringFill = True
mySQLDA2.Fill(myDataSet)

Dim myDataRow
For Each myDataRow In myDataSet.Tables("table").Rows()
   For iLoop = 0 To myDataRow.Table.Columns.Count() - 1
                    Console.Write(myDataRow.Item(iLoop))
                    Console.Write(Chr(9))
   Next
   Console.WriteLine("")
Next
```

Our next example does exactly the same, except we do not populate the `DataSet` with the primary key information for our `DataTable`. This results in the subsequent population being appended to the existing rows within the `DataTable`, and the changes we had previously made still remain in effect:

```
Dim mySQLConn As New SqlConnection _
                    ("Server=MyServer;Database=pubs;User ID=sa;Password=;")
Dim myDataSet As New DataSet()
Dim iLoop As Integer

Dim mySQLDA As New SqlDataAdapter("SELECT * FROM dbo.employee", mySQLConn)
Dim mySQLDA2 As New SqlDataAdapter("SELECT * FROM dbo.employee", mySQLConn)
```

```
mySQLDA.MissingSchemaAction = MissingSchemaAction.Add
mySQLDA.AcceptChangesDuringFill = True
mySQLDA.Fill(myDataSet)

'Make changes to a row
myDataSet.Tables("table").Rows(0).Item("emp_id") = "BBBBB"
myDataSet.Tables("table").Rows(1).Item("lname") = "Glucina"
myDataSet.AcceptChanges()
```

Now instead of updating the existing rows, the subsequent fill simply appends all its rows to the end of the existing rows. This also leaves both of our changes in place:

```
mySQLDA2.MissingSchemaAction = MissingSchemaAction.Add
mySQLDA2.AcceptChangesDuringFill = True
mySQLDA.Fill(myDataSet)

Dim myDataRow
For Each myDataRow In myDataSet.Tables("table").Rows()
    For iLoop = 0 To myDataRow.Table.Columns.Count() - 1
                    Console.Write(myDataRow.Item(iLoop))
                    Console.Write(Chr(9))
    Next
    Console.WriteLine("")
Next
```

Updating Data

While selecting data for your application is of great importance, there will be many occasions when the data will have to be modified. At first the process of updating the data may seem complex, as there is no simple Update command to update the data source as there was in ADO. However the new approach in ADO.NET, where you define a command object for each type of data modification, is considerably more powerful since this allows you to write custom T-SQL or stored procedures to handle these events.

We need to define the T-SQL command for each type of data modification that can occur which include INSERTs, UPDATEs, and DELETEs. This could be as simple as T-SQL INSERT, UPDATE, or DELETE commands, or it may be passing parameters to stored procedures that we have defined to do custom updating of the underlying tables. For our example we will use the simple T-SQL commands to INSERT, UPDATE, and finally DELETE a row from our data source.

In the following example we populate a DataSet from a T-SQL SELECT command, then proceed to add, update, and finally delete a row within the DataSet and also at our data source. Now let's take a closer look at how the code actually does this.

First we define our connection to SQL Server and also create SqlCommand objects that will be used for performing the SELECT, INSERT, UPDATE, and DELETE operations against the data source:

```
Dim Conn As New SqlConnection _
                ("Server=MyServer;Database=Pubs;User ID=sa;Password=;")
Dim dtDataAdapter As New SqlDataAdapter()
```

```
Dim dsDataSet As New DataSet()

Dim cmdSelect As New SqlCommand()
Dim cmdInsert As New SqlCommand()
Dim cmdUpdate As New SqlCommand()
Dim cmdDelete As New SqlCommand()

Dim drDataRow As DataRow
Dim arArray(3) As Object
```

Next we set the `MissingSchemaAction` and `AcceptChangesDuringFill`. This ensures that the schema within the `DataSet` is created with primary key constraints corresponding to those within the data source, and also that the `AcceptChanges` is run for each row after the `Fill`, so the initial state the rows are in is `Unchanged`:

```
dtDataAdapter.MissingSchemaAction = MissingSchemaAction.AddWithKey
dtDataAdapter.AcceptChangesDuringFill = True
```

The first command we define is our `SELECT` command. This will be used to populate our `DataSet`. Here it is simply a `SELECT` of a selection of columns from all rows within the store's table:

```
' Add the Select command
cmdSelect.CommandText = "SELECT stor_id,stor_name,stor_address,city" _
                        & "FROM dbo.stores"
cmdSelect.Connection = Conn
dtDataAdapter.SelectCommand = cmdSelect
```

Next we define the command that will be used to `Insert` a record at the data source. We must create parameters for every column that will be inserted and map these parameters to the column within the data adapter that will be used to populate the parameter:

```
' Add the Insert command
cmdInsert.CommandText = "INSERT" _
& "dbo.stores(stor_id,stor_name,stor_address,city) VALUES(@p1,@p2,@p3,@p4)"
cmdInsert.Parameters.Add("@p1", SqlDbType.Char, 4, "stor_id")
cmdInsert.Parameters.Add("@p2", SqlDbType.VarChar, 40, "stor_name")
cmdInsert.Parameters.Add("@p3", SqlDbType.VarChar, 40, "stor_address")
cmdInsert.Parameters.Add("@p4", SqlDbType.VarChar, 20, "city")
cmdInsert.Connection = Conn
dtDataAdapter.InsertCommand = cmdInsert
```

We also have a similar requirement for the `Update` command:

```
' Add the Update command
cmdUpdate.CommandText = "UPDATE dbo.stores" _
        & "SET stor_name=@p2,stor_address=@p3,city=@p4 WHERE stor_id=@p1"
cmdUpdate.Parameters.Add("@p1", SqlDbType.Char, 4, "stor_id")
cmdUpdate.Parameters.Add("@p2", SqlDbType.VarChar, 40, "stor_name")
cmdUpdate.Parameters.Add("@p3", SqlDbType.VarChar, 40, "stor_address")
cmdUpdate.Parameters.Add("@p4", SqlDbType.VarChar, 20, "city")
cmdUpdate.Connection = Conn
dtDataAdapter.UpdateCommand = cmdUpdate
```

And again for the `Delete` command. As we only require the value of the `stor_id` column for the `DELETE`, we only map a single parameter that corresponds to this column:

```
'Add the Delete command
cmdDelete.CommandText = "DELETE dbo.stores WHERE stor_id=@p1"
cmdDelete.Parameters.Add("@p1", SqlDbType.Char, 4, "stor_id")
cmdDelete.Connection = Conn
dtDataAdapter.DeleteCommand = cmdDelete
```

The next piece of code creates a mapping between the resultset that is returned by the `SelectCommand`, which has a default table name of `Table`, and a table named `Store`. As this mapped `Store` table doesn't exist within the `DataSet`, this will be created during the `Fill`. Which is precisely what happens next:

```
dtDataAdapter.TableMappings.Add("Table", "Store")
dtDataAdapter.Fill(dsDataSet)
```

Next we call the `Rows.Add` method of our `DataSet` to add a row to the `DataTable` within the `DataSet`. We are specifying the values of the row within an object array. The members of the array don't correspond directly to particular columns, but we use their ordinal reference to decide what array member is for which `DataColumn`:

```
'Add a new row to the table, and update the source database
arArray(0) = "CHCH"
arArray(1) = "Book Superstore"
arArray(2) = "Cashel Street"
arArray(3) = "Christchurch"

drDataRow = dsDataSet.Tables("Store").Rows.Add(arArray)
dtDataAdapter.Update(dsDataSet)
```

The call to `dtDataAdapter.Update` is what causes the changes to be propagated to the data source. Until this is called, changes are only made locally within our `DataSet` object. When the `Update` method is called, the various `INSERT`, `UPDATE`, and `DELETE` commands associated with the `SqlDataAdapter` are called to change the data source so it is consistent with the `DataSet`.

Next, as with the insert, we update our newly created row and propagate these changes to the data source:

```
'Update the row, and update the source database
drDataRow.Item("stor_id") = "CHCH"
drDataRow.Item("stor_name") = "MegaBooks Superstore"
drDataRow.Item("stor_address") = "Manchester Street"
drDataRow.Item("city") = drDataRow.Item("city")
dtDataAdapter.Update(dsDataSet)
```

Finally we delete our recently created row and ensure that the row is also deleted at the data source:

```
'Delete the row, and update the source database
drDataRow.Delete()
dtDataAdapter.Update(dsDataSet)
```

Notice we don't call the AcceptChanges method on our DataSet object. Doing so would set the row state to Unchanged and this would prevent the DataAdapter from updating the data source with the changes, as previously discussed in Chapter 1.

RowUpdating / RowUpdated

The RowUpdating and RowUpdated events allow you to monitor and react to changes made to the data source. The RowUpdating method is fired before any data modification is made at the data source, the RowUpdated event is fired after the data modification has been made.

The RowUpdating and RowUpdated events are passed by the SqlRowUpdatingEventArgs and the SqlRowUpdatedEventArgs arguments respectively. These arguments have the following properties:

Properties	Description
Command	References the Command object being used to perform the update.
Errors	Gets errors that have occurred during the update.
Row	References a DataRow object that contains the updated rows being sent to the data source.
StatementType	The type of update that is being carried out (INSERT, UPDATE, or DELETE)
Status	The current status of the RowUpdating or RowUpdated event.
TableMapping	Provides a mapping to the table that is being updated within the DataSet.

The Status property can be both read to determine the current state of the row update, and modified to affect how the update operation will continue. The values of the status property can be:

❑   Continue – Continue the update. This is the default value.

❑   ErrorsOccured – The update for the row has been unsuccessful. The update is aborted and an exception is thrown.

❑   SkipCurrentRow – Do not update the current row, but continue updating subsequent rows.

❑   SkipAllRows – Do not update the remaining rows and no exception will be thrown.

The following example uses the OnRowUpdating event to skip over rows that contain errors:

```
Add Handler dtDataAdaper.RowUpdating, _
        New SqlRowUpdatingEventHandler(AddressOf OnRowUpdatingEvt)

Private Shared Sub OnRowUpdatingEvt _
        (ByVal sender as Object, ByVal args as SQLRowUpdatingEventArgs)
    If args.Status = UpdateStatus.ErrorsOccured then
        args.Status = UpdateStatus.SkipCurrentRow
    End if
End Sub
```

Having completed our look at the SqlDataAdapter, let's move on to take a closer look at the DataSet object that we have already been using to hold the data resulting from our queries.

DataSet Object

As you read in Chapter 1, it is now much simpler to work with disconnected DataSets. In fact, disconnected Recordsets are the crux of the design for ADO.NET. When working with data, it is the DataSet object that will hold the data that you will work with. The DataSet is very similar to a database definition because once a DataSet is defined you have access to the tables that exist, the columns within it, and so on.

The following diagram reminds us of how a DataSet is made up:

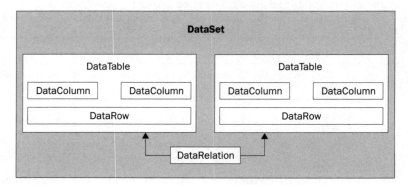

Let's take a look at the properties of this object.

Properties

Properties	Description
CaseSensitive	A Boolean setting that can be altered and is used for functions within DataSets and their related objects. A setting of True defines that all operations are case-sensitive. The default value is False. CaseSensitive is explored in more detail below.
DataSetName	Retrieves or sets the name of the DataSet.
DefaultViewManager	Returns a custom view of the data within the DataSet. Used for filtering, searching, and navigating when using a custom DataViewManager.
EnforceConstraints	Set to True if when performing data modifications, constraints are enforced. The default value is True. See the *Constraints* section later in this chapter.
ExtendedProperties	A collection of additional properties assigned to the DataSet. We'll return to this property towards the end of the chapter.
HasErrors	Set to True if any row (in any DataTable) has an error. You cannot determine which row at this level.

Properties	Description
Locale	Gets or sets the locale information used to compare strings within the table. The default value is a NULL reference.
Namespace	Gets or sets the namespace of the DataSet. Used when working with XML.
Prefix	Sets or retrieves an XML prefix used to alias the namespace.
Relations	This property is a DataRelations collection that contains the relationships between parent and child tables. DataRelations are discussed later in this chapter.
Tables	A collection of all the tables contained within the DataSet.

CaseSensitive

This property specifies if string comparisons made against character columns within the table are case-sensitive or case-insensitive. This property affects sorting, filtering, and comparisons on string columns.

If you have a character column that you are using as a key within a relation, you will need to set the CaseSensitive property for the child table to the same setting as for the parent table. Failure to do so will result in an exception being thrown when the relation is created. DataRelations are covered in detail later in this chapter.

Now let's take a look at the methods of the DataSet object.

Methods

Method	Description
AcceptChanges	Inserts, modifies, or removes any changes pending either since the start or since the last AcceptChanges. This applies to every row within all of the DataTables contained in the DataSet. This method is examined in more detail overleaf.
Clear	Clears the DataSet of any data by removing all rows in all tables.
Clone	Used to clone the structure of one DataSet object for another DataSet object. No data is copied.
Copy	Similar to Clone, but this will also copy the data.
GetChanges	Returns a new DataSet containing all of the changed rows (whether created, updated, or deleted). For more on this method, see later.
GetXml	Returns the XML representation of the data stored in the DataSet.
GetXmlSchema	Returns the XSD schema for the XML representation of the data stored in the DataSet. For more on this, see Chapter 10.

Table continued on following page

Method	Description
HasChanges	A Boolean setting indicating if there are changes to any DataRows (within any DataTable) pending update.
InferXmlSchema	Infers the XML schema from the specified TextReader or file into the DataSet. This can be used to make an XML structure available as a DataTable without an XSD file.
Merge	Merges this DataSet with another DataSet object.
ReadXml	Reads XML schemas and data into the DataSet from a file.
ReadXmlSchema	Only reads an XML schema into the DataSet.
RejectChanges	Similar to a database rollback. This will undo all the changes made to the DataSet since it was created, or since the last time AcceptChanges was called. See later in the chapter.
Reset	Resets the DataSet to its original state. Examined in greater detail later.
WriteXml	Writes XML schemas and data from the DataSet.
WriteXmlSchema	Writes the DataSet structure as an XML schema to a file. For more on this, please see Chapter 10.

A DataSet on its own is nothing greatly exciting. It is the equivalent of an empty database in SQL Server. However, like a database, it can be populated with tables, columns, rows, relationships, and constraints. All of these can be defined to collectively form the schema, or structure, of the DataSet and we will look at each of these in turn. Before then we'll examine some of the methods of the DataSet object more closely.

To get us started let's look at the following example. When this code is executed a new DataSet is created. The call to the SqlDataAdapter.Fill method is used to populate our empty DataSet with a new table that contains the columns and rows that are taken from the resultset of our query:

```
Dim sqlConn As New SqlClient.SqlConnection _
                ("Server=MyServer;User ID=sa;Password=;Database=northwind")
Dim myDataSet As New DataSet()
Dim myDataTable As DataTable

Dim myDataAdapter1 As New SqlDataAdapter("SELECT * FROM Orders", sqlConn)

myDataAdapter1.Fill(myDataSet)
```

AcceptChanges

AcceptChanges accepts any modifications to rows changed within a DataSet, but will not make changes at the data source. Since AcceptChanges will set the RowState to Unchanged, any calls to the DataAdapter Update method will not result in the changes being made at the data source. Also, once the DataSet is repopulated these changes will be lost. If you want the changes to be reflected at the data source then AcceptChanges must not be called directly. Use the Update method, which will automatically accept the changes after the data source has been updated.

GetChanges

The GetChanges method populates a new DataSet with the rows of DataTables that have been altered after AcceptChanges was last called. This allows for the modified rows to easy be reviewed and validated before deciding to make the changes stick by calling AcceptChanges.

The following example populates a DataSet from a simple SELECT query:

```
Dim sqlConn As New SqlClient.SqlConnection _
("Server=MyServer; User ID=sa; Password=; Database=pubs")
Dim myDataSet As New DataSet()
Dim myDataTable As DataTable
Dim myDataRow As DataRow
Dim iLoop As Integer

Dim mySQLDA As New SqlDataAdapter("SELECT * FROM dbo.employee", sqlConn)
mySQLDA.Fill(myDataSet)
```

Next we modify the first three rows within this table to have different values:

```
myDataSet.Tables("table").Rows(0).Item("lname") = "Glucina"
myDataSet.Tables("table").Rows(0).Item("fname") = "Linda"
myDataSet.Tables("table").Rows(1).Item("lname") = "Major"
myDataSet.Tables("table").Rows(1).Item("fname") = "Laura"
myDataSet.Tables("table").Rows(2).Item("lname") = "Bain"
myDataSet.Tables("table").Rows(2).Item("fname") = "Stephanie"
```

Then we create a new DataSet and populate it from our original DataSet by calling the GetChanges method. Finally, we output all the rows within our new DataSet to the console window. As our new DataSet only contains the rows that had been modified within the original DataSet, just these three rows are outputted:

```
Dim myChangesDataSet As DataSet = myDataSet.GetChanges

For Each myDataRow In myChangesDataSet.Tables("table").Rows()
    For iLoop = 0 To myDataRow.Table.Columns.Count() - 1
        Console.Write(myDataRow.Item(iLoop))
        Console.Write(Chr(9))
    Next
        Console.WriteLine("")
Next
```

RejectChanges

RejectChanges is very similar to AcceptChanges in that it does not make changes to the data source. You would call this if you want all changes removed from the DataSet. This will return the data to the state it was in when it was retrieved, or when the last AcceptChanges took place.

If we add the following code to the end of our GetChanges example, above, we can see the effect RejectChanges will have. As shown in the previous example, after GetChanges was called our new DataSet was populated with our three modified rows. However, if we now call RejectChanges before the call to GetChanges:

```
    myDataSet.RejectChanges()
    Dim myChangesDataSet As DataSet = myDataSet.GetChanges

    For Each myDataRow In myChangesDataSet.Tables("table").Rows()
        For iLoop = 0 To myDataRow.Table.Columns.Count() - 1
            Console.Write(myDataRow.Item(iLoop))
            Console.Write(Chr(9))
        Next
            Console.WriteLine("")
    Next
```

our code will generate an exception because our new DataSet remains empty. This is as a result of all changes being undone by calling RejectChanges.

Reset

Reset is used to empty a DataSet of all objects from within its various collections. This is an easy way to purge a DataSet it you wish to use it with a new task that it wasn't previously used for.

This example populates a DataSet with a DataTable generated from a resultset retrieved from SQL Server. The first call to Tables.Count() returns the value 1, indicating one DataTable exists within the DataSet. After the Reset method has been called this returns 0 as all DataTables have been removed:

```
    Dim sqlConn As New SqlClient.SqlConnection("Server=MyServer;" _
                                             & "User ID=sa;" _
                                             & "Password=;Database=pubs")
    Dim myDataSet As New DataSet()

    Dim myDataAdapter As New SqlDataAdapter("SELECT * FROM employee", sqlConn)
    myDataAdapter.TableMappings.Add("Table", "employee")
    myDataAdapter.MissingSchemaAction = MissingSchemaAction.AddWithKey
    myDataAdapter.Fill(myDataSet)

    Console.WriteLine("# Tables : " & myDataSet.Tables.Count().ToString)
    myDataSet.Reset()
    Console.WriteLine("# Tables : " & myDataSet.Tables.Count().ToString)
```

Now we've looked at the DataSet itself, let's examine its component parts in more detail, beginning with DataTables.

DataTable Object

A DataTable is in essence a set of records returned from a query built from the SqlDataAdapter. If you have multiple sets of records, in other words you have more than one SELECT query passed in to the SelectCommand property, then you will have a collection of DataTables returned to you (which we cover later on). In this section of the chapter, we will concentrate on cases where only a single table is returned.

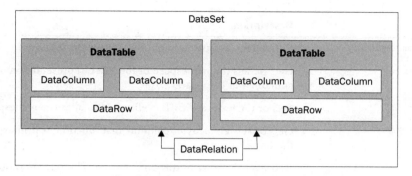

At this point we need to examine the properties and methods of the DataTable object. Once we have this completed, we can look at more complex examples.

Properties

Property	Description
CaseSensitive	A Boolean setting that can be altered and is used for functions within DataTables. A setting of True defines that all operations are case-sensitive. It defaults to the CaseSensitive property of the DataSet. If the DataTable has been created independently of a DataSet, then this will default to False.
ChildRelations	A collection of relations between this table and any child tables. We cover DataRelations later in this chapter.
Columns	A collection defining every column contained within this table. DataColumns are covered shortly in this chapter.
Constraints	Any constraints assigned to the table can be referenced through this collection. Constraints are also covered later in this chapter.
DataSet	Retrieves the DataSet object that is related to this table. This will be empty if the DataTable was created independently of a DataSet.
DefaultView	Returns a custom view of the data. Very similar to views within SQL Server. This property is discussed in further detail overleaf.
ExtendedProperties	A collection of additional properties assigned to the DataTable. More on this towards the end of this chapter.
HasErrors	Set to True if any row has an error. You cannot determine which row at this level.
Locale	Gets or sets the locale information used to compare strings within the table. Defaults to the Locale property of the DataSet.

Table continued on following page

Property	Description
MinimumCapacity	Either gets or sets the initial size for the DataTable.
Namespace	Gets or sets the namespace of the XML representation of the data contained in the DataTable.
Prefix	Sets or retrieves an XML prefix used to alias the namespace.
PrimaryKey	Gets or sets an array of columns that function as primary keys for the DataTable.
Rows	Retrieves the rows of this DataTable. The DataRow object is covered in our next main section.
Tablename	Gets or sets the name of this DataTable.

DefaultView

The DefaultView returns a DataView object containing the DataRows that exist within the DataTable. This DataView can then have criteria applied to restrict and customize what DataRows are returned.

The following example obtains the DataView object returned by the DefaultView property and uses this to apply a RowFilter that specifies that only return rows where the lname column begins with the letter A should be returned:

```
Dim sqlConn As New SqlClient.SqlConnection _
                ("Server=MyServer;User ID=sa;Password=;Database=pubs")
Dim myDataSet As New DataSet()
Dim iLoop As Integer

Dim myDataAdapter As New SqlDataAdapter("SELECT * FROM employee", sqlConn)
myDataAdapter.Fill(myDataSet)

Dim myDataView As DataView
Dim myDataRowView As DataRowView
myDataView = myDataSet.Tables("table").DefaultView
myDataView.RowFilter = "lname LIKE 'A%'"
```

When we cycle through the rows in the DataView, we only receive rows matching this criterion:

```
For Each myDataRowView In myDataView 'myDataSet.Tables("table").Rows()
    For iLoop = 0 To myDataView.Table.Columns.Count - 1
        Console.Write(myDataRowView.Item(iLoop))
        Console.Write(Chr(9))
    Next
        Console.WriteLine("")
Next
```

Having looked at the properties of the DataTable object, let's move on to examine its methods.

Methods

Method	Description
AcceptChanges	Inserts, modifies, or removes any changes made to every row within the DataTable that are pending since the last call to AcceptChanges.
BeginLoadData	Switches off all data constraints while loading data. This is discussed in further detail overleaf.
Clear	Clears the DataTable of any data by removing all rows in all tables.
Clone	Used to clone the structure (including all schemas and constraints) of one DataTable object within another DataTable object. No data is copied.
Copy	Similar to Clone but this will also copy the data.
EndLoadData	Following the loading of data, this will switch on all index maintenance and constraints. See overleaf for a further discussion of this method.
GetChanges	Gets a copy of the DataTable containing all changes made to it since it was last loaded, or since AcceptChanges was last called.
GetErrors	Retrieves DataRow objects containing errors.
ImportRow	Copies a DataRow into a DataTable, preserving any property settings, as well as original and current values. See later on for further discussion and an example.
LoadDataRow	Locates and updates a specific row. If no matching row is found, a new row is created using the given values. An example is included overleaf showing the use of this method.
NewRow	Creates a new row with the same schema as the table. This is discussed in further detail later on.
RejectChanges	Similar to a database rollback. This will undo all the changes made to the DataTable since it was created, or since the last time AcceptChanges was called.
Reset	Resets the DataTable to its original state.
Select	Retrieves an array of DataRow objects. Please see the further discussion and example later in the chapter.

You can create a DataTable within a DataSet in several different ways. First we can call the Add method of the DataSet.Table property:

```
Dim cDataSet As New DataSet()
cDataSet.Tables.Add("MyTable1")
```

Secondly we could define our DataTable object first and then subsequently add it to our DataSet object:

```
Dim cDataSet As New DataSet()
Dim cDataTable As New DataTable("MyTable1")
cDataSet.Tables.Add(cDataTable)
```

Or thirdly we can create a `DataTable` object by filling the `DataSet` from a SQL Server query:

```
Dim sqlConn As New SqlClient.SqlConnection _
                ("Server=MyServer;User ID=sa;Password=;Database=northwind")
Dim myDataSet As New DataSet()
Dim myDataTable As DataTable

Dim myDataAdapter1 As New SqlDataAdapter("SELECT * FROM Orders", sqlConn)
myDataAdapter1.TableMappings.Add("Table", "Orders")

myDataAdapter1.Fill(myDataSet)

myDataTable = myDataSet.Tables("Orders")
```

The `TableMappings.Add` method of the `SqlDataAdapter` object allows us to specify the table names that will be within the `DataSet` when it is filled from this SQL command.

BeginLoadData / EndLoadData / LoadDataRow

`BeginLoadData` provides a high-speed means of adding rows to a table by not checking constraints when the row is added. It disables constraints and index maintenance, allowing rows to be added without the constraints being checked. When the `EndLoadData` method is called, index updating and constraints are re-enabled. The constraints also validate the data contained within the `DataTable`; if any of the rows violate these constraints an exception is thrown at this point.

`LoadDataRow` can be used to add a row from any array of values. If a primary key constraint exists, it will first check to see if the row that it is attempting to load already exists within the table. If a matching row is found then this is updated, otherwise the row is inserted.

The following example uses `LoadDataRow` to inserted two rows within our `DataTable` while the constraints have been disabled using `BeginLoadData`:

```
Dim sqlConn As New SqlClient.SqlConnection _
                ("Server=MyServer;User ID=sa;Password=;Database=pubs")
Dim myDataSet As New DataSet()
Dim iLoop As Integer

Dim myDataAdapter As New SqlDataAdapter("SELECT * FROM employee", sqlConn)
myDataAdapter.TableMappings.Add("Table", "employee")
myDataAdapter.MissingSchemaAction = MissingSchemaAction.AddWithKey
myDataAdapter.Fill(myDataSet)

Dim MyValues(7) As Object

MyValues(0) = "GLU55555F"
MyValues(1) = "Linda"
MyValues(2) = "M"
```

```
    MyValues(3) = "Glucina"
    MyValues(4) = 1
    MyValues(5) = 10
    MyValues(6) = "0736"
    MyValues(7) = Now()

    myDataSet.Tables("employee").BeginLoadData()
    myDataSet.Tables("employee").LoadDataRow(MyValues, True)
    MyValues(1) = "Laura"
    MyValues(3) = "Major"
    myDataSet.Tables("employee").LoadDataRow(MyValues, True)
```

At this point no constraints have been checked, but the call to EndLoadData enables the constraints and checks that the data in the table conforms. If there are any constraint violations then an exception will be thrown at this point:

```
myDataSet.Tables("employee").EndLoadData()
```

```
Dim myDataRow As DataRow
For Each myDataRow In myDataSet.Tables("employee").Rows()
   For iLoop = 0 To myDataRow.Table.Columns.Count - 1
       Console.Write(myDataRow.Item(iLoop))
       Console.Write(Chr(9))
   Next
       Console.WriteLine("")
Next
```

NewRow / ImportRow

Both NewRow and ImportRow can be used to add a row to an existing DataTable. The difference is in the state and property settings assigned to the rows after they have been added.

NewRow will add the row and set the row state to Added. The row will also inherit the property settings of the DataTable in which it was added. ImportRow, on the other hand, will set the row state to that of the existing row that is being imported and also leave the property setting to the imported row's existing property settings.

This example shows the difference between these methods. Both are used to add a new row, from an existing row, to a DataSet:

```
    Dim sqlConn As New SqlClient.SqlConnection _
                   ("Server=MyServer;User ID=sa;Password=;Database=pubs")
    Dim myDataSet As New DataSet()

    Dim myDataAdapter As New SqlDataAdapter("SELECT * FROM employee", sqlConn)
    myDataAdapter.TableMappings.Add("Table", "employee")
    myDataAdapter.MissingSchemaAction = MissingSchemaAction.AddWithKey
    myDataAdapter.Fill(myDataSet)

    Dim myNewDataTable As DataTable = myDataSet.Tables("employee").Clone
    Dim myDataRow As DataRow
```

For the first row within our new `DataTable` we use the `ImportRow` method, for the second we use the `NewRow` method.

```
myNewDataTable.ImportRow(myDataSet.Tables("employee").Rows(0))
myDataRow = myNewDataTable.NewRow()
myDataRow.ItemArray = myDataSet.Tables("employee").Rows(1).ItemArray
myNewDataTable.Rows.Add(myDataRow)
```

Next we output the current `RowState` for each of these newly inserted rows. The row that we added using `NewRow` shows a current row state of `Added` and the row state of the row inserted using `ImportRow` shows as `Unchanged`:

```
Console.WriteLine("Row 0 state: " & myNewDataTable.Rows(0).RowState.ToString)
Console.WriteLine("Row 1 state: " & myNewDataTable.Rows(1).RowState.ToString)
```

Select

The `Select` method can be used to return an array of `DataRows` that match a specified selection criterion. This criterion may be a column predicate clause, or a request for rows of a particular row state such as `Added`.

Our example uses the `Select` method to return an array of `DataRows` in which the `lname` column begins with the letter `A`:

```
Dim sqlConn As New SqlClient.SqlConnection _
                ("Server=MyServer;User ID=sa;Password=;Database=pubs")
Dim myDataSet As New DataSet()
Dim iLoop As Integer

Dim myDataAdapter As New SqlDataAdapter("SELECT * FROM employee", sqlConn)
myDataAdapter.TableMappings.Add("Table", "employee")
myDataAdapter.MissingSchemaAction = MissingSchemaAction.AddWithKey
myDataAdapter.Fill(myDataSet)
```

```
Dim myDataRow As DataRow
Dim myDataRows As DataRow()

myDataRows = myDataSet.Tables("employee").Select("lname like 'A%'")
```

```
For Each myDataRow In myDataRows
    For iLoop = 0 To myDataRow.Table.Columns.Count - 1
        Console.Write(myDataRow.Item(iLoop))
        Console.Write(Chr(9))
    Next
    Console.WriteLine("")
Next
```

Moving down a level of granularity, let's now examine the `DataRow` object contained within a `DataTable`.

DataRow Object

In previous versions of ADO the records returned from a query were held in a `Recordset`. This `Recordset` was still connected to the data source and could be updated when running. A `DataRow` object is similar to a `Recordset` because it holds the data pertinent to a query, however this data is held in memory as a disconnected `recordset`, therefore any modifications to the data require further work.

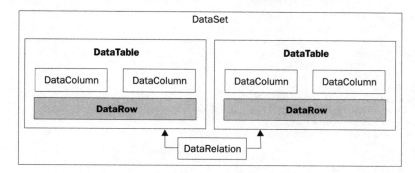

It is possible to check whether a row has errors and to then decide on an action to perform if errors are found. For example by checking the `HasErrors` property, you can then rollback the changes with `CancelEdit` or commit the changes with `EndEdit`. Let's take a closer look at these and other properties of the `DataRow` object now.

Properties

Property	Description
HasErrors	A Boolean value indicating if the row has any errors. If `True`, then we can use the `RowError` property to find out what the error is.
Item	Gets or sets data stored in a given column.
ItemArray	When building a row programmatically, we can assign an array to this property to set the columns. This property can also be used to return all the columns in a row as an array. Please see the further discussion below.
RowError	If `HasErrors` is set to `True`, then this property will have the details of the errors for the row.
RowState	Gets the current state of the row in terms of its relationship to the `DataRowCollection`. Discussed in more detail overleaf.
Table	Returns the `DataTable` object relating to the `DataRow`.

ItemArray

This property can be used to assign values to the columns in a particular `DataRow`. The values contained within the array are mapped to the `DataColumn` in the corresponding ordinal position within the `DataRow`. If you are inserting a row that contains an `AutoIncrement` column, or a column with a default value, then specifying a `NULL` reference in the array will cause the automatic values to be used.

The following example assigns the values for the columns in a soon-to-be-added row to an array before assigning the values within the array to the corresponding columns within the DataRow using the ItemArray property:

```
Dim cDataSet As New DataSet()
Dim cRow As DataRow
Dim rowValues(1) As Object

cDataSet.Tables.Add("myTable")
cDataSet.Tables("myTable").Columns.Add _
                ("IDCol", Type.GetType("System.Int32"))
cDataSet.Tables("myTable").Columns.Add _
                ("TextCol", Type.GetType("System.String"))

rowValues(0) = 1
rowValues(1) = "ABC"
cRow = cDataSet.Tables("myTable").NewRow
cRow.ItemArray = rowValues
cDataSet.Tables("myTable").Rows.Add(cRow)

rowValues(0) = 2
rowValues(1) = "DEF"
cRow = cDataSet.Tables("myTable").NewRow
cRow.ItemArray = rowValues
cDataSet.Tables("myTable").Rows.Add(cRow)
```

The ItemArray property can also be used in reverse to assign the values from all the DataColumns for a particular DataRow to an array. Adding the following code to our example above uses the ItemArray property to assign the columns within each row to the rowValues array before these are then outputted to the console:

```
For Each cRow In cDataSet.Tables("myTable").Rows()
    rowValues = cRow.ItemArray
    Console.Write(rowValues(0))
    Console.WriteLine(rowValues(1))
Next
```

RowState

When it comes to modifying the data within a table, whether this is removing, adding, or modifying a row, each row will have a property called RowState that will determine the state of the row in comparison to its original value. From this value it is possible to see what has occurred within that row.

We will see soon how to add rows to a DataTable object, but firstly we should note that there are two actions involved. The first action, NewRow, creates a DataRow item but does not add this to the DataRow collection. If you check the RowState property at this point, it will return a value of Detached. It is not until you call the Add method of the DataTable.Rows collection that the item is added to the collection and you will see Added.

Any row within the collection will initially have a RowState of Unchanged. As soon as any data is altered, this state will changed to Modified. A row removed will have a RowState of Deleted.

Let's now take a look at the methods of DataRow.

Methods

Method	Description
AcceptChanges	Inserts, modifies, or removes any changes made to this specific DataRow within the DataTable that are pending since the last AcceptChanges.
BeginEdit	You call this method to commence an edit a specific row.
CancelEdit	Cancels the edit that is in progress on the current row and returns the row to its original state.
ClearErrors	If the row has errors, then you can clear out those errors within this row.
Delete	Deletes the DataRow from the DataTable once AcceptChanges is called.
EndEdit	Used in conjunction with the BeginEdit function to complete the editing of the row.
GetChildRows	When a DataRelation exists, the GetChildRows method will return the child rows of the specified relationship for this row. See the discussion of DataRelations later in this chapter.
GetColumnError	Returns the error description for a column.
GetColumnInError	Returns an array of columns that contain errors.
GetParentRow	Gets the ParentRow for the data row using a specified DataRelation. See the discussion of DataRelations later in this chapter.
GetParentRows	Gets the ParentRows for the data row using a DataRelation. See the discussion of DataRelations later in this chapter.
HasVersion	Determines if the current RowVersion exists. See later for an explanation.
IsNull	Returns True if the specified column contains a NULL value.
RejectChanges	Undoes the changes that have been made and set the RowState property back to Unchanged.
SetColumnError	Sets the error description for the specified column.
SetParentRow	Sets a parent row for the DataRow.

RowVersion

While the columns within a row are being edited, the values of the column in the pre- and post- updated state are available by specifying the RowVersion. The following RowVersions may be available, depending on the current status of the modification to the DataRow:

RowVersion	Description
Current	The row's current values.
Default	The default row version, dependent on RowState.
Original	The original value of the row.
Proposed	The proposed value of the row.

The RowVersion is specified when using the Item property of a DataRow to retrieve the value of a column.

The following example shows adding a row to a DataTable, then updating the column in this row to a new value:

```
Dim cDataSet As New DataSet()
Dim cRow As DataRow
Dim rowValues(1) As Object

cDataSet.Tables.Add("myTable")
cDataSet.Tables("myTable").Columns.Add _
              ("IDCol", Type.GetType("System.Int32"))
cDataSet.Tables("myTable").Columns.Add _
              ("TextCol", Type.GetType("System.String"))

rowValues(0) = 1
rowValues(1) = "My text value"
cRow = cDataSet.Tables("myTable").NewRow
cRow.ItemArray = rowValues

cDataSet.Tables("myTable").Rows.Add(cRow)
cRow.AcceptChanges()
cRow(0) = 3
```

By accessing the column using a RowVersion we can determine both the current value, and the value of the column in this row before it was updated. The following code outputs 3, the current value, and 1, the previous value, to the console window:

```
Console.WriteLine(cRow(0, DataRowVersion.Original))
Console.WriteLine(cRow(0, DataRowVersion.Current))
```

HasVersion

As we mentioned above, some of the RowVersions are only available depending on the status of a modification to a row. An exception will be raised if you request a DataRow with a RowVersion that does not exist. Fortunately the HasVersion method can be used first to determine if a DataRow has a certain RowVersion before requesting it.

This example retrieves some rows from SQL Server, before proceeding to modify a row. At various stages during the modification process we output all the currently available RowVersions, determined using HasVersion:

```
Dim mySQLConn As New SqlConnection _
                    ("Server=MyServer;Database=pubs;User ID=sa;Password=;")
Dim myDataSet As New DataSet()
Dim iLoop As Integer

Dim mySQLDA As New SqlDataAdapter("SELECT * FROM dbo.employee", mySQLConn)

mySQLDA.MissingSchemaAction = MissingSchemaAction.Add
mySQLDA.AcceptChangesDuringFill = True
mySQLDA.Fill(myDataSet)

'Make changes to a row
Dim myDataRow As DataRow
```

Next we output the row versions before the edit begins:

```
myDataRow = myDataSet.Tables("table").Rows(0)
Console.WriteLine("Before Edit")
ShowColumnRowVersions(myDataRow, "lname")

myDataRow.BeginEdit()

myDataRow.Item("lname") = "Glucina"
Console.WriteLine("During edit, after column change")
ShowColumnRowVersions(myDataRow, "lname")
```

Then we output the RowVersions after the edit has taken place, but before the EndEdit method is called:

```
myDataRow.EndEdit()
Console.WriteLine("After EndEdit, before AcceptChanges")
ShowColumnRowVersions(myDataRow, "lname")
```

Now we output the RowVersions available after the EndEdit method has been called, but before AcceptChanges is called:

```
myDataRow.AcceptChanges()
Console.WriteLine("After AcceptChanges")
ShowColumnRowVersions(myDataRow, "lname")
```

Finally, we display the RowVersions available after the AcceptChanges method has been called. We use the following function to output the various RowVersions. Notice how HasVersion is used to request a particular version of a row only if it exists:

```
Private Sub ShowColumnRowVersions _
                    (ByVal DR As DataRow, ByVal ColName As String)
   If DR.HasVersion(DataRowVersion.Current) Then
      Console.WriteLine("Current: " & DR(ColName, DataRowVersion.Current))
   End If
   If DR.HasVersion(DataRowVersion.Default) Then
      Console.WriteLine("Default: " & DR(ColName, DataRowVersion.Default))
```

```
      End If
      If DR.HasVersion(DataRowVersion.Original) Then
          Console.WriteLine("Original: " & DR(ColName, DataRowVersion.Original))
      End If
      If DR.HasVersion(DataRowVersion.Proposed) Then
          Console.WriteLine("Proposed: " & DR(ColName, DataRowVersion.Proposed))
      End If
      Console.WriteLine("")
  End Sub
```

The above code will produce the following results:

Before BeginEdit has been called, the Current, Default, and Original RowVersions are available and they have the following values. The value Accorti is the column value before we updated it:

Current: Accorti
Default: Accorti
Original: Accorti

Next the result of the RowVersions after the modification has taken place. Notice how the default row version has changed to be the proposed value:

Current: Accorti
Default: Glucina
Original: Accorti
Proposed: Glucina

Next we view the various RowVersions after the EndEdit method has been called. The proposed RowVersion is no longer available as this is not the current RowVersion. The original value is still available, as this edit is not yet confirmed.

Current: Glucina
Default: Glucina
Original: Accorti

Finally, after a call has been made to AcceptChanges, the Current, Default, and Original RowVersions all reflect the modified value within our column:

Current: Glucina
Default: Glucina
Original: Glucina

The other component of a DataTable is the DataColumn, so we'll look at that next.

DataColumn Object

The DataColumn object is used to define the structure of the DataTable object. Every DataRow that is added to the DataTable must provide values for each of the columns that are presented within that DataTable.

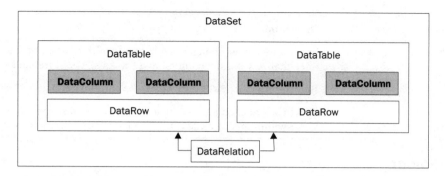

It is important to realize that column values within a row are not accessed through the `DataColumn` collection of a `DataTable` object. The `DataColumns` relate purely to structure and individual row values are accessed through the `DataRow.Item` property.

Properties

Property	Description
AllowDBNull	Specifies if NULL values are allowed within this column.
AutoIncrement	Specifies that an auto-incremented number should be generated in this column after every new row containing it is created. This is equivalent to an Identity column in SQL Server. This property is discussed in further detail overleaf.
AutoIncrementSeed	Specifies the initial value of the incrementing column.
AutoIncrementStep	Specifies the value by which the column will increment after each new row is created.
ColumnName	The name of the column.
DataType	Specifies the data type of the column. See later for a discussion of the values this can take.
DefaultValue	A column may have a default value property specified. If no value is explicitly specified for this column when a row is inserted, the default value will be used.
Expression	Used to create a calculated or aggregated column. See the example given later in the chapter.
MaxLength	The maximum number of characters allowed in a text column.
Ordinal	Returns the ordinal position of the DataColumn within a DataColumnCollection.

Table continued on following page

Property	Description
ReadOnly	Specifies whether changes can be made to this column for a row, once that row has been added to a DataTable. More later on.
Table	Returns the DataTable to which the column belongs.
Unique	Specifies that each row within a DataTable must contain a unique value within this DataColumn. See later for further information.

AutoIncrement

The AutoIncrement property allows a column to be incremented automatically after every row containing this DataColumn is inserted. The AutoIncrementSeed and AutoIncrementStep properties are used in conjunction with AutoIncrement to customize how the incrementing occurs.

Our example here defines a DataTable having an automatically incrementing column (IDCol). We specify the AutoIncrementStep as being 10, which means every time a row is inserted 10 will be added to the value that was last inserted:

```
Dim cDataSet As New DataSet()
Dim cRow As DataRow
Dim cCol As DataColumn

cDataSet.Tables.Add("myTable")

cCol = cDataSet.Tables("myTable").Columns.Add _
                    ("IDCol", Type.GetType("System.Int32"))
cCol.AutoIncrement = True
cCol.AutoIncrementSeed = 1
cCol.AutoIncrementStep = 10

cCol = cDataSet.Tables("myTable").Columns.Add _
                    ("TextCol", Type.GetType("System.String"))


cRow = cDataSet.Tables("myTable").NewRow
cRow.Item("TextCol") = "Row1"
cDataSet.Tables("myTable").Rows.Add(cRow)

cRow = cDataSet.Tables("myTable").NewRow
cRow.Item("TextCol") = "Row2"
cDataSet.Tables("myTable").Rows.Add(cRow)

cRow = cDataSet.Tables("myTable").NewRow
cRow.Item("TextCol") = "Row3"
cDataSet.Tables("myTable").Rows.Add(cRow)

For Each cRow In cDataSet.Tables("myTable").Rows()
   Console.Write(cRow.Item("IDCol") & ", ")
   Console.WriteLine(cRow.Item("TextCol"))
Next
```

This code produces the following output to the console in VS.NET. The first value is the automatically incremented IDCol followed by our TextCol column:

```
1, Row1
11, Row2
21, Row3
```

Unlike identity columns within SQL Server, you can insert an explicit value into a DataColumn defined as AutoIncrement. If you do this the value of the AutoIncrementSeed is automatically updated to be the maximum value contained with the DataColumn for a given DataTable, plus the AutoIncrementStep. For example the following code explicitly specifies a value for the IDCol on the second row being added:

```
Dim cDataSet As New DataSet()
Dim cRow As DataRow
Dim cCol As DataColumn

cDataSet.Tables.Add("myTable")

cCol = cDataSet.Tables("myTable").Columns.Add _
                    ("IDCol", Type.GetType("System.Int32"))
cCol.AutoIncrement = True
cCol.AutoIncrementSeed = 1
cCol.AutoIncrementStep = 10

cCol = cDataSet.Tables("myTable").Columns.Add _
                    ("TextCol", Type.GetType("System.String"))


cRow = cDataSet.Tables("myTable").NewRow
cRow.Item("TextCol") = "Row1"
cDataSet.Tables("myTable").Rows.Add(cRow)

cRow = cDataSet.Tables("myTable").NewRow
cRow.Item("IDCol") = 110
cRow.Item("TextCol") = "Row2"
cDataSet.Tables("myTable").Rows.Add(cRow)

cRow = cDataSet.Tables("myTable").NewRow
cRow.Item("TextCol") = "Row3"
cDataSet.Tables("myTable").Rows.Add(cRow)

For Each cRow In cDataSet.Tables("myTable").Rows()
   Console.Write(cRow.Item("IDCol") & ", ")
   Console.WriteLine(cRow.Item("TextCol"))
Next
```

This results in the following values being inserted into the DataColumns for the DataTable:

```
1, Row1
110, Row2
120, Row3
```

DataType

The `DataType` property specifies the data type for the `DataColumn` and can be set to one of the following values:

Data Type	Description
Boolean	Can be set to either True or False.
Byte	An unsigned integer between 0 and 255.
Char	A single Unicode character.
DateTime	A date and time combination that can be in the range 00:00:00 01-Jan-0001 to 11:59:59 31-Dec-9999.
Decimal	A decimal number in the range of -2^{96} to 2^{96}. It is an approximate numeric data type as the fractional portion of the number may be rounded to a lesser number of decimal places.
Double	Double precision 64-bit number.
Int16	Integer values from -32768 to 32768.
Int32	Integer values from -2,147,483,647 to 2,147,483,647.
Int64	Integer values from -9,223,372,036,854,775,808 to 9,223,372,036,854,775,808.
SByte	Signed integer from -128 to 127.
Single	Single precision 32-bit number.
String	A series of characters.
TimeSpan	Measure of time elapsed between two DateTimes. Stored in ticks, and represented in the following format "days:hours:minutes:seconds".
UInt16	Unsigned integer from 0 to 65535.
UInt32	Unsigned integer from 0 to 4,294,967,295.
UInt64	Unsigned integer from 0 to 184,467,440,737,095,551,615.

Expression

`Expression` allows for computed columns, or aggregate columns, to be added to a `DataTable` and used in the same way as an ordinary column that contains a value.

The following code shows an `Expression` being used to create a `FullName` column within our `DataTable`. This `FullName` column contains no data itself, but instead it is calculated by concatenating the `fname`, `minit`, and `lname` columns that are specified in the `Expression` property:

```
Dim mySQLConn As New SqlConnection _
                ("Server=MyServer;Database=pubs; User ID=sa;Password=;")
Dim myDataSet As New DataSet()
Dim iLoop As Integer
```

```
Dim mySQLDA As New SqlDataAdapter("SELECT * FROM dbo.employee", mySQLConn)
mySQLDA.TableMappings.Add("Table", "employee")
mySQLDA.Fill(myDataSet)

Dim myCol As New DataColumn()
myCol.DataType = Type.GetType("System.String")
myCol.ColumnName = "FullName"
myCol.Expression = ("fname + ' ' + minit +' '+lname")

myDataSet.Tables("employee").Columns.Add(myCol)

Dim myDataRow
For Each myDataRow In myDataSet.Tables("employee").Rows()
   Console.Write(myDataRow.Item("emp_id"))
   Console.Write(Chr(9))
   Console.WriteLine(myDataRow.Item("FullName"))
Next
```

The next example performs a similar query, except this time the calculated column uses an aggregate function to determine the maximum value of the price column within the table, and subtracts the price column from the current row to get the MaxPriceDiff column:

```
Dim mySQLConn As New SqlConnection _
                  ("Server=MyServer; Database=pubs; User ID=sa;Password;")
Dim myDataSet As New DataSet()
Dim iLoop As Integer

Dim mySQLDA As New SqlDataAdapter("SELECT * FROM dbo.titles", mySQLConn)
mySQLDA.TableMappings.Add("Table", "titles")
mySQLDA.Fill(myDataSet)

Dim myCol As New DataColumn()
myCol.DataType = Type.GetType("System.Decimal")
myCol.ColumnName = "maxpricediff"
myCol.Expression = ("MAX(price) - price")

myDataSet.Tables("titles").Columns.Add(myCol)

Dim myDataRow
For Each myDataRow In myDataSet.Tables("titles").Rows()
   Console.Write(myDataRow.Item("title_id"))
   Console.Write(Chr(9))
   Console.Write(myDataRow.Item("title"))
   Console.Write(Chr(9))
   Console.Write(myDataRow.Item("price"))
   Console.Write(Chr(9))
   Console.WriteLine(myDataRow.Item("maxpricediff"))
Next
```

ReadOnly

The ReadOnly property specifies that the column value cannot be changed after the DataRow has been added to a DataTable.

The following example demonstrates the use of ReadOnly. We create a DataSet containing a DataTable and add a ReadOnly DataColumn to this DataTable:

```
Dim cDataSet As New DataSet()
Dim cRow As DataRow
Dim cCol As DataColumn

cDataSet.Tables.Add("myTable")

cCol = cDataSet.Tables("myTable").Columns.Add _
                     ("IDCol", Type.GetType("System.Int32"))
cCol.ReadOnly = True
```

Next we add a new DataRow to our table:

```
cRow = cDataSet.Tables("myTable").NewRow
cRow.Item("IDCol") = 1
cDataSet.Tables("myTable").Rows.Add(cRow)
```

Finally, we attempt to update the value contained within our DataColumn within this DataRow. As this is prevented by the ReadOnly property an exception is raised:

```
' Throws an exception
cDataSet.Tables("myTable").Rows(0).Item("IDCol") = 2
```

Unique

A Unique DataColumn prevents more than one DataRow having the same value contained in the column for a given DataTable. An attempt to add a DataRow with a column that violates this Unique restriction, will result in an exception been thrown.

In our example, we create a DataTable within our DataSet, this time defining our column as Unique:

```
Dim cDataSet As New DataSet()
Dim cRow As DataRow
Dim cCol As DataColumn

cDataSet.Tables.Add("myTable")

cCol = cDataSet.Tables("myTable").Columns.Add _
                     ("IDCol", Type.GetType("System.Int32"))
cCol.Unique = True
```

The first two DataRows are added successfully because they both contain unique values within our DataColumn:

```
cRow = cDataSet.Tables("myTable").NewRow
cRow.Item("IDCol") = 1
cDataSet.Tables("myTable").Rows.Add(cRow)
```

```
cRow = cDataSet.Tables("myTable").NewRow
cRow.Item("IDCol") = 2
cDataSet.Tables("myTable").Rows.Add(cRow)
```

However the third attempt to add a `DataRow` fails as there is already an existing row containing the same value for this `DataColumn`:

```
' Throws an exception
cRow = cDataSet.Tables("myTable").NewRow
cRow.Item("IDCol") = 1
cDataSet.Tables("myTable").Rows.Add(cRow)
```

Finally, in our examination of the components of the `DataSet` object, we need to understand the `DataRelation`, which provides us with a means of creating relationships between our `DataTables`.

DataRelation

As we have previously mentioned, a `DataSet` can be thought of as an in-memory copy of a database. There is one major difference, however. While the `DataTable` objects will reflect the structure of the underlying database tables, relationships between `DataTables` will not be implicitly established from database referential integrity constraints when they are populated using the `Fill` method. You can use `DataRelations` to create the relationships between `DataSet` `DataTables` thereby protecting data integrity while located in the `DataSet`, as well as allowing for changes to be cascaded to child `DataTables`.

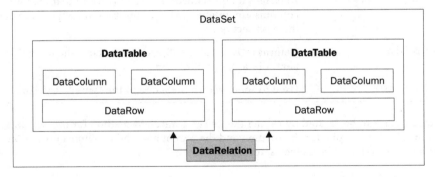

`DataRelations` differ from foreign key constraints defined at the database level, as they allow you to create relationships between `DataTables` that may have originated from many independent data sources. This allows you to ensure referential integrity of the data while it is within the `DataSet`, even when your application is working with data sources that, at the database level, have no such constraints.

Properties

Property	Description
ChildColumns	Returns an array of DataColumn objects, which make up the child columns of the relation. The child columns are columns contained within the table that has been specified as the child table for a DataRelation.
ChildKeyConstraint	Returns a ForeignKeyConstraint object that represents the foreign key for the DataRelation. The ForeignKeyConstraint object is detailed in the next section.
ChildTable	Returns a DataTable object containing the table that is the child in a DataRelation.
DataSet	Returns the DataSet that the DataRelation belongs to. All tables used within the DataRelation must also be contained in this DataSet because a DataRelation cannot span DataSets.
ExtendedProperties	Stores custom information about the DataRelation. We will discuss this in more detail shortly.
Nested	When set to True the child relations are nested within their parents when the DataSet is exposed as XML.
ParentColumns	Returns an array of DataColumn objects, which make up the parent columns of the DataRelation.
ParentKeyConstraint	Returns a unique constraint used to ensure that the parent columns are unique. UniqueConstraint objects are detailed in the next section.
ParentTable	Returns a DataTable object that contains the table that is the parent in a DataRelation.
RelationName	Used to set or return the name of the DataRelation.

A DataRelation can be created by calling the Relations.Add method for the DataSet. Using this method you specify the name for the relation and the parent and child columns for the DataRelation in the form of two DataColumn objects, for example:

```
Dim ConnString As String = _
     "Server=MyServer; User ID=sa;Password=;Database=Northwind"

Dim sqlcmd As New SqlClient.SqlCommand()
Dim sqlConn As New SqlClient.SqlConnection(ConnString)

Dim myDataAdapter1 As New SqlDataAdapter("SELECT * FROM Employees", sqlConn)

myDataAdapter1.TableMappings.Add("Table", "Employees")

Dim myDataAdapter2 As New SqlDataAdapter _
```

```
                          ("SELECT * FROM Orders", sqlConn)

myDataAdapter2.TableMappings.Add("Table", "Orders")

Dim myDataSet As New DataSet()

myDataAdapter1.Fill(myDataSet)
myDataAdapter2.Fill(myDataSet)

Dim myParentColumns As DataColumn = _
                    myDataSet.Tables("Employees").Columns("EmployeeID")
Dim myChildColumns As DataColumn = _
                    myDataSet.Tables("Orders").Columns("EmployeeID")

myDataSet.Relations.Add("FK_Departments", myParentColumns, myChildColumns)
```

In this code you can see we have created two `DataColumn` objects, one for the column that is the parent key and one for the column that is the child key in the relationship. If we were using multi-key columns, we would create an array of `DataColumn` objects and specify these when creating the `DataRelation`, for example:

```
Dim cDataSet As New DataSet()

Dim cCol(1) As DataColumn
cDataSet.Tables.Add("mypktable")
cCol(0) = cDataSet.Tables("mypktable").Columns.Add _
                        ("col1", System.Type.GetType("System.Int32"))
cCol(1) = cDataSet.Tables("mypktable").Columns.Add _
                        ("col2", System.Type.GetType("System.Int32"))

Dim cCol2(1) As DataColumn
cDataSet.Tables.Add("myfktable")
cCol2(0) = cDataSet.Tables("myfktable").Columns.Add _
                        ("col1", System.Type.GetType("System.Int32"))
cCol2(1) = cDataSet.Tables("myfktable").Columns.Add _
                        ("col2", System.Type.GetType("System.Int32"))

cDataSet.Relations.Add("MyRelation", cCol, cCol2)
```

Using DataRelations

You cannot explicitly join tables within the `DataSet` using the `DataRelation` object. Instead you can call the `GetChildRows` or `GetParentRows` methods of the `DataRow` object to return the related rows. This differs from the typical use of relationships in SQL Server, where you would normally use a join to return the related rows within a single resultset. For example:

```
Dim ChildRows() as DataRow
ChildRows = MyParentTable.Rows(0).GetChildRows("MyFKConstraint")
```

In this example the call to `GetChildRows` will return a collection of `DataRows`. This collection consists of all the rows from the child table in the foreign key relationship that are related to the first row, `Rows(0)`, within our parent table.

81

Lastly, we need to examine how we can use constraints to maintain the integrity of the data we hold in our DataSets.

Constraints

In order for the DataRelation to maintain data integrity between DataTables, a constraint is created to protect the relationship between the parent and child DataColumns, so long as the EnforceConstraints property of the DataSet object is set to True. If this is set to False then constraints will exist but they will be ignored.

This constraint is implemented as a UniqueConstraint constraint for ParentRelation tables and as a ForeignKey constraint for child tables. These constraints will be generated when you create the relationship or they can be created independently of the DataRelation object to enforce non-referential integrity, such as a unique constraint on a candidate key.

UniqueConstraint

A UniqueConstraint stipulates that every row must contain a different value in the column, or set of columns, it refers to.

UniqueConstraint has the following properties:

Properties	Description
Columns	An array of columns that are used to form the constraint.
ConstraintName	The name of the constraint.
ExtendedProperties	Used to hold custom information. See later in this chapter for further explanation and examples.
IsPrimaryKey	Value that when True, specifies that this UniqueConstraint is the primary key for the table.
Table	Table to which the constraint belongs.

The following example demonstrates the use of UniqueConstraint by creating a table with a single column and creating a unique constraint on this column:

```
Dim cDataSet As New DataSet()
Dim cTable1 As New DataTable("mytable")

Dim cCol As New DataColumn("col1", System.Type.GetType("System.Int32"))
cTable1.Columns.Add(cCol)
cDataSet.Tables.Add(cTable1)

cDataSet.Tables("mytable").Constraints.Add("CandidateKey", cCol, False)

Dim MyArray(0) As Object
MyArray(0) = 1

cDataSet.Tables("mytable").Rows.Add(MyArray)
```

The initial insert will work as expected as this is the only row within the table so far, however any subsequent attempts to insert a row with the same value contained in the unique constraint column, such as:

```
cDataSet.Tables("mytable").Rows.Add(MyArray)
```

will result in a System.Data.ConstraintException being thrown. We can also see how setting the EnforceConstraints property of the DataSet object to False, disables constraint checking, as rerunning the code with this change:

```
Dim cDataSet As New DataSet()
Dim cTable1 As New DataTable("mytable")

Dim cCol As New DataColumn("col1", System.Type.GetType("System.Int32"))
cTable1.Columns.Add(cCol)
cDataSet.Tables.Add(cTable1)

cDataSet.Tables("mytable").Constraints.Add("CandidateKey", cCol, False)

Dim MyArray(0) As Object
MyArray(0) = 1
```

```
cDataSet.EnforceConstraints = False
```

```
cDataSet.Tables("mytable").Rows.Add(MyArray)
cDataSet.Tables("mytable").Rows.Add(MyArray)
```

will execute fine without throwing an exception. As we mentioned in the DataSet *Properties* section previously, if you disable constraint checking and insert rows that violate constraints you will not be able to set EnforceConstraints back to True until these constraints' violations have been manually resolved. Doing so will only result in a System.Data.ConstraintException exception being thrown.

ForeignKeyConstraint

A ForeignKeyConstraint should be created when the value of a column in a row in one table must exist as a value of a column, in a row, in another table. Enforcing this type of constraint ensures that errors in application logic will not result in data being inserted into one table that is dependent on a non-existent row within another table.

The properties of ForeignKeyConstraint are:

Properties	Description
AcceptRejectRule	Affects how a constraint behaves when AcceptChanges is invoked.
Columns	The child columns for this constraint.
ConstraintName	The name of the ForeignKeyConstraint.
DeleteRule	How the constraint behaves when a row is deleted in the parent table.

Table continued on following page

Properties	Description
RelatedColumns	The columns in the parent table to which this constraint relates.
RelatedTable	The parent table for which this constraint is applied.
Table	The child table of this constraint.
UpdateRule	How the constraint behaves when a row is updated in the parent table.

The AcceptRejectRule can be set to the following values:

❑ None – No action occurs. This is the default.

❑ Cascade – Changes are cascaded across the relationship.

The AcceptRejectRule affects whether or not the AcceptChanges or RejectChanges methods are also applied to the child table when applied to the parent table. Remember, when a row is changed its state becomes Added, Modified, or Deleted until the Accept(Reject)Changes method is called, at which point the state reverts to Unchanged. The AcceptRejectRule defaults to None, so a call to accept or reject changes in the parent table won't automatically call the accept or reject for the child table.

> Note: if you cascade updates from a parent to a child table, and you're not automatically cascading **AcceptReject** changes, make sure you don't get into the situation where you accept the changes for the parent table and reject them for the child table. Doing so will result in a constraint violation exception being thrown.

The DeleteRule and UpdateRule can be set to one of the following values:

❑ None – No action occurs on related rows.

❑ Cascade – The changes are cascaded from the parent to the child tables. This is the default.

❑ SetDefault – Sets the values in the related rows to their default value.

❑ SetNull – Sets the values in the related rows to NULL.

DeleteRule and UpdateRule dictate how the relation will apply changes made in the parent table to the child table. The default is to cascade the changes from the parent to the child, which is usually appropriate when replicating the primary / foreign key constraints held with SQL Server. However the DataRelation also supports the SetDefault and SetNull actions that are not possible with SQL Server constraints.

Using Foreign Key Constraints

As with the UniqueConstraint, a foreign key constraint will automatically be created to enforce the integrity of any data relations you may define. We can highlight this by reusing the code we used earlier to create our DataRelation, and displaying the constraints that exist after the DataRelation is created:

```
Dim ConnString As String = _
        "Server=MyServer;User ID=sa;Password=;Database=Northwind"
Dim sqlcmd As New SqlClient.SqlCommand()
Dim sqlConn As New SqlClient.SqlConnection(ConnString)

Dim myDataAdapter1 As New SqlDataAdapter("SELECT * FROM Employees", sqlConn)
myDataAdapter1.TableMappings.Add("Table", "Employees")

Dim myDataAdapter2 As New SqlDataAdapter _
                        ("SELECT * FROM Orders", sqlConn)
myDataAdapter2.TableMappings.Add("Table", "Orders")

Dim myDataSet As New DataSet()
myDataAdapter1.Fill(myDataSet)
myDataAdapter2.Fill(myDataSet)

Dim myParentColumns As DataColumn = _
                    myDataSet.Tables("Employees").Columns("EmployeeID")

Dim myChildColumns As DataColumn = _
                    myDataSet.Tables("Orders").Columns("EmployeeID")

myDataSet.Relations.Add("FK_Departments", myParentColumns, myChildColumns)
```

```
Console.Write _
        (myDataSet.Tables("Employees").Constraints(0).ConstraintName() + " ")

Console.WriteLine(myDataSet.Tables("Employees").Constraints(0).GetType)

Console.Write _
    (myDataSet.Tables("Departments").Constraints(0).ConstraintName() + " ")

Console.WriteLine(myDataSet.Tables("Departments").Constraints(0).GetType)
```

When we run this code we see that two constraints have now been created on our tables. The first is named FK_Departments and is of the type ForeignKeyConstraint and the second is named Constraint1 as is of the type UnqiueConstraint.

As with the UniqueConstraint, ForeignKeyConstraints can be created manually, for example:

```
Dim cDataSet As New DataSet()
Dim cTable1 As New DataTable("mytable")

Dim cCol As New DataColumn("col1", System.Type.GetType("System.Int32"))
cTable1.Columns.Add(cCol)
cDataSet.Tables.Add(cTable1)

cDataSet.Tables("mytable").Constraints.Add("CandidateKey", cCol, False)

Dim MyArray(0) As Object
MyArray(0) = 1

cDataSet.Tables("mytable").Rows.Add(MyArray)
```

```
Dim cCol2 As DataColumn
cDataSet.Tables.Add("myfktable")
cDataSet.Tables("myfktable").Columns.Add _
              ("col1", System.Type.GetType("System.Int32"))
cCol2 = cDataSet.Tables("myfktable").Columns("col1")
cDataSet.Tables("myfktable").Constraints.Add("FK_MyFK1", cCol, cCol2)
```

While the constraints will be enforced when manually created using the method above, no corresponding DataRelation object is created. This can be seen if we count the number of DataRelations within our DataSet using:

```
Console.Writeline(cDataSet.Relations.Count) ' Returns 0
```

While the integrity of the data is maintained without the DataRelation object, you will not be able to navigate between tables using the relations collection for the DataSet, or the ChildRelations and ParentRelations properties of the data tables.

ExtendedProperties Property

There may be times with a DataSet, DataTable, or DataRelation that you wish to hold extra information that is not defined as a property within the DataSet object itself.

The ExtendedProperties property can be used to hold information such as a record of the number of times the DataSet has been used, or perhaps a description of the data that the DataSet is holding. There is no limit to what can be stored as long as it can be kept as a String data type. If you wish to store a numeric value, then it has to be converted to a string prior to storing within the property. Retrieval of the value does allow a reverse conversion back to the original data type and can be performed with the inbuilt data conversion functions, such as Val.

The ExtendedProperties property collection is a very useful addition to the assigned objects that will allow such information to be held as a String data type. To use this is very simple indeed and a code example is detailed below.

```
myDataSet.ExtendedProperties.Add("Description", _
                "This data set details the Employees records")
```

Each Add statement will add a new extended property to the collection built. It is then a simple matter to retrieve the item from the collection as demonstrated below. The example returns the value using the ToString method. To return a numeric value, you would surround the whole right-hand side of the argument with the Val function.

```
aString = myDataSet.ExtendedProperties("Description").ToString()
```

Summary

In this chapter we have taken a whistle-stop tour of the `SqlClient` namespace. We have discussed not only how to open a connection to a SQL Server instance, but also how to retrieve and manipulate data from the database itself. We have considered the nature of the `DataSet` object, which contains our data, and how we can make use of its component parts.

We looked at how `DataSet`, `DataTable`, `DataRow`, and `DataColumn` objects relate to one another, and how referential integrity constraints within the database can be enforced in the data retrieved in each `DataSet` object.

In the next chapter we will look at a sample application, where we put to use many of the objects, and their associated properties and methods, discussed here.

3

HR Sample Application

In this chapter we'll create and populate the database that we will use throughout the rest of this book. We'll also create a Windows Form application, which we can use to verify that our database is working as we wish it to. This application gives us a chance to illustrate the use of a number of the data objects that we discussed in the previous chapter.

All the code discussed in this chapter is available for download at www.wrox.com.

The HumanResources Database

No doubt like many developers, you will have seen `Northwind` and `Pubs` and the examples associated with these two databases. To compliment these we are going to build a new example surrounding a database you might find in a Human Resources department. This is not a complex example and will in fact only hold a few tables.

It is not the intention of this book to discuss areas such as normalization or database design techniques, since these are covered in more detail in titles such as *'Professional SQL Server 2000 Database Design'* (*Wrox Press, ISBN 1861004761*). What we will do here is concentrate purely on working with **VB.NET** and SQL Server, focusing on the T-SQL code required to build the database solution, and the **VB.NET** code we'll use to create our Windows Form application.

The database is designed so as to hold the following details about employees:

❑   Which departments they have worked in

❑   The salary payments they have received

❑   Any other payments they have received

❑   Any courses that they have attended

A diagram of the database structure can be seen in the figure below, which includes the relationships between the various tables.

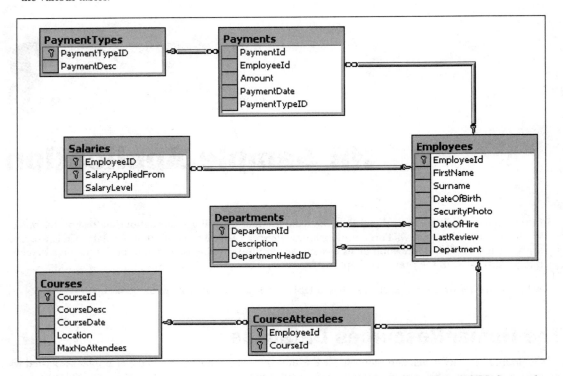

Note that if you wish to create your database data files in a location other than the default SQL Server data directory, you will need to specify the FILENAME parameter as part of the CREATE DATABASE command. You should consult SQL Server Books Online for more information on using CREATE DATABASE with the FILENAME parameters.

To create the database, open **SQL Server Query Analyzer** and connect with a login that has the system administrator (or the CREATE DATABASE) privilege.

For more information on these privileges see Chapter 11 later in this book.

Now you can either enter the following code section by section and execute it, or enter all the code sections and execute it once at the end.

```
CREATE DATABASE [HumanResources]
GO
```

If no errors are encountered, then a new empty database will have been created within SQL Server and you will see something like the following in the query pane:

The CREATE DATABASE process is allocating 0.63 MB on disk 'HumanResources'.
The CREATE DATABASE process is allocating 0.49 MB on disk 'HumanResources_log'.

You could also use the Wizard in SQL Server Enterprise Manager to create the database. To access the **Create Database Wizard** connect to the server on which you wish to create the new database using SQL Server Enterprise Manager, select the **Tools | Wizards** menu item and choose **Create Database Wizard**, as shown in the following diagram:

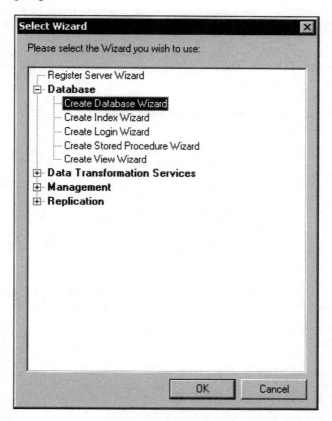

Having created the database, let's now take a look at the T-SQL code we'll use to insert the required tables, including the appropriate keys and relationships. Some of the tables have a PRIMARY KEY column that specifies an IDENTITY property, which has a starting point of 1 and is incremented by 1. Other tables without the IDENTITY property will either have the primary key values generated manually by our application, or have this inherited from a foreign key relationship.

The tables we'll create here can be summarized as follows:

- ❑ Departments – the name of departments within the organization and a link to the Employees table detailing which employee is the department head.

- ❑ Employees – a list of employees and their essential details.

- ❑ Salaries – a history of employees' salaries, including when salary increases were applied.

- ❑ Courses – holds the description of each of the courses, as well as details regarding when and where the course is being held, and the maximum class size for students.

❑   CourseAttendees – contains an ID for each of the courses held, and the EmployeeID of the attendees at each course.

❑   PaymentTypes – for holding details of all the different types of payments.

❑   Payments – every payment each employee has received, when, how much, and what type of payment (for example salary, bonus), is held in this table.

Now let's start running the T-SQL to create these tables. As I mentioned above you can either create all of these tables individually or all at once in a single batch. Connect to your SQL Server using SQL Server Query Analyzer and run the following code:

```sql
-- Use our newly created HumanResources database
USE  [HumanResources]
GO


-- First we create our departments table used for storing
-- a list of departments within our database

CREATE TABLE dbo.Departments (
   DepartmentId   int      NOT NULL
   IDENTITY (1, 1) PRIMARY KEY,

   Description   varchar(256) NOT NULL
)


-- Next we create our Employees table. This is the core table of
-- our database and will contain a list of the organization's employees

CREATE TABLE dbo.Employees (

   EmployeeId   int      NOT NULL
   IDENTITY (1, 1) PRIMARY KEY,

   FirstName   varchar(30)   NOT NULL ,

   Surname   varchar(30)   NOT NULL ,

   DateOfBirth   smalldatetime NOT NULL
   -- The check constraint ensures that the employee is
   -- over 15 years old but younger than 100 years old.

   CHECK(   DateOfBirth > DateAdd(yy,-100,getdate())
      AND   DateOfBirth < DateAdd(yy,-15,getdate()) ),

   SecurityPhoto   image      NULL ,

   DateOfHire   smalldatetime NOT NULL
   -- The check constraint ensures that the employee
   -- was hired in the last 100 years or is intended to
   -- be hired in the next five years.

   CHECK(   DateOfHire>DateAdd(yy,-100,getdate())
      AND   DateOfHire<DateAdd(yy,5,getdate()) ),
```

```
    LastReview   smalldatetime NOT NULL ,
    -- This check constraint ensures that the employee's last
    -- review was in the previous 10 years and not in the future

    CHECK(   LastReview>DateAdd(yy,-10,getdate())
      AND    LastReview<=getdate() ),

    Department   int      NOT NULL
    REFERENCES Departments(DepartmentID)
)
GO

-- Next we create the Salaries table. This is used to store
-- the salary records, current and historical, for the employees

CREATE TABLE dbo.Salaries (

    EmployeeID   int      NOT NULL
    REFERENCES Employees(EmployeeID),

    SalaryAppliedFrom smalldatetime NOT NULL ,
    -- The check constraint ensures that the salary was applied
    -- within the last 100 years, but is not scheduled to be
    -- applied more than 1 year into the future.

    CHECK(   SalaryAppliedFrom>DateAdd(yy,-100,getdate())
      AND    SalaryAppliedFrom<=DateAdd(yy,1,getdate()) ),

    SalaryLevel   money       NOT NULL,
    -- The check constraint ensures that the Salary is more than 0
    -- but less than 10000000

    CHECK(   SalaryLevel>0
      AND    SalaryLevel<10000000 ),

    PRIMARY KEY(EmployeeID, SalaryAppliedFrom)
)

-- Now we create the Courses tables. This contains training courses
-- available for our employees.

CREATE TABLE dbo.Courses (
    CourseId   int          NOT NULL
    IDENTITY (1, 1) PRIMARY KEY,

    CourseDesc   varchar(50)   NOT NULL ,

    CourseDate   smalldatetime NOT NULL
    -- The check constraint ensures the Course is scheduled for
    -- sometime in the next five years

    CHECK( CourseDate<=DateAdd(yy,5,getdate()) ),
```

```
    Location    varchar(100)    NOT NULL ,

    MaxNoAttendees int       NOT NULL
    -- The Check constraint ensures that the maximum number of
    -- attendees on the course is at least 1.

    CHECK (MaxNoAttendees>0)
)

-- Next we create our CourseAttendees table. This associates an
-- Employee with a specific course that they are attending.

CREATE TABLE dbo.CourseAttendees (
    EmployeeId    int       NOT NULL
    REFERENCES Employees(EmployeeID),

    CourseId     int        NOT NULL
    REFERENCES Courses(CourseID),

    PRIMARY KEY (EmployeeID,CourseID)
)


-- Our PaymentTypes table contains a list of different types of
-- payments that can be made to employees

CREATE TABLE dbo.PaymentTypes (
    PaymentTypeID    tinyint    NOT NULL
    IDENTITY (1, 1) PRIMARY KEY,

    PaymentDesc    varchar(30) NOT NULL
)
GO

-- Our final table created is Payments. This table will
-- contain a list of payments that have been made to employees

CREATE TABLE dbo.Payments (

    PaymentId    int       NOT NULL,

    EmployeeId    int       NOT NULL
    REFERENCES Employees(EmployeeID),

    Amount        money    NOT NULL
    CHECK(    Amount>0
        AND    Amount<=100000 ),

    PaymentDate    smalldatetime NOT NULL
    -- The check constraint ensures that the payment was made
    -- at some stage during the last 100 years or is scheduled 1
    -- year into the future.

    CHECK(    PaymentDate>DateAdd(yy,-100,getdate())
```

```
        AND     PaymentDate<=DateAdd(yy,1,getdate()) ),

    PaymentTypeID tinyint       NOT NULL
    REFERENCES PaymentTypes(PaymentTypeID),

    PRIMARY KEY(EmployeeID, PaymentID)
)
GO


-- Finally we add a foreign key to our Departments table
-- that references an employee row.

ALTER TABLE dbo.Departments
    ADD DepartmentHeadID int NULL
    REFERENCES Employees(EmployeeID)
GO
```

Every table has a **clustered index** created implicitly on the primary key column(s) in each table. What this means is that the data is physically stored on disk in the sort order defined by the index, making queries that use this index more efficient. We also created some **foreign keys**, which will be used to build relationships between the necessary tables ensuring that referential integrity of the data is maintained within the database.

We will create additional non-clustered indexes on several of the tables. Unlike clustered indexes, non-clustered indexes are stored separately from the table data within the SQL Server database. They store the copies of the index keys, the values contained in the columns you choose to participate in the index, and pointers to the actual rows that contain those values, in a separate hierarchical tree structure. This allows a row containing a particular value in the indexed columns to be easily identified by navigating the index structure. This all happens internally in SQL Server; however it is up to us to create the appropriate indexes first.

We should note here that every index on a table will slow down the insert time, or for that matter, the updates and deletes later in your projects cycle. This is because SQL Server not only inserts data into a table, but also updates the table indexes to reflect any changes made to the base table. However the creation of indexes on frequently referenced columns can significantly improve database querying performance, and if the number of indexes on a table is kept low the impact of row changes is usually minimal.

```
CREATE NONCLUSTERED INDEX ix_employees_department
ON dbo.Employees(Department)

CREATE NONCLUSTERED INDEX ix_department_departmentheadid
ON dbo.Departments(DepartmentHeadID)

CREATE NONCLUSTERED INDEX ix_payments_paymenttypeid
ON dbo.Payments(PaymentTypeID)
```

Once the above code is executed we are ready to move on to working with the raw data. At this point we will not discuss restricting access to the tables by only using stored procedures or views to perform data manipulation and retrieval. We will look at stored procedures in more detail in Chapter 5. However, the stored procedures we will discuss there are included in the installation script, which accompanies this chapter, and is available for download at **www.wrox.com**.

Now we can insert the test data that we will use within our `HumanResources` database. While we will include sufficient data to prove useful in our subsequent examples, this is nowhere near the amount of data that would be stored in a real HR database.

As with the examples above, run the following T-SQL code within SQL Server Query Analyzer:

```
-- INSERT our Departments rows

INSERT Departments(Description)
VALUES('Personnel')

INSERT Departments(Description)
VALUES('Orders')

INSERT Departments(Description)
VALUES('Stock Control')

INSERT Departments(Description)
VALUES('Deliveries')

INSERT Departments(Description)
VALUES('Incoming Orders')

-- INSERT our Employee rows

INSERT dbo.Employees
(      FirstName, SurName, DateOfBirth,
      DateOfHire, LastReview, Department )
VALUES
(      'Robin','Johnson','Jun 19 1963 10:47AM',
      'May  3 2000 10:47AM','Mar  9 2002 10:47AM', 1)

INSERT dbo.Employees
(      FirstName, SurName, DateOfBirth, DateOfHire,
      LastReview, Department )
VALUES
(      'Denise', 'Samson', 'Nov  6 1972 10:47AM',
      'Oct 19 2002 10:47AM', 'May 10 2001 10:47AM', 1 )

INSERT dbo.Employees
(      FirstName, SurName, DateOfBirth, DateOfHire,
      LastReview, Department )
VALUES
(      'Jack', 'Jones', 'Feb 22 1945 10:47AM',
      'Apr 16 1999 10:47AM', 'Mar 15 2002 10:47AM', 2 )

INSERT dbo.Employees
(      FirstName, SurName, DateOfBirth, DateOfHire,
      LastReview, Department )
VALUES
(      'John', 'Doe', 'Sep 18 1986 10:47AM',
      'Mar  6 1998 10:47AM', 'Mar  9 2002 10:47AM', 3 )

INSERT dbo.Employees
```

```
(       FirstName, SurName, DateOfBirth,
      DateOfHire, LastReview, Department )
VALUES
(       'Linda', 'Glucina', 'Apr  9 1944 10:47AM',
      'Feb  9 2000 10:47AM', 'Mar 11 2002 10:47AM', 1 )

INSERT dbo.Employees
(       FirstName, SurName, DateOfBirth,
      DateOfHire, LastReview, Department )
VALUES(   'Laura', 'Wright', 'Feb  7 1978 12:00AM',
      'Feb 23 1999 12:00AM','Apr 13 2002 11:23PM',1 )

INSERT dbo.Employees
(       FirstName, SurName, DateOfBirth,
      DateOfHire,LastReview,Department)
VALUES(   'Stephanie', 'Glucina', 'May 16 1963 12:00AM',
      'May 21 2001 12:00AM','Apr 12 2002 11:23PM',2)

INSERT dbo.Employees
(       FirstName, SurName, DateOfBirth,
      DateOfHire, LastReview, Department)
VALUES(   'Linda','Anderson','Dec 10 1981 12:00AM',
      'Jul  9 2000 12:00AM','Apr 13 2002 11:23PM',1)

INSERT dbo.Employees
(       FirstName, SurName, DateOfBirth,
      DateOfHire, LastReview, Department)
VALUES(   'Graham', 'Brown', 'Jun  7 1945 12:00AM',
      'Aug 11 1999 12:00AM','May 16 2001 11:23PM',3)

INSERT dbo.Employees
(       FirstName, SurName, DateOfBirth,
      DateOfHire, LastReview, Department)
VALUES(   'Suzanne', 'Smith', 'Nov  2 1960 12:00AM',
      'Jan  6 1998 12:00AM', 'Mar 14 2002 11:23PM', 1)

INSERT dbo.Employees
(       FirstName, SurName, DateOfBirth,
      DateOfHire, LastReview, Department)
VALUES(   'David', 'Allan', 'Sep 22 1973 12:00AM',
      'Nov 21 1999 12:00AM', 'Mar 13 2002 11:23PM',2)

-- Now INSERT our Salary rows

INSERT dbo.Salaries
(       EmployeeID, SalaryAppliedFrom, SalaryLevel )
VALUES(   1, 'Jan 29 2002 12:00AM', 119948 )

INSERT dbo.Salaries
(       EmployeeID,SalaryAppliedFrom,SalaryLevel )
VALUES(   2, 'Jan 25 2002 12:00AM', 119896 )

INSERT dbo.Salaries
(       EmployeeID,SalaryAppliedFrom,SalaryLevel )
```

```
VALUES(    3, 'Jan 17 2002 12:00AM', 119792 )

INSERT dbo.Salaries
(      EmployeeID,SalaryAppliedFrom,SalaryLevel )
VALUES(    4, 'Jan  1 2002 12:00AM', 119584)

INSERT dbo.Salaries
(      EmployeeID, SalaryAppliedFrom, SalaryLevel )
VALUES(    5, 'Nov 30 2001 12:00AM',119168)

INSERT dbo.Salaries
(      EmployeeID, SalaryAppliedFrom, SalaryLevel )
VALUES(    6, 'Sep 27 2001 12:00AM', 118336)

INSERT dbo.Salaries
(      EmployeeID, SalaryAppliedFrom, SalaryLevel )
VALUES(    7, 'May 22 2001 12:00AM', 116672)

INSERT dbo.Salaries
(      EmployeeID, SalaryAppliedFrom, SalaryLevel )
VALUES(    8,'Sep  8 2000 12:00AM',113344)

INSERT dbo.Salaries
(      EmployeeID,  SalaryAppliedFrom, SalaryLevel )
VALUES(    9, 'Apr 15 1999 12:00AM', 106688)

INSERT dbo.Salaries
(      EmployeeID, SalaryAppliedFrom, SalaryLevel )
VALUES(    10, 'Jun 25 1996 12:00AM', 93376 )

INSERT dbo.Salaries
(      EmployeeID, SalaryAppliedFrom, SalaryLevel )
VALUES(    11, 'Nov 16 1990 12:00AM', 66752)

-- Now INSERT our Course rows

INSERT dbo.Courses
(      CourseDesc, CourseDate, Location, MaxNoAttendees)
VALUES(   'TechFest','11/10/2002','Auckland',100)

INSERT dbo.Courses
(      CourseDesc, CourseDate, Location, MaxNoAttendees)
VALUES(   'Time Management','8/8/2002','Wellington',15)

-- Now INSERT our PaymentType rows

INSERT dbo.PaymentTypes (PaymentDesc)
VALUES('Expense Claim')

INSERT dbo.PaymentTypes (PaymentDesc)
VALUES('Milage')
```

HumanResources Project

Now that we have the database in place, we can start writing the code for our test application. As we mentioned in the introduction this is a sample application that will be used to demonstrate our database design, and more importantly, the numerous ADO.NET objects for dealing with data that we covered in the previous chapter. The goal is not to produce a production quality application, but rather a practical example of how these objects can be used together to create data-based applications.

Open up the Visual Studio .NET IDE and create a new **Visual Basic Project** based on a **VB.NET Windows Application**. Call the project `HumanResources` and select a location to place the source. This location should be a local drive if it is available, or a network drive (one that you have administrative rights to). The **Location** shown in the **New Project** window in the screenshot below is the default location created on our local machine.

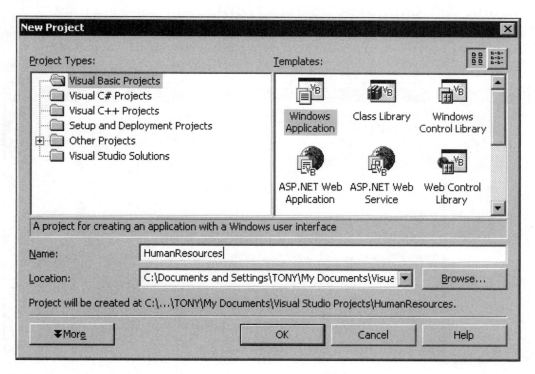

Within this project we will create a single form for use in maintaining our `Employee` records. This `EmployeeDetails` form will have controls for adding and deleting an employee, as well as fields for editing the various details associated with an employee, including their department assignment and their current salary.

This application will make use of the following ADO.NET objects we discussed in the previous chapter.

- ❑ `SqlConnection`
- ❑ `SqlCommand`
- ❑ `DataSet`
- ❑ `DataTable`
- ❑ `DataRow`
- ❑ `DataRelation`
- ❑ `DataView`

Creating the EmployeeDetails Form

Within the project create a form (name it `frmEmployeeDetail`) so that it looks similar to the one shown below. I have created two `GroupBoxes` in order to separate the navigation and editing areas of the `EmployeeDetail` form.

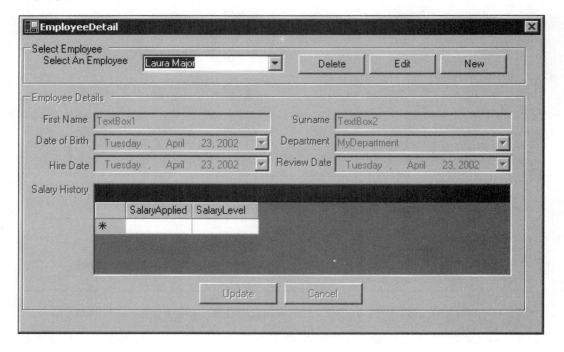

Create the two GroupBoxes as follows:

Control	Comment	Properties
grpControls	The GroupBox seen in the top portion of the form. This will house our control objects	Text = Select Employee Size = 600,48 Location = 0,8
grpEmployeeDetails	The GroupBox seen in the bottom portion of the form. This will look after items such as our employee editing fields	Text = Employee Details Size = 600,248 Location= 0,64

Now within each of these group boxes we need to add in several other controls. First in the grpControls GroupBox add the following:

Control	Comment	Properties
cboEmployeeList	A ComboBox list used to select our current employee for editing	Size = 160,21 Location= 135,23
lblEmployeeList	Label for ComboBox	Text = Select An Employee
btnDelete	A Button used for deleting unnecessary employee records	Text = Delete Size = 75,23 Location = 336,24
btnEdit	A button used for enabling the editing of an existing employee record	Text = Edit Size = 75,23 Location = 424,24
btnNew	A button used for adding a new employee record to our database	Text = New Size = 75,23 Location = 512,23

Now within the `grpEmployeeDetails` GroupBox we need to create the following controls on our form:

Control	Comment	Properties
txtFirstName	A `TextBox` used for displaying and editing the first name of an employee	Size = 200,20" Location = 90,24
lblFirstName	Label for `txtFirstName` textbox	Text = First Name Size = Location =
txtSurName	A `TextBox` used for displaying and editing the surname of an employee	Size = 200,20 Location = 392,24
lblSurName	Label for `txtSurName` TextBox	Text = Surname Size = Location =
dtpDateOfBirth	A `DateTimePicker` used for displaying and editing the date of birth for an employee	Size = 200,20 Location = 392,48
lblDateOfBirth	Label for `dtpDateOfBirth` DateTimePicker	Text = Date Of Birth Size = Location =
cboDepartment	A `ComboBox` used for displaying and editing the department for an employee	Size = 200,20 Location = 392,48
lblDepartment	Label for `cboDepartment` ComboBox	Text = Department Size = Location =
dtpDateOfHire	A `DateTimePicker` used for displaying and editing the date of employment for an employee	Size = 200,20 Location = 90,72
lblDateOfHire	Label for `dtpDateOfHire` DateTimePicker	Text = Hire Date Size Location =
dtpLastReview	A `DateTimePicker` used for displaying and editing the date of the last review of an employee	Size = 200,20 Location = 392,72

Table continued on following page

Control	Comment	Properties
lblLastReview	Label for dtpLastReview DateTimePicker	Text = Review Date
		Size =
		Location =
dgSalaries	A DataGrid used for displaying and editing the salary details of an employee	Size = 472,104
		Location = 95,104
lblSalaries	Label for dgSalaries DataGrid	Text = Salary History
		Size =
		Location =
btnUpdate	A button used for updating the database with the changes that took place during the edit	Text = Update
		Size = 88,24
		Location = 200,216
btnCancel	A button used for canceling the current edit taking place and discarding changes made	Text = Cancel
		Size = 88,24
		Location = 296,216

EmployeeDetails Code

We'll now take a look at each piece of the code in turn. The first line of code defines the form as a publicly accessible class. Forms have been a specialized type of class for a long time now, but up until now this has been hidden from us as VB developers. Now that full inheritance exists within .NET it makes more sense for such detail to be exposed to you. This form will inherit functionality from the Windows base form, hence why the Inherits statement is placed within the code.

```
Imports System.Data.SqlClient

Public Class frmEmployeeDetail
    Inherits System.Windows.Forms.Form

    Private dsDataSet As New DataSet()
    Private dvEmployees As New DataView()
    Private dvSalaries As New DataView()

    Private daEmployees As New SqlDataAdapter()
    Private daSalary As New SqlDataAdapter()
    Private daDepartments As New SqlDataAdapter()
```

We then move on to take a look at how we code events, since this has been altered from previous versions of Visual Basic. There are two new parameters as well as a new keyword called Handles. In previous versions of Visual Basic you would simply code Object_Event(). In .NET however, it is possible to create a subroutine by any name, and use two parameters as shown below:

```
Private Sub GeneralSub(ByVal sender As Object, _
        ByVal e As System.EventArgs) Handles cmdTest.Click, _
        cmdTest2.Click, txtTextBox.TextChanged
```

Both of the parameters that are passed in by the common events within VB.NET can tell you all there is to know about what has occurred. The first parameter (sender) will contain the actual object that has caused the event to be raised. Looking at the code snippet above, this object would either be one of the two command buttons (cmdTest or cmdTest2) or the textbox (txtTextBox). The second parameter (e) deals with the arguments that are associated with the raised event. These arguments in the main match previous parameters that were associated with an event, but there isn't a one-to-one match; for example the KeyPress event has no parameter to indicate if the *Shift* key was pressed.

By using the Handles keyword, you are informing the CLR that this routine is specifically looking at the named object and the event named, in this case the cmdConnect button's Click event. Another major advancement with the Handles keyword is that you can use one method to deal with several events that accept these two named parameters. This could be several button Click events or in fact any object's Click event. If you wish to deal with more than one event, then you create a comma-separated list. In the code snippet above you can see that this one routine deals with three events.

> **All of the common events within VB.NET pass in the two parameters that you see above, which could lead you to build single generic code-handling routines for every event. You should take great care if you decide to do this however, since you will find that there is little common code between a Click event and a TextChanged event. Even if there is common code, you may find that in a later release, the code needs to be separated out due to other coding considerations.**

Having looked at how events are dealt with, let's begin adding code to our project. Our first code listing handles the Load method of our fmEmployeeDetails form. This procedure is quite large so we will split it up into sections and cover these individually.

```
Private Sub frmEmployeeDetail_Load(ByVal sender As System.Object, _
                                   ByVal e As System.EventArgs) _
                                   Handles MyBase.Load
```

First we define our connection string and use this to create a new SqlConnection object. This is the connection that we will use to execute all commands made against SQL Server within this application.

```
'Change the connection string to your own SQL Server details
Dim strConnection As String = "Server=MyServer;" _
                            & "Database=HumanResources;" _
                            & "User Id=sa;Password=;"

Dim cnSqlServer As New SqlConnection(strConnection)
```

Next, using the daEmployees SqlDataAdapter object that we declared earlier, we begin to create SqlCommand objects that contain the actual T-SQL commands for selecting, inserting, updating, and deleting rows from the Employees table within our HumanResources database.

We create a new instance of a SqlCommand object and assign this to the .SelectCommand property of our daEmployees SqlDataAdapter.

```
' Create the SELECT, INSERT, UPDATE, and DELETE command
' objects to be used with the Employees SqlDataAdapter.
With daEmployees

    ' The SELECT command used to retrieve and return employee rows.
    .SelectCommand = New SqlCommand()

        With .SelectCommand
```

Now we assign the `cnSqlServer` object we created above to this new `SqlCommand` object. This connection will be used to retrieve the rows from our `Employees` table in the database.

```
            .Connection = cnSqlServer
```

The `CommandText` property of our `SqlCommand` object contains the actual T-SQL command used to retrieve the rows from our `Employees` table. Here we define a `SELECT` command that will retrieve all the columns (excluding the `SecurityPhoto` column as we don't use it in this example) for all the rows within our `Employees` table.

```
            .CommandText = " SELECT EmployeeID, FirstName, Surname,"
            .CommandText += " DateOfBirth, DateOfHire, LastReview, "
            .CommandText += " Department FROM dbo.Employees"

        End With
```

Following this we define the `INSERT` command used to add a new row to our `Employees` table within the `HumanResources` database. Once again we create a new `SqlCommand` object and assign this to our `daEmployees SqlDataAdapter`.

```
    ' The INSERT command to create new Employee rows
    .InsertCommand = New SqlCommand()

        With .InsertCommand

            .Connection = cnSqlServer

            .CommandText = "INSERT dbo.Employees(FirstName, Surname,"
            .CommandText += " DateOfBirth, DateOfHire, LastReview"
            .CommandText += ", Department) VALUES(@FirstName, "
            .CommandText += "@Surname, @DateOfBirth, @DateOfHire, "
            .CommandText += "@LastReview,@Department)"
```

This `INSERT` command differs from the `SELECT` command in that it uses `SqlParameters` to assign the values to be inserted by the `INSERT` statement.

```
            With .Parameters

                .Add("@FirstName", SqlDbType.VarChar, 30, "FirstName")
```

In Add parameters we give them a name (for example @FirstName) followed by a data type and size, and finally a column mapping. When creating the T-SQL command within the CommandText property, you can refer to these parameters by name. When the SqlCommand is later executed, the parameters that you have referenced within the CommandText are replaced with the value of the actual column from the table within the DataSet (as specified by the column mapping), for the particular row being modified.

```
            .Add("@Surname", SqlDbType.VarChar, 30, "Surname")

            .Add("@DateOfBirth", SqlDbType.SmallDateTime, 8, _
                "DateOfBirth")

            .Add("@DateOfHire", SqlDbType.SmallDateTime, 8, _
                "DateOfHire")

            .Add("@LastReview", SqlDbType.SmallDateTime, 8, _
                "LastReview")

            .Add("@Department", SqlDbType.Int, 4, "Department")

        End With

    End With
```

The SqlCommand object that will be used to update rows with our Employees table is as follows:

```
    ' The UPDATE command to modify existing Employee rows.
    .UpdateCommand = New SqlCommand()

        With .UpdateCommand

            .Connection = cnSqlServer

            .CommandText = "UPDATE dbo.Employees Set
            .CommandText += "FirstName=FirstName, "
            .CommandText += "Surname=@Surname, "
            .CommandText += "DateOfBirth=@DateOfBirth,"
            .CommandText += "DateOfHire=@DateOfHire, "
            .CommandText += " LastReview=@LastReview,"
            .CommandText += "Department=@Department "
            .CommandText += "WHERE EmployeeID=@EmployeeID"

            With .Parameters

                .Add("@FirstName", SqlDbType.VarChar, 30, "FirstName")

                .Add("@Surname", SqlDbType.VarChar, 30, "Surname")

                .Add("@DateOfBirth", SqlDbType.SmallDateTime, 8, _
                    "DateOfBirth")

                .Add("@DateOfHire", SqlDbType.SmallDateTime, 8, _
                    "DateOfHire")
```

```
                    .Add("@LastReview", SqlDbType.SmallDateTime, 8, _
                        "LastReview")

                    .Add("@Department", SqlDbType.Int, 4, "Department")

                    .Add("@EmployeeID", SqlDbType.Int, 4, "EmployeeID")

            End With

    End With
```

In order to DELETE a row within our Employees table we create the following SqlCommand object. This only requires one parameter to be assigned, the @EmployeeID parameter, which is the primary key of our Employees table.

```
        ' The DELETE command, to delete existing rows
        .DeleteCommand = New SqlCommand()

            With .DeleteCommand

                .Connection = cnSqlServer

                .CommandText = "DELETE dbo.Salaries "
                .CommandText += " WHERE EmployeeID=@EmployeeID"
                .CommandText += " DELETE dbo.Employees "
                .CommandText += " WHERE EmployeeID=@EmployeeID"

                .Parameters.Add("@EmployeeID", SqlDbType.Int, 4, _
                                "EmployeeID")

            End With
```

Before we finish defining our daEmployees object there are three more properties that we need to assign. First we have the AcceptChangesDuringFill property. This is used to set the row state of the rows added to our Employees DataTable within the DataSet. The row state will be set to Unchanged after the Fill has completed.

```
        ' Set AcceptChangesDuringFill to True so the rows
        ' that are added to the DataSet by the Fill operation
        ' have an inital row state of Unchanged

            .AcceptChangesDuringFill = True
```

The table mappings property adds a name mapping the resultset returned by our SELECT command to a DataTable. This DataTable is created from the rows in the resultset, using the table mapping name, and is contained within the DataSet. By default the name of the table returned by a SELECT command will be simply 'Table'. This is obviously not very suitable for referencing our employees details so instead we add a TableMapping object to the SqlDataAdapter. This specifies that during a Fill, we create a DataTable named Employees (within the DataSet).

```
' Map the resultset returned by our SELECT command to
' a DataTable within the DataSet named Employees

    .TableMappings.Add("Table", "Employees")
```

The `MissingSchemaAction` property determines what the `SqlDataAdapter` does during a `Fill` when the destination schema for the resultset, in this case the `Employees DataTable`, does not exist (such as on the first `Fill` operation). By setting this to `MissingSchemaAction.AddWithKey`, our `daEmployees` object will create the table schema within the `DataSet` and include the primary key information gathered from the SQL Server database schema.

```
' Set the MissingSchemaAction to AddWithKey, so during
' the inital FILL operation any schema that is missing
' is added with its primary key information.
.MissingSchemaAction = MissingSchemaAction.AddWithKey

    End With
```

We continue our code, by carrying out a very similar task for the `Salaries` table. We define `SELECT`, `INSERT`, `UPDATE`, and `DELETE SqlCommands` and assign these to our `daSalary` object.

```
' Define the SELECT, INSERT, UPDATE, and DELETE commands
' used to retrieve and modify salary data.
With daSalary

    ' The SELECT command for our Salary data
    .SelectCommand = New SqlCommand()

    With .SelectCommand

        .Connection = cnSqlServer

        .CommandText = "SELECT EmployeeID, SalaryAppliedFrom, "
        .CommandText += "SalaryLevel FROM Salaries"

    End With

    ' The INSERT command for our Salary data
    .InsertCommand = New SqlCommand()

    With .InsertCommand

        .Connection = cnSqlServer

        .CommandText = "INSERT dbo.Salaries(EmployeeID, "
        .CommandText += " SalaryAppliedFrom, SalaryLevel) "
        .CommandText += " VALUES(@EmployeeID, @SalaryAppliedFrom,"
        .CommandText += " @SalaryLevel)"

            With .Parameters
```

```
            .Add("@EmployeeID", SqlDbType.Int, 4, "EmployeeID")

            .Add("@SalaryAppliedFrom", SqlDbType.SmallDateTime, 8, _
                "SalaryAppliedFrom")

            .Add("@SalaryLevel", SqlDbType.Money, 8, "SalaryLevel")

        End With

      End With

    ' The UPDATE command for our Salary data
    .UpdateCommand = New SqlCommand()

    With .UpdateCommand

       .Connection = cnSqlServer

        .CommandText = "UPDATE Salaries SET
        .CommandText += " SalaryAppliedFrom=@NewSalaryAppliedFrom,"
        .CommandText += " SalaryLevel=@SalaryLevel "
        .CommandText += " WHERE EmployeeID=@EmployeeID"
        .CommandText += " AND SalaryAppliedFrom= "
        .CommandText += " @OldSalaryAppliedFrom"

       With .Parameters

        .Add("@NewSalaryAppliedFrom", SqlDbType.SmallDateTime, 8, _
            "SalaryAppliedFrom")

        .Add("@SalaryLevel", SqlDbType.Money, 8, "SalaryLevel")

        .Add("@EmployeeID", SqlDbType.Int, 4, "EmployeeID")

        .Add("@OldSalaryAppliedFrom", SqlDbType.SmallDateTime, 8, _
            "SalaryAppliedFrom")

       End With

    End With
```

The following parameter assignment is a little different from those we have looked at up to this point. The SalaryAppliedFrom column is used as part of the primary key in our Salaries table, and is therefore required to uniquely identify the row that we are updating. However for a given employee salary record, this column can also be updated to a new value.

When updating this column we need to know not only the new value, but also the old value so that we can identify the existing row within our Salaries table before we update it. Fortunately the DataSet provides support for this using DataRowVersions. Even though we create two parameters using the same source column, by specifying the DataRowVersion.Original as the SourceVersion of our first parameter, the value of this first parameter will be set to the SalaryAppliedFrom DataColumn before it was updated. Our second parameter using this DataColumn on the other hand uses the current value of this column, which will be the value of the DataColumn after being edited.

```
            ' The original value of the SalaryAppliedFrom column,
            ' before the update
              .Parameters("@OldSalaryAppliedFrom").SourceVersion = _
                          DataRowVersion.Original

            ' The value of the SalaryAppliedFrom column, after
            ' the update
              .Parameters("@NewSalaryAppliedFrom").SourceVersion = _
                          DataRowVersion.Current
    End With
```

We continue by defining the DELETE command for our Salaries table.

```
      ' The DELETE command for our Salary data
      .DeleteCommand = New SqlCommand()

      With .DeleteCommand

            .Connection = cnSqlServer

            .CommandText = "DELETE Salaries "
            .CommandText = " WHERE EmployeeID = @EmployeeID"
            .CommandText += " AND SalaryAppliedFrom=@SalaryAppliedFrom"

              .Parameters.Add("@EmployeeID", SqlDbType.Int, 4, _
                          "EmployeeID")

              .Parameters.Add("@SalaryAppliedFrom", _
                          SqlDbType.SmallDateTime, 8, "SalaryAppliedFrom")

      End With

        ' Set AcceptChangesDuringFill to True so the rows
        ' that are added to the DataSet by the Fill operation
        ' have an inital row state of Unchanged
        .AcceptChangesDuringFill = True

        ' Map the resultset returned by our SELECT command to
        ' a DataTable within the DataSet named Salaries
        .TableMappings.Add("Table", "Salaries")

        ' Set the MissingSchemaAction to AddWithKey, so during
        ' the inital FILL operation any schema that is missing
        ' is added with its primary key information.
        .MissingSchemaAction = MissingSchemaAction.AddWithKey

      End With
```

The final table that we define the SELECT SqlCommand object for is our Departments table. However since we are not making any changes to this table within this application we do not need to define INSERT, UPDATE, or DELETE SqlCommand objects.

```
' Add the SqlCommand objects that will handle the SELECT
' statement for the Departments table within the DataSet.
' As we do not modify the Departments table within this
' sample application the INSERT, UPDATE, and DELETE
' commands are not required.
With daDepartments

    .SelectCommand = New SqlCommand()

    With .SelectCommand

        .Connection = cnSqlServer
        .CommandText = "Select DepartmentID, Description"
        .CommandText += " FROM dbo.Departments"

    End With

    ' Set AcceptChangesDuringFill to True so the rows
    ' that are added to the DataSet by the Fill operation
    ' have an inital row state of Unchanged
    .AcceptChangesDuringFill = True

    ' Map the resultset returned by our SELECT command to
    ' a DataTable within the DataSet named Salaries
    .TableMappings.Add("Table", "Departments")

    ' Set the MissingSchemaAction to AddWithKey, so during
    ' the inital FILL operation any schema that is missing
    ' is added with its primary key information.
    .MissingSchemaAction = MissingSchemaAction.AddWithKey

End With
```

Now we call the `Fill` methods for all three of our `SqlDataAdapter` objects. This in turn populates our `DataSet` with the `Employees`, `Salaries`, and `Departments` tables. We encase these `Fill`s within exception-handling code, as they will each attempt to connect to SQL Server to retrieve the results of their respective SELECT commands. If the connection to SQL Server or the `SqlCommand` should fail, we output the exception message so we can determine what the cause of the failure was.

```
' Now we populate our DataSet using the FILL method for each
' of the SqlDataAdapters we created above.
Try

    daEmployees.Fill(dsDataSet)
    daSalary.Fill(dsDataSet)
    daDepartments.Fill(dsDataSet)

Catch oSqlException As SqlException

    MsgBox("The following SQL Server error occured: " _
            & oSqlException.Message)
    End

Finally

    ' Default error handling code goes here

End Try
```

Having populated our `DataSet` we add a calculated column to our `Employees` table that is used to return an employee's full name within one column. This `FullName` column is calculated based on the concatenation of the `FirstName` and `Surname` columns. We add the calculated column as we wish to provide a ComboBox selector that allows the user of the application to select existing employees for editing. As the ComboBox can only display a `DataColumn`, we use the calculated column in order to display the employee's full name in the drop-down list.

```
' Add a Calculated Column to our Employees DataSet
' that contains the Full Name of an Employee. This
' is used within our Employee Picker ComboBox.
dsDataSet.Tables("Employees").Columns.Add _
    ("FullName", System.Type.GetType("System.String"), _
    "FirstName + ' '+ Surname")
```

Next we create `DataRelations` between the `DataTables` within our `DataSet`. These `DataRelations` enforce the relationship between the `Employees` `DataTable` and the `Departments` `DataTable`, as well as the `Salaries` `DataTable` and the `Employees` `DataTable`. These `DataRelations` ensure that, for example, the values inserted into the `Department` column in the `Employees` table correspond to an existing value in the `Departments` parent table.

```
' Create DataRelation objects that will enforce the
' relationships between the various tables within our
' DataSet.

With dsDataSet

    ' Relationship between the Salaries table
    ' and the Employees table
    .Relations.Add("FK_Salaries_Employees", _
        .Tables("Employees").Columns("EmployeeID"), _
        .Tables("Salaries").Columns("EmployeeID"), _
        True)

    ' Relationship between the Employees table
    ' and the Employees table
    .Relations.Add("FK_Employees_Departments", _
        .Tables("Departments").Columns("DepartmentID"), _
        .Tables("Employees").Columns("Department"), _
        True)

End With
```

Now we can assign the `Employees` table as the base table of our `dvEmployees` `DataView` object. This view of the `Employees` table will be used to filter the specific employee that is being edited from the `Employees` table.

```
' Create a DataView of our Employees Table. We will use this
' DataView for locating specific employee rows for editing
dvEmployees.Table = dsDataSet.Tables("Employees")
```

Following on from this, we set the `DataSource` of our `cboEmployeeList` ComboBox to the `Employees` table. The `DisplayMember` property is set to the `FullName` column, and the `ValueMember` property to the `EmployeeID` column. This allows the user to select the row from the ComboBox based on the employees `FirstName`, and allows us to identify the selected row within our code based on the value of the selected `EmployeeID`.

```
' Assign the EmployeeID and FullName columns from the Employees
' DataTable to our cboEmployeeList ComboBox.
With cboEmployeeList

    .DataSource = dsDataSet.Tables("Employees")

    ' This specifies the column that the value property will return
    ' for a selected row
    .ValueMember = "EmployeeID"

    ' This specifies the column that is displayed in the
    ' ComboBox.
    .DisplayMember = "FullName"

End With
```

We do a similar thing with our `cboDepartment` ComboBox. We will display the `Description` column from our `Departments` table and use the `DepartmentID` column within the code to identify the row in the ComboBox selected by the user.

```
' Assign our Departments DataTable as the DataSource for
' our Departments ComboBox.
With cboDepartment

    .DataSource = dsDataSet.Tables("Departments")

    .ValueMember = "DepartmentID"

    .DisplayMember = "Description"

End With
```

Within our `FormLoad` method we define a `DataView` object based on our `Salaries` table. By setting the `RowFilter` property to -1 initially, rows will be retrieved by the `dvSalaries` `DataView` when the form is first loaded.

```
' Create a DataView on our Salaries table. This will be
' used for locating salary rows for the specific employee
' that is being edited.
dvSalaries.Table = dsDataSet.Tables("Salaries")

' Set the inital row filter to -1, so now rows will be
' displayed within the Salaries DataGrid initially.
dvSalaries.RowFilter = "EmployeeId=-1"
```

After this we assign our `dvSalaries` DataView as the `DataSource` of our `dgSalaries` DataGrid object. We then create a `DataGridTableStyle` object that will be mapped to our `Salaries` table when added to the `dgSalaries` DataGrid object.

```
' Create a DataGridTable style, this will be used to
' hide our EmployeeID from the Salaries DataGrid.
Dim dgSalariesTableStyle As New DataGridTableStyle()

' Map this TableStyle to the Salaries table that
' will be assigned to the DataGrid
dgSalariesTableStyle.MappingName = "Salaries"

' Using the DataView that we created above, assign the Salaries
' table to our DataView. Also assign the TableStyle to the
' DataGrid. Once the TableStyle has been assigned GridColumnStyle
' objects are implicitly created. Use a GridColumnStyle object
' to set the Width of our EmployeeID column to 0. This ensures
' it won't show within the DataGrid.
With dgSalaries

    .DataSource = dvSalaries

    .TableStyles.Add(dgSalariesTableStyle)
```

Once the `DataGridTableStyle` has been added to the `DataGrid`, `GridColumnStyles` objects are implicitly added for each column within our `Salaries` table. By setting the `Width` property of the `EmployeeID` to 0 we prevent the `EmployeeID` column from being displayed within the `dgSalaries` DataGrid.

```
    .TableStyles("Salaries").GridColumnStyles("EmployeeID"). _
    Width = 0

End With
```

Finally in this section of code, we set the `Enabled` property of our `grpEmployeeDetails` control group to `False`, essentially disabling all the editing items on the form when initially loaded.

```
    grpEmployeeDetails.Enabled = False

End Sub
```

Now we need to consider the `Click` event for the **Edit** button. First we set the `RowFilter` property of the `dvSalaries` DataView to display only salary rows that have an `EmployeeID` matching that which is currently selected in our `cboEmployeeList` ComboBox.

We also set the default value of the `EmployeeID` column within the `DataSet` to the currently selected `EmployeeID`. This ensures that the user can only edit the salary of the currently selected `EmployeeID`.

```
Private Sub btnEdit_Click(ByVal sender As System.Object, _
                    ByVal e As System.EventArgs) Handles _
                    btnEdit.Click

    ' Set the RowFilter property of or Salaries DataView to only
    ' return rows that match the currently selected EmployeeID

    dvSalaries.RowFilter = "EmployeeId=" & cboEmployeeList.SelectedValue

    ' Set the default value of the Employee column within our
    ' DataSet to the currently selected employee. As we have
    ' hidden our EmployeeID column we need the default value
    ' As this is part of the Primary Key it must contain a value
    ' when new rows are inserted.

    dvSalaries.Table.Columns.Item("EmployeeID").DefaultValue = _
        cboEmployeeList.SelectedValue

    ' Next restrict the rows within our Employees DataView
    ' to the currently selected Employee within the Employees
    ' ComboBox.

    dvEmployees.RowFilter = "EmployeeId=" & _
    cboEmployeeList.SelectedValue
```

Finally we enable the editing control group, and disable the navigation control group while the edit is in progress. After this we update our form to display the values of the currently selected employee.

```
    ' Enable the EmployeeDetails editing section of the main window
    ' Disable the Employee selections section of the main window
    ' while the edit is in progress.

    grpEmployeeDetails.Enabled = True

    grpControls.Enabled = False

    ' Populate the editing fields on the form with the values retrieved
    ' from our current employee record.

    Refresh_EmployeeDetails()

End Sub
```

Our `Refresh_EmployeeDetails` code assigns the values of the first row within the `DataView` to the fields of the form. As the filter on our `DataView` only allows one row to be returned by the `DataView` we can be confident that this corresponds to the currently selected employee's details.

As we will learn in Chapter 7 there is a more efficient method of assigning values from a DataSet to fields within a form using data binding methods.

```
Private Sub Refresh_EmployeeDetails()
    ' Assign the Employee details from our DataView to
    ' the fields of our Form.
    With dvEmployees(0)

        txtFirstName.Text = .Item("FirstName")

        txtSurName.Text = .Item("Surname")

        dtpDateOfBirth.Value = .Item("DateOfBirth")

        dtpDateOfHire.Value = .Item("DateOfHire")

        dtpLastReview.Value = .Item("LastReview")

        cboDepartment.SelectedValue = .Item("Department")

    End With
End Sub
```

Next we define the `Click` event for our `Cancel` button. As edits within a `DataSet` can be undone at any time until `AcceptChanges` has been called, calling `RejectChanges` will undo any modifications made within the `DataSet` since the last `AcceptChanges` had occurred. This effectively cancels the changes made during the current edit.

Once the `RejectChanges` has been called we disable the editing part of the form, and enable the navigating part of our form.

```
Private Sub btnCancel_Click(ByVal sender As System.Object, _
                            ByVal e As System.EventArgs) _
                            Handles btnCancel.Click
    ' If the cancel button has been clicked we call the RejectChanges
    ' method of our DataSet to undo the changes made during the edit.
    dsDataSet.RejectChanges()

    ' Disable the EmployeeDetails editing section of the main window
    ' Enable the Employee selections section of the main window
    grpControls.Enabled = True

    grpEmployeeDetails.Enabled = False
```

Finally in this section of code, we update the fields within the form to be the values of the currently selected employee, making sure that the values of the canceled edit do not remain on screen. Once again setting the `RowFilter` of the `dvSalaries` object to -1 clears the `dgSalaries` DataGrid of all rows.

```
    ' Next restrict the rows within our Employees DataView
    ' to the currently selected Employee within the Employees
    ' ComboBox.
    dvEmployees.RowFilter = "EmployeeId=" & cboEmployeeList.SelectedValue

    ' Reset fields within our form back to their previous values
    Refresh_EmployeeDetails()

    ' Set the RowFilter to -1 so no Salary rows show within the
    ' Salary DataGrid.
    dvSalaries.RowFilter = "EmployeeId=-1"

End Sub
```

A user clicking on the **Update** button has the completely opposite effect of the **Cancel** button. In this case the dvEmployees DataView is updated to reflect the values contained within the form. As the DataView is merely presenting the data contained within the underlying table, any update on the DataView is actually updating the underlying DataTable.

```
Private Sub btnUpdate_Click(ByVal sender As System.Object, _
                            ByVal e As System.EventArgs) _
                            Handles btnUpdate.Click

    ' Update the Employee row within the DataView to
    ' reflect the values contained within our form.
    With dvEmployees(0)

        .Item("FirstName") = txtFirstName.Text
        .Item("Surname") = txtSurName.Text
        .Item("DateOfBirth") = dtpDateOfBirth.Value
        .Item("DateOfHire") = dtpDateOfHire.Value
        .Item("LastReview") = dtpLastReview.Value
        .Item("Department") = cboDepartment.SelectedValue

    End With
```

After the DataSet has been modified to reflect the changes contained within our form, the Update methods of both the Employees and Salaries SqlDataAdapters are called to carry out the necessary SQL commands, in order to make the HumanResources database reflect the changes present in the DataSet.

```
    ' Update the Employees table via the Employees SqlDataAdapter
    daEmployees.Update(dsDataSet)

    ' Update the Salaries table via the Employees SqlDataAdapter
    daSalary.Update(dsDataSet)

    ' Disable the EmployeeDetails editing section of the main window
    ' Enable the Employee selections section of the main window
    grpControls.Enabled = True

    grpEmployeeDetails.Enabled = False

    ' Set the RowFilter to -1 so no Salary rows show within the
    ' Salary DataGrid.
    dvSalaries.RowFilter = "EmployeeId=-1"
End Sub
```

If the **New** button is clicked we actually add a new row to our Employees table located within our DataSet. This new employee row has FirstName and Surname columns that are empty, and default values assigned to the various date and department columns of the row.

```
Private Sub btnNew_Click(ByVal sender As System.Object, _
                         ByVal e As System.EventArgs) _
                         Handles btnNew.Click

    ' Declare a DataRow object to be used for the row that
    ' we are about to insert.
    Dim drDataRow As DataRow
```

```
        ' Create our new DataRow in the same schema as our
        ' existing Employees table.
        drDataRow = dsDataSet.Tables("Employees").NewRow()

        ' Reset the Departments ComboBox to the first Department
        ' in the department list.
        cboDepartment.SelectedIndex = 1

        ' Populate the new row with empty or default values
        drDataRow("FirstName") = ""
        drDataRow("SurName") = ""
        drDataRow("DateOfBirth") = DateAdd(DateInterval.Year, -15, Now)
        drDataRow("DateOfHire") = Now
        drDataRow("LastReview") = Now
        drDataRow("Department") = cboDepartment.SelectedValue

        ' Add our new row to our DataSet.
        dsDataSet.Tables("Employees").Rows.Add(drDataRow)

        ' Update our Database with the newly created
        ' DataRow.
        daEmployees.Update(dsDataSet)
```

As the `EmployeeID` within our `DataSet` may not reflect the `EmployeeID` created within the base table (remember the `Employees` table has an identity column defined on it), we retrieve the row with the maximum `EmployeeID` from the `Employees` table and use this as our currently selected `Employee` row following the insert.

```
        ' Retrieve the newest created Employee row.
        dvEmployees.RowFilter = "EmployeeID=MAX(EmployeeID)"

        ' Set our currently selected employees drop-down combo
        ' to our newly created row.
        cboEmployeeList.SelectedValue = dvEmployees(0).Item("EmployeeID")

        ' Set the default value of the Employee column within our
        ' Salaries DataSet to the currently selected employee. As we have
        ' hidden our EmployeeID column we need the default value.
        ' As this is part of the Primary Key it must contain a value
        ' when new rows are inserted.
        dvSalaries.Table.Columns.Item("EmployeeID").DefaultValue = _
           cboEmployeeList.SelectedValue

        ' Enable the EmployeeDetails editing section of the main window
        ' Disable the Employee selections section of the main window
           grpEmployeeDetails.Enabled = True

           grpControls.Enabled = False

        ' Set fields within our form back to those of the new row,
        ' these are currently empty
        Refresh_EmployeeDetails()

    End Sub
```

Finally we create the `Click` event used to delete rows from within our `Employees` table. We identify the row to be deleted using the `RowFilter` property of the `dvEmployees` `DataView`, and modify the `HumanResources` database to reflect this delete using the `Update` method of our `daEmployees` object.

```
Private Sub btnDelete_Click(ByVal sender As System.Object, _
                        ByVal e As System.EventArgs) _
                        Handles btnDelete.Click
    ' Reset the row filter to current rows.
    dvEmployees.RowStateFilter = DataViewRowState.CurrentRows

    ' Restrict our DataView to only return the row where the
    ' EmployeeID is equal to the selected employee in our
    ' ComboBox.
    dvEmployees.RowFilter = "EmployeeId=" & cboEmployeeList.SelectedValue

    ' Delete this employee row.
    dvEmployees(0).Delete()

    ' Update our Employees table within the database by calling
    ' the Update method of our Employees SQLDataAdapter.
    daEmployees.Update(dsDataSet)

End Sub
```

Debugging

If you are running in a client/server environment where your SQL Server is on a remote machine, it is necessary to set up your project and the server to allow SQL Debugging within .NET to take place. There are 3 specific DLLs and one EXE that have to be installed either on the client or the server for debugging to successfully take place. Without this installation you may find that debugging either does not work, or is at best sporadic. If you need to debug SQL Server-side code on a remote machine, then there is no other option than to install .NET on your server.

The debugging components that need to be installed are as follows:

Component	Location	Description
SQLLE.DLL	Client `\Microsoft Visual Studio.NET\Common7\Packages\Debugger`	SQL Language Engine used for debugging
SQLDBG.DLL	Client and Server `\Program Files\Common Files\Microsoft Shared\SQL Debugging`	Proxy stub used for processing
MSSDI98.DLL	Server within the `\Binn` directory of the SQL Server install	SQL Debugging Interface
SQLDBREG.EXE	Client `\Program Files\Common Files\Microsoft Shared\SQL Debugging`	SQ Debugging registry

The client-side components should be installed when .NET is set up on your client computer, but you may find that on the SQL Server .NET has not been installed. If this is the case, then you have to install **Remote Debugging** from the Visual Studio .NET installation media. You can gain access to this install either from the Visual Studio .NET setup screen (as you can see in the screenshot below), or from the foot of the **Welcome** screen when you first start the set-up process (as you can see in the screenshot opposite). Clicking the **Remote Components Setup** link at the foot of this screen opens up an HTML document in which you will see a button for installing the **Remote Debugging** options.

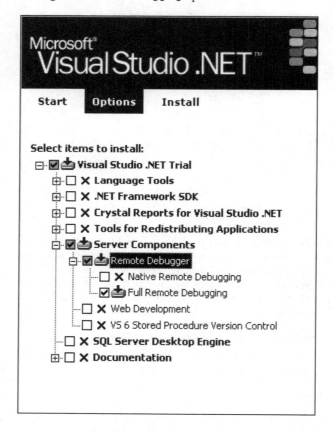

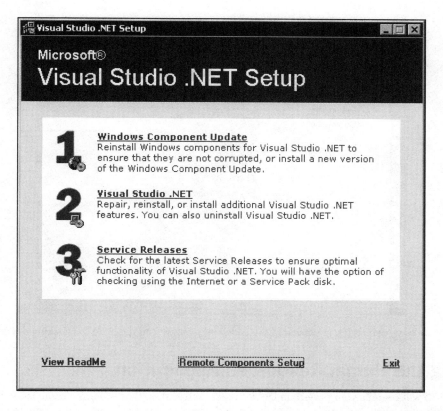

Note that in order to install the Full Remote Debugging option, you may have to complete upgrades on certain components so that the .NET Framework can function. This will entail installing service packs, Internet Explorer 6, and MDAC 2.7 amongst other items. Such components should ideally be installed on a development server, rather than a production server, so as to give the developer more control.

By selecting the Full Remote Debugging option you will install the debug components for SQL Server, as well as other debugging components that are unnecessary for any VB.NET or SQL Server code. It is not possible just to select the SQL Server debug components themselves.

Moving back to the client computer that you are developing your .NET solution on, you also have to inform the Visual Studio .NET IDE that you wish to debug a SQL solution. To do this you need to move the highlight in the Solution Explorer to the project to debug (in this example the HumanResources project), instead of the project group. Then from the menu select View | Property Pages, or press *Shift+F4*, which will bring up the Property Page. From there you can get access to the Configuration Properties | Debugging area where you can find the checkbox to enable debugging SQL Server solutions.

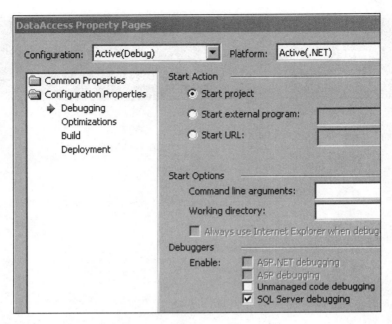

Now that we have debugging in place and the code complete we can move on to checking out our work.

Testing the HumanResources Application

Pressing *F5* will compile your project, in Debug mode, and start up the test form if compilation is successful. Your application should be similar to that shown in the figure below. You can see the form up and running with details already populated and a successful connection having taken place.

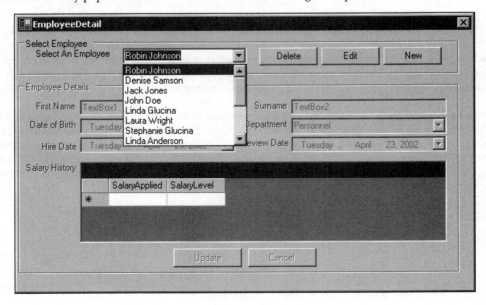

Selecting an employee from the drop-down list, and clicking the Edit button will allow you to make changes to the employee details. At this stage these changes are only being carried out locally within the DataSet. Not until you click the Update button are the changes then propagated back to our HumanResources database.

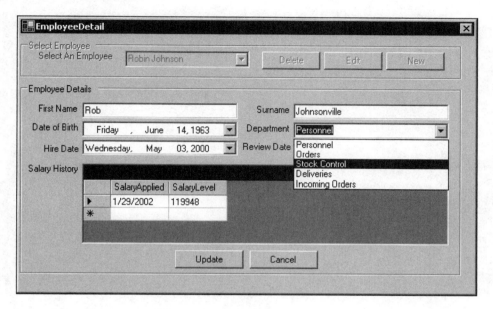

Summary

In this chapter we have looked at the HumanResources sample database, which we will come back to throughout the rest of this book. We began by showing the design of the database, and the script required to create it.

We then moved on to build our example HumanResources application code, which can be used to manipulate the data held within the Employees table of our HumanResources database. To achieve this we demonstrated practical usage of the following ADO.NET objects:

- ❑ SqlConnection
- ❑ SqlCommand
- ❑ DataSet
- ❑ DataTable
- ❑ DataRow
- ❑ DataRelation
- ❑ DataView

Handling Streams of Data with ADO.NET

In Chapter 1, we learned the basic definition of a `DataReader` and saw a simple example of how to use one to retrieve data from a data store. This chapter will look at `DataReader`s in much more detail, by covering the following points:

- ❑ Using a `DataReader` to retrieve data from a data store
- ❑ Using a `DataReader` to retrieve multiple resultsets
- ❑ Using a `DataReader` to update data in a data store
- ❑ Filling controls with the results of a `DataReader`

Introduction

The ADO.NET `DataReader` allows you to retrieve a read-only, forward-only data stream from a data store. The `DataReader` is faster than the `DataSet` and should be used whenever an in-memory copy of the data is not needed. In many ways, a `DataReader` is similar in concept to cursors within stored procedures. It doesn't really dictate the data to be retrieved, but just acts upon the data provided to it from somewhere else (in this case, the `Command` object). The reason that the `DataReader` is so fast is because only one record of data is ever in memory at a given time. Since this is a book about SQL Server, we will focus on the `SqlDataReader` object for retrieving data. However, as you learned in Chapter 1, there is also a .NET `OleDb` provider that provides similar functionality. All of the topics discussed in this chapter will also work with the `OleDb` data provider and the `OleDbDataReader`.

As a reminder here, the `SqlDataReader` exposes five public properties, as shown below:

- ❑ `Depth` – indicates how deeply nested the current row is. The outermost table has a depth of zero. Note that nesting is not supported by the `SqlDataReader` (only by the `OleDbDataReader`) so will always return zero for this property

- ❑ `FieldCount` – indicates the number of columns in the current row

- ❑ `IsClosed` – indicates whether the `DataReader` is closed

- ❑ `Item` – retrieves the value of a specified column in its native format

- ❑ `RecordsAffected` – indicates the number of rows affected by the SQL statement

The `SqlDataReader` also exposes a number of public methods, with the most common ones shown below:

- ❑ `Close` – Closes the `SqlDataReader`

- ❑ `IsDbNull` – Indicates whether a specified column contains values that are missing or non-existent

- ❑ `NextResult` – Advances the `DataReader` to the next resultset, when multiple results were returned from the batch

- ❑ `Read` – Moves the `SqlDataReader` to the next record

- ❑ `ToString` – Returns a string value that represents the current object

> **Note that the `SqlDataReader` object does not have any constructors (in other words will not accept any parameters when creating the object). The `SqlDataReader` object is created by calling the `ExecuteReader` method of the `SqlCommand` object. We will see more of this demonstrated throughout the remainder of this chapter.**

Using a DataReader To Retrieve Data

Let's first look at the overall process by which you retrieve data using a `DataReader`, and then we'll look at some actual code examples to demonstrate how it works. The first thing we need to do is to declare `Connection` and `Command` objects. The `Connection` object will specify the necessary information for connecting to the database. The `Command` object will communicate with the database over the connection to take whatever action is being requested. You then populate a `DataReader` by calling the `ExecuteReader` method of the `Command` object. There are two constructors for the `ExecuteReader` method, one that doesn't accept any parameters, and one that accepts a `CommandBehavior` parameter. These two examples are shown below:

```
drReader = cmd.ExecuteReader()
```

or

```
drReader = cmd.ExecuteReader(CommandBehavior.SingleResult)
```

In the second constructor opposite, you could specify any of the CommandBehavior values as the parameter. Or, if you use the first constructor above and do not pass a parameter to ExecuteReader, then the CommandBehavior.Default value will be used by default. The key point for us to understand then is what impact the CommandBehavior value has on how the ExecuteReader method is executed, and ultimately on what gets populated in the DataReader. To this end, let's now take a look at all of the possible values for CommandBehavior.

❑ CloseConnection – Automatically closes the associated Connection when the command is executed and the DataReader is closed.

❑ Default – The query can return one or more resultsets. Execution of the query may update the database.

❑ KeyInfo – The query returns column and primary key details and runs without locking any selected rows.

❑ SchemaOnly – The query returns column details only and does not change anything in the database.

❑ SequentialAccess – This is a way that the DataReader can handle rows that have columns with large binary values. This allows data to be loaded as a stream instead of the entire row. As a result, you can use the GetBytes or GetChars methods to specify a byte location to start the read.

❑ SingleResult – The query can return only one resultset. Execution of the query may update the database.

❑ SingleRow – The query is expected to return a single row. Execution of the query may update the database.

As you can see from the above list, the CommandBehavior values allow you to specify the type of command you are executing, ensuring that the DataReader will know what to expect.

So let's briefly recap the high-level process of retrieving data from a database using a DataReader. First, you declare Connection and Command objects and associate them with each other. Then, you call the ExecuteReader method of the Command object and return the results to a DataReader. You specify the value for the CommandBehavior parameter of the ExecuteReader constructor, or leave it blank so that the default value is used. Note that the default value allows you to update or retrieve data from a database.

Let's now get straight into the details of seeing how this works in action. For starters, make sure you have the System.Data and System.Data.SqlClient namespaces imported into any source file (outside of the class declaration) where you're wanting to access SQL Server databases with the SQL-managed provider:

```
Imports System.Data
Imports System.Data.SqlClient
```

Remember that the use of these Imports statements is optional, but saves us having to type in the fully qualified name of each namespace.

Now, let's have a look at how to use a SqlDataReader to retrieve data with a SQL statement.

Retrieving Data with a SELECT Statement

To open a `SqlDataReader` stream of data with the results of a SELECT statement, you first must declare a connection string and associate it with a new `SqlConnection` object:

```
Dim strConnection As String = "Server=MyServer; " _
    & "Database=HumanResources;" _
    & "User Id=sa;Password=;"

Dim cnSqlServer As New SqlConnection(strConnection)
```

Next, you specify the SELECT statement that you want to run against the database. The example below shows the SQL statement as a string variable called `strSQL`:

```
Dim strSQL As String = "SELECT * FROM Employees"
```

After defining the connection and SQL statement, you are ready to declare a `SqlDataReader` object and a new `SqlCommand` object. Recall that a `SqlCommand` object is what you use to send commands to the database:

```
Dim drReader As SqlDataReader
Dim cmd As New SqlCommand(strSQL, cnSqlServer)
```

Notice that the SQL statement and `Connection` object are being passed as parameters to the new `SqlCommand` object. This ensures that the `CommandText` and `Connection` properties are associated with the new `SqlCommand` object created.

We could of course simply use the `SqlCommand()` constructor with no parameters instead, in which case we would need to specify the properties separately as follows:

```
Dim cmd As New SqlCommand()

'set the SQL Statement to be executed
cmd.CommandText = strSQL
'set the Connection
cmd.Connection = cnSqlServer
```

The next step is to open the connection to the database:

```
Try

    'open the connection
    cnSqlServer.Open()
```

Then, you're ready to call the `ExecuteReader` method of the `SqlCommand` object to populate the `DataReader`:

```
'open the DataReader
drReader = cmd.ExecuteReader()
```

Notice how we're calling the ExecuteReader method without passing a CommandBehavior parameter to the constructor. This means that the default value will be used, allowing us to make database updates or selects. After calling the ExecuteReader method of the SqlCommand object, you have a live connection to the database and no other code can use this connection until this DataReader is closed. You can stream through the results one record at a time, as shown below:

```
'loop through the results and do something
Do While drReader.Read
    Console.WriteLine(drReader("Surname"))
Loop
```

Note that the Read method of the DataReader will retrieve the next record. When the DataReader is first opened, the position is one before the first record, so we have to do a read before we actually get any data from the database. The line of code inside the While loop will only be executed when there are remaining records. In this case, the line is writing the value of the Surname column to the console window. There are several ways that you can reference a column in the DataReader. The first one is the one shown above, which uses this syntax:

```
Console.WriteLine(drReader("Surname"))
```

We should note in passing here that the Item property of the DataReader is used by default in this example. However, you can also be explicit and specify the Item property, as shown below, which is the recommended approach:

```
Console.WriteLine(drReader.Item("Surname"))
```

> The **Item()** method will return the value converted to its native data type regardless of which syntax you use.

Note that it is possible to replace the column name with the numerical ordinal position of that column. Not only that, but you can also explicitly call a method, if you know what data type you are dealing with. For example:

```
Console.WriteLine(drReader.GetString(2))
```

In this case, we call the GetString method and pass the ordinal position of the Surname column in the DataReader. This corresponds to the order in which the column gets returned. While there is a performance gain in explicitly specifying the data type when retrieving the value, since you save the time that ADO.NET would otherwise spend converting the column value into the appropriate data type, this syntax is not recommended. The problem lies in the difficulty in maintaining code that isn't explicit in what value it is retrieving. Imagine the nightmare problems you will encounter if you change the order of columns, or add new columns to your SQL statements, and then your code breaks because of the 'hard-coded' column numbers.

At this point, you can add your closing error handling to catch any errors and then perform any cleanup:

```
        Catch

            'error handling code goes here

        Finally

            'cleanup code that needs to run no matter what

            'close the data reader
            drReader.Close()

            'close the connection
            cnSqlServer.Close()

            If Not cnSqlServer Is Nothing Then
                cnSqlServer.Dispose()
            End If
        End Try
```

It is absolutely critical that you make sure to close the DataReader when finished, since it will maintain a connection to the database until it is closed. The example above has the Close in the Finally block of the error handler. The code in the Finally block will run in all cases, whether the method runs successfully or if it encounters errors. As a result, it is a good place to consider putting your Close statement for the DataReader. Furthermore, in the example above, the Dispose() method of the Connection object is called to free all resources being used for it, in the event that it isn't already 'nothing'.

It is worth mentioning here that in the Catch statement you can add error handlers to take different actions depending on the type of errors that occur. For example, suppose you want to catch the scenario where an error is raised due to a field being missing. You could handle that something like this:

```
        Catch e as MissingFieldException

            'error handling code goes here to handle missing field
```

The complete code listing for the sample we just looked at is shown below:

```
    Dim strConnection As String = "Server=MyServer; " _
                              & "Database=HumanResources;" _
                              & "User Id=sa;Password=;"

    Dim cnSqlServer As New SqlConnection(strConnection)
    Dim strSQL As String = "SELECT * FROM Employees"
    Dim drReader As SqlDataReader
    Dim cmd As New SqlCommand(strSQL, cnSqlServer)

        Try

            'open the connection
            cnSqlServer.Open()

            'open the Data Reader
            drReader = cmd.ExecuteReader()
```

```
                    'loop through the results and do something
                    Do While drReader.Read
                        Console.WriteLine(drReader("Surname"))
                    Loop

            Catch

                    'error handling code goes here

            Finally

                    'cleanup code that needs to run no matter what

                    'close the data reader
                    drReader.Close()

                    'close the connection
                    cnSqlServer.Close()

                    If Not cnSqlServer Is Nothing Then
                        cnSqlServer.Dispose()
                    End If

            End Try
```

As you can see, it is really quite simple to retrieve data using a `DataReader`. You just have to handle the code at the receiving end to deal with looping through and acting upon the data returned.

GET Methods

In Chapter 2 we listed the large number of methods available to the developer when utilizing a `SqlDataReader` object. While we won't illustrate the use of every single method, we will look at some of the more common ones here.

GetDataTypeName

This is used when you need to determine the SQL Server database type for a particular column. The following code lists all of the data types of the columns within the `Employee` table from the `Pubs` database:

```
Dim sqlCon As New SqlConnection _
         ("Server=MyServer; Database=HumanResources;User ID=sa;Password=;")
Dim sqlCmd As New SqlCommand()
Dim sqlDR As SqlDataReader
Dim iLoop As Integer

sqlCmd.Connection = sqlCon
sqlCmd.CommandText = "SELECT * FROM dbo.employees"

sqlCon.Open()
```

```
sqlDR = sqlCmd.ExecuteReader

If sqlDR.Read Then
   For iLoop = 0 To sqlDR.FieldCount - 1
      Console.WriteLine(sqlDR.GetName(iLoop) & ": " _
                       & sqlDR.GetDataTypeName(iLoop))
   Next
End If

sqlDR.Close()
sqlCon.Close()
```

Executing this code produces the following results in the console window:

```
EmployeeId: int
FirstName: varchar
Surname: varchar
DateOfBirth: smalldatetime
SecurityPhoto: image
DateOfHire: smalldatetime
LastReview: smalldatetime
Department: int
```

GetSchemaTable

The GetSchemaTable method returns a DataTable object. This contains rows and columns describing the meta data of the ResultSet returned when the SqlCommand object is executed. The meta data describes the structure of the columns within the ResultSet. This can be particularly useful when executing stored procedures on remote servers where the underlying structure of the columns returned is unknown.

The following code executes the same SELECT against the Employee table within the Pubs database that we used in our previous example:

```
Dim sqlCon As New SqlConnection _
         ("Server=MyServer; Database=HumanResources;User ID=sa;Password=;")
Dim sqlCmd As New SqlCommand()
Dim sqlDR As SqlDataReader
Dim iLoop As Integer

sqlCmd.Connection = sqlCon
sqlCmd.CommandText = "SELECT EmployeeId,Surname,DateOfHire,Department" _
                   & "FROM dbo.employees"

sqlCon.Open()
sqlDR = sqlCmd.ExecuteReader
```

However, instead of displaying the values returned within the columns and rows, we show the meta data associated with the ResultSet by making a call to the GetSchemaTable method:

```
Dim myDataTable As DataTable
Dim myDataRow As DataRow
```

```
myDataTable = sqlDR.GetSchemaTable

For iLoop = 0 To myDataTable.Columns.Count() - 1
   Console.Write(myDataTable.Columns(iLoop).ColumnName & Chr(9))
   For Each myDataRow In myDataTable.Rows()
      Console.Write(myDataRow.Item(iLoop))
      Console.Write(Chr(9))
   Next
   Console.WriteLine("")
Next
```

```
sqlDR.Close()
sqlCon.Close()
```

The output written to our console windows will look similar to the table shown here. This is all meta data, data describing the columns within the ResultSet, not the values within those columns themselves:

ColumnName	EmployeeId	Surname	DateOfHire	Department
ColumnOrdinal	0	1	2	3
ColumnSize	4	30	4	4
NumericPrecision	10	255	5	23
NumericScale	255	255	16	10
IsUnique	False	False	False	False
BaseColumnName	EmployeeId	Surname	DateOfHire	Department
DataType	System.Int32	System.String	System.DateTime	System.Int32
AllowDBNull	False	False	False	False
ProviderType	8	22	15	8
IsIdentity	True	False	False	False
IsAutoIncrement	True	False	False	False
IsRowVersion	True	False	False	False
IsLong	False	False	False	False
IsReadOnly	False	False	False	False

GetValues / GetSqlValues

The GetValues or GetSqlValues methods can be used to populate an array with the values from all the columns contained within the current row of the SqlDataReader. Use the GetSqlValues method if you want the array to be populated with Type objects that correspond to the column's native SQL Server data type, alternatively use GetValues to populate the array with Type objects using .NET data types.

The following code, once again, does a simple `SELECT` from the `Employees` table within our `HumanResources` database:

```
Dim sqlCon As New SqlConnection _
        ("Server=MyServer; Database=HumanResources;User ID=sa;Password=;")
Dim sqlCmd As New SqlCommand()
Dim sqlDR As SqlDataReader
Dim iLoop As Integer

sqlCmd.Connection = sqlCon
sqlCmd.CommandText = "SELECT * FROM dbo.employees"

sqlCon.Open()
sqlDR = sqlCmd.ExecuteReader
```

Now, to output the row's column values, we populate our array and then cycle through this array outputting each value to the console window:

```
Dim MyColumns(sqlDR.FieldCount - 1) As Object

While sqlDR.Read
   sqlDR.GetValues(MyColumns)
   For iLoop = 0 To sqlDR.FieldCount - 1
      Console.Write(MyColumns(iLoop) & Chr(9))
   Next
      Console.WriteLine("")
End While
```

```
sqlDR.Close()
sqlCon.Close()
```

Retrieving Multiple Resultsets

Having seen how to populate a `DataReader` from a single SQL statement, it's time to look at how you can retrieve multiple resultsets by running SQL statements in a batch:

```
Dim strConnection As String = "Server=MyServer; " _
                            & "Database=HumanResources;" _
                            & "User Id=sa;Password=;"

Dim cnSqlServer As New SqlConnection(strConnection)
Dim strSQL As String = "SELECT * FROM Employees;" & _
                       "SELECT * FROM Departments;"
```

Notice how the SQL statement contains two `SELECT` statements, separated by semi-colons (the proper syntax for sending multiple statements to SQL Server). This code also functions in exactly the same way as if we were using a stored procedure to return multiple resultsets. The next section of our code is similar to the other examples we have already seen. We begin by opening the database connection and populating the `DataReader`:

```
Dim drReader As SqlDataReader
Dim cmd As New SqlCommand(strSQL, cnSqlServer)

    Try

        'open the connection
        cnSqlServer.Open()

        'open the Data Reader
        drReader = cmd.ExecuteReader()
```

Here is where the biggest difference comes in. Since you sent two commands to the database, there are two sets of results that your DataReader will be scrolling through:

```
        'loop through the first set of results
        Do While drReader.Read
            'write the Surname to the console
            Console.WriteLine(drReader("Surname"))
        Loop
```

You loop through the first one in the same manner as before. Then, in order to access the results in the second ResultSet, you execute the NextResult method of the DataReader object:

```
        'Move to the next set of results
        drReader.NextResult()
```

After you move to the next resultset, you loop through it in the same fashion as the first one:

```
        'loop through the second set of results
        Do While drReader.Read
            'write the Department Description to the console
            Console.WriteLine(drReader("Description"))
        Loop

    Catch

        'error handling code goes here

    Finally

        'cleanup code that needs to run no matter what

        'close the data reader
        drReader.Close()

        'close the connection
        cnSqlServer.Close()

        If Not cnSqlServer Is Nothing Then
            cnSqlServer.Dispose()
        End If

    End Try
```

The output of this query will look something like the following:

Johnson
Samson
Jones
Doe
Glucina
Wright
Glucina
Anderson
Brown
Smith
Allan
Personnel
Orders
Stock Control
Deliveries
Incoming Orders

For the sake of completeness here let's now briefly take a look at how to use a `DataReader` to execute a stored procedure.

Retrieving Data By Executing a Stored Procedure

Populating a `DataReader` from a stored procedure is slightly different from doing it with a SQL string. The lines that differ from what you have already seen are shown highlighted in the code sample below:

```
Dim strConnection As String = "Server=MyServer; " _
                            & "Database=HumanResources;" _
                            & "User Id=sa;Password=;"

Dim cnSqlServer As New SqlConnection(strConnection)
    Dim strSPName As String = "EmployeesDepartments"
    Dim drReader As SqlDataReader
    Dim cmd As New SqlCommand(strSPName, cnSqlServer)

    Try

        'open the connection
        cnSqlServer.Open()

        'set the Type to Stored Procedure
        cmd.CommandType = CommandType.StoredProcedure


        'open the Data Reader
        drReader = cmd.ExecuteReader()

        'loop through the results and do something
        Do While drReader.Read
            Console.WriteLine(drReader("Name"))
        Loop
```

```
    Catch

        'error handling code goes here

    Finally

        'cleanup code that needs to run no matter what

        'close the data reader
        drReader.Close()

        'close the connection
        cnSqlServer.Close()

        If Not cnSqlServer Is Nothing Then
            cnSqlServer.Dispose()
        End If


    End Try
```

Notice that in this case, instead of specifying the SQL string, we specify the name of the stored procedure that we want to execute. In this case, our `EmployeesDepartments` stored procedure will return a list of the employees and their corresponding departments. We also have to specify that the `CommandType` property of the `SqlCommand` object is a stored procedure, unlike in the previous example, where we used the default value (a SQL statement). The other lines of code are the same as in our prior examples.

Since in this case we're calling our `EmployeesDepartments` stored procedure, which concatenates the `Surname` and `FirstName` values together into a new field called `Name`, we will write the value to the `Name` column to the console for each record returned:

```
            Console.WriteLine(drReader("Name"))
```

Note that there are further details regarding the use of stored procedures in Chapter 6.

Using a DataReader To Update Data

All of our examples up to this point have just been reading data from the database. At this point, we're ready to see how you can use the `DataReader` to actually update data in the underlying database. Here is an example of how you can insert a new record into the `Departments` table of our `HumanResources` database:

```
    Dim strConnection As String = "Server=MyServer; " _
                            & "Database=HumanResources;" _
                            & "User Id=sa;Password=;"

    Dim cnSqlServer As New SqlConnection(strConnection)
```

```
Dim strSQL As String = "INSERT INTO Departments " & _
                       "(Description) VALUES ('Management')"
Dim drReader As SqlDataReader
Dim cmd As New SqlCommand(strSQL, cnSqlServer)

    Try

        'open the connection
        cnSqlServer.Open()

        'open the Data Reader
        drReader = cmd.ExecuteReader()

        drReader.Close()

        Console.WriteLine(drReader.RecordsAffected())

    Catch

        'error handling code goes here

    Finally

        'cleanup code that needs to run no matter what
        If drReader.IsClosed = False Then
            drReader.Close()
        End If
        'close the connection
        cnSqlServer.Close()

        If Not cnSqlServer Is Nothing Then
            cnSqlServer.Dispose()
        End If
    End Try
```

Notice how there are only a few differences. First, the SQL statement contains the INSERT statement instead of the SELECT statement we have used previously. Second, notice how the DataReader object is being closed immediately after calling the ExecuteReader method. The reason for closing it at this point, in addition to within the Finally block, is because we want to get an accurate value in the RecordsAffected property. Since the RecordsAffected property will give the number of records in the database that were affected by the SQL statement, we need to close the database connection immediately after our INSERT statement, so as to get a meaningful value. You will also note the absence of any results. If you invoke the drReader.Read() method it will immediately return False with any kind of SQL statement that updates a database (versus returning data).

Just one line of code above would need to be modified if we wanted to perform an update or delete on records in the database. All we have to do is modify the SQL statement to make this perform an update or a delete. For example, the following statement would delete the record we just added.

```
Dim strSQL As String = "DELETE FROM Departments " & _
                       "WHERE Description = 'Management'"
```

Populating Controls Using a DataReader

In all of our prior examples to this point, we have not really done anything other than display the values we have returned from the DataReader to the console. In a real-world case, you would most likely use the DataReader to load data onto a web page, or to populate a control being displayed on a form or page. In this section, we will look at an example of how to loop through a DataReader and populate a ComboBox with its contents. Note that this concept applies to pretty much any control you choose, since you just loop through the DataReader stream of data and add the value(s) to the control one record at a time.

The example below will select all employees in the Employees table in our HumanResources database. It will then display the Surname and FirstName fields to the user in a combo box. It will have the EmployeeId stored as the ValueMember property so that you will be using a key the database understands if you need to update the database later. To run the example create a new Windows Application and add a ComboBox control to the form. Clear the Text property of this control and then add the following code to the form's Load event:

```
Dim strConnection As String = "Server=MyServer; " _
                            & "Database=HumanResources;" _
                            & "User Id=sa;Password=;"

Dim cnSqlServer As New SqlConnection(strConnection)
Dim strSQL As String = "SELECT * FROM Employees"
Dim drReader As SqlDataReader
Dim cmd As New SqlCommand(strSQL, cnSqlServer)

    Try

        'open the connection
        cnSqlServer.Open()

        'open the Data Reader
        drReader = cmd.ExecuteReader()

        'loop through the results and do something
        Do While drReader.Read

            'populate a combo box with employee names

            'display the name
            ComboBox1.Items.Add(drReader("Surname") & _
                    ", " & drReader("FirstName"))

        Loop

    Catch

        'error handling code goes here

    Finally

        'cleanup code that needs to run no matter what
```

```
            'close the data reader
            drReader.Close()

            'close the connection
            cnSqlServer.Close()

            If Not cnSqlServer Is Nothing Then
                cnSqlServer.Dispose()
            End If
        End Try
```

Notice how we loop through the DataReader and use it to populate the ComboBox with employee names. The names are being added to the ComboBox in the order they were retrieved from the DataReader. An example of what the screen might look like after running this code is shown below:

This is a simple example of how to use a DataReader to fill data in a control. Let's look at another example. DataReaders are a good approach for a lot of the data retrieval scenarios you will encounter in web applications, since you can quickly get data to display on a page. So our next data-binding example will demonstrate how to use a DataGrid to display data from a DataReader in a web application. Let's create an ASP.NET Web Application and place a Button and a DataGrid control on the form. Place the following code under the Click event of the Button control:

```
        Private Sub Button1_Click(ByVal sender As System.Object, ByVal e _
                As System.EventArgs) Handles Button1.Click

        Dim strConnection As String = "Server=MyServer; " _
                                & "Database=HumanResources;" _
                                & "User Id=sa;Password=;"

        Dim cnSqlServer As New SqlConnection(strConnection)
        Dim strSQL As String = "SELECT * FROM Employees"
        Dim drReader As SqlDataReader
        Dim cmd As New SqlCommand(strSQL, cnSqlServer)
```

```
Try
    'open the connection
    cnSqlServer.Open()

    'open the Data Reader
    drReader = cmd.ExecuteReader()

    'Bind the Data Reader to the DataGrid
    DataGrid1.DataSource = drReader
    DataGrid1.DataBind()

Catch
    'error handling code goes here

Finally

    'cleanup code that needs to run no matter what

    'close the data reader
    drReader.Close()

    'close the connection
    cnSqlServer.Close()

    If Not cnSqlServer Is Nothing Then
        cnSqlServer.Dispose()
    End If
End Try


End Sub
```

Notice that this time we have two lines of code that bind the DataGrid to the DataReader, as follows:

```
'Bind the Data Reader to the DataGrid
DataGrid1.DataSource = drReader
DataGrid1.DataBind()
```

Not only that but we also removed the loop to move through the DataReader one record at a time and take some action. In this case, by binding the DataReader to the DataGrid, VB.NET automatically handles this looping for us when it sets up the binding. If you by habit happen to leave the loop in your code and put the data-binding code shown above in that loop, then you will only see one row in the Datagrid, which will be the last record returned by the DataReader. That is because it will redo the binding for each record that it fetches and will end up just displaying the last row. You can see why it is important in this situation to make sure you don't use a loop to retrieve the data one by one.

Now, when you run this program, you will see a web page with a button. After clicking the button, you should see the results in the DataGrid, similar to that shown overleaf:

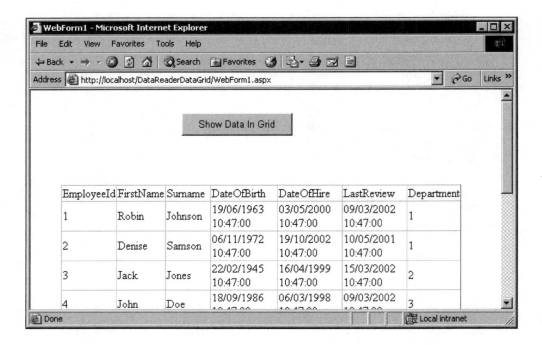

Summary

In this chapter we have looked at several examples of how to use a `DataReader` to return a forward-only, read-only stream of data from the database. As you have seen firsthand, the `DataReader` is really easy to work with and provides a lot of performance advantages because it processes one row at a time. We specifically learned:

❑   How to populate a `DataReader` with the results of a SQL statement

❑   How to populate a `DataReader` with multiple resultsets

❑   How to populate a `DataReader` with the results of a stored procedure

❑   How to update a database using a `DataReader` and determine the number of records that were affected

❑   How to stream through the `DataReader` and take action, such as populate the contents of a control

Now that we have a good understanding of how to use a `DataReader` to retrieve data, we will move on to another topic, that of writing good stored procedures.

5

Writing Good Stored Procedures

Stored procedures are the heart and lungs of any database application. Well-written procedures are fast, utilize T-SQL to its full capacity, enable a well-designed database to perform efficiently, respond quickly, and compute at an optimum level. Many developers can perform reasonable T-SQL but what separates excellent developers from the pack is their ability to utilize T-SQL commands efficiently. Stored Procedures allow a group of T-SQL commands to be compiled and stored within SQL Server for reuse whenever necessary. This means that we do not have to recode each time we need to do the same thing, and that we only have to make changes in one place if they are required. Throughout this chapter we will see how they provide a convenient, high-performance means of utilizing data within your database.

This chapter will focus on how to use stored procedures to create more secure, effective, well-performing, scaleable code that is robust enough for production applications. We will demonstrate how to work with more complex areas of code and how to optimize your code so that you write clean, fast, and efficient T-SQL in your stored procedures. To that end we will look at:

- ❑ Data Security and stored procedures
- ❑ The structure of stored procedures
- ❑ How to join data from multiple tables
- ❑ Control of flow
- ❑ Passing resultsets and XML into and out of stored procedures
- ❑ User-defined functions
- ❑ Handling errors

It should be stated here that this chapter is by no means an introduction to creating stored procedures or an introduction to T-SQL programming. It is assumed that you have a good understanding of the basics of these topics and this chapter is intended to build on that knowledge.

Stored Procedures and Performance

As you have seen in previous chapters, we can execute T-SQL commands in order to return data to the calling VB.NET program. Each call has been sent across the network via ADO.NET and TCP/IP to the server, processed by SQL Server, and then returned to the client by the same route. In the case of a large number of T-SQL commands processing a large amount of data, this results in heavy network loading, especially if there is additional data processing performed by the VB.NET program itself (manipulating user input values for example). Stored procedures can help to significantly reduce network traffic for two reasons:

- ❏ Once created, stored procedures are stored in the database. This reduces the number of calls required between client and server, and will significantly reduce the processing load when dealing with large tables within the database. For complex data logic routines the saving can be very significant because some require hundreds or thousands of queries. By embedding these into a stored procedure, we need to pass only one T-SQL command (the command to execute the stored procedure) to the server, saving network bandwidth and reducing response times.

- ❏ When a stored procedure is executed for the first time, it is parsed and optimized by SQL Server, to ensure that the most efficient execution plan is performed, and then compiled. After that first execution it is likely to be cached in memory for any repeated calls required. This improves the speed of any subsequent executions, since SQL Server simply calls the already optimized stored procedure from memory, rather than passing the T-SQL commands over the network once again. In Chapter 6 we will look at how we can get similar speed advantages by calling any T-SQL code from VB.NET.

Security

Perhaps one of the biggest security mistakes people make is to allow access to the raw data, either to all users, or to specific groups of people. The only SQL Server login that should have access to the raw data is someone with database owner privileges. Even this can be seen as questionable if there is no other auditing in place, such as recording alterations to existing data, or monitoring additions and deletions to crucial areas of the system. Without such auditing the user will be free to modify data without any record of this being made. This can make a full recovery of the database, in the event of a security breach or system failure for example, very difficult to achieve, without significant data loss.

While careful monitoring of login authority, through the use of roles, and password protection of login IDs, are of most immediate concern in maintaining a secure application, we will focus here on how writing stored procedures to complete application tasks can assist with this protection. Such stored procedures not only allow the underlying tables to be inspected or manipulated in a controlled manner, but also the setting up of audit routines to track any data changes, especially to sensitive corporate information.

In Chapter 3 we created our database but we did not alter the access rights on the tables we created. At this point only users who are defined as dbos (database owners) will have access to that data. So how do users access the data within applications? While we could make every user a dbo this would mean that we'd lose all control of the data, since every user would be able to modify the database. The neater solution to this problem is to create roles, containing users, which are given specific access rights to data. What we can then do is write stored procedures against each table and grant execution rights on these stored procedures to those roles deemed necessary.

We'll talk about roles and authentication in Chapter 11, and you can also read more about them in 'Professional SQL Server 2000 Programming' (Wrox Press, ISBN 1861004486).

In our HumanResources database we should build stored procedures that access our tables, but restrict access to some of the stored procedures to specific roles. In this way we can restrict access to the more sensitive information, such as salary details. So, for example, if we have a stored procedure called PaymentsMade, used to return payments received and made by employees, then we can restrict access to it (in Query Analyzer) as follows:

```
GRANT EXECUTE ON PaymentsMade TO Payroll
```

This explicitly allows permissions to execute the procedure to the Payroll role. Payroll is a user-defined role, which in this case would only include those users with permission to access financial details. Under no circumstances should you ever complete a command granting access to the Public role (defined within SQL Server), no matter what the stored procedure is processing, because this role:

❑   has all users and roles assigned to it by default.

❑   cannot be dropped.

❑   captures all default permissions for users in the database.

In other words, you will lose all control of your data by granting execute to Public.

We can also explicitly prevent users from accessing the stored procedure, even if they are a member of the Payroll role, by using DENY:

```
DENY EXECUTE ON PaymentsMade TO DodgyJack
```

This prevents the user DodgyJack from executing the PaymentsMade stored procedure even if he is a member of the Payroll user-defined role we granted permissions to above. An explicit DENY always takes precedence over a GRANT.

To complete the same action in Enterprise Manager, find the relevant stored procedure, right mouse click, and select **All Tasks | Manage Permissions**. This will bring up the **Permissions** dialog.

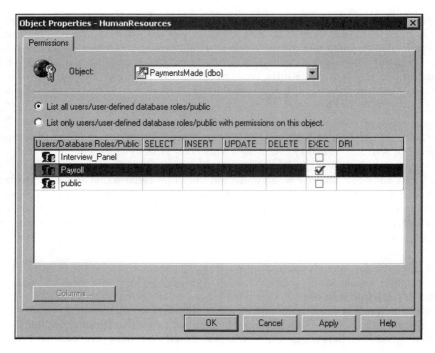

Selecting the role(s) that you wish to grant execution authority on is completed by a simple click, followed by pressing the Apply button.

> **Only one user should be set up as dbo, and use of this should be strictly controlled. While you might consider giving several users dbo access rights during the development of a system, this should never be done in production. Data and data structures in production are sacrosanct. In many organizations any changes to data will need to be audited. Allowing direct access to the data will never provide the auditing required.**

Now that we have covered some of the security issues surrounding stored procedures, it's time to take a look at how to work with them and ensure that we get optimum performance from them.

Executing Stored Procedures

Perhaps one of the greatest overlooked performance issues relates to the way in which you execute a stored procedure. Although not a large gain, when it comes to running large numbers of procedures every millisecond can count. By specifying the owner of the stored procedure, which will in most cases be dbo, as the prefix to the stored procedure name, you will avoid SQL Server having to search through its system catalog for this information. For example:

```
EXEC dbo.ShowMeTheMoney
```

This command identifies a unique and specific occurrence of the stored procedure, whereas SQL Server has to first identify the owner when you execute the following:

```
EXEC ShowMeTheMoney
```

When you call an unqualified stored procedure, SQL Server first of all tries to find it by looking under the name of the current login. If you are logged in as Joe Bloggs, it will begin by searching the sysobjects table for the stored procedure under that login. If it is not found, it is only then that SQL Server will search for a stored procedure owned by dbo.

> The sysobjects table is a system table, existing within every database, which should not be modified. It holds a list of all the objects within a database from tables through to stored procedures. There is no problem inspecting sysobjects and there will be times when there are advantages when searching for a specific item, however do take care.

When deciding on your naming convention for use with stored procedures it is best not to use the sp_ prefix for your own procedures. This is because stored procedures prefixed with sp_ are treated specially by SQL Server. The master database is first searched to find a matching procedure name, not the currently selected database for the connection. If no stored procedure with a matching name is found in master then, and only then, the current database is searched to locate a matching procedure. This is extra processing overhead that is unnecessary and can easily be avoided by using a different naming convention. Some common naming conventions include prefix stored procedures with usp_ or company name abbreviation such as ssl_ or wrx_. It is also common for stored procedures not to be prefixed at all and named simply on function, such as ShowCurrentEmployees.

Dynamic SQL

This section could really come under the *Security* or *Performance* parent topics as it affects both. Dynamic SQL refers to building up a T-SQL command in a character variable, and executing it using the EXEC function. For example:

```
CREATE PROCEDURE dbo.ExecuteDynamicSQL(@SQLCommand varchar(512))
AS
    EXEC(@SQLCommand)
GO
```

This is effectively a dumb procedure, since it knows nothing about the command it is going to execute other than it will be passed at run-time as a parameter.

```
EXEC dbo.ExecuteDynamicSQL 'SELECT * FROM dbo.Employees'
```

This will return a list of all rows from the Employees table by passing SELECT * FROM dbo.Employees as a parameter to the stored procedure. The stored procedure takes that parameter and runs it using the EXEC function, without ever knowing what is contained in it.

Using dynamic SQL in stored procedures is a bad idea, from both a security and performance point of view. As we mentioned above you can grant a user the ability to access a stored procedure without granting that user the rights to have direct access to the tables used by the procedure. This means that code running within a stored procedure is executed within the security context of the user who *created* the procedure, rather than the user *running* the stored procedure. This is not true, however, in the case of dynamic SQL. EXEC runs dynamic T-SQL commands you pass to it outside of the security context of the stored procedure, within the security context of the user calling the stored procedure. For the dynamic SQL command to be successful the user running the stored procedure must have appropriate permissions on all of the tables used within that dynamic SQL command. This is unacceptable when the security of data is a concern and somewhat negates the point of using stored procedures in the first place. For example:

```
CREATE PROCEDURE dbo.ListEmployees
AS
    SELECT EmployeeId,
        FirstName,
        Surname
    FROM    Employees
GO
EXEC dbo.ListEmployees
```

The user who executes this procedure requires absolutely no permissions on the Employees table, other than EXECUTE permission on the stored procedure. The stored procedure could then be expanded to include auditing and authority checking logic, making access to the Employees table very secure. However when using a Dynamic SQL alternative such as:

```
CREATE PROCEDURE dbo.ListTable @Columns varchar(255) ,
                                @Table as varchar(255)
AS
    DECLARE @sql varchar(8000)
    SELECT @sql='SELECT  ' + @columns +'
    FROM '+@Table

    EXEC (@sql)
GO

EXEC dbo.ListTable 'EmployeeId, FirstName,Surname','Employees'
```

the user requires permissions to both the stored procedure and permissions to the Employees table. In fact there is no reason at all for the user to execute this procedure as they can go directly to the table without invoking any of the auditing or authority checking logic, which may be built in.

The second point about dynamic SQL relates to performance. As dynamic SQL is exactly that, dynamic, SQL Server will need to generate a new query plan for each execution. Once again this negates a main benefit of using stored procedures, namely that the query plan is generated the first time the procedure is run and held in memory for subsequent executions of it.

SET NOCOUNT

After each T-SQL statement has finished executing, the number of rows affected by that statement is sent over the network to the client. By default this also happens for statements contained within stored procedures. While this may not be a concern for small procedures, or for low-use databases, the added overhead of this unnecessary network traffic can be significant when dealing with large procedures that execute many T-SQL statements, or when you have a high number of users executing code simultaneously.

By setting the SET NOCOUNT option to ON you disable the sending of row modified information back to the client, improving the efficiency of the stored procedure call. We can demonstrate how SET NOCOUNT works by executing the following batch of queries in Query Analyzer:

```
SELECT COUNT(*) FROM dbo.Courses
SELECT COUNT(*) FROM dbo.PaymentTypes
SELECT COUNT(*) FROM dbo.CourseDetails
SELECT COUNT(*) FROM dbo.Departments
SELECT COUNT(*) FROM dbo.Employees
SELECT COUNT(*) FROM dbo.Payments
```

Ignoring the actual resultsets for a moment, and taking a look at the messages pane, we see something similar to that shown below. This is SQL Server informing our client of the number of rows affected after each statement in the batch:

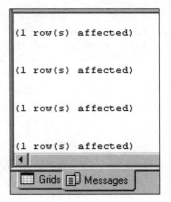

Simply by adding SET NOCOUNT ON to the start of this query batch and re-executing it, you will see that you no longer get this information as SQL Server is now not bothering to send the affected rows across the network to our client. When executed as a T-SQL command the SET NOCOUNT option applies for the duration of a connection and remains in effect for all T-SQL commands executed on that connection. However, if SET NOCOUNT is executed within a stored procedure itself, this setting only applies for commands executed within that stored procedure. When the stored procedure has completed the NOCOUNT option is changed back to its previous setting.

Parameters in Stored Procedures

Many stored procedures are built, not to be executed as they are, but rather so as to accept information in order to make selections on the data and produce results. Building parameters onto a stored procedure, as you would do on a subroutine within VB.NET, is just as crucial. There are a number of performance considerations to take into account when building stored procedures, as well as some good coding techniques.

First of all parameters can be used to input a value, output a value, or in fact both. As you move through this chapter you will see this in action. By default a parameter is defined as an input parameter.

Do not create a parameter to have a defined size that is not the same as the definition for the column of data that it will be working with. Too small can cause erroneous output, while too large can be a waste of network traffic. For example if you are inserting data into a table that has a varchar(500) column for a notes field; for security and performance purposes you use a stored procedure to insert the notes into the base table, however the stored procedure has a parameter defined as varchar(255). If you attempt to insert a string value of 400 characters, the string will be truncated at 255 characters when it is passed to the stored procedure parameter, even though the table itself would have no problem with this amount of data.

Default Values

Some parameters passed into stored procedures will, in the majority of passes, have an identical value. Such parameters become prime candidates for setting a default value, which will then allow the calling program to avoid passing this information across the network. While this does not make a large reduction in network traffic when applied to one parameter, if you have several parameters and you are looking to insert a volume of records, this can engineer a large and useful saving.

Setting a default value for a parameter in a stored procedure is very similar to VB.NET, since you simply place an equals sign after the data type declaration and then the value. An example of this is shown below where we believe that in most cases people will be interested in payment type of 1:

```
CREATE PROCEDURE dbo.PaymentsMade @PaymentType INT = 1,
                                  @Month INT,@Year INT
AS
SELECT SUM(Amount)
FROM Payments
WHERE PaymentType = @PaymentType
AND DATEPART(mm,PaymentDate) = @Month
AND DATEPART(yy,PaymentDate) = @Year
```

In order to execute the above procedure we simply need to name the stored procedure, then name and pass in a value for each of the two required parameters:

```
EXEC dbo.PaymentsMade @Month=2,@Year=2002
```

Or you could pass values for all three parameters:

```
EXEC dbo.PaymentsMade @PaymentType=1, @Month=2,@Year=2002
```

If you are specifying all the parameters, then you do not need to supply the parameter name as part of the execute statement. However, this makes the code dependent on the order of the parameters as declared in the stored procedure:

```
EXEC dbo.PaymentsMade 1, 2, 2002
```

It is a much better coding to supply parameter names when executing stored procedures as this allows for the order of parameters in the stored procedure definition to change at a later point without breaking existing code that calls the procedure. It also helps to ensure that the values you are providing are being used for the stored procedure parameters you intend.

We should note that it is not possible to extend the defaults within this example stored procedure further. So, for example, if you wish to set the default for Year to the current year, you would have to actually code the default value directly as part of your procedure logic, not include it as a default for the parameter. Functionality such as DATEPART, which will take part of a date and return a specific portion, as demonstrated previously where we return the month and year part of date, cannot be placed within the definition of a default value. Only a constant can be specified as default for a parameter. This is because the default value would become a "moving target" which would necessitate recompilation of the stored procedure for each execution just in case that value had altered.

SELECT * Statements

Many developers will use the SELECT * command in order to inspect data, while remaining unaware of the performance implications that using the SELECT command in this way incurs, as well as being unaware of the side-effects that may occur in their applications when columns are added to a table.

The SELECT * command will return every column from every table used in the query into the resultset that has been requested. You may well think this is an ideal scenario and perfect for what you wish to do. From a performance viewpoint, you have to sit back and consider whether having every column returned is, in fact, an appropriate use of network traffic and server resources. In many cases I have come across developers who have simply completed this command to avoid having to type in the handful of columns they want to see. This is not quite as bad in a straight T-SQL command as it is within a stored procedure (although it's bad enough).

It is recommended that you avoiding coding a SELECT * statement within a stored procedure whenever possible. The reason for this is that the command will return all columns in the table you are accessing, many of which will be of no interest to you. Maybe not a major concern you might think, but you may end up returning a sensitive item of information to a calling program and therefore breaching security, especially as you should keep in mind that any number of columns could be added to this table days, weeks, or years from the time that you wrote your original procedure.

Deferred Name Resolution

SQL Server 2000 uses a slightly different form of name resolution than earlier versions when creating stored procedures. It now uses a **deferred** scheme for resolving object names. Deferred name resolution allows stored procedures to be created that refer to objects that don't exist at the time of procedure creation. This allows these referenced objects to be created at a later time obviating the requirement to create objects in a strict order. This can be of great assistance to project teams that include developers working on different parts of a single database. It also makes automatic deployment of SQL Server objects easier to manage. Unfortunately this also makes run-time errors, as opposed to compile-time errors, more likely to occur. These errors are much more difficult to track down and resolve than compile-time errors, and may appear worse since it is often customers who discover them.

153

As an example of this, earlier versions of SQL Server would complain that an object didn't exist if a typo was made in an object name when trying to create the procedure. This allowed us to go back and fix the error and compile the code again. If I have a typo in an object name under SQL Server 2000's deferred name resolution process, my stored procedure will compile successfully and I won't know about my error until I, or someone else, tries to execute it.

This is also significant when rolling changes from a development environment to production. While your procedure may have compiled and tested fine in your development environment, a successful compilation in a production environment does not guarantee that the code will run equally successfully there. Some database objects that the procedure relies on may exist within your development database, but may not have yet made it into your production database. If this is the case your stored procedure will compile fine in production but will generate an error when it is executed.

This rule does however only apply to objects that don't exist, not column names in objects that do exist. To summarize, the rules are:

❑   If you reference an object that doesn't exist at the time of creating the stored procedure, the creation will succeed and no error message will be generated.

❑   If you reference a column that doesn't exist, in an object that does exist, at the time of creating the stored procedure the creation will fail and a 'Unknown column' error will be thrown.

A simple way to check that the procedure is referencing objects that exit without actually executing it, is to generate an estimated execution plan. The generation of the estimated execution plan prepares the execution plan, which requires the validation of whether objects exist or not, but does not actually run the code. To do this highlight the execute statement for your procedure in Query Analyzer and select the Tools/Display Estimated Execution Plan menu item. Alternatively you use the SET SHOWPLAN_TEXT option to do this within your code itself. For example:

```
CREATE PROCEDURE selectfromtable
AS
    SELECT * FROM dbo.IDontExist
GO
SET SHOWPLAN_TEXT ON
GO
EXEC selectfromtable
GO
SET SHOWPLAN_TEXT OFF
```

which produces the following error message:

Server: Msg 208, Level 16, State 1, Procedure selectfromtable, Line 3
Invalid object name 'dbo.IDontExist'

However, the actual SELECT statement within the procedure isn't actually attempted, the code and object names are only validated. If there are no errors, instead of the message above you will get a textual representation of the query plan to be used for this code returned. This can be ignored for testing purposes.

Joins

One of the ways that tables used to be joined in T-SQL was by using the WHERE statement. This is no longer the best option when joining tables within SQL Server, although it is still possible. You will find that the WHERE statement is used more to filter rows within your query, which is what it is really designed for. Using the WHERE statement for joining tables is difficult to follow as joining logic gets mixed up with the logic being used to filter the rows being returned. Also this use is not part of the ANSI SQL-92 standard, so it cannot be recommended because support for this type of join may not continue. In fact the old way of specifying outer joins *= and =* has been dropped from SQL Server 2000.

Within the FROM clause you can use the keyword JOIN, in conjunction with other keywords such as INNER, OUTER, CROSS, LEFT, and RIGHT, to accomplish the joining of the tables. Each of these keywords has special functionality and is discussed in detail below.

Every JOIN condition has to name the two tables involved in the join, as well as the name of the column, or columns, from each table that the join will use for combining the two data sources. There is usually a logical operator between the two named columns, although with CROSS JOINs this is not the case.

When executing queries that require rows from multiple tables you are still only joining two tables at a time using the JOIN syntax. However, a table can be joined to more than one other table within a single query, for example TableA can be joined to TableB. TableB can also be joined to TableC. TableC can be joined to TableD. If this example were to be specified as INNER JOINs for a SELECT statement, it would be represented similarly to this:

```
SELECT *
FROM TableA
JOIN TableB ON TableA.AJoinColumn = TableB.AJoinColumn
JOIN TableC ON TableB.BJoinColumn = TableC.BJoinColumn
JOIN TableD ON TableC.CJoinColumn = TableD.CJoinColumn
```

Another common method of joining involves a central **fact table** to which all, or most, other tables are joined. This is especially common in data warehouses. In this case, all of our tables may join to TableA, which is a fact table, for example:

```
SELECT *
FROM TableA
JOIN TableB ON TableA.BJoinColumn = TableB.BJoinColumn
JOIN TableC ON TableA.CJoinColumn = TableC.CJoinColumn
JOIN TableD ON TableA.DJoinColumn = TableD.DJoinColumn
```

Notice the slight change in the way we specify our JOIN syntax, however either method, or a combination of the two, is valid and this will be entirely driven from the physical design of your SQL Server database.

INNER JOIN

This is probably the most common of type of join and is a direct "replacement" for the WHERE statement. While there is no performance degradation or gain either way at the moment, this is unlikely to remain the case in future releases of SQL Server, since use of the JOIN keyword is now a SQL standard.

So the old way of performing this type of join between two tables may have looked something like:

```
SELECT *
FROM TableA, TableB
WHERE TableA.AColumn = TableB.AColumn
```

but the ANSI standard way of performing this type of join is:

```
SELECT *
FROM TableA
INNER JOIN TableB ON TableA.AColumn = TableB.AColumn
```

While it is hard to appreciate how much more intuitive the ANSI syntax is over the older method in this simple example, the first time you write a query that joins over 5 tables you will begin to understand. The new syntax easily allows you to identify what is being joined to what, as opposed to the old syntax where this information was all mixed up as part of the WHERE clause.

An INNER JOIN is the only join that will return all of the rows from the tables named in the join where there is a full match concerning the columns and the operator defining the joining statement. If a particular row, in the first table being joined, has no matching row based on the join columns, then in the second table this row will not be returned. Only rows from both tables that have columns used in the join criteria match will be returned.

The keyword INNER is an optional word as this is the default when using the keyword JOIN. In the example below, we perform a simple join between the Employees table and the Departments table. The two join columns are defined as indexes within their respective tables so we have already optimized our query.

> **Whenever possible use columns from defined indexes. If you do have to use columns in a join that are not part of an index, then review your indexes and see if it is worthwhile creating indexes to support the join, by questioning the number of times the procedure will run.**

Let's look at an example of an inner join in the following stored procedure:

```
CREATE PROCEDURE dbo.EmployeesDepartments
AS

    SELECT emp.EmployeeId,
        RTRIM(emp.FirstName) + ' ' + RTRIM(emp.Surname) as Name,
        dep.Description
    FROM dbo.Employees emp
    INNER JOIN dbo.Departments dep ON emp.Department = dep.DepartmentId

GO
```

A simple SELECT statement is joining the Employees and the Departments tables through the department IDs. Notice we are also specifying table aliases for both the Employees (emp) and Departments (dep) tables, which allows us to only specify these aliases instead of the full table names in the join and selection criteria.

If there is no index on the Employees table for the departmentId the table will be scanned from start to finish. Each record found will then be tested against the Departments table to check if a matching record exists there. If it does then we move on to printing it out. You may think that this is a waste and an index would improve results but it may not. SQL Server may perform a full table scan on the Employees table, as the index will not reduce the number of matches by a significant number. There is no magic figure as to when a table scan is chosen over an index but as a rule of thumb, an index will be chosen if around 15% or less of the records in the table will be returned by using that index.

To show a join of several tables, the following example will return details of employees and their departments with the payments they have received and their salary history. The procedure is detailed below.

```
CREATE PROCEDURE dbo.EmployeesFullDetails
AS
    SELECT    emp.FirstName, emp.Surname, dep.Description,
              pay.paymentId, pay.Amount, pay.PaymentDate,
              payt.PaymentDesc, sal.SalaryAppliedFrom, sal.SalaryLevel
    FROM      Employees emp
    JOIN      Departments dep       on emp.Department=dep.DepartmentID
    JOIN      Payments pay       on pay.EmployeeID=emp.EmployeeID
    JOIN      PaymentTypes payt       on payt.PaymentTypeID=pay.PaymentTypeID
    JOIN      Salaries sal       on sal.EmployeeID=emp.EmployeeID
GO
```

The SELECT statement in this procedure is joining five tables to produce one resultset. All five join types are INNER JOINs, which means only the rows from each of the tables that match the join criteria will be included in the resultset returned by this query.

We can specify any valid expression as part of our join criteria. If it evaluates to True for any given row combination between the two tables, then the join will be made. While almost all of the joins you see in SQL code will use two columns being checked for equality, or multiple columns being checked for equality separated by the AND operand, this is by no means always the case. Complex join requirements may join on several possible columns by specifying OR, instead of AND, or in special circumstances functions may be used to evaluate the join criteria. While we will not be covering these complex joins in this chapter, it is important you are aware of the possibilities in case you come across, or need, these types of joins in the future.

If we look at the execution plan generated for our example above, as shown in the following diagram, we can see that this code requires a great deal of processing by our SQL Server instance:

This diagram may appear a little daunting if you are unfamiliar with execution plans, but it isn't really. It is simply a graphical representation of the logical steps used by SQL Server to take the query you have submitted, then identify and return the data you have requested. Over time you will become familiar with this syntax and will find these diagrams extremely helpful in identifying and resolving query performance issues.

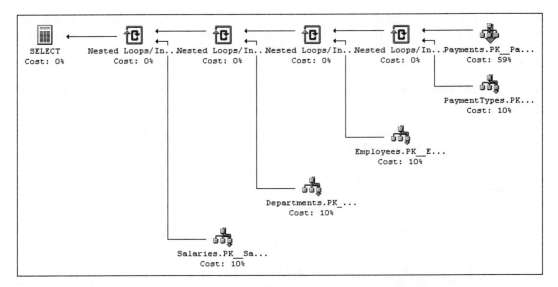

This execution plan is showing the five tables being joined together, and the internal method SQL Server is using to join the tables. `Payments` and `PaymentTypes` are joined, then `Employees`, then `Departments` and finally the `Salaries` table is joined into the resultset.

> **As understanding execution plans is critical for developing highly efficient T-SQL code, I strongly advise that you review the execution plans for all T-SQL queries that you construct for use in your applications.**

While it is perfectly possible for SQL Server to cope with this, it is crucial to reduce the numbers of records passed on down the process chain, by as many records as you can, when working with a number of joins. Placing the `Departments` table join at the end rather than at the beginning, makes no difference, as SQL Server will re-order the joins as it sees fit. In this instance it does move the `Departments` join to become the first process to take place.

It will not always be the case that you wish to return only matched rows, so let's take a look at working with **OUTER JOIN**s.

OUTER JOIN

OUTER JOIN is used to join two tables where we still require records for a table to be listed even if there are no joined records within the second table. Employing either a RIGHT or LEFT OUTER JOIN determines which table is seen as the driving force for the query, and where the records to be returned are expected to be found. A RIGHT OUTER JOIN is used where the records you definitely want to return will be found on the right-hand side of the JOIN statement. The result of this is that, where there is no match, any columns listed from the left-hand side of the join will have a value of NULL. A LEFT OUTER JOIN is the same but is used where conditions are reversed.

Here are some examples to demonstrate the syntax. The following query:

```
SELECT Col1, Col2
FROM table1
LEFT OUTER JOIN table2
    ON table1.Col1 = table2.Col2
```

will return all the rows from `table1` but only the rows from `table2` where `Col2` is equal to `table1`'s `Col1`. On the other hand:

```
SELECT Col1, Col2
FROM table1
RIGHT OUTER JOIN table2
    ON table1.Col1 = table2.Col2
```

will return all the rows from `table2`, but only the rows from `table1` that match the join criteria, `Col1=Col2`.

There is also a third option, the FULL OUTER JOIN where you wish to list records that would be missing in both tables.

```
SELECT Col1, Col2
FROM table1
FULL OUTER JOIN table2
    ON table1.Col1 = table2.Col2
```

All the rows from both tables will be returned, matched based on the join criteria `Col1=Col2` where possible. NULL values will be used as placeholders where no matching rows are found, as we see shortly.

Let's now take a look at more complex examples of all these types of join.

RIGHT OUTER JOIN

In this following query, we are dealing with a RIGHT OUTER JOIN. This is informing SQL Server that we want to list every record from the right-hand table (Departments) and where no matching records are found in the left-hand table (Employees) we expect to see the value NULL instead. Create the following stored procedure in the HumanResources database.

```
CREATE PROCEDURE DepartmentsWithEmployees
AS
    SELECT dep.Description, emp.EmployeeId,
        RTRIM(emp.FirstName) + ' ' + RTRIM(emp.Surname) as Name
    FROM Employees emp
    RIGHT OUTER JOIN Departments dep ON emp.department = dep.departmentId
GO
```

To prove the query works, execute it by running the following command:

```
EXEC dbo.DepartmentsWithEmployees
```

You will see output similar to that below. As expected, all the Departments records are listed and where there are no employees, there is a NULL value.

	EmployeeId	Name	Description
1	1	Robin Johnson	Personnel
2	2	Denise Samson	Personnel
3	3	Jack Jones	Orders
4	4	John Doe	Stock Control
5	5	Linda Glucina	Personnel
6	6	Laura Wright	Personnel
7	7	Stephanie Glucina	Orders
8	8	Linda Anderson	Personnel
9	9	Graham Brown	Stock Control

Again a table scan takes place because we are providing no filtering criteria, which would reduce the number of rows significantly.

LEFT OUTER JOIN

A variation on the theme is a LEFT OUTER JOIN. This tells SQL Server we wish to list all the records from the table on the left side of the join, the Employees table in our example. All matching records from the right-side table, in this case the Department table, will be listed and if no matching rows are found then NULL will be used for the column values instead:

```
CREATE PROCEDURE dbo.EmployeesWithDepartments
AS
    SELECT emp.EmployeeId,
        RTRIM(emp.FirstName) + ' ' + RTRIM(emp.Surname) as Name,
        dep.Description
    FROM Employees emp
    LEFT OUTER JOIN Departments dep ON emp.department = dep.departmentId

GO
```

Once again we execute the procedure by using the EXEC command:

```
EXEC dbo.EmployeesWithDepartments
```

You should see a result similar to that shown below. The EmployeeID and Name column are taken from the Employee table and we get a full listing of rows from this table. The Description column is taken from the Department table and we only get values for where there is a match.

	EmployeeId	Name	Description
1	1	Robin Johnson	Personnel
2	2	Denise Samson	Personnel
3	5	Linda Glucina	Personnel
4	6	Laura Wright	Personnel
5	8	Linda Anderson	Personnel
6	10	Suzanne Smith	Personnel
7	3	Jack Jones	Orders
8	7	Stephanie Glucina	Orders
9	11	David Allan	Orders
10	12		Orders
11	4	John Doe	Stock Control
12	9	Graham Brown	Stock Control
13	NULL	NULL	Deliveries
14	NULL	NULL	Incoming Orders

FULL OUTER JOIN

A FULL OUTER JOIN is really the combination of both the LEFT and RIGHT OUTER JOINs. This will show the full listing of tables on both side of the JOIN statement, matching rows where possible and listing NULL for the column values when no match is found.

```
CREATE PROCEDURE dbo.AllEmployeesWithAllDepartments
AS
    SELECT emp.EmployeeId,
        RTRIM(emp.FirstName) + ' ' + RTRIM(emp.Surname) as Name,
        dep.Description
    FROM Employees emp
    FULL OUTER JOIN Departments dep ON emp.department = dep.departmentId

GO
```

Executing this procedure returns the following resultset. You can see that all the Employees records have been returned as well as all the Departments records. When no match has been made on the joining column, DepartmentId, NULL values have been listed:

	EmployeeId	Name	Description
1	1	Robin Johnson	Personnel
2	2	Denise Samson	Personnel
3	3	Jack Jones	Orders
4	4	John Doe	Stock Control
5	NULL	NULL	Deliveries
6	NULL	NULL	Incoming Orders
7	5	Linda Glucina	NULL

There is one final type of join to examine, namely the CROSS JOIN.

CROSS JOIN

A CROSS JOIN is sometimes also referred to as a **Cartesian product**. It differs from the three other join types that we have just looked at, since you don't specify a joining column with the CROSS JOIN. Instead all rows in one of the joining tables are combined with all of the rows in the other table producing a resultset with all the possible combinations of rows from both tables. For example:

```
CREATE PROCEDURE dbo.AllEmployeesInAllDepartments
AS

    SELECT emp.EmployeeId,
        RTRIM(emp.FirstName) + ' ' + RTRIM(emp.Surname) as Name,
        dep.Description
    FROM Employees emp
    CROSS JOIN Departments dep
GO
```

The formula for working out the number of rows returned by a CROSS JOIN is:

Number of rows returned = rows in left table x rows in right table.

Obviously the number of rows returned is going to get pretty big, pretty quickly, so restraint should be used when deciding to use a CROSS JOIN with large tables.

We can execute our procedure by issuing the following command:

```
EXEC dbo.AllEmployeesInAllDepartments
```

We will only show a few of the rows returned from this procedure, but you get the idea.

	EmployeeId	Name	Description
1	1	Robin Johnson	Personnel
2	2	Denise Samson	Personnel
3	3	Jack Jones	Personnel
4	4	John Doe	Personnel
5	5	Linda Glucina	Personnel
6	1	Robin Johnson	Orders
7	2	Denise Samson	Orders

Temporary Tables

A temporary table is a subset of data that is created from a T-SQL command and placed into a table that resides in **tempdb**. tempdb is a special system database that is used to hold temporary information. This can be either explicitly created temporary information such as the temp tables that we are examining here, or information created internally by SQL Server where the database is used as a temporary location for storing results of queries etc before returning the resultset to the client.

There are two types of temporary tables, **local** and **global**. The way in which you wish to use a temporary table determines which to define. A local temporary table is defined by using one pound (#) mark before the table name. To define a global temporary table you would use two pound marks (##) instead. Temporary tables can be used in the same way as permanent tables, and can also have indexes, primary keys, constraints, and so on, defined on them. What makes temporary tables different from permanent tables is their scope.

Local temporary tables are available for use only by the connection that created them, and can only be used by the session that created them and its child batches. They cannot be shared with other SQL Server connections, even if these other connections use the same temporary table name.

Global temporary tables are available to all connections as long as the connection that created the global temporary table remains connected to SQL Server. Once this connection is closed, the temporary table is dropped. To highlight this, open two SQL Server Query Analyzer windows with connections to the same SQL Server.

In the first query window run the following code. This creates a global temporary table and inserts a value:

```
CREATE TABLE ##GlobalTemp(Message VARCHAR(255))

INSERT ##GlobalTemp VALUES('Why, hello there!')
```

Now in the second Query Analyzer window execute the following code. This loops around, outputting the rows of the global temporary table as long as an error does not occur:

```
WHILE @@Error=0
BEGIN
    SELECT * FROM ##GlobalTemp
    WAITFOR DELAY'000:00:05'
END
```

Now close your original query window, the one in which you created the global temporary table, and soon the looping query in your second window will halt. This is because the global temporary table was dropped automatically when its creating connection was closed.

To define a temporary table you simply use the keyword INTO within your T-SQL statement as follows:

```
SELECT column1, column2, column3
INTO #temptable
FROM table1
WHERE column1 = value1
```

The above code would create a local temporary table called #temptable using data from table1 that met the filter criteria defined within the WHERE clause (namely that column1 = value1). The temporary table is created with the column structure and data types of the columns chosen in the SELECT statement, and can be treated and used like any permanent SQL Server table including being used in joins with other permanent or temporary tables.

If you just wish the data to be available for the connection that created the temporary table, then you would define a local temporary table. When you disconnect, which could be when a stored procedure finishes executing, or when you close the query pane in Query Analyzer, the temporary table is removed. However, it is always considered best programming practice to clean up temporary objects within your code explicitly as soon as possible to free those resources, rather than simply letting them go out of scope. In the case of temporary tables this means dropping the temporary tables using the DROP TABLE command.

On the other hand, if you wish the data to be available for other connections and it is only when all of the connections are finished with the data that the temporary table needs to be removed, then you would define a global temporary table. You would also use this type of temporary table if you wish it to be shared between query panes in Query Analyzer, or if you have stored procedures calling other stored procedures and you want to pass a volume of data.

> Whether you choose local or global temporary tables, it is standard practice to also drop the tables once you have finished with them rather than relying on SQL Server to clean up after you. By controlling when the table is dropped, you can avoid a temporary table still existing when you expect it to be removed.

Table Variables

SQL Server 2000 introduced a variation on the temporary table, the **table variable**. These can be used as short-term, session-specific tables to build up a resultset during the course of execution of a stored procedure like temporary tables, but they differ from temporary tables in the following ways:

❑ Scope – A table variable only remains in scope for the batch that is currently being executed. Temporary tables remain in scope while the connection they were created on remains open.

❑ Transaction support – Temporary tables are fully transactional and participate in user-defined transactions. Table variables do not participate in user-defined transactions. Please see later in this chapter for more on user-defined functions.

❑ Syntax – Temporary tables are created using the CREATE TABLE syntax, as per normal tables within SQL Server. Table variables are defined using the DECLARE syntax, as per normal variables within SQL Server.

We can demonstrate the differences more clearly by executing a few simple examples in Query Analyzer. First we can see the difference in scope for temporary tables:

```
CREATE TABLE #MyTempTable(idcol INT)
GO
INSERT #MyTempTable VALUES(1)
```

The GO keyword is a Query Analyzer command used to separate batches. If you run the above code in query analyzer it will complete successfully even though we have submitted two separate batches. This is because the temporary table remains in scope for the duration of a connection (or until explicitly dropped) so it will be available for both batches.

A table variable on the other hand will not complete successfully:

```
DECLARE @MyTable TABLE(idcol INT)
GO
INSERT @MyTable VALUES(1)
```

As variables only remain in scope for the duration of the batch, the @MyTable table variable will go out of scope when the end of the batch in which it was created, indicated by the GO keyword, is encountered.

Next we can demonstrate the differences in transactional support by executing another simple example.

Please note: the following three code fragments should be run as one block of T-SQL.

First we create both a temporary table and a table variable:

```
CREATE TABLE #MyTable(idcol INT)
DECLARE @MyTable TABLE(idcol INT)
```

Then within the scope of a user-defined transaction we insert three values into these tables:

```
BEGIN TRANSACTION

INSERT #MyTable VALUES(1)
INSERT @MyTable VALUES(1)

INSERT #MyTable VALUES(2)
INSERT @MyTable VALUES(2)

INSERT #MyTable VALUES(3)
INSERT @MyTable VALUES(3)
```

Next the transaction is rolled back, and we SELECT all the data from both the temporary table and the table variable:

```
ROLLBACK TRANSACTION

SELECT * FROM #MyTable
SELECT * FROM @MyTable
```

So, our complete T-SQL block looks like this:

```
CREATE TABLE #MyTable(idcol INT)
DECLARE @MyTable TABLE(idcol INT)

BEGIN TRANSACTION

INSERT #MyTable VALUES(1)
INSERT @MyTable VALUES(1)

INSERT #MyTable VALUES(2)
INSERT @MyTable VALUES(2)

INSERT #MyTable VALUES(3)
INSERT @MyTable VALUES(3)

ROLLBACK TRANSACTION

SELECT * FROM #MyTable
SELECT * FROM @MyTable
```

The first resultset, the one returned from the temporary table, contains no rows as the temporary table participated within the user-defined transaction. The second resultset, the one returned from the table variable returns all three rows that we inserted. This is because the inserts that took place on the table variable were not participating within the user-defined transaction. We discuss transactions in more detail in Chapter 8.

While it is somewhat similar in functionality to a temporary table, the table variable does have some limitations that may restrict its use, which are:

❑   You cannot insert the resultset returned from a stored procedure execution into a table variable as you can with a temporary table. For example, `INSERT @MyTableV EXEC MyProc` will fail.

❑   You cannot create a table variable using `SELECT INTO` as you can with a temporary table. For example this will also fail: `SELECT * INTO @MyTableVar FROM MyTable`.

❑   You cannot create indexes on a table variable.

❑   You cannot execute DDL statements, such as `ALTER TABLE`, on a table variable.

> **Despite these limitations you should use table variables as opposed to temporary tables whenever you can, as these should generally produce better performing stored procedures than a temporary table alternative.**

Cursors

A **cursor** is a temporary subset of data, created within a query or stored procedure, which can be used to process each record found one at a time. It is only at cursor initiation that any filtering can take place; once the cursor has been defined, it is only possible to move the record pointer to a specific record number within the set. The `FETCH` command allows you to move to the next, previous, first or last record, or to a record relative to the record number you are at.

When building a cursor you can define whether the data retrieved is static or will be updated as the underlying data is being modified. All of this sounds quite powerful, so there are a number of issues that you have to be aware of.

Cursors within queries should be avoided whenever possible. While cursors do give the developer the ability to perform one-record-at-a-time processing, in most cases (though not all), it is possible to look at a different method of processing. You should approach all T-SQL coding requirements with the intention of developing a cursor-less, batch-based solution. Only if you run into trouble should a cursor be considered, as they are usually many times less efficient.

SQL Server is designed and tuned for set processing, where a set of data is taken and dealt with in one process. By moving to a record each time, SQL Server cannot perform any performance tuning on the data retrieval. Even when working with cursors through API calls, via languages such as VB.NET, when you request a block of records SQL Server is still performing record-at-a-time processing to retrieve that data. This type of processing can hamper you application's ability to scale in both data and users volumes, so an alternative set-based approach should be identified whenever possible. Take the following cursor for example:

```
DECLARE @RunningSubTotal TABLE(
    IDCol          INT   IDENTITY(1,1) PRIMARY KEY,
    OrderID        INT,
    OrderTotal     MONEY,
    SUBTOTAL       MONEY
```

```
   )

DECLARE @OrderID    INT,
    @OrderTotal     MONEY,
    @SubTotal       MONEY

SELECT   @OrderTotal=0,
         @SubTotal=0

DECLARE totallying_cursor CURSOR FAST_FORWARD FOR
    SELECT OrderID
    FROM dbo.Orders
    ORDER BY OrderID ASC

OPEN totallying_cursor
FETCH NEXT FROM totallying_cursor INTO @OrderID

WHILE @@fetch_status=0
BEGIN

    SELECT @OrderTotal=SUM((UnitPrice * Quantity)-Discount)
    FROM dbo.[Order Details]
    WHERE OrderID = @OrderID

    SELECT @SubTotal=@SubTotal+@OrderTotal

    INSERT @RunningSubTotal(OrderID, OrderTotal, SubTotal)
    VALUES (@OrderID, @OrderTotal, @SubTotal)


    FETCH NEXT FROM totallying_cursor INTO @OrderID
END

SELECT * FROM @RunningSubTotal ORDER BY IDCOL ASC

CLOSE totallying_cursor
DEALLOCATE totallying_cursor
```

This produces a resultset that contains a running total for the summation of order amounts within the Northwind database. Even though this is a very simplistic comparison you can see that the cursor method is much more complex than the equivalent set-based method shown below. While this is not always true, and it is possible for a set-based solution to be much more complex than the equivalent code using a cursor, the difference in execution times will almost always be in favor of the set-based method. The actual execution times will vary from machine to machine, but the set-based method will produce better performance. More importantly, because our operation requires the execution of three commands within the cursor loop, as the Orders table grows to thousands or maybe hundreds of thousands of rows, the set-based method below will prove to be a much more scalable solution than the cursor example shown previously:

```
SELECT od.OrderID,SUM((od.UnitPrice * od.Quantity)-od.Discount),
    (SELECT SUM((od2.UnitPrice * od2.Quantity)-od2.Discount)
     FROM dbo. [Order Details] od2
     WHERE od2.OrderID<=od.OrderID
    )

FROM dbo. [Order Details] od
GROUP BY od.OrderID
ORDER BY od.OrderID ASC
```

This query is using a correlated subquery (a query within a query) to create the subtotal column. Logically, for every row that is retrieved from the main SELECT statement, a second SELECT statement takes place retrieving the SUM of all the orders that have a lower OrderID than the OrderID for the current row. However, if this was how SQL Server physically resolved this query, it would be effectively repeating our cursor-based solution internally and we would get little or no performance gain. But SQL Server is smarter than this. While logic dictates that for every row retrieved by our main SELECT we are asking for the summation of every previous row, the Query Optimizer is able to work out a more efficient means of achieving this result without using row-by-row processing. Instead SQL Server builds a work table in memory that contains the summations required for all rows and then internally joins this to our main SELECT statement, resulting in a much more efficient set-based solution.

To take this point to the extreme, I have disallowed the use of cursors within any online application code on very high transaction databases, due to the huge impact they can have on the concurrency of a SQL Server database. By online application code I mean any code that is executed by users as a typical and regular function of the application. When a developer has come to me with code containing a cursor it is usually possible to rewrite it, so as to use a more efficient SQL set-based method. While this may seem heavy-handed, there is good reason for this approach.

Firstly, while cursors will generally perform adequately when used by a single user, or over small data volumes, they tend not to scale well. If the application code makes extensive use of cursors, it is likely to suffer from scalability issues as the application grows.

Secondly, a regular requirement to use cursors is a good indication of database design issues. If your relational database cannot be queried and manipulated by using the standard SQL commands, SELECT, INSERT, UPDATE, and DELETE, there is a good chance that it is suffering normalization issues. Such issues should have been identified early on in the development process and rectified. It is always easier to prevent the cause than to try and fix the problem, especially if the problem is performance-related and it occurs in 12 months time in your production environment.

All this doom and gloom surrounding cursors should not be misinterpreted. They have their place and there are a number of situations that require their use. These are almost always maintenance or data extraction / importing routines that do actually require row-by-row processing, therefore I do allow the use of cursors in batch overnight jobs and system maintenance if necessary. The impact of the cursor is not so important for these tasks and they can often only be completed in this way.

Decision Making In-Line

It is possible to embed logic within a T-SQL query, such as SELECT or an UPDATE, which can conditionally change the data processed by these commands on a per-row basis. By using the CASE statement you can achieve different results within a column depending on the values retrieved. Working with a CASE statement is just like using an in-line IF statement where there are several routes that can be taken. It is also possible to have nested CASE statements if you need to make a second decision, in the event of the first decision being found to be True.

There are two ways to use a CASE statement. You can either define a column or a variable immediately after the CASE keyword (so that all tests are against this object), or test an object in the WHEN statement. Both of these options are demonstrated in the example that follows.

Let's take a look at how to create and use a CASE statement.

CASE...WHEN...ELSE...END

A T-SQL CASE statement has a quite different purpose than the traditional VB CASE statement, because it cannot be used to change the execution order of the stored procedure. CASE can only be used in-place of a column reference to conditionally select an alternative value to be used.

The first example we will look at is where we will be testing the value of the same variable each time. We will use the EmployeesFullDetails stored procedure we created earlier and change the type of join that we are using with the Payments and PaymentTypes tables to be LEFT OUTER JOINs instead of INNER JOINs. This allows us to view the full employee list even if an employee hasn't received a payment. If an employee has not received a payment the pay.paymentID, pay.Amount, pay.PaymentDate and payt.PaymentDesc columns will be NULL within the resultset. Instead of having a NULL value for the payment description, we would prefer that the payment description contained the 'No payment made' value. This should also be the case if the payment amount is 0. To do this we include a CASE evaluation as part of the PaymentDesc column definition.

```
ALTER PROCEDURE EmployeesFullDetails
AS

SELECT    emp.FirstName, emp.Surname, dep.Description,
          pay.paymentId, pay.Amount, pay.PaymentDate,

       CASE   WHEN pay.Amount IS NULL THEN 'No payment made'
          WHEN pay.Amount=0 THEN 'No payment made'
       END as PaymentDesc
       , sal.SalaryAppliedFrom, sal.SalaryLevel
FROM      Employees emp
JOIN      Departments dep       on emp.Department=dep.DepartmentID

LEFT OUTER JOIN Payments pay          on pay.EmployeeID=emp.EmployeeID
LEFT OUTER JOIN   PaymentTypes payt on payt.PaymentTypeID=pay.PaymentTypeID

JOIN      Salaries sal       on sal.EmployeeID=emp.EmployeeID
GO
```

This procedure returns the Employee's information as with our earlier procedure, except that instead of simply returning the payt.PaymentDesc column we now introduce the CASE conditional logic. This CASE statement is essentially saying "Look at the pay.Amount column, and when the value is NULL, or when it equals 0, then return 'No payment made' as the column value for the payment type description column". However, as we are only explicitly checking for the amount column value being NULL or 0, if any other value is retrieved from the pay.Amount column the CASE evaluation would actually return a NULL, since there is no corresponding logic currently within our CASE statement to handle other values. Fortunately we can define an unspecific catch-all for a CASE statement by using ELSE. If ELSE is present then this will be used if none of the criteria specified in the WHEN clauses are True. So for our previous example we could add the ELSE statement as follows:

```
SELECT    emp.FirstName, emp.Surname, dep.Description,
          pay.paymentId, pay.Amount, pay.PaymentDate,

       CASE   WHEN pay.Amount IS NULL THEN 'No payment made'
          WHEN pay.Amount=0 THEN 'No payment made'
```

```
        ELSE payt.PaymentDesc
    END as PaymentDesc

    , sal.SalaryAppliedFrom, sal.SalaryLevel
FROM    Employees emp
JOIN    Departments dep        on emp.Department=dep.DepartmentID

LEFT OUTER JOIN Payments pay      on pay.EmployeeID=emp.EmployeeID
LEFT OUTER JOIN    PaymentTypes payt on payt.PaymentTypeID=pay.PaymentTypeID

JOIN    Salaries sal      on sal.EmployeeID=emp.EmployeeID
```

If pay.Amount evaluates to any other value than NULL or 0, the ELSE clause will be used to return the actual payt.PaymentDesc column value.

END must be specified to indicate the end of the CASE statement. As we are now using an expression (the CASE statement) in place of a specific table column to return the value for this column within our resultset, we must also give this column a name using a **column alias**. Without this alias our results would be returned as an unnamed column within the resultset.

In our next example we wish to examine the same values each time, but here we are looking for a range of values rather than individual specific values. Within our CASE statement we can use any comparison operators that we are able to use elsewhere in T-SQL code. The important point to remember is the first WHEN clause that evaluates to True will be used. If none of the WHEN clauses evaluate to True then the ELSE clause will be used, if present.

The following code will create a stored procedure listing every payment made for a particular month. By using the CASE statement to test the Amount column in the Payments table, we can see if the payment was a debit or a credit:

```
CREATE PROCEDURE dbo.MonthlyPayments @PaymentDate DATETIME
AS
    SET NOCOUNT ON

    SELECT emp.FirstName + ' ' + emp.Surname , PaymentDate,
        CASE
            WHEN pmt.Amount < 0 THEN "Debit"
            WHEN pmt.Amount > 0 THEN "Credit"
            ELSE "No movement"
        END AS "Money Movement",
        pmt.Amount
    FROM Employees emp
    LEFT OUTER JOIN Payments pmt ON pmt.EmployeeId = emp.EmployeeId
    WHERE DATEPART(month,PaymentDate) = DATEPART(month,@PaymentDate)
    AND DATEPART(year,PaymentDate) = DATEPART(year,@PaymentDate)

GO
```

Once this has been created, it is now possible to test out the example. If we are looking for the payments for February, 2002 then we need to issue the following command:

```
EXEC dbo.MonthlyPayments 'Feb 28 2002'
```

Any expression that can be used to return a value from a column with a T-SQL statement, such as a column name, a constant, a function, a subquery or any combination of these, can be used within the CASE statement. When used with aggregate functions, such as SUM, AVG, or COUNT, CASE is evaluated after the aggregation has been calculated for all rows that the aggregation is running over, as opposed to being evaluated for each individual row on columns that are not being aggregated.

```
CREATE PROCEDURE dbo.EmployeePayments
AS
    SET NOCOUNT ON
SELECT emp.FirstName + ' '+ emp.Surname , PaymentDate,
        CASE
            WHEN SUM(pmt.Amount) < 0 THEN "Debit"
            WHEN SUM(pmt.Amount) > 0 THEN "Credit"
            ELSE "No movement"
        END AS "Money Movement",SUM(pmt.Amount) AS Amount
    FROM Employees emp
    RIGHT OUTER JOIN Payments pmt ON pmt.EmployeeId = emp.EmployeeId
    GROUP BY emp.FirstName + " " + emp.Surname, PaymentDate

GO
```

While both of these examples use the CASE in the column list of a SELECT statement, it is important to realize that CASE can be used anywhere a column name can be used. This includes WHERE clauses, JOIN predicates, and even ORDER BY clauses. The next procedure does exactly this; it returns a list of all the employees contained in our Employees table and, depending on the parameter we pass in, will sort the list by surname either in ascending order or descending order:

```
CREATE PROCEDURE dbo.ListEmployeesOrdered @OrderBy char(1)='A'
AS
    SET NOCOUNT ON

    IF @OrderBy NOT IN ('A','D')
    BEGIN
        PRINT 'Only A or D are valid options for this procedure'
        RETURN 1
    END

    SELECT FirstName + ' ' + Surname
    FROM Employees
    ORDER BY
        CASE @Orderby
            WHEN 'A' THEN Surname
            ELSE NULL
        END ASC,
        CASE @Orderby
            WHEN 'D' THEN Surname
            ELSE NULL
        END DESC
GO
```

As stated above, the CASE statement can only be used to replace a column value within a T-SQL statement conditionally, not parts of the statement itself. So to achieve our conditional ORDER BY we need two columns within our ORDER BY statement, one ordered ascending and the other descending. If the value of the parameter passed to the procedure is A then the resultset is first ordered by the Surname column ascending, then NULL descending. Obviously ordering by NULL for every row in a table isn't going to change the output of the ordering established by the first column in the ORDER BY clause in any way. In fact, SQL Server is smart enough to realize this so it doesn't bother doing anything at all when ordering by NULL. We would execute this stored procedure as follows:

```
EXEC dbo.ListEmployeesOrdered 'A'
```

If, however, the parameter passed to the procedure is D then our resultset is first ordered by NULL ascending, which applies no order (once again SQL Server doesn't bother doing anything), then by our Surname column descending, giving us the list of employees in descending order:

```
EXEC dbo.ListEmployeesOrdered 'D'
```

Control of Flow

There are several methods of controlling the flow throughout a stored procedure or a query. The two main methods for control-of-flow statements are IF...ELSE and WHILE...BREAK...CONTINUE. Within these sets of statements we can specify T-SQL that we wish to be executed conditionally, based on a specified criterion evaluating to True. In this section we will take a look at how they can control the way your stored procedure will flow while being processed.

Stored procedures are not simply a method for security as you read earlier in the chapter, or a means of allowing queries to run faster through compiled code, but also contain complex processing where decisions will be made regarding the content of the data you return. The first method we will take a look at is the IF...ELSE statement.

IF...ELSE

There will be times, when working with a stored procedure, that either a local or global variable setting has to be tested, or the details of a query need to be evaluated. The only decision-making process within SQL Server when working with code post query execution is the IF...ELSE statement. Just as with VB.NET, this is a simple true or false test against two parts of an equation.

Once the criteria of the IF statement have been evaluated we are able to execute a different group of T-SQL commands based on the outcome of the evaluation, either True or False. We'll take a look at an example of doing this shortly, and we'll also take this example as an opportunity to examine the code blocks we need to use for this type of conditional processing at the same time. First we need to understand what code blocks are.

Code Blocks

When working with IF...ELSE statements, or WHILE loops, there will be times when more than one T-SQL statement has to be processed for either of the decisions made. Within SQL Server, since there is no End If statement, you need a means of informing SQL Server where the start and end of a segment of code lies. In this way you can write T-SQL code that only executes if our conditional criterion evaluates to True, or write T-SQL code that only executes if the conditional criteria evaluates to False, and once the conditional logic has completed continue to process further code no matter what the decision was in the IF...ELSE statement.

BEGIN...END

The keywords BEGIN and END are used to surround a block of code. This signifies to SQL Server where the **batch** of code specific to that branch of the decision starts and ends. In the following example only the first statement of code lies within the actual decision process because, without a BEGIN and END block, only the SQL statement immediately preceding the conditional statement is executed based on the outcome of that condition. Therefore, the second and third PRINT statements will always run no matter what value is placed in the two variables. This is obviously not our desired outcome and it highlights how easy it is to introduce bugs within T-SQL code by incorrectly using conditional execution statements:

```
DECLARE @Value1 INT
DECLARE @Value2 INT
SET @Value1 = 1
SET @Value2 = 2

IF @Value1 = @Value2
    PRINT 'The Value is true'
    PRINT 'Is it still true?'
    PRINT 'This statement always prints'
```

However by placing BEGIN and END statements around the appropriate code you will get the desired results. In other words, only the third PRINT statement executes:

```
DECLARE @Value1 INT
DECLARE @Value2 INT
SET @Value1 = 1
SET @Value2 = 2

IF @Value1 = @Value2
BEGIN
    PRINT 'The value is true'
    PRINT 'Is it still true?'
END
PRINT 'This statement always prints'
```

If there was an ELSE statement included in this code, then it would be placed after the END statement and would continue with the alternative processing:

```
DECLARE @Value1 INT
DECLARE @Value2 INT
SET @Value1 = 1
SET @Value2 = 2
```

```
IF @Value1 = @Value2
    BEGIN
        PRINT 'The value is true'
        PRINT 'Is it still true?'
    END
ELSE
    BEGIN
        Print 'The value is false'
        Print 'It is still false'
    END
PRINT 'This statement always prints'
```

Finally if there is only one line of code as explained earlier, then there is no need for a BEGIN...END statement. This next section demonstrates this in practice.

```
DECLARE @Value1 INT
DECLARE @Value2 INT
SET @Value1 = 1
SET @Value2 = 2

IF @Value1 = @Value2
    BEGIN
        PRINT 'The value is true'
        PRINT 'Is it still true? '
    END
ELSE
    BEGIN
        Print 'The value is false'
        Print 'It is still false'
    END
PRINT 'This statement always prints'
PRINT ' '
PRINT ' '
IF @Value1 = @Value2
    PRINT 'The value in the second test is true'
ELSE
    PRINT 'The value in the second test is false'
PRINT 'This will always print too'
```

While this works as expected, it is considered best practice to always encase your conditional logic within BEGIN and END code blocks. A less informed developer than yourself may be making changes to your code one day and not realize the importance specifying BEGIN and END with more than one line, thereby potentially introducing difficult-to-isolate bugs within an application.

WHILE...BREAK...CONTINUE

There will be times when it is necessary to loop around a section of code a number of times. To build a loop you are required to use the WHILE statement which evaluates a supplied expression to either True or False. If the expression evaluates to True the WHILE statement will execute the conditional T-SQL code that makes up this command before evaluating the expression once again. This process continues until the expression evaluates to False, at which point the next statement within the T-SQL batch is executed.

This requires the use of a BEGIN...END code block as there is bound to be more than one line of code to execute within the loop. The END statement will also determine where the end of the loop code is. If there is no END statement then it will only be the first line of code after the WHILE statement which is executed.

Just as with any programming language, the sooner you can get out of a loop the better, and if the condition you are checking for has occurred, then stop processing any more of the loop at that point and exit. This is accomplished by the use of the BREAK command:

```
DECLARE    @WhatIveGot         int,
           @WhatIThinkIWant    int,
           @WhatIReallyWant    int

SELECT     @WhatIveGot    =0,
           @WhatIThinkIWant=1000,
           @WhatIReallyWant=10

WHILE @WhatIveGot < @WhatIThinkIWant
BEGIN
   SELECT @WhatIveGot=@WhatIveGot+1
   PRINT 'Got one more thanks!'

   IF @WhatIveGot=@WhatIReallyWant
      BREAK
END
```

In this example we add some conditional logic within the code that is executed as part of the WHILE loop, to BREAK out of the loop early if the condition is satisfied.

RETURN

RETURN is used to exit a stored procedure or function, returning control of execution to the calling process. It can be used by itself, or with an integer value to pass a return parameter back to the calling process.

From a control-of-flow viewpoint, it is possible and acceptable to place a RETURN statement at any point within your stored procedure, and this is preferable to using a GOTO statement to move control to a single RETURN statement placed at the end of the T-SQL.

Let's take a closer look at returning from a stored procedure:

```
CREATE PROCEDURE dbo.CountEmployeesForDepartment(@departmentid int)
AS
   SET NOCOUNT ON
   IF NOT EXISTS(SELECT departmentid FROM departments
        WHERE departmentid=@departmentid)
   BEGIN
      PRINT    'This department does not exist'
      RETURN
   END

   SELECT   count(*)
   FROM     Employees
   WHERE    department=@departmentid
   GROUP    BY department
GO
```

When we execute this procedure we pass a `DepartmentID` as a parameter as follows:

```
EXEC dbo.CountEmployeesForDepartment 8
```

The procedure first checks to see if the department exists, if it doesn't then it prints a message letting us know. At this point the `RETURN` statement will ensure that no subsequent code is executed. If the department does exist then the rest of the procedure, following the `BEGIN...END` block, will be executed.

Returning Success or Failure

There will be many times when a stored procedure will be built purely to process information. There may be no data returned, just pure number crunching. Even if there is no data to be returned, it may be necessary to return a value to the calling stored procedure or program to indicate whether or not the procedure's execution has been successful.

Let's consider the previous example above. While outputting a message telling us the procedure has failed is useful to a user who may be executing the procedure interactively, it isn't much use to a piece of application logic if we are executing the procedure from within a code routine. Unless we are prepared to write code that does string comparisons to check for every possible error message that may be returned from subroutines, we are better off using `RETURN` to pass back a value that indicates whether the procedure execution has been successful or not.

```
ALTER PROCEDURE dbo.CountEmployeesForDepartment(@departmentid int)
AS
    SET NOCOUNT ON
    IF NOT EXISTS(SELECT departmentid FROM departments
            WHERE departmentid=@departmentid)
    BEGIN
        PRINT   'This department does not exist'
        RETURN 1 -- Not successful
    END

    SELECT COUNT(*)
    FROM    Employees
    WHERE    department=@departmentid
    GROUP BY department

    RETURN 0 -- Successful
```

Now when executing the stored procedure we need to define a variable to store the value that's passed back from the `RETURN` statement:

```
DECLARE @ReturnVal int

EXEC @ReturnVal = dbo.CountEmployeesForDepartment 8

IF @ReturnVal=0
    PRINT 'Success'
ELSE
    PRINT 'Failure'
```

SQL Server's own internal stored procedures use 0=Success and 1 and above=Failure as return values (each value greater than 0 could correspond to a particular error you are checking for). TO avoid confusing the heck out of your developers, I strongly recommend that you stick to this convention when implementing success/failure return values in your stored procedures, unless your development team has an existing standard that they are happy with.

Passing Resultsets

As we have seen, passing parameters between stored procedures is a trivial task. However, what happens when we want to pass many values, or even an entire resultset, between stored procedures? SQL Server 2000 did introduce a new table variable but even these cannot be used as parameters with stored procedures. In fact the only effective method of passing resultsets between procedures is to create a temporary table in the calling procedure and insert the results from the stored procedure execution into it. For example:

```
CREATE PROCEDURE sp_FiveRandomEmployees
AS
    SELECT top 5 EmployeeId, FirstName, Surname
    FROM dbo.Employees
    ORDER BY NEWID()
GO
```

To have the results available for further processing we execute the procedure as shown:

```
CREATE TABLE #TempEmployees
(   EmployeeId  BigInt,
    FirstName   Varchar(30),
    Surname     varchar(30)
)

-- Inserts the first resultset returned by the
-- stored procedure into the temporary table

INSERT #TempEmployees
EXEC sp_FiveRandomEmployees

SELECT EmployeeId, FirstName, Surname FROM #TempEmployees
```

Note that there are some limitations here, in particular that the stored procedure being called can only return a single resultset. More precisely, only the first resultset will be inserted into the temporary table; any others will be ignored.

> You cannot insert multiple returned resultsets into a temporary table using the
> INSERT table EXEC stored procedure syntax, only the first returned resultset.

Passing resultsets into a stored procedure is a little more interesting, but is also possible through the use of a temporary table. To understand how to achieve this, we need to discuss the scope of a temporary table in relation to the nesting of procedures. A temporary table's scope is limited to the scope of the procedure in which it was created, and to any stored procedures executed from this procedure. Let's consider the following example:

```
CREATE PROC sp_scope1
AS    EXEC dbo.sp_scope2
      SELECT * FROM #temp1
GO


CREATE PROC sp_scope2
AS    CREATE TABLE #temp1(procname sysname)
      INSERT #temp1 values('sp_scope2')
      EXEC dbo.sp_scope3
      SELECT * FROM #temp1
GO


CREATE PROC sp_scope3
AS    INSERT #temp1 values('sp_scope3')
      EXEC dbo.sp_scope4
      SELECT * FROM #temp1
GO


CREATE PROC sp_scope4
AS    INSERT #temp1 values('sp_scope4')
      SELECT * FROM #temp1
GO
```

The temporary table created in sp_scope2, #temp1, is also available for use by sp_scope3 and sp_scope4 as these procedures are executed as children of the process that create the procedure (namely sp_scope2). When the execution of sp_scope2 is complete the temporary table goes out of scope and is dropped, so becoming unavailable for use by the parent procedure, sp_scope1. If you run this script you will get three resultsets generated by the SELECT statements in sp_scope2, sp_scope3 and sp_scope4 and finally an error message stating "Invalid object name #temp1" which is caused by the SELECT statement in sp_scope1.

So coming back to our original goal, to pass resultsets into stored procedures, we can see now that to do this we should populate a temporary table, which our child stored procedure will expect to exist and utilize. For example:

```
CREATE PROC sp_ShowEmployees
AS    SELECT EmployeeID, FirstName, Surname
      FROM   #TempEmployees
GO
```

Now to execute this procedure we first create and populate the temporary table:

```
CREATE TABLE #TempEmployees
(   EmployeeId   BigInt,
    FirstName    Varchar(30),
    Surname      varchar(30)
)
INSERT #TempEmployees VALUES(1,'Linda','Glucina')
INSERT #TempEmployees VALUES(2,'Laura','Major')
INSERT #TempEmployees VALUES(3,'Stephanie','Bain')

EXEC dbo.sp_ShowEmployees
```

> Note that if the temporary table does not exist prior to calling the child procedure,
> then you will return an invalid object name error.

Passing XML

XML is absolutely everywhere, especially now with the release of the Microsoft .NET Framework. SQL
Server 2000, as the back-end storage component of the .NET Framework, has the built-in ability to pass
XML in and out of stored procedures. Some XML tools are now available for SQL Server 7.0, but they
are not integrated within the database platform itself, as they are with SQL Server 2000.

FOR XML

The easiest way to get XML out of a stored procedure is to use the FOR XML clause on a SELECT
statement. FOR XML returns an XML **stream** to the calling application, not a resultset which is what we
have been dealing with so far in this chapter. For more information on this topic see both the next
chapter, and Chapter 10.

FOR XML has three modes of operation which are:

❑   FOR XML AUTO – SQL Server returns an XML stream in a format that it automatically
    determines from the tables and their joining columns. This mode is discussed shortly.

❑   FOR XML EXPLICIT – SQL Server returns an XML stream in a format that the developer
    specifies in the structure of the SELECT statement.

❑   FOR XML RAW – SQL Server returns an XML stream in a generic format.

*FOR XML EXPLICIT and FOR XML RAW require a much greater understanding of the structure of
XML documents than we can provide in this chapter. However, an in-depth look at both of these
commands is included in Chapter 10.*

FOR XML AUTO

FOR XML AUTO is the fastest and easiest way to extract XML from a SQL Server database. In fact it
usually only requires the addition of a FOR XML AUTO clause to the end of existing queries. For example:

```
SELECT    EmployeeId,
          RTRIM(FirstName) + ' ' + RTRIM(Surname) as "Name"
FROM      Employees
FOR XML AUTO
```

Will return a basic XML stream similar to this:

```
<Employees EmployeeId="1" Name="Robin Johnson"/>
<Employees EmployeeId="2" Name="Denise Samson"/>
<Employees EmployeeId="3" Name="Jack Jones"/>
<Employees EmployeeId="4" Name="John Doe"/>
<Employees EmployeeId="5" Name="Linda Glucina"/>
...
```

The XML node name (in this case `Employees`) is determined by either the table name, or the table alias name if used. The attributes for each XML node are derived from the columns in the `SELECT` list.

But `FOR XML AUTO` doesn't stop there! When using this clause with multiple tables in a join, SQL Server automatically devises a structured XML format, based on the columns you are using to join your tables. The format is also dependent on the order of the columns within the `SELECT` statement itself. So, for example, the following query:

```
SELECT      e.EmployeeId,
            RTRIM(e.FirstName) + ' ' + RTRIM(e.Surname) as "Name",
            d.DepartmentID,
            d.Description
FROM dbo.Employees e
INNER JOIN dbo.Departments d ON e.Department = d.DepartmentID
FOR XML AUTO
```

will produce an XML stream similar to that shown below, where the `Employees` element is the parent with each `Employees` element having a child `Department` element that contains the details of the department that this employee is a member of. Notice that because we are now using table aliases, `Employees` has been replaced with e and `Departments` with d:

```
<e EmployeeId="1" Name="Robin Johnson">
  <d DepartmentID="1" Description="Personnel"/>
</e>
<e EmployeeId="2" Name="Denise Samson">
  <d DepartmentID="1" Description="Personnel"/>
</e>
<e EmployeeId="3" Name="Jack Jones">
  <d DepartmentID="2" Description="Orders"/>
</e>
<e EmployeeId="4" Name="John Doe">
  <d DepartmentID="3" Description="Stock Control"/>
</e>
```

However simply by changing the order of the columns within our `SELECT` statement we get an entirely different XML structure, as seen next. This is because `XML AUTO` uses the physical order of the columns within the `SELECT` list to determine the structure of the XML that it will create.

If our query now looked like this:

```
SELECT      d.DepartmentID,
            d.Description,
            e.EmployeeId,
            RTRIM(e.FirstName) + ' ' + RTRIM(e.Surname) as "Name"
FROM  dbo.Employees e
INNER JOIN dbo.Departments d ON e.Department = d.DepartmentID
FOR XML AUTO
```

then the following XML stream would be produced:

```
<d DepartmentID="1" Description="Personnel">
  <e EmployeeId="1" Name="Robin Johnson"/>
  <e EmployeeId="2" Name="Denise Samsonl"/>
  <e EmployeeId="5" Name="Linda Glucina"/>
</d>
<d DepartmentID="2" Description="Orders">
  <e EmployeeId="3" Name="Jack Jones"/>
</d>
<d DepartmentID="3" Description="Stock Control">
  <e EmployeeId="4" Name="John Doe"/>
</d>
...
```

OPENXML

OPENXML is used to make an XML document available for use by T-SQL code within SQL Server. It allows an XML stream to be opened as a resultset, which can then be treated the same as any other SQL Server table and used in queries, joins, INSERT statements, and so on.

For our example we will take the XML result that we created using the first FOR XML AUTO clause above, pass this back into SQL Server, and return this in a column/row format once again.

```
CREATE PROCEDURE dbo.XMLInEmployeesAndDepartments
    @XMLInput AS Text
AS
```

Normally you cannot declare a variable of type Text, but this is a special type of variable that is only allowed as a parameter of a stored procedure. XML is plain text and can be very large in size, much larger than the 8000 maximum possible characters of the varchar data type. By using this special Text parameter we can handle very large amounts of XML (up to 2GB, limited by the size of text variable) being passed into this procedure.

Executing sp_xml_preparedocument passes the XML input to the XMLDOM (the Microsoft XML parser), which in turn checks that the XML document is valid and then loads it into memory and passes back a document ID that we will use when querying the XML data:

```
SET NOCOUNT ON

DECLARE   @docid   int
EXEC sp_xml_preparedocument @docid OUTPUT, @XMLInput
```

The remainder of the stored procedure makes calls to the OPENXML function, each time passing in the document ID and the node from which we wish to retrieve the data. The WITH clause specifies which attributes from this node we wish to make available to the SELECT statement, and the format and layout of the resultset that we return from OPENXML. If we do not specify the WITH clause we get a generic resultset returned that contains all of the elements of our XML document in a flat structure.

```
SELECT DISTINCT
    e.Name,
    d.Description
FROM    OPENXML(@docid, '/ROOT/Employee',1)
WITH    (EmployeeID   bigint,
         Name         varchar(512),
```

If the attribute we require is in a different node to the default node that was specified with OPENXML ('/ROOT/Employee' in this example) we can navigate through the XML hierarchy from the default node by specifying the path to the attribute as part of the attribute mapping, for example:

```
Department   int './Department/@DepartmentID') e
```

As OPENXML returns a resultset, we can use the output as we would any other table in SQL Server. The whole OPENXML statement, including the WITH clause, can be used as an alternative to a table name within a T-SQL query, and can be joined with ordinary SQL Server tables using the standard JOIN syntax we are used to.

In this case we have chosen to join the employee information retrieved with the first OPENXML statement, with the department information returned with the second OPENXML statement:

```
INNER JOIN   OPENXML(@docid, '/ROOT/Employee/Department',1)
WITH   (DepartmentID   bigint,
   Description   varchar(512)) d on e.department = d.DepartmentID
```

When we pass the XML document to the XMLDOM using sp_xml_preparedocument the DOM loads the XML document into memory and it remains there until a call to remove it is made using sp_xml_removedocument. It is therefore very important to remember to release this document from memory by calling sp_xml_removedocument with the appropriate document ID. As some XML documents can be very large, it is particularly important to release the resources used to cache the XML as soon as possible.

```
EXEC sp_xml_removedocument @docid
```

Putting this altogether we get the code to create our procedure:

```
CREATE PROCEDURE dbo.XMLInEmployeesAndDepartments
   @XMLInput as Text
AS
   SET NOCOUNT ON

   DECLARE   @docid   int
   EXEC sp_xml_preparedocument @docid OUTPUT, @XMLInput

   SELECT DISTINCT
      e.Name,
      d.Description
   FROM   OPENXML(@docid, '/ROOT/Employee',1)
   WITH   (EmployeeID   bigint,
      Name      varchar(512),
      Department   int './Department/@DepartmentID') e
   INNER JOIN   OPENXML(@docid, '/ROOT/Employee/Department',1)
   WITH   (DepartmentID   bigint,
      Description   varchar(512)) d on e.department = d.DepartmentID

   EXEC sp_xml_removedocument @docid
```

To pass the XML into this procedure we have added an extra node to the XML structure, the <ROOT> node. This is because the XML handlers within SQL Server only allow a single root node within the XML document. This check is performed as part of the validation processes because a valid XML structure can only have one root node, as per the XML standards.

Executing our procedure:

```
EXEC XMLInEmployeesAndDepartments '<ROOT>
    <Employee EmployeeID="1" Name="Robin Johnson">
        <Department DepartmentID="1" Description="Personnel"/>
    </Employee>
    <Employee EmployeeID="2" Name="Denise Samson">
        <Department DepartmentID="1" Description="Personnel"/>
    </Employee>
    <Employee EmployeeID="3" Name="Jack Jones">
        <Department DepartmentID="2" Description="Orders"/>
    </Employee>
    <Employee EmployeeID="4" Name="John Doe">
        <Department DepartmentID="3" Description="Stock Control"/>
    </Employee><Employee EmployeeID="5" Name="Linda Glucina">
        <Department DepartmentID="1" Description="Personnel"/>
    </Employee></ROOT>'
```

results in the following XML:

```
<ROOT>
  <Employee EmployeeID="1" Name="Robin Johnson">
    <Department DepartmentID="1" Description="Personnel"/>
  </Employee>
  <Employee EmployeeID="2" Name="Denise Samson">
    <Department DepartmentID="1" Description="Personnel"/>
  </Employee>
  <Employee EmployeeID="3" Name="Jack Jones">
    <Department DepartmentID="2" Description="Orders"/>
  </Employee>
  <Employee EmployeeID="4" Name="John Doe">
    <Department DepartmentID="3" Description="Stock Control"/>
  </Employee><Employee EmployeeID="5" Name="Linda Glucina">
    <Department DepartmentID="1" Description="Personnel"/>
  </Employee></ROOT>'
```

Note the root node need not be named <ROOT>; this was chosen for clarity. The root node can have any name, for example <MyYellowTrousers> would have been equally valid just so long as there is only one occurrence of this node at the root level with all the other XML nodes being children of this node. More on this in Chapter 10.

In our example, without the root node each <Employee> node is in the root of the document and the following error will occur:

```
Server:Msg 6603, Level 16, State 1, Procedure sp_xml_preparedocument, Line 4
XML parsing error: Only one top level element is allowed in an XML document.
```

Navigating Trees

One of the most common types of poorly performing T-SQL code introduced into production databases is code designed for navigating tree hierarchies. Take the example of an employee who is also a manager. They may manage X number of employees, who in turn may manage X number of employees and so on. For large organizations you may have numerous levels of management with each layer having a number of employees associated with each manager. Typically this would be implemented as a self-join on the `Employees` table, with a column called `ManagerID`, which references another `Employee` row.

To add this new structure to our existing `Employees` table execute the following code to add the `ManagerID` column:

```
ALTER TABLE dbo.employees
ADD ManagerID int REFERENCES dbo.employees(employeeID)
```

Now we wish to populate this column with the ID of another employee to act as the manager for this employee. You don't need to worry about what the following code is doing too much, other than to know it is creating three levels of management by selecting random employees at each level. Our head honcho will be `employeeid=1`:

```
UPDATE employees
   SET managerid=1
WHERE employeeid between 2 and 10

UPDATE employees
   SET managerid=(   select top 1 employeeid from employees e1
           where e.employeeid=e.employeeid
           and e1.employeeid between 2 and 10
           order by NEWID())
FROM employees e
WHERE employeeid between 11 and 50

UPDATE employees
   SET managerid=(   select top 1 employeeid from employees e1
           where e.employeeid=e.employeeid
           and e1.employeeid between 11 and 50
           order by NEWID())
FROM employees e
WHERE employeeid >50
```

Now, if I am near the top of the tree and I wish to survey my empire, I need a query that travels down the branching hierarchy right to the bottom, returning all employees in the various branches along the way. As there could be *n* number of levels in this hierarchy we cannot do this effectively using SQL joins, since each level would require the joining of another table, and we cannot pre-determine the number of joins that will be required.

An alternative approach is to use a loop within T-SQL to populate a temporary table with the list of employees in the tree that directly or indirectly report to our selected employee:

```
CREATE PROCEDURE dbo.ShowEmployeesWhoReportToManager @ManagerID int
AS
   SET NOCOUNT ON

   CREATE TABLE #EmployeeTree
   (
       EmployeeID   int
   )

   INSERT #EmployeeTree
   SELECT EmployeeID
   FROM Employees
   WHERE ManagerID=@ManagerID

   WHILE    @@ROWCOUNT>0
   BEGIN
      INSERT #EmployeeTree
      SELECT e.EmployeeID
      FROM      Employees e
      INNER JOIN    #EmployeeTree et on e.ManagerID=et.EmployeeID
      LEFT OUTER JOIN #EmployeeTree et2 on e.EmployeeID=et2.EmployeeID
      WHERE et2.EmployeeID IS NULL
   END

   SELECT     e.EmployeeId,
              RTRIM(e.FirstName) + ' ' + RTRIM(e.Surname) as "Name"
   FROM       Employees e
   INNER JOIN   #EmployeeTree et on e.EmployeeID = et.EmployeeID

   DROP TABLE #EmployeeTree

GO
```

As this is quite a complicated batch of T-SQL code, we will step through it piece by piece, explaining what is happening. First we create a temporary table and populate this with one row, the row of our known `ManagerID`:

```
CREATE TABLE #EmployeeTree
(
    EmployeeID   int
)

INSERT #EmployeeTree
SELECT EmployeeID
FROM Employees
WHERE ManagerID=@ManagerID
```

Next we check the `@@ROWCOUNT` global variable and determine if this is greater than zero (see the later section entitled *@@ROWCOUNT* for further details of this variable). As our last statement, our insert of our `ManagerID` into our temporary table, affected 1 row then the contents of the `WHILE` statement will be executed:

```
WHILE    @@ROWCOUNT>0
```

Now, within the WHILE statement itself, we insert all the rows from our Employees table where the Manager is in our temporary #EmployeesTree table. On the first pass through this WHILE statement, only one row, the ManagerID we inserted above, is within our #EmployeesTree table so this only inserts Employees rows that have a ManagerID corresponding to this value. The LEFT OUTER JOIN back to the #EmployeesTree table is used to prevent duplicates. The et2.EmployeeID IS NULL clause in the WHERE statement only allows the SELECT to return rows where there are matching EmployeeID's between our Employees table and the rows that have already been inserted into the #EmployeesTree table.

```
BEGIN
    INSERT #EmployeeTree
    SELECT e.EmployeeID
    FROM       Employees e
    INNER JOIN  #EmployeeTree et on e.ManagerID=et.EmployeeID
    LEFT OUTER JOIN #EmployeeTree et2 on e.EmployeeID=et2.EmployeeID
    WHERE et2.EmployeeID IS NULL
END
```

Now after the first pass, @@ROWCOUNT is checked again. As an insert did take place, this is greater than zero once again. So the contents of the WHILE statement are executed once again. This time our #EmployeesTree table contains a number of rows, the employees who directly report to our manager. The second pass then, in turn, inserts all the employees who report to employees who report to our manager. This cycle continues until there are no more levels within the hierarchy, at which point no more records will be inserted. As @@ROWCOUNT will then evaluate to 0, the WHILE loop will end and the procedure will proceed to outputting the results.

```
SELECT     e.EmployeeId,
           RTRIM(e.FirstName) + ' ' + RTRIM(e.Surname) as "Name"
FROM       Employees e
INNER JOIN   #EmployeeTree et on e.EmployeeID = et.EmployeeID
```

Executing this procedure with the EmployeeID for any employee that is a manager (passed in as a parameter) will return a list of employees which that manager has control over.

```
EXEC dbo.ShowEmployeesWhoReportToManager 5
```

At first this may think this looks slightly inefficient, and you are right. Like relational databases in general, SQL Server does not support hierarchal structures naturally. The best that you can come up with is a crude fit. The above method of working with hierarchical trees will work most efficiently for short trees that contain many values at each level. As an INSERT statement is generated for each level in the hierarchy, it isn't optimal to use this method for trees that contain more than 5-10 levels, unless absolutely necessary. However, as a single T-SQL statement gathers all the values at a single level, its scalability won't be adversely affected by a minor change in the number of values at each level in the tree.

Nesting Procedures

As with VB, SQL Server stored procedures can be nested. There is, however, a limit to the depth of the nesting; we are restricted to 32 levels in SQL Server 2000. Usually this is not a problem since you typically only execute through a handful of stored procedure levels for normal application logic. If, on the other hand, you are performing some form of mathematical or recursive processing, this limit of 32 nested procedures approaches fast and you need to ensure that you do not exceed it so as to avoid throwing an exception.

Fortunately SQL Server at least provides a way to determine how many levels deep you are with the @@NESTLEVEL global variable. Using it in your procedures allows you to determine your ability to call another recursion of the procedure if you haven't reached the level limit, or exit gracefully with a useful error to the user if you have.

```
CREATE PROCEDURE dbo.ShowNestLevel
AS
    SET NOCOUNT ON
    SELECT 'Current at nesting level: ' + CAST(@@NestLevel as varchar(2))

    IF @@NESTLEVEL=32
        RETURN

    EXEC DBO.ShowNestLevel
GO

EXEC dbo.ShowNestLevel
```

When executed this stored procedure will recursively execute itself until the value of @@NESTLEVEL is equal to 32, at which point the procedure will exit. If we change the procedure to allow just one more level it will throw an error when executed, complaining that stored procedures and triggers can only be nested to a depth of 32:

```
ALTER PROCEDURE dbo.ShowNestLevel
AS
    SET NOCOUNT ON
    SELECT 'Current at nesting level: ' + cast(@@NestLevel as varchar(2))

    IF @@NESTLEVEL=33
        RETURN

    EXEC dbo.ShowNestLevel
GO

EXEC dbo.ShowNestLevel
```

> The nesting level relates the number of procedures executed between the current stored procedure, and the stored procedure that was executed first. For example **ProcA** executes **ProcB**, which in turn executes **ProcC**, and this executes **ProcD**, and so on. This does not affect the number of procedures that can be executed at each level, for example **ProcA** may execute **ProcB**, **ProcC**, and **ProcD**. There is no limit to the number of procedures that can be executed at each level in the nesting hierarchy.

User-Defined Functions

User-defined functions (**UDF**s) are a new addition to SQL Server 2000. They allow developers to construct routines that can be used to return a value, or a set of values in table format, based on parameters passed into them. They differ from stored procedures in the way they are called and in the way they return values, which we will look at next.

There are three types of user-defined functions, each with a different syntax and different purpose to fulfill. These are:

- ❏ The Scalar UDF
- ❏ The Inline UDF
- ❏ The Table Valued UDF

Functions offer a new dimension to T-SQL that had been greatly desired by SQL Server developers in previous versions. Functions allow developers to cut down on code duplication and complexity by separating out common operations into self-contained units that are accessible from within core SELECT, INSERT, UPDATE, and DELETE operations.

Scalar UDF

A scalar function accepts zero or more parameters and returns a single value of pre-determined data type to the caller of the function. These behave very much like the system functions built into SQL Server for string manipulation, mathematical calculations and so on.

A scalar UDF can be used wherever an expression can be used within SQL Server, such as a column list or a WHERE clause of a SELECT statement or in the IF statement used to evaluate conditional logic.

The following example of a scalar UDF is used to convert degrees Fahrenheit to degrees Celsius:

```
CREATE FUNCTION dbo.fn_FahrenheitToCelsius(@Farenheit INT)
RETURNS INT
AS
BEGIN
    DECLARE @Celsius INT

    SELECT @Celsius = (@Farenheit-32) * 5/9

    RETURN @Celsius
END
```

To make use of this function we could utilize it from within a conditional WHILE loop:

```
WHILE dbo.fn_FahrenheitToCelsius(@MyFarenheitVar) <32
BEGIN
    ...
END
```

or from within the SELECT list of a T-SQL query:

```
SELECT MyFarenheitCol
       dbo.fn_FahrenheitToCelsius(MyFarenheitCol) as MyCelsiusCol
FROM   dbo.MyTemperatureTable
```

Once again, the power of the Query Optimizer shines when using scalar functions. While we would logically think that the function is being called for each row retrieved by the SELECT statement, this is not actually how it physically takes place. Instead, the Query Optimizer integrates the scalar function into the query plan for the SELECT resulting in a set-based solution as opposed to row-based execution.

Inline UDF

An inline UDF returns a single resultset to the caller of the function, as opposed to the singular value we saw above. As a result of this difference, inline UDFs cannot be used directly within expressions, but they can be used in the FROM clause of a SELECT or UPDATE statement. They cannot be inserted or updated though, as they are read-only. An inline UDF can return the resultset from a single query.

This type of UDF is sometimes called a parameterized view by those used to other platforms. Normal views in SQL Server do not accept parameters that restrict the values they return, instead you apply a WHERE clause to achieve the same result. Inline UDFs, on the other hand, do accept parameters and these are then used to determine what rows are returned to the caller of the function.

Let's have a look at one:

```
CREATE FUNCTION dbo.fn_DepartmentsForEmployee(@EmployeeID INT)
RETURNS TABLE
AS
RETURN
(
SELECT d.DepartmentID,
       d.Description
FROM Departments d
INNER JOIN Employees e ON d.DepartmentID = e.Department
WHERE e.EmployeeID=@EmployeeID
)
```

To execute this inline function we would place a call to it within a FROM clause of a T-SQL query. For example:

```
DECLARE @EmployeeID INT

SELECT @EmployeeID=1

SELECT *
FROM dbo.fn_DepartmentsForEmployee(@EmployeeID)
```

Table Valued UDF

A table valued UDF, like an inline UDF, returns a single resultset to the caller of the function. But unlike an inline UDF, many T-SQL statements embedded within the function may build up this resultset.

Table valued UDFs resemble stored procedures most closely, however they can be used within the FROM clause of T-SQL statements and be joined against, which stored procedures cannot. This is because they have a defined output schema.

A good way to compare the two is to re-examine the stored procedure we used earlier in this chapter to display all the employees that report directly, or indirectly, to a manager. While this stored procedure was useful for its one purpose, displaying this information in its entirety, it is of little use if we wish to use the list of reporting employees to join to other tables for further processing. By rewriting this stored procedure as a table valued UDF, we can now make use of the list of reporting users in other queries rather than simply listing the employees:

```
CREATE FUNCTION dbo.fn_EmployeesWhoReportToManager(@ManagerID int)
RETURNS @EmployeeTree TABLE(EmployeeID INT PRIMARY KEY)
AS
BEGIN
   INSERT @EmployeeTree(EmployeeID)
   SELECT EmployeeID
   FROM Employees
   WHERE ManagerID=@ManagerID

   WHILE    @@rowcount>0
   BEGIN
      INSERT @EmployeeTree(EmployeeID)
      SELECT e.EmployeeID
      FROM    Employees e
      INNER JOIN    @EmployeeTree et on e.ManagerID=et.EmployeeID
      LEFT OUTER JOIN @EmployeeTree et2 on e.EmployeeID=et2.EmployeeID
      WHERE et2.EmployeeID IS NULL
   END
   RETURN
END
```

We can now get a list of the employee's information from this UDF by joining to our Employees table to determine the name of the employee and so on:

```
DECLARE @ManagerID INT

SELECT @ManagerID=1

SELECT e.EmployeeID, e.FirstName, e.SurName
FROM dbo.fn_EmployeesWhoReportToManager(@ManagerID) r
INNER JOIN employees e ON r.EmployeeID=e.EmployeeID
```

Having this information available within a function not only allows us to perform the original requirement that was carried out by the procedure (listing this information) we can also make this information available to be used by any other queries within our database.

Global Variables

SQL Server has the ability to return certain results of actions that have been taken within code. It is possible to find out the number of rows that have been modified within a query, whether the T-SQL has produced an error, or the number of the last automatically generated identity number, to give but a few examples. The results of these actions are placed for inspection within **global variables** and can be inspected by viewing the relevant identifier.

Global variables are defined within SQL Server and have @@ as a prefix. The provision of these variables and the values they can contain, removes the necessity to write code to find out such information from other sources.

@@ERROR

Perhaps the most useful global variable is @@ERROR. This variable holds a numeric value of any error generated from the last T-SQL statement that executed, whether this was a SELECT, INSERT, call to execute to a stored procedure, the creation of a database object or any T-SQL statement. We'll see this in action in a few moments.

> The main thing to note about the @@ERROR global variable is that it is set at the end of each T-SQL statement. As a result, it is crucial that you store any value you wish to test in a variable before it alters its state and will give a **False** value.

@@ROWCOUNT

@@ROWCOUNT is used to return the number of rows affected by the last T-SQL statement that was executed. This is reset for every T-SQL statement so if you wish to retain its value it must be moved to a local variable, as shown in the following examples.

If you run the following query

```
SELECT * FROM dbo.Employees
SELECT @@ROWCOUNT
```

every row in the Employees table will be returned, along with a value representing that number of rows. However, if you change this query slightly and add a conditional check between the SELECT from the table and the SELECT @@ROWCOUNT, we get a very different result:

```
SELECT * FROM dbo.Employees
IF 1=1
    SELECT @@ROWCOUNT
```

In this case you will get all the rows from the Employees table as before, but now the @@ROWCOUNT value returned is 0. Remember we said that @@ROWCOUNT is set for every T-SQL command so in this example the IF statement has set the @@ROWCOUNT last. As the IF statement doesn't affect any rows this sets @@ROWCOUNT to 0, the value that we return.

The more useful way to have constructed this particular query is as shown next:

```
DECLARE @MyRowCount INT
SELECT * FROM dbo.Employees
SELECT @MyRowCount=@@ROWCOUNT

IF 1=1
    SELECT @MyRowCount
```

Now we store the actual @@ROWCOUNT value that we are interested in, the number of rows returned by SELECT * FROM dbo.Employees, within a variable for later use. This way @@ROWCOUNT can be changed by subsequent T-SQL commands but we retain the value that we are interested in.

@@SERVERNAME

@@SERVERNAME is used to return the name of the current SQL Server instance. The server name will either be in the format ServerName or ServerName\InstanceName for SQL Server 2000 named instances.

Here are a few examples of how you can access the @@SERVERNAME global variable:

```
SELECT @@SERVERNAME
```

```
DECLARE @LocalServer sysname
SELECT @LocalServer=@@SERVERNAME
```

```
INSERT MyTestTable VALUES(1, @@SERVERNAME)
```

If no server name is returned then for some reason SQL Server has lost the local server row from the sysservers table. This can sometimes happen if the server is renamed. To fix this issue, execute the following stored procedure:

```
EXEC sp_addserver 'YourServerNameHere',local
```

This re-adds the local server name to the appropriate system table, and should result in the @@SERVERNAME variable returning correctly.

@@IDENTITY

An identity column is a special type of column within a table that increases in value with each insert that is made into the table. When inserting into such a table, it is not possible to insert an explicit value for the identity column itself, or to determine what this value is going to be before, or during the insert. SQL Server determines the value that is to be used for a particular row when it receives the request to do the insert, and after it has been made it makes the value inserted available in the @@IDENTITY global variable. The @@IDENTITY global variable is unique to a connection, so the value you get returned from @@IDENTITY is going to be from the last insert you did and not necessarily the last insert made on this table by all users.

The following example shows the use of @@IDENTITY to determine the key value of the last row inserted:

```
CREATE TABLE #MyTestTable
(
    IDCol        INT IDENTITY(1,1) PRIMARY KEY,
    VarCharCol   VARCHAR(255)
)

INSERT #MyTestTable(VarCharCol)
VALUES('Test 1')
```

```
SELECT @@IDENTITY -- Returns the value of the last identity column inserted

DROP TABLE #MyTestTable
```

Handling Errors

As with every programming platform, there will be times when errors occur. These could be the result of anything from bad data through to unexpected circumstance. No matter what the reason, you have to create a stored procedure strong enough to cater for as many possibilities as possible. However, don't be caught out by thinking that the only error is one that might cause some sort of exception to occur. An error could also be an incorrect number of rows processed, a transaction that has not been dealt with, or even an unusual computed value for a set of data. In these latter cases there is not much SQL Server can do to help, and it's down to you as a developer to ensure that your data is valid.

> If you know the bounds of the command you are executing, you should be checking that the command is operating within these bounds and raising an error if the execution falls out of these bounds.

Typically you will want to check the @@ERROR and @@ROWCOUNT global variables after every T-SQL statement that performs some form of data modification. If an error has occurred or if the number of rows affected are not what is expected, then you should cause the data modification to fail, for example:

```
CREATE PROCEDURE UpdateEmployee
    @FirstName varchar(30),
    @Surname varchar(30),
    @EmployeeID int
AS
BEGIN TRANSACTION

    DECLARE   @Error      int,
              @Rowcount   int

    UPDATE Employees
    SET   FirstName  = @FirstName,
          Surname    = @Surname
    WHERE EmployeeID = @EmployeeID

    SELECT @Error    =@@ERROR,
       @Rowcount     =@@ROWCOUNT

    IF @Error<>0
    BEGIN
        ROLLBACK TRANSACTION
        RAISERROR('An error occurred updating the Employee record.
                The error number is: %d ',16,1, @Error)
        RETURN 0
    END
```

```
    IF @Rowcount<>1
    BEGIN
        ROLLBACK TRANSACTION
        RAISERROR('The update on the employees table did not update
        1 row.  The number of rows affected were: %d',16,1, @Rowcount)
        RETURN 0
    END

    COMMIT TRANSACTION
    RETURN 1
```

In this example, within a user-defined transaction (for more on these, see Chapter 8), we update our Employees table using the values passed by the executor of the stored procedure. Let's now step through this code and examine all our error handling routines.

The first thing we do after the physical update statement is to assign the value of the @@ERROR and @@ROWCOUNT variables to temporary storage variables because, as we discussed above, these change after every T-SQL statement that is executed:

```
    SELECT @Error      =@@ERROR,
           @Rowcount   =@@ROWCOUNT
```

Next we check the value of the @Error variable that is holding the returned @@ERROR value from the UPDATE statement. For this UPDATE to occur successfully we expect the @@ERROR value to be 0, which indicates that no error occurred. If any error has occurred then we undo our UPDATE by calling ROLLBACK TRANSACTION, then exit out of our stored procedure after returning an error message to our client application:

```
    IF @Error<>0
    BEGIN
        ROLLBACK TRANSACTION
        RAISERROR('An error occurred updating the Employee record.
                The error number is: %d ',16,1, @Error)
        RETURN 0
    END
```

But error checking doesn't end there with checking for physical operation errors. For robust, reliable code we should also be checking the number of rows affected. In most T-SQL data modification operations you usually have an idea of the number of rows that will be affected by a given statement. If you do then you should be checking that this number of rows is actually being affected. We do this in the next code snippet. We check our @Rowcount (the value of @@ROWCOUNT from our UPDATE) and, if more or less than 1 row was updated, we undo our transaction and return an error to our client application because we have an unexpected result:

```
    IF @Rowcount<>1
    BEGIN
        ROLLBACK TRANSACTION
        RAISERROR('The update on the employees table did not update
        1 row.  The number of rows affected were: %d',16,1, @Rowcount)
        RETURN 0
    END
```

Checking the rows affected is probably the method of validation within stored procedures most underused by developers. However, as it is so simple to do, and it provides such a useful early warning mechanism for data integrity issues, I recommend everyone writing stored procedures for production use to perform this sort of validation whenever possible. Just imagine our example above without this form of validation. If our database had developed data integrity issues and the `employeeid` record that we believed we were updating no longer existed, we would be in trouble. Without row count validation, our stored procedure would have updated 0 rows without raising any error, leaving the client application thinking the update was successful.

RAISERROR

`RAISERROR` provides a convenient and powerful mechanism for informing a client application of an error occurring within, or status information relating to, the processing of a stored procedure or T-SQL batch.

`RAISERROR` has the following syntax:

```
RAISERROR MSGID | MSG, Severity, State, Arguments, Arguments... WITH option
```

We'll look at the differences between using a **message ID** (`MSGID`) and an **ad hoc** message shortly, but first let's talk about severity, state, and the arguments as they relate to the syntax we have just seen.

Severity and State

Severity is used to indicate the type of error that has occurred. Generally, all user-defined error messages should have a severity of 16. Severity 16 refers to an application error. Higher severities are used to indicate problems within SQL Server itself, and should not be generated within your code to indicate application error.

State is an integer value in the range of 1 through 127, but this has no real impact on user-defined error messages. This wide range is provided more for use by SQL Server's own internally generated error messages. If you have no use for state, then setting it to 1 is the most common option.

Arguments

Arguments are used to substitute run-time values as part of the error message when the error is being raised. Within the error message you insert placeholders for where you wish the run-time values to go, and then, when raising the error, you specify the values for these placeholders in the form of an argument list.

The placeholders you can insert within your error message take the following format:

```
% flag width precision h | l type
```

for example:

```
RAISERROR('Error: %061d',16,1,@@ERROR)
```

There are various types of placeholders, used on the basis of the type of information you wish them to take. Here are the different indicators:

Type	Description
%d	Display argument as signed integer (for example -1234 or 1234)
%o	Display argument as an octal (base 8 number)
%p	Display argument as a pointer (8 digital hex number for example 0000001A)
%s	Display argument as a string (for example Hello!)
%u	Display argument as an unsigned integer
%x	Display argument as an unsigned hex number (for example 6E)

Additionally, the flag parameter can have one of the following values:

Flag	Description
–	Left justify within the given width.
+	If the parameter is a signed numeric type, then prefix with plus or minus.
0	Pad the argument with leading 0's until the width parameter has been reached.
#	Prefix with 0x for hexadecimal type.
' ' (space)	Prefix argument with spaces.

The width parameter can be used to specify the minimum width (in characters) of the outputted argument. If you specify * then the next parameter, the precision, is used to determine the width.

The precision determines the maximum number of characters output within the error message from the argument supplied.

h or l are used to specify short int or long int values.

Some more examples of using arguments within RAISERROR are shown here:

```
RAISERROR('Error: %#08x',16,1,10)
```

produces:

Error: 0x00000a

and:

```
RAISERROR('Error: %+d',16,1,10)
```

produces:

Error: +10

and:

```
RAISERROR('Error: %s',16,1,'Exception')
```

produces:

Error: Exception

Arguments can be specified within both user-defined error messages and ad hoc error messages as we will see shortly.

Ad Hoc Error Messages

Ad hoc error messages are generated using the RAISERROR command directly, within procedures. We saw several of them in the previous section. Another example might be:

```
RAISERROR('The following error occurred: %d',16,1, @@Error)
```

Ad hoc error messages have the advantage that they do not require us to set up user-defined error messages (we'll take a look at these next). However, they have the disadvantage of binding error text within your code, which makes changing the text of an error message, or changing the language of all error messages a difficult process.

User-Defined Error Messages

User-defined error messages are messages that can be defined at the server level (stored in the sysmessages table in the master database), for use within any of your procedures in any of your databases on that server. Each user-defined error message has a message ID, which is a number assigned by the developer. You can use error numbers 50001 and above for the purpose of creating user-defined error messages. SQL Server reserves the error numbers 0-50000 for use internally.

To access a user-defined error message that you created previously, you can specify its message ID in your code via the MSGID parameter. This method can be used to replace ad hoc messages in your application code with the result that you now only have to change the error message in one place if your needs change, rather than in each piece of stored procedure code itself.

User-defined errors also allow a message per language to be defined which is of great advantage when working with multilingual applications. Instead of needing to code the application to check the current language for a given user, SQL Server will determine the language of that user from the language assigned to their login, and return the user-defined error message in the language of the login.

User-defined error messages are added using the sp_addmessage system stored procedure. For example:

```
EXEC sp_addmessage @msgnum=70000,
                   @severity=16,
                   @msgtext='A problem has occured.',
                   @lang='us_english'
```

```
EXEC sp_addmessage @msgnum=70000,
                   @severity=16,
                   @msgtext=' Ima Problema',
                   @lang='Croatian'

SET LANGUAGE 'us_english'
RAISERROR(70000,16,1)

SET LANGUAGE 'Croatian'
RAISERROR(70000,16,1)

EXEC sp_dropmessage @msgnum=70000,@lang='Croatian'
EXEC sp_dropmessage @msgnum=70000,@lang='us_english'
```

SET LANGUAGE is used in this example to change the language setting of the current session, first to us_english, and then to Croatian, so you can see the way in which the appropriate error message is returned based on what the current language for that session is. Normally you wouldn't set the language explicitly in code like this but instead you would associate a default language with the user's login using the master.dbo.sp_defaultlanguage system stored procedure.

The only danger with using user-defined error messages is that they are server specific, not database specific. If your database is sharing a server with other databases, this means that there is a potential conflict between the error message IDs that you decide to use and the error message IDs other developers decide to use. The worst case is if you both select the same IDs for completely different error messages as only one application can store its custom messages for the duplicated error IDs. This would lead to confusing (and interesting) responses from the second application when it raises these errors expecting to present the user with the appropriate error message, but instead returning a completely different error message created by the other application.

If your server is only running one database, or if it is running databases that you or your development team have developed, then duplicate IDs are less of a concern as you can come up with an internal register for error message IDs to ensure you don't use the same one twice for different purposes. However, if you are mixing your applications with other vendors' applications there is a higher potential for conflict. In practice the risk of this happening is low due to the huge number of potential user-defined error numbers available, 2147433646 in fact.

If you do make use of user-defined error numbers, there are a couple of things you can do to minimize the risk of conflicts, both with other developers and with other vendors:

❑   Choose a range of numbers unlikely to be chosen by another vendor. Avoid choosing numbers that are multiples of 1000 such as 60000-61000, instead choose a range like 834220-834420.

❑   Create an internal register for error messages that is accessible by all your development teams. While you cannot specifically control conflicts that may occur between your applications and those developed by external vendors, you can at least prevent conflicts between database applications developed within your own organization.

❑   Standardize errors between the applications you develop. Instead of just creating new error messages, developers should first check the register for existing matching errors. This way new applications instantly benefit from multilingual error messages that may have previously been created.

> Due to this risk of conflicts, if you are developing off-the-shelf database applications where you will have no control over which other database applications will be sharing a server with your own, you should consider using only ad hoc error messages.

Handling Raised Errors

The error raised with T-SQL is returned to our client application in the form of a `SqlException` where it can be dealt with appropriately. For example:

```
Dim mySQLConn As New SqlConnection("Server=MyServer; Database=pubs;" _
                                    & "User Id=sa;Password=;"
Dim mySQLCmd As New SqlCommand()
```

```
With mySQLCmd
    .Connection = mySQLConn
    .CommandText = "RAISERROR('This is an error',16,1)"
End With
```

```
mySQLConn.Open()
```

```
Try
    mySQLCmd.ExecuteNonQuery()
Catch oSQLException As SqlException
    With oSQLException
        Console.WriteLine("Error Number: " & .Number)
        Console.WriteLine("Error State: " & .State)
        Console.WriteLine("Error Message: " & oSQLException.Message)
    End With
End Try
mySQLConn.Close()
```

Within this code we execute a T-SQL statement that does nothing but raise an error from SQL Server to our client application. Within our client VB.NET application we catch the `SqlException` and output the details of the error to our console window.

Summary

This chapter has focused on topics that will help you develop more effective stored procedures. By harnessing the power available you will be able to build more scalable, better performing database applications.

Important topics we covered in this chapter include:

- ❑ Why and how to prefix stored procedures by their owner
- ❑ Why dynamic SQL is not a great idea in stored procedures
- ❑ Joins, aggregation, and conditional logic
- ❑ Passing parameters, resultsets, and XML in and out
- ❑ Navigating hierarchies using T-SQL
- ❑ Defining and using user-defined functions
- ❑ Handling errors

I have deliberately concentrated solely on the SQL Server side of the application in this chapter. In the next chapter we will cover how we can harness the power of our stored procedures in VB.NET to produce quality application code.

6

Using Stored Procedures in VB.NET

Now we have learned about writing great stored procedures it is time to move on and discuss how we can use them from within our .NET applications. There are a number of different ways in which we can utilize stored procedures in VB.NET and each method is suited for a particular situation. With the introduction of SQLXML, an add-on component to SQL Server released by Microsoft, there are now three managed classes available for use when working with stored procedures, above and beyond those already provided within the .NET Framework.

In this chapter we will cover all the major ways of utilizing stored procedures so that you can make an informed choice of the best method for your applications. We will discuss:

- ❑ Creating stored procedures in Visual Studio .NET
- ❑ Executing a stored procedure by using a `DataReader` object
- ❑ Returning multiple resultsets from a stored procedure
- ❑ Passing parameters in and out of stored procedures
- ❑ Using return parameters within stored procedures
- ❑ Retrieving and passing XML in stored procedures

Creating Stored Procedures in VS.NET

Visual Studio .NET's combination of most of the Microsoft development tools into one IDE has included tools used for designing SQL Server database objects. While not meant as a replacement for SQL Server Query Analyzer, or indeed SQL Server Enterprise Manager, the integration achieved is a godsend for most people used to developing applications that access SQL Server with Visual Studio 6.

To create or edit objects contained within your database you first need to register the database as a data connection within the Server Explorer. The Server Explorer is one of the tool windows shown by default in VS.NET, but if it is not visible you can easily open it by selecting View | Server Explorer or by pressing *Ctrl+Alt+S*.

From within the Server Explorer right-click and select Add Connection and the DataLink Properties window will be opened as shown in the figure below. Enter the server name, security information, and database you wish to connect to:

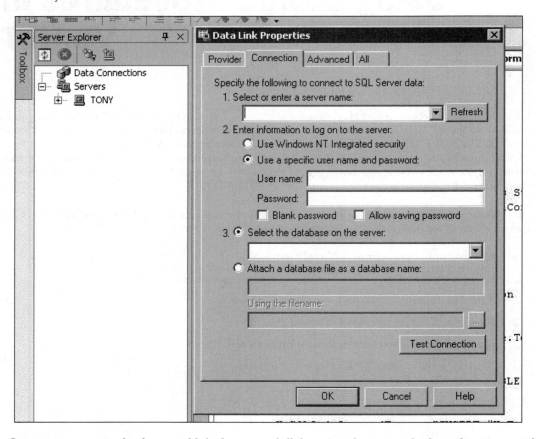

Once your connection has been established, you can drill down into the various database object types and either select existing objects for deletion/editing or create new objects to be included within your database. For use within this chapter, create a Data Connection to our HumanResources database on the SQL Server where this database is located.

To create stored procedures within the database drill down into this connection, right-click **Stored Procedures** and select **New Stored Procedure**. Once you have entered the T-SQL code you wish to include in your stored procedure, click the **Save** button on the VS.NET toolbar in order to create your stored procedure within the selected SQL Server database. Note however that this will not save a local copy of the stored procedure to a disk file.

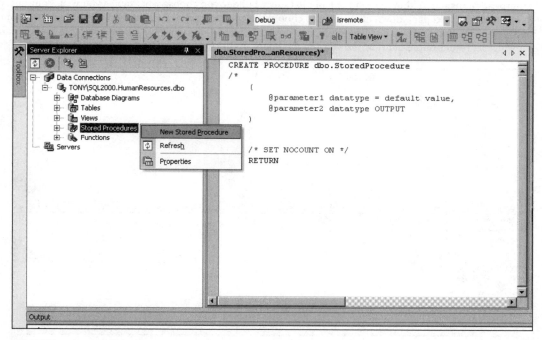

VS.NET makes it easy to generate simple stored procedures by including a SQL builder utility. While you cannot create complex conditional control-of-flow logic with the SQL Query builder, you can easily create simple queries to be used within your stored procedures. To use the Query builder right-click within the stored procedure definition where you wish the query to be placed and select **Insert SQL**.

Once created these statements will appear surrounded by a blue border, which highlights that these can be edited with the Query builder at a later time.

The Query builder itself has an interface that will be familiar to those people who have worked with Microsoft Access, or those who have created views using the GUI interface provided by SQL Server Enterprise Manager. Within the top pane of the Query builder you choose what tables you wish your query to contain. The next pane down allows you to choose the columns, predicates, and ordering clause that you wish to be included in the query. The next pane down shows the query in SQL syntax, with the bottom pane showing the results of the query when you run the query (right-click, select Run).

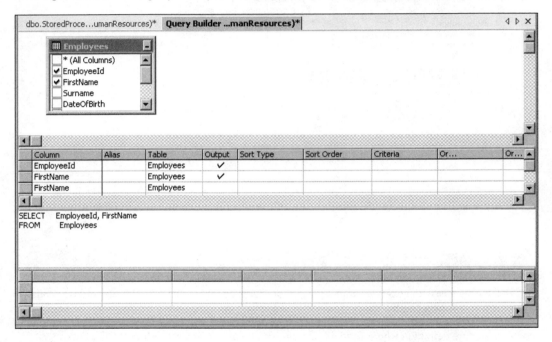

Note that, in addition to creating SELECT statements, by right-clicking within the Query Builder, and choosing the **Change Type** menu item, you can select from the follow types of SQL statements:

- ❑ **Select** – A SQL SELECT statement, used for returning rows from one or more tables
- ❑ **Insert Results** – An INSERT statement that inserts rows based on the results of a SELECT statement
- ❑ **Insert Values** – An INSERT statement that inserts rows based on a set of values
- ❑ **Update** – An UPDATE statement that updates a table based on a set of values
- ❑ **Delete** – A DELETE statement

These statements are part of the basic SQL syntax so we won't go into further detail here. To learn more about these SQL statements you can read 'Beginning SQL Programming' (Wrox Press, ISBN 1861001800) or 'Beginning SQL Server 2000 Programming', (Wrox Press, ISBN 1861005237).

DataReader

Having seen how to create stored procedures within VS.NET, we begin our discussion of using them by looking at a simple execution of one using the `SqlDataReader` object. The stored procedure we'll consider here accepts no parameters and produces a list of employees from our `HumanResources` sample database for use by our client application. While this list of employees may have multiple rows, all of these rows will be returned within a single resultset. As the application has no ability to control what values the stored procedure returns, this type of procedure is used infrequently within database applications.

In the previous chapter we created a procedure named `ListEmployees`, which returned the `EmployeeID`, `FirstName`, and `Surname` columns from all rows contained in the `Employees` table of our `HumanResources` database.

To call this procedure within a VB.NET application, we begin by adding the usual references to the `System.Data` and `System.Data.SqlClient` namespaces at the head of the code module:

```
Imports System.Data
Imports System.Data.SqlClient
```

The rest of the code is as follows:

```
'Change the connection string to your own SQL Server details
Dim strConnection As String = "Server=MyServer; " _
                    & "Database=HumanResources;" _
                    & "User Id=sa;Password=;"

Dim cnSqlServer As New SqlClient.SqlConnection(strConnection)
Dim cmdSqlServer As New SqlClient.SqlCommand()

    With cmdSqlServer

        .Connection = cnSqlServer
        .CommandText = "dbo.ListEmployees"
        .CommandType = CommandType.StoredProcedure

    End With

    cmdSqlServer.CommandType = CommandType.StoredProcedure

    'open the connection
    cnSqlServer.Open()

    Dim drSqlServer As SqlDataReader = cmdSqlServer.ExecuteReader
    Dim iLoop As Integer

        While drSqlServer.Read

            For iLoop = 0 To drSqlServer.FieldCount() - 1

                Console.Write(drSqlServer(iLoop))

                Console.Write(vbTab)
```

```
            Next
        End While

    drSqlServer.Close()

    cnSqlServer.Close()
```

The first section of code provides the connection string for our SQL Server instance, and creates the `SqlConnection` and `SqlCommand` objects we require:

```
'Change the connection string to your own SQL Server details
Dim strConnection As String = "Server=MyServer; " _
                        & "Database=HumanResources;" _
                        & "User Id=sa;Password=;"

Dim cnSqlServer As New SqlClient.SqlConnection(strConnection)
Dim cmdSqlServer As New SqlClient.SqlCommand()

    With cmdSqlServer

        .Connection = cnSqlServer
        .CommandText = "dbo.ListEmployees"
        .CommandType = CommandType.StoredProcedure

    End With
```

We then call the stored procedure:

```
    cmdSqlServer.CommandType = CommandType.StoredProcedure

    'open the connection
    cnSqlServer.Open()
```

Finally we create our `DataReader` object, and output the results to the console window:

```
    Dim drSqlServer As SqlDataReader = cmdSqlServer.ExecuteReader
    Dim iLoop As Integer

        While drSqlServer.Read

            For iLoop = 0 To drSqlServer.FieldCount() - 1

                Console.Write(drSqlServer(iLoop))

                Console.Write(vbTab)

            Next
        End While
```

If you set the `CommandType` property to `StoredProcedure` instead of `Text`, the stored procedure will be executed directly with SQL Server rather than being packaged within a prepared SQL statement. Whichever way the stored procedure executes however, an execution plan is compiled and cached for reuse.

Multiple Resultsets

A stored procedure is not limited to returning the results of a single query. In fact the stored procedure can return an unlimited number of resultsets, although it doesn't make good design sense to have more than a few for performance reasons. Typically you would use SQL joins to create query resultsets that contain the information you need, however there may be times where you are returning multiple independent resultsets from one stored procedure. This has a performance impact, since the higher the number of resultsets you wish to return, the higher the number of queries that are executed on SQL Server to produce them. Keeping query activity as low as possible per connection, helps to improve the overall scalability of your database application so you should only return multiple resultsets when absolutely necessary.

Create the following procedure that could be used to populate various drop-down lists on an application screen, allowing for the assignment of employees to departments for example.

```
CREATE PROCEDURE dbo.EmployeesAndDepartments
AS
    SET NOCOUNT ON

    SELECT    EmployeeID,FirstName,Surname
    FROM      Employees


    SELECT    DepartmentID, Description
    FROM      Departments
GO
```

As there are two independent queries contained with this stored procedure, two resultsets will be returned. There is a different method for accessing the multiple resultsets depending on whether we are accessing this stored procedure using a DataReader or a DataAdapter object. We have extensively discussed in previous chapters the differences between the DataReader and DataAdapter and the reasons to choose between the two. Basically it boils down to what happens to the data once it is at the client application. If the data is simply to be displayed before being thrown away, then the DataReader object provides the best performance. However if you need to display the data repeatedly, or modify the data within the application and maybe update the original data source, then storing the data within a DataSet via a DataAdapter is your best option. We will look at both methods, beginning with the use of a DataReader object.

```
'Change the connection string to your own SQL Server details
Dim strConnection As String = "Server=MyServer; " _
                            & "Database=HumanResources;" _
                            & "User Id=sa;Password=;"

Dim cnSqlServer As New SqlClient.SqlConnection(strConnection)
Dim cmdSqlServer As New SqlClient.SqlCommand()

    With cmdSqlServer
        .Connection = cnSqlServer
        .CommandText = "dbo.EmployeesAndDepartments"
        .CommandType = CommandType.StoredProcedure
    End With

'open the connection
cnSqlServer.Open()
```

```
Dim drSqlServer As SqlDataReader

drSqlServer = cmdSqlServer.ExecuteReader

Dim iLoop As Integer

    Do
        While drSqlServer.Read

                For iLoop = 0 To drSqlServer.FieldCount() - 1
                    Console.Write(drSqlServer(iLoop))
                    Console.Write(vbTab)

                Next
                    Console.WriteLine("")

        End While

    Loop While drSqlServer.NextResult

drSqlServer.Close()

cnSqlServer.Close()
```

This code listing is, in the main, now familiar to us. The key section in this case is the following:

```
Do
    While drSqlServer.Read

            For iLoop = 0 To drSqlServer.FieldCount() - 1
                Console.Write(drSqlServer(iLoop))
                Console.Write(vbTab)

            Next
                Console.WriteLine("")

    End While
```

```
    Loop While drSqlServer.NextResult
```

The drSqlServer.NextResult moves our SqlDataReader object to the next resultset and returns True, if there have been additional resultsets returned from SQL Server. Using this method we loop around displaying the values from all of the columns, for all of the rows within the current resultset. When there are no more resultsets to move forward to then the NextResult method returns False.

The second method we'll look at uses a DataAdapter to populate a DataSet object in order to make the various resultsets available. This method is a bit more involved than using the DataReader, however it does allow us to retain the data within a DataSet for further processing once the connection to SQL Server has been closed.

```vbnet
'Change the connection string to your own SQL Server details
Dim strConnection As String = "Server=MyServer; " _
                           & "Database=HumanResources;" _
                           & "User Id=sa;Password=;"

Dim cnSqlServer As New SqlClient.SqlConnection(strConnection)
Dim cmdSqlServer As New SqlClient.SqlCommand()

    With cmdSqlServer

        .Connection = cnSqlServer
        .CommandText = "dbo.EmployeesAndDepartments"
        .CommandType = CommandType.StoredProcedure

    End With

'open the connection
cnSqlServer.Open()

    Dim daSqlServer As New SqlDataAdapter(cmdSqlServer)
    Dim dsDataSet As New DataSet()

    daSqlServer.Fill(dsDataSet)

    Dim iLoopTable As Integer
    Dim iLoopRow As Integer
    Dim iLoopColumn As Integer

    For iLoopTable = 0 To dsDataSet.Tables.Count - 1

        With dsDataSet.Tables(iLoopTable)

            Console.WriteLine(.TableName)

            For iLoopRow = 0 To .Rows.Count - 1

                For iLoopColumn = 0 To .Columns.Count - 1

                    Console.Write(.Rows(iLoopRow).Item(iLoopColumn))
                    Console.Write(vbTab)

                Next

                Console.WriteLine()

            Next
        End With
    Next

    dsDataSet.Dispose()
    daSqlServer.Dispose()

    cnSqlServer.Close()
```

Having established our connection to SQL Server, we then create the `DataAdapter` and `DataSet` objects and populate the `DataSet` as follows:

```
Dim daSqlServer As New SqlDataAdapter(cmdSqlServer)
Dim dsDataSet As New DataSet()

daSqlServer.Fill(dsDataSet)
```

We allow for any number of `resultsets` being returned by the stored procedure, by looping through the `DataSet` writing out to the console window the values for all the columns, in all of the rows, in all of the tables.

```
Dim iLoopTable As Integer
Dim iLoopRow As Integer
Dim iLoopColumn As Integer

   For iLoopTable = 0 To dsDataSet.Tables.Count - 1

      With dsDataSet.Tables(iLoopTable)

         Console.WriteLine(.TableName)

         For iLoopRow = 0 To .Rows.Count - 1

            For iLoopColumn = 0 To .Columns.Count - 1

               Console.Write(.Rows(iLoopRow).Item(iLoopColumn))
               Console.Write(vbTab)

            Next

            Console.WriteLine()

         Next
      End With
   Next
```

Passing Parameters

While executing a simple stored procedure is useful, as we discovered in Chapter 5, stored procedures can become really useful when we start passing parameters to them. In fact almost all stored procedures that you find in production applications, will have one or more parameters that control what data is returned or modified.

As an example here, the stored procedure shown opposite accepts an `EmployeeID` as an input parameter and it returns a resultset containing the details for that employee as well as the IDs for the previous and next employees as output parameters. This procedure could now be used within an application that has an employee detail screen with a Next and Previous button to scroll through the list of employees, for example.

```
CREATE PROCEDURE dbo.ScrollEmployeeDetail
   @EmployeeID          int,
   @PreviousEmployeeID  int   OUTPUT,
   @NextEmployeeID      int   OUTPUT
AS
   SET NOCOUNT ON

   SELECT EmployeeId, FirstName, Surname, DateOfBirth,
      SecurityPhoto, DateOfHire, LastReview, Department
   FROM   dbo.Employees
   WHERE  EmployeeID = @EmployeeID

   SELECT @PreviousEmployeeID = MAX(EmployeeID)
   FROM   dbo.Employees
   WHERE  EmployeeID < @EmployeeID

   if @@ERROR<>0
     RETURN 1

   SELECT @NextEmployeeID = MIN(EmployeeID)
   FROM   dbo.Employees
   WHERE  EmployeeID > @EmployeeID

   if @@ERROR<>0
     RETURN 1

   RETURN 0
GO
```

We'll utilize this stored procedure following a discussion of the SqlParameter object.

SqlParameter Object

The SqlParameter object is used to both pass and retrieve parameter values between T-SQL and .NET languages such as VB.NET. These may be used to pass parameter values to and from stored procedures, as well as passing parameters within standard T-SQL code. While we will just take a look at using the SqlParameter object with stored procedures within this chapter you should bear in mind that they can be used to pass parameters with any valid parameterized SQL statement.

A SqlParameter gets associated with a SqlCommand object using either of two methods. The first uses the SqlCommand object to create the SqlParameter object, as follows:

```
Dim prmSQLParameter As SqlClient.SqlParameter
prmSQLParameter = cmdSqlServer.Parameters.Add("@Name", "Value")
```

The second creates a new SqlParameter object and adds this object to the SqlCommand's SqlParameter collection:

```
Dim prmSQLParameter As New SqlClient.SqlParameter
cmdSqlServer.Parameters.Add(prmSQLParameter)
```

Some of the `SqlParameter`'s object properties that we will be using in this chapter are:

Property	Description
Direction	Specifies if the parameter is input, output, input & output, or a return value. If you do not specify a direction this will default to being an input parameter.
ParameterName	The name of the parameter. If not a return value this should correspond to the name of the parameter in the stored procedure.
Size	Defines the maximum size of the parameter data type. This is set in bytes for non-unicode for non-string and ANSI string types, and in characters for Unicode string types. This determines the maximum size of the value of the parameter.
SqlDbType	Defines the parameter's data type as a SQL Server data type.
Value	The actual value of the parameter. It may be set by the application, the SQL command, or both for Input/Output parameters.

SqlDataReader and Parameters

If you are executing a stored procedure that returns a `resultset` and you use the `ExecuteReader` method of the `SqlDataReader` object, such as in our example earlier, the values for the output parameters and return value parameters will be `NULL` within the first resultset. The output parameters are actually treated like an additional resultset by the `SqlDataReader` and you must execute `NextResult` before you can access these. This is a limitation of the `ExecuteReader` method and one you should be well aware of as it can easily lead to difficulty in attempts to isolate problems within your application code.

For example, using our `ScrollEmployeeDetail` stored procedure that we created above, we can execute the following code to run our stored procedure using a `SqlDataReader` object:

```
'Change the connection string to your own SQL Server details
Dim strConnection As String = "Server=MyServer; " _
                        & "Database=HumanResources;" _
                        & "User Id=sa;Password=;"

Dim cnSqlServer As New SqlClient.SqlConnection(strConnection)
Dim cmdSqlServer As New SqlClient.SqlCommand()
Dim prmSQLParameter As SqlClient.SqlParameter

    With cmdSqlServer
        .Connection = cnSqlServer
        .CommandText = "dbo.ScrollEmployeeDetail"
        .CommandType = CommandType.StoredProcedure
    End With

prmSQLParameter = cmdSqlServer.Parameters.Add("@EmployeeID", 2)
prmSQLParameter.Direction = ParameterDirection.Input
prmSQLParameter.SqlDbType = SqlDbType.Int

prmSQLParameter = _
        cmdSqlServer.Parameters.Add("@PreviousEmployeeID", Nothing)
```

```
prmSQLParameter.Direction = ParameterDirection.Output
prmSQLParameter.SqlDbType = SqlDbType.Int

prmSQLParameter = _
        cmdSqlServer.Parameters.Add("@NextEmployeeID", Nothing)
prmSQLParameter.Direction = ParameterDirection.Output
prmSQLParameter.SqlDbType = SqlDbType.Int

'open the connection
cnSqlServer.Open()

Dim drDataReader As SqlDataReader = cmdSqlServer.ExecuteReader

    Console.WriteLine("Parameter values in first resultset")
    Console.WriteLine("Previous Employee:" _
            & cmdSqlServer.Parameters("@PreviousEmployeeID").Value)
    Console.WriteLine("Next Employee:" _
            & cmdSqlServer.Parameters("@NextEmployeeID").Value)

    While drDataReader.Read

        Console.Write(drDataReader("EmployeeID") & ",")
        Console.Write(drDataReader("FirstName") & ",")
        Console.WriteLine(drDataReader("SurName") & ",")

    End While

drDataReader.NextResult()

    Console.WriteLine("Parameter values in second resultset")

    Console.WriteLine("Previous Employee:" _
            & cmdSqlServer.Parameters("@PreviousEmployeeID").Value)
    Console.WriteLine("Next Employee:" _
            & cmdSqlServer.Parameters("@NextEmployeeID").Value)

drDataReader.Close()
cnSqlServer.Close()
```

In this example we create our `SqlConnection`, `SqlCommand`, and `SqlParameter` objects. Then we associate the `SqlConnection` with our `SqlCommand` object, and populate the `CommandText` property with the name of the stored procedure that we wish to call.

```
'Change the connection string to your own SQL Server details
Dim strConnection As String = "Server=MyServer; " _
                    & "Database=HumanResources;" _
                    & "User Id=sa;Password=;"

Dim cnSqlServer As New SqlClient.SqlConnection(strConnection)
Dim cmdSqlServer As New SqlClient.SqlCommand()
Dim prmSQLParameter As SqlClient.SqlParameter

    With cmdSqlServer
        .Connection = cnSqlServer
        .CommandText = "dbo.ScrollEmployeeDetail"
        .CommandType = CommandType.StoredProcedure
    End With
```

Next we add three new `SqlParameters` to our `SqlCommand` object. First the `@EmployeeID` parameter that is used to retrieve the selected employee details in a resultset.

```
prmSQLParameter = cmdSqlServer.Parameters.Add("@EmployeeID", 2)
prmSQLParameter.Direction = ParameterDirection.Input
prmSQLParameter.SqlDbType = SqlDbType.Int
```

Second, the `@PreviousEmployeeID` and `@NextEmployeeID` output parameters. These will contain the next lowest and next highest `EmployeeID`s within our `Employees` table.

```
prmSQLParameter = _
        cmdSqlServer.Parameters.Add("@PreviousEmployeeID", Nothing)
prmSQLParameter.Direction = ParameterDirection.Output
prmSQLParameter.SqlDbType = SqlDbType.Int

prmSQLParameter = _
        cmdSqlServer.Parameters.Add("@NextEmployeeID", Nothing)
prmSQLParameter.Direction = ParameterDirection.Output
prmSQLParameter.SqlDbType = SqlDbType.Int
```

Now we open our connection and execute our `SqlCommand` object, returning a `SqlDataReader` object that will contain our results.

```
'open the connection
cnSqlServer.Open()

Dim drDataReader As SqlDataReader = cmdSqlServer.ExecuteReader
```

The values of our output parameters should be 1 and 3 respectively. However on our first attempt to display these we get `NULL` values returned. The reason for this is that we have returned a resultset, namely the `SELECT` statement within the stored procedure, which means that the values of our output parameters are not contained within this initial result.

```
Console.WriteLine("Parameter values in first resultset")
Console.WriteLine("Previous Employee:" _
        & cmdSqlServer.Parameters("@PreviousEmployeeID").Value)
Console.WriteLine("Next Employee:" _
        & cmdSqlServer.Parameters("@NextEmployeeID").Value)
```

Next we iterate through the returned rows and output those to our console window.

```
While drDataReader.Read

    Console.Write(drDataReader("EmployeeID") & ",")
    Console.Write(drDataReader("FirstName") & ",")
    Console.WriteLine(drDataReader("SurName") & ",")

End While
```

Once we have output all the rows contained within the initial resultset we can move to the second one by calling the `NextResult` method. Now when we display our output parameters to the console window we get the expected results.

```
drDataReader.NextResult()

Console.WriteLine("Parameter values in second resultset")

Console.WriteLine("Previous Employee:" _
            & cmdSqlServer.Parameters("@PreviousEmployeeID").Value)
Console.WriteLine("Next Employee:" _
            & cmdSqlServer.Parameters("@NextEmployeeID").Value)
```

> The only time that output parameters are accessible when using a `SqlDataReader` object and then calling `NextResult`, is when you are calling a stored procedure that does not return a resultset, or you are using the `ExecuteNonQuery` method.

If we were only interested in retrieving the return parameters from the stored procedure above, and not the actual resultset, we can change our code to use the `ExecuteNonQuery` method. While this gives us direct access to the output parameters, it obviously means that we are no longer able to access the `resultset`.

```
cmdSqlServer.ExecuteNonQuery()

Console.WriteLine("Previous Employee:" _
    & cmdSqlServer.Parameters("@PreviousEmployeeID").Value)

Console.WriteLine("Next Employee:" _
    & cmdSqlServer.Parameters("@NextEmployeeID").Value)
```

This limitation does not apply to the `SqlDataAdapter`. All parameter values are available via the `SqlCommand` object immediately after the stored procedure has been executed, even when returning multiple `resultsets` from within your stored procedure.

Of course, as we have seen in earlier chapters, the stored procedures called by the `SqlDataReader` can perform a variety of tasks within a SQL Server database including the updating of data. The next procedure is designed to do just that. This procedure can be passed an `EmployeeID`, and optionally `FirstName` and `Surname` parameters.

```
CREATE PROCEDURE dbo.UpdateEmployeeName
    @EmployeeID     int,
    @FirstName      varchar(30)=Null,
    @Surname        varchar(30)=Null
AS
    SET NOCOUNT ON

    Update Employees
    SET   Firstname=IsNull(@FirstName,FirstName),
        Surname=IsNull(@Surname,Surname)
    WHERE   EmployeeID=@EmployeeID

GO
```

217

The employee row specified by the EmployeeID is then updated to reflect the new FirstName and Surname values passed in the parameters. If either of these parameters isn't passed then the original value contained within the FirstName or Surname column is maintained. This is achieved using the IsNull function on the following lines:

```
SET    Firstname=IsNull(@FirstName,FirstName),
    Surname=IsNull(@Surname,Surname)
```

This statement tells SQL Server to set the column to the value currently in the column if the value of the parameter is NULL. In other words there will be no change in the column value. Within a real application this procedure would normally be created to update all of the columns in the Employees table that are updateable. But for our example the FirstName and Surname columns will be acceptable.

Now back within VB.NET we can call our update procedure to change our employee record.

```
'Change the connection string to your own SQL Server details
Dim strConnection As String = "Server=MyServer; " _
                            & "Database=HumanResources;" _
                            & "User Id=sa;Password=;"

Dim cnSqlServer As New SqlClient.SqlConnection(strConnection)
Dim cmdSqlServer As New SqlClient.SqlCommand()
Dim prmSQLParameter As SqlClient.SqlParameter

    With cmdSqlServer
        .Connection = cnSqlServer
        .CommandText = "dbo.UpdateEmployeeName"
        .CommandType = CommandType.StoredProcedure
    End With

    Dim iEmployeeToUpdate As Integer = 1
    Dim strNewFirstName As String = "Laura"
    Dim strNewSurname As String = "Major"

    prmSQLParameter = _
        cmdSqlServer.Parameters.Add("@EmployeeID", iEmployeeToUpdate)
    prmSQLParameter.Direction = ParameterDirection.Input
    prmSQLParameter.SqlDbType = SqlDbType.Int

    prmSQLParameter = _
        cmdSqlServer.Parameters.Add("@FirstName", strNewFirstName)
    prmSQLParameter.Direction = ParameterDirection.Input
    prmSQLParameter.SqlDbType = SqlDbType.VarChar

    prmSQLParameter = _
        cmdSqlServer.Parameters.Add("@Surname", strNewSurname)
    prmSQLParameter.Direction = ParameterDirection.Input
    prmSQLParameter.SqlDbType = SqlDbType.VarChar

    'open the connection
    cnSqlServer.Open()

    cmdSqlServer.ExecuteNonQuery()

    cnSqlServer.Close()
```

In addition to the parameters that are passed into the stored procedures as seen in both of these examples, parameters can be returned from the stored procedure as well.

The following stored procedure is used to insert a new row into the `Departments` table. As this `Departments` table has an identity column on the primary key, the `DepartmentID` column, we do not explicitly insert a value into this column, but instead generate it automatically when the new row is created.

```
CREATE PROCEDURE dbo.AddNewDepartment
    @DepartmentID int=Null OUTPUT,
    @Description varchar(256)
AS
    SET NOCOUNT ON

    INSERT dbo.Departments( Description)
    VALUES(@Description)

    SELECT @DepartmentID = @@IDENTITY
GO
```

This stored procedure has two parameters defined, however only one of these is an input parameter. The `@DepartmentID` variable has been defined as an output parameter and the value of this variable, when the execution of the stored procedure has completed, will be returned to the application that called it.

```
CREATE PROCEDURE dbo.AddNewDepartment
    @DepartmentID int=Null OUTPUT,
    @Description varchar(256)
```

To determine the value of this automatically generated column we use the `@@IDENTITY` function. As discussed in the previous chapter this returns the last identity value that was generated for this connection.

```
    SELECT @DepartmentID = @@IDENTITY
```

By assigning it to our output variable this will be returned to our application when the stored procedure execution has compiled. This is exactly what we require when we run our next piece of VB.NET code.

```
    'Change the connection string to your own SQL Server details
    Dim strConnection As String = "Server=MyServer; " _
                    & "Database=HumanResources;" _
                    & "User Id=sa;Password=;"

    Dim cnSqlServer As New SqlClient.SqlConnection(strConnection)
    Dim cmdSqlServer As New SqlClient.SqlCommand()
    Dim prmSQLParameter As SqlClient.SqlParameter

        With cmdSqlServer
            .Connection = cnSqlServer
            .CommandText = "dbo.AddNewDepartment"
            .CommandType = CommandType.StoredProcedure
        End With

    Dim strNewDepartment As String = "Distribution"
```

```
        prmSQLParameter = _
            cmdSqlServer.Parameters.Add("@DepartmentID", Nothing)
        prmSQLParameter.Direction = ParameterDirection.Output
        prmSQLParameter.SqlDbType = SqlDbType.Int

        prmSQLParameter = _
            cmdSqlServer.Parameters.Add("@Description", strNewDepartment)
        prmSQLParameter.Direction = ParameterDirection.Input
        prmSQLParameter.SqlDbType = SqlDbType.VarChar

        'open the connection
        cnSqlServer.Open()

        cmdSqlServer.ExecuteNonQuery()

        cnSqlServer.Close()

        Console.WriteLine("The new DepartmentID is : " _
                    & cmdSqlServer.Parameters("@DepartmentID").Value)
```

This code executes a stored procedure in much the same way as the other examples we have seen so far. The difference is that the value of the new row that has been inserted into the Departments table is returned to us in the form of an output parameter defined in this section of code:

```
    prmSQLParameter = _
        cmdSqlServer.Parameters.Add("@Description", strNewDepartment)
    prmSQLParameter.Direction = ParameterDirection.Input
    prmSQLParameter.SqlDbType = SqlDbType.VarChar
```

Once the stored procedure has been executed, we output the value of our new Department row to the console window.

A special type of output parameter, called a **Return Parameter**, is used to return status information between a SQL Server stored procedure and the executor of the stored procedure, as we will look at now.

Return Parameters

In the last chapter we described how a return value can be used to indicate the success or failure state of a stored procedure. In ADO.NET, return values are exposed like the stored procedure Input and Output parameters, by using the SqlParameter object. Instead of setting the parameter direction to Input or Output we use the special direction option ReturnValue. As a stored procedure can only return a single return value, it makes sense to only define one return value parameter. If you do define multiple return value parameters only the first will be populated; the others will be left empty.

The same limitations that exist when using other parameter types with the SqlDataReader exist for return parameters. That is, if you are using the SqlDataReader to return a resultset by calling the ExecuteReader method, the value of the ReturnValue parameter will likely be set to NULL, until you cycle through all resultsets using the NextResult method.

The following example shows returning the return value from a stored procedure that is executed via a SqlDataAdapter object.

```
'Change the connection string to your own SQL Server details
Dim strConnection As String = "Server=MyServer; " _
                    & "Database=HumanResources;" _
                    & "User Id=sa;Password=;"

Dim cnSqlServer As New SqlClient.SqlConnection(strConnection)
Dim cmdSqlServer As New SqlClient.SqlCommand()
Dim prmSQLParameter As SqlClient.SqlParameter

    With cmdSqlServer
        .Connection = cnSqlServer
        .CommandText = "dbo.ScrollEmployeeDetail"
        .CommandType = CommandType.StoredProcedure
    End With

    prmSQLParameter = cmdSqlServer.Parameters.Add("@EmployeeID", 1)
    prmSQLParameter.Direction = ParameterDirection.Input
    prmSQLParameter.SqlDbType = SqlDbType.Int

    prmSQLParameter = _
        cmdSqlServer.Parameters.Add("@PreviousEmployeeID", Nothing)
    prmSQLParameter.Direction = ParameterDirection.Output
    prmSQLParameter.SqlDbType = SqlDbType.Int

    prmSQLParameter = _
        cmdSqlServer.Parameters.Add("@NextEmployeeID", Nothing)
    prmSQLParameter.Direction = ParameterDirection.Output
    prmSQLParameter.SqlDbType = SqlDbType.Int

    prmSQLParameter = _
        cmdSqlServer.Parameters.Add("RETURN_VALUE", Nothing)
    prmSQLParameter.Direction = ParameterDirection.ReturnValue
    prmSQLParameter.SqlDbType = SqlDbType.Int

    Dim daSqlDataAdapter As New SqlDataAdapter(cmdSqlServer)
    Dim dsDataSet As New DataSet()

    daSqlDataAdapter.Fill(dsDataSet)

        Console.WriteLine("Stored Procedure Result:" _
            & cmdSqlServer.Parameters("RETURN_VALUE").Value)

    dsDataSet.Dispose()
    daSqlDataAdapter.Dispose()
    cnSqlServer.Close()
```

In this example we pass the same parameters into the stored procedure as in the previous example, but we also now pass the `ReturnValue` parameter:

```
prmSQLParameter = _
        cmdSqlServer.Parameters.Add("RETURN_VALUE", Nothing)
prmSQLParameter.Direction = ParameterDirection.ReturnValue
prmSQLParameter.SqlDbType = SqlDbType.Int
```

We use the `SqlDataAdapter` object as opposed to the `SqlDataReader` object to call our stored procedure, as this allows both the parameter values and the `resultset` to be correctly passed back to our application. Once the stored procedure is executed the value sent back by the `RETURN` command within the stored procedure is entered into our `ReturnValue` parameter. This value will be 0, to indicate success, under normal circumstances.

Retrieving XML

One of the fundamental benefits of developing within a .NET language is the XML functionality ingrained within the .NET framework. Instead of just returning flat resultsets, our stored procedures can return structured XML back to our client application for further processing. We have already touched on generating the XML within SQL Server in the last chapter, using the `FOR XML AUTO` clause and we will look at this again in the next example. However, first we should discuss how this is handled from within VB.NET, or more importantly how we get the XML being generated by SQL Server into VB.NET so we can utilize it.

In addition to the `ExecuteReader` and `ExecuteNonQuery` methods of the `SqlDataReader` object that we have taken a look at so far, the `SqlDataReader` also supports the `ExecuteXMLReader` method. This is used to return an `XMLReader` object. Similar to the `DataReader` object returned by the `ExecuteDataReader` method, the `XMLReader` object returned by the `ExecuteXMLReader` method provides a cached forward-only, read only copy method of accessing the XML being returned from SQL Server.

The `XMLReader` object is known as an abstract class. You can utilize implementations of the `XMLReader` class based on what you need to use the `XMLReader` for, as we will discuss in chapter 10. However for the purpose of the following example we will be using the `XMLTextReader` implementation to retrieve our XML as simple character output so we can easily display this to our console window.

The following stored procedure encapsulates a query, which returns a structured XML representation of our `Employee` and `Department` tables from our `HumanResources` database:

```
CREATE PROCEDURE dbo.XMLEmployeeListing
AS
    SELECT Employees.EmployeeId,
        RTRIM(Employees.FirstName) + ' ' +
        RTRIM(Employees.Surname) as "Name",
        Departments.DepartmentID,
        Departments.Description
    FROM    Employees
    INNER JOIN    Departments
        ON Employees.Department = Departments.DepartmentID
    FOR XML AUTO
GO
```

As the FOR XML option within the stored procedure causes an XML stream to be returned, rather than a table resultset, we do not use our SqlDataAdapter or SqlDataReader objects to call our stored procedures. Instead we must use the ExecuteXmlReader method of our SqlCommand object to return an XmlReader object to our client application.

```
'Change the connection string to your own SQL Server details
Dim strConnection As String = "Server=MyServer; " _
                            & "Database=HumanResources;" _
                            & "User Id=sa;Password=;"

Dim cnSqlServer As New SqlClient.SqlConnection(strConnection)
Dim cmdSqlServer As New SqlClient.SqlCommand()

    With cmdSqlServer
        .Connection = cnSqlServer
        .CommandText = "dbo.XMLEmployeeListing"
        .CommandType = CommandType.StoredProcedure
    End With

'open the connection
cnSqlServer.Open()

Dim xrXmlTextReader As Xml.XmlTextReader

xrXmlTextReader = cmdSqlServer.ExecuteXmlReader

    Console.WriteLine(xrXmlTextReader.GetRemainder.ReadToEnd.ToString())

xrXmlTextReader.Close()

cnSqlServer.Close()
```

All of the code in this example will be familiar to you, except the following lines:

```
Dim xrXmlTextReader As Xml.XmlTextReader

xrXmlTextReader = cmdSqlServer.ExecuteXmlReader

    Console.WriteLine(xrXmlTextReader.GetRemainder.ReadToEnd.ToString())

xrXmlTextReader.Close()
```

First we declare our XMLTextReader object and then execute our stored procedure returning the XML into our XMLTextReader object. The final line shown above uses the GetRemainder.ReadToEnd.ToString method to read all the XML returned by the XMLReader in string format.

Passing in XML

Now we have XML being produced by our stored procedures let's take a look at the opposite situation, namely feeding XML into our stored procedures where it can be processed and then treated as a resultset within SQL Server. First let's create the following procedure in our HumanResources database, that will act as the consumer of the XML we pass in. As you will remember, OPENXML takes a cached XML document (placed into cache by calling sp_xml_preparedocument) and returns the data contained within the XML in a specified resultset format. For a description of the various T-SQL commands used in this example see the discussion of OPENXML in the previous chapter.

```
CREATE PROCEDURE dbo.AddEmployeeFromXML
    @XMLInput as NTEXT
AS
    DECLARE    @DocID    int

    EXEC sp_xml_preparedocument @DocID OUTPUT, @XMLInput

    INSERT Employees(FirstName, Surname, DateOfBirth, SecurityPhoto,
            DateOfHire, LastReview, Department)
    SELECT FirstName,
        Surname,
        DateOfBirth,
        Cast(0 as binary(1)),
        DateOfHire,
        GetDate(),
        Department
    FROM    OPENXML(@DocID, '/NewEmployees/Employee',1)
    WITH    (
            FirstName    varchar(30),
            Surname      varchar(30),
            DateOfBirth  smalldatetime,
            DateOfHire   smalldatetime,
            Department   int
        )

    EXEC sp_xml_removedocument @DocID
GO
```

Now we need to create some XML to pass to our stored procedure. For the purpose of this example we will be passing in XML from a file, but this could very well be generated by a VB.NET application or a web service somewhere on the Internet. Create a new file called C:\NewEmployees.xml and enter the following XML into this file:

```
<NewEmployees>
    <Employee FirstName="Laura" Surname="Wright" DateOfBirth="19780207"
        DateOfHire="20020201" Department="1"/>
    <Employee FirstName="Stephanie" Surname="Glucina"
        DateOfBirth="19630516" DateOfHire="20020321" Department="2"/>
    <Employee FirstName="Linda" Surname="Anderson" DateOfBirth="19811210"
        DateOfHire="20020112" Department="1"/>
    <Employee FirstName="Graham" Surname="Brown" DateOfBirth="19450607"
        DateOfHire="20020110" Department="3"/>
    <Employee FirstName="Suzanne" Surname="Smith" DateOfBirth="19601102"
```

```
        DateOfHire="20020306" Department="1"/>
    <Employee FirstName="David" Surname="Allan" DateOfBirth="19730922"
        DateOfHire="20020311" Department="2"/>
</NewEmployees>
```

Now within the client application we must open the XML file and pass the XML to our stored procedure. To do this we use an `XmlDocument` object to load the XML file and then pass a text representation of the XML document to our stored procedure input parameter:

```vbnet
'Change the connection string to your own SQL Server details
Dim strConnection As String = "Server=MyServer; " _
                            & "Database=HumanResources;" _
                            & "User Id=sa;Password=;"

Dim cnSqlServer As New SqlClient.SqlConnection(strConnection)
Dim cmdSqlServer As New SqlClient.SqlCommand()

    With cmdSqlServer
            .Connection = cnSqlServer
            .CommandText = "dbo.AddEmployeeFromXML"
            .CommandType = CommandType.StoredProcedure
    End With

Dim xXmlDocument As New Xml.XmlDocument()
xXmlDocument.Load("c:\NewEmployees.xml")

Dim prmSQLParameter As SqlParameter

    prmSQLParameter = _
            cmdSqlServer.Parameters.Add("@XMLInput", SqlDbType.NText)
    prmSQLParameter.Value = xXmlDocument.OuterXml

cnSqlServer.Open()

cmdSqlServer.ExecuteNonQuery()

cnSqlServer.Close()
```

When run, this application code connects to SQL Server and checks the rows contained within the Employees table. The employees listed in our `NewEmployees.xml` should have been added to the Employees table. Now we will examine what each section of code is doing.

First we create our connection and command objects as in previous examples.

```vbnet
'Change the connection string to your own SQL Server details
Dim strConnection As String = "Server=MyServer; " _
                            & "Database=HumanResources;" _
                            & "User Id=sa;Password=;"

Dim cnSqlServer As New SqlClient.SqlConnection(strConnection)
Dim cmdSqlServer As New SqlClient.SqlCommand()

    With cmdSqlServer
            .Connection = cnSqlServer
            .CommandText = "dbo.AddEmployeeFromXML"
            .CommandType = CommandType.StoredProcedure
    End With
```

Next we create an XMLDocument object and load our NewEmployees.xml file into this object.

```
Dim xXmlDocument As New Xml.XmlDocument()
xXmlDocument.Load("c:\NewEmployees.xml")
```

We now create a Text parameter that will be used to pass our XML file into SQL Server.

```
Dim prmSQLParameter As SqlParameter

prmSQLParameter = _
        cmdSqlServer.Parameters.Add("@XMLInput", SqlDbType.NText)
prmSQLParameter.Value = xXmlDocument.OuterXml
```

Now we use the OuterXml method of our xXMLDocument object to return the XML structure that has been loaded into our object as text, and pass this text into our Text parameter:

```
prmSQLParameter.Value = xXmlDocument.OuterXml
```

Finally we make a call to execute the SqlCommand object, passing the XML contained within the parameter to our stored procedure for processing.

```
cnSqlServer.Open()

cmdSqlServer.ExecuteNonQuery()

cnSqlServer.Close()
```

If you run the ListEmployees procedure, demonstrated in the first SqlDataReader example earlier in this chapter, you will now see that all the employees contained within the NewEmployees.xml data file have been added to our Employees table.

SQLXML

When SQL Server 2000 was released it came packaged with XML-handling functionality, some of which we have already seen in this book. Microsoft also promised at release time that it would be developing future improvements in the XML functionality as it evolved its own .NET Framework as well as keeping up with the latest XML standards as they also evolved. Microsoft has kept its promise and has delivered increased XML integration functionality in a series of SQLXML add-on packages for SQL Server. At the time of writing the latest SQLXML version is 3.0 and this can be obtained from http://msdn.microsoft.com/sqlxml.

Depending on the functionality you wish to use from the SQLXML package, you may need to install the SQLXML package on more than just your development machine. For example if you wish to utilize the Web Services functionality you need to install SQLXML on the IIS server that you will be using to publish the web services from. If you wish to run all of the examples provided in the rest of this book you will need to install SQLXML on both your development computer and your development IIS server, if this is located on a separate computer.

The installation order for a fully functional implementation of the SQLXML package is:

❑   .NET Framework

❑   SOAP Toolkit

❑   SQL XML Package

Installing the .NET Framework

To install the SQLXML .NET managed classes you will first need to install the Microsoft .NET Framework. When installing the SQLXML package on your local development machine, this shouldn't be an issue as the .NET Framework is installed as part of the Visual Studio .NET installation. However if you are installing this on a machine that currently does not have the .NET Framework this will need to be installed, and can be downloaded from http://msdn.microsoft.com/net.

> **If you have installed SQLXML before installing the .NET Framework, you will need to uninstall and reinstall SQLXML before you can use the .NET Managed Classes functionality provided.**

Installing the SOAP Toolkit

To use the SQLXML you also need the SOAP Toolkit installed. If you are unsure if the SOAP Toolkit has been installed on your machine don't fret, if the SQLXML installation (covered next) detects that the SOAP Toolkit hasn't been installed you will receive the following message during the setup procedure.

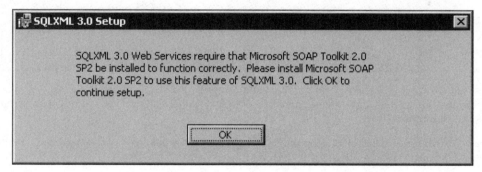

While you can continue to install the SQXML components without the SOAP Toolkit you will not be able to run all the examples shown in this book, so your best option is to cancel the installation of the SQLXML package and first install the SOAP Toolkit.

If you do not have a copy of the SOAP Toolkit you can download a copy of this from http://msdn.microsoft.com/soap.

The installation for the SOAP Toolkit is quite straightforward and should complete without any issues. Once you have the SOAP Toolkit successfully installed you can proceed to install the SQLXML package.

> **If you have installed SQLXML 3.0 before installing the SOAP Toolkit, you will need to uninstall and reinstall SQLXML before you utilize the Web Services functionality provided.**

Installing the SQLXML Package

Now we have both the .NET Framework and the SOAP Toolkit installation we can install the SQLXML package. The only option we have available during this installation is whether we wish to perform a complete or a custom install. As we will be making use of some of the additional functionality provided by the SQLXML package in a later chapter, you can simply select the Install Now button to do a complete install.

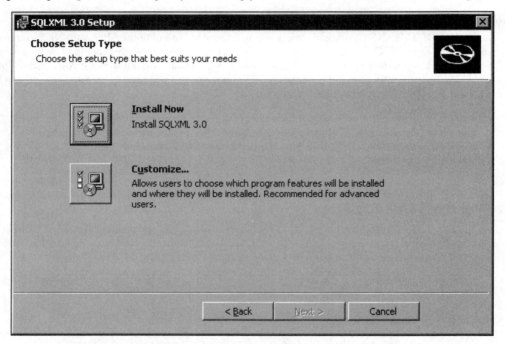

Once again this should install without problems and complete in a couple of minutes or less. As mentioned above, if the IIS you use for your development is located on a different machine you will need to repeat these steps on that machine.

Once you have this installed on the appropriate computers we can then move on to beginning to utilize some of the .NET functionality provided by this SQLXML package.

SQLXML Managed Classes

The SQLXML package contains three new .NET managed classes for integrating XML with SQL Server 2000. These managed classes expand on the functionality provided by the built in .NET SQL Server Managed providers, the SqlDataAdapter and SqlDataReader that we have looked at extensively so far in this book. These new managed classes are:

- ❑ SqlXmlCommand object – Used for executing commands that process XML against SQL Server.
- ❑ SqlXmlParameter object – Used for passing parameters to and from SQL Server using the SqlXmlCommand object.
- ❑ SqlXmlAdapter object – Used as an interface to a DataSet object. Performs a similar function to a regular SqlDataAdapter, except that it deals with the XML to and from the SqlXmlCommand objects.

The `SqlClient` objects, namely the `SqlDataAdapter` and `SqlDataReader`, use a direct low-level protocol to communicate with SQL Server known as the Tabular Data Stream (TDS). While this is a proprietary interface (when compared to the open OLE DB standard), it provides a higher level of performance than has commonly been experienced in the earlier communication protocols used by traditional ADO.

However the SQLXML managed classes use `SqlOleDb` to connect to the SQL Server data source so you will need to add the `PROVIDER=SqlOleDb` option into your connection string, as shown in the following examples. This is necessary as the functionality provided by these managed classes isn't directly accessible via the TDS stream described above. This will result in slightly longer query times than directly accessing SQL Server using the `SqlClient` objects, however this is not to say that connecting through the SQL OLE DB provider is greatly inefficient. In fact the `SQLOLEDB` provider was the preferred method of connection to SQL Server in previous versions of ADO.

While the main functionality of the SQLXML Managed classes will be discussed in a later chapter, we'll look at how we can exploit some of the classes when calling stored procedures.

For the examples that we cover next, you need to add a reference to the `SqlXml` component from within VS.NET. To do this, from within your project in VS.NET, select **References | Add Reference** and choose the **Microsoft.Data.SqlXml** component as shown in the diagram below.

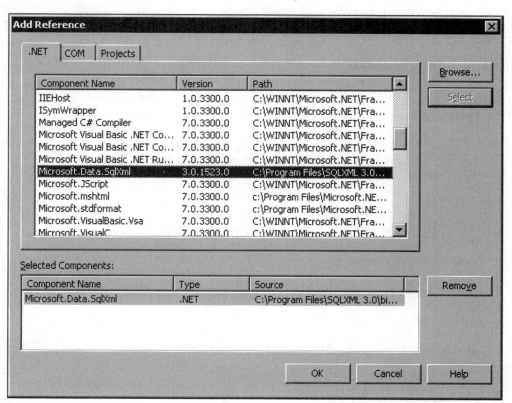

We also need to change the namespaces that we import to include the `SqlXml` namespace. As we also utilize functionality provided by the `System.IO` namespace, we should add the appropriate `Imports` statement for this also.

So, for the remainder of the examples in this chapter, ensure you have the following `Imports` statements located within your code declarations section.

```
Imports System.Data
Imports System.Data.SqlClient
Imports Microsoft.Data.SqlXml
Imports System.IO
```

SqlXmlCommand

The `SqlXmlCommand` is the first managed class provided by the SQLXML package that we will look at. This is similar to the `SqlCommand` object we have been using so far, except the `SqlXmlCommand` object is designed and optimized for retrieving and submitting XML data to and from SQL Server (instead of dealing with `resultsets`).

The `SqlXmlCommand` has two methods of executing and retrieving XML from our stored procedures, which we will look at here, namely `ExecuteStream` and `ExecuteToStream`. The `SqlXmlCommand` object also provides an `ExecuteXmlReader` method, which returns the XML from our stored procedure within a `XmlReader` object. This is a more complex type of object that we will cover later in Chapter 10.

SqlXmlCommand.ExecuteStream

The `ExecuteStream` method calls our SQL command and returns a new `Stream` object that contains our XML output. As the `Stream` object is just a collection of bytes, this is useful when you wish to deal with the XML structure as a whole without additional XML validation or processing:

```
'Change the connection string to your own SQL Server details
Dim strConnection As String = "Provider=SQLOLEDB;" _
                            & "Server=MyServer; " _
                            & "Database=HumanResources;" _
                            & "User Id=sa;Password=;"

Dim xcmdSqlServer As New SqlXmlCommand(strConnection)

xcmdSqlServer.CommandText = "dbo.XMLEmployeeListing"

Dim ioStream As IO.Stream

ioStream = xcmdSqlServer.ExecuteStream

Dim ioStreamReader As New StreamReader(ioStream)

   Console.WriteLine(ioStreamReader.ReadToEnd)

ioStreamReader.Close()
ioStream.Close()
```

After defining our connection string we create our new `SqlXmlCommand` object that will use the parameters provided by our connection string to connect to SQL Server.

```
Dim xcmdSqlServer As New SqlXmlCommand(strConnection)
```

Next we populate the `CommandText` property of our `xcmdSqlServer` object to contain the name of the stored procedure that we wish to execute and retrieve the results from.

```
xcmdSqlServer.CommandText = "dbo.XMLEmployeeListing"
```

The next section of code returns a `Stream` object by calling the `ExecuteStream` method of our `xcmdSqlServer` object. This `Stream` is then passed to a `StreamReader` object, which allows us to output the data contained in the `Stream` object as character format.

```
Dim ioStream As IO.Stream

ioStream = xcmdSqlServer.ExecuteStream

Dim ioStreamReader As New StreamReader(ioStream)
```

The `ReadToEnd` method of the `StreamReader` object is called to return all the character information contained in the `Stream` to our console window.

```
Console.WriteLine(ioStreamReader.ReadToEnd)
```

SqlXmlCommand.ExecuteToStream

The `ExecuteToStream` method will write the XML returned from our command to an existing `Stream` object. In the following example we create a file system `Stream` object and then using the `ExectuteToStream` method we write the XML returned from SQL Server directly to this file.

```
'Change the connection string to your own SQL Server details
Dim strConnection As String = "Provider=SQLOLEDB;" _
                            & "Server=MyServer; " _
                            & "Database=HumanResources;" _
                            & "User Id=sa;Password=;"

Dim xcmdSqlServer As New SqlXmlCommand(strConnection)
Dim ioFileStream As New _
    IO.FileStream("c:\AllEmployees.xml", IO.FileMode.OpenOrCreate)

    With xcmdSqlServer

        .CommandText = "dbo.XMLEmployeeListing"
        .RootTag = "AllEmployees"
        .ExecuteToStream(ioFileStream)

    End With

ioFileStream.Close()
```

In this code example we declare our connection string and `SqlXmlCommand` object as previously. However, we also create a new `IO.FileStream` object that will create the specified file on our local machine file-system.

```
Dim ioFileStream As New _
        IO.FileStream("c:\AllEmployees.xml", IO.FileMode.OpenOrCreate)
```

Next we populate the `CommandText` property of our `xcmdSqlServer` object with the name of the stored procedure that we wish to execute. In this example we also make use of the `RootTag` property. This allows us to specify an XML node that the XML we retrieve will be encased in. As well-formed XML requires a single root node, this is a useful option since it allows us to produce valid XML documents directly from SQL Server without writing additional code to add the root node around our retrieved XML.

```
With xcmdSqlServer

        .CommandText = "dbo.XMLEmployeeListing"
        .RootTag = "AllEmployees"
```

Finally we call the `ExecuteToStream` method of our `xcmdSqlServer` object in order to output the XML returned by our stored procedure to our newly created file.

```
        .ExecuteToStream(ioFileStream)

End With
```

If you browse the root of your C:\ drive you should be able to find the `AllEmployees.xml` file we have just created. You can open this file with Internet Explorer to view the XML returned by this procedure, which should look similar to the following:

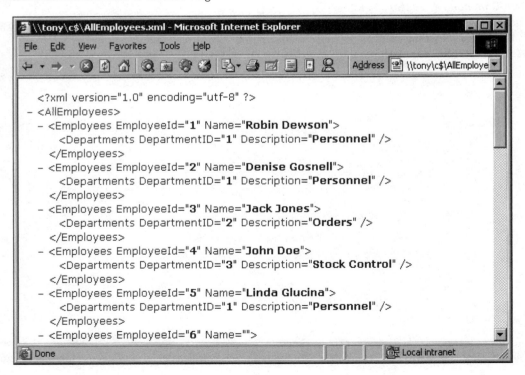

SqlXmlCommand.ClientSideXml property

The `SqlXmlCommand` object expects to execute a SQL Server command that returns XML using the `FOR XML` T-SQL option, and it will raise an exception if the SQL command attempts to return a `resultset`. The only exception to this is if you set the `ClientSideXml` property of the `SqlXmlCommand` object to `True`. Once this has been set the `SqlXmlCommand` object will accept a `resultset` from SQL Server and actually convert this to XML on the client where the application is running. This can provide increased performance on a busy SQL Server by offloading the creation of the XML to the client.

The code you execute against SQL Server must not return data in XML format when you set the `ClientSideXml` to `True`. It must return a traditional resultset, as we demonstrated earlier in this chapter. If you do try to return XML from SQL Server and you have the `ClientSideXml` property set to `True` then an exception will be thrown.

As well as setting the `ClientSideXml` property to `True` for the `SqlXmlCommand` object, you must also append the `FOR XML NESTED` parameter to the end of the `CommandText` property. This `FOR XML NESTED` parameter, unlike the `FOR XML AUTO` parameter that we looked at in an earlier chapter, is not sent to SQL Server to process but is interpreted and stripped off by the `SqlXmlCommand` object.

In the following example we are using our `EmployeesDepartments` stored procedure, which we created in the previous chapter.

```
ALTER   PROCEDURE dbo.EmployeesDepartments
AS
    SELECT e.EmployeeId,
        RTRIM(e.FirstName) + ' ' + RTRIM(e.Surname) as "Name",
        d.DepartmentID,
        d.Description
    FROM    Employees e
    INNER JOIN    Departments d ON e.Department = d.DepartmentID

GO
```

Within our client application we call our stored procedure using the `SqlXmlCommand` object as we have done in the previous examples, but with notable differences. The `CommandText` property contains the `FOR XML NESTED` clause, which instructs the `SqlXmlCommand` object to generate a nested XML structure from the `resultset` returned by our stored procedure. The `ClientSideXml` parameter tells the `SqlXmlCommand` object that this XML is to be generated on the client rather than on the SQL Server. If you are running your application and SQL Server on the same machine for development purposes, the actual difference you may notice will be minimal. However you should still recognize that this is a significant change in behavior as it is no longer SQL Server that is generating the XML as in previous examples. Instead SQL Server is simply passing a resultset to our client machine where it is being turned into XML.

```
'Change the connection string to your own SQL Server details
Dim strConnection As String = "Provider=SQLOLEDB;" _
                            & "Server=MyServer; " _
                            & "Database=HumanResources;" _
                            & "User Id=sa;Password=;"


Dim xcmdSqlXmlCommand As New SqlXmlCommand(strConnection)
```

```
Dim ioFileStream As New _
    IO.FileStream("c:\AllEmployees.xml", IO.FileMode.OpenOrCreate)

With xcmdSqlXmlCommand

    .RootTag = "AllEmployees"
    .CommandText = "dbo.EmployeeListing FOR XML NESTED"
    .ClientSideXml = True
    .ExecuteToStream(ioFileStream)

End With

ioFileStream.Close()
```

If we examine the trace of the command that is actually sent to SQL Server, we can see that the SqlXmlCommand object has indeed interpreted and stripped off the FOR XML NESTED clause and this is not actually passed to SQL Server.

EventClass	TextData
TraceStart	
SQL:BatchCompleted	exec sp_oledb_ro_usrname
SQL:BatchCompleted	select collationname(0x0904D00034)
SQL:BatchCompleted	SET NO_BROWSETABLE ON
SQL:BatchCompleted	exec dbo.EmployeeListing

This trace information has been captured using SQL Server Profiler, which is run from the Start Menu under the SQL Server program group. The default settings are fine for monitoring the interaction between our SqlXmlCommand object and SQL Server so, once authenticated, you can just choose the Run button to begin the trace.

If you leave the trace running while executing your VB.NET application, you will see all the calls being made to SQL Server from client applications, including your VB.NET application.

You can read more about SQL Server Profiler in Chapter 11.

SqlXmlAdapter

The SqlXmlAdapter is used to populate a DataSet with XML data retrieved from SQL Server. Note that although we are using XML generated by SQL Server to populate the DataSet, we are still using our standard DataSet object seen throughout this book. In fact once populated the DataSet is no different to a DataSet populated using a normal SQL query.

In contrast to the standard SqlClient Adapters, we only have two methods available to us when using a SqlXmlAdapter object. These are Fill and Update. Both of these methods accept a DataSet object as a parameter. We can use a CommandType of SqlXmlCommand.Sql to execute a stored procedure directly to Fill the DataSet, however we cannot use this stored procedure to perform the Update method.

```vbnet
'Change the connection string to your own SQL Server details
Dim strConnection As String = "Provider=SQLOLEDB;" _
                            & "Server=MyServer; " _
                            & "Database=HumanResources;" _
                            & "User Id=sa;Password=;"

Dim xcmdSqlXmlCommand As New SqlXmlCommand(strConnection)

    With xcmdSqlXmlCommand

        .CommandType = SqlXmlCommandType.Sql

        .CommandText = "dbo.XMLEmployeeListing"

    End With

    Dim xdaSqlXmlAdapter As New SqlXmlAdapter(xcmdSqlXmlCommand)
    Dim dsDataSet As New DataSet()

    xdaSqlXmlAdapter.Fill(dsDataSet)

    Dim iLoopTable As Integer
    Dim iLoopRow As Integer
    Dim iLoopColumn As Integer

        For iLoopTable = 0 To dsDataSet.Tables.Count - 1

            With dsDataSet.Tables(iLoopTable)

                Console.WriteLine(.TableName)

                For iLoopRow = 0 To .Rows.Count - 1

                    For iLoopColumn = 0 To .Columns.Count - 1

                        Console.Write( _
                            .Rows(iLoopRow).Item(iLoopColumn) & Chr(9))

                    Next

                    Console.WriteLine()

                Next
            End With
        Next
```

Let's break this down in more detail. First we define our connection to SQL Server and create a
`SqlXmlCommand` object as in previous examples. The `SqlXmlCommand` object `CommandText` property
contains the name of the stored procedure that we wish to execute.

```
Dim xcmdSqlXmlCommand As New SqlXmlCommand(strConnection)

    With xcmdSqlXmlCommand

        .CommandType = SqlXmlCommandType.Sql

        .CommandText = "dbo.XMLEmployeeListing"

    End With
```

Next we create our `SqlXmlDataAdapter` object, assign our `SqlXmlCommand` object to it, and fill our `DataSet` using it. Remember that the `SqlXmlDataAdapter` is the interface between our `SqlXmlCommand` (the object that retrieves the data from SQL Server), and our `DataSet`.

```
Dim xdaSqlXmlAdapter As New SqlXmlAdapter(xcmdSqlXmlCommand)
Dim dsDataSet As New DataSet()

xdaSqlXmlAdapter.Fill(dsDataSet)
```

The `DataSet` has now been populated in the same way as we saw demonstrated earlier in this chapter, populated with `DataTable`, `DataColumn`, and `DataRow` objects that make up a structured representation of the data retrieved from SQL Server. And just like our previous `DataSet` examples we can use the same looping code to output every column, from every row in every `DataTable` to our console window.

Summary

From the last chapter we already know how powerful stored procedures are for developing database applications. In this chapter we have learned how this power can be further built on by the diversity of methods available for calling them.

In particular we have looked at how we can perform the following tasks using stored procedures:

- ❑ Executing using the `SqlDataReader` object
- ❑ Passing parameters in and out of stored procedures
- ❑ Using return values
- ❑ Passing XML in and out of stored procedures
- ❑ Returning streams using the `SqlXmlCommand` object
- ❑ Converting a `ResultSet` to XML on the client using the `SqlXmlCommand.ClientSideXml` parameter
- ❑ Populating a `DataSet` from XML using the `SqlXmlAdapter`

In general you will commonly use only one or two methods of calling stored procedures. However being aware of all the methods available helps prepare you for difficult situations, when the standard options are not suitable.

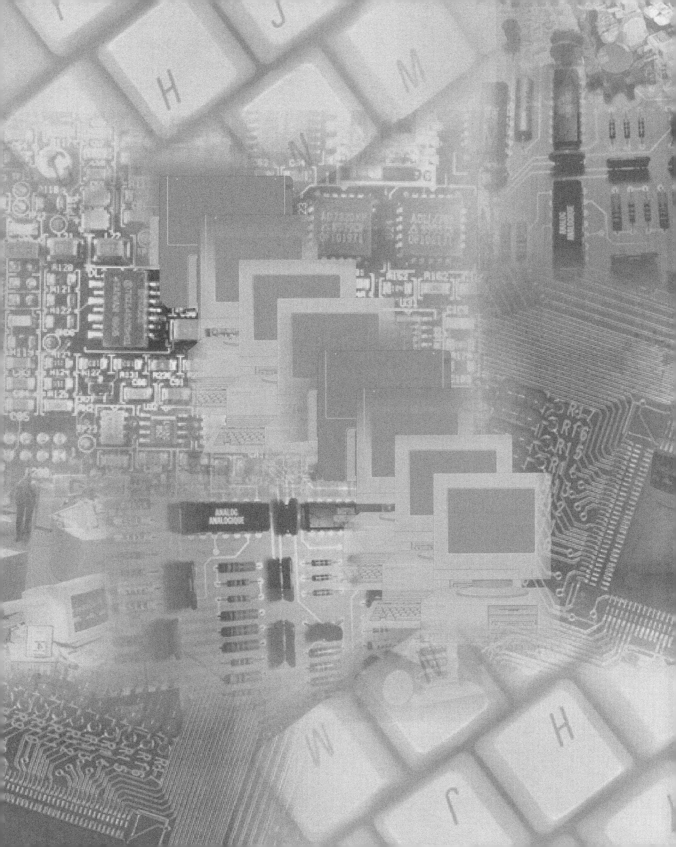

7

Data Binding

In this chapter, we will learn about binding data in various formats to the properties of several controls. To data bind a control to a source you simply assign a property of the control, such as the `Text` property, to nearly any type of data structure. This chapter will specifically cover the following:

❑   Simple data binding versus complex data binding

❑   Single-value versus multi-record controls

❑   Using the `BindingContext` object to manage data-bound controls

❑   Using the `TextBox`, `DataGrid`, and `ComboBox` controls to bind data on a Windows Form

❑   Using the `DataGrid` and `ListBox` controls to bind data on a Web Form

Finally, we will summarize the concepts covered as a checkpoint to ensure that you mastered them.

Introduction

A lot of people think of data binding in terms of a form with fields displaying data from a database. In many cases these fields are then automatically updated as you move to the next record. **Data binding** takes on a different meaning in the .NET world. Data binding is the idea that you assign properties of a control to some piece of data that may or may not be coming directly from a database. For example, you can:

❑   Assign the display (`Text`) property of a `TextBox` control to a field in a `DataSet`

❑   Assign the size properties of a control to some values in an array

❑   Populate a drop-down list with the values from a `DataReader`

All of these are examples of data binding. In both Windows Forms and Web Forms applications, you can bind any control's properties to nearly any structure that contains data.

In the .NET world of disconnected data, the idea of binding to a database and automatically updating records as you move from one record to the next has changed. For example, you might return results from a database into a local `DataSet`, that you then display on the screen and allow the user to navigate through. That `DataSet` is disconnected from its underlying data store. As the user navigates on the screen and makes changes to the data, the data is being changed in that local `DataSet`. More steps have to be taken to have those changes updated in the database. One possible way is to use the `DataSet`'s built-in update capabilities. Thus, the idea of data binding fields on a form to a database is a bit different from the concept you may be used to in ADO. While it will be more common to write applications in such a disconnected fashion, you can still write an application that will update data as you move from one record to the next, but there are additional steps you have to take.

Hopefully you now have the idea that data binding is much more than just binding data, and displaying this data to the user. Data can be bound to controls in ways that may or may not ever be seen by the user. For example, you could bind the `Tag` property of a control to a `DataSet` or array element to store custom-defined data that your application uses, but that the user never sees. As another example, perhaps you bind the `CausesValidation` property of a control to a source that will specify whether that control should fire the validation events for checking user input and other such validation actions. In both of these situations, the user is not aware these data bindings even exist. Yet another example is demonstrated later in this chapter, which is to bind the `ValueMember` property of a control to an ID that is meaningful to the database, but that the user never sees, while binding the `DisplayMember` property of a control to the corresponding value that a user would see and find meaningful.

Since the most common use for data binding is to show data to the user, let's focus most of our attention in this chapter to the controls that display data. The ideas presented will apply equally to those controls that do not display data.

It is important to mention that we have at our disposal both **single-value controls**, which allow you to display single values, and **multi-record controls** that allow you to display multiple records. For example, the `TextBox` control only displays a single value at a time, while the `DataGrid`, on the other hand, can display multiple records at a time.

In the next section, we will look at examples of data binding in Windows Forms applications, and then move on to look at examples of data binding in Web Forms applications. There are many more controls than what we cover in this chapter that you may want to use in your applications. These examples are meant to give you ideas on how data binding works so you can employ the same techniques for whatever controls you choose to use.

You can read more about data binding in Windows Forms applications in 'Professional Windows Forms' (Wrox Press, ISBN 1861005547).

Data Binding with Windows Forms

Having seen in the previous section that many controls can take advantage of data binding to assign a property value from data, in this section we will look at several of the more common controls that you are likely to use in building a Windows Forms application.

Simple Data Binding

With **simple data binding**, a control is bound to a single data element. A common example of simple data binding is to bind a TextBox or Label control to a single value in a DataSet or other data source.

Let's walk through an example of binding a label and some textboxes to a DataSet to further demonstrate how simple binding works. We will base this example on data from our Employees table in the HumanResources database we have been using throughout this book. First, create a new Windows Forms application, which will be named Form1 by default. Set the Size property of the Form to 450,450 (Width 450, Height 450) or something large enough to display all the controls we'll be adding next. Place 7 labels, 5 text boxes, and 2 buttons on the Form, as shown below:

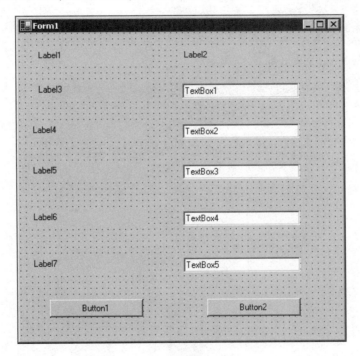

Set the control properties as follows:

Default Name	Name	Text
Label1	lblEmployeeId	Employee ID:
Label2	lblEmployeeIdData	
Label3	lblFirstName	First Name:
TextBox1	txtFirstName	
Label4	lblSurname	Last Name:
TextBox2	txtSurname	

Table continued on following page

Default Name	Name	Text
Label5	lblDateOfBirth	Date of Birth:
TextBox3	txtDateOfBirth	
Label6	lblDateOfHire	Date of Hire:
TextBox4	txtDateOfHire	
Label7	lblLastReview	Last Review:
TextBox5	txtLastReview	
Button1	btnMovePrevious	Move Previous
Button2	btnMoveNext	Move Next

At this point, the Form should look as follows:

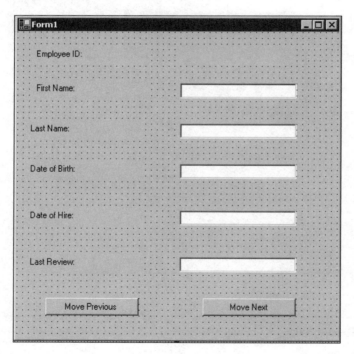

Add the following statements to the class above the `Public Class Form1` declaration:

```
Imports System.Data
Imports System.Data.SqlClient
```

These two lines of code above import the ADO.NET data access libraries that will allow us to communicate with SQL Server and populate our `DataSet`. At the top of the class, and immediately following the line that inherits from the base Form, add the following class-level declaration:

```
        Dim dsEmployees As New DataSet()
```

Next, let's add a class module to the project into which we will put a function to connect to the database and populate a `DataSet`. We will be able to reuse this function from other Forms in our application. To insert a new class, select **Project | Add Class** and specify `clsCommon.vb` for the name. Double-click on **clsCommon** to open the code window for it.

Add the following statements to the class above the `Public Class clsCommon` declaration:

```
    Imports System.Data
    Imports System.Data.SqlClient
```

We already know that these two lines of code import the ADO.NET data access libraries that will allow us to manipulate our `DataSet`. Next, add the `PopulateDataSet` function that accepts a SQL string as a parameter and returns a populated `DataSet` to `clsCommon`:

```
    Public Function PopulateDataSet(ByVal strSQL As String) As DataSet

        'populate a DataSet based on the SQL statement passed in

        Dim dsResults As New DataSet()

        Dim strConnection As String = "Server=MyServer;" _
                                    & "Database=HumanResources;" _
                                    & "User Id=sa;Password=;"

        Dim Conn As New SqlConnection(strConnection)

            Try
                Dim dtAdapter As New SqlDataAdapter(strSQL, Conn)

                'open the connection
                Conn.Open()

                'populate the DataSet
                dtAdapter.Fill(dsResults)

            Finally
                'close the connection
                Conn.Close()

                PopulateDataSet = dsResults
            End Try

    End Function
```

The above procedure can be used generically (by changing the connection string details as necessary) and will populate a `DataSet` based on the SQL string passed to it. We will be able to use this procedure in other examples later in this chapter too.

At this point, we have a form with the controls that we want to display data in, and a function to populate a DataSet based on a SQL statement passed to it. We still need a way of populating the DataSet with the specific Employees data we desire and then binding that data to the controls on our form. Let's now look at how to achieve this. Add the following code to the Form1_Load event:

```
Private Sub Form1_Load(ByVal sender As System.Object, ByVal e _
         As System.EventArgs) Handles MyBase.Load

    'declare a new instance of the common class
    Dim cCommon As New clsCommon()

    'call the PopulateDataSet function in the common
    'classand pass it the SQL statement to retrieve
    'the records from the database
    dsEmployees = cCommon.PopulateDataSet("SELECT EmployeeId, " & _
        "FirstName, Surname, DateOfBirth, DateOfHire, LastReview " & _
        "FROM dbo.Employees")

    'bind the Text property of the EmployeeId label to the EmployeeId
    'field in the DataTable
    lblEmployeeIdData.DataBindings.Add("Text", dsEmployees.Tables(0), _
                              "EmployeeId")

    'bind the Text property of the FirstName textbox to the FirstName
    'field in the DataTable
    txtFirstName.DataBindings.Add("Text", dsEmployees.Tables(0), _
                            "FirstName")

    'Bind the Text property of the Surname textbox to the Surname
    'field in the DataTable
    txtSurname.DataBindings.Add("Text", dsEmployees.Tables(0), _
                          "Surname")

    'Bind the Text property of the DateOfBirth textbox to the
    'DateOfBirth field in the DataTable
    txtDateofBirth.DataBindings.Add("Text", dsEmployees.Tables(0), _
                           "DateOfBirth")

    'Bind the Text property of the DateOfHire textbox to the
    'DateOfHire field in the DataTable
    txtDateOfHire.DataBindings.Add("Text", dsEmployees.Tables(0), _
                           "DateOfHire")

    'Bind the Text property of the LastReview textbox to the
    'LastReview field in the DataTable.
    txtLastReview.DataBindings.Add("Text", dsEmployees.Tables(0), _
                           "LastReview")

End Sub
```

Note that the first line of code will declare a new instance of the common class so that we can use the PopulateDataSet function we created earlier:

```
'declare a new instance of the common class
Dim cCommon As New clsCommon()
```

The next lines of code will populate the dsEmployees class-level DataSet with the results of the Select statement:

```
'call the PopulateDataSet function in the common
'class and pass it the SQL statement to retrieve
'the records from the database
dsEmployees = cCommon.PopulateDataSet("SELECT EmployeeId, " & _
    "FirstName, Surname, DateOfBirth, DateOfHire, LastReview " & _
    "FROM dbo.Employees")
```

Immediately following are the lines that bind the results in the DataSet to each appropriate control on the Form:

```
'bind the Text property of the EmployeeId label to the EmployeeId
'field in the DataTable
lblEmployeeIdData.DataBindings.Add("Text", dsEmployees.Tables(0), _
                                   "EmployeeId")
```

The DataBindings.Add method is called for each control, specifying the following parameters:

- ❑ the property of the control that is to be bound
- ❑ the data source it is to be bound to
- ❑ the name of the field or item in the data source that it is to be bound to

This single line of code will bind a control to a data source.

In a Windows Forms application, when you bind to a control, the data will automatically be written from the control back to the underlying source you bound it to (such as the DataSet, array, and so on). In our case, we are binding the Text property (which is what gets displayed to the user) of each control to a DataTable in our DataSet. We could just as easily bind the value to any other property on the control that matches the data type. When the user makes a change to one of the bound textbox fields, the underlying data in the DataTable is updated automatically. As we learned earlier, the underlying database that this data came from does not get updated automatically, however. At this point, if you run the application, you should see that the first record in your Employees table is displayed on the screen, as shown overleaf:

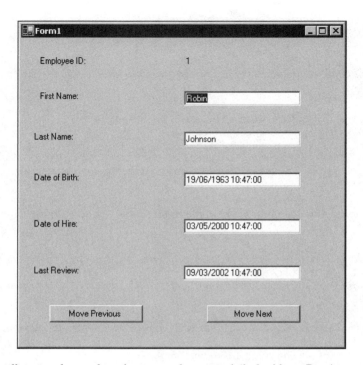

However, you will notice that nothing happens when you click the **Move Previous** or **Move Next** buttons. That is because we haven't added the code to make use of the `BindingContext` object to move to the relevant data record when you click a button. Let's do that now. Add the following code to the form:

```
Private Sub btnMoveNext_Click(ByVal sender As System.Object, ByVal e _
        As System.EventArgs) Handles btnMoveNext.Click

    Me.BindingContext(dsEmployees.Tables(0)).Position += 1

End Sub

Private Sub btnMovePrevious_Click(ByVal sender As System.Object, _
        ByVal e As System.EventArgs) Handles btnMovePrevious.Click

    Me.BindingContext(dsEmployees.Tables(0)).Position -= 1

End Sub
```

Notice that both procedures are coded in a similar fashion, with the `Position` value altered appropriately for the next or previous records:

```
Me.BindingContext(dsEmployees.Tables(0)).Position += 1
```

The `BindingContext` object is associated with each form and keeps track of all of the bound controls on the form and what position the records are in. The `BindingContext` object can be used with different bindings on the form, and the parameter specified allows us to specify which binding we're changing the location of. In our example above, it is the table containing our SQL results that we're changing. Unlike ADO, you do not have to check for `BOF` and `EOF`, since the binding context takes care of your position. If you move one too far, an error will not occur like it would in ADO. The above is an example using the `BindingContext` object of the form (`Me`) to change the position of the first table in the `dsEmployees` `DataSet` to one more (or less) than the previous position. The first and only table in the `dsEmployees` `DataSet` is the one that contains the results of our query. If you run the program again and click the **Move Next** and **Move Previous** buttons, you will find that the controls are advanced to the previous or next records in the `DataSet`.

Now that we have seen an example of how easy it can be to implement simple binding, let's move on to learning about more complex binding types.

Complex Data Binding

With **complex data binding**, a control is bound to more than one data element, such as binding a `DataGrid` to an entire `DataSet`. Another example of complex data binding is to bind a `ComboBox` to more than one field in a data source, such as binding the value that is displayed to the user to one field and the value used to update the appropriate record in the database in another field. Let's now take a look at an example of how you can bind a `ComboBox` to multiple fields.

Binding To a DataSet

Add a new Windows Form to our project, accepting the default name `Form2`. Select the project name in the Solution Explorer and right-click so you see the pop-up menu. Select the **Set As Startup Project** from the pop-up menu. Next, we need to make `Form2` the form that will load when the application runs. To do so, select the project name in Solution Explorer again, and this time select **Properties** from the pop-up menu. From the Property Pages window that appears, change the `Startup Object` to `Form2` and click **OK**. Next, add a `Label` and a `ComboBox` control to the form, as shown below:

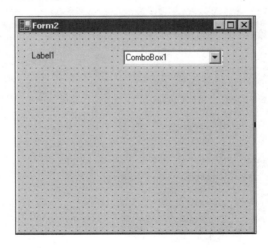

Set the following properties of the two objects:

Default Name	Name property	Text property
Label1	lblDepartment	Description:
ComboBox1	cboDepartment	

Now add the following statements to the form code above the `Public Class Form2` declaration:

```
Imports System.Data
Imports System.Data.SqlClient
```

Next, at the top of the class and immediately following the line that inherits from the base form, add the following class level declaration:

```
Dim dsDepartments As New DataSet()
```

This declares the class-level `DataSet` that we will use to store the departments.

At this point, you are ready to add the following code to the `Form2_Load` event to load the `DataSet` and bind it to the `ComboBox`:

```
Private Sub Form2_Load(ByVal sender As System.Object, ByVal e As _
                    System.EventArgs) Handles MyBase.Load

    'specify the SQL statement to retrieve the data
    'from the database
    Dim strSQL As String = _
            "SELECT DepartmentId, Description " & _
            "FROM dbo.Departments ORDER BY Description"

    'declare a new instance of our common class with the
    'function for populating the DataSet
    Dim cCommon As New clsCommon()

    'populate the dataset
    dsDepartments = cCommon.PopulateDataSet(strSQL)

    'set the data source of the cboDepartment to the
    'data table in the DataSet with the values
    cboDepartment.DataSource = dsDepartments.Tables(0)

    'set the Value member of the cboDepartment to the
    'DepartmentId value. This is data to help correspond
    'to a value the database would understand
    cboDepartment.ValueMember = _
            dsDepartments.Tables(0).Columns("DepartmentId").ToString

    'set the Display member of the cboDepartment to the
    'Description value. This is data that the user will
    'see and understand.
```

```
        cboDepartment.DisplayMember = _
            dsDepartments.Tables(0).Columns("Description").ToString

    End Sub
```

In this instance, we first declare a new instance of our `clsCommon` class and populate the `dsDepartments` `DataSet` with the results of the SQL statement. Next, we assign the `DataSource` property of `cboDepartment` to the table in `dsDepartments` that contains our data. The `ValueMember` and `DisplayMember` properties are assigned to fields in the table. The `ValueMember` property is the value that you want stored as the identifier for the data, such as the ID that the database will understand for retrieving and updating the particular record or value. The `DisplayMember` property is the value that you want displayed to the user. After assigning the `DataSource`, `ValueMember`, and `DisplayMember` properties, you are ready to bind the control to the column in the table.

Let's run the application and see what happens. You should see a form that has the combo box populated with values such as the following:

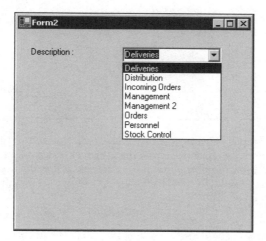

What you see above in the drop-down lists are the `DisplayMember` values for the `Department` `Description` that the user sees. Notice how you do not see anything for the `ValueMember` that stores the `DepartmentId`, since it is hidden. Just to prove to you that the `DepartmentId` is really there, let's add a label to the form that we will populate with the `ValueMember` value when the user selects an item from the combo box. That way, you can see that it really does exist. So go ahead and add another label to the form, calling it `lblValueMember`. Then place the following code within the `Form 2` class:

```
    Private Sub cboDepartment_SelectedIndexChanged(ByVal sender _
            As System.Object, ByVal e As System.EventArgs) _
            Handles cboDepartment.SelectedIndexChanged

        'if an item in the list is selected, display the SelectedValue
        '(that is in the ValueMember property) in the label to prove it
        'is really there.
        If cboDepartment.SelectedIndex >= 0 Then
            lblValueMember.Text = cboDepartment.SelectedValue.ToString
```

```
        End If

    End Sub
```

Now, when you run the program and choose an item in the combo box, you should see the corresponding `DepartmentId` from the database for the selected department description. An example of what this might look like is shown below:

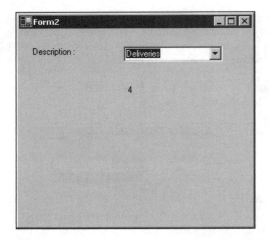

As you can see, in this example we were able to bind a `ComboBox` to two fields in a table. The `DisplayMember` property of the `ComboBox` that the user sees was bound to the `Description` field in the `DataTable`. The `ValueMember` property of the `ComboBox` that the user doesn't typically see was bound to the `DepartmentId` field. We added the label to show you that the value really does exist.

Binding to an Array

It is important to note that you could also bind this `ComboBox` to an array instead of a `DataSet`. Here is a simple example:

```
    Dim DepartmentArray() As String = {"Maintenance", _
                                "Information Systems", "Management"}

        cboDepartment.DataSource = DepartmentArray
```

This code declares a new array, and sets the data source of the `ComboBox` to the array instead of a `DataSet`. This is a simplified example to show you how it works, but you should get the idea. You could expand the example to employ complex data binding to have a multi-dimensional array that contains the values for `DepartmentId` and `Description` and assign them to the `ComboBox` just as we did before.

Binding to a DataGrid

Let's now look at another example of complex data binding, by binding data to a `DataGrid`.

On `Form2`, you can delete the `ComboBox` and `Labels` we were using in the prior example and you can also delete the `cboDepartment_SelectedIndexChanged` event. You can leave the `Form2_Load` event code there for now as we will modify it momentarily. Add a `DataGrid` to the form and name it `dgResults`. An example of what it should look like is shown below:

Modify the `Form2_Load` event so that it looks as follows:

```
Private Sub Form2_Load(ByVal sender As System.Object, ByVal e As _
                    System.EventArgs) Handles MyBase.Load

    'specify the SQL statements to retrieve the data
    'from the database. Note that we are sending two
    'different SQL statements separated by a semicolon.
    'Results from both of these will be populated in the
    'DataSet
    Dim strSQL As String = _
            "SELECT DepartmentId, Description " & _
            "FROM dbo.Departments ORDER BY Description;" & _
            "SELECT FirstName, Surname, " & _
            "DateOfHire FROM dbo.Employees ORDER BY " & _
            "Surname, FirstName"

    'declare a new instance of our common class with the
    'function for populating the DataSet
    Dim cCommon As New clsCommon()

    'populate the DataSet
    dsDepartments = cCommon.PopulateDataSet(strSQL)

    'bind the DataSet containing the results
    'to the DataGrid
```

```
          dgResults.DataSource = dsDepartments


   End Sub
```

Notice how we are setting the `DataSource` property of the `DataGrid` to our `DataSet` containing the results of the SQL statement. This is the only line of code we need in order to set up the data-binding functionality. Unlike with Web Forms, we do not have to explicitly call a `DataBind` method here.

If you run this code, you should see something similar to the following:

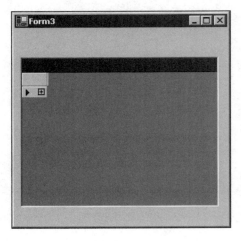

Notice how there is a plus sign next to the arrow. If you click the plus sign, it will expand the results so you can see which tables contained in the `DataSet`. In our case, there are two tables in the `DataSet` since we populated it with the results of two different `SELECT` statements:

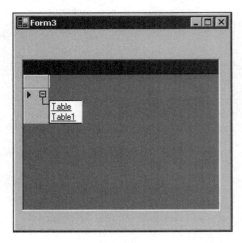

If you click on the first table called Table, then you will see the actual data values, similar to that shown here:

Notice how the fields that came from the Departments table are shown, since these are the values we populated the first table in the DataSet with.

You can navigate back up the hierarchy in the DataSet and look at the values in Table1 to see the other table we populated in the DataSet. You are probably wondering if there is an easier way to have the DataGrid automatically expand to a certain table. The answer is 'yes'. Let's look at how to do that. You can set the DataMember property of the DataGrid to a particular table in the DataSet and then that table will automatically be displayed without having to navigate through the hierarchy. Modify the code in Form2_Load to add this line at the end after the line of code that sets the data source property:

```
'Set the first table (called Table by default if
'you didn't specify otherwise) as the DataMember.
'This will show data in that table expanded.
dgResults.DataMember = "Table"
```

Now, run the application again and notice how the first table containing the Department information is displayed automatically expanded:

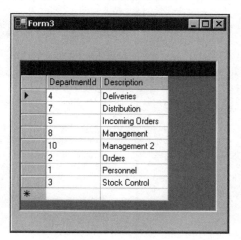

The reason it is expanded automatically this time is because we set the `DataMember` property to `Table`, which is the name of the table that contains the `Departments` data from the database. Recall that `Table1` contains the `Employees` information. The reason the tables have this name is because we populated them from a SQL statement, and didn't specify a table name to call them in the `DataSet`.

Suppose that you want to allow the user to modify data in the `DataGrid` and then update those changes in the underlying data store. You already learned that a `DataSet` is an in-memory copy of the data, and that as users change the `DataGrid` which is bound to the `DataSet`, the underlying database is not automatically updated. So, let's look at an example of how we can allow the user to modify the data in the `DataGrid`, and then click a button to save those changes back to the database. Let's start by adding a button to `Form2`. Name the button `btnUpdate` and set its `Text` property to `Update Database`.

Next, open the `clsCommon.vb` class module. We are going to add a new function in a moment but first need to make sure we have a connection string defined. Recall that in the `PopulateDataSet` function in this class, we already defined the connection string. Instead of copying it again into our new function, let's move it from the `PopulateDataSet` function and place it within the class declaration immediately following the `Public Class clsCommon` statement, but outside of the `PopulateDataSet` function declaration. That line should look like this:

```
Dim strConnection As String = "Server=MyServer; " _
                            & "Database=HumanResources;" _
                            & "User Id=sa;Password=;"
```

Now that we have our connection string available, we're ready to add the new function to the `clsCommon` class. This new function will accept a SQL statement and a `DataSet` containing changes and will update those changes to the underlying database. Place the following code in `clsCommon.vb`:

```
Public Function UpdateDbFromDataSet(ByVal dsChanges As DataSet, _
                                    ByVal strSQL As String) As Boolean

    Dim Conn As New SqlConnection(strConnection)

        Try
            'declare a new DataAdapter but assign it to the
            'same SQL statement that was used to retrieve the
            'data from before
            Dim dtAdapter As New SqlDataAdapter(strSQL, Conn)

            'build the commands automatically to update the database
            'for the DataAdapter
            Dim custCB As SqlCommandBuilder = _
                New SqlCommandBuilder(dtAdapter)

            'open the connection
            Conn.Open()

            'save the DataSet changes back to the database
            dtAdapter.Update(dsChanges)

            'return success
            UpdateDbFromDataSet = True
```

```
        Finally
            'close the connection
            Conn.Close()

        End Try

    End Function
```

Let's take a quick look at what this newly created function will do. First, it will accept a SQL statement and a `DataSet` as parameters. The SQL statement needs to be the same SQL statement that was used to retrieve the data to begin with. That is how we can use the `DataAdapter` to automatically generate the INSERT, UPDATE, and DELETE statements for us. The `DataSet` passed to this function should contain those records that are changed, and thus those needing to be updated in the database. The first line of code takes care of declaring the `DataAdapter`, assigning the SQL statement and connection to the `DataAdapter`:

```
        'declare a new data adapter but assign it to the
        'same SQL statement that was used to retrieve the
        'data from before
        Dim dtAdapter As New SqlDataAdapter(strSQL, Conn)
```

The next line of code uses the `SqlCommandBuilder` to generate automatically the appropriate SQL statements for INSERT, UPDATE, and DELETEs to make the changes in the database. If we didn't use the `SqlCommandBuilder`, then we would have to specify each of those statements manually. But here, since we have specified the SQL statements that specify where our data came from, the `SqlCommandBuilder` will try to determine automatically how to update the database appropriately:

```
        'build the commands automatically to update the database
        'for the DataAdapter
        Dim custCB As SqlCommandBuilder = _
            New SqlCommandBuilder(dtAdapter)
```

Next, we opened the connection to the database and called the `Update` method of the `DataAdapter` passing the `DataSet` that contains only the changed records. Finally, we closed the connection:

```
        'open the connection
        Conn.Open()

        'save the DataSet changes back to the database
        dtAdapter.Update(dsChanges)

        'return success
        UpdateDbFromDataSet = True

    Finally
        'close the connection
        Conn.Close()

    End Try

    End Function
```

Now that we have created the function that will save the changes back to the database, let's re-open Form2 and place the code for the button so that our new function will be called to update the changes in the database from the DataSet. Add the following code to the Form2 class:

```
Private Sub btnUpdate_Click(ByVal sender As System.Object, ByVal e _
                        As System.EventArgs) Handles btnUpdate.Click

    ' Check for changes with the HasChanges method first.
    If Not dsDepartments.HasChanges(DataRowState.Modified) Then Exit Sub

    ' Create temporary DataSet variable to store
    'the records that have changed (and thus need
    'updating in the database.
    Dim ChangesDataSet As DataSet

    ' GetChanges for modified rows only.
    ChangesDataSet = dsDepartments.GetChanges(DataRowState.Modified)

    'Use the same SQL string that you populated the DataSet
    'with the first time
    Dim strSQL As String = _
            "SELECT DepartmentId, Description " & _
            "FROM dbo.Departments ORDER BY Description;" & _
            "SELECT FirstName, Surname, " & _
            "DateOfHire FROM dbo.Employees ORDER BY " & _
            "Surname, FirstName"

    'Update the database with the changes.
    Dim cCommon As New clsCommon()
    cCommon.UpdateDbFromDataSet(ChangesDataSet, strsql)

End Sub
```

Now, run the program, modify the data in the DataGrid, and then click the **Update Database** button. Close the program and run it again, and you should see that the data that gets loaded again reflects the changes you made to the database. See how easy it was to let the user make changes interactively to the DataGrid and then with one click update all of the changes in the database from the changed DataSet!

At this point, we have seen examples of binding data to a DataSet as well as to arrays and other data sources. In the next section, we will look at data binding with Web Forms and we'll see how to bind controls to a DataReader and to an array, as two of many possibilities.

Data Binding with Web Forms

Data binding to controls on Web Forms is similar in many ways to binding to data on Windows Forms. Both are very flexible and you can bind many properties of a control to data from many sources. However, there are some differences between the two types of form that we should note here. First of all, the nature of a Web Form is typically read-only. In other words, once the page is built, it is rendered to the browser in a format such as HTML, and typically presents read-only information, which the user cannot modify. The Web Forms architecture for data binding does not automatically write data from the control back to the data source. This is very unlike the example we created in the previous section where the DataSet was automatically updated based on changes in the textboxes or in the DataGrid. To implement such functionality in a web environment, we would have to implement the update logic ourselves.

In this section, we will look at a detailed example of how you can bind data to a web control. We will first look at an example of binding to a `DataGrid` so you can see how it differs from our prior `DataGrid` example. We will then enhance the `DataGrid` example to add updating capabilities.

Binding to a DataGrid

To get started, you need to close the previous project and create a new Web Forms (ASP.NET Web Application) project. Place a `DataGrid` control on `WebForm1`. Name the `DataGrid` `dgResults`. It should look similar to what you see below:

Start Page	**WebForm1.aspx***

Column0	Column1	Column2
abc	abc	abc
abc	abc	abc
abc	abc	abc
abc	abc	abc
abc	abc	abc

Just as we did before in the other examples, you need to add the `Imports` statements to the top of the class (outside the class declaration) so that you can make use of the ADO.NET data access libraries:

```
Imports System.Data
Imports System.Data.SqlClient
```

Within the class declaration (such as beneath the `Public Class WebForm1` line), add the connection string variable so that it can be used throughout the form:

```
'specify the Connection String
Dim strConnection As String = "Server=MyServer; " _
                            & "Database=HumanResources;" _
                            & "User Id=sa;Password=;"
```

Next, add the following procedure to the form:

```
Private Sub LoadData()
    Dim dr As SqlDataReader
    Dim oCommand As New SqlCommand()
    Dim oConnection As New SqlConnection()

    'specify the SQL statement
    Dim strSQL As String = _
            "SELECT DepartmentId, Description " & _
            " From dbo.Departments ORDER BY Description"
```

```
        'assign the connection string to the Connection object
        oConnection.ConnectionString = strConnection

        'specify the SQL statement as the CommandText of the
        'command object that will be used to retrieve the
        'data from the database
        oCommand.CommandText = strSQL

        'assign the Connection property of the
        'command object to the Connection object
        oCommand.Connection = oConnection

        'open the connection
        oConnection.Open()

        'execute the SQL statement through the Command object
        'and populate the DataReader with the results
        dr = oCommand.ExecuteReader()

        'bind the DataGrid to the DataReader
        dgResults.DataSource = dr
        dgResults.DataBind()

        'Close the DataReader and database Connection
        dr.Close()
        oConnection.Close()
End Sub
```

The code for retrieving data using a DataReader should look familiar to you, as it has been covered in prior chapters, Chapter 4 in particular. The DataReader gets populated through using the Command object, which communicates with the database over a Connection. After populating the DataReader, we then bind the values in the DataReader to our DataGrid:

```
        dgResults.DataSource = dr
        dgResults.DataBind()
```

What happens behind the scenes with these two lines of code is that ASP.NET will stream through the DataReader and build the DataGrid based on those values.

Now we are ready to add the code that will call the LoadData method when the page loads. In the Page_Load event, add the following code:

```
Private Sub Page_Load(ByVal sender As System.Object, ByVal e As _
                    System.EventArgs) Handles MyBase.Load

        'if the page isn't a postback
        If Not Page.IsPostBack Then

                'load the data from the database onto
                'the DataGrid
```

```
        LoadData()

    End If
...End Sub
```

If you run the application, you will see a Web Form similar to the following:

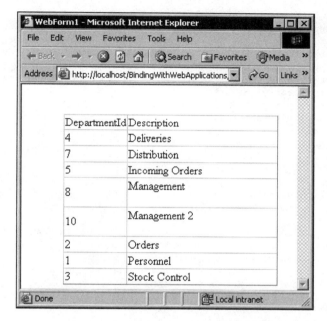

Notice how this isn't nearly as fancy as the `DataGrid` we saw in the Windows Forms examples. If you want to update or otherwise interact with the data, you have to create the code for that yourself. Let's expand our example to show you how this works.

Updating Data Using a DataGrid

First, you need to open the form in design view, and then switch to the HTML view. We need to modify the HTML code to read like this:

```
<HTML>
   <HEAD>
      <title>WebForm1</title>
      <meta content="Microsoft Visual Studio.NET 7.0" name="GENERATOR">
      <meta content="Visual Basic 7.0" name="CODE_LANGUAGE">
      <meta content="JavaScript" name="vs_defaultClientScript">
      <meta content="http://schemas.microsoft.com/intellisense/ie5"
         name="vs_targetSchema">
   </HEAD>

<body MS_POSITIONING="GridLayout">
```

```
<form id="Form1" method="post" runat="server">
  <asp:datagrid id="dgResults" style="Z-INDEX: 101; LEFT: 51px;
  POSITION: absolute; TOP: 43px" runat="server"
  OnUpdateCommand="OnUpdateCommand"
  onDeleteCommand="OnDeleteCommand"
  OnCancelCommand="OnCancelCommand"
  OnEditCommand="OnEditCommand"
  AutoGenerateColumns="False" GridLines="Horizontal">
  <SelectedItemStyle HorizontalAlign="Center"></SelectedItemStyle>
  <EditItemStyle HorizontalAlign="Center"></EditItemStyle>
  <AlternatingItemStyle HorizontalAlign="Center" ForeColor="Black"
  BackColor="DarkSalmon"></AlternatingItemStyle>
  <ItemStyle HorizontalAlign="Center" ForeColor="Black"
  BackColor="White"></ItemStyle>
  <HeaderStyle Font-Bold="True" ForeColor="Black"
  BackColor="LightSteelBlue"></HeaderStyle>
  <Columns>
      <asp:EditCommandColumn ButtonType="LinkButton"
          UpdateText="Update" CancelText="Cancel"
          EditText="Edit"></asp:EditCommandColumn>

      <asp:ButtonColumn Text="Delete"
          CommandName="Delete"></asp:ButtonColumn>

      <asp:BoundColumn DataField="DepartmentId" ReadOnly="True"
                  HeaderText="Department Id">
        <HeaderStyle HorizontalAlign="Center"
                  Width="150px"></HeaderStyle>
        <ItemStyle HorizontalAlign="Center"></ItemStyle>
      </asp:BoundColumn>

      <asp:BoundColumn DataField="Description"
                  HeaderText="Description">
        <HeaderStyle HorizontalAlign="Left"
                  Width="150px"></HeaderStyle>
        <ItemStyle HorizontalAlign="Left"></ItemStyle>
      </asp:BoundColumn>
  </Columns>
</asp:datagrid></form>
  </body>
</HTML>
```

Here, we have specified several important aspects in the HTML code, which we will need to examine one by one. First, we have specified the Commands that should be fired whenever the particular action is chosen:

```
OnUpdateCommand="OnUpdateCommand"
onDeleteCommand="OnDeleteCommand"
OnCancelCommand="OnCancelCommand"
OnEditCommand="OnEditCommand"
```

Whenever the user clicks the Update hyperlink on the Form, a method called OnUpdateCommand will be executed. We will create this and the other methods shortly. For now, just understand that these lines of code specify what method gets called when the user clicks on one of the editing hyperlinks.

Next we have a lot of formatting code to display the DataGrid in a fancier way than we did before. Then, of particular importance, we find the Columns that are displayed in the DataGrid:

```
<Columns>
    <asp:EditCommandColumn ButtonType="LinkButton"
        UpdateText="Update" CancelText="Cancel"
        EditText="Edit"></asp:EditCommandColumn>
    <asp:ButtonColumn Text="Delete"
        CommandName="Delete"></asp:ButtonColumn>

    <asp:BoundColumn DataField="DepartmentId" ReadOnly="True"
                    HeaderText="Department Id">
        <HeaderStyle HorizontalAlign="Center"
                    Width="150px"></HeaderStyle>
        <ItemStyle HorizontalAlign="Center"></ItemStyle>
    </asp:BoundColumn>

    <asp:BoundColumn DataField="Description"
                    HeaderText="Description">
        <HeaderStyle HorizontalAlign="Left"
                    Width="150px"></HeaderStyle>
        <ItemStyle HorizontalAlign="Left"></ItemStyle>
    </asp:BoundColumn>
</Columns>
```

Notice how the EditCommandColumns are defined first, with the names that are to appear to the user specified:

```
<asp:EditCommandColumn ButtonType="LinkButton"
    UpdateText="Update" CancelText="Cancel"
    EditText="Edit"></asp:EditCommandColumn>
```

Then, a ButtonColumn is defined for the Delete capability. The text to be displayed to the user and the command name are specified:

```
<asp:ButtonColumn Text="Delete"
    CommandName="Delete"></asp:ButtonColumn>
```

The column defining the DepartmentId is next. The DataField that it's bound to is specified, and its ReadOnly property is set to True so the user cannot modify this field. Some formatting properties are set, such as to center the text horizontally and to set the column size:

```
<asp:BoundColumn DataField="DepartmentId" ReadOnly="True"
                HeaderText="Department Id">
    <HeaderStyle HorizontalAlign="Center"
                Width="150px"></HeaderStyle>
    <ItemStyle HorizontalAlign="Center"></ItemStyle>
</asp:BoundColumn>
```

Lastly, the Description column definition is defined. It is very similar to the DepartmentId column, only it is not read-only and can be updated by the user:

```
<asp:BoundColumn DataField="Description"
                 HeaderText="Description">
    <HeaderStyle HorizontalAlign="Left"
                 Width="150px"></HeaderStyle>
    <ItemStyle HorizontalAlign="Left"></ItemStyle>
</asp:BoundColumn>
```

So now that we have the HTML code for our DataGrid, we are ready to put the update code behind the form so that when the user clicks on the different hyperlinks (Edit, Delete, Cancel, Update), the appropriate action will be taken.

You should switch back to the design view of the form if you are still in HTML view. Double-click so the code window opens up, and place the following ExecuteSQL procedure in the form:

```
Private Sub ExecuteSQL(ByVal strSQL As String)

    'This method will run the SQL statement
    'that is passed in to update the
    'database

    Dim oCommand As New SqlCommand()
    Dim oConnection As New SqlConnection()

    'assign the connection string to the Connection object
    oConnection.ConnectionString = strConnection

    'specify the SQL statement as the CommandText of the
    'command object that will be used to retrieve the
    'data from the database
    oCommand.CommandText = strSQL

    'assign the Connection property of the
    'command object to the Connection object
    oCommand.Connection = oConnection

    'open the connection
    oConnection.Open()

    'execute the SQL statement through the Command object
    oCommand.ExecuteNonQuery()

    'close the database connection
    oConnection.Close()

End Sub
```

The purpose of this procedure is to execute a SQL statement that is passed in against the database. We are going to use it to run our UPDATE and DELETE statements against the database when the user selects the appropriate hyperlink.

Next, let's add the four procedures that will be fired when the respective hyperlinks are clicked. Recall in our HTML code that we specified that the OnEditCommand event would be called "OnEditCommand". Well, that means that we need to create a procedure with that exact name and create within it the code that we want to run when the user clicks the Edit hyperlink. That method looks like this:

```
    Public Sub OnEditCommand(ByVal sender As Object, _
                            ByVal e As DataGridCommandEventArgs)

        'This fires when the user clicks the
        'Edit hyperlink

        'select the item to edit
        dgResults.EditItemIndex = e.Item.ItemIndex

        'load the data
        LoadData()

    End Sub
```

The OnEditCommand procedure will select the item in the DataGrid based on the record the user was positioned on when the Edit hyperlink was clicked. When changing to Edit mode, any bound column that is not read only will be displayed as a textbox so the user can change the value. You can also create template columns instead that allow you more flexibility, such as ComboBoxes and other such controls. Those are beyond the scope of this example, but you should know that they exist, in case you find a need for them.

Next, add the OnUpdateCommand procedure, as shown below:

```
    Public Sub OnUpdateCommand(ByVal sender As Object, _
                            ByVal e As DataGridCommandEventArgs)

        'This fires when the user clicks the
        'Update hyperlink

        'retrieve the department ID value
        Dim DepartmentId As Integer
        DepartmentId = e.Item.Cells(2).Text

        'declare a local textbox variable to
        'allow us to get the value in the one
        'the user just edited
        Dim txtDesc As New TextBox()
        txtDesc = e.Item.Cells(3).Controls(0)

        'retrieve the Description value the user
        'just edited in the textbox
        Dim Desc As String = txtDesc.Text

        'define the SQL statement and include the
        'DepartmentId and Description of the record
        'to be updated
        Dim strSQL As String
        strSQL = "UPDATE dbo.Departments SET Description = '" & _
                    Desc & "' WHERE DepartmentId = " & DepartmentId

        'save the updates to the database
        ExecuteSQL(strSQL)
```

```
        'return to viewing mode
        dgResults.EditItemIndex = -1

        'load the data to show
        'the changes to the database
        LoadData()

    End Sub
```

The OnUpdateCommand procedure will retrieve the value of the DepartmentId for the record that the user is editing. It will also retrieve the Description from the Edit textbox that is displayed on the form. After retrieving those values, the SQL statement with the proper values is created and executed against the database. The DataGrid is returned to view mode so the edit controls are no longer displayed and the DataGrid is also updated with the current data from the database.

At this point, we are ready to add the OnDeleteCommand procedure to the form. It should look like this:

```
    Public Sub OnDeleteCommand(ByVal sender As Object, _
                               ByVal e As DataGridCommandEventArgs)

        'This fires when the user clicks the
        'Delete hyperlink

        'retrieve the department ID value
        Dim DepartmentId As Integer
        DepartmentId = e.Item.Cells(2).Text

        'define the SQL statement and include the
        'DepartmentId of the record to be
        'deleted
        Dim strSQL As String
        strSQL = "DELETE FROM dbo.Departments " & _
                 "WHERE DepartmentId = " & DepartmentId

        'delete the record from the database
        ExecuteSQL(strSQL)

        'return to viewing mode
        dgResults.EditItemIndex = -1

        'load the data to show
        'the changes to the database
        LoadData()

    End Sub
```

Very similar to the OnUpdateCommand, the OnDeleteCommand procedure retrieves the value of the DepartmentId for the record currently selected. It then creates the proper SQL statement and executes that statement against the database. Again, the DataGrid is returned to view mode and refreshed with current data.

Lastly, we are ready to add the code for the `OnCancelCommand` procedure. This procedure will run when the user clicks the **Cancel** hyperlink to cancel out of edit mode. Place this code on the form:

```
Public Sub OnCancelCommand(ByVal sender As Object, _
                           ByVal e As DataGridCommandEventArgs)

    'This fires when the user clicks the
    'Cancel hyperlink

    'deselect all items
    dgResults.EditItemIndex = -1

    'load the data
    LoadData()
End Sub
```

This procedure deselects everything and reloads the data on the form, which in effect cancels whatever edit the user was doing.

Now that we have our HTML code and our procedures in place, we're ready to try everything out and see our new, improved, more professional looking `DataGrid` that allows our users to edit data. If you run the web application, a page similar to below should be shown:

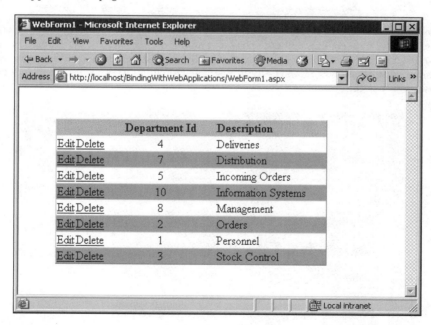

Wow! Notice how we now see **Edit** and **Delete** hyperlinks, as well as some fancier formatting that has improved the `DataGrid`'s looks. If we click the **Edit** link, then we can modify the `Description` and update the data in the database, or alternatively, cancel the update by using the **Cancel** link. Let's click the **Edit** hyperlink for a record we wish to edit. After doing so, the screen should look something like this:

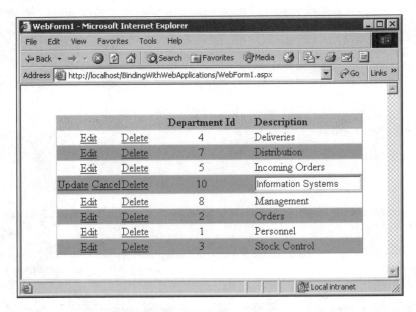

Notice how a textbox is displayed in the grid to allow you to update the Description column. The Update and Cancel hyperlinks are also displayed in addition to the Delete hyperlink. Go ahead and modify the textbox to a different value, and then click the Update link. In our example above, we are going to modify Information Systems to Information Technology. After clicking the Update link, our screen now looks like this:

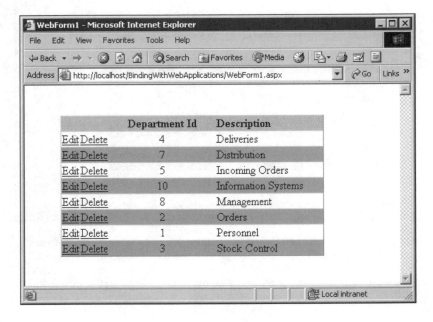

Notice that when the page reloads, our updated value, Information Technology, is displayed appropriately in the Department column. Go ahead and play around with the features to see how the Cancel and Delete hyperlinks work too. As we mentioned earlier, there is more work involved in working with DataGrids in a web application than in a Windows application. Now that we have worked through examples in both environments, you should have a decent feel for the different levels of effort required for each one.

Congratulations, you have now successfully bound a Web Form to data and provided the user with the ability to update the data in the DataGrid.

Summary

In this chapter, we looked at several examples of how to bind controls to different data sources. We saw how you would go about binding any property of a control to nearly any type of data source. At this point, you should have a good understanding of:

- ❑ The difference between simple versus complex binding to a Windows Form
- ❑ How to bind a control to a DataSet
- ❑ How to bind a control to a DataReader
- ❑ How to bind a control to an array
- ❑ Binding a TextBox, Label, DataGrid, and ComboBox to a data source from a Windows Form
- ❑ Updating a data source based on changes made to the DataSet
- ❑ Binding a DataGrid to a data source from a Web Form
- ❑ How to design a DataGrid in a Web Form that allows the user to update data in the data source
- ❑ Some differences between data binding on Windows Forms versus Web Forms

Now that you have a familiarity with how to bind controls to various data sources, it is time to move on to an equally important topic, namely handling database transactions.

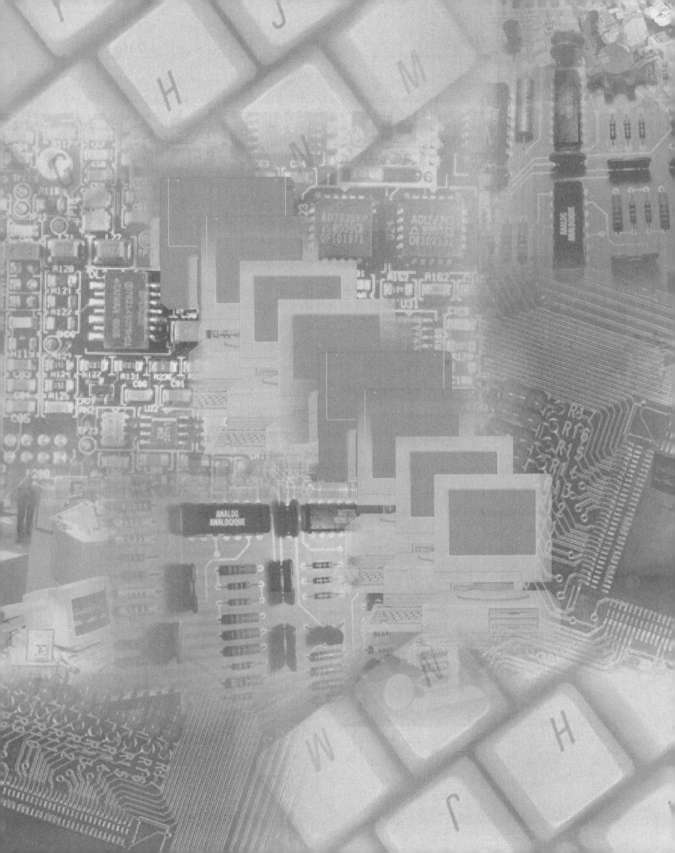

Transactions and Locking

Now that we have seen how we can efficiently utilize the data contained within our SQL Server database, we need to get serious about protecting the integrity of this data. A database that cannot ensure that the information it contains is valid, is virtually useless.

Transactions are an important aspect of preserving data consistency since they allow multiple SQL statements to be considered as a single unit of work. The classic example of a transaction is when transferring funds from one bank account to another. This is a two-stage process, with the funds being deducted from one account, and then credited to another. As these transactions are taking place in the real world, it is possible that external factors could cause this process to fail between the two steps. What if the computer processing the transaction was to crash between the debit and credit? An account would have funds deducted, but no other account would then be credited with this amount, resulting in the funds essentially being lost into the ether.

Transactions are used to prevent this sort of thing happening by combining all the operations that occur within the process into a single unit of work. This means that either all the steps in the process are carried out, or none of them are carried out. They stick together, through thick and thin, for better or worse. Transactions support the ability to undo the changes that have occurred within them, right up to the point when they are explicitly told to make the changes stick. Once this has happened the changes made within the transaction cannot and will not be undone by any external influence, such as computer failure.

In considering transactions here we will look at:

❑ The properties of transactions
❑ How we can use transactions from SQL Server and ADO.NET
❑ How locks are used to enforce the various transaction isolation levels
❑ Some best practice advice on using transactions
❑ Deadlock prevention

The ACID Test

How could we possibly discuss an IT topic such as transactions without introducing an acronym? It just wouldn't be right. The term **ACID** has been used to refer to the properties of a transaction for a long, long time, in fact well before meaningless acronyms were fashionable. No discussion of transactions would be complete without a discussion of the ACID transaction properties, so let's look at each one in turn:

(A)tomicity

This is the transaction property that people are most familiar with. A transaction must be an **atomic** unit of work, that is to say it must be applied fully or not applied at all. Or in even less geek-speak, as your mother used to say, "If you are going to take that, make sure you eat it all; otherwise put it back".

If a transaction is to complete successfully then all the changes made in the transaction must be applied. If a transaction does not complete successfully then all the changes made in the transaction must be undone, leaving the database as it was before the transaction began.

(C)onsistency

If a transaction is committed, explicitly rolled back or rolled back due to failure of some kind, the transaction must leave the database in a consistent, error-free, useable state. For example an update to a table that is interrupted halfway through, and ends up being rolled back, isn't allowed to leave that table all messed up. It must be returned to the state which it was in before the transaction began.

(I)solation

One transaction that is modifying data cannot be affected by another transaction that is modifying data. For example, if one transaction changes column y in row x, and while this transaction is still running another concurrent transaction begins and tries to look at the value of column y in row x, it will be forced to wait until after the updating transaction has finished to see the value of this column. The point here is that the second transaction won't be able to see the new value for column y in row x until after this first transaction has completed.

(D)urability

Transactions must stick. Once they have been committed they must not be undone at all, not by anyone or anything. Even if the server fails a mere second after the commit has completed, when the database eventually becomes available again you can sleep easy knowing the changes made within the transaction are still applied within the database.

Okay, this is a fairly universal definition of a transaction but we are starting to get the feeling of how transactions can be useful. Let us now begin learning about how we can actually create transactions using VB.NET and SQL Server 2000. To do this let's first talk about when and where transactions are present and after this we will move on to how we actually create them.

Implicit & Explicit Transactions

As we will see in the following sections, you can explicitly specify where to use transactions by making use of the various transaction commands to surround SQL statements that you want to combine into a single unit of work. However, even when you don't explicitly specify that a transaction is to take place through the use of the BEGIN TRANSACTION...COMMIT TRANSACTION commands (as we'll look at in more detail shortly), SQL Server still uses transactions to maintain data consistency. In other words SQL Server uses an implicit transaction for each and every command that you execute. You can think of this in another way, namely that every command in SQL Server is contained within a transaction, and you have the ability to explicitly control how many SQL commands are included within a single transaction.

Why is this? Surely if it's only one command then it's either going to succeed or fail? Not quite. A single SQL command has the ability to modify large amounts of data. It is not unusual for a single UPDATE command to modify thousands of rows. If the server was to fail while this single SQL UPDATE command was halfway through updating several thousand rows, and a transaction had not been used, when SQL Server was available again some of the rows would have been updated and some wouldn't have been. Who would know which rows had been updated successfully? So to stress the point once again, SQL Server avoids this situation completely by using an implicit transaction for every command unless told to use an explicit transaction.

Using Transactions

When you are using the SqlClient objects within ADO.NET there are two different ways in which you can handle transactions in SQL Server. Firstly you can define the transaction and control its behavior using SQL Server's T-SQL transaction commands, which are:

- ❑ BEGIN TRANSACTION
- ❑ SAVE TRANSACTION
- ❑ ROLLBACK TRANSACTION
- ❑ COMMIT TRANSACTION

Alternatively you can define and control the behavior of your transactions using a SqlTransaction object.

The difference between using T-SQL transaction commands and the SqlTransaction object is purely implementation. That is, both methods actually utilize transactions in the same way. The methods of the SqlTransaction object actually just send SQL Server T-SQL commands to define and control the transaction, the same commands you would have used yourself if you had chosen to implement transactions using T-SQL directly.

SqlTransaction or T-SQL?

So if the `SqlTransaction` sends T-SQL transaction commands that you could send yourself anyway, why bother using it? Surely this is just another annoying layer of abstraction? The method you select should be the one that provides the best code consistency for your application, depending on how it has been structured. What I mean is, if you are passing single SQL commands to your database and performing all of your data logic and error checking within the application code, use of the `SqlTransaction` objects fits more cleanly with the overall code structure. If, on the other hand, you have built stored procedures within your database to abstract all the data logic away from your application code, including the transaction commands within the stored procedures themselves is a much more desirable approach. You can then confidently call the stored procedure and let it take care of all the 'data stuff' itself.

As far as performance goes there is no major difference in using these methods, except that calls to the various methods of the `SqlTransaction` object require extra roundtrips to your database server, which are not required when embedding the transaction control within stored procedures. The slight difference is more a result of the way in which you design your application architecture than a direct result of the way in which you choose to implement the transactions themselves.

Now let's stop talking about it and actually take a look at how we create and use these wonderful things we now know as transactions.

BEGIN TRANSACTION

To start an explicit transaction within SQL Server we must issue the BEGIN TRANSACTION command. For those who like to save on valuable keystrokes, this can be shortened to BEGIN TRAN and it can be used to create a named or unnamed transaction. First let's look at unnamed transactions.

To initiate an unnamed transaction from T-SQL use BEGIN TRANSACTION. Every SQL statement after the BEGIN TRANSACTION will be included within the one explicitly defined user transaction, such as:

```
BEGIN TRANSACTION

    UPDATE dbo.Employees
        SET Surname='Smith'
    WHERE EmployeeID=1

    UPDATE dbo.Employees
        SET Surname='Jones'
    WHERE EmployeeID=2
```

Now let's look at doing this with ADO.NET from VB.NET. Notice how the command to begin the transaction is a method of the `SqlConnection` object, not the `SqlCommand` object. This helps to remind us that a transaction is defined for a connection and many commands may be submitted on that connection, each of which will be included as part of that transaction until it is either committed or rolled back.

First we create our `SqlConnection` and `SqlCommand` objects that we will use to execute our commands against our SQL Server database.

```
'Change the connection string to your own SQL Server details
Dim strConnection As String = "Server=MyServer; " _
                            & "Database=HumanResources;" _
                            & "User Id=sa;Password=;"

Dim cnSqlServer As New SqlConnection(strConnection)
Dim cmdSqlServer As New SqlCommand()

cnSqlServer.Open()
```

Next we create a new `SqlTransaction` object. This is assigned a new transaction that is created on our `SqlConnection` by calling the `BeginTransaction` method.

```
Dim trnSqlServer As SqlTransaction = cnSqlServer.BeginTransaction
```

Now using these objects we execute an UPDATE statement against our SQL Server that modifies two rows within our dbo.Employees table.

```
With cmdSqlServer

    .Connection = cnSqlServer

    'Assign our SqlTransaction to our SqlCommand object
    .Transaction = trnSqlServer

    .CommandType = CommandType.Text

    .CommandText = " UPDATE dbo.Employees SET Surname='Smith'"
    .CommandText += " WHERE EmployeeID=1"

    ' Execute our first SQL command
    ' this occurs as part of our transaction
    .ExecuteNonQuery()

    .CommandText = " UPDATE dbo.Employees SET Surname='Jones'"
    .CommandText += " WHERE EmployeeID=2"

    ' Execute our second SQL command
    ' this also occurs as part of our transaction
    .ExecuteNonQuery()

End With
```

We have initiated a transaction in both the SQL and ADO.NET examples, but as we have not yet learned how to complete the transaction, we do not commit or roll-back the transaction, nor do we actually close the connection to SQL Server. This is very bad. If it were to happen within an actual application, this transaction would still be in progress, holding resources and blocking access to the rows that we have modified right now. Our transaction would continue to stay in this state until either we explicitly ended it (which we will look at shortly), or the connection to SQL Server was closed. If the connection to SQL Server that has transactions in progress is closed, all those transactions in progress are automatically canceled and rolled back. This is true if you have defined your transaction using either the T-SQL transaction commands, or the `SqlTransaction` object.

A slight variation on these examples is to name our transactions. While naming transactions is not particularly useful when dealing with single transactions, when we deal with nested transactions later naming transactions is essential.

We begin a named transactions using T-SQL like this:

```
BEGIN TRANSACTION OurTransaction
```

To do the same thing using ADO.NET we use:

```
Dim trnSqlServer As SqlTransaction _
        = cnSqlServer.BeginTransaction("OurTransaction")
```

Now we know how to create a transaction we need to learn how to complete a transaction. One way, especially useful when errors or unexpected results have occurred with the SQL statements within your transaction, is to ROLLBACK the transaction.

ROLLBACK TRANSACTION

A ROLLBACK TRANSACTION command can fulfill two purposes, to either roll back an entire transaction or roll back to a savepoint as we will see shortly. Rollback undoes any changes made by the transaction and leaves things as they were before the transaction began. A roll-back is usually called when things within a transaction do not go to plan and all the changes need to be undone.

Using a ROLLBACK command from T-SQL is very straightforward:

```
BEGIN TRANSACTION

  UPDATE dbo.Employees
     Set Surname='Smith'
  WHERE EmployeeID=1

  UPDATE dbo.Employees
     Set Surname='Jones'
  WHERE EmployeeID=2

ROLLBACK TRANSACTION
```

As well as when using ADO.NET from VB.NET:

```
'Change the connection string to your own SQL Server details
   Dim strConnection As String = "Server=MyServer; " _
                          & "Database=HumanResources;" _
                          & "User Id=sa;Password=;"

   Dim cnSqlServer As New SqlConnection(strConnection)
   Dim cmdSqlServer As New SqlCommand()

   cnSqlServer.Open()
```

```
Dim trnSqlServer As SqlTransaction = cnSqlServer.BeginTransaction

    With cmdSqlServer

        .Connection = cnSqlServer

        'Assign our SqlTransaction to our SqlCommand object
        .Transaction = trnSqlServer

        .CommandType = CommandType.Text

        .CommandText = " UPDATE dbo.Employees SET Surname='Smith'"
        .CommandText += " WHERE EmployeeID=1"

        ' Execute our first SQL commmand
        ' this occurs as part our transaction
        .ExecuteNonQuery()

        .CommandText = " UPDATE dbo.Employees SET Surname='Jones'"
        .CommandText += " WHERE EmployeeID=2"

        ' Execute our second SQL commmand
        ' this also occurs as part our transaction
        .ExecuteNonQuery()

    End With
```

```
    trnSqlServer.Rollback()
```

If we are using named transactions, we can also specify the name as part of the ROLLBACK command. However as you will see in the section discussing nested transactions, there is little point in doing so as a rollback will roll back all nested transactions regardless of whether you specify the name or not.

```
ROLLBACK TRANSACTION OurTransaction
```

To perform a named ROLLBACK from ADO.NET we issue the following:

```
    trnSqlServer.Rollback("OurTransaction")
```

A rollback specifying the name of a savepoint is slightly more useful, and we will get to this soon. However, first we need to discuss how we complete a transaction after everything has taken place as we intended.

COMMIT TRANSACTION

To commit a transaction is to make a transaction stick. When we set off creating transactions we usually intend the changes that we make within these transactions to take place without problem, and at the end of the transaction for the changes to be applied to the database. This should be how the transaction operates most of the time and only if something unexpected occurs do we roll back the changes that have been made.

Once COMMIT TRANSACTION (or COMMIT TRAN) has been called, the changes we have made in our transaction are applied and cannot be undone, even if our server decides to crash one millisecond after the commit has completed.

This example shows COMMIT TRANSACTION from T-SQL:

```
BEGIN TRANSACTION

   UPDATE dbo.Employees
      Set Surname='Smith'
   WHERE EmployeeID=1

   UPDATE dbo.Employees
      Set Surname='Jones'
   WHERE EmployeeID=2

COMMIT TRANSACTION
```

And again the equivalent example in ADO.NET is as follows:

```
'Change the connection string to your own SQL Server details
   Dim strConnection As String = "Server=MyServer; " _
                               & "Database=HumanResources;" _
                               & "User Id=sa;Password=;"

   Dim cnSqlServer As New SqlConnection(strConnection)
   Dim cmdSqlServer As New SqlCommand()

   cnSqlServer.Open()

   Dim trnSqlServer As SqlTransaction = cnSqlServer.BeginTransaction

      With cmdSqlServer

         .Connection = cnSqlServer

         'Assign our SqlTransaction to our SqlCommand object
         .Transaction = trnSqlServer

         .CommandType = CommandType.Text

         .CommandText = " UPDATE dbo.Employees SET Surname='Smith'"
         .CommandText += " WHERE EmployeeID=1"

         ' Execute our first SQL commmand
         ' this occurs as part our transaction
         .ExecuteNonQuery()

         .CommandText = " UPDATE dbo.Employees SET Surname='Jones'"
         .CommandText += " WHERE EmployeeID=2"

         ' Execute our second SqlCommmand
         ' this also occurs as part our transaction
         .ExecuteNonQuery()

      End With

   trnSqlServer.Commit()
```

If you are using named transactions you can also specify the name as part of the commit, such as:

```
COMMIT TRANSACTION OurTransaction
```

for T-SQL or the following for ADO.NET:

```
sqlCmd.Transaction.Commit("OurTransaction")
```

As a developer it is absolutely essential that you write code that will correctly terminate transactions, and terminate them as quickly as possible, rather than leaving them in progress until later on, maybe waiting until just before the user closes the application. If you have written a client-server application for example, a user may make a modification to some data within a SQL Server database via your application using a transaction. Unless you successfully close that transaction after the modification has completed, it is possible for that user to wander off to lunch leaving their application open, which in turn keeps the connection to the database open, which has an open transaction blocking every other user from accessing the changed data. In addition the longer the transaction remains open the greater the chance some sort of failure (Client PC, Server, Network, Application…) may occur causing the transaction to be rolled back. By getting them over with as soon as possible you reduce the likelihood of the unexpected occurring.

SAVE TRANSACTION

SAVE TRANSACTION (or SAVE TRAN) is one of those commands that's nice to know is there but won't actually end up getting using too often. This command allows you to define a point in a transaction that you can roll back to later, called a **savepoint**.

It really requires a special kind of circumstance to need savepoints within your transactions, as by definition a transaction is a logical unit of work. Without getting too academic you need to consider the purposes of transactions when implementing them within your code. If it is a logical unit of work, in other words, something that must be fully completed or fully undone, then why would only one part need rolling back using savepoints? You hopefully see my point.

Let's first look at creating a savepoint within T-SQL:

```
BEGIN TRANSACTION

    UPDATE dbo.Employees
        Set Surname='Smith'
    WHERE EmployeeID=1

SAVE TRANSACTION AfterFirstUpdate

    UPDATE dbo.Employees
        Set Surname='Jones'
    WHERE EmployeeID=2

ROLLBACK TRANSACTION AfterFirstUpdate
COMMIT TRANSACTION
```

And now creating a savepoint within ADO.NET:

```vb
'Change the connection string to your own SQL Server details
   Dim strConnection As String = "Server=MyServer; " _
                              & "Database=HumanResources;" _
                              & "User Id=sa;Password=;"

   Dim cnSqlServer As New SqlConnection(strConnection)
   Dim cmdSqlServer As New SqlCommand()

   cnSqlServer.Open()

   Dim trnSqlServer As SqlTransaction _
           = cnSqlServer.BeginTransaction("OurTransaction")

      With cmdSqlServer

         .Connection = cnSqlServer

         'Assign our SqlTransaction to our SqlCommand object
         .Transaction = trnSqlServer

         .CommandType = CommandType.Text

         .CommandText = " UPDATE dbo.Employees SET Surname='Smith'"
         .CommandText += " WHERE EmployeeID=1"

         ' Execute our first SQL commmand
         ' this occurs as part our transaction
         .ExecuteNonQuery()

         trnSqlServer.Save("AfterFirstUpdate")

         .CommandText = " UPDATE dbo.Employees SET Surname='Jones'"
         .CommandText += " WHERE EmployeeID=2"

         ' Execute our second SQL commmand
         ' this also occurs as part our transaction
         .ExecuteNonQuery()

      End With

   trnSqlServer.Rollback("AfterFirstUpdate")

   trnSqlServer.Commit()
```

In both of these examples a new transaction is created, an update is performed then a savepoint is created. After the savepoint another update takes place. At this point a ROLLBACK command rolls the transaction back to the point where the savepoint occurred and finally the transaction is committed. The actual changes applied by this transaction are only those made by the first update, the second update effectively never happened.

If we don't specify a savepoint name with the ROLLBACK command then this behaves as in earlier examples and rolls back the entire transaction, even if savepoints have been defined throughout the transaction.

You can have many savepoints within your transaction. If you specify a different name for the savepoints, then you create several points that can be rolled back to. For example:

```
BEGIN TRANSACTION

    UPDATE dbo.Employees
        SET Surname='Smith'
    WHERE EmployeeID=1

SAVE TRANSACTION AfterUpdate1

    UPDATE dbo.Employees
        SET Surname='Jones'
    WHERE EmployeeID=2

SAVE TRANSACTION AfterUpdate2

    UPDATE dbo.Employees
        SET Surname='Jeeves'
    WHERE EmployeeID=3

SAVE TRANSACTION AfterUpdate3

    UPDATE dbo.Employees
        SET Surname='Regan'
    WHERE EmployeeID=4

ROLLBACK TRANSACTION AfterUpdate3

    UPDATE dbo.Employees
        Set Surname='Thompson'
    WHERE EmployeeID=5

ROLLBACK TRANSACTION AfterUpdate1

COMMIT TRANSACTION
```

As each of our savepoints has a different name, we can choose to roll back to any of the previous savepoints. In this example only our first UPDATE:

```
    UPDATE dbo.Employees
        SET Surname='Smith'
    WHERE EmployeeID=1
```

will be applied to our database once the COMMIT TRANSACTION command has been called. This is because the ROLLBACK TRANSACTION AfterUpdate1 command effectively undid all SQL statements that occurred after the SAVE TRANSACTION AfterUpdate1 took place.

Note however, that once you have rolled back past a savepoint, you cannot then choose to roll forward to a following savepoint again. For example, replacing the ROLLBACK statements in our example above with the ROLLBACK statements below will result in an error:

```
ROLLBACK TRANSACTION AfterUpdate1

ROLLBACK TRANSACTION AfterUpdate3
```

Once we have rolled back to our `AfterUpdate1` savepoint, we can't then roll forward to our `AfterUpdate3` savepoint.

If you create multiple savepoints with the same name, each savepoint effectively replaces the previous savepoint of the same name. For example:

```
BEGIN TRANSACTION

    UPDATE dbo.Employees
        SET Surname='Smith'
    WHERE EmployeeID=1
```

```
SAVE TRANSACTION AfterUpdate
```

```
    UPDATE dbo.Employees
        SET Surname='Jones'
    WHERE EmployeeID=2
```

```
SAVE TRANSACTION AfterUpdate
```

```
    UPDATE dbo.Employees
        SET Surname='Jeeves'
    WHERE EmployeeID=3
```

```
SAVE TRANSACTION AfterUpdate
```

```
    UPDATE dbo.Employees
        SET Surname='Regan'
    WHERE EmployeeID=4
```

```
ROLLBACK TRANSACTION AfterUpdate
```

```
COMMIT TRANSACTION
```

When the transaction is committed (assuming no errors), all of the updates, except the very last, are committed to the database. Each SAVE TRANSACTION command is replacing the previously created savepoint, therefore the ROLLBACK command only rolls back to the last place the savepoint was created. So in the example above, all but our very last UPDATE statement are applied to the database.

Transaction Scope

A transaction is not associated with a particular SQL statement or batch of statements. A transaction is created for a connection and once created it will continue to remain open until it is either committed, rolled back, or the connection is closed (which initiates an implicit roll-back). Once you have created a transaction on a SQL Server connection, many SQL commands or batches can be submitted, and all of these commands will be included as part of the transaction. In fact in VS.NET after you have created a transaction on a connection to SQL Server, all `SqlCommand` objects that use this connection must have their `Transaction` property assigned to the transaction active for the connection. If it isn't assigned then an exception will be thrown, as in the following example:

```
        Dim trnSqlServer As SqlTransaction _
                = cnSqlServer.BeginTransaction("OurTransaction")

        With cmdSqlServer

            .Connection = cnSqlServer

            .CommandType = CommandType.Text

            .CommandText = " UPDATE dbo.Employees SET Surname='Smith'"
            .CommandText += " WHERE EmployeeID=1"

            .ExecuteNonQuery()

        End With
```

This will throw an exception since the `SqlCommand` object hasn't been assigned the `SqlTransaction` object that is active on the connection to SQL Server. The following code on the other hand will not throw this exception as the `SqlCommand` object is assigned the `SqlTransaction` object that is active on the connection.

```
        Dim trnSqlServer As SqlTransaction _
                = cnSqlServer.BeginTransaction("OurTransaction")

        With cmdSqlServer

            .Connection = cnSqlServer

            'Assign our SqlTransaction to our SqlCommand object
            .Transaction = trnSqlServer

            .CommandType = CommandType.Text

            .CommandText = " UPDATE dbo.Employees SET Surname='Smith'"
            .CommandText += " WHERE EmployeeID=1"

            .ExecuteNonQuery()

        End With
```

You cannot therefore define a `SqlTransaction` object and elect for some commands to participate within this user-defined transaction and some not to. All `SqlCommand` objects using the connection on which the transaction has been defined, must participate in the transaction until it is either committed or rolled back.

Commands within Transactions

In SQL Server 2000 all commands execute within a transaction, either implicitly or explicitly. This includes not only our familiar SELECT, INSERT, UPDATE, and DELETE commands, but also all DDL commands such as CREATE TABLE and ALTER PROCEDURE. For example:

```
BEGIN TRANSACTION

CREATE TABLE TranTestTable1
(
    IDCol       Int,
    VarCharCol  Varchar(255)
)

INSERT TranTestTable1 VALUES(1,'abc')
INSERT TranTestTable1 VALUES(2,'def')
INSERT TranTestTable1 VALUES(3,'ghi')

SELECT * FROM TranTestTable1
```

This code will begin a transaction, create a new table and populate this table with data. If we retrieve the data using a SELECT command, we find that indeed we have a new table that contains the data we have just inserted. However, if we continue and execute the following T-SQL:

```
ROLLBACK TRANSACTION

SELECT * FROM TranTestTable1
```

we undo our changes made within the transaction, the table creation, and data insertion, and the SELECT statement now fails with an invalid object name error.

Nested Transactions

A transaction can be nested within another transaction, but the rules associated with doing this require some explanation. And before we discuss these rules there is one thing I want to make clear.

> **You do not, and should not, design your code to use nested transactions within a single routine, such as a stored procedure or batch.**

This is because, as we will see when we look at the rules, they don't offer you anything beyond that which can be achieve, with a single transaction. However nesting transactions between procedures can allow for effective reuse of existing code, as we will see in the next example.

However, let's first discuss the rules of nested transactions. A nested transaction effectively becomes part of the overall outermost transaction. The important rules are:

❑ A COMMIT TRANSACTION will only commit the transaction if the transaction is the outermost transaction of the nested hierarchy. Even if you specify an inner transaction by name, the commit will be ignored (though the nesting level value will be decreased to reflect the number of nested stored procedures).

❑ A ROLLBACK TRANSACTION will roll back all transactions in the nested hierarchy. Even if you specify an inner transaction by name, this will be ignored and all transactions will be rolled back.

❑ By design stored procedures must exit with the same number of transactions in progress as when they were called. This means when you are nesting transactions by calling nested stored procedures, you must ensure a COMMIT is called in each stored procedure in the nested hierarchy that commences a transaction by issuing a BEGIN TRANSACTION statement.

So when should transactions be nested? They may be useful when grouping existing stored procedures into a new transactional requirement, for example, if you have a stored procedure for updating employees and another for updating departments. While each of these may utilize transactions within their own right, you may have a unique requirement to update both an employee and a department with a single transaction. Rather than create another stored procedure you can make use of the two existing procedures and add a top-level transaction within the application.

To illustrate this we'll create a procedure that updates our employee records. This could be used independently as a stand-alone procedure from our application, and creates an explicitly named user-defined transaction to either COMMIT on success, or ROLLBACK our transaction on error.

```
CREATE PROCEDURE UpdateEmployees
@EmployeeId int =null,
@FirstName varchar(30) = null,
@Surname varchar(30) = null,
@DateOfBirth smalldatetime=null,
@DateOfHire smalldatetime=null,
@LastReview smalldatetime=null,
@Department int=null
AS
    BEGIN TRAN UpdateEmployees

-- Update the Employees table
-- The IsNull function is used to set the column to its current value
-- if a NULL value is passed as a parameter for that column.
-- This allows us to update a single column without losing existing
-- values in other columns.
    UPDATE Employees
    SET    FirstName = IsNull(@FirstName,FirstName),
        Surname = IsNull(@Surname,Surname),
        DateOfBirth = IsNull(@DateOfBirth,DateOfBirth),
        DateOfHire= IsNull(@DateOfHire,DateOfHire),
        LastReview= IsNull(@LastReview,LastReview),
        Department = IsNull(@Department,Department)
    WHERE EmployeeID = @EmployeeID

    IF @@ERROR<>0
```

```
    BEGIN
       ROLLBACK TRAN
       RETURN -1
    END
    ELSE
    BEGIN
       COMMIT TRAN UpdateEmployees
       RETURN 0
    END
GO
```

Next we create our stored procedure that updates our Departments table. Once again this commits on success and rolls back on failure:

```
CREATE PROCEDURE UpdateDepartments
@DepartmentID int,
@Description varchar(30)
AS
    BEGIN TRAN UpdateDepartments

    UPDATE Departments
    SET Description=@Description
    WHERE DepartmentID=@DepartmentID

    IF @@ERROR<>0
    BEGIN
       ROLLBACK TRAN
       RETURN -1
    END
    ELSE
    BEGIN
       COMMIT TRAN UpdateDepartments
       RETURN 0
    END
GO
```

However for our unique requirement we can combine both of these transactions into a nested transaction that will require both of these stored procedures to complete successfully or both be rolled back.

```
'Change the connection string to your own SQL Server details
    Dim strConnection As String = "Server=MyServer; " _
                            & "Database=HumanResources;" _
                            & "User Id=sa;Password=;"

    'Define our new SqlConnection object
    Dim cnSqlServer As New SqlConnection(strConnection)

    'Define our new SqlCommand object.
    Dim cmdSqlServer As New SqlCommand()

    'Open the connection to SQL Server.
```

```
cnSqlServer.Open()

'Define the transaction that is to be used
'as the parent transaction for those contained in the
'stored procedures
Dim trnSqlServer As SqlTransaction _
        = cnSqlServer.BeginTransaction()

    With cmdSqlServer
        .Connection = cnSqlServer

        .CommandType = CommandType.Text

        .Transaction = trnSqlServer

        .CommandText = "EXEC UpdateEmployees "
        .CommandText += " @EmployeeID=1, @Surname='Glucina'"

        .ExecuteNonQuery()

        .CommandText = "EXEC UpdateDepartments "
        .CommandText += " @DepartmentID=1, @Description='Service'"

        .ExecuteNonQuery()

    End With

trnSqlServer.Rollback()

'Close our connection
cnSqlServer.Close()
```

Each of the stored procedures executes successful, thereby committing their respective transactions, as they have been nested in the transaction we began from VB.NET using:

```
Dim trnSqlServer As SqlTransaction _
        = cnSqlServer.BeginTransaction()
```

The control of whether these transactions are actually committed or not remains within our application, as the holder of the top-level transaction. Our subsequent call to roll back the transaction:

```
trnSqlServer.Rollback()
```

rolls back all changes made by the stored procedures. The important concept here is that this is not rolling back committed transactions. When a transaction is nested, when you call COMMIT on the nested transaction SQL Server only pretends that the transaction has been committed. Not until the outermost transaction is committed do any of the changes made in the various nested transactions get permanently applied to the database. So when used in this way the COMMIT TRANSACTION commands within the stored procedures do not actually COMMIT the transaction. They simply decrease the transaction count by one, and leave the matter of actually committing or rolling back the transaction to the outermost transaction that we defined from VB.NET.

Transactions and Locks

Transactions and locks are two topics that are closely related. So far we have concentrated on why transactions are needed and how we can use them. In the following sections we start discussing the properties of transactions in detail and how you can customize these properties to improve the overall concurrency of your applications.

A lock is a mechanism used in SQL Server to control access to data for the purpose of enforcing transactional consistency. When one process is using a particular set of data, locks are applied to that set, restricting what other processes can do with that particular set of data while the first process continues to use it. What the first process intends to do with the set of data, whether simply looking at it or making changes to it, affects what types of lock are applied and this in turn affects what other processes can also do.

Transactions rely on locking to enforce the isolation of a transaction. Out of all the ACID characteristics of a transaction the isolation property is the only one that we can influence, as we will see next.

Why Have Locks?

If SQL Server were simply a single user database there would be little need for locks. We could quite happily retrieve and update data knowing that the changes we are making are not going to be affected by anyone else. However SQL Server is definitely not a single-user database, in fact some large implementations have many thousands of concurrent users all accessing and updating a single database. With this large number of users, or in fact with only two users, it is possible for more than one user to be utilizing the same data at the same time. Locks are then required to allow for the prevention of the following concurrency issues:

❑ **Dirty Reads** – When a transaction is in progress the data modifications made by that transaction are said to be **in doubt**. This is because they have yet to be confirmed, by issuing a COMMIT command, or canceled by issuing a ROLLBACK command. If another user reads the data that has been changed by the transaction while it is in progress, this is said to be a **dirty read**. This is because the changes are not yet confirmed, and could be further changed or rolled back completely by the transaction.

❑ **Unrepeatable Reads** – An **unrepeatable read** occurs when a transaction reads a set of data on more than one occasion and gets different values on these separate occasions. Unrepeatable reads can occur when one transaction is reading a set of data concurrently with another transaction that is updating rows within the same set of data.

❑ **Phantoms** – These occur when one transaction reads a set of data on more than one occasion and it receives a different number of rows on each occasion. These phantoms occur when the transaction reading the data set is running concurrently with another transaction that is inserting or deleting rows that would fall within the data set.

❑ **Lost Updates** – A **lost update** occurs when two transactions running concurrently retrieve a set of data based on criteria, then both update the data set. As each update is not aware of the other concurrent update, the one that is applied last will overwrite the previous update. The first update is considered lost.

Locks To the Rescue

Locks prevent these situations from occurring by blocking transactions from accessing data that is in use by another transaction. Locks are held by one process, and used to block the continuing execution of another process. When the process completes, it releases the locks that it held, allowing the process that was blocked to then continue its execution. While blocking is a normal and required trait of multi-user transactional databases, the goal in writing database applications is to create transactions that keep the duration for which other transactions are blocked as short as possible.

There are a number of different types of locks that SQL Server uses to block other processes, each having different characteristics.

Shared Locks

Whenever we read data, in other words when executing a SELECT statement, a **shared lock** is placed on the set of data that we retrieve. When a shared lock exists on a set of data, concurrent processes can read this data. However no data modifications can be made to the set of data for the duration of the shared lock.

For a shared lock to be obtained there must not be any exclusive locks currently in use by other processes on the data set that we requested. However, shared locks can be taken even if other processes have shared locks or update locks currently is use on the dataset..

Exclusive Locks

An **exclusive lock** must be obtained before modifications to a particular set of data can be made. An exclusive lock prevents any other concurrent processes from reading or modifying the dataset by blocking any requests for any type of lock made on this set of data by any other processes. Once an exclusive lock has been obtained all other processes must wait for the process that has the exclusive lock to release it before they can gain access to the set of data.

For an exclusive lock to be obtained, no other locks must currently exist on the data set.

Update Locks

A condition known as a **deadlock** occurs when two transactions attempt to convert their locking mode, and each transaction is blocked by the other. An example of this is where there are two transactions, A and B, which have shared locks on a set of data and Transaction A attempts to convert its shared locks into exclusive locks so it can make modifications to this data set. To acquire the exclusive lock there must not be any other locks on a data set, so at this point Transaction A is blocked by the shared locks held by Transaction B. If Transaction B now also attempts to convert its locks to exclusive locks, a deadlock has occurred, since not only is Transaction A blocked by Transaction B, but Transaction B is blocked by Transaction A.

Update locks can be used to prevent deadlocks from occurring, as we discuss later in this chapter. If a transaction requires a shared lock on a set of data but knows that it will need to acquire an exclusive lock on this data set at some point during the transaction, an update lock can be obtained. An update lock allows other processes to take shared locks, but does not allow any other process to take an exclusive lock, or another update lock, on the set of data. An update lock can then itself be upgraded to an exclusive lock when changes are made on the data set by the holder of the update lock. As only one update lock can be present at a time, other requests for update locks will be blocked until the current transaction has completed.

Update locks improve concurrency but prevent you shooting yourself in the foot by being overly generous. They do this by allowing multiple transactions to take shared locks. In other words, they allow them to read the data set, while preventing anyone other than yourself from changing the data for the course of your transaction. This way if you know you are going modify a set of data later in your transaction you can reserve the right to do so later in your transaction, without preventing anyone else from reading this data in the meantime.

To use an update lock you must specify a locking hint when retrieving the data set. An example of this is also shown later in this chapter.

Intent Locks

Intent locks are used by SQL Server to indicate the locks that are in place on a resource. They are used in conjunction with all three lock types we described above and improve the performance of locking by removing the need for a lock request to check for blocking locks at the table, page, and row level before being granted. For example, if a transaction takes out a shared lock at the row level, SQL Server will also take out intent shared locks at the page and table level. If another transaction requests an exclusive page or table lock, SQL Server just checks for locks at the same level as the request. The intent lock lets SQL Server know immediately that a shared lock currently exists on the requested resource, albeit at a different locking level.

Schema Locks

There are two schema locking modes but these aren't used in relation to changing data contained within a table. Instead these are used to control making modifications to the table structure itself. When changing a table's schema, for example adding columns, a schema modification lock is taken on the table. This schema modification lock prevents any other type of lock being taken on the table for the duration of the schema modification.

When running queries on a table a schema stability lock is taken on the table. This does not prevent any of the standard locks that we looked at above from being created, but it does prevent the schema modification lock from being granted. The net result is that, when the schema is being modified, no queries can access it and when it is being accessed by a query the schema cannot be modified. It's nice when things make sense, isn't it?

Lock Granularity

In the old days, when SQL Server 6.5 reigned supreme, locks could be taken at the page, extent, or table level. Pages were the smallest unit on which locks could be obtained and, as many rows could potentially be on one page, this level of locking was a bit of a concurrency limiter. In more modern times, since the release of SQL Server 7 and now SQL Server 2000, data can be locked right at the row level which allows for higher numbers of transactions to run concurrently, when these transactions are modifying data that is stored internally near other data currently involved in transactions.

However SQL Server doesn't only take row-level locks. Imagine the overhead needed to allocate a lock for every row when updating 10,000,000 rows in a table. Instead SQL Server has different granularities of locks and, based on the number of rows being affected by the data modification, can choose what level of granularity is needed.

The lock granularity levels available in SQL Server are:

Row Lock	The lock is applied on a single row.
Key Lock	Used to lock rows, or a range of rows within an index.
Page Lock	The lock is applied at a data page level. A page is a unit of storage in SQL Server that is 8k in size. Depending on the size of the individual rows, one or more rows will exist within a page.
Extent Lock	An extent is a series of eight pages.
Table	The lock is applied on the entire table.

SQL Server dynamically determines at which level it should apply the locks, and can escalate to less granular locks during a transaction if the number of locks granted at the current level exceeds an internal limit. The level at which locks are applied is automatic but we can influence the level that SQL Server decides upon by specifying a locking hint, as we discuss shortly.

Isolation Levels

The isolation property of our ACID transaction definition clearly states that one transaction cannot be affected by another transaction. This setting has a profound effect on concurrency, which is the ability to support simultaneous users. To adhere to this rule strictly, all reads and modifications of data would occur without any changes from another user affecting the data that is used by the transaction in any way. This is called **serializing** transactions, each transaction on a particular set of data must wait for the previous transaction on that set of data to finish before proceeding.

Often strict serialized transactions are not required, and a reduced level of isolation would be acceptable. Reducing the level of isolation makes it more likely that transactions working with the same set of data will be able to run at least partly simultaneously, which will improve the overall concurrency, and therefore performance, of a database. SQL Server allows us to control isolation with the SET TRANSACTION ISOLATION LEVEL command, which can take any one of the parameters detailed below.

The default isolation level for a connection is READ COMMITTED, which we discuss in this section. Unless you explicitly change the isolation level for your connection, you will always be using READ COMMITTED.

Throughout this section we will be creating example code to demonstrate the behavior of each of these isolation levels. To use these examples, first create a new VB.NET Console Application project and include the following statements to import the appropriate namespaces:

```
Imports System.Data
Imports System.Data.SqlClient
```

READ UNCOMMITTED

READ UNCOMMITTED essentially breaks the isolation rule completely by allowing the current transaction to read data that has not been committed by another transaction. In other words the current transaction can carry out dirty reads. This level of isolation should be avoided unless you have a special type of database in which errors in the data don't matter.

Too often I see production database applications using the READ UNCOMITTED isolation level when it is not at all appropriate. Typically this happens because the application is created in a development environment and tested with one or two users and works fine. The application is then rolled out to production, with maybe 100 or 200 users. If the developer has not concentrated on writing efficient transactions, the database will often grind to a halt as the numerous users are all trying to access and modify data at the same time. The developer, now in a mad panic, desperately tries to improve concurrency by changing settings, rather than rewriting code. One of the first settings to be changed is to set the isolation level to READ UNCOMMITTED, which will result in a slight increase in concurrency. The developer wanders off feeling happier that their code is performing a little better, completely unaware that they have just allowed their database application to use erroneous data. This has potentially disastrous results for users, in manipulating items such as incorrect salary figures, or incorrect tax codes.

> **Concentrate on writing efficient transactions from the start of your application development process, rather than try and do a quick fix when going into production.**

To set the isolation level to READ UNCOMMITTED in T-SQL:

```
SET TRANSACTION ISOLATION LEVEL READ UNCOMMITTED
```

And using ADO.NET from VB.NET:

```
cnSqlServer.BeginTransaction(IsolationLevel.ReadUncommitted)
```

In this example we create two connections to simulate two users connecting to the database concurrently.

```
'Change the connection string to your own SQL Server details
   Dim strConnection As String = "Server=MyServer; " _
                      & "Database=HumanResources;" _
                      & "User Id=sa;Password=;"

   'Define two new SqlConnection objects, both created
   'using the same connection string from above.
   Dim cnSqlServer As New SqlConnection(strConnection)
   Dim cnSqlServer2 As New SqlConnection(strConnection)

   'Define two new SQLCommand objects.
   Dim cmdSqlServer As New SqlCommand()
   Dim cmdSqlServer2 As New SqlCommand()

   Dim drSqlServer As SqlDataReader

   'Open both the first and second connections to SQL Server.
   cnSqlServer.Open()
   cnSqlServer2.Open()
```

Next we define our transaction objects. The trnSqlServer transaction is created on our first connection and uses the default READ COMMITTED isolation level, while our second transaction, trnSqlServer2, is created on our second connection to SQL Server and uses the READ UNCOMMITTED isolation level.

```
' Define the transaction on our first connection to use the
' default isolation level, which is READ COMMITTED
Dim trnSqlServer As SqlTransaction = cnSqlServer.BeginTransaction()

'Define the transaction on our second connection to use the
'READ UNCOMMITTED isolation level.
Dim trnSqlServer2 As SqlTransaction = cnSqlServer2.BeginTransaction _
                                    (IsolationLevel.ReadUncommitted)
```

Using the first connection we insert three values into our `Departments` table within our `HumanResources` database.

```
'On our first connection to SQL Server define our
'command object, then use it to INSERT three rows
'into our SQL Server database.
With cmdSqlServer

        .Connection = cnSqlServer

        .CommandType = CommandType.Text

        .Transaction = trnSqlServer

        .CommandText = "INSERT dbo.Departments(Description)"
        .CommandText += " VALUES('HR')"

        .ExecuteNonQuery()

        .CommandText = "INSERT dbo.Departments(Description)"
        .CommandText += " VALUES('Finance')"

        .ExecuteNonQuery()

        .CommandText = "INSERT dbo.Departments(Description)"
        .CommandText += " VALUES('Information Technology')"

        .ExecuteNonQuery()

End With
```

Now, while leaving the first transaction in progress, on the second connection we utilize our other transaction. This time we are using a transaction that has the isolation level explicitly set to `ReadUncomitted` so this will allow the reading of dirty data. We SELECT all the rows from our `Departments` table and output the results to our console window:

```
'Set our ISOLATION LEVEL to READ UNCOMMITTED and retrieve
'the rows from our dbo.Departments table.
With cmdSqlServer2
        .Connection = cnSqlServer2

        .CommandType = CommandType.Text
```

```
            .Transaction = trnSqlServer2

            .CommandText = "SELECT * FROM dbo.Departments"

        drSqlServer = .ExecuteReader
    End With

        'Output rows within the Departments table
        'to our console window
        While drSqlServer.Read

            Console.WriteLine(drSqlServer(1))

        End While

        'Close the DataReader
        drSqlServer.Close()
```

The SELECT statement executed on the second connection returns the rows that were initially inserted using the first connection, which is still currently uncommitted. If we now choose to roll back the transaction on the first connection, like this:

```
    ' Undo the INSERTS that we have performed on our
    ' first connection to SQL Server.
    trnSqlServer.Rollback()
```

we see that a subsequent SELECT from this table results in no rows being returned. This is because when the previous SELECT took place, the rows that had been inserted were not committed and therefore not guaranteed to remain within the database. As the transactions in which the inserts were made have been rolled back then these rows no longer exist within our database.

```
    'Execute the SELECT again on our second connection to
    'SQL Server.  Return results as a DataReader.
    drSqlServer = cmdSqlServer2.ExecuteReader

        'Output rows within the Departments table
        'to our console window
        While drSqlServer.Read

            Console.WriteLine(drSqlServer(0))

        End While

        'Close the DataReader
        drSqlServer.Close()

        'Complete the transaction on our second connection
        trnSqlServer2.Commit()

        'Close both of our connections
        cnSqlServer.Close()
```

You can imagine how having rows present one minute, viewable from our second READ UNCOMMITTED transaction, and then gone completely without trace another minute, could cause problems within production databases.

Be sure not to use the READ UNCOMMITTED isolation level within your VB.NET, SQL, or stored procedure code unless the quality of the data you are working with is not of concern.

READ COMITTED

READ COMMITTED is a commonly used isolation level as it provides a balance between concurrency and consistency. When the isolation level is set to READ COMMITTED, a transaction will read data that has been committed, however subsequent reads of that data within the transaction may return different results if modifications have been made by other users transactions. This gives a true picture of data within a table at any given time.

To set the isolation level to READ COMMITTED in T-SQL:

```
SET TRANSACTION ISOLATION LEVEL READ COMMITTED
```

And using ADO.NET from VB.NET:

```
cnSqlServer.BeginTransaction(IsolationLevel.ReadCommitted)
```

When a command within a transaction selects data from a table, it takes shared locks on the rows it examines. As shared locks can only be taken when no exclusive locks are held on the rows being examined, this prevents data being retrieved that is still in an uncommitted form. An exclusive lock cannot be taken on a row while a shared lock is in place, so this prevents the data being modified while the SELECT is in progress. Once the SELECT has finished the shared locks are released, leaving the data available to be modified by other transactions. Therefore, if the same set of data is retrieved at a later point within our transaction, it is possible for the data to have changed from the previous SELECT.

To help explain this, let's look at an example of using READ COMMITTED. Once again for simplicity we are using two separate connections within our VB.NET code to simulate two separate database users.

```
'Change the connection string to your own SQL Server details
Dim strConnection As String = "Server=MyServer; " _
                            & "Database=HumanResources;" _
                            & "User Id=sa;Password=;"

'Define two new SqlConnection objects, both created
'using the same connection string from above.
Dim cnSqlServer As New SqlConnection(strConnection)
Dim cnSqlServer2 As New SqlConnection(strConnection)

'Define two new SQLCommand objects.
Dim cmdSqlServer As New SqlCommand()
Dim cmdSqlServer2 As New SqlCommand()

Dim drSqlServer As SqlDataReader

'Open both the first and second connections to SQL Server.
cnSqlServer.Open()
cnSqlServer2.Open()
```

On our first connection we insert three rows into our Departments table. As we have not explicitly defined a transaction for these inserts, each insert will run in an implicit transaction and be committed on completion:

```
'On our first connection to SQL Server define our
'command object, then use it to INSERT three rows
'into our SQL Server database.
With cmdSqlServer

    .Connection = cnSqlServer

    .CommandType = CommandType.Text

    .CommandText = "INSERT dbo.Departments(Description)"
    .CommandText += " VALUES('HR')"

    .ExecuteNonQuery()

    .CommandText = "INSERT dbo.Departments(Description)"
    .CommandText += " VALUES('Finance')"

    .ExecuteNonQuery()

    .CommandText = "INSERT dbo.Departments(Description)"
    .CommandText += " VALUES('Information Technology')"

    .ExecuteNonQuery()

End With
```

Now on our second database connection we create a new transaction, and set the isolation level to ReadCommitted. Within this transaction we select and display all the rows within the table, the rows that we inserted above:

```
'Define the transaction on our second connection to use the
'READ COMMITTED isolation level.
Dim trnSqlServer2 As SqlTransaction = cnSqlServer2.BeginTransaction _
                                    (IsolationLevel.ReadCommitted)

'Set our ISOLATION LEVEL to READ COMMITTED and retrieve
'the rows from our dbo.Deparments table.
With cmdSqlServer2

    .Connection = cnSqlServer2

    .CommandType = CommandType.Text

    .Transaction = trnSqlServer2

    .CommandText = "SELECT * FROM dbo.Departments"

    drSqlServer = .ExecuteReader

End With
```

```
'Output rows within the Departments table to our console window
While drSqlServer.Read

    Console.WriteLine(drSqlServer(1))

End While

'Close the DataReader
drSqlServer.Close()
```

Next on the first database connection we execute a command to update one of the rows of our Departments table, changing the description of one of our departments from 'Information Technology' to 'IT Operations'. While the previous SELECT used shared locks on the rows contained within this table, as we are using the ReadCommitted isolation level these shared locks were released once the SELECT had completed, so they don't block our UPDATE and it completes successfully.

```
With cmdSqlServer

    .CommandText = "UPDATE dbo.Departments SET "
    .CommandText += " Description='IT Operations' "
    .CommandText += " WHERE Description ='Information Technology'"

    .ExecuteNonQuery()

End With
```

A subsequent SELECT from the table within the transaction on our first database connection retrieves the rows that now contain the updated values. This is an example of an unrepeatable read, as two retrievals of the same set of data within a transaction returned different values each time.

```
'Execute the SELECT again on our second connection to
'SQL Server. Return results as a DataReader.
drSqlServer = cmdSqlServer2.ExecuteReader

'Output rows within the Departments table
'to our console window
While drSqlServer.Read

    Console.WriteLine(drSqlServer(1))

End While

'Close the DataReader
drSqlServer.Close()

'Complete the transaction on our second connection
trnSqlServer2.Commit()

'Close both of our connections
cnSqlServer.Close()
cnSqlServer.Close()
```

As READ COMMITTED provides the best concurrency of all isolation levels, apart from READ UNCOMITTED, you should first evaluate whether the isolation provided by READ COMMITTED will be sufficient for your transaction before considering a more isolated transaction level. Choosing the right isolation level can have dramatic effects on the performance of your database application, so we will discuss how you should select the isolation level a little later in this chapter.

REPEATABLE READ

The REPEATABLE READ isolation level takes the READ COMMITTED isolation level a step further, by guaranteeing that subsequent reads of a set of data will always result in the same values being returned for the duration of the transaction. Shared locks are taken on the data set when it is being read, just as for READ COMMITTED; however the difference is that these shared locks are not released after the data retrieval has finished. Instead they are held for the entire duration of the transaction. We can see how this instantly impacts concurrency because now once a set of data has been read, it cannot be modified by any other user until this transaction has completed.

To set the isolation level to REPEATABLE READ in T-SQL:

```
SET TRANSACTION ISOLATION LEVEL REPEATABLE READ
```

And using ADO.NET from VB.NET:

```
sqlConn.BeginTransaction(IsolationLevel.RepeatableRead)
```

REPEATABLE READ does not, however, completely isolate the current transaction from other transactions. Even though rows within a data set that has been previously read cannot be changed, rows that are valid within this data set can be inserted by other transactions and will appear on subsequent reads of the data set, at which time the shared locks will be placed on these new rows. These conditions make phantom reads possible, as rows can appear out of the mist of other transactions. To demonstrate these points let's look at the following example:

```
'Change the connection string to your own SQL Server details
    Dim strConnection As String = "Server=MyServer; " _
                          & "Database=HumanResources;" _
                          & "User Id=sa;Password=;"

    'Define two new SqlConnection objects, both created
    'using the same connection string from above.
    Dim cnSqlServer As New SqlConnection(strConnection)
    Dim cnSqlServer2 As New SqlConnection(strConnection)

    'Define two new SQLCommand objects.
    Dim cmdSqlServer As New SqlCommand()
    Dim cmdSqlServer2 As New SqlCommand()

    Dim drSqlServer As SqlDataReader

    'Open both the first and second connections to SQL Server.
    cnSqlServer.Open()
    cnSqlServer2.Open()
```

On the first connection we begin a `RepeatableRead` transaction and retrieve and display all the rows within our test table:

```
'Define the transaction on our second connection to use the
'READ COMMITTED isolation level.
Dim trnSqlServer2 As SqlTransaction = cnSqlServer2.BeginTransaction _
                                      (IsolationLevel.RepeatableRead)

With cmdSqlServer2

    .Connection = cnSqlServer2

    .CommandType = CommandType.Text

    .Transaction = trnSqlServer2

    .CommandText = "SELECT * FROM dbo.Departments"

    drSqlServer = .ExecuteReader

End With

'Output rows within the Departments table
'to our console window
While drSqlServer.Read

    Console.WriteLine(drSqlServer(1))

End While

'Close the DataReader
drSqlServer.Close()
```

Next on our first connection we insert a new row into our test table. As the `RepeatableRead` isolation level allows new (or phantom) rows to be created this `INSERT` is successful. Since we have not explicitly defined a `SqlTransaction` object for this first connection, the `INSERT` will only be running within its own implicit transaction:

```
'On our first connection to SQL Server define our
'command object, then use it to INSERT a row
'into our SQL Server database.
With cmdSqlServer

    .Connection = cnSqlServer

    .CommandType = CommandType.Text

    .CommandText = "INSERT dbo.Departments(Description)"
    .CommandText += " VALUES('Produce')"

    .ExecuteNonQuery()

End With
```

However we now try and update the rows within our `Departments` table, as we did using the `ReadCommitted` isolation level. As the `RepeatableRead` isolation level blocks other processes' attempts to make changes on any of the rows that have been read within the first transaction, our `UPDATE` is blocked.

```
'Now on our first connection attempt to UPDATE a row within
'our Departments table.
With cmdSqlServer

    .CommandText = "UPDATE dbo.Departments SET "
    .CommandText += " Description='IT Department' "
    .CommandText += " WHERE Description ='IT Operations'"

    .ExecuteNonQuery()

End With
```

```
'Close the DataReader
drSqlServer.Close()

'Complete the transaction on our second connection
trnSqlServer2.Commit()

'Close both of our connections
cnSqlServer.Close()
cnSqlServer2.Close()
```

Our `UPDATE` statement would continue to be blocked until the `RepeatableRead` transaction was completed. As we are running these examples from within the same piece of code, this would not happen and our code would appear to hang while the `UPDATE` continues to wait for the `RepeatableRead` transaction to complete. So in this example we add the `CommandTimeout` parameter, which causes our `UPDATE` to time out after waiting 5 seconds. You should not specify a `CommandTimeout` within your application code, as the `UPDATE` would normally continue once the other transaction has completed: this is normal blocking behavior.

SERIALIZABLE

`Serializable` is the isolation level that strictly adheres to the letter of the law specified by our ACID transaction definition. When we are using this level of isolation no other transaction is going to bother us. `Serializable` has all the properties of `RepeatableRead` except that we will not get phantom rows, because other transactions will be blocked from inserting rows that fall within data sets retrieved by our transaction.

`Serializable` works by taking shared locks on the range of rows that would fall within the data set retrieved within our transaction. Any new row that is being inserted that is in this range of values will be blocked until our transaction has been completed. This allows our retrievals to be repeated throughout the transaction without the risk of phantom rows popping up.

While this level of isolation gives us the least to worry about, in terms of data changes during our transaction, `Serializable` should really only be considered if we are sure that `ReadCommitted` or even `RepeatableRead` simply will not do. Using it when it is not strictly necessary may be imposing an unnecessary stranglehold on our database concurrency.

Now let's look at the `Serializable` example:

```
'Change the connection string to your own SQL Server details
   Dim strConnection As String = "Server=MyServer; " _
                         & "Database=HumanResources;" _
                         & "User Id=sa;Password=;"

   'Define two new SqlConnection objects, both created
   'using the same connection string from above.
   Dim cnSqlServer As New SqlConnection(strConnection)
   Dim cnSqlServer2 As New SqlConnection(strConnection)

   'Define two new SqlCommand objects.
   Dim cmdSqlServer As New SqlCommand()
   Dim cmdSqlServer2 As New SqlCommand()

   Dim drSqlServer As SqlDataReader

   'Open both the first and second connections to SQL Server.
   cnSqlServer.Open()
   cnSqlServer2.Open()
```

The only difference in the code between the `RepeatableRead` example and this `Serializable` example is the isolation level that we specify when beginning the transaction:

```
   'Define the transaction on our second connection to use the
   'READ COMMITTED isolation level.
   Dim trnSqlServer2 As SqlTransaction = cnSqlServer2.BeginTransaction _
                                     (IsolationLevel.Serializable)

      With cmdSqlServer2

         .Connection = cnSqlServer2

         .CommandType = CommandType.Text

         .Transaction = trnSqlServer2

         .CommandText = "SELECT * FROM dbo.Departments"

         drSqlServer = .ExecuteReader

      End With

      'Output rows within the Departments table
      'to our console window
      While drSqlServer.Read

         Console.WriteLine(drSqlServer(1))

      End While

   'Close the DataReader
   drSqlServer.Close()
```

However unlike our `RepeatableRead` example, where the `INSERT` was successful, `Serializable` prevents any rows that fall within the range of our `SELECT` statement from being inserted or modified.

```
'On our first connection to SQL Server define our
'command object, then use it to INSERT a row
'into our SQL Server database.
With cmdSqlServer

    .Connection = cnSqlServer

    .CommandType = CommandType.Text

    .CommandText = "INSERT dbo.Departments(Description)"
    .CommandText += " VALUES('Produce')"

    .ExecuteNonQuery()

End With
```

As we have specified a command timeout, our `INSERT` will eventually time out after 5 seconds. In the real world the blocking transaction would likely be executed by another user process and at some stage it would complete (by either committing or rolling back). Once this had happened the code would continue executing.

```
'Now on our first connection attempt to UPDATE a row within
'our Departments table.
With cmdSqlServer

    .CommandText = "UPDATE dbo.Departments SET "
    .CommandText += " Description='IT Department' "
    .CommandText += " WHERE Description ='IT Operations'"

    .ExecuteNonQuery()

End With

'Close the DataReader
drSqlServer.Close()

'Complete the transaction on our second connection
trnSqlServer2.Commit()

'Close both of our connections
cnSqlServer.Close()
cnSqlServer.Close()
```

Having discussed the various modes of locking it is now an appropriate time to discuss how you can influence the type of locks SQL Server will take during a particular transaction by using locking hints.

Locking Hints

Locking hints affect isolation in a similar way to the SET TRANSACTION ISOLATION LEVEL setting. However while the SET TRANSACTION statement specifies the isolation level for all transactions that occur on a connection, locking hints specify the isolation level required by individual statements.

> *Note that there is no property or method of the* SqlTransaction *object to set a locking hint directly. Instead you include these locking hints within your T-SQL commands being sent to SQL Server.*

By default SQL Server does a pretty good job of selecting the most appropriate lock type, and lock granularity. If you wish to specifically alter the locking behavior you can do this with lock hints. You may wish to do this for several reasons, which include:

❑ You know your code will be making changes to the data set at a later point in the transaction. In this case you may wish to acquire an update lock instead of a shared lock. This is useful for preventing deadlocks.

❑ You are writing a task that runs as a batch job and it will be the only user accessing the database when it is run. Here you may wish to acquire table-level locks. Using table level locks, instead of row-or page level-locks for a transaction can greatly improve the performance of single-user tasks by reducing the locking overhead.

❑ You have a number of data sets retrieved within your transaction that require a more stringent level of locking than others. Locking hints allow you to customize the isolation level for individual sets of data within a transaction. This may allow you to use locks more efficiently. For example if a small number of data sets retrieved within your transaction require the RepeatableRead isolation level, whereas the majority of data sets only require ReadCommitted, then you can set the isolation level for the connection to ReadCommitted, and specify the RepeatableRead locking hint for those data sets that require a higher level of isolation. Or you could use this example in reverse, setting the isolation level for your connection to RepeatableRead and specifying the ReadCommitted isolation level for specific transactions.

SQL Server includes many lock hints that you can choose to specify. By default you should **not** use locking hints, unless you have a specific reason. Incorrect use of locking hints can seriously impact your database's ability to process concurrent transactions.

The locking hints available are:

HOLDLOCK or SERIALIZABLE	Holds shared locks on the range of rows that would fall within the data set. These locks are then held for the duration of the transaction preventing any other transaction from inserting, deleting, or updating any rows that would fall in this range, while the transaction holding this locking hint is in progress.
NOLOCK or READUNCOMMITTED	This locking hint does not create shared locks on the rows returned in its data set, nor does it take any notice of existing exclusive locks which may be in place. It allows the reading of uncommitted data, which is usually a bad thing, as we have already discussed.

PAGELOCK	Takes locks at the page level, instead of the table or row level.
READCOMMITTED	Specifies that shared locks are obtained for the duration of the data set retrieval, and are released once the data retrieval has completed.
READPAST	When you are using the READ COMMITTED isolation level setting, you have the option of specifying a READPAST locking hint. This causes the retrieval of the data set to skip over rows that currently have exclusive locks in place from other transactions, rather than the default behavior, which is to be blocked. As rows can be missed this should only be used when you do not require an exact data set.
REPEATABLEREAD	Holds shared locks on the data that has been retrieved for the duration of the transaction, however it does not hold these locks on the data range. This allows new rows to be inserted that will fall into the range of values retrieved by this data set, but prevents rows that have previously been retrieved from being modified.
ROWLOCK	Specifies that the locks be taken at the row level. Care should be taken using this option when updating a large number of rows.
TABLOCK	Takes a shared lock at the table level. By specifying the TABLOCK locking hint within your queries, if you know that the table is only ever read by your application code, you will increase the performance of the data retrieval. This is because SQL Server does not need to create more costly locks at the row or page level.
TABLOCKX	Holds an exclusive lock on a table for the duration of the transaction. This prevents any other user from obtaining any other form of lock, so this is normally only used for single-user processes, such as batch jobs.
UPDLOCK	Tells SQL Server to take an update lock instead of a shared lock. As only a single update lock can be taken on a data set this can help prevent deadlocks occurring when two processes that hold shared locks are both trying to convert these to exclusive locks.
XLOCK	Holds an exclusive lock on the data set for the duration of the transaction. This will block any other transaction from accessing this data until the transaction holding the exclusive lock has completed.

To specify a locking hint we use the WITH construct in T-SQL, for example:

```
BEGIN TRANSACTION
    SELECT EmployeeID, FirstName, Surname
    FROM Employees WITH (UPDLOCK)
    WHERE EmployeeID>10
```

This command retrieves a list of employees but instead of acquiring the default shared lock, we instruct SQL Server to lock the data set using an update lock instead, since we intend to make changes to the data set at a later point in the transaction.

Displaying Lock Information

To demonstrate intent locks in one Query Analyzer window, run the following commands to begin a transaction and take a row-level lock on our `Employees` table:

```
USE HumanResources

SET TRANSACTION ISOLATION LEVEL REPEATABLE READ

BEGIN TRANSACTION

SELECT *
FROM dbo.employees
WHERE Surname='Allan'

EXEC master.dbo.sp_lock

ROLLBACK TRANSACTION
```

The `sp_lock` stored procedure returns information about locks within the current database. It is located in the `master` database and is provided as a DBA monitoring tool, although it is also of great use for developers creating applications. `sp_lock` displays locks that are currently active on a SQL Server, and displays the object, indexes, type, and mode of these locks. Using `sp_lock` it is possible to determine the types of locks that your code is acquiring.

You should get results similar to the following (you may get more results than shown here depending on the activity of your server):

SPID	DBID	ObjectID	IndID	Type	Resource	Mode	Stats
52	13	0	0	DB		S	GRANT
52	13	389576426	1	PAG	1:113	IS	GRANT
52	13	389576426	1	KEY	(75004d705a82)	S	GRANT
52	13	389576426	0	TAB		IS	GRANT

The columns within this resultset include:

❏ `SPID` - The process that required the lock.

❏ `DBID` – The ID of the database in which the lock is present.

❏ `ObjectID` – The ID of the object on which the lock is held.

❏ `IndID` – The index on which the lock is held.

❏ `Type` – The type of lock, such as Row, Page, Key, Table, or Database.

❏ `Resource` – Textual description of the lock, safely ignorable.

❏ `Mode` – The mode of lock, such as Shared, Intent Shared, Exclusive, Intent Exclusive, Update, and so on.

❏ `Status` – The status of the lock. `GRANT` means the lock has been granted, `WAIT` means the lock is waiting (or has been blocked) to be granted, and `CNVRT` means the lock is being converted (or escalated).

From this resultset we can see that our transaction has taken a key lock. As our table contains a clustered index an index key is used to identify a row within the table. This is indicated by the `Type` and `Mode` columns within our resultset:

```
52      13      389576426    1        KEY     (75004d705a82)   S      GRANT
```

However, there are also several others. SQL Server has also taken an intent lock on the database page in which this row is stored which prevents other transactions from taking an exclusive lock at the page level:

```
52      13      389576426    1        PAG     1:113            IS     GRANT
```

We can also see that SQL Server has taken an intent lock at the table level, which will prevent other transactions from taking an exclusive lock at the table level while our transaction is in progress:

```
52      13      389576426    0        TAB                      IS     GRANT
```

If you have been paying attention, you will also notice another type of lock that we haven't discussed. This is the database-level shared lock:

```
52      13      0            0        DB                       S      GRANT
```

All connections to a database hold a shared database lock. This prevents any exclusive database operations, such as a database restore, from taking place while connections are present to the database.

Transaction Best Practices

Now that we have had a reasonably in-depth discussion on SQL Server transactions, I hope you have a good feel for why they are required and how they work. For every data modification that you need to code during the development of your database applications, you have to make decisions about what the transactional requirements of this data modification are, and how you are going to implement them.

To assist you with making these decisions, we have compiled a list of best practices to consider when designing SQL Server transactions within your database.

Only When You Have To

Transactions are absolutely critical for data consistency in multi-user databases and should always be used when necessary. However, they should **only** be used when necessary. As we have seen, transactions have serious impacts on the concurrency of multiple users so their use needs to be kept to a minimum. For every modification you perform in a transaction you should ask the following question:

"Is the success or failure of this modification really dependent on the success or failure of other data modifications within the transaction?"

If the answer is no, you may wish to reconsider having this modification contained within that transaction. Perhaps it's a separate transaction or perhaps it doesn't require an explicit transaction at all.

> **Remember, you can do a lot to improve concurrency by having a higher number of shorter transactions, rather than a smaller number of larger transactions.**

Keep Them Brief

Once you have made changes within a transaction, locks are being held that prevent other users from reading or writing the data you have touched within that transaction. It makes good sense to keep the number of commands and amount of logic to process within the transaction to an absolute minimum. Do as much of this as possible beforehand, and get in and out of the transaction as quickly as possible.

Use Lowest Isolation Level

As we have already discussed, the isolation level of a transaction has a direct impact on the concurrency of transactions within a database. To keep concurrency at its optimal level you should select the lowest level of isolation possible **without sacrificing data consistency**. If you only need `ReadCommitted` why use `Serializable`? Start at `ReadCommitted` and work your way up the isolation level tree until you find a level that will satisfy the needs of your transaction.

Build Transactions To Succeed

Since you can easily roll back transactions, you may be tempted to be lazy on your validation checking before entering into a transaction and instead perform this validation on the fly. To explain what I mean let's once again revisit the now famous banking transaction example. For a transfer of funds to be successful you need two valid accounts, one from which the funds are being drawn and one to which the funds are being credited. You may be tempted to write the transaction as:

```
BEGIN TRANSACTION

    UPDATE BankAccount
        SET balance = balance - @transfer_ammount
    WHERE AccountNumber = @DebitAccount

    IF @@ERROR<>0 or @@ROWCOUNT<>1
    BEGIN

        ROLLBACK TRANSACTION

        RAISERROR ('Either the debit account number is invalid ' +
                   ' or an error occured',16,1)

        RETURN -1

    END

    UPDATE BankAccount
        SET balance = balance + @transfer_ammount
    WHERE AccountNumber = @CreditAccount

    IF @@ERROR<>0 or @@ROWCOUNT<>1
    BEGIN

        ROLLBACK TRANSACTION

        RAISERROR ('Either the credit account number is invalid ' +
```

```
                     'or an error occured',16,1)

     RETURN -1

   END

 COMMIT TRANSACTION

 RETURN 0
```

This is a valid transaction and would protect funds from being debited without being credited, but what would happen if the `@CreditAccount` number is invalid? While this doesn't generate an error, our check to `@@ROWCOUNT<>1` will pick up that no rows (or more than one row) have been updated causing the transaction to be rolled back. As part of this rollback of the previous update, the update to debit the funds is obviously also rolled back. What a waste of resources! While this is a simplistic example, imagine if we had 5, 10, or more data modification statements within our transaction which all had to be undone because the account number was not validated. A much better, more efficient method is to perform validation manually before entering into the transaction. This prevents us even getting started on modifying data if all the values passed don't stack up. So rewriting this example to be more efficient would give us:

```
IF NOT EXISTS
(
   SELECT AccountNumber
   FROM BankAccount
   WHERE AccountNumber=@DebitAccount
)
BEGIN

   RAISERROR ('The debit account number is invalid ',16,1)

   RETURN -1

END

IF NOT EXISTS
(
   SELECT AccountNumber
   FROM BankAccount
   WHERE AccountNumber=@CreditAccount
)
BEGIN

   RAISERROR ('The credit account number is invalid ',16,1)

   RETURN -1
END

BEGIN TRANSACTION

   UPDATE BankAccount
      SET balance = balance - @transfer_ammount
   WHERE AccountNumber = @DebitAccount

   IF @@ERROR<>0 or @@ROWCOUNT<>1
   BEGIN
```

```
        ROLLBACK TRANSACTION

        RAISERROR ('Either the debit account number is invalid '+
                ' or an error occured',16,1)
        RETURN -1
    END

    UPDATE BankAccount
        SET balance = balance + @transfer_ammount
    WHERE AccountNumber = @CreditAccount

    IF @@ERROR<>0 or @@ROWCOUNT<>1
    BEGIN

        ROLLBACK TRANSACTION

        RAISERROR ('Either the credit account number is invalid ' +
                'or an error occured',16,1)
        RETURN -1
    END

COMMIT TRANSACTION

RETURN 0
```

The keen of wit may be thinking that we now have unnecessary checking with the transaction, as we still have our original logic to check if a row is updated, even though we now check this before the transaction. However, we do actually need the logic within the scope of the transaction, and you should never remove it. Since an initial check of account numbers occurs outside the transaction there is a teeny-weeny chance that the account numbers could change between our initial checks and the actual account balance updates. Agreed, it's very unlikely, but you try being a bank that tells its customers they have a teeny-weeny chance of losing their money into a void, and see how successful you are. To the purists this may seem like duplication of code, but what you are actually ending up with is more efficient database processing by doing additional checks to ensure everything is valid before entering into a resource-costly transaction.

Preventing Deadlocks

As we have previously discussed, a deadlock occurs when two transactions are each trying to escalate the type of lock that the transaction holds, and each of these transactions is blocking the other from doing it. This is known as a **conversion deadlock**. To prevent these processes from blocking each other for eternity, SQL Server uses an algorithm to select one of the transactions to be killed. This may not happen instantaneously as SQL Server only periodically checks to see if any deadlocks have occurred. However they are usually discovered within seconds of occurring. Once one of the transactions has been killed, the remaining transaction can then escalate its locks and continue.

Deadlocks can also occur when you access objects in two transactions using a different order. This is known as a **cycle deadlock**. To illustrate how these occur, let's assume one transaction takes an exclusive lock on TABLEA and performs a modification, then takes an exclusive lock on TABLEB and performs another modification. A second transaction takes an exclusive lock on TABLEB and makes a change, then takes an exclusive lock on TABLEA and makes a change. Each of these transactions work fine independently, but imagine if these transactions occur in a highly concurrent environment where it would be possible for them to be executed at the same time. The following table shows the progress of these transactions if they happened to be executed at the same time:

Connection 1	Connection 2	SQL Server
BEGIN TRANSACTION		Begins a new user-defined transaction on Connection 1
	BEGIN TRANSACTION	Begins a new user-defined transaction on Connection 2
Requests exclusive lock on rows in range EmployeeID BETWEEN 1 AND 10 for the Employees table		Grants exclusive lock on the Employees table to Connection 1.
	Requests exclusive lock on rows in range EmployeeID BETWEEN 1 AND 10 for the Salaries table	Grants exclusive lock on the Salaries table to Connection 2.
Requests exclusive lock on rows in range EmployeeID BETWEEN 1 AND 10 for the Salaries table		Cannot grant exclusive lock on rows in Salaries table to Connection 1, as Connection 2 is still holding its exclusive lock on these rows in this table. Connection 1 is blocked from proceeding at this point.
	Requests exclusive lock on rows in range EmployeeID BETWEEN 1 AND 10 for the Employees table	Cannot grant exclusive lock on rows in Employees table to Connection 2, as Connection 1 is still holding its exclusive lock on these rows in this table. Connection 2 is blocked from proceeding at this point.
	Connection Killed	As both Connection 1 and Connection 2 are blocking each other from proceeding, once again we have transactions in a stalemate position. SQL Server does the humane thing and chooses one transaction to put out of its misery. For this example let's assume that Connection 2 is chosen to be killed.
Commits transaction	Transaction rolled back	Connection 1 completes successfully, while Connection 2 is rolled back to undo the changes it has made.

SQL Server uses an internal algorithm for deciding which transaction to kill. This generally calculates which transaction requires the least amount of effort to roll back and selects this one as the deadlock victim. You can influence which transaction SQL Server selects by setting the deadlock priority option, which we'll discuss shortly.

Deadlocks are the result of poor code design. There are no 'if's, 'but's, or 'maybe's about it. If you have transactions that are designed to work perfectly with all other transactions then deadlocks will not occur. In the real world this is an extremely difficult, if not impossible, thing to achieve especially when working with large development teams. However, there are best practices that can be used by developers to help reduce the likelihood of deadlocks occurring. These best practices include all best practices we have previously discussed, along with each of the following:

Document Object Access Order

An important process you should undertake in the design of your database is to document the order in which your objects must be accessed during transactions. This will go a long way to preventing cycle deadlocks from occurring.

If logic dictates that a transaction needs to access the objects in a different order than what you have documented, then the developer can build in pre-locking mechanisms to ensure that their code complies with your object access order policy. For example, if you policy states the Employees table must be modified before the Departments table, and the developer has a situation where the Departments table must be modified before the Employees table, they can use a hold lock to gather the necessary locks so that their code complies with the access order, such as:

```
BEGIN TRANSACTION

--Take and hold a SHARED lock on the Employees table by touching every
--row within the table, even though we don't require the use of these
--rows at this point. By specifying @NullVar=@NullVar we prevent an empty
--resultset being returned to our client application

DECLARE @NullVar INT
SELECT @NullVar=@NullVar FROM dbo.Employees WITH(HOLDLOCK)

UPDATE Departments

UPDATE Employees

COMMIT TRANSACTION
```

This SELECT statement, in conjunction with the HOLDLOCK hint, takes and holds shared locks on the Employees table, which prevents any other transaction from taking an exclusive lock on the table until after this transaction has completed.

Use UPDLOCK Hint

If you are retrieving data in a transaction, and you know you are going to modify this data later in the transaction, then specify an update lock hint with the initial retrieval. This is especially important if you are using an isolation level of REPEATABLE READ or above, as these isolation levels are particularly prone to lock conversion deadlocks. For example, open two Query Analyzer windows with connections to our HumanResources database.

In both Query Analyzer windows run the following T-SQL commands:

```
SET TRANSACTION ISOLATION LEVEL REPEATABLE READ

BEGIN TRANSACTION

CREATE TABLE TestTrans1
(
    IDCol       Int,
    VarCharCol  Varchar(255)
)
SELECT * FROM TestTrans1
```

Once this is done, run the following T-SQL command in both of these Query Analyzer windows.

```
UPDATE TestTrans1 SET IDCOL=IDCOL*3
```

Oops, one of these updates has just been killed with the following error message being returned.

Server: Msg 1205, Level 13, State 50, Line 1
Transaction (Process ID 60) was deadlocked on {lock} resources with another process and
has been chosen as the deadlock victim. Rerun the transaction.

As I said, it is really easy for deadlocks to occur when using REPEATABLE READ or above isolation levels. The correct way to write this transaction would have been:

```
SET TRANSACTION ISOLATION LEVEL REPEATABLE READ

BEGIN TRANSACTION

SELECT * FROM TestTrans1 WITH(UPDLOCK)
```

When we try to run this in the second Query Analyzer window, the second transaction is blocked at this point. Once the first transaction has completed then the second transaction will proceed.

Deadlock Priority Level

I consider the SET DEADLOCK PRIORITY command more of a band-aid to a deadlocking problem than a preventative measure you can take. This essentially makes a connection volunteer to be killed if a deadlock situation arises. While this may be an honorable thing to do, it is not actually doing anything to reduce the likelihood of deadlocks occurring.

Nonetheless, you should be aware of this if you are experiencing difficulties with deadlocks, and the syntax of this command is:

```
SET DEADLOCK PRIORITY LOW | NORMAL
```

However, be aware that this will be set for the entire connection and not just a specific command. Therefore all transactions you execute on this connection will run under the deadlock priority you set. If you only wish to set this for a particular command, then set it to LOW before the command, and make sure you set it back to NORMAL after the command has completed.

Summary

The aim of this chapter was to not only introduce SQL Server transactions, but also provide examples of, and insight into, how you can use transactions optimally in creating applications capable of supporting high numbers of concurrent users. To this end we have looked at:

- ❑ The nature of transactions, and why we use them

- ❑ The properties that a transaction must have to protect data consistency, namely atomicity, consistency, isolation, and durability

- ❑ How we can use transactions from SQL Server, through the use of the BEGIN, COMMIT, ROLLBACK, and SAVE TRANSACTION commands

- ❑ How we can use transactions in ADO.NET by utilizing the SqlTransaction object

- ❑ How transactions and locking are interrelated

- ❑ How locks are used to enforce the various transaction isolation levels

- ❑ Some best practice advice on writing transactions, namely to keep them brief, only use them when necessary, and include error handling in your coding

- ❑ Deadlock prevention, through the use of the HOLDLOCK and UPDLOCK hints, or the SET DEADLOCK PRIORITY command

Transactions, like so many database topics, are easy to use but hard to get right. The most important point I would like to make is that you should spend a reasonable amount of your development time designing how your transactions should be structured, detailing both the level of isolation and granularity that these transactions require. Spending time on this process will help you to write significantly better transactional code.

9

Component Services

In this chapter we will learn about the `System.EnterpriseServices` namespace and how to use it for distributed transactions, object pooling, and other COM+ features. The `System.EnterpriseServices` namespace takes advantage of COM+ behind the scenes. We will specifically explore the following topics:

❑ The nature of serviced components and the `System.EnterpriseServices` namespace.

❑ Creating a serviced component – we will follow through a detailed example of doing this.

❑ Creating a client application that uses a serviced component – again, we'll step through creating an example client for our example serviced component.

❑ Object pooling.

Let's begin by finding out exactly what is meant by a serviced component.

Serviced Components

You may or may not be familiar with **COM+**, also called **Component Services**, already. If COM+ is a new concept to you, then you may be wondering what a **serviced component** is. A serviced component is one that gets managed by a coordinating tool that will keep track of components across processes and machines.This can allow for more sophisticated applications in many cases. Take, for example, a scenario where you have multiple database updates that need to take place on different databases. Not only that, but you want them all to succeed or fail together as a unit. Since this requires a **distributed transaction**, in other words one that spans more than one system or process, then Component Services come into play. It provides you with the ability to create robust components that can be managed from outside a process or system boundary.

It is important to note that you should only use this functionality when you need it, as it will always cost an additional performance overhead. This is because there are extra costs associated with a resource manager having to keep track of activities going on across processes and to then commit or rollback all of those activities together as a unit.

In the .NET world, there is a `System.EnterpriseServices` namespace, which exposes all of the COM+ functionality to you in an easy-to-use fashion. In addition to distributed transactions there are several other COM+ features supported in .NET including:

❑ **Just-In-Time Activation** – This feature allows you to configure a component to have instances of itself kept active in a pool, and ready for use by any client that executes a method on the component. The client still holds an active reference to the object and when the client calls the method on the object, the object will be activated just-in-time. The creation (and deletion) of components takes time, so Just-In-Time (**JIT**) activation is a feature that allows a component to remain in memory, having been used once, in case another instance is required. JIT is frequently used in conjunction with **Object Pooling**, as discussed next.

❑ **Object Pooling** – Objects get pooled so they can be reused without overhead of constant recreation. The `ObjectPoolingAttribute` attribute determines how the pool will operate. When the pooled object is garbage collected by the CLR, it returns to the object pool. This raises a problem that there may be a delay between when the object is no longer needed and when the CLR garbage collects it. This can have a serious impact on the scalability and throughput of your application and can negate the benefits of object pooling. One way to solve this problem is to use JIT in conjunction with object pooling so the pooled object returns to the pool when every method call from the client completes.

❑ **Queued Components** -In standard component use, we invoke a method and wait for a response. Every method call is termed synchronous, since a further method isn't invoked until a response from the current method call is received. However, in the distributed computing world there will be times when it does not make sense to wait on a method call response, before moving on to the next task. Queued components are those where a method is invoked and processing continues, without waiting for a response to the call. This means that method calls can be made asynchronously. The means by which these asynchronous method calls are managed is **MSMQ** (**Microsoft Message Queue**), which will monitor the number of requests outstanding, the responses received, and so on.

❑ **Role-Based Security** – Security permissions can be applied based on role. You can enforce security for an application based on a flexible model of security roles that can be configured administratively, versus programmatically. In other words, you don't have to write security logic into your components when you use role-based security at the method level. Please see Chapter 11 for more on ways to implement roles, and security in general.

Now that you have a basic idea of what a serviced component is, let's look at how to actually build one in Visual Basic .NET.

Building Serviced Components

Taking advantage of COM+ features within .NET applications is very easy. As you already learned, by using the `System.EnterpriseServices` namespace, COM+ is used automatically behind the scenes. In this section, we will walk through the steps of creating a serviced component and we'll implement an example that uses distributed transactions. As you will see, you can easily adapt this to use object pooling or some other COM+ feature instead of, or in addition to, distributed transactions.

Creating Serviced Components

There are four key steps to creating a serviced component in Visual Basic .NET:

1. Creating one or more classes for the new assembly.

2. Assigning a **strong name** to the assembly.

3. Compiling the assembly.

4. Registering the assembly with Component Services.

Let's walk through each of those steps now.

Creating the Class for the New Assembly

The first step is to create a new project that will contain the code for your serviced component. In our case, we are going to create the most common type of assembly for a serviced component, which is a **Class Library**.

Select File | New | Project | Class Library, then specify a name (ServicedComponentDemo) and location and click the OK button. Rename Class1 in the code window to DemoComponentServices. Next, from the Project Explorer, select the Class1.vb file, right-click, and from the pop-up menu choose Rename. Change the filename from Class1.vb to ServicedComponentDemo.vb.

Before you can use any serviced component features, you must add a reference in your project to the System.EnterpriseServices namespace. To do so, select Project | Add Reference and add a reference to the System.EnterpriseServices namespace as shown in the graphic below:

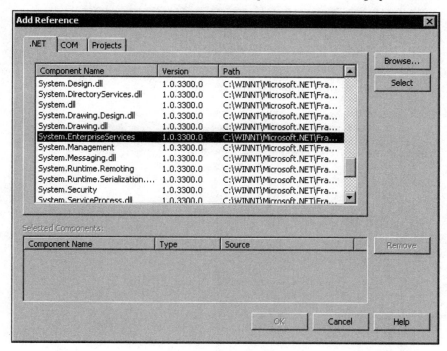

Now we are ready to add the code that contains the logic describing what we want our serviced component to do. In our case, we'll implement a function that will accept a Boolean as a parameter and attempt to update the database either once or twice, depending on the Boolean value passed in. If it attempts to update the database twice, then we will code it so that the second update will fail. This will demonstrate that both the first and second updates were not made in the event of an error, and that the transactions were all rolled back in such an instance.

Here is the complete code listing that you should add to your class module (in place of the existing empty class). We will walk through each section in more detail after the complete code listing:

```
Option Explicit On

Imports System.EnterpriseServices
Imports System.Reflection
Imports System.Data.SqlClient

<Assembly: AssemblyKeyFile("C:\YourAppPath\bin\ServicedComponentDemo.snk")>
<Assembly: ApplicationNameAttribute ("ServicedComponentDemo")>
<Assembly: Description("Serviced Component Demonstration")>

<Transaction(TransactionOption.Required)> Public Class DemoComponentServices
    Inherits ServicedComponent

    Public Function DemoTransactions(ByVal bCauseError As Boolean) As String

        'Add a new record to the payments table in our HR database

        Dim StatusMsg As String = "Transaction Not Attempted Yet"

        Dim strConnection As String = "Data Source=localhost; " _
            & "Initial Catalog=HumanResources;" _
            & "User Id=sa;Pwd=xxxxxx"

        Dim Conn As New SqlConnection(strConnection)

        Dim strSQL As String = "INSERT INTO dbo.Departments " & _
            "(Description) VALUES ('Management " & Now & "')"

        Dim cmd As New SqlCommand(strSQL, Conn)

            Try

                'Open the connection
                Conn.Open()

                'Insert the record into the database
                cmd.ExecuteNonQuery()

                'If the CauseError parameter is set to true,
                'demonstrate a failure because of a key violation
                'to show that the transaction fails.
                If bCauseError Then
```

```
                    'this statement will cause an error since you can't insert
                    'explicit value into identity column and because this is a
                    'string, not numeric.
                    strSQL = "INSERT INTO dbo.Departments (DepartmentId) " & _
                             "VALUES ('BadValue')"

                    cmd.CommandText = strSQL

                    'Attempt to insert the record.
                    'An error will occur on this line.
                    cmd.ExecuteNonQuery()

                End If

                    'Mark the transaction a success
                    ContextUtil.SetComplete()
                    StatusMsg = "Transaction Success"

            Catch e As Exception
                'Mark the transaction a failure
                ContextUtil.SetAbort()
                StatusMsg = "Transaction Failure"

            Finally

                'Cleanup code that needs to run no matter what

                'Close the connection
                Conn.Close()

            End Try

            Return StatusMsg
        End Function

    End Class
```

We begin by setting the `Option Explicit` option on, which requires all variables to be declared, and follow it with three `Imports` statements. Both the `System.EnterpriseServices` and `System.Reflection` namespaces are required for our serviced component. The `System.Reflection` namespace has classes and interfaces that allow you to determine information about an assembly, and dynamically invoke its types. It also provides you with the ability to add details to describe an assembly. In our example, we are using the `System.Reflection` namespace to describe the `AssemblyKeyFile` attribute. We will discuss this attribute momentarily. The `System.Data.SqlClient` namespace is being imported so that we can connect to SQL Server and update the database.

```
Option Explicit On

Imports System.EnterpriseServices
Imports System.Reflection
Imports System.Data.SqlClient
```

Next, we specify some details about the assembly, such as where the **key file** can be found, the name of the application, and the description. The key file is used as part of the encryption process. It is important to mention that encryption allows two parties to communicate with each other over an insecure channel while protecting the data integrity during transmission and ensuring that the data originated from the particular party. The key file is a file that contains keys for encryption and decryption of your assembly. A public key is made public and distributed widely whereas a private key is always kept secret. If the assembly is encrypted with the public key, it can only be decrypted with the private key. Or, if the assembly is encrypted with the private key it can only be decrypted with the public key. In a later step we will be assigning the assembly a strong name (which is a unique identifier of the assembly) and the `AssemblyKeyFile` setting specified below will let .NET know where to look for the required key when assigning that strong name.

```
<Assembly: AssemblyKeyFile("C:\YourAppPath\bin\ServicedComponentDemo.snk")>
<Assembly: ApplicationNameAttribute ("ServicedComponentDemo")>
<Assembly: Description ("Serviced Component Demonstration")>
```

The `ApplicationNameAttribute` is what the assembly will be called in the Component Services Tool and the `Description` attribute describes the component.

> *Note that these three assembly attributes above could also have been placed in the `AssemblyInfo.vb` file that Visual Studio .NET creates for you automatically. The advantage to putting these attributes in the `AssemblyInfo.vb` file is that you can list all assembly attributes in a common place, regardless of how many class modules you have in your solution. You would have to add an `Imports` statement to import the `System.EnterpriseServices` namespace in the `AssemblyInfo.vb` code for this to work. To keep our example simple, we are placing all of the code in a single class module but you can see an example of doing it the other way in our case study, Chapter 12.*

The `Class` declaration follows the `Assembly` attributes. Immediately preceding the `Class` declaration is where you place any attribute declarations to specify which Enterprise Services (and thus COM+) features you want to use. In our example, we have specified the `Transaction` attribute with the `Required` property. This indicates that a transaction is required when this component runs; if one already exists when this component is created, it will participate in that existing transaction; if one doesn't already exist it will be created.

```
<Transaction(TransactionOption.Required)> Public Class DemoComponentServices
```

These are the possible values for `TransactionOption`:

- ❑ `Disabled` – Ignore any transaction. The object never gets created in a Component Services (COM+) transaction. This is the default setting.

- ❑ `NotSupported` – Create the component without a transaction. The object is never created in any transaction.

- ❑ `Required` – Share a transaction if one already exists; create a new transaction if one doesn't already exist.

- ❑ `RequiresNew` – Create the component in a new transaction no matter what. The object requires a transaction and is created within a new transaction.

- ❑ `Supported` – Share a transaction if one already exists; create a new non-transacted component if one doesn't already exist.

After the `Class` declaration, we need an `Inherits` statement so we can inherit from the `ServicedComponent` base class. The `ServicedComponent` class is the base class for all COM+ services and is required when using serviced components in .NET.

```
Inherits ServicedComponent
```

Then, we have the code for our function to demonstrate the distributed transaction functionality. Notice that several variables are declared, such as the connection string, connection variable, and command object. Remember that you will need to set these to appropriate values for your own system.

```
Public Function DemoTransactions(ByVal bCauseError As Boolean) As String

    'Add a new record to the payments table in our HR database

    Dim StatusMsg As String = "Transaction Not Attempted Yet"

    Dim strConnection As String = "Data Source=localhost; " _
        & "Initial Catalog=HumanResources;" _
        & "User Id=sa;Pwd=xxxxxx"

    Dim Conn As New SqlConnection(strConnection)

    Dim strSQL As String = "INSERT INTO dbo.Departments " & _
        "(Description) VALUES ('Management " & Now & "')"

    Dim cmd As New SqlCommand(strSQL, Conn)
```

After the variable declarations, we get into the meat of our code, where the SQL statement to insert a record into the `Departments` table of our `HumanResources` database gets executed against the database:

```
    Try

        'Open the connection
        Conn.Open()

        'Insert the record into the database
        cmd.ExecuteNonQuery()
```

After executing the first `INSERT` statement, the second one gets executed if the `CauseError` Boolean is passed in as `True`. If the statement executes, it will generate an error and thus roll back the entire transaction, which includes rolling back the effect of both SQL statements.

```
        'If the CauseError parameter is set to true,
        'demonstrate a failure because of a key violation
        'to show that the transaction fails.
        If bCauseError Then

            'this statement will cause an error since you can't insert
            'explicit value into identity column and because this is a
            'string, not numeric.
            strSQL = "INSERT INTO dbo.Departments (DepartmentId) " & _
```

```
                    "VALUES ('BadValue')"

         cmd.CommandText = strSQL

         'Attempt to insert the record.
         'An error will occur on this line.
         cmd.ExecuteNonQuery()

    End If
```

If all goes well, we want to set the context to complete, so that the transaction will be committed. We also want to return a success to the calling function:

```
         'Mark the transaction a success
         ContextUtil.SetComplete()
         StatusMsg = "Transaction Success"
```

The ContextUtil class exists in the System.EnterpriseServices namespace and exposes the functionality to retrieve and modify the context of the serviced component, such as determining whether it is currently participating in a transaction or modifying its status to success or failure. The SetComplete method will mark the transaction as a success so that it will be committed. The SetAbort method will mark the transaction as a failure so that all of the SQL statements in the transaction will be rolled back. In our example, we placed the SetAbort code in the error handler because, if all does not go well, we want to abort the entire transaction and return a failure message:

```
     Catch e As Exception
         'Mark the transaction a failure
         ContextUtil.SetAbort()
         StatusMsg = "Transaction Failure"
```

The Finally section contains the code that we want to run in either case, such as for closing the database connection:

```
     Finally

         'Cleanup code that needs to run no matter what

         'Close the connection
         Conn.Close()

     End Try
```

The last portion of code returns the StatusMsg string value back to the calling routine to indicate success or failure:

```
         Return StatusMsg
    End Function

End Class
```

Note that if you prefer to have Visual Basic.NET automatically handle the SetCompletes and SetAborts for you, there is an <AutoComplete()> attribute you can specify to turn this functionality on. This means that as long as an exception isn't encountered in the function, SetComplete will be called automatically. In the event of an exception, SetAbort will be called automatically. When you don't want to have to explicitly set SetComplete and SetAbort, you can enable the AutoComplete feature. In most cases it is better to explicitly commit or abort, but in the event that you need the commits and aborts to be handled for you, the functionality is available. Here is an example of how you might enable this functionality for a given function or procedure:

```
<AutoComplete()> Public Function DemoTransactions() As String
```

<AutoComplete()> is used in our case study, Chapter 12.

Assigning a Strong Name To the Assembly

Now that we have created the code for the Serviced Component, we need to assign a strong name to the assembly. A strong name for an assembly provides details about the assembly, such as its name, version, and public key. Recall from earlier in this chapter that the public and private keys allow encryption and decryption to take place in a manner that helps protect the data and to verify its origin. A component that runs as a serviced component is required to have a strong name and to thus be associated with a public key as well.

> Make sure to save all of your changes in the project. Note that at this point we haven't yet compiled the assembly.

Next, we are going to use a command line-tool to generate a strong key. You can open a command window by selecting the Start | Programs | Microsoft Visual Studio.NET 7.0 | Visual Studio.NET Tools | Visual Studio.NET Command Prompt menu. Alternatively you can select Start | Run and type Cmd in the box.

Once this command window has opened, you then need to move to the directory where you want the strong name key to be created (in our example it is the Bin directory of our project). Execute the strong name utility (sn.exe) and create a key called ServicedComponentDemo.snk for the ServicedComponentDemo project. If you're writing software for a company, the company would most likely want to have their own strong key so that all code can be marked as from that company or department, as appropriate. In this example, we're just creating the strong name for a specific application, and can generate the key by running the following code in the command window:

```
Sn -k "ServicedComponentDemo.snk"
```

If you get an error about it not recognizing the sn program, then you may need to type the explicit path where it is located, from the directory where you want the file created, which should be similar to that shown below:

```
"C:\Program Files\Microsoft Visual Studio .Net\FrameworkSDK\bin\sn.exe" -k
"ServicedComponentDemo.snk"
```

The -k option generates a new key file, which is created in the directory specified after the -k option. After executing the strong name utility, you should get similar results to the following:

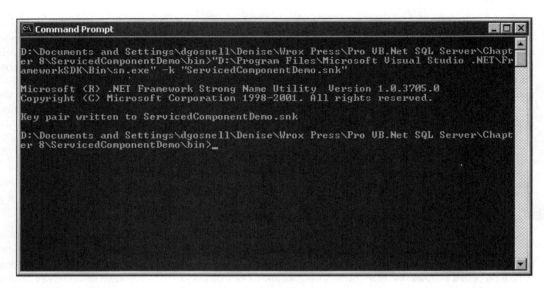

Notice that a message appears indicating that the key pair was written to the ServicedComponentDemo.snk file. Type the directory (dir) command to verify that this file was indeed created in the current directory:

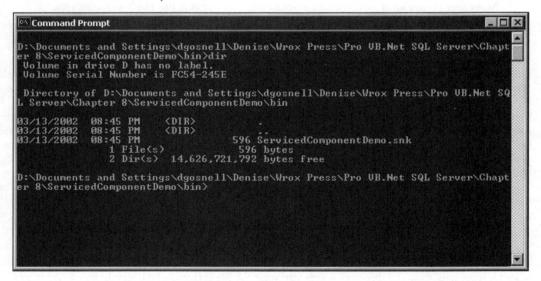

Make sure to keep the command window open but minimized, as you will need to use it again in the next step. Now that we have created the key pair to be used to sign the assembly, let's move on to the actual compilation of the assembly.

Compiling the Assembly

Return to your Visual Studio project and save all of your changes if you have not done so already. Select Build | Build Solution to create the assembly. If the build was successful, and it was able to associate the strong name key you created with the assembly, then you will get the following results in your output window:

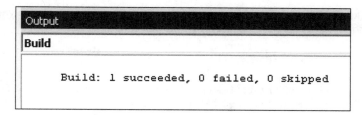

If the build failed, one possible reason is if the key file you specified in the AssemblyKeyFile attribute did not exist. To verify that the DLL indeed got created, maximize your command window and execute a directory listing command against the Bin directory. You should see something like the following:

```
Command Prompt                                                          _ □ X
D:\Documents and Settings\dgosnell\Denise\Wrox Press\Pro VB.Net SQL Server\Chapt
er 8\ServicedComponentDemo\bin>dir
 Volume in drive D has no label.
 Volume Serial Number is FC54-245E

 Directory of D:\Documents and Settings\dgosnell\Denise\Wrox Press\Pro VB.Net SQ
L Server\Chapter 8\ServicedComponentDemo\bin

03/13/2002  08:59 PM    <DIR>          .
03/13/2002  08:59 PM    <DIR>          ..
03/13/2002  08:59 PM             8,192 ServicedComponentDemo.dll
03/13/2002  08:59 PM            13,824 ServicedComponentDemo.pdb
03/13/2002  08:45 PM               596 ServicedComponentDemo.snk
               3 File(s)         22,612 bytes
               2 Dir(s)  14,626,148,352 bytes free

D:\Documents and Settings\dgosnell\Denise\Wrox Press\Pro VB.Net SQL Server\Chapt
er 8\ServicedComponentDemo\bin>_
```

Notice that we now have three files in the directory, the dll, pdb, and snk files. Keep the command window open, as you will need it one more time.

Registering the Assembly with Component Services

The next step is to register the assembly with Component Services, which is a resource manager that manages serviced components. This is not a required step but is highly recommended. When I say it is not required, I mean that if you do not do this, Visual Basic .NET will register the component with Component Services for you automatically the first time it runs. You sometimes hear this called **Lazy Registration**. The reason this is not recommended is because you don't get as much control over how and when the component gets registered. For example, if you want to correct any component registration errors before a client first uses the component, then you would want to manually register it to ensure there are no errors. Another example of where lazy registration will not work is if the serviced component is being called from unmanaged code. In such cases, you must manually register the component with Component Services.

Let's go ahead and register the assembly ourselves so we have more flexibility. To do so, first maximize your command window and navigate to the Bin directory where your project is saved. If you still have the command window from before open, you should still be in the Bin directory.

We are going to use the `RegSvcs` tool of the .NET Framework to register the assembly with Component Services. To do so, from your project directory, type the following command:

```
RegSvcs ServicedComponentDemo.Dll
```

If an error is thrown stating that it has not been possible to find `RegSvcs`, then you will need to use the complete path, which should look something like the following:

```
"C:\WINDOWS\Microsoft.NET\Framework\v1.0.3705\RegSvcs.exe"
ServicedComponentDemo.Dll
```

or alter your `PATH` environment variable to include the directory where `RegSvcs` is located.

After executing the `RegSvcs` command, you should see results similar to the following indicating that the assembly was installed with Component Services:

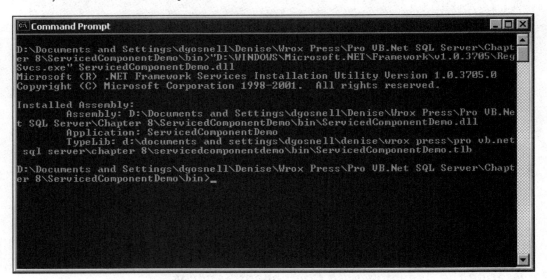

Note that you could have specified a different name for it to be identified within Component Services, by specifying an additional command-line parameter as shown below.

```
RegSvcs ServicedComponentDemo.Dll ServicedComponentDemoApp
```

> **Note that registering the assembly will fail if you didn't previously give the assembly a strong name.**

In the event that you need to uninstall the assembly from Component Services, you can execute the following command:

```
RegSvcs /u ServicedComponentDemo.Dll
```

Assuming you received a message indicating your assembly was installed, we next need to verify that it was indeed added to Component Services. Open your Control Panel and select the **Administrative Tools | Component Services** menu, in order to open up the Component Services Management Console.

Navigate through the tree to see the nodes under the computer you installed the component on, and then see if you can locate it under COM+ applications as shown below:

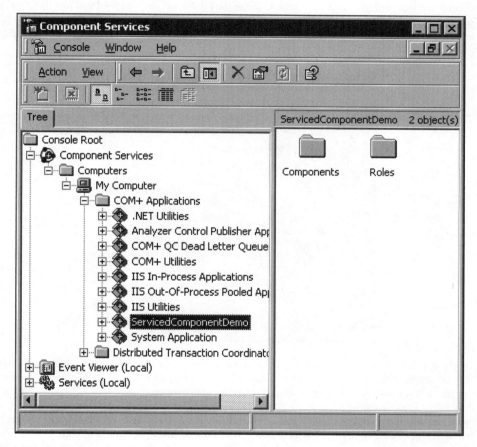

As you can see our `ServicedComponentDemo` serviced component has been created and registered successfully. If you compare the properties for the application as shown in Component Services with the attributes specified in the class, you will see that they are the same. Now that we have created our serviced component, we need to create a test client application that will make use of it.

Creating the Client Component

Select **File | Close Solution** to close the other solution you already have open. Then, select **File | New | Project | Windows Application**, specify a name (`ServicedComponentClientDemo`) and path where you want it saved and click the **OK** button, in order to create the new Windows Application project.

In Solution Explorer, rename Form1.vb to Main.vb. In the properties for Main.vb, change the Name property to Main and the Text property to Serviced Component Client Demo. Also, highlight the project name (not the Solution) and right-click to view its **Properties**. Make sure that Main is set as the startup form (and not Form1 or Sub Main).

Now, we are ready to place a few controls on the form. From the toolbox, drag and drop two command buttons and one label control on to the form. Change the **Name** property of the label to lblResults and the **Text** property to Results Will Go Here. Change the Text properties of the two buttons to Run and Run and Cause Error, and set their Name properties to btnRun and btnError, respectively. At this point, the form should look similar to that shown below:

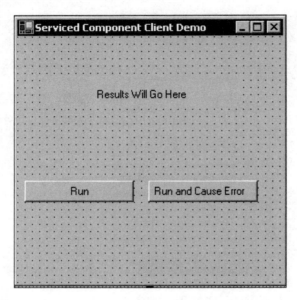

We are going to have the Run button call our component and pass a False value so that it will only run the first INSERT statement. Under the **Run and Cause Error** button, we will call our component and pass a True value so that it will generate an error and abort the entire transaction.

Before we can add the code to call our component, we need to add two references. The first reference is to the System.EnterpriseServices namespace, while the second reference is to your ServicedComponentDemo assembly created in the previous steps. You can add these references by simply selecting **Project | Add Reference**. Note that your assembly will not be in the list that you see when the dialog box opens, since it is not in the global assembly cache. To locate the ServicedComponentDemo.dll file, you should click the **Browse** button and browse to the Bin directory of your ServicedComponentDemo project, as shown opposite:

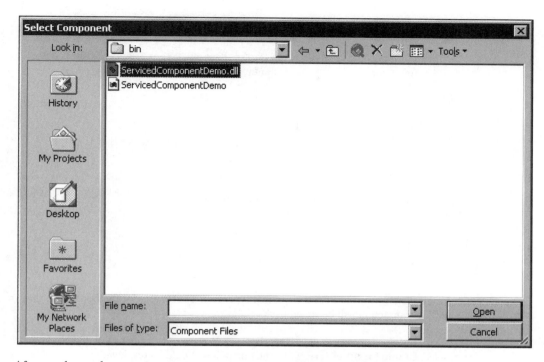

After you locate the ServicedComponentDemo.dll file, click the **Open** button. The ServicedComponentDemo.dll will now be listed as the **Selected Component**. Click the **OK** button to add a reference to your serviced component to the client project.

Next, place the following code under the click event for btnRun:

```
Private Sub btnRun_Click(ByVal sender As System.Object, ByVal e As _
        System.EventArgs) Handles btnRun.Click

    lblResults.Text = "Results Will Go Here"

    'Declare the serviced component
    Dim objDemo As New ServicedComponentDemo.DemoComponentServices()

    Dim blnCauseError As Boolean = False

    'Execute the component
    lblResults.Text = objDemo.DemoTransactions(blnCauseError)

    objDemo = Nothing

End Sub
```

The code above will declare a new instance of your serviced component, call the DemoTransactions method with a False value, and will then display the return value in the label on the form to indicate the success or failure.

Place the following code under the click event for the btnError:

```
Private Sub btnError_Click(ByVal sender As System.Object, ByVal e As _
        System.EventArgs) Handles btnError.Click

    lblResults.Text = "Results Will Go Here"

    'Declare the serviced component
    Dim objDemo As New ServicedComponentDemo.DemoComponentServices()

    Dim blnCauseError As Boolean = True

    'Execute the component and generate an error
    lblResults.Text = objDemo.DemoTransactions(blnCauseError)

    objDemo = Nothing

End Sub
```

This code works in the same way other than the fact that it passes a True value for the Boolean so that an error will occur and the transaction will be rolled back.

Save and build your project by selecting **Build | Build Project**. We are now ready to test and see how it works. To do so, select **Debug | Start**. A screen like the one below should be displayed:

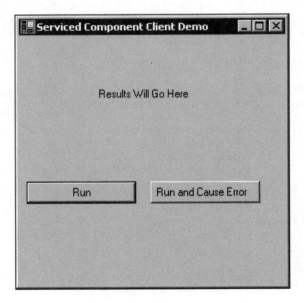

If you click the Run button, you should get a Transaction Success message, as you can see below:

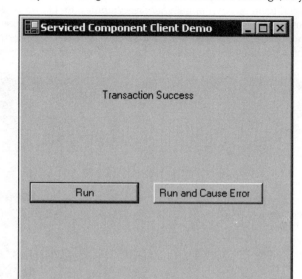

At this point, if you open your underlying database and view the Departments table, you should see that your record just got inserted for the description of the department. Next, click the Run and Cause Error button. You should get a Transaction Failure message as shown below:

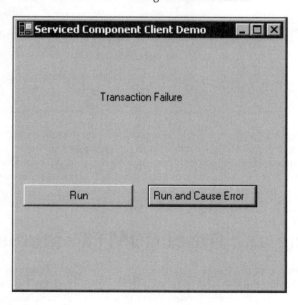

After clicking this button, the serviced component was called and attempted to run both INSERT statements. When the second INSERT statement failed, the transaction was aborted.

If you would like to verify that your component really is running under the control of the Component Services resource manager, open the Component Services graphical tool again by going into your Control Panel and selecting **Administrative Tools | Component Services**. Navigate in the hierarchy until you find the **Distributed Transaction Coordinator**. If you click on the **Transaction Statistics** node under **Distributed Transaction Coordinator**, you will see a window similar to the following:

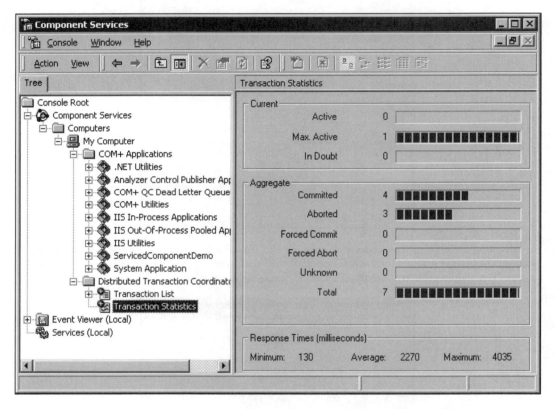

This window will tell you how many components are active at the present moment, how many transactions have been committed, how many were aborted, and so on. Open up your test client program and run it a few more times and watch these numbers change. That is your proof that your component is running under a transaction manager. Now that we have learned how to create a serviced component using transactions, let's learn about how easy it is to modify the code for other COM+ features.

Object Pooling and Other COM+ Features

We learned at the beginning of this chapter that there are several COM+ features supported in Visual Basic .NET. Regardless of which of these features you want to use, you follow the basic steps in this chapter to create the serviced component and a client component that uses it. You can also monitor and view settings using the Component Services graphical tool.

Let's look at a simple example to see how easy it is to add other features to a serviced component. Suppose you want to take advantage of **object pooling**, which will maintain a pool of objects and activate them whenever required and deactivate them when no longer needed. By pooling objects, there is no need to recreate objects over and over again, which can reduce the performance overhead of object creation. Objects that are expensive to create are good candidates for object pooling, because those objects will be maintained in the pool and will be made quickly available when needed. This can improve your application's performance, even drastically in some situations. Implementing object pooling is very similar to implementing transactions like we've looked at throughout this chapter. You start by adding the `ObjectPoolingAttribute` to your class. After adding this attribute, you can then set the object pooling properties of a serviced component: `CreationTimeOut`, `Enabled`, `MinPoolSize`, and `MaxPoolSize`. Each of these properties is described below:

- ❑ `CreationTimeOut` – The length of time, in milliseconds, to wait for an object to become available in the pool before an exception should be raised.

- ❑ `Enabled` – Whether object pooling is enabled.

- ❑ `MinPoolSize` – The minimum number of objects that will be maintained in the pool and ready for activation.

- ❑ `MaxPoolSize` – The maximum number of objects that will be maintained in the pool.

Once a component is marked as a pooled object, COM+ will call the `Activate`, `Deactivate`, and `CanBePooled` methods of the serviced component's base class. The `Activate` and `Deactivate` methods are used to perform the appropriate initialization and cleanup of the pooled object. The `CanBePooled` method allows you to designate whether or not your object can be pooled.

To take advantage of object pooling in the example we already created, all you would have to do is modify the class declaration to add the object pooling attribute. Here is an example of how that might look:

```
<Transaction(TransactionOption.Required), ObjectPoolingAttribute (5, 10)> _
    Public Class DemoComponentServices
```

In the above example, the `MinPoolSize` is set to 5 and the `MaxPoolSize` is set to 10. This means that 5 objects will be kept in the pool at all times and that no more than 10 will be kept at any one time. These settings should vary based on how many clients you expect to use the component at a given time. One possible approach is to set the `MinPoolSize` to the average number of clients you expect to need the component at a given time and the `MaxPoolSize` to the maximum number you ever expect to need the component.

Next, add the following methods to your serviced component:

```
Protected Overrides Sub Activate()

    'add code here that you want to run when the
    'component is activated (such as initialization code).

End Sub

Protected Overrides Function CanBePooled() As Boolean
```

```
            'set the CanBePooled attribute to true
        Return True

    End Function

    Protected Overrides Sub Deactivate()

            'add code here that you want to run when
            'the component is deactivated.

    End Sub
```

By adding this simple attribute to the Class declaration and assigning the CanBePooled property to True, your object will now be pooled. Any code that you inserted in the Activate and Deactivate methods will run when each object is activated and deactivated, respectively.

To complete the revision of our example to use object pooling, save and recompile the serviced component by selecting Build | Build Solution. Unregister the prior component as described in the *Registering the Assembly with Component Services* section. Then, rerun the registration step to register this newly compiled component with Component Services. Finally, open and run your client application and test to see if you can notice any difference in the application's performance when you click between the Run and the Run and Cause Error options. With such a simple example, you may not notice any difference in performance visually. With larger applications where the object is very resource consuming, you would be more likely to notice a significant difference in performance.

Implementing the other COM+ features is very similar, since it is basically a matter of adding the relevant attributes to the class declaration and setting their properties.

Summary

In this chapter, we explored the world of serviced components and learned how to create one from scratch. At this point, you should know:

❑   What a serviced component is

❑   The role that the System.EnterpriseServices namespace plays in serviced components

❑   How to create a serviced component

❑   How to implement transactions in a serviced component

❑   How to use the Component Services graphical tool to verify installation and monitor statistics

❑   How to implement object pooling in a serviced component

You got to see firsthand how using the System.EnterpriseServices namespace in .NET allows you to implement nearly any COM+ feature.

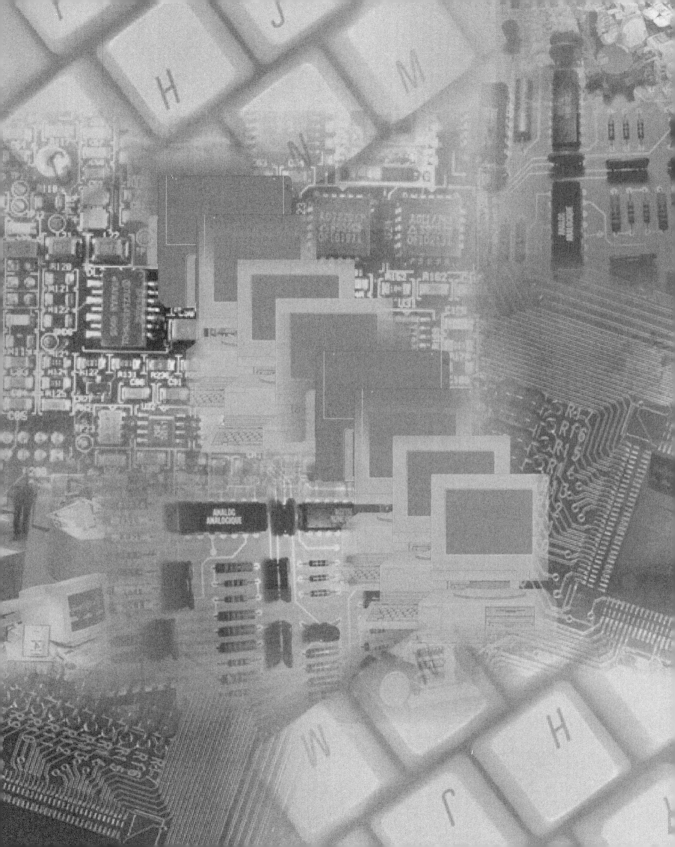

10

SQL Server and XML

XML has fast become the *de facto* standard for any form of inter-application communication and, since the release of SQL Server 2000, interacting with the database directly using XML has been possible. There are many means by which you can utilize SQL Server via XML, and we have seen some of the simpler ones in earlier chapters, such as SELECT FOR XML AUTO and the ClientSideXML property of the .NET SqlXmlCommand managed class.

In this chapter we describe some of the more advanced methods, so you can make an informed choice when assessing whether or not XML will meet your needs for particular purposes.

More specifically, within this chapter we will be discussing:

❑   Using the FOR XML EXPLICIT clause

❑   Some of the inherent problems associated with FOR XML EXPLICIT

❑   Transforming XML using XSL and the SqlXmlCommand .NET managed class

❑   Creating and using Stored Procedure Web Services with SQLXML 3.0

Let's begin this chapter with an in-depth look at FOR XML EXPLICIT.

> *Note that throughout this chapter we use the following terms to describe the different parts of an XML document:*

```
<ELEMENT Attribute="Attribute Value">Element Value</ELEMENT>
```

FOR XML EXPLICIT

In Chapter 5 we described how we could use the FOR XML AUTO option as part of our SELECT query to return an XML stream to our client application instead of a standard resultset. The format of the XML structure generated by FOR XML AUTO is automatically determined by SQL Server based on the tables you use in your SELECT statement, the way in which the tables are joined, and the order of columns that you specify in the SELECT list.

While this is a relatively easy option to use, it doesn't give us a great deal of control over the resulting XML structure. We may need the XML document to be structured in a particular way so that it can be integrated with other applications, perhaps requiring columns from one of our database tables to map to different elements within our XML document. For example, with our Employees and Departments tables we could produce a basic parent-child hierarchy by using a FOR XML AUTO clause in a simple SQL query:

```
SELECT   Employees.EmployeeID,
         Employees.FirstName,
         Employees.Surname,
         Departments.DepartmentID,
         Departments.Description
FROM    Employees
INNER JOIN Departments ON Employees.Department=Departments.DepartmentID
FOR XML AUTO
```

This query would produce the following XML document:

```
<Employees EmployeeID="1" FirstName="Robin" Surname="Johnson">
  <Departments DepartmentID="1" Description="Personnel"/>
</Employees>
<Employees EmployeeID="2" FirstName="Denise" Surname="Samson">
  <Departments DepartmentID="1" Description="Personnel"/>
</Employees>
<Employees EmployeeID="3" FirstName="Jack" Surname="Jones">
  <Departments DepartmentID="2" Description="Orders"/>
</Employees>
...
```

However, it would not be possible to use the FOR XML AUTO option if we wanted to use the same underlying database tables to create a vastly different XML document such as:

```
<Employee>
  <EmployeeID>1</EmployeeID>
  <FirstName>Robin</FirstName>
  <Surname>Johnson</Surname>
  <Department>Personnel</Department>
</Employee>
<Employee>
  <EmployeeID>2</EmployeeID>
  <FirstName>Denise</FirstName>
  <Surname>Samson</Surname>
  <Department>Personnel</Department>
```

```
</Employee>
<Employee>
  <EmployeeID>3</EmployeeID>
  <FirstName>Jack</FirstName>
  <Surname>Jones</Surname>
  <Department>Orders</Department>
</Employee>
...
```

To build such complex XML structures from our SELECT queries we can use the FOR XML EXPLICIT option instead. This is a much more complicated command than FOR XML AUTO because you must explicitly specify how the resultset is converted to XML, but along with this complexity comes a great deal of power and control. In using a FOR XML EXPLICIT clause the syntax is similar to that of FOR XML AUTO:

```
SELECT column_list FROM table_name FOR XML EXPLICIT
```

However, the way in which the query is constructed is usually vastly different to the FOR XML AUTO equivalent, since FOR XML EXPLICIT takes the resultset from our SELECT query and converts it to XML. Having the resultset in the correct format required by FOR XML EXPLICIT is the key to getting a correctly formatted XML document created. For this reason it is common to develop queries without specifying the FOR XML EXPLICIT clause initially. This allows the developer to concentrate on getting the resultset logic correct and is very useful for debugging purposes. Once this has been done, FOR XML EXPLICIT can be added to ensure the actual XML is created as we planned.

The resultset that is converted to XML using the FOR XML EXPLICIT option must be structured appropriately both horizontally (using columns) and vertically (using rows) with the following requirements:

❑ Every attribute to be contained within the XML document must have a column within the resultset.

❑ Every element that doesn't contain attributes within the XML document must have at least one column in the resultset.

❑ Every occurrence of an element in the XML document must have a corresponding row within the resultset.

❑ The first two columns in the resultset must be TAG and PARENT. These are special columns, which we'll discuss shortly.

These requirements allow the overall structure of the XML document to be highly customizable and the formatting of this document can be controlled in three ways:

❑ By using the TAG and PARENT columns to define element hierarchy within the XML document.

❑ Ordering the resultset to ensure the correct parent-child relationship between appropriate elements.

❑ Using column name mappings to associate the appropriate values with XML attributes or element values.

Each of these controls must be specified appropriately for the XML document to be created correctly. If they aren't then the FOR XML EXPLICIT clause is likely to cause an error and you won't get any XML at all.

Most of the examples we present in this section will relate to the following XML document derived from our HumanResources database. While this is a simple XML document that could be produced using the FOR XML AUTO option, we will use it in drawing comparisons between these two methods.

```
<Departments>
    <Department DepartmentID="1" Name="Personnel">
        <Employee EmployeeID="1" FirstName="Robin" Surname="Johnson"/>
        <Employee EmployeeID="2" FirstName="Denise" Surname="Samson"/>
    </Department>
    <Department DepartmentID="2" Name="Orders">
        <Employee EmployeeID="3" FirstName="Jack" Surname="Jones"/>
    </Department>
    <Department DepartmentID="3" Name="Stock Control">
        <Employee EmployeeID="4" FirstName="John" Surname="Doe"/>
    </Department>
</Departments>
```

We begin by discussing how the resultsets need to be structured for successful conversion to XML.

Resultset Structure

For every resultset that you wish to convert to an XML structure using FOR XML EXPLICIT, you must specify both a TAG and a PARENT column. These are both integer columns and are used by SQL Server to position elements in the resulting XML document structure.

The TAG value is a unique number per element (not per instance of an element, just per element) that we define, which allows an element to be positioned within the XML document structure. For example, as each of the following XML elements are unique within the XML document they all require a unique TAG value to be specified in the resultset to be converted into XML.

```
<ELEMENT_A>              <--! Unique Tag value -->
    <ELEMENT_B>          <--! Unique Tag value -->
        <ELEMENT_C/>     <--! Unique Tag value -->
    </ELEMENT_B>
</ELEMENT_A>
```

Multiple occurrences of an element within the XML document do not require a unique TAG number; all occurrences use the same TAG number in the resultset. For example, while the <ELEMENT_A>, <ELEMENT_B>, and <ELEMENT_C> elements would each require a unique TAG value in the resultset, each occurrence of the <ELEMENT_C> element would use the same TAG value.

```
<ELEMENT_A>
    <ELEMENT_B>
        <ELEMENT_C/>     <--! All occurrences have the same tag value -->
        <ELEMENT_C/>     <--! All occurrences have the same tag value -->
        <ELEMENT_C/>     <--! All occurrences have the same tag value -->
        <ELEMENT_C/>     <--! All occurrences have the same tag value -->
    </ELEMENT_B>
</ELEMENT_A>
```

To define an element's position in the XML document the TAG value is referenced from the second column we have mentioned, the PARENT column. The PARENT column contains a value that relates to a TAG value of another XML element that will serve as the parent for this current element. Let's look at an example to explain this.

```
<ELEMENT_A>        <--! TAG=1 and PARENT=Null -->
    <ELEMENT_B/>   <--! TAG=2 and PARENT=1 -->
</ELEMENT_A>
```

Don't worry about how the TAG and PARENT values relate to the actual name of the element at the moment, as we will come back to this later in the chapter. What we are discussing here is how the TAG and PARENT values represent the desired hierarchal structure of the XML document. Obviously XML documents can be considerably more structured than the previous examples, but the basic parent-child relationship described above still applies. For example:

```
<ELEMENT_A>              <-- TAG=1 and PARENT=Null -->
    <ELEMENT_B>          <-- TAG=2 and PARENT=1 -->
       <ELEMENT_C/>      <-- TAG=3 and PARENT=2 -->
    </ELEMENT_B>
    <ELEMENT_B>          <-- TAG=2 and PARENT=1 -->
        <ELEMENT_C/>     <-- TAG=3 and PARENT=2 -->
        <ELEMENT_C/>     <-- TAG=3 and PARENT=2 -->
            <ELEMENT_D/> <-- TAG=4 and PARENT=3 -->
            <ELEMENT_E/> <-- TAG=5 and PARENT=3 -->
            <ELEMENT_F/> <-- TAG=6 and PARENT=3 -->
        </ELEMENT_C>
    </ELEMENT_B>
    <ELEMENT_B/>         <-- TAG=2 and PARENT=1 -->
</ELEMENT_A>
```

Now if we take the XML sample generated from our HumanResources database that we introduced at the beginning of this chapter, and (ignoring the attribute values for the time being) associate the XML elements with appropriate TAG and PARENT values we see the following:

```
<Departments>         <-- TAG=1 and PARENT=Null -->
    <Department>      <-- TAG=2 and PARENT=1 -->
       <Employee/>    <-- TAG=3 and PARENT=2 -->
       <Employee/>    <-- TAG=3 and PARENT=2 -->
    </Department>
    <Department>      <-- TAG=2 and PARENT=1 -->
       <Employee/>    <-- TAG=3 and PARENT=2 -->
    </Department>
    <Department>      <-- TAG=3 and PARENT=2 -->
       <Employee/>    <-- TAG=3 and PARENT=2 -->
    </Department>
</Departments>
```

While each of the various elements may exist many times within the XML, the actual number of XML elements does not change the fact that there are still only three element levels throughout the entire XML document.

Ordering

What becomes apparent, when looking at the TAG and PARENT relationship, is that there is a third factor that is also holding information relating to the XML structure. Let's zoom in on a section of our example XML:

```
<Departments>
    <Department DepartmentID="1" Name="Personnel">
        <Employee EmployeeID="1" FirstName="Robin" Surname="Johnson"/>
        <Employee EmployeeID="2" FirstName="Denise" Surname="Samson"/>
    </Department>
    <Department DepartmentID="2" Name="Orders">
        <Employee EmployeeID="3" FirstName="Jack" Surname="Jones"/>
    </Department>
```

We can see that we have three levels of elements in this XML document. Not only that, but we see that the first <Department> element has two child elements:

```
<Department DepartmentID="1" Name="Personnel">
    <Employee EmployeeID="1" FirstName="Robin" Surname="Johnson" />
    <Employee EmployeeID="2" FirstName="Denise" Surname="Samson" />
```

The next <Department> element on the other hand has one child element.

```
<Department DepartmentID="2" Name="Orders">
        <Employee EmployeeID="3" FirstName="Jack" Surname="Jones" />
```

Even though the three child elements are at the same level in the XML document's hierarchy, they are also logically dependent on (or related to) their specific parent element.

So how do we represent this relationship in a resultset format? FOR XML EXPLICIT requires the resultset to be ordered in such a way that each row (remember a row represents each occurrence of an element) follows the row which will be converted into its parent element in the resulting XML document. The following rules relate to how element relationships are created using the TAG, PARENT, and ordering information:

❑ If the PARENT value of the next row in the resultset is equal to the current row's TAG value, then the current element is left open and subsequent elements are created as child elements.

❑ An open element remains open for all subsequent rows in the resultset until a row specifies a PARENT value of an element higher in the XML hierarchy than this open element (or the PARENT value is NULL).

❑ The PARENT value must be the TAG value of an element that is currently open. Setting the PARENT value to the TAG value of an element that is considered closed will generate an error.

❑ When FOR XML EXPLICIT reaches the end of the resultset all open elements are closed.

So if we represent the structure of the example XML above in resultset form, showing the action that would be taken when FOR XML EXPLICIT interpreted the TAG and PARENT column values for each row of the resultset in turn, we see the following:

Tag	Parent	Parent column Evaluation	Action
1		Is Null.	Create and open a new element.
2	1	Equals previous rows TAG	Create and open a new child element of the previous element.
3	2	Equals previous rows TAG	Create and open a new child element of the previous element.
3	2	Equals TAG of higher element	Close previous element and create a new element as a child of the TAG=2 element.
2	1	Equals TAG of higher element	Close previous element and create a new element as child of the TAG=1 element.
3	2	Equals previous rows TAG	Create and open a new child element of the previous element.

Alternatively, we can map our sample XML to this same TAG and PARENT structure showing the actual XML elements corresponding to each action:

Tag	Parent	Corresponding XML Element
1		<Departments>
2	1	<Department DepartmentID="1" Name="Personnel">
3	2	<Employee EmployeeID="1" . . ./>
3	2	<Employee EmployeeID="2" . . ./>
2	1	<Department DepartmentID="2" Name="Orders">
3	2	<Employee EmployeeID="3".../>

If we look at two sections of this resultset we can see how the order of the resultset is now relevant. In our first section we have our first set of parent-child elements represented here:

2	1	<Department DepartmentID="1" Name="Personnel">
3	2	<Employee EmployeeID="1" .../>
3	2	<Employee EmployeeID="2" .../>

While in our second section another set of parent child elements is represented:

2	1	<Department DepartmentID="2" Name="Orders">
3	2	<Employee EmployeeID="3" .../>

341

The interesting point, though it's somewhat difficult to come to terms with, is that we cannot create this ordering simply by specifying the TAG and PARENT columns in an ORDER BY clause. An ORDER BY PARENT ASC, TAG ASC statement would produce a resultset in the following format:

Tag	Parent	Corresponding XML Element
1		<Departments>
2	1	<Department DepartmentID="1" Name="Personnel">
2	1	<Department DepartmentID="2" Name="Orders">
3	2	<Employee EmployeeID="1" .../>
3	2	<Employee EmployeeID="2" .../>
3	2	<Employee EmployeeID="3" .../>

Converting this to the full XML document format would produce:

```
<Departments>
    <Department DepartmentID="1" Name="Personnel"/>
    <Department DepartmentID="2" Name="Orders">
        <Employee EmployeeID="1" FirstName="Robin" Surname="Johnson"/>
        <Employee EmployeeID="2" FirstName="Denise" Surname="Samson"/>
        <Employee EmployeeID="3" FirstName="Jack" Surname="Jones"/>
    </Department>
```

This is obviously not our desired output. We need to ORDER BY some other columns within the resultset to achieve the correct XML structure. These will be other columns that we'll include within the resultset, and we'll come back to them again shortly.

Attributes and Element Values

We are beginning to understand how we must form our resultset so that it is converted to XML with the correct hierarchal structure using FOR XML EXPLICIT. Now we need to discuss how we populate the elements and attributes of this XML document with actual data from our database.

As we have mentioned the way FOR XML EXPLICIT works is that each of the element attributes requires a column within the resultset, effectively flattening out the XML structure horizontally. From this flat structure we need to tell FOR XML EXPLICIT which element, and which attribute within this element, the column value will be used to populate. We do this by naming the columns in our resultset using a special mapping format understood by FOR XML EXPLICIT.

This column name mapping has the following format:

```
ElementName!TagNumber!AttributeName!Directive
```

We will take a look at each part of this column identifier separately. The ElementName is used to specify the name of the element that this particular column will map to. For example, if we take our sample XML once again:

```
<Departments>
   <Department DepartmentID="1" Name="Personnel">
      <Employee EmployeeID="1" FirstName="Robin" Surname="Johnson" />
      <Employee EmployeeID="2" FirstName="Denise" Surname="Samson" />
   </Department>
   <Department DepartmentID="2" Name="Orders">
      <Employee EmployeeID="3" FirstName="Jack" Surname="Jones" />
   </Department>
   < Department DepartmentID="3" Name="Stock Control">
      <Employee EmployeeID="4" FirstName="John" Surname="Doe" />
   </Department>
</Departments>
```

We can take the columns that we have already identified as being required for our resultset, and map them to their XML element as follows:

Resultset Source Column	XML Element	Mapping Column Name
NULL	<Departments>	Departments!...
DepartmentID	<Department>	Department!...
Description	<Department>	Department!...
EmployeeID	<Employee>	Employee!...
FirstName	<Employee>	Employee!...
Surname	<Employee>	Employee!...

You may notice that our <Departments> element has a column mapping name in the resultset but it is not populated from a table column within our database. Instead we assign it a constant NULL value. To help explain this recall one of the rules of the resultset that we specified earlier, which was:

❑   Every element within the XML document must have at least one column in the resultset.

If you are specifying an element that does not contain any attributes you still need to specify at least one column for this element in the resultset. As there is no value for this element we can assign a constant NULL value for this column in the resultset. It is not the value within this column that is needed for this element; rather it is the actual column name mapping.

The TagNumber component of our naming identifier specifies which tag (or at what level in the XML hierarchy) this column's values will be used for. If we recall our TAG and PARENT values that we previously determined for our XML structure:

Tag	Parent	Corresponding XML Element
1		<Departments>
2	1	<Department>
3	2	<Employee>

We can now map each of our column values to the appropriate TAG, or level, in our XML hierarchy. This would give us:

Resultset Source Column	TAG	Mapping Column Name
NULL	1	Departments!1!...
DepartmentID	2	Department!2!...
Description	2	Department!2!...
EmployeeID	3	Employee!3!...
FirstName	3	Employee!3!...
Surname	3	Employee!3!...

The next component of our mapping identifier is the AttributeName. This specifies the attribute name that the column value will be contained within. The attribute will be part of the specified element in the XML document. Usually this is simply a name that we wish to display but this can also be skipped if there is no attribute, such as when the column value is to be used for the actual element value (as with our <Departments> element). So if we continue and add the AttributeNames to our column name mapping we get:

Resultset Source Column	Attribute Name	Mapping Column Name
NULL		Departments!1!!
DepartmentID	ID	Department!2!DepartmentID
Description	Name	Department!2!Name
EmployeeID	ID	Employee!3!EmployeeID
FirstName	FirstName	Employee!3!FirstName
Surname	Surname	Employee!3!Surname

The last remaining component of our column identifier is the Directive. This is optional and provides special functions for our XML attribute. It can contain the following values:

Directive	Description
ID	Specifies that this is a unique attribute for an element. This enables the element to be referenced by an IDREF attribute of another element. This is similar to creating primary key/foreign key relationships within a database schema.
IDREF & IDREFS	Used to specify the attribute which is linked to an ID attribute. Allows inter-document linking.

Directive	Description
hide	The attribute is not contained within the XML returned by FOR XML EXPLICIT. Some complicated XML documents may require special columns to be added to the resultset purely for ordering the elements needed to produce the desired XML document. As these 'ordering' columns are not needed in the XML itself you can specify the hide directive to prevent these from being included in the XML document outputted by FOR XML EXPLICIT.
element	Tells FOR XML EXPLICIT that this is not an attribute but rather an element. If the column value contains a NULL then an empty element is created, such as <ELEMENT></ELEMENT>. However, if the column contains a value this will be used as the element value, such as <ELEMENT>value</ELEMENT>. The name of the element is still determined from the ElementName component of the column identifier we discussed above.
xml	When using the element Directive special characters (such as < and >) are encoded so that they will not corrupt the XML structure. When using the xml directive, this encoding doesn't take place. This allows you to add XML elements that may be stored as XML within a column. For example: `<Element> `**`<ColumnValue> A </ColumnValue>`**`</Element>`
xmltext	If you have an XML element stored within a column, you can merge the attributes of that element into the current element. For example, if the column value is <Tag A="1" B="2"> and the attribute you specify with the xmltext is part of the <Letters> element, the resulting XML output would be <Letters A="1" B="2"/>. The attributes of the XML stored within our column are stripped from their element and included within our new Letters element.
cdata	Specifying cdata will not encode the column value but will wrap the value with the CDATA tags. For example <Element><![CDATA][Value]></ELEMENT>. The values contained within the CDATA tag can contain special characters such as < and > but these will be interpreted as plain text, not as markup characters, when interpreting the XML. CDATA is useful when XML is being used to transport non-text data between applications as in these situations the actual data usually cannot be altered. Using CDATA prevents modification of the data by not requiring encoding of special characters while still allowing the XML to be interpreted correctly.

So applying the directive gives us our final column names to be used within our SELECT FOR XML EXPLICIT command (notice we only require the use of one directive).

Resultset Source Column	Attribute Name	Mapping Column Name
NULL		Departments!1!!element
DepartmentID	ID	Department!2!DepartmentID
Description	Name	Department!2!Name
EmployeeID	ID	Employee!3!EmployeeID
FirstName	FirstName	Employee!3!FirstName
Surname	Surname	Employee!3!Surname

Now we need to discuss the final step in preparing our resultset to be converted to XML, namely populating the resultset.

Populating the Resultset

While we have determined both the appropriate TAG and PARENT columns and the appropriate column names for mapping our results to XML, we still haven't populated our resultset. As a general rule, every element (or multiple occurrences of an element) requires a separate SQL query to retrieve the appropriate resultset to populate the attributes within our XML structure. So for our example XML, once again, we will require 3 queries to retrieve the information needed from our HumanResources database.

Why is this? Well, each element (or multiple occurrences of this element) corresponds to a unique TAG value. As these TAG values are not automatically generated, we enter them as constants within our SELECT queries. Since our sample XML has three different TAG values, we need to use three queries to generate the appropriate values for our resultset.

The attributes within our XML structure have been flattened out into a single column list. For each row we return in the resultset, we only populate the appropriate columns corresponding to attributes for our current element. It's getting confusing again, so let's go back into example mode.

First we must return a row for our TAG=1 element, which corresponds to the <Departments/> element within our XML:

Tag	Parent	Corresponding XML Element
1		<Departments>

But hang on, why do we need a query to be associated with this element? Well, remember another of the rules we stated earlier in this chapter:

❑   Every occurrence of an element in the XML document must have a corresponding row within the resultset.

Even though this element doesn't contain any values, it is still an element so we must have a row within our resultset for it. But we don't need to return a row from any of our database tables for this element. Instead we just return a single row containing the constants that we need.

For every row we return we must SELECT all the columns even if we don't need to use them. We need to do this because it facilitates the concatenating of resultsets, as we will see next. So, for this first XML element, we would write a SELECT statement that looked like:

```
SELECT
    1    AS TAG, -- Our first level element
    NULL    AS PARENT,      -- At the first level there is no parent

    NULL    AS "Departments!1!!element", --Element without a value

    NULL    AS "Department!2!DepartmentID",  --Not used yet, but must include
    NULL    AS "Department!2!Name",  --Not used yet, but must include
    NULL    AS "Employee!3!EmployeeID",  --Not used yet, but must include
    NULL    AS "Employee!3!FirstName",  --Not used yet, but must include
    NULL    AS "Employee!3!Surname"  --Not used yet, but must include

FOR XML EXPLICIT
```

If we expand what exactly is going on here, we begin by selecting the TAG and PARENT columns that tell the FOR XML EXPLICIT clause where to place this element in the XML hierarchy.

```
    1    AS TAG, -- Our first level element
    NULL    AS PARENT,      -- At the first level there is no parent
```

Next we are specifying NULL as the element value of the element name Departments. As we discussed above every element must have at least one column mapping in the resultset.

```
    NULL    AS "Departments!1!!element", --Element without a value
```

We then specify the column mappings of the remaining elements and attributes in the XML structure, even though we don't require (or populate) them within this first query.

Finally we tell SQL Server to convert this resultset to XML by specifying FOR XML EXPLICIT:

```
    FOR XML EXPLICIT
```

Notice that there was no FROM clause in this query. You will commonly see this in queries used to generate XML using FOR XML EXPLICIT, because it is often necessary to generate elements that are not derived from any table in particular, such as the <Departments> element.

If you now run this query from Query Analyzer, you get the following XML structure returned to you:

```
<Departments/>
```

UNION and Resultsets

FOR XML EXPLICIT can only process a single resultset. But, as we mentioned above, different element levels (or each unique TAG value) usually require a separate query to retrieve the values required for the element's attributes. As a result, we must concatenate each of these individual queries into a single resultset using the UNION ALL SQL operator.

UNION ALL is specified between two queries, and effectively adds the resultset produced by the second query to the end of the resultset produced by the first query. For this to work however, both resultsets must produce matching column lists of matching (or compatible) data types. This is why in our first SQL statement used to retrieve our XML structure we had to specify all the column mappings to be used throughout the resultset, even though we didn't use them specifically. If we had left them out and later tried to UNION with a query that did specify these columns, an error would be raised telling us that our query column definitions do not match.

So now we can retrieve our second level of elements within our sample XML, which are:

```
<Departments>
    <Department DepartmentID="1" Name="Personnel"/>
    <Department DepartmentID="2" Name="Orders"/>
    <Department DepartmentID="3" Name="Stock Control"/>
</Departments>
```

To do this we first create a query that retrieves our department information, and also contains all the mapping columns needed by FOR XML EXPLICIT:

```
SELECT
    2    AS TAG, -- Our second level ELEMENT
    1    AS PARENT,     -- TAG level 1 is the PARENT

    NULL   AS "Departments!1!!element", --Not used, but must be included

    DepartmentID   AS "Department!2!DepartmentID",  -- Our Department ID's
    Description    AS "Department!2!Name", -- Our Department Description

    NULL   AS "Employee!3!EmployeeID",  --Not used yet, but must be included
    NULL   AS "Employee!3!FirstName",  --Not used yet, but must be included
    NULL   AS "Employee!3!Surname"  --Not used yet, but must be included

FROM dbo.Departments
```

We now combine this with our first query producing the SQL query shown here:

```
SELECT
    1    AS TAG, -- Our first level element
    NULL   AS PARENT,    -- At the first level there is no parent

    NULL   AS "Departments!1!!element", --Element without a value

    NULL   AS "Department!2!DepartmentID", --Not used yet, but needs included
    NULL   AS "Department!2!Name",  --Not used yet, but needs included
```

```
      NULL    AS "Employee!3!EmployeeID",  --Not used yet, but must be included
      NULL    AS "Employee!3!FirstName",   --Not used yet, but must be included
      NULL    AS "Employee!3!Surname"  --Not used yet, but must be included
```

```
UNION ALL
```

```
SELECT
   2    AS TAG, -- Our second level ELEMENT
   1    AS PARENT,     -- TAG level 1 is the PARENT

   NULL   AS "Departments!1!!element", --Not used, but must be included

   DepartmentID    AS "Department!2!DepartmentID",  -- Our Department ID's
   Description     AS "Department!2!Name", -- Our Department Description

   NULL    AS "Employee!3!EmployeeID",  --Not used yet, but must be included
   NULL    AS "Employee!3!FirstName",   --Not used yet, but must be included
   NULL    AS "Employee!3!Surname"  --Not used yet, but must be included

FROM dbo.Departments
```

```
FOR XML EXPLICIT
```

You will notice the use of UNION ALL to concatenate these queries together, and that FOR XML EXPLICIT is specified at the end of the UNION query (not for each query) further highlighting that it operates on the resultset as a whole after the UNION has been performed. If you execute this query you will get the following XML output:

```
<Departments>
  <Department DepartmentID="1" Name="Personnel"/>
  <Department DepartmentID="2" Name="Orders"/>
  <Department DepartmentID="3" Name="Stock Control"/>
  <Department DepartmentID="4" Name="Deliveries"/>
  <Department DepartmentID="5" Name="Incoming Orders"/>
</Departments>
```

Now we must add in the query for the third level (TAG=3) within our XML structure, the query to retrieve the employee information for each department:

```
<Departments>
   <Department DepartmentID="1" Name="Personnel">
      <Employee EmployeeID="1" FirstName="Robin" Surname="Johnson" />
      <Employee EmployeeID="2" FirstName="Denise" Surname="Samson" />
   </ Department>
   < Department DepartmentID="2" Name="Orders">
      <Employee EmployeeID="3" FirstName="Jack" Surname="Jones" />
   </ Department>
   < Department DepartmentID="3" Name="Stock Control">
      <Employee EmployeeID="4" FirstName="John" Surname="Doe" />
   </ Department>
</Departments>
```

Before you think "Another query right? Not a problem just union it in" and decide to skip the next section, I urge you to continue reading as this is when things start to get a bit more interesting. Why don't we just do as we have implied and add in the query to retrieve the employee information as follows:

```
SELECT
    3    AS TAG, -- Our third level ELEMENT
    2   AS PARENT,    -- TAG level 2 is the PARENT

    NULL   AS "Departments!1!!element", --Not used, but must be included

    Null   AS "Department!2!DepartmentID",  -- Not needed right?
    Null   AS "Department!2!Name",  -- Not needed right?

    EmployeeID AS "Employee!3!EmployeeID",  --Our Employee ID
    FirstName AS "Employee!3!FirstName",  --Our Employees FirstName
    Surname AS "Employee!3!Surname"  --Our Employees Surname

FROM dbo.Employees
```

and expand our full query, used to retrieve the resultset that is processed by FOR XML EXPLICIT, to:

```
SELECT
    1    AS TAG, -- Our first level ELEMENT
    NULL   AS PARENT,    -- At the first level there is no parent

    NULL   AS "Departments!1!!element", --Element without a value

    NULL   AS "Department!2!DepartmentID", --Not used yet, but needs included
    NULL    AS "Department!2!Name",  --Not used yet, but must be included

    NULL   AS "Employee!3!EmployeeID",  --Not used yet, but must be included
    NULL    AS "Employee!3!FirstName",  --Not used yet, but must be included
    NULL    AS "Employee!3!Surname"  --Not used yet, but must be included

UNION ALL

SELECT
    2    AS TAG, -- Our second level ELEMENT
    1   AS PARENT,    -- TAG level 1 is the PARENT

    NULL   AS "Departments!1!!element", --Not used, but must be included

    DepartmentID   AS "Department!2!DepartmentID",  -- Our Department ID's
    Description    AS "Department!2!Name",-- Our Department Descriptions

    NULL   AS "Employee!3!EmployeeID",  --Not used yet, but must be included
    NULL    AS "Employee!3!FirstName",  --Not used yet, but must be included
    NULL    AS "Employee!3!Surname"  --Not used yet, but must be included

FROM dbo.Departments

UNION ALL
```

```
SELECT
    3    AS TAG, -- Our third level ELEMENT
    2    AS PARENT,      -- TAG level 2 is the PARENT

    NULL   AS "Departments!1!!element", --Not used, but must be included

    Null   AS "Department!2!DepartmentID",  -- Not needed right?
    Null    AS "Department!2!Name",  -- Not needed right?

    EmployeeID AS "Employee!3!EmployeeID",  --Our Employee ID
    FirstName AS "Employee!3!FirstName",  --Our Employees FirstName
    Surname AS "Employee!3!Surname"  --Our Employees Surname

FROM dbo.Employees
```

```
FOR XML EXPLICIT
```

Great, now we have everything we need to return our desired XML structure, so let's move on to a topic that's more interesting. Well, not quite. Run this query and have a look at the XML that is produced:

```
<Departments>
  <Department DepartmentID="1" Name="Personnel"/>
  <Department DepartmentID ="2" Name="Orders"/>
  <Department DepartmentID ="3" Name="Stock Control"/>
  <Department DepartmentID ="4" Name="Deliveries"/>
  <Department DepartmentID ="5" Name="Incoming Orders">
    <Employee EmployeeID="1" FirstName="Robin" Surname="Johnson"/>
    <Employee EmployeeID ="2" FirstName="Denise" Surname="Samson"/>
    <Employee EmployeeID ="3" FirstName="Jack" Surname="Jones"/>
    <Employee EmployeeID ="4" FirstName="John" Surname="Doe"/>
    <Employee EmployeeID ="5" FirstName="Linda" Surname="Glucina"/>
    <Employee EmployeeID ="6" FirstName="Laura" Surname="Wright"/>
    <Employee EmployeeID ="7" FirstName="Stephanie" Surname="Glucina"/>
    <Employee EmployeeID ="8" FirstName="Linda" Surname="Anderson"/>
    <Employee EmployeeID ="9" FirstName="Graham" Surname="Brown"/>
    <Employee EmployeeID ="10" FirstName="Suzanne" Surname="Smith"/>
    <Employee EmployeeID ="11" FirstName="David" Surname="Allan"/>
  </Department>
</Departments>
```

Hmm, this doesn't look right. So what has gone wrong? Recall a statement I made near the beginning of the chapter that went something along the lines of "To debug FOR XML EXPLICIT, remove this clause and concentrate on getting the resultset right first". So let's do this, producing the following results (we only show an extract). To make things clearer I have added codes within the TAG column to help remind us which TAG refers to what element. Note that (DS) means the <Departments> element, (D) means the <Department> element and (E) means the <Employee> element:

TAG	PARENT	Departments!1!element	Department!2!DepartmentID	Department!2!Name	Employee!3!EmployeeID
1 (DS)	NULL	NULL	NULL	NULL	NULL
2 (D)	1	NULL	1	Personnel	NULL
2 (D)	1	NULL	2	Orders	NULL
2 (D)	1	NULL	3	Stock Control	NULL
2 (D)	1	NULL	4	Deliveries	NULL
2 (D)	1	NULL	5	Incoming Orders	NULL
3 (E)	2	NULL	NULL	NULL	1
3 (E)	2	NULL	NULL	NULL	2
3 (E)	2	NULL	NULL	NULL	3
3 (E)	2	NULL	NULL	NULL	4
3 (E)	2	NULL	NULL	NULL	5
3 (E)	2	NULL	NULL	NULL	6
3 (E)	2	NULL	NULL	NULL	7
3 (E)	2	NULL	NULL	NULL	8
3 (E)	2	NULL	NULL	NULL	9
3 (E)	2	NULL	NULL	NULL	10
3 (E)	2	NULL	NULL	NULL	11

By looking at the TAG and PARENT columns we can tell that something is wrong with the way the resultset is being ordered. All the Employee rows retrieved in the resultset are simply being added to the end of the resultset (normal behavior for UNION ALL), instead of each Employee row being correctly positioned under its respective Department parent element.

Using the column values that we currently have, there is no way to actually achieve the correctly ordered resultset. Instead of this, what we need to do is include a column value within the Employee query result that is related to, and orderable by, the parent Department's query result. The only relationship between the Departments and Employees tables is on the Department column, so this is our only option for fixing this resultset. To do this we specify the Department column as part of the Employees query:

```
SELECT
    3    AS TAG, -- Our third level ELEMENT
    2    AS PARENT,     -- TAG level 2 is the PARENT

    NULL   AS "Departments!1!!element", --Not used, but must be included

    Department AS "Department!2!DepartmentID",   -- Not needed right?
    Null    AS "Department!2!Name",   -- Not needed right?

    EmployeeID AS "Employee!3!ID",   --Our Employee ID
    FirstName AS "Employee!3!FirstName",   --Our Employees FirstName
    Surname AS "Employee!3!Surname"   --Our Employees Surname

FROM dbo.Employees
```

This column is purely in the query for us to order on. As this value has been placed in a column that is
mapped to a different level in the XML hierarchy (TAG=2 whereas this query is returning rows where
TAG=3) it will actually be ignored by the FOR XML EXPLICIT option. However, thankfully, the ORDER
BY clause of a SELECT statement is processed before FOR XML EXPLICIT gets a hold of the resultset, so
even though it is ignored in the final XML output, it is still available for us to ORDER on. Making this
addition and adding an ORDER BY clause to our original query:

```
SELECT
    1    AS TAG, -- Our first level ELEMENT
    NULL   AS PARENT,     -- At the first level there is no parent

    NULL   AS "Departments!1!!element", --Element without a value

    NULL   AS "Department!2!DepartmentID", --Not used yet, but needs included
    NULL    AS "Department!2!Name",  --Not used yet, but must be included

    NULL    AS "Employee!3!EmployeeID",  --Not used yet, but must be included
    NULL     AS "Employee!3!FirstName",  --Not used yet, but must be included
    NULL     AS "Employee!3!Surname"  --Not used yet, but must be included

FROM dbo.Departments

UNION ALL

SELECT
    2    AS TAG, -- Our second level ELEMENT
    1    AS PARENT,     -- TAG level 1 is the PARENT

    NULL    AS "Departments!1!!element", --Not used, but must be included

    DepartmentID    AS "Department!2!DepartmentID",  -- Our Department ID's
    Description     AS "Department!2!Name",  -- Our Department Descriptions

    NULL    AS "Employee!3!EmployeeID",  --Not used yet, but must be included
    NULL     AS "Employee!3!FirstName",  --Not used yet, but must be included
    NULL     AS "Employee!3!Surname"  --Not used yet, but must be included

FROM dbo.Departments
```

```
UNION ALL

SELECT
    3    AS TAG, -- Our third level ELEMENT
    2    AS PARENT,    -- TAG level 2 is the PARENT

    NULL   AS "Departments!1!!element", --Not used, but must be included

    Department AS "Department!2!DepartmentID",  -- Is needed, right!
    Null   AS "Department!2!Name",  -- Not needed right?

    EmployeeID AS "Employee!3!EmployeeID",  --Our Employee ID
    FirstName AS "Employee!3!FirstName",  --Our Employees FirstName
    Surname AS "Employee!3!Surname"  --Our Employees Surname

FROM dbo.Employees

ORDER BY "Department!2!DepartmentID"
```

This will produce a very different resultset:

TAG	PARENT	Departments!1!! element	Department!2! DepartmentID	Department!2! Name	Employee!3! EmployeeID
1(DS)	NULL	NULL	NULL	NULL	NULL
2 (D)	1	NULL	1	Personnel	NULL
3 (E)	2	NULL	1	NULL	1
3 (E)	2	NULL	1	NULL	2
3 (E)	2	NULL	1	NULL	5
3 (E)	2	NULL	1	NULL	6
3 (E)	2	NULL	1	NULL	8
3 (E)	2	NULL	1	NULL	10
3 (E)	2	NULL	2	NULL	11
3 (E)	2	NULL	2	NULL	7
3 (E)	2	NULL	2	NULL	3
2 (D)	1	NULL	2	Orders	NULL
2 (D)	1	NULL	3	Stock Control	NULL

TAG	PARENT	Departments!1! element	Department!2! DepartmentID	Department!2! Name	Employee!3! EmployeeID
3 (E)	2	NULL	3	NULL	4
3 (E)	2	NULL	3	NULL	9
2 (D)	1	NULL	4	Deliveries	NULL
2 (D)	1	NULL	5	Incoming Orders	NULL

Unfortunately this is still not quite right. Take a look at the following rows from this resultset:

3 (E)	2	NULL	2	NULL	11
3 (E)	2	NULL	2	NULL	7
3 (E)	2	NULL	2	NULL	3
2 (D)	**1**	**NULL**	**2**	**Orders**	**NULL**

Our <Employee> elements are coming before the related <Department> element. These <Employee> elements would then simply be included in the previous department's element, leaving the <Department> element where the Description="Orders" empty. We need an additional ordering column to order on the EmployeeID column. As rows containing NULL values in the ORDER BY columns are returned at the top of the resultset, the following clause:

```
ORDER BY "Department!2!DepartmentID", "Employee!3!EmployeeID"
```

will first order by the Department!2!ID column, and when multiple rows have the same DepartmentID then the order will be determined by the Employee!3!ID column. As rows with NULL values will be ordered first again, the Department rows (that don't contain an EmployeeID value) will be placed at the top of the rows for their respective DepartmentID, followed by the Employee rows for that department. And once again we show our resultset output:

TAG	PARENT	Departments!1!! element	Department!2! DepartmentID	Department!2! Name	Employee!3!Employee ID
1 (DS)	NULL	NULL	NULL	NULL	NULL
2 (D)	1	NULL	1	Personnel	NULL
3 (E)	2	NULL	1	NULL	1
3 (E)	2	NULL	1	NULL	2
3 (E)	2	NULL	1	NULL	5
3 (E)	2	NULL	1	NULL	6
3 (E)	2	NULL	1	NULL	8
3 (E)	2	NULL	1	NULL	10
2 (D)	1	NULL	2	Orders	NULL
3 (E)	2	NULL	2	NULL	11
3 (E)	2	NULL	2	NULL	7
3 (E)	2	NULL	2	NULL	3
2 (D)	1	NULL	3	Stock Control	NULL
3 (E)	2	NULL	3	NULL	4
3 (E)	2	NULL	3	NULL	9
2 (D)	1	NULL	4	Deliveries	NULL
2 (D)	1	NULL	5	Incoming Orders	NULL

Or better yet, by adding the FOR XML EXPLICIT clause to the end of this query, we can see it as XML output:

```
<Departments>
  <Department DepartmentID="1" Name="Personnel">
    <Employee EmployeeID="1" FirstName="Robin" Surname="Johnson"/>
    <Employee EmployeeID ="2" FirstName="Denise" Surname="Samson"/>
    <Employee EmployeeID ="5" FirstName="Linda" Surname="Glucina"/>
    <Employee EmployeeID ="6" FirstName="Laura" Surname="Wright"/>
    <Employee EmployeeID ="8" FirstName="Linda" Surname="Anderson"/>
    <Employee EmployeeID ="10" FirstName="Suzanne" Surname="Smith"/>
  </Department>
  <Department DepartmentID ="2" Name="Orders">
    <Employee EmployeeID ="3" FirstName="Jack" Surname="Jones"/>
```

```
      <Employee EmployeeID ="7" FirstName="Stephanie" Surname="Glucina"/>
      <Employee EmployeeID ="11" FirstName="David" Surname="Allan"/>
    </Department>
    <Department DepartmentID ="3" Name="Stock Control">
      <Employee EmployeeID ="4" FirstName="John" Surname="Doe"/>
      <Employee EmployeeID ="9" FirstName="Graham" Surname="Brown"/>
    </Department>
    <Department DepartmentID ="4" Name="Deliveries"/>
    <Department DepartmentID ="5" Name="Incoming Orders"/>
</Departments>
```

As you are probably now well aware, FOR XML EXPLICIT is very powerful. This power certainly doesn't come without problems though. These include:

❑   FOR XML EXPLICIT queries get very big, very fast. As each level within the XML hierarchy requires a separate query, complex structures require many queries to produce the output. This has many detrimental effects, including a performance cost (large number of queries), the ability to understand and modify the code, and the ability to debug the code. I have found myself writing FOR XML EXPLICIT queries over 1000 lines long. It's not for the faint-hearted.

❑   The column list for queries used with FOR XML EXPLICT gets wide very quickly. By wide I mean the number of columns in the resultset. This is because each attribute, and any elements without attributes, requires a column in the resultset for mapping purposes.

❑   Ordering gets to be a real pain. You can see from our relatively simple example above, what an important part the ordering of the resultset plays on the outputted XML. Now imagine an XML structure with many different elements at many different levels. In this situation the ORDER BY statement required to get all the rows in the correct order can be very complicated and not always intuitive to understand.

Despite these limitations it is still a great way to extract custom XML structures from SQL Server 2000. Fortunately there is an easier way to produce more complex XML document structures by using an XSL stylesheet with our SQXML .NET provider we introduced in Chapter 6.

Transforming with Style

When using FOR XML EXPLICIT the queries that we use to retrieve the data needed for each element are typically fairly basic; it's the formatting and ordering of these queries to produce the required resultset where the complexity gets introduced. If we take a step back and think about what we are actually trying to achieve, we realize that trying to create complex hierarchical structures using a relational language (SQL) isn't very practical. Instead we should concentrate on getting SQL Server to do what it does best, retrieve the data, and convert it to a simple flat XML structure. Then we can use something that is better suited for manipulating complex XML structures, such as XSL, to create our hierarchies.

Someone at Microsoft must have also been thinking this way, as the SqlXmlCommand object included with the SQLXML 3.0 release (refer to Chapter 6 for instructions on installation) has the ability to apply an XSL stylesheet to the XML stream returned to it by SQL Server. This is particularly useful as the XML returned by executing multiple SQL statements (using the FOR XML option) is contained in a single stream, with the XML results of each SELECT FOR XML statement concatenated together.

In this section we will be creating a VB.NET application that takes a flat (non-structured) XML result returned by SQL Server and transforms it, using XSL, into the same hierarchical XML structure that we created in the FOR XML EXPLICIT example above.

Open up a new VB.NET Windows Application project and add a reference to the Microsoft.Data.SqlXml .NET component. We also need to import the following namespaces within the code:

```
Imports Microsoft.Data.SqlXml
Imports System.IO
```

Now we can make use of the SqlXmlCommand object to execute the following two queries within a single command:

```
SELECT * FROM dbo.Departments FOR XML AUTO
SELECT * FROM dbo.Employees FOR XML AUTO
```

To do this add the following VB.NET code to an event such as the Form Load event, or a Click event for a button:

```
'Change the connection string to your own SQL Server details
Dim xcmdSqlServer As _
        New SqlXmlCommand("Provider=SQLOLEDB; " _
                        & "Data Source=localhost; " _
                        & "Initial Catalog=HumanResources;" _
                        & "User Id=sa;Password=;")

'Create a new File stream that we will use to output the
'XML returned from our queries to.
Dim strmXMLFile As _
    New IO.FileStream("c:\OurTestXML.xml", _
                        FileMode.Create, FileAccess.Write)

With xcmdSqlServer

    ' Add a generic Root tag as well formed XML only
    ' has one root tag, and our returned XML
    ' will have two.
    .RootTag = "Root"

    ' Add the two SELECT commmands for our SqlXmlCommand
    ' to execute
    .CommandText = "SELECT DepartmentID,Description " _
        & "FROM Departments as Department FOR XML AUTO"

    .CommandText += " SELECT EmployeeID,FirstName, Surname, " _
        & "Department FROM Employees as Employee " _
        & "FOR XML AUTO"

    ' Execute our queries and output the result to our
    ' c:\OurTestXML.XML file
    .ExecuteToStream(strmXMLFile)
```

```
    End With

  'Close our test XML File
strmXMLFile.Close
```

This code declares our `SqlXmlCommand` object first. Notice how we need to specify the `Provider=SQLOLEDB` because the `SqlXmlCommand` object connects through OLEDB, not directly through TDS as the `SqlClient` .NET managed class does.

```
'Change the connection string to your own SQL Server details
Dim xcmdSqlServer As _
      New SqlXmlCommand("Provider=SQLOLEDB; " _
             & "Data Source=localhost; " _
             & "Initial Catalog=HumanResources;" _
             & "User Id=sa;Password=;")
```

We then define our `FileStream` object that we will output the XML returned by the `SqlXmlCommand` object to a file called `C:\OurTestXML.xml`:

```
'Create a new File stream that we will use to output the
'XML returned from our queries to.
 Dim strmXMLFile As _
     New IO.FileStream("c:\OurTestXML.xml", _
                       FileMode.Create, FileAccess.Write)
```

Next we set the `RootTag` property so that the `SqlXmlCommand` object will automatically encase the XML returned by SQL Server with an outermost XML element. Well-formed XML, as per the XML standard, only allows one outer (or root) element. We will be executing more than one SQL statement using the `FOR XML AUTO` clause, so each will return XML that has multiple elements within the root of the XML document. By adding this `<Root>` element, which encases our returned XML, we prevent any potential processing problems by ensuring the XML is well formed:

```
With xcmdSqlServer

    ' Add a generic Root tag as well formed XML only
    ' has one root tag, and our returned XML
    ' will have two.
    .RootTag = "Root"
```

Now we add the `SELECT` commands that we wish to execute with our `SqlXmlCommand` object. In this example we are executing two independent SQL queries, both of which convert their resultset to a simple XML structure by way of the `FOR XML AUTO` clause:

```
    ' Add the two SELECT commmands for our SqlXmlCommand
    ' to execute
    .CommandText = "SELECT DepartmentID,Description " _
        & "FROM Departments as Department FOR XML AUTO"

    .CommandText += " SELECT EmployeeID,FirstName, Surname, "_
        & "Department FROM Employees as Employee "_
        & "FOR XML AUTO"
```

We execute the `SqlXmlCommand` object by calling the `ExecuteToStream` method, passing our `FileStream` object as a parameter. The XML results of these `SELECT` queries are written to our `C:\OurTestXml.xml` file:

```
' Execute our queries and output the result to our
   ' c:\OurTestXML.XML file
    .ExecuteToStream(strmXMLFile)
```

Finally we close the `FileStream` so our newly populated XML file can be used:

```
'Close our test XML File
strmXMLFile.Close
```

If you open the `C:\OurTestXML.xml` file, you will see the resulting XML that looks similar to the XML shown below:

```xml
<?xml version="1.0" encoding="utf-8" ?>
<Root>
  <Department DepartmentID="1" Description="Personnel"/>
  <Department DepartmentID="2" Description="Orders"/>
  <Department DepartmentID="3" Description="Stock Control"/>
  <Department DepartmentID="4" Description="Deliveries"/>
  <Department DepartmentID="5" Description="Incoming Orders"/>
  <Employee EmployeeID="1" FirstName="Robin" Surname="Johnson"
    Department="1"/>
  <Employee EmployeeID="2" FirstName="Denise" Surname="Samson"
    Department="1"/>
  <Employee EmployeeID="3" FirstName="Jack" Surname="Jones"
    Department="2"/>
  <Employee EmployeeID="4" FirstName="John" Surname="Doe"
    Department="3"/>
  <Employee EmployeeID="5" FirstName="Linda" Surname="Glucina"
    Department="1"/>
  <Employee EmployeeID="6" FirstName="Laura" Surname="Wright"
    Department="1"/>
  <Employee EmployeeID="7" FirstName="Stephanie" Surname="Glucina"
    Department="2"/>
  <Employee EmployeeID="8" FirstName="Linda" Surname="Anderson"
    Department="1"/>
  <Employee EmployeeID="9" FirstName="Graham" Surname="Brown"
    Department="3"/>
  <Employee EmployeeID="10" FirstName="Suzanne" Surname="Smith"
    Department="1"/>
  <Employee EmployeeID="11" FirstName="David" Surname="Allan"
    Department="2"/>
</Root>
```

This is essentially a flat XML structure with each element located on the same level with no hierarchical arrangement, except our automatically added `<Root>` element. This was very simple to get out of SQL Server and all we need do is transform it into our desired XML structure. In this case we want the same structure that we created earlier using the `FOR XML EXPLICIT` clause:

```
<Departments>
   <Department>
      <Employees>
         <Employee></Employee>
      </Employees>
   </Department>
</Departments>
```

This is where the `XslPath` property of our `SqlXmlCommand` object becomes useful. The `XslPath` property allows us to specify the location of an XSL stylesheet (that we create for the `SqlXmlCommand` object) to apply against the XML structure that it receives from SQL Server, before passing the resulting XML to our client application. This is really powerful. While, in theory, we could transform the XML manually ourselves once we have received the XML back from SQL Server, being able to apply the stylesheet directly before we receive the XML stream is a very easy and clean way of achieving our aim.

So what does applying an XSL stylesheet to the XML returned by SQL Server allow us to do? XSL is a transformation language. It takes XML as input and applies the transformations specified in the XSL stylesheet to output a **result-tree**, the transformed result. XSL can transform from XML to XML, or it can transform XML into other types of markup such as HTML. We will just be looking at transforming XML to XML with a different structure here. However, you should also be aware that, by simply creating a different XSL stylesheet, you can just as easily output HTML from SQL Server queries.

> You can find more details about this at **http://www.w3.org/Style/XSL/** and in *'Professional XSL'* (Wrox Press, ISBN 1861003579).

Let's create our own stylesheet now. In a file named `C:\OurTransform.xsl` enter the following as plain text:

```
<?xml version="1.0" encoding="UTF-8" ?>
<xsl:stylesheet xmlns:xsl="http://www.w3.org/1999/XSL/Transform" version="1.0">

<xsl:output method="xml"/>

<xsl:template match="/">

<Departments>

   <xsl:for-each select="/Root/Department">

      <xsl:variable name="DepartmentID" select="@DepartmentID"/>

      <Department>
         <xsl:attribute name="ID">
            <xsl:value-of select="$DepartmentID"/>
         </xsl:attribute>

         <xsl:attribute name="Name">
            <xsl:value-of select="@Description"/>
         </xsl:attribute>
```

```
        <Employees>

            <xsl:apply-templates
                        select="/Root/Employee[@Department=$DepartmentID]"/>

        </Employees>

    </Department>

  </xsl:for-each>

</Departments>

</xsl:template>


<xsl:template match="Employee">

  <Employee>

    <xsl:attribute name="ID">
       <xsl:value-of select="@EmployeeID"/>
     </xsl:attribute>

    <xsl:attribute name="FirstName">
       <xsl:value-of select="@FirstName"/>
    </xsl:attribute>

    <xsl:attribute name="Surname">
       <xsl:value-of select="@Surname"/>
    </xsl:attribute>

  </Employee>

</xsl:template>

</xsl:stylesheet>
```

You will have probably noticed that this XSL is itself an XML document. Not only that, but this XSL document consists of a series of templates, and these templates are matched against the elements of our XML input. During transformation, when a match is found, the matching template is applied. Any XML element that begins with <xsl:...> will be interpreted as XSL and the appropriate actions will be carried out. Any element without the XSL prefix, such as <Department> will simply be passed to the XML result without being modified.

Our XML file consists of the following sections. First we have the header and namespace information, followed by the output method attribute. As we want XML to be outputted from the stylesheet we set this to XML; however, it could also be HTML or another XML document type:

```
<?xml version="1.0" encoding="UTF-8" ?>
<xsl:stylesheet xmlns:xsl="http://www.w3.org/1999/XSL/Transform" version="1.0">

<xsl:output method="xml"/>
```

Our first template matches / or all XML elements within the XML document. Basically the XSL processor takes each element from the XML source and iterates through the XSL file looking for a matching XSL template. As our generic "/ " parameter will match all elements within our XML file, this template will be called for every element.

```
<xsl:template match="/">
```

We then specify an XML node, which will simply be passed through the XSL file and included within our outputted XML document:

```
<Departments>
```

Now we specify a `for-each select`. This is a loop that is repeated for each XML element matching our `/Root/Department` clause (in other words all our departments elements):

```
<xsl:for-each select="Root/Department">

    <xsl:variable name="DepartmentID" select="@DepartmentID"/>

    <Department>
       <xsl:attribute name="ID">
          <xsl:value-of select="$DepartmentID"/>
       </xsl:attribute>

       <xsl:attribute name="Name">
          <xsl:value-of select="@Description"/>
       </xsl:attribute>

       <Employees>

          <xsl:apply-templates
                        select="/Root/Employee[@Department=$DepartmentID]"/>

       </Employees>

    </Department>

</xsl:for-each>

</Departments>

</xsl:template>
```

All the `<Department>` elements we had originally will match this clause, so the XSL contained within this loop will be repeated for each of these elements:

```
<Root>
  <Department DepartmentID="1" Description="Personnel"/>
  <Department DepartmentID="2" Description="Orders"/>
  <Department DepartmentID="3" Description="Stock Control"/>
  <Department DepartmentID="4" Description="Deliveries"/>
  <Department DepartmentID="5" Description="Incoming Orders"/>
```

Our loop first takes the value of the DepartmentID attribute and assigns this to an XSL variable named DepartmentID:

```
<xsl:variable name="DepartmentID" select="@DepartmentID"/>
```

Next it passes through another XML element tag (which will appear in the resulting XML output):

```
<Department>
```

and then creates attributes for this <Department> element. First it creates an attribute named ID, based on the value of the DepartmentID variable:

```
<xsl:attribute name="ID">
    <xsl:value-of select="$DepartmentID"/>
</xsl:attribute>
```

It then creates an attribute called Name based on the value of the currently selected element's Description attribute:

```
<xsl:attribute name="Name">
    <xsl:value-of select="@Description"/>
</xsl:attribute>
```

Finally our loop passes through another XML element tag, <Employees>, and then makes a call to another XSL template. This time it passes out the /Root/Employee elements where the DepartmentID attribute matches the value of the DepartmentID stored in the XML variable that we defined earlier. In this case it is the DepartmentID of the currently selected <Department> element within our loop:

```
<Employees>

    <xsl:apply-templates
              select="/Root/Employee[@Department=$DepartmentID]"/>

</Employees>
```

We then close the passed-through <Department> tag and the for-each loop, our passed-through <Departments> tag, and the current XSL template itself:

```
    </Department>

  </xsl:for-each>

</Departments>

</xsl:template>
```

Our call to apply a template to the /Root/Employee elements where the employee DepartmentID equals the current DepartmentID is matched by the following XSL template:

```
<xsl:template match="Employee">

    <Employee>

        <xsl:attribute name="ID">
          <xsl:value-of select="@EmployeeID"/>
         </xsl:attribute>

        <xsl:attribute name="FirstName">
          <xsl:value-of select="@FirstName"/>
        </xsl:attribute>

        <xsl:attribute name="Surname">
          <xsl:value-of select="@Surname"/>
        </xsl:attribute>

    </Employee>

</xsl:template>
```

Within this template we pass through another XML element tag, the `<Employee>` tag:

```
<xsl:template match="Employee">

    <Employee>
```

Then we output the `ID` attribute that is determined from the `EmployeeID` attribute within the source XML:

```
        <xsl:attribute name="ID">
          <xsl:value-of select="@EmployeeID"/>
         </xsl:attribute>
```

and the `FirstName` and `Surname` attributes that are also determined from the source XML:

```
        <xsl:attribute name="FirstName">
          <xsl:value-of select="@FirstName"/>
        </xsl:attribute>

        <xsl:attribute name="Surname">
          <xsl:value-of select="@Surname"/>
        </xsl:attribute>
```

Next we close our passed-through `<Employee>` XML element, before closing the current template:

```
    </Employee>

</xsl:template>
```

Finally we close the XSL stylesheet element itself:

```
</xsl:stylesheet>
```

Once this file has been saved to C:\OurTransform.xsl we can easily apply this XSL stylesheet to the XML returned from SQL Server by simply assigning the XslPath property of our SqlXmlCommand object to point to our newly created XSL file:

```
' Add a generic Root tag as well formed XML only
' has one root tag, and our returned XML
' will have two.
.RootTag = "Root"

'Add the XSL file path to our SqlXmlCommand object
'This XSL sytlesheet will be applied against the XML
'returned by SQL Server before being passed to our application
.XslPath = "C:\OurTransform.xsl"

' Add the two SELECT commmands for our SQLXMLCommand
' to execute
.CommandText = "SELECT DepartmentID,Description " _
    &   "FROM Departments as Department FOR XML AUTO"

        ...
```

The rest of the VB.NET code, and the queries made to SQL Server itself, remain unchanged. However, this time when we execute our application we get the following, very different, XML output in our C:\OurTestXml.xml file:

```
<?xml version="1.0" encoding="utf-8" ?>
<Departments>
  <Department ID="1" Name="Personnel">
    <Employee ID="1" FirstName="Robin" Surname="Johnson" />
    <Employee ID="2" FirstName="Denise" Surname="Samson" />
    <Employee ID="5" FirstName="Linda" Surname="Glucina" />
    <Employee ID="6" FirstName="Laura" Surname="Wright" />
    <Employee ID="8" FirstName="Linda" Surname="Anderson" />
    <Employee ID="10" FirstName="Suzanne" Surname="Smith" />
  </Department>
  <Department ID="2" Name="Orders">
    <Employee ID="3" FirstName="Jack" Surname="Jones" />
    <Employee ID="7" FirstName="Stephanie" Surname="Glucina" />
    <Employee ID="11" FirstName="David" Surname="Allan" />
  </Department>
  <Department ID="3" Name="Stock Control">
    <Employee ID="4" FirstName="John" Surname="Doe" />
    <Employee ID="9" FirstName="Graham" Surname="Brown" />
  </Department>
  <Department ID="4" Name="Deliveries"></Department>
  <Department ID="5" Name="Incoming Orders"></Department>
</Departments>
```

As you can see our XSL transform has taken each `<Department>` element, along with the related `<Employee>` elements and nested them within it. While this is a relatively simple example of using an XSL stylesheet, you should recognize that creating highly structured XML using XSL transforms does not get exponentially more complicated, in contrast to using the FOR XML EXPLICIT clause of the SELECT statement within SQL Server.

Multiple "XML Views"

Another advantage of using XSL transformations comes into play when you have multiple applications (or different components within an application) that need XML documents with a different structure but containing the same data. With FOR XML EXPLICIT each **XML view** of the data would require a different stored procedure with a different query to return the data in the required format.

Using XSL, on the other hand, doesn't require any additional queries or stored procedures to be created. The one stored procedure (or set of queries) can be optimized for retrieval of the data and different XSL stylesheets can then be applied to transform the base XML into the appropriate formats. To understand what I mean, let's rename our existing XSL transform file and create a new `C:\OurTransform.xsl` file containing the following XSL definition:

```
<?xml version="1.0" encoding="UTF-8" ?>
<xsl:stylesheet xmlns:xsl="http://www.w3.org/1999/XSL/Transform" version="1.0">

<xsl:output method="xml"/>

<xsl:template match="/">

<Employees>

<xsl:for-each select="/Root/Employee">

<xsl:variable name="Department" select="@Department"/>

   <Employee>

      <xsl:attribute name="ID">

      <xsl:value-of select="@EmployeeID"/>

   </xsl:attribute>
      <xsl:attribute name="First">
      <xsl:value-of select="@FirstName"/>
   </xsl:attribute>

   <xsl:attribute name="Last">
      <xsl:value-of select="@Surname"/>
   </xsl:attribute>

   <xsl:attribute name="Dept">
      <xsl:value-of select=
         "/Root/Department[@DepartmentID=$Department]/@Description"/>
   </xsl:attribute>

   </Employee>
```

```
    </xsl:for-each>

    </Employees>

    </xsl:template>

    </xsl:stylesheet>
```

In this example we only have a single template. This template first outputs an <Employees> element, then an <Employee> element for each /Root/Employee element matched from the XML stream returned by SQL Server. The attributes of this Employee element are then outputted.

```
    <Employees>

    <xsl:for-each select="/Root/Employee">

    <xsl:variable name="Department" select="@Department"/>

        <Employee>

            <xsl:attribute name="ID">

            <xsl:value-of select="@EmployeeID"/>

        </xsl:attribute>
            <xsl:attribute name="First">
            <xsl:value-of select="@FirstName"/>
        </xsl:attribute>

        <xsl:attribute name="Last">
            <xsl:value-of select="@Surname"/>
        </xsl:attribute>
```

As we only require a single attribute from our <Departments> element, we can do this within our existing template by using the following xsl select syntax:

```
    <xsl:value-of select=
        "/Root/Department[@DepartmentID=$Department]/@Description"/>
```

This specifies that we wish to select the Description attribute from the Departments element where the DepartmentID attribute is equal to the value of the $Department variable (this is holding the DepartmentID of the current employee element).

Also notice that in this example we do not change either our VB.NET code, or the SQL queries themselves, only the XSL stylesheet. When we run this code, the file outputted from our queries is very different to previous examples, as you can see:

```
<?xml version="1.0" encoding="utf-8"?>
<Employees>
  <Employee ID="1" First="Robin" Last="Johnson" Dept="Personnel"/>
```

```
<Employee ID="2" First="Denise" Last="Samson" Dept="Personnel"/>
<Employee ID="3" First="Jack" Last="Jones" Dept="Orders"/>
<Employee ID="4" First="John" Last="Doe" Dept="Stock Control"/>
<Employee ID="5" First="Linda" Last="Glucina" Dept="Personnel"/>
<Employee ID="6" First="Laura" Last="Wright" Dept="Personnel"/>
<Employee ID="7" First="Stephanie" Last="Bain" Dept="Orders" />
<Employee ID="8" First="Linda" Last="Anderson" Dept="Personnel" />
<Employee ID="9" First="Graham" Last="Brown" Dept="Stock Control" />
<Employee ID="10" First="Suzanne" Last="Smith" Dept="Personnel" />
<Employee ID="11" First="David" Last="Allan" Dept="Orders"/>
</Employees>
```

Once you have come to terms with XSL, creating complicated structures (such as the example we saw earlier) will prove to be much more effective using the XSL method as opposed to FOR XML EXPLICIT clauses.

Stored Procedures As Web Services

A common definition of a **web service** is a software service that is exposed on the Internet using a common protocol. More specifically, it is a software component made available on the web that can be utilized by applications communicating using the **Simple Object Access Protocol** (**SOAP**) over HTTP.

SOAP is a messaging protocol that sends and receives messages using XML. An example of an XML SOAP message sent from a client application to a web service is shown below. After receiving this XML message from a client the web service would perform the required processing and respond with an XML SOAP response message.

```
<?xml version="1.0" encoding="utf-8" ?>
<soap:Envelope xmlns:soap="http://schemas.xmlsoap.org/soap/envelope/"
  xmlns:xsi="http://www.w3.org/2001/XMLSchema-instance"
  xmlns:xsd="http://www.w3.org/2001/XMLSchema">
  <soap:Body>
      <ListAsXML xmlns="http://MyServer/EmployeeListing/EmployeeList" />
  </soap:Body>
</soap:Envelope>
```

Web services are typically created to provide one of two types of solution. First they can provide new services across the Internet to be harnessed by application developers for integration into their applications. Microsoft Passport, as discussed in Chapter 12, is an example of a new authentication service that can be used by developers to provide user authentication for applications they develop. Secondly, web services address the age-old problem of application integration. Different protocols and different information formats have made it difficult for applications to interoperate. While there have been attempts to develop standards for many years, these have typically been limited in scope to a particular type of application (such as EDI) rather than a global solution to the problem. Web services provide a common standard for interacting between all types of applications, and even legacy applications can benefit from this new standard because it is often possible to build an interface that talks to the legacy application using its own language. Put these benefits together with the fact that web services communicate over HTTP, so can very easily be accessed through firewalls, and this makes them a very accessible and easy to utilize solution.

Typically a developer would build a web service using a language such as VB.NET because such services often require business rules and processing logic to be built in, to ensure that the information being provided by the consumer of the web service is valid. However, you may also wish to provide lower-level data services via a web service and when doing so you may find that all the validation you require is contained within a SQL Server stored procedure. All the VB.NET application would be doing in this situation, in effect, is acting as a web service wrapper for your stored procedure.

> **For more information on creating Microsoft .NET Web Services visit http://msdn.microsoft.com/webservices or read '*Professional ASP.NET Web Services*' (Wrox Press, ISBN 1861005458)**

Microsoft has supplied a way to do away with this wrapper with the release of SQLXML 3.0, which provides support for exposing SQL Server stored procedures directly as web services. By simply adding the necessary configuration to an IIS web server, the SQLXML 3.0 components will effectively act as the wrapper between your stored procedure and the web services interface.

Configuring a Stored Procedure Web Service

Before you can configure a web service you must first ensure that the SQLXML components are installed on the web server you wish to make the web services available from (see Chapter 6 for installation information).

The web server must be running IIS, however this does not necessarily need to be the same machine as your SQL Server. In fact, in production environments, it is desirable to separate SQL Server and IIS onto different physical machines. If you didn't install SQLXML on your web server in Chapter 6 please do so now.

> **In production environments it is recommended that you install IIS and SQL Server on different physical servers. This allows you to configure security and performance factors to the most appropriate settings for each of these server applications.**

To demonstrate the web service functionality included with the SQLXML 3.0 release, we are going to create a simple web service that provides the consumer of the service with a list of employees. While this is only a simple example, it is a practical example of a web service that may be deployed internally within an organization. Many applications within an organization require a list of employees, such as a web-based telephone directory, or a staff skills database for example. The HR database is usually considered the most accurate repository of employee information, so being able to easily interface with it to gain this employee information is valuable.

In our example we will be exposing the following procedure from our web service. Connect to our HumanResources sample database using Query Analyzer, and create the following stored procedure:

```
CREATE PROCEDURE dbo.EmployeeListWebService
AS
    SET NOCOUNT ON
```

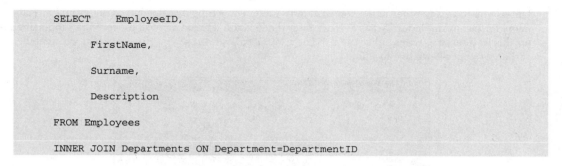

```
SELECT     EmployeeID,

       FirstName,

       Surname,

       Description

FROM Employees

INNER JOIN Departments ON Department=DepartmentID
```

Now we can start configuring our web service, but before we do this we need to create some directories that will be used to store the supporting web service files. Unless you have an alterative preferred location then create the following directory:

`C:\InetPub\EmployeeListing`

If you use an alternative path you will need to use it throughout the following example.

To configure the web service virtual directory in IIS, you need to use the special Microsoft Management Console (MMC) plug-in provided by the SQLXML install. You can find this **Configure IIS support** utility on the **Start Menu** under the **SQLXML 3.0** folder.

First we need to create and configure a new virtual directory. To do so right-click the default web site and select **New | Virtual Directory**.

The virtual directory, along with the server name, forms the URL path that the web service will be accessible from (for example http://myserver/EmployeeListing/).

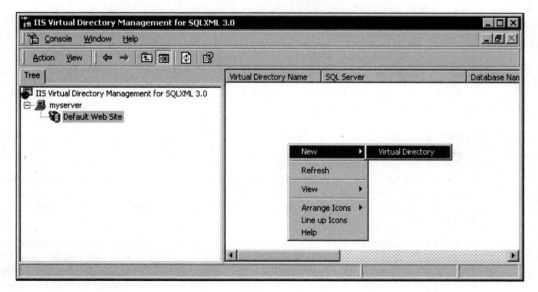

Unless you have any other name you wish to use then enter EmployeeListing as the virtual directory name for our example web service. Next enter the location where you wish to store the supporting files for this web service. Enter either the C:\InetPub\EmployeeListing directory that we created earlier, or your alternative location.

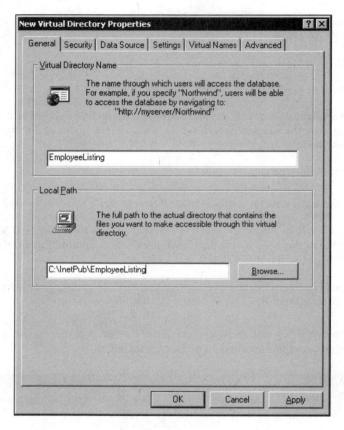

Click on the Security tab and select the security mode that users of the web service will need to utilize when accessing it. We have three security modes available in this screen, and they are:

❑ Always Log on as – This option allows you to specify an account with which the web service will automatically authenticate against SQL Server. If you specify this option you are making the web service anonymous, or in other words, available for use by everyone. The account that you specify here can either be a SQL Server Authentication account or a Windows User account. If you select Windows authentication you can either set this to the IIS anonymous user, or to a Windows User that you specify (by unselecting Enable Windows account synchronization).

❑ Use Windows Integrated Authentication – This option uses the Windows user account of the user who is connecting to the web service to authenticate to SQL Server. This option may be suitable if you are deploying your stored procedure web service internally on your corporate LAN, and have a suitable domain structure in place.Use Basic Authentication – This requires the user to enter a SQL Server authenticated login to gain access to the web service.

For our example, we will select **Always Log on as:** and choose **SQL Server**. Here we enter a valid SQL Server authenticated login that has permissions to execute the stored procedures within our HumanResources database. By setting this option, every user of the web service, including anonymous users, will be authenticated both with our web service and SQL Server.

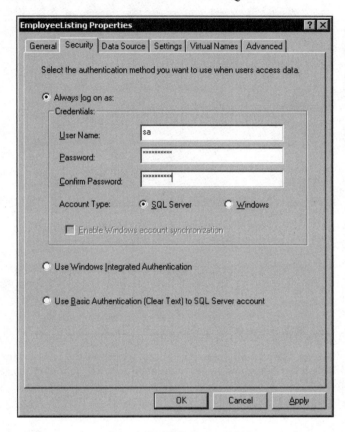

On the **Data Source** tab enter the name of the SQL Server 2000 server that you wish to provide the web service from. Uncheck the **Use default database for current login** option, and select a database that contains the stored procedures to be exposed as web services from the drop-down list below. In this example select our HumanResources sample database:

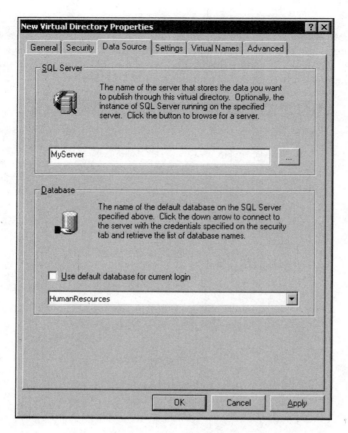

Moving on to the **Settings** tab, the only option required to support the web service is **Allow Post**. Unless you are utilizing other functionality provided by SQLXML, configure the settings as shown in the following diagram:

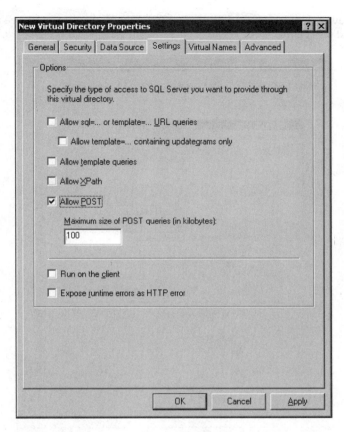

Next click on the Virtual Names tab because we need to add a new virtual name to support our web service. A virtual name is used within the URL when accessing our Virtual Directory and informs SQLXML what type of functionality we wish to use.

Enter EmployeeList as the name, and also select soap as the type. There are a number of different types of virtual name, however soap is the only type used by the web services functionality of SQLXML.

Enter a path to a directory location where the Web Services Description Language (WSDL) file will be created. A WSDL file is an XML file that describes, using a common standard, the service and operations provided by the web service. This file is provided by the web service to tell clients how to utilize it correctly. The web service will only accept requests from client applications that follow the instructions provided within the WSDL file.

The WSDL file is automatically created by SQLXML for our stored procedure, however we need to specify a path for it to be stored. For this example we simply specify our existing directory, C:\InetPub\EmployeeListing.

Ensure the web service name is also set to EmployeeList. If you intend to expose this web service on the Internet then the Domain Name field should be set to the public URL used to access this web service, such as http://www.tonybain.com/EmployeeListing/EmployeeList. For our example we will leave this set to its default.

Click the **Save** button, but don't close this window yet. Next we have to configure the mappings to our SQL Server stored procedure.

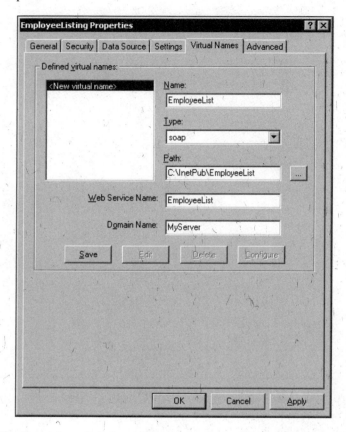

To do this click Configure then click the ... button next to the SP/Template box. On the Soap Virtual Name configuration screen we enter the methods that will be available for our web service, and each method maps to a SQL Server stored procedure:

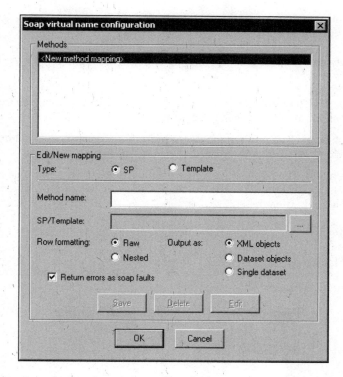

There are several options that can be configured on this screen. First of all we set the type of mapping to one of the following values:

❑ **Stored Procedure** – A regular SQL Server stored procedure that returns a resultset (in other words not using the FOR XML options).

❑ **Template** – Allows you to use an annotated XSD schema template instead of a stored procedure to access SQL Server. We are not covering such templates in this chapter, but they are discussed in *'Professional SQL Server XML'* (Wrox Press, ISBN 1861005466) if you want to learn more.

The **Method name** is the method that the client application calls to execute the appropriate stored procedure. We will see an example of this later when we make use of our stored procedure from a VB.NET application.

The **SP/Template** field is used to select the stored procedure (or template) that will be executed for this method of our web service.

The **Row Formatting** option specifies how the results of the stored procedure execution should be converted to XML. As web services communicate using XML only, the way SQLXML does this conversion depends on the selection of the following options:

❑ Raw – Use the Raw option if you want the XML to be passed to the client using a flat XML structure. Generic <row> tags will be used to mark up each row as XML.

❏   Nested – Use the Nested option to instruct SQLXML to create a nested XML structure, based on the tables and columns within the query.

Next we can specify how the output of our stored procedure can be utilized by the client application. We have three **Output as** options which are:

❏   **XML objects** – The result of the stored procedure execution invoked by the method call from the client application is returned as an array of XMLElement objects.

❏   **Dataset objects** – The result of the stored procedure execution invoked by the method call from the client application is returned as an array of DataSet objects.

❏   **Single dataset** – The result of the stored procedure execution is returned as a single DataSet to our client application. This is only possible when our stored procedure returns a resultset, rather than XML using the FOR XML option.

For our example we will create two methods, using the stored procedure that we created earlier.

Ensure that the **Type** option is set to **Stored Procedure**, then select the EmployeeListWebService stored procedure using the ... button next to the **SP/Template** field. The stored procedure should be listed in this pop-up dialog as shown:

Once this has been selected enter ListAsXML as the method name. Set the **Output formatting** option to be **Raw** and set the **Output as** option to XMLObjects. Your configuration of this first method should look similar to this:

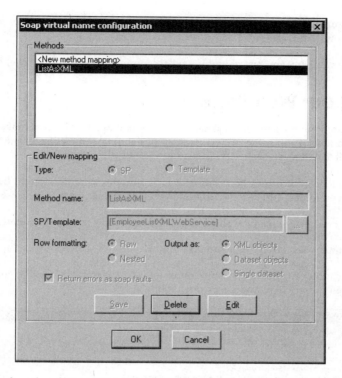

Click **Save** then select the **<New method mapping>** item in the **Methods** listbox. This time select our `EmployeeListWebService` stored procedure and enter `ListAsDS` as the method name. Now set the **Row formatting** option to **Nested** and the **Output as** option to **Single dataset**. Click **Save** and then click **OK** to save our Virtual Name configuration.

Clicking OK a further time will save our new web service virtual directory, and this should appear as a new virtual directory within the main window of the configuration tool, as shown:

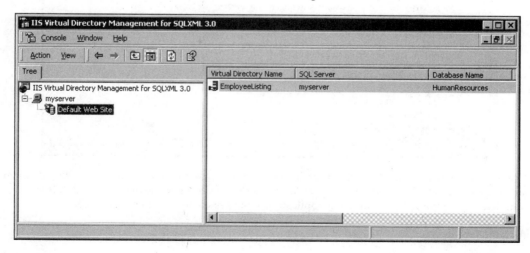

SQLXML has automatically created the WSDL file needed for accessing the web service, and this will be located within our `C:\InetPub\EmployeeListing` directory.

Our web service has now been created and is available to be accessed by our client applications.

Referencing Our Web Service

Now we have created our web service, we can create a client application that makes use of it. Create a new VB.NET Windows Application project. Instead of defining connecting to our SQL Server using ADO.NET we will use our new web service.

First we need to reference it from within our project. To do this use the Solution Explorer window, right click the References folder, and choose the Add Web Reference menu item.

Enter the URL to our newly created web service, followed by the WSDL parameter. For example:

http://localhost/EmployeeListing/EmployeeList?wsdl

If our client application can successfully communicate with the web service, the contents of the WSDL file will be returned to our client and displayed as shown:

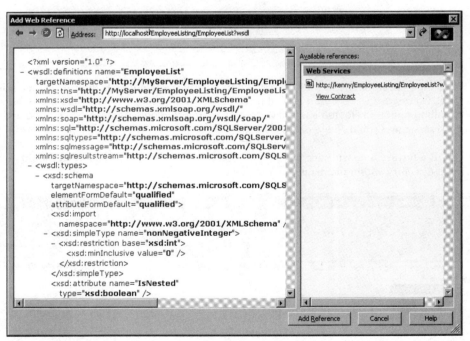

This WSDL file isn't particularly user friendly, but if you browse through it you will see that it contains the various methods that we defined earlier for our web service. As we have mentioned, this is a complete description of how our client application should make use of the web service.

We can now click the Add Reference button to add our web service to our application.

Using our Web Service

It is easy to make use of web services using VS.NET, since the .NET Framework takes care of understanding the rules and requirements specified within the WSDL file. From our application we make use of the web service as we would any other object.

Within our project, create a form and add four objects as follows:

- ❑ txtXML – A TextBox control used to display the XML result returned from our web service. Set the MultiLine property to True.
- ❑ dgDataSet – A DataGrid control used to display the DataSet returned by our web service.
- ❑ btnXML – The button used to populate the txtXML TextBox
- ❑ btnDataSet – The button used to populate the dgDataSet DataGrid.

Organize these in a layout similar to that shown in this screenshot:

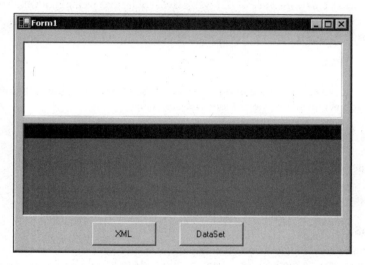

Now we can begin adding the code that uses our web service. But first we should add the following Imports statement to our application:

```
Imports ProjectName.WebServerName
```

This adds the namespace of the web service to our project. As I named my project EmployeeListing, I need to add:

```
Imports EmployeeListing.localhost
```

You should alter this based on both what your project is called, and the name of the web server that you are accessing your web service from.

Web Service XML

We only need a few lines of code to retrieve the XML output from our stored procedure via our web service. This code will be invoked when the Click event of the btnXML button occurs:

```
Private Sub btnXML_Click(ByVal sender As System.Object, _
          ByVal e As System.EventArgs) Handles btnXML.Click

    Dim EmployeeList As New EmployeeList()

    Dim xmlElement As Xml.XmlElement

    xmlElement = EmployeeList.ListAsXML(0)

    txtXML.Text = xmlElement.OuterXml

End Sub
```

This code first creates a new instance of our web service object, as well as an XMLElement object:

```
    Dim EmployeeList As New EmployeeList()

    Dim xmlElement As Xml.XmlElement
```

We then call the ListAsXML method of our web service and pass the return XMLElement object (in position 0 of the object array returned by our web service):

```
    xmlElement = EmployeeList.ListAsXML(0)
```

Lastly we add the XML to the text property of our textbox, to display on our form:

```
    txtXML.Text = xmlElement.OuterXml
```

Web Service DataSet

Next we add similar code to handle populating our DataGrid control from the DataSet returned by our ListAsDS web service method. This time we add code to handle the Click event of our btnDataSet button:

```
Private Sub btnDataSet_Click(ByVal sender As System.Object, _
          ByVal e As System.EventArgs) Handles btnDataSet.Click

    Dim EmployeeList As New EmployeeList()

    Dim dsDataSet As DataSet

    dsDataSet = EmployeeList.ListAsDS(0)

    dgDataSet.DataSource = dsDataSet

End Sub
```

As in the previous code, we declare our `EmployeeList` web service object, but this time we also create a `DataSet` object:

```
Dim EmployeeList As New EmployeeList()

Dim dsDataSet As DataSet
```

Next we assign the `DataSet` returned by our web service (position 0 in the object array) to our `DataSet` object:

```
dsDataSet = EmployeeList.ListAsDS(0)
```

before assigning this to our `DataGrid` control:

```
dgDataSet.DataSource = dsDataSet
```

If we execute our application and click each of the buttons, our controls should both be populated with the data returned from our web service, as shown.

Note you will need to drill down (using the + sign) into the DataGrid object to view the retrieved rows within each DataTable object.

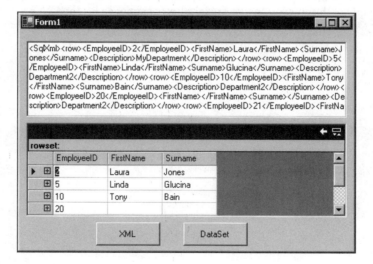

Summary

In this chapter we have looked at three important areas of XML integration with SQL Server. These were the FOR XML EXPLICIT query option, directly applying XSL transformations via the SqlXmlCommand object, and exposing stored procedures as web services.

During our detailed look at FOR XML EXPLICIT, we discovered that it is powerful. Yet this power doesn't come without a price, and that price is complexity. For every element and every attribute you add to your XML structure, FOR XML EXPLICIT queries get larger and more complicated. We saw how three factors influence the XML result of a FOR XML EXPLICIT query, namely the TAG/PARENT assignments, the column naming, and the resultset ordering. Each must be correct before the desired XML structure will be produced.

Using XSL is another approach to creating highly structured XML documents directly from SQL Server. We can use the basic XML functionality provided, such as the FOR XML AUTO clause, to easily and efficiently mark up the results of our queries into an XML stream. Then by applying an XSL stylesheet directly when we retrieve this XML stream, we can transform the simple XML into almost any XML hierarchy that we require, without adding greatly to the complexity of the solution. The drawback of using XSL is that there is another language to learn.

Finally we discovered how to directly expose SQL Server stored procedures using the SQLXML 3.0 release. We could use this to provide a generic application access to data services, and we looked at a real-world example of this in exposing an organization's employee list through a web service for consumption by various directory applications throughout the organization.

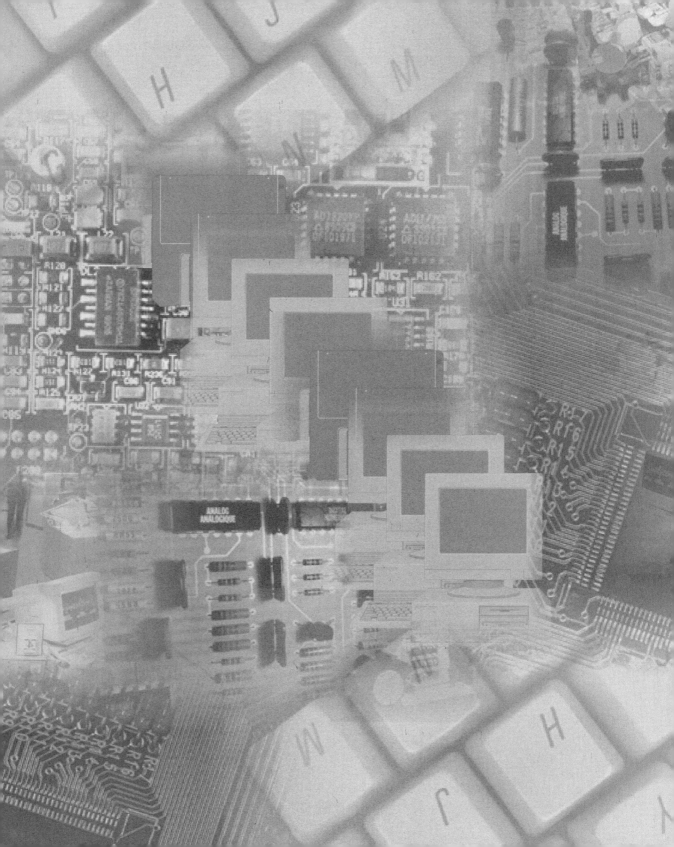

11

Effective Administration for Developers

Well done. You are braver than some developers. I know several developers who, after reading the title of this chapter, would have put this book down and run away from fear of being turned into a DBA! You can rest assured that is not our intention. Instead what we are concerned with is developer-focused administration issues. While the topics covered in this chapter may be the ultimate responsibility of a dedicated Database Administrator in a production environment, they have been chosen especially to benefit SQL Server developers, particularly those who create applications in independent development teams.

The topics we will cover in this chapter are:

- ❑ Managing Database and Server Security
- ❑ Profiling your Server activity
- ❑ Auditing Database Security
- ❑ Using the Index Tuning Wizard
- ❑ Moving a Database
- ❑ Scripting database objects

Let's begin with an issue that is getting a higher priority throughout the industry recently, namely security.

Managing Security

While the security of a corporate LAN, and physical security surrounding network servers, may be the responsibility of the network administrator and/or DBA, the security associated with your database application is a shared responsibility between its developers and its administrators. As a developer it is up to you to design and build your database application to use appropriate security policies. Once you have done so, it is the administration staff that have the responsibility of implementing these security policies. Having an understanding of the issues and requirements of both roles will lead to the development of more secure applications.

SQL Server Log ins

Log ins control who can gain access to an instance of SQL Server, rather than particular databases. As we will see later log ins get associated with database users, but on their own they do not provide access past authenticating a physical connection to SQL Server.

This is an important and fundamental security concept so please forgive me for spelling it out but log ins are not the same as database users, or to put it in developer terms:

```
[SQL Server Log ins] <> [SQL Server Database Users]
```

Log in authentication can be achieved with SQL Server using one of two 'modes' of security. The first mode is using **Windows Authentication**, sometimes called **Trusted Connections**. The second mode is called **SQL Server authentication**.

Before we consider these different modes, we should introduce the three terms that we need to use in this context, namely:

- ❑   GRANT – To explicitly allow a permission.

- ❑   DENY – To explicitly disallow a permission.

- ❑   REVOKE – To remove an explicitly allowed or an explicitly disallowed permission.

It is particularly important to note the difference between the DENY and REVOKE keywords, as these are used extensively throughout this section.

Setting Authentication Mode

We will take a look at each of these modes next, but now is an opportune time to demonstrate how SQL Server can be configured to use them. SQL Server 2000 and SQL Server 7 can be configured to accept either Windows Authenticated users only or Windows and SQL Server Authenticated users. There isn't a mode for SQL Server Authenticated users only.

To change the security mode you need to use **SQL Server Enterprise Manager**, since this setting is recorded in the registry, and as a result there is no command to change this directly from T-SQL. Open Enterprise Manager, right-click on your instance name, and select the **Properties** menu on your SQL Server registration. Choose the **Security** tab and from here you can select the security mode that you require:

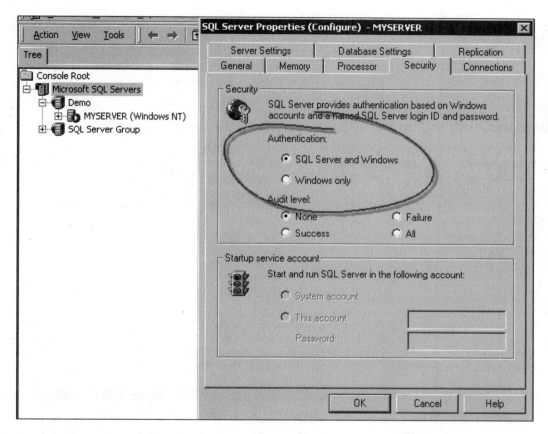

Those purists who believe UIs are for wimps and prefer to do all their administration from code, should note that SQL Server exposes a lot of its administration and configuration functions through an API known as **SQL-DMO** (SQL Distributed Management Objects). Through SQL-DMO you can change almost any of the SQL Server configuration options, including the log in security mode. From VB.NET this would look something like (after adding a COM reference to the Microsoft SQLDMO Object Library):

```
Dim oServer As New SQLDMO.SQLServer()

oServer.Log inSecure = True

'Replace with your own SQL Server Name
oServer.Connect("localhost")

oServer.IntegratedSecurity.SecurityMode = _
SQLDMO.SQLDMO_SECURITY_TYPE.SQLDMOSecurity_Mixed

oServer.Close
```

This code uses SQL-DMO to connect to SQL Server and change the log in security mode to Mixed Mode Security, which means SQL Server will accept both Windows authentication and SQL Server authentication.

SQL-DMO is a powerful API that can be utilized to automate and control the administration of SQL Server. This chapter does not go into detail but if you would like more information see 'Professional SQL Server 7.0 development using SQL-DMO, SQL-NS & DTS' (Wrox Press, ISBN 1861002807). While this book was written for the version of SQL-DMO provider in SQL Server 7.0, this will certainly give you a good starting point to understanding SQL-DMO in SQL Server 2000.

Windows Authentication

As we have mentioned, Windows Authentication (or Trusted Security as it used to be called) allows users to be authenticated with SQL Server based on their Windows user account. This Windows user could be a NT Domain account, an Active Directory Account, or a local Windows NT/2000 account.

To grant the log in privilege to a Windows user account from within T-SQL, execute the following command:

```
EXEC sp_grantlog in DomainName\WindowsUserName
```

For example:

```
EXEC sp_grantlog in 'MyDomain\GlucinaL'
```

You can also do this from SQL Server Enterprise Manager. As this is fairly straightforward we only need to go through it once. From within SQL Server Enterprise Manager, drill down into the server you wish to create the log in for, then drill down into the Security node and right-click the Log ins node and select New Log in. From here you can enter the details of the log in you wish to grant the ability to connect to SQL Server to:

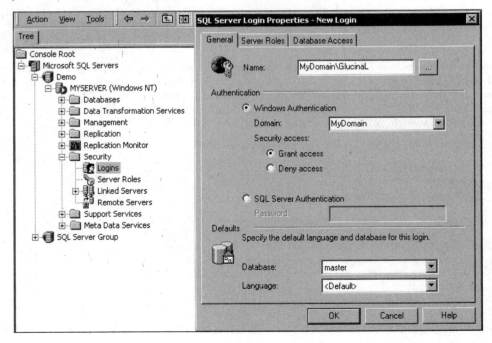

In this screen you enter the Windows user account in the format `Domain\AccountName` in the **Name** field. You can also launch the domain account picker by clicking the "…" button next to the **Name** field. The **Password** field will be disabled, since you only need to enter a password for a SQL Server authenticated log in (as we will see next). Make sure you choose **Grant access** for the moment, although we will discuss denying access shortly.

A third method of carrying this out is once again using SQL-DMO from VB.NET. The object model for SQL-DMO is in SQL Server Books Online, but to add and remove log ins we use the `SQLDMO Log in` object as shown.

```
Dim oServer As New SQLDMO.SQLServer()

    oServer.Log inSecure = True

    'Replace with your own SQL Server Name
    oServer.Connect("localhost")
```

```
    Dim oLog in As New SQLDMO.Log in()

        With oLog in

            'Specifies that the log in type is that of a Domain User
            .Type = SQLDMO.SQLDMO_LOG IN_TYPE.SQLDMOLog in_NTUser

            'Specifies the log in name of the Windows User to be added
            'as a log in to SQL Server. You will need to change this
            'to a valid Windows user in your own domain.
            .Name = "MyDomain\GlucinaL"

        End With

        oServer.Log ins.Add(oLog in)
```

```
    oServer.Close
```

Windows user accounts can be added to Windows Domain (or local) groups to simplify administration. These Windows groups themselves can be granted the log in to SQL Server privilege. For example the `BUILTIN\Administrators` Windows group is granted log in access by default after you have installed SQL Server, which allows everyone who is a member of this `Administrators` group, log in privilege to SQL Server. The `BUILTIN` term means that the group is a local machine group rather than a domain group (this could also be specified as `LocalMachine\UserAccount`). Using this method you do not need to grant that log in privilege to every person wanting to connect to SQL Server explicitly. You simply grant the log in privilege to the appropriate Windows group, and members of that group inherit it.

We still use the same `sp_grantlog in` procedure (or the same Enterprise Manager UI if you so wish) to allow members of a Windows group access to SQL Server. For example:

```
EXEC sp_grantlog in 'MyDomain\MyWindowsGroup'
```

Using SQL-DMO from VB.NET would look like this:

```
Dim oServer As New SQLDMO.SQLServer()

oServer.Log inSecure = True

'Replace with your own SQL Server Name
oServer.Connect("localhost")

Dim oLog in As New SQLDMO.Log in()

    With oLog in

        'Specifies that the log in type is that of a Domain Group
        .Type = SQLDMO.SQLDMO_LOG IN_TYPE.SQLDMOLog in_NTGroup

        'Specifies the Windows group to be added as a SQL Server log in
        'You will need to change this to a valid group in your own
        'Windows domain.
        .Name = "MyDomain\MyWindowsGroup"

    End With

    oServer.Log ins.Add(oLog in)

oServer.Close
```

All the members of the `MyWindowsGroup` from `MyDomain` now have the permission to establish a connection with this SQL Server.

A particular Windows user account may authenticate with SQL Server using one of the following methods:

- ❑ No Authentication – SQL Server knows nothing about the Windows user account, so any connection request from this user is disallowed.
- ❑ Direct Granted Authentication – The Windows user account has been explicitly granted the permission to log in to SQL, so a request to establish a connection is granted.
- ❑ Indirect Granted Authentication – The Windows user account is not granted log in to SQL Server permissions explicitly, but it is a member of a Windows group that has been granted log in permission.
- ❑ Direct Denied Authentication – The Windows user account has been directly denied the log in permission to SQL Server. All requests to establish a connection with SQL Server from this log in are disallowed.

❑ Indirect Denied Authentication – The Windows user account has not been explicitly denied the ability to log in to SQL Server, but it is a member of a Windows group that has been denied permission to log in. All requests to establish a connection with SQL Server from this log in are disallowed.

To revoke the log in we use the `sp_revokelog in` command (or the **Delete** option from within Enterprise Manager), for example:

```
EXEC sp_revokelog in 'MyDomain\MySQLUsersGroup'
```

Using SQL-DMO from VB.NET would look something like:

```
Dim oServer As New SQLDMO.SQLServer()

oServer.Log inSecure = True

'Replace with your own SQL Server Name
oServer.Connect("localhost")

oServer.Log ins.Item("MyDomain\MySQLUsersGroup").Remove()

oServer.Close
```

> **Revoking a log in does not necessarily deny permission to log in to SQL Server. Revoke is used to remove existing log ins, whether they be an existing granted log in or an existing denied log in.**

We introduced a new concept in the previous list, namely that of **denied authentication**. Denied is not the same as removing a Windows user or Windows group log in information from SQL Server. Denied permission is explicitly denying a Windows user connection to SQL Server, overriding any log in permission that may have been directly applied to them. It will also override any log in permission that has been indirectly applied to this user by inheriting the log in permission from a Windows group that they are member of.

If you are only using Windows user accounts within SQL Server to assign log in permissions, rather than Windows user groups, then there is little point using Deny. If you simply Revoke the Windows user account, then they will not be able to connect. However, if you are using Windows user groups, or a combination of Windows user groups and Windows user accounts, to assign log in permissions, then using Deny will prevent a user who may have received the log in permission from a Windows user group from establishing a connection. This is true no matter which way around you do it. So, for example, if you grant the user log in permissions and then deny a group the user is a member of log in permissions, the user will be prevented from logging in. A deny, even a deny inherited from a group, always prevents the user logging in.

To help explain this, imagine we are a delivery company and we have a Windows users group, named CorporateUsers. Within this group we have the users from our corporate head office. This group may be used for many different purposes and may be assigned permissions to a variety of resources on our network, including file shares and perhaps public folders on a Microsoft Exchange server.

The CorporateUsers Windows group also has the permission to log in to our SQL Server because all members of this group from Head Office require access to carry out their daily tasks. All the users that is, except for Dodgy Pete. Dodgy Pete has recently joined our organization and is not yet trusted with access to our core systems until he has completed corporate training.

As our CorporateUsers group is also assigned permissions on other network resources amongst the organization's various file, print, and mail servers (all resources that Dodgy Pete is allowed to access) we don't particularly want to take Dodgy Pete out of this group. Dodgy Pete is the only user who doesn't require log in access to SQL Server, so we don't particularly wish to set up another Windows group for users who are allowed to connect to SQL Server, exclude Dodgy Pete from it, and then change SQL Server to use this new group instead of our existing CorporateUsers group, as this instantly increases our Domain administration overhead. Thankfully SQL Server has the ability to cope with this situation by being able to deny the log in permission to a particular Windows User.

An explicit Deny will always take precedence over an explicit, or inherited, Grant on the ability to log in to SQL Server. As a result of denying the ability to log in to Dodgy Pete, he can still remain in the CorporateUsers group whilst all the other members of this group will continue to be able to establish connections with our SQL Server.

In this case, in order to avoid administration overhead we denied log in permission on a per Windows user basis. However, if the situation developed where we had a number of new employees, such as DodgyDave and DodgySusan, to whom we wished to deny access then denying the log in permission on a per user basis would once again start to increase administration overhead. A more administration-friendly approach would be to set up a second Windows Group called NoSQLServerAccess and specifically deny log in permission to this group. The Windows Users we add to this group will not be able to access SQL Server, even if they are members of other Windows Groups that have been granted the log in permission. Once DodgyPete, DodgyDave, and DodgySusan had received their training they could simply be removed from the NoSQLServerAccess Windows Group and they would be free to log in to SQL Server once more.

To deny a log in we use the sp_denylog in command, so for our example above we would execute:

```
EXEC sp_denylog in 'MyDomain\GlucinaL'
```

Or from VB.NET using SQL-DMO we would issue:

```
Dim oServer As New SQLDMO.SQLServer()

oServer.Log inSecure = True

'Replace with your own SQL Server Name
oServer.Connect("localhost")

Dim oLog in As New SQLDMO.Log in()

   With oLog in

       'Specifies that the log in type is that of a Domain User
       .Type = SQLDMO.SQLDMO_LOG IN_TYPE.SQLDMOLog in_NTUser

       .Name = "MyDomain\GlucinaL"

       .DenyNTLog in = True

   End With

oServer.Log ins.Add(oLog in)

oServer.Close
```

The DenyNTLog in property of our Log in object specifically creates a denied log in with SQL Server.

SQL Server Authentication

SQL Server also has its own built-in authentication system called, understandably enough, SQL Server authentication. SQL Server authentication stores usernames and passwords within the master database, and these are compared to the username and password submitted by a person requesting a connection; if they match the connection is allowed.

SQL Server authentication comes from long ago in SQL Server's past, before integration with the operating system security was achieved. Due to this long history there are an awful lot of applications out there today that use SQL Server authentication to establish connections to the database server.

The interesting thing is that people are still using SQL Server authentication for *new* database application deployments instead of using Windows authentication. It is intriguing for a couple of reasons. Firstly, Microsoft announced a few years back that SQL Server authentication would be dropped in a future version of SQL Server, although they haven't announced a specific version yet. Secondly, SQL Server authentication is a particularly poor means of security for corporate data for the following reasons:

❑   It doesn't support password aging. A user may have the same password for years.

❑   It doesn't support minimum password lengths. A user could set their password to be just the letter a if they wanted.

❑   It doesn't support account lockouts. A hacker could submit hundreds or thousands of log in attempts for a given SQL Server authentication account without the account being disabled.

❑   Windows uses a much more secure method of passing log in credentials across the network in comparison to SQL Server Authentication.

So, if all these issues are counting against SQL Server authentication, why is it still being used? Well, there are several reasons for this, which include:

❑   It is easy to set up and manage. You can add, remove, or change the password of SQL Server users by either using Enterprise Manager or T-SQL.

❑   It is easy to deploy. You can give the same SQL Server log in account to five, five hundred, or more people who can then log in to SQL Server. This only leaves you with one SQL Server user to manage.

❑   SQL Server authentication can be used to log in to SQL Server from other client operating systems that do not use Windows authentication.

❑   Windows Authentication is not supported by SQL Server when it is running on either the Windows 98 or Windows Millennium editions.

Now, do any of these reasons sound like they benefit security? Indeed the second reason greatly reduces security of your SQL Server. The only valid reasons for using SQL Server security are the last two, and they are really the exception. SQL Server authentication, no matter how easy to set up and manage, does not offer you a highly secure mechanism for protecting your SQL Server from unauthorized log ins. The only truly secure method is integrating with the operating system using Windows Authentication.

However, if you are supporting legacy applications or deploying a SQL Server for which security isn't really a concern, you still need to know how to create SQL Server users. As I mentioned above, this can be done both from Enterprise Manager and from T-SQL. When using Enterprise Manager you simply select the SQL Server authentication radio button in the New Log in window that we used when creating Windows Authenticated log ins. Once you have clicked on SQL Server authentication you will be able to enter a password for the SQL Server user.

To do this from T-SQL we can execute the `sp_addlog in` system stored procedure from within Query Analyzer. The `sp_addlog in` stored procedure is used in the following format:

```
EXEC sp_addlog in UserName, Password
```

For example:

```
EXEC sp_addlog in 'GlucinaL','mypassword'
```

Using SQL-DMO from VB.NET we would issue:

```
Dim oServer As New SQLDMO.SQLServer()

oServer.Log inSecure = True

'Replace with your own SQL Server Name
oServer.Connect("localhost")

Dim oLog in As New SQLDMO.Log in()

    With oLog in

        'Specifies that the log in type is SQL Standard Log in
        .Type = SQLDMO.SQLDMO_LOG IN_TYPE.SQLDMOLog in_Standard

        .Name = "GlucinaL"

        'Set the initial log in password
        .SetPassword("", "MyPassword")

    End With

oServer.Log ins.Add(oLog in)

oServer.Close
```

To remove a SQL Server log in we use `sp_droplog in`. This uses the following syntax:

```
EXEC sp_droplog in Log inName
```

For example:

```
EXEC sp_droplog in 'MajorL'
```

And again using SQL-DMO from VB.NET we would issue the following:

```
Dim oServer As New SQLDMO.SQLServer()

oServer.Log inSecure = True

'Replace with your own SQL Server Name
oServer.Connect("localhost")

oServer.Log ins.Item("MajorL").Remove()

oServer.Close
```

Note that we also use the Remove *method with SQL Server Authenticated log ins to drop them from our SQL Server.*

There is no concept of a specific denied log in with SQL Server authentication, as opposed to Windows authentication. This is because a log in is either granted permission to log in, or it is dropped. There is no grouping or inheritance of permissions for SQL Server log ins.

The only management of the account you can do other than adding or removing a SQL Server log in is to change the password, to do this we use sp_password which has the following syntax:

```
EXEC sp_password OldPassword, NewPassword, Log inName
```

For example:

```
EXEC sp_password 'Password1', 'Password2', 'GlucinaL'
```

Or using the SetPassword method from SQL-DMO:

```
Dim oServer As New SQLDMO.SQLServer()

oServer.Log inSecure = True

'Replace with your own SQL Server Name
oServer.Connect("localhost")

oServer.Log ins.Item("GlucinaL"). _
        SetPassword("MyPassword", "MyNewPassword")

oServer.Close
```

Remember adding a log in doesn't allow the ability to access a database, it only allows a connection to SQL Server to be established. We cover allowing access to a database a little later in this chapter.

Copying SQL Server Log ins

From time to time databases get moved between servers within an organization either due to the replacement of old hardware, or in an attempt to even out the use of resources if a database has increased in usage. While we haven't looked at how log ins are associated with databases yet, we all understand that a user logs into SQL Server to gain access to one or more databases. If one of the databases that they are accessing has moved to a new SQL Server, then the user will need an appropriate log in on the new SQL Server before they can regain access to the moved database.

It is easy to copy or move Windows authentication log ins between SQL Servers, since these are just an association with an account managed by the Windows domain. You can add a particular Windows user account to many SQL Servers without concern that any account details, such as the password, will differ between SQL Servers. This is because the Windows domain looks after these details and all that SQL Server stores is a reference to the domain account, in the form of the SID (Security Identifier).

However, when dealing with SQL Server log ins things are not quite as straightforward. While you can add the same log in name on multiple servers, you cannot determine what the SQL Server user account password is currently set to. This means if you are just adding SQL Server log ins with the same name to your new server, you have to set a new password for each of these log ins and then communicate the new password to each of the users individually. This may not be so much of an issue for five or ten SQL Server log ins, but what if you are dealing with 500 or 1000 SQL Server log ins? Are you going to set a new password for each of these then phone or e-mail 1000 people with their new password? Fortunately there is a way to add log ins to another SQL Server whilst maintaining an existing password, without even knowing what it is.

SQL Server stores a SQL Server Authenticated Log in's password internally in a system table in an encrypted `varbinary` column. However, as I have mentioned above, the security around SQL Server authentication is quite poor, since the same routine used to encrypt a password on one SQL Server can be used to resolve the original user password on another SQL Server.

As we can easily access the encrypted password, we can also insert it directly into another SQL Server. The SQL Server log in created on the new server will have the same password as the original log in. To do this we make use of an extra property of the `sp_addlog in` command, by utilizing the syntax:

```
EXEC sp_addlog in @log inname=Log in, @passwd=Pasword,
@encryptopt=EncryptionOption
```

The `@encryptopt` parameter is used to tell SQL Server that the password we are submitting for this new log in is already encrypted, so it shouldn't go encrypting it again. This can take one of three possible values:

- ❑   `NULL` – The default when adding a new log in. The password isn't encrypted, it's just plain text.

- ❑   `skip_encryption` – The password is already encrypted so just use it as is.

- ❑   `skip_encryption_old` – The password is already encrypted, however it was encrypted with an earlier version of SQL Server. Allows us to add a log in using the encrypted password created on a previous version of SQL Server and have it function correctly on SQL Server 2000 (in other words allow the user to log in with their original password).

Log in information, including this encrypted password, is stored within the `master.dbo.sysxlog ins` table. From this table we can generate the necessary `sp_addlog in` commands to be run on the SQL Server where we wish to create the new (copied) log ins.

399

To do this we can use a common administration technique; we use a query to generate a script. The result of this query is a valid T-SQL script that can be run against SQL Server. This script simply extracts the log inname and password from the master.dbo.syxlog ins table and adds the appropriate text around these values to form a valid T-SQL sp_addlog in command.

```
SET NOCOUNT ON

-- For each row in our syslog ins table select the actual
-- text string "exec sp_addlog in @log inname=" then
-- concatenate the log in name to the string for example
-- "exec sp_addlog in @log inname='GlucinaL' "
SELECT N'exec sp_addlog in @log iname=N''' + name + ''''

-- Next check to see if the password in this row is NULL
-- If it isn't then script the added @password='encrypted password' to
-- the text we created above.
-- If the password is Null then set it to be NULL in our text string
+ ',@passwd=' + IsNull('N'''+[password]+'''','Null')

-- Finally add the "@encryptopt=skip_encryption" parameter to
-- our text string.
+ ', @encryptopt= ''skip_encryption '''

FROM master.dbo.syslog ins

WHERE isntname=0
```

If you ensure you have the output mode of Query Analyzer set to text (Query | Results In Text menu item), this T-SQL query will produce a script that can be run against other SQL Servers to recreate these log ins. The above query may result in the following output, for example:

```
EXEC sp_addlog in       @log iname=N'SQLLog in1',
                 @passwd=N'·沚(6)□ê撑峏殴·賜軼鐇双音□□□簿殳16.□□□',
                 @encryptopt='skip_encryption'
EXEC sp_addlog in       @log iname=N'SQLLog in2',
                 @passwd=N'·沚(6)翻□□·낟□□膺□罜□□ペ燻□□肵□诓□',
                 @encryptopt='skip_encryption'
EXEC sp_addlog in @log iname=N'SQLLog in3',
                 @passwd=N'·沚(6)·□姣□□欲"捽씾藲칡诙鈚□ض□□□刭猨',
                 @encryptopt='skip_encryption'
```

If you wish to limit the log ins you copy to a certain few, then simply add this WHERE clause and alter the IN list to include the log ins you wish to generate sp_addlog in commands for:

```
AND log inname IN ('SQLLog in1', 'SQLLog in2, 'SQLLog in3')
```

Everyone who connects to SQL Server, be it a database application user or a SQL Server DBA, does so through a SQL Server log in. Obviously the log ins used for administration purposes require higher level privileges than standard database users, and what gives these log ins the necessary additional privileges is their Server Role membership.

Log in Roles

Whatever way you decided to create your log ins, either SQL Server Authenticated log ins or Windows authenticated log ins, you can assign these log ins to Server Roles if required. While most normal users will not be members of a Server Role, such roles can be useful for assigning certain privileges to administration staff, or indeed special log ins. The permissions that a Server Role allows apply to the SQL Server and all databases that exist within it.

There are no permissions to apply against a log in in SQL Server, other than assigning the log in to one of the predefined Server Roles. All log ins not within a Server Role are treated equally although, as we will see shortly, these log ins may gain vastly different permissions within a database. Remember we are still talking server log ins in SQL Server, and that log ins are not database users.

There are eight Server Roles in SQL Server 2000. Each of these roles offers a slightly different level of privileges to their members. These are:

Server Role	Description
sysadmin	This role assigns privileges to perform any task in SQL Server, including configuration tasks. Members of this role can access all the data within every database and can perform any tasks with these databases. This role is equivalent to the Administrators group within the operating system's security, and as such only select administration staff should be a member of this role.
serveradmin	Can change SQL Server configuration options and shut down the service, but being a member of this server role alone does not allow any permissions within the user databases.
setupadmin	Can configure linked servers and configure a stored procedure to run at server startup, but is more restrictive than serveradmin.
securityadmin	Can grant, revoke, and deny log ins to SQL Server.
processadmin	Can execute the KILL command to terminate SQL Server processes.
dbcreator	Can create and alter database options for any of the databases on this SQL Server. Can also restore databases but, once again, does not specifically allow any permission within a database.
diskadmin	Manages disk files. Can increase the size of database files, and add additional files to a database as required.
bulkadmin	Can execute the bulk insert command, as long as they have the INSERT permission on the table into which they are bulk inserting.

If you are using Enterprise Manager to assign log ins to Server Roles, you do this from the **Server Roles** tab of the **Log in** property box that we used above, or from the **Server Roles** node in SQL Server Enterprise Manager as shown in the diagram below.

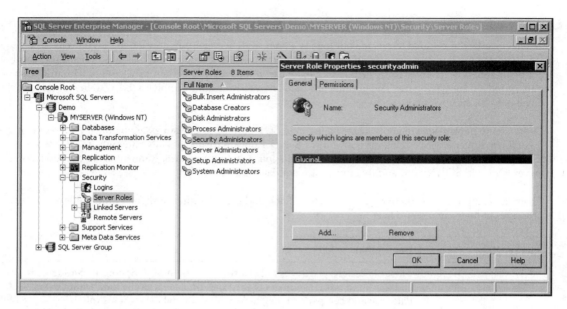

From T-SQL, log ins are assigned to ServerRoles using the sp_addsrvrolemember command. This has the following syntax:

```
EXEC sp_addsrvrolemember Log inName, RoleName
```

For example:

```
EXEC sp_addsrvrolemember 'GlucinaL', 'sysadmin'
```

When using SQL-DMO we make use of the ServerRoles collection of ServerRole objects that is associated with the SQLServer object. The AddMember method is called to add a SQL Server log in to the server role, as in the following example:

```
Dim oServer As New SQLDMO.SQLServer()

oServer.Log inSecure = True

'Replace with your own SQL Server Name
oServer.Connect("localhost")

'Adds a SQL Server log in to a fixed server role.
oServer.ServerRoles.Item("sysadmin").AddMember("MajorL")

oServer.Close
```

These log ins can be removed from a role by using sp_dropsrvrolemember:

```
EXEC sp_dropsrvrolemember Log inName, RoleName
```

For example:

```
EXEC sp_dropsrvrolemember 'GlucinaL', 'sysadmin'
```

To remove a SQL Server log in from a fixed server role using SQL-DMO we use:

```
Dim oServer As New SQLDMO.SQLServer()

oServer.Log inSecure = True

'Replace with your own SQL Server Name
oServer.Connect("localhost")

'Removes a SQL Server log in to a fixed server role.
oServer.ServerRoles.Item("sysadmin").DropMember("MajorL")

oServer.Close
```

An important point here is that there is no command to deny a particular log in from a `ServerRole`. You should be very careful, when adding Windows groups as members of a `ServerRole`, in ensuring that all the members of this Windows group really ought to have all the privileges that you are assigning. You must be sure of this, since there is no way to block an individual group member from inheriting every privilege within a `ServerRole`; the only way to do this would be to deny them access to log in to SQL Server entirely.

Giving users the ability to create a database is a bit of an anomaly, since this is not controlled by assigning log ins to particular server roles. Instead it is assigned to specific database users of the `master` database. To learn more about this, we'll now move to the database user level and the permissions that can be assigned with a SQL Server database.

Database Permissions

Permissions within a SQL Server database do not get assigned to log ins; rather they get assigned to **database users**, or **database roles**. A database user is a user created within each database, and is unique to each database. While you can have a database user of the same name in multiple databases, each of these users is completely independent of one another.

All database permissions get assigned to these database users (or roles) and the only link between database users and server log ins is that a database user is associated with a server log in internally. A SQL Server database user may be associated with one and only one SQL Server Log in. A server log in may only be associated with one database user within a given database. However, a Server log in may be associated with database users in multiple databases. This association is based on an internal ID so there is no need for a SQL Server log in and a database user to have the same name, although it does make administration easier to manage.

We add database users using the `sp_grantdbaccess` command, which has the following syntax:

```
EXEC sp_grantdbaccess Log inName, DBUserName
```

Log inName is the server log in that this database user is to be associated with. DBUserName is the name of the database user to be created and is unique within the current database. For example:

```
USE HumanResources
EXEC sp_grantdbaccess 'GlucinaL','dbGlucinaL'
```

It is important to remember that you must be currently connected to the database that you wish to grant access to, as shown in the above example, which changes to the HumanResources database before granting access to the specified log in.

To grant database access using SQL-DMO we use the Database.Users collection:

```
Dim oServer As New SQLDMO.SQLServer()

oServer.Log inSecure = True

'Replace with your own SQL Server Name
oServer.Connect("localhost")
```

```
Dim oUser As New SQLDMO.User()

    With oUser

        ' Specifies the name of the Database user
        .Name = "dbGlucinaL"

        ' Specifies the log in which this
        ' database user is mapped to
        .Log in = "GlucinaL"

    End With

    oServer.Databases.Item("HumanResources").Users.Add(oUser)

    oServer.Close()
```

And to remove a database user we execute the sp_revokedbaccess command, which has the syntax:

```
EXEC sp_revokedbaccess DBUserName
```

For example:

```
USE HumanResources
EXEC sp_revokedbaccess 'dbGlucinaL'
```

while our SQL-DMO example looks like this:

```
Dim oServer As New SQLDMO.SQLServer()

oServer.Log inSecure = True

'Replace with your own SQL Server Name
oServer.Connect("localhost")

' Remove the existing database user.
oServer.Databases.Item("HumanResources"). _
         Users.Item("dbGlucinaL").Remove()

oServer.Close()
```

Before we look at assigning permissions to these database users, we first need to talk about database roles, which can be used to group them together.

Database Roles

A database role is a means of grouping users together for the purpose of assigning permissions. A database role can contain many database users and a database user can be the member of one or more database roles. However, database roles cannot be nested, so a database role cannot be the member of another database role.

There are two types of database roles, there are **fixed database roles** and **user-defined database roles**. First let's cover the fixed database roles.

Fixed Database Roles

All databases have ten built-in database roles that cannot be removed. Nine of these (shown in the table below) have special privileges associated with the role that cannot be changed and are inherited by the members of these database roles:

Fixed Database Role	Description
db_owner	Has full permission to perform any activity within a database. Can view, update, or delete all data and create or drop all objects.
db_accessadmin	Can add or remove all users within a database.
db_datareader	Can view data contained within all tables in the database. Cannot change the data by being a member of this fixed database role alone.
db_datawriter	Can modify all the data in every table within a database. However, a user cannot change the object structures by being a member of this fixed database role alone. Being a member of this fixed role does not allow the reading of data. More on this overleaf.

Table continued on following page

Fixed Database Role	Description
db_ddladmin	Can add, modify, or drop all objects within a database. A user cannot view or change the data within the database tables through being a member of this role alone.
db_securityadmin	Can modify role membership and grant/revoke and deny all statement and object permissions within the database.
db_backupoperator	Can back up the database. A user doesn't have permissions to view any of the data by being a member of this role alone.
db_denydatareader	Cannot view any data within any of the tables in the database. This overrides any permission that may have been granted to the database user.
db_denydatawriter	Cannot modify any of the data within any of the tables in the database. This also overrides any permission that may have been granted to the database user.

The db_datawriter fixed database role allows the writing of data to all tables within the SQL Server database but does not allow the reading of data when used alone. This does not simply mean you cannot SELECT from the tables but instead means any command that requires the reading of existing data will fail. Take the following command:

```
UPDATE dbo.Employees
SET Surname='Major'
WHERE EmployeeID=2
```

If the database user is only a member of the db_datawriter database role this will fail, since the EmployeeID=2 clause requires the data within the Employees table to be read to determine what rows match this condition. The following statement on the other hand will succeed as this can INSERT the row without retrieving information from existing rows.

```
INSERT dbo.Departments(Description)
VALUES('Credit Control')
```

As we will see in the next section, an explicitly denied permission overrides any permissions inherited from the fixed database roles by a particular user.

The tenth fixed database role, public, is slightly different in that it does not have permissions defined by default and always contains all the users within a database. Also, unlike the other fixed database roles, the permissions on public can be changed. The public role is useful when you wish to assign a permission, such as the permission to execute a certain stored procedure, to everyone within a database. We will look at assigning these permissions shortly.

User-Defined Database Roles

The other type of role is the user-defined database role. Any number of these can be created so that users can be grouped and simultaneously acquire the set of permissions you choose to assign to the role. This prevents the need for the same permissions to be explicitly granted to multiple database users. By granting the permissions throughout the database to the database role, any database users that are the member of that role will inherit the permissions that have been granted.

To add a user-defined role we use the sp_addrole command and this has the following syntax:

```
EXEC sp_addrole RoleName
```

For example:

```
EXEC sp_addrole 'UsersWhoViewData'
```

To add a role from VB.NET with SQL-DMO we use the DatabaseRole object. This is accessible from the Database collection.

```
Dim oServer As New SQLDMO.SQLServer()

oServer.Log inSecure = True

'Replace with your own SQL Server Name
oServer.Connect("localhost")

Dim oDBRole As New SQLDMO.DatabaseRole()

oDBRole.Name = "UsersWhoViewData"

' Add the new database role to the database
oServer.Databases.Item("HumanResources"). _
          DatabaseRoles.Add(oDBRole)

oServer.Close()
```

To remove a user-defined role we execute sp_droprole and its syntax is:

```
EXEC sp_droprole RoleName
```

For example:

```
EXEC sp_droprole 'UsersWhoViewData'
```

Dropping the database role with SQL-DMO will look something like:

```
Dim oServer As New SQLDMO.SQLServer()

oServer.Log inSecure = True

'Replace with your own SQL Server Name
oServer.Connect("localhost")

' Remove the database role from the database
oServer.Databases.Item("HumanResources"). _
          DatabaseRoles.Item("UsersWhoViewData").Remove()

oServer.Close()
```

407

Adding and Removing Role Members

We add database users to a database role, either fixed or user defined, by using the sp_addrolemember command, which has the following syntax:

```
EXEC sp_addrolemember RoleName, MemberName
```

If you add the UsersWhoViewData database role again (using the method we have just outlined above) then you can add members to this role by executing sp_addrolemember, as follows:

```
EXEC sp_addrolemember 'UsersWhoViewData' , 'GlucinaL'
```

The AddMember method allows a DatabaseUser to be added to a DatabaseRole from SQL-DMO, as follows:

```
Dim oServer As New SQLDMO.SQLServer()

oServer.Log inSecure = True

'Replace with your own SQL Server Name
oServer.Connect("localhost")

' Add the database user dbGlucinaL
' as a member of the UsersWhoViewData database role
oServer.Databases.Item("HumanResources"). _
    DatabaseRoles.Item("UsersWhoViewData"). _
        AddMember("dbGlucinaL")

oServer.Close()
```

To remove a member from a role we execute sp_droprolemember, which has the same syntax as sp_addrolemember:

```
EXEC sp_droprolemember RoleName, MemberName
```

For example:

```
EXEC sp_droprolemember 'UsersWhoViewData' , 'GlucinaL'
```

As with the previous task we also have a SQL-DMO method to take care of business from VB.NET:

```
Dim oServer As New SQLDMO.SQLServer()

oServer.Log inSecure = True

'Replace with your own SQL Server Name
oServer.Connect("localhost")

oServer.Databases.Item("HumanResources"). _
    DatabaseRoles.Item("UsersWhoViewData"). _
        DropMember("dbGlucinaL")

oServer.Close()
```

Assigning Permissions

When a database user is created it is a member of the `public` database role but has no permissions granted by default. Unless you have granted permissions to the `public` role, then they cannot do or access anything. Until permissions are explicitly granted, or the user is added to a database role that has been granted permissions, this is how they will stay.

The type of permissions that can be granted to a database user or database role can be broken up into **statement permissions** or **object permissions**. Statement permissions affect what database-related commands the user is allowed to execute, object permissions affect what database objects (table, view, stored procedure, or function) a user can access and the way in which they can be accessed.

The statement permissions are:

Statement Permission	Description
CREATE DATABASE	Can create a database within SQL Server. Can only be granted to users of the `master` database.
CREATE DEFAULT	Can create a user-defined default within the current database. A default is a pre built expression that can be assigned to tables as the default value for a column. See SQL Server Books Online for more information on defaults.
CREATE FUNCTION	Can create user-defined functions within the current database.
CREATE PROCEDURE	Can create stored procedures within the current database.
CREATE RULE	Can create a rule within the current database.
CREATE TABLE	Can create tables within the current database.
CREATE VIEW	Can create views within the current database.
BACKUP DATABASE	Can perform a full or differential backup of the database.
BACKUP LOG	Can perform a transaction log backup for the database.

And the object permissions that are grantable within a SQL Server database are:

Object Permission	Description
SELECT	Can retrieve rows from a specified table or view.
INSERT	Can insert rows into a specified table.
UPDATE	Can update rows within a specified table.
DELETE	Can delete rows from a specified table.
REFERENCES	If also granted the CREATE TABLE statement permission, the database user can create a table that has a foreign key constraint against the specified table.
EXECUTE	Is allowed to execute a specified stored procedure or user-defined function.

So now we know what they are, how do we assign them?

GRANT / REVOKE / DENY

Both statement and object permissions are granted, removed, or explicitly prevented using the GRANT, REVOKE, and DENY T-SQL commands. These do have slightly different formats depending upon whether you are referring to statement or object permissions, so let's take a look at the appropriate syntax.

For statement permissions the syntax is:

```
GRANT StatetementPermission TO DatabaseUser/DatabaseRole
```

To illustrate this, create the database user dbGlucinaL again using one of the methods described above, and then grant the CREATE TABLE statement permission as follows:

```
GRANT CREATE TABLE TO dbGlucinaL
GRANT CREATE TABLE TO PowerUsersRole
```

When using SQL-DMO statement permissions are granted using the Grant method of the Database object.

```
Dim oServer As New SQLDMO.SQLServer()

oServer.Log inSecure = True

'Replace with your own SQL Server Name
oServer.Connect("localhost")

' Grant the Create table permission to our
' dbGlucinaL database user.
oServer.Databases.Item("HumanResources"). _
Grant(SQLDMO.SQLDMO_PRIVILEGE_TYPE.SQLDMOPriv_CreateTable, _
                      "dbGlucinaL")

oServer.Close()
```

For object permissions the syntax is:

```
GRANT ObjectPermission ON Object TO DatabaseUser/DatabaseRole
```

For example:

```
GRANT EXECUTE ON MyNewStoredProcedure TO dbGlucinaL
GRANT EXECUTE ON MyNewStoredProcedure TO ApplicationUsersRole
```

From SQL-DMO object permissions are granted using the GRANT method of the object for which you wish to grant the permission, such as:

```
Dim oServer As New SQLDMO.SQLServer()

oServer.Log inSecure = True

'Replace with your own SQL Server Name
```

```
oServer.Connect("localhost")

' Grant the ability to execute our ListEmployees
' stored procedure
oServer.Databases.Item("HumanResources"). _
    StoredProcedures.Item("ListEmployees"). _
        Grant(SQLDMO.SQLDMO_PRIVILEGE_TYPE.SQLDMOPriv_Execute, _
                        "dbGlucinaL")

oServer.Close()
```

If the database user inherits permissions from a database role, these permissions can be overridden by explicitly denying them. As with log ins, an explicitly denied permission will always override an inherited grant of that permission.

A statement permission can be denied using the following syntax:

```
DENY StatetementPermission TO DatabaseUser/DatabaseRole
```

while for object permissions the syntax is:

```
DENY ObjectPermission ON Object TO DatabaseUser/DatabaseRole
```

Using our previous example, we can now deny these permissions to our database user:

```
DENY CREATE TABLE TO dbGlucinaL
DENY CREATE TABLE TO SloppyUsersRole
DENY EXECUTE ON MyNewStoreProcedure TO dbGlucinaL
```

In the case of SQL-DMO we use the DENY method of either our object, for object permissions, or the database object for statement permissions, as follows:

```
Dim oServer As New SQLDMO.SQLServer()

oServer.Log inSecure = True

'Replace with your own SQL Server Name
oServer.Connect("localhost")

' Deny the ability to execute our ListEmployees
' stored procedure
oServer.Databases.Item("HumanResources"). _
    StoredProcedures.Item("ListEmployees"). _
        Deny(SQLDMO.SQLDMO_PRIVILEGE_TYPE.SQLDMOPriv_Execute, _
                    "dbGlucinaL")

' Deny the ability to Create Tables to dbGlucinaL
oServer.Databases.Item("HumanResources"). _
    Deny(SQLDMO.SQLDMO_PRIVILEGE_TYPE.SQLDMOPriv_CreateTable, _
                    "dbGlucinaL")

oServer.Close()
```

If a database role is denied permissions then all the members of that database role are also denied those permissions, even if they have been explicitly granted to a database user, or the database user has inherited these permissions from another database role of which it is also a member.

We can also remove permissions from a database user or role with the REVOKE command. REVOKE can be used to remove an explicit GRANT or DENY of permissions.

```
REVOKE CREATE TABLE FROM dbGlucinaL
REVOKE CREATE TABLE FROM SloppyUsersRole
REVOKE EXECUTE ON MyNewStoreProcedure FROM dbGlucinaL
```

This leaves the dbGlucinaL user and SloppyUsersRole role with no explicit permissions on the objects specified in the revoke statements.

Revoking from SQL-DMO looks like this:

```
Dim oServer As New SQLDMO.SQLServer()

oServer.Log inSecure = True

'Replace with your own SQL Server Name
oServer.Connect("localhost")
```

```
' Revoke the ability to execute our ListEmployees
' stored procedure
oServer.Databases.Item("HumanResources"). _
    StoredProcedures.Item("ListEmployees"). _
        Revoke(SQLDMO.SQLDMO_PRIVILEGE_TYPE.SQLDMOPriv_Execute, _
                        "dbGlucinaL")

' Revoke the ability to Create Tables to dbGlucinaL
oServer.Databases.Item("HumanResources"). _
    Revoke(SQLDMO.SQLDMO_PRIVILEGE_TYPE.SQLDMOPriv_CreateTable, _
                        "dbGlucinaL")
```

```
oServer.Close()
```

To help explain GRANT, REVOKE, and DENY let's take at look at an example. First connect to SQL Server using Query Analyzer, and log in as sa (or a user with db_owner privileges to the HumanResources database). Ensure that your currently selected database is HumanResources.

Next add the Managers and Employees database roles:

```
EXEC sp_addrole 'Managers'
EXEC sp_addrole 'Sales'
```

What we'll do now is grant the ability to SELECT from our table to our first database role, and explicitly deny the ability to SELECT from this database table to our second database role:

```
GRANT SELECT ON dbo.Salaries TO Managers
DENY SELECT ON dbo.Salaries TO Sales
```

Now we create a new SQL Server log in, along with a new database user that is associated with this new log in.

```
EXEC sp_addlog in 'MyTestLog in','password'
EXEC sp_grantdbaccess 'MyTestLog in','dbMyTestUser'
```

After this we add this new database user as a member of both of our newly created database roles:

```
EXEC sp_addrolemember 'Managers','dbMyTestUser'
EXEC sp_addrolemember 'Sales','dbMyTestUser'
```

Finally, we use the SETUSER command to change the security context of the current session to that of the database user we have just created, the dbMyTestUser, and SELECT everything in MyTestTable:

```
SETUSER 'dbMyTestUser' --Change to this users security context

SELECT * FROM dbo.Salaries
```

While we may have been logged in as a user with full database privileges, after the SETUSER command we only have the permissions we have granted to dbMyTestUser. The SELECT from MyTestTable fails with the following error message:

Server: Msg 229, Level 14, State 5, Line 1
SELECT permission denied on object 'Salaries', database 'HumanResources', owner 'dbo'.

This is because the DENY permission granted on the second database role has overridden any GRANT permission that may also have been given.

Monitoring SQL Server

If everything always ran fine, 100% of the time, there would be little point in monitoring SQL Server's activity. However, in the 'real' world things don't happen like this. As the size, structure, and code surrounding a database is usually in a constant state of flux, sooner or later unexpected issues are bound to occur, and more often than not these unexpected issues are performance or security related.

SQL Server provides a number of methods for monitoring the activity that is occurring within it. One of the most useful tools is the **SQL Server Profiler**.

SQL Server Profiler

SQL Server Profiler is one of the most under-utilized tools in the SQL Server application set. It is extremely valuable to both DBAs and developers because it assists in the isolation of issues that have occurred between a client application and SQL Server.

Unfortunately a lot of database applications are created in development environments that have a fraction of the data, and a fraction of the number of users, that they are exposed to once they have gone live. Unless you have created some very sloppy T-SQL code, almost all SQL statements will perform acceptably when executing operations on a few hundred rows.

However, this is not necessarily the case once the data volume increases tenfold. All too often, after these database applications have been deployed and running for a few months, they begin to suffer from performance problems. The symptoms include screens that used to take seconds to appear, now taking tens of seconds to appear. Clicking the update button used to return in seconds, now it times out 2 out of 3 times, and so on.

The nice thing about SQL Server Profiler is that it allows you to identify the cause of these sorts of issues very easily. SQL Server Profiler monitors every interaction between a client application and a server and, as part of this task, tracks the duration and resources used by a particular request from a particular client connection.

If an application is performing poorly we can set up a profiler trace to capture all the statements that are taking place between the client and SQL Server. If we are trying to isolate a particular problem we can set up filters to exclude events that we are not interested in. Let's take a look at how to use this tool.

Capturing a Trace

First we need to run SQL Server Profiler and connect to the server for which you wish to capture a SQL Profiler trace. SQL Server Profiler can be found on the Start menu, in the SQL Server program group. Enter the server and authentication information needed to connect to your SQL Server.

On the General tab of the Trace Properties window you can enter the name for the trace and where you would like the trace data to be saved (if at all).

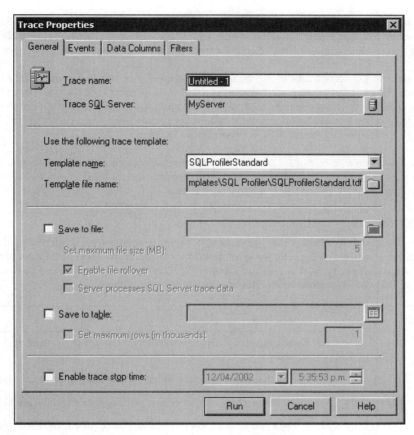

By default the trace will only be captured to the screen, however you can also choose to save the trace data into a disk file and/or a database table. Saving the trace data into a database table is particularly useful as you can easily query the resulting table to identify events that match or exceed criteria you specify. If you are monitoring to identify performance issues, just make sure that you are not logging the trace data to the same server from which you are capturing events. Doing so will only skew your results as the impact on the trace logging can be noticeable on busy servers.

If you are logging to a file, you have a couple more options to consider. The first is file rollover. Trace files can get big, and this can happen fast for busy servers. Instead of creating a trace file that is many gigabytes in size that grinds your machine to a halt later when you try and examine it, you can tell the Profiler to create a new file every time the file reaches a specified size. The filenames of each of these rollover files will be appended with a number indicating their rolled-over order.

The second option you have is whether you wish SQL Server to guarantee that every event is captured into the log file. By default the Profiler will capture all the events that it can. Its ability to do this can however be affected if SQL Server gets busy, and in such conditions the Profiler may miss some events. By turning off the **Server Processes SQL Server Trace Data** option, you can ensure that every event is logged. However, if your server gets busy it may be forced to slow down so that the Profiler can keep up. Also, if the Profiler is forced to stop logging to the file, because it runs out of disk space for example, then SQL Server will be shut down. These factors make this option only suitable when tracing security auditing information, as opposed to performance-related information.

The third option available on the General tab allows you to specify a date and time that the Profiler trace should automatically stop. This is useful if you only wish to trace overnight, for example, and don't wish to get up early to come into work by 10am to stop the trace (we are in IT after all).

The Event and Data Columns tabs allow you to select the specific events, and information generated by those events, to be included in your trace output. You will see a lot more than the ones we will discuss below, however these will be the ones you'll see most often. The others are usually used in special circumstances, or when using the Profiler to audit security activity rather than performance issues. You can find an explanation of all the SQL Server Profiler events in SQL Server Books Online.

The last tab allows you to specify filter criteria. This is where you can choose to monitor only those events that are being generated by a particular user, or a particular database, or those events that were running over a particular duration. We'll return to this tab in a later section.

Profiler Events

Every interaction that occurs between a client and SQL Server generates what is referred to as an **event**. These events are what the Profiler is listening for. It will capture and store them as they occur on the basis of the event criteria you specify. SQL Server can monitor the following event classes, and there are a number of specific events that you can choose to monitor specifically for each of them:

Event Class	Description
Cursors	Events raised by cursor operations, such as the opening and closing of a cursor.
Database	Events that occur when a database is changing in physical size.
Errors and Warnings	Occurs when SQL Server errors, warnings, or exceptions are thrown.
Locks	These events occur whenever a lock is acquired, released, escalated, or deadlocked.
Objects	Occur whenever an object (such as a table) is accessed.
Performance	These events are raised to show the degree of parallelism (number of CPUs being used to execute the query) and the execution plan of a query being executed by SQL Server.
Scans	Occur whenever a table or index scan takes place.
Security Audit	Security auditing events, we will take a look as these in more detail in a moment.
Server	A single event that occurs when SQL Server changes memory configuration.
Sessions	An event that only occurs when SQL Server Profiler starts a trace. This shows what connections are established between clients and SQL Server when the trace began. This doesn't get fired when any new sessions are established. To detect this you should use the Security Audit events instead.

Event Class	Description
Stored Procedures	Used to monitor the execution of stored procedures, and T-SQL submitted over an RPC connection.
Transactions	Events that occur whenever Distributed Transactions or Local SQL Server transaction are initiated, or whenever the transaction log is written to.
TSQL	Events that occur when T-SQL is submitted by a client application to SQL Server over a standard connection.
User configurable	10 Profiler events that you can use for your own purposes.

As I said, each of these event classes has numerous events within it that can be monitored. In terms of tracing actual server performance some of the most valuable events that you can use are:

Class	Event	Description
Locks	Lock: Deadlock	Identifies when a deadlock has occurred. For more information on deadlocks see Chapter 8.
Performance	Execution Plan	Shows the execution plan the current T-SQL batch is using to execute.
Stored Procedures	SP: Recompile	This shows that the stored procedure being executed was recompiled.
Stored Procedures	SP: RPC Completed	Occurs when a command executed over RPC has completed.
Stored Procedures	SP: SP Completed	Occurs when a stored procedure has completed execution.
Stored Procedures	SP: Stmt Completed	Occurs when each individual T-SQL statement within a stored procedure has completed.
TSQL	SQL: Batch completed	Occurs when a T-SQL batch has been completed.

However, the Profiler doesn't just end there with monitoring the events that have occurred. It also monitors the CPU, disk, and other activity for these events. There are a number of data columns that hold information about the event that has been generated. Here are some of the more useful event data columns:

Data Column	Description
Application Name	The name of the client application that creates the connection to SQL Server on which the event was generated.
Binary Data	The binary data representation of the event.
CPU	The amount of CPU time consumed by the event.
DatabaseName	The database in which the statement that generated the event is running.
Duration	The length of time in milliseconds that the statement that generated the event was running.
End Time	The date and time when the event was completed.
Log inName	The SQL Server authenticated, or Windows authenticated, log in from which the event was generated.
Reads	The number of logical I/O reads generated by the event.
SPID	The SQL Server process ID of the connection that generated the event.
TextData	The text of the statement that generated the event. For events that are generated by SQL statements (such as SQL: Batch completed and SP: RPC Completed for example) this contains the text of the actual SQL statements being executed by SQL Server.
Writes	The number of physical disk writes that were generated by the event.

Not all data columns are available for all events. If the data column isn't available, a NULL will just appear in the data columns place within the Profiler output.

Profiling Long Running Queries

To demonstrate how we can identify long running queries open the Profiler, connect to your SQL Server and create a new SQL Server trace (don't worry about logging it to file or table) and select only the **Stored Procedures SP: Completed** event. The default data columns are acceptable for this demonstration. Leaving the filter blank at this stage, click **Run**.

Now open a SQL Server Query Analyzer window with a connection to your SQL Server. Select our HumanResources test database and create the following two stored procedures. Both of them use the WAITFOR DELAY command to pause the execution of the stored procedure for a number of seconds:

```
CREATE PROCEDURE RunsQuickly
AS
SET NOCOUNT ON
WAITFOR DELAY '000:00:01'
GO

CREATE PROCEDURE RunsSlowly
AS
SET NOCOUNT ON
WAITFOR DELAY '000:00:10'
GO
```

Now open two more Query Analyzer windows and select the `HumanResources` database to be the current database. In the first Query Analyzer window, execute our first procedure in an infinite loop by issuing the following:

```
WHILE 1=1
    EXEC RunsQuickly
```

In the second Query Analyzer window run the following command to run our second stored procedure in an infinite loop:

```
WHILE 1=1
    EXEC RunsSlowly
```

Returning now to our Profiler trace you will see the events being generated. Most of the events listed are the completion of our `RunsQuickly` stored procedure, since this is running 10 times as often as our `RunsSlowly` stored procedure. This is similar to the type of trace output you would get if you monitored most production databases without a Profiler filter. While they wouldn't all be the same stored procedure, as in our example, most of the executions listed will be from stored procedures that run`very quickly and run often. These are not usually of interest to us when attempting to isolate slow performing queries.

However, by adding a filter to the trace properties, we can leave out information that we're not interested in. In our example, stop the trace in the Profiler and add a filter in the trace properties (**File | Properties**). The filter we wish to add is on the **Duration** column and our filter criteria is '**Duration is Greater than or equal to 5000**' to only show events that take over 5 seconds to execute:

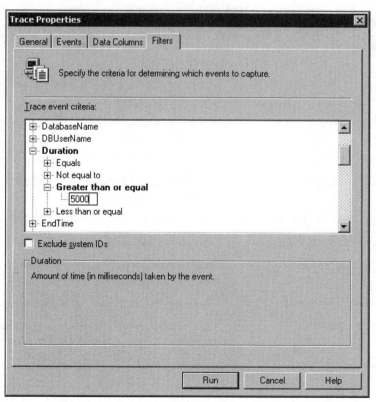

419

Now when we rerun the trace, only those stored procedure executions that are not performing within our criteria (in other words our `RunsSlowly` procedure) are captured in our trace results allowing us to easily identify code that is performing poorly.

You can now stop the trace by clicking the red stop button in the SQL Server Profiler window, and also stop both of our queries from running by clicking the red stop button in each query's respective Query Analyzer window.

Auditing Database Security

While the interface looks much the same, the Profiler in SQL Server 2000 is much different from the first release in SQL Server 7.0. The number of events generated by SQL Server has increased dramatically with the Profiler now being able to collect database security auditing information. It is a reliable tool for collecting security information because, as we described above, it can now be configured to guarantee that it will collect all events generated by SQL Server, something that's critical when collecting security information.

There are a large number of security auditing events available in the Profiler and these provide a means of customizing the density at which you audit, from a low level of auditing such as log in and logout events, to a high level of auditing that gathers auditing information for every object that is accessed.

The auditing events are members of the `Security Audit` event class. Here are some of the more important and useful ones:

Security Event	Description
Audit Add DB User Event	Raised when a user is added to or removed from a SQL Server database.
Audit Add Log in to Server Role Event	Raised when a log in is added or removed from a `ServerRole` within SQL Server.
Audit Add Member to DB Role Event	This event occurs when a database user is either added or removed from a database role.
Audit Add Role Event	Occurs when a database role is created or deleted.
Audit Addlog in Event	Occurs when a SQL Server authenticated log in is either created or removed.
Audit Backup/Restore Event	Occurs when a backup or restore of a database has begun.
Audit Log in Event	This event is raised when a client logs into SQL Server.
Audit Log in Change Password Event	Raised when a SQL Server authenticated log in has its password changed.
Audit Log in Failed Event	This event occurs when a log in attempt is unsuccessful.
Audit Log in GDR Event	Occurs whenever a Windows authenticated user is granted, revoked, or denied permission to log in to SQL Server.

Security Event	Description
Audit Logout Event	Occurs when a user with a current connection to SQL Server closes their connection.
Audit Object GDR Event	Records object Grant, Deny, or Revoke events. This would include the granting of SELECT, INSERT, UPDATE, DELETE, and REFERENCE on a table or view, and EXECUTE on stored procedures, for example.
Audit Object Permission Event	This event occurs whenever an object is accessed. This could be triggered by a SELECT, INSERT, UPDATE, DELETE, or EXECUTE.
Audit Statement GDR Event	This event occurs when a specific statement Grant, Revoke or Deny takes place. This will occur when CREATE TABLE, or CREATE PROCEDURE statement permissions are managed, for example.
Audit Statement Permission Event	Occurs when a statement that can be secured by using statement permissions is utilized. This event occurs irrespective of whether the use of the statement was successful or not.

To create an audit trace start up SQL Server Profiler as before (if you haven't already) and connect to the server that you wish to audit for security information. This time create the trace so that you output the trace information to a file and enable file rollover, so that you will not have to interrogate excessively large trace files. The default of 5Mb is a bit small though; a setting of 100Mb is more practical. You will also want to enable the **Server processes SQL Server trace data** option to ensure that you capture all security-related events.

Since SQL Server will be taking the responsibility of inserting the audit events directly into the log file, we must specify a Universal Naming Convention (UNC) path to a file share that is accessible to the account that the SQL Server service is running under. If the SQL Server Service account is running under the local system account security context, then this will not be able to access file shares on other computers on your network. But the path you specify still has to be a UNC path, though this will be a UNC path to a share on the local machine instead of a network share. To find out what account SQL Server is running under, right-click the Server node in Enterprise Manager and select **Properties**. The **Security** tab will have the name of the Windows account that the SQL Server service is running under.

Once you have the UNC path sorted, you can enter it and continue setting up your audit trace.

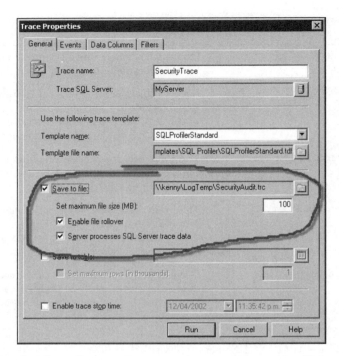

On the Events tab, select the audit events that you are interested in capturing. Unless you are monitoring a particularly sensitive database, good choices are usually Log in, Logout, and Statement events.

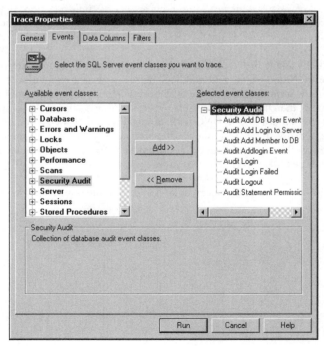

We have chosen a number of events, as you can see from this screenshot, and this may seem like a lot. But almost all of these events are required to monitor a SQL Server at a reasonably secure level:

❑ Audit Add DB User – Allows us to detect users that are added to a database. We can then check that the user is authorized and the permissions for the user are valid.

❑ Audit Add Log in to Server Role – Server roles allow varying levels of administrative privileges right up to full permissions to do everything for the sysadmin role. By auditing the assignment of log ins to server roles we can detect the unauthorized assignment of such privileges.

❑ Audit Add Member to DB Role – As we have discussed, database roles are used for the assignment of permissions. Some of the fixed database roles allow the user to access all database objects, or change permissions on objects within the database. By tracking the assignment of users to roles we can detect potential inappropriate or unauthorized assignments of permissions.

❑ Audit AddLog in – Allows us to detect the authorized creation or deletion of SQL Server Authenticated log ins.

❑ Log in & Logout – When used in conjunction with each other Log in & Logout allows us to record those who are connected to our SQL Server at any given point in time.

❑ Audit Log in Failed -This is a useful event to monitor as repeated or continuous failures may indicate a client application problem, or someone attempting to 'crack' a SQL Server authenticated log in password.

❑ Audit Statement Permission – Allows us to detect the unauthorized use of statement permissions, such as the creation or deletion of a table, view, producer, or function in a production database.

The more events you choose to audit, the more load you are going to place on your server. Try to strike a balance between sensible auditing and an acceptable increase in server load from the auditing process. While the load that this type of auditing places on SQL Server is relatively low, any wasted resource affects the overall throughput and scalability of a system.

For our example trace, the default data columns and filter settings are fine, except that we must remove the default **SQL Profiler** text from the application filter. This is placed as a filter by default so SQL Server Profiler doesn't fill up with events generated within SQL Server by the Profiler application itself, but this isn't needed for a security trace. What's more, as you may remember from Chapter 2, the application name is picked up from the connection string and is completely customizable within code on the client computer. The primary reason for a security audit is to detect unauthorized access. Anyone serious about making unauthorized changes, and with half a brain, would configure the application name of the tool they are using to make these unauthorized changes to, wait for it, SQL Profiler, as there would be a good chance that this default filter has been left on in a lot of environments. They are then free to make unauthorized data changes undetected, leaving DBAs scratching their heads wondering how things managed to get so messed up. But not on our servers!

Once we click **Run**, SQL Server profiler will begin capturing our audit events to our trace files.

Background Profiling

To gather meaningful trace data, whether performance or security, we usually have to leave the profiler running for long periods of time. If we performed traces using the SQL Profiler UI tool this would turn out to be a bit of a pain, since we would either have to leave our server logged in with the SQL Profiler tool running locally, or have a client machine dedicated to running SQL Profiler also kept logged in.

A much better approach is to use the background tracing functionality provided by SQL Server. Without going into too much detail here, we should mention that SQL Profiler itself is just a GUI tool for displaying the trace information. It is SQL Server that generates the trace events themselves, and we can capture these with our own applications, or log them directly to a table by using several stored procedures within SQL Server. More specifically these procedures are:

❑ sp_trace_create – Used for creating a new trace

❑ sp_trace_setevent – Adds or removes both an event and data columns from our trace definition

❑ sp_trace_setfilter – Adds a filter to our trace definition, specifying under what conditions an event is captured

❑ sp_trace_setstatus – Used to start, stop, and delete our trace

In the following example we use all four of these system-stored procedures to create our trace log file.

```
DECLARE @TraceID INT,
    @return int,
    @On   bit

SELECT @On=1
```

Now we create the new trace definition and get passed back the TraceID for use when calling the remainder of the trace procedures. We do this using the sp_trace_create stored procedure (for more information see SQL Server Books Online).

```
    -- Create the new trace and return its ID
EXEC sp_trace_create @TraceID OUTPUT, @options=0,
            @tracefile=N'c:\MyNewTrace'
```

To add the SQL:BatchCompleted event, and TextData, DatabaseID, NTUser Name, Duration, CPU, and Database Name data columns to our trace output we issue the following:

For a full list of event IDs and data column IDs see sp_trace_setevent in SQL Server Books Online.

```
    -- Event SQL:BatchCompleted, column TextData
EXEC sp_trace_setevent   @TraceID, @eventid=12, @columnid=1, @on=@On

    -- Event SQL:BatchCompleted, column DatabaseID
EXEC sp_trace_setevent   @TraceID, @eventid=12, @columnid=3, @on=@On

    -- Event SQL:BatchCompleted, column NTUser Name
```

```
      EXEC sp_trace_setevent    @TraceID, @eventid=12, @columnid=6, @on=@On

      -- Event SQL:BatchCompleted, column Duration
      EXEC sp_trace_setevent    @TraceID, @eventid=12, @columnid=13, @on=@On

      -- Event SQL:BatchCompleted, column CPU
      EXEC sp_trace_setevent    @TraceID, @eventid=12, @columnid=18, @on=@On

      -- Event SQL:BatchCompleted, column Database Name
      EXEC sp_trace_setevent    @TraceID, @eventid=12, @columnid=35, @on=@On
```

Now we set the filter of our trace to only capture events that occur within our HumanResources database. We do this using the sp_trace_setfilter stored procedure (once again see SQL Server Books Online for more details).

```
      -- Add a filter to only capture events that occurred within our
      -- HumanResources database.
      EXEC sp_trace_setfilter @TraceID, @columnid=35, @logical_operator=1,
             @comparison_operator=0, @value=N'HumanResources'
```

At this point we can start the trace.

```
      -- Start our trace
      EXEC sp_trace_setstatus @TraceID, @status=1 -- Status 1=Start Trace
```

The remaining code keeps the trace running for 60 seconds. During this time we need to generate some events that we can observe in our trace file once the capturing of events has completed. The easiest way to achieve this is to use SQL Server Enterprise Manager in order to browse or review the properties of the HumanResources database, since this will generate a reasonable number of SQL: StatementCompleted events.

```
      WAITFOR DELAY '00:01:00'
```

After running for 60 seconds we stop and remove the trace and return a message to let us know it has completed.

```
      -- Stop and delete our trace
      EXEC sp_trace_setstatus @TraceID, @status=0 -- Status 2=Stop Trace
      EXEC sp_trace_setstatus @TraceID, @status=2 -- Status 3=Remove Trace

      SELECT 'Trace has completed'
```

Before you run this code, ensure that the trace file you are creating doesn't already exist; if it does then a new trace will not be created (though no error message will be displayed).

If we wanted to execute this trace whenever SQL Server was running we would wrap the code that starts the trace within a stored procedure. If we create this stored procedure in the master database, we can set this stored procedure to be run every time SQL Server starts up. See sp_procoption in SQL Server Books Online for more information.

To see what traces are currently running on your SQL Server execute the following function:

```
SELECT * FROM :: fn_trace_getinfo(default)
```

Now we have captured our trace data let's learn how we can view the captured output.

Reviewing Trace Output

No matter how you capture your trace output, at some stage you will want to view it and see what events you have actually caught. There are two ways in which you can do this.

The first method uses SQL Server Profiler. From the File menu select the Open | Trace File menu item. Navigate to where the trace file that we created above is located. Select this trace file to be opened. You should see trace data within your SQL Server Profiler window similar to that show in the diagram below.

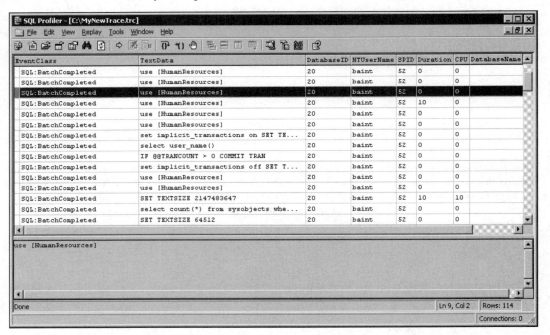

From within SQL Server Profiler you can navigate within your saved trace file to locate any events or issues that may be of concern. Even though the trace is a saved file you can still apply a filter to limit what you actually see on the screen. You can also, if you wish, remove events and data columns (out of a list of those you captured) from the trace display. To do this click File | Properties and click on the Events, Data Columns, or Filters tab.

The second method of reviewing the contents of the trace file involves loading this into a SQL Server database table. Microsoft has provided an inbuilt function with SQL Server to make this really easy, which is named fn_trace_gettable. If you supply a trace filename parameter when calling this function it will return the contents of the trace file in table format. This can then be inserted into a table for long-term storage, while facilitating easy reviewing of the trace data using SQL queries. For example, to load the trace file we create earlier into a new table named MyTraceTable execute the following T-SQL command from Query Analyzer:

```
USE HumanResources
GO
SELECT *
INTO MyTraceTable
FROM ::fn_trace_gettable('C:\MyNewTrace.trc',default)
```

Our trace information is now located within the `MyTraceTable` table and we can query this using standard SQL commands just like every other database table. For example if we wish to list all the `SELECT` commands within our trace results, we could run the following query:

```
SELECT *
FROM dbo.MyTraceTable
WHERE TextData LIKE 'SELECT%'
```

A more common use would be to return the top 10 longest running queries as follows:

```
SELECT TOP 10 TextData,Duration
FROM dbo.MyTraceTable
ORDER BY Duration DESC
```

Or the top 10 most commonly executed queries, such as:

```
SELECT TOP 10 Cast(TextData as varchar(8000)), Count(*) AS Executions
FROM dbo.MyTraceTable
GROUP BY Cast(TextData as varchar(8000))
ORDER BY Executions DESC
```

Note that since the `TextData` column is text we must convert this to the `varchar` data type before we can use this in the `GROUP BY` clause.

Hopefully you are beginning to see the power and potential of SQL Server Profiler not only for production implementations, but also for developing applications. Being able to monitor the interaction between your application and SQL Server is an invaluable tool. Another invaluable tool to include in your development toolbox is the automated index recommendation tool, the Index Tuning Wizard.

Index Tuning Wizard

The third impressive and useful feature of SQL Server Profiler is the ability to capture server activity and then replay this activity through the **Index Tuning Wizard (ITW)**.

The ITW is a tool that was introduced with SQL Server 7.0. It analyzes a snapshot of server activity and uses that analysis to recommend indexes that a database should have to achieve optimum performance.

> *Even though it is very easy to use this tool, behind the scenes there is a lot of complex decision making going on. There is a research paper available on the Web that describes some of the processes and algorithms used to come up with the recommendations. You can access this information at* ftp://ftp.research.microsoft.com/users/AutoAdmin/vldb00.pdf *and also* ftp://ftp.research.microsoft.com/users/AutoAdmin/SIG01-AQP.pdf.

Thankfully the tool protects us from complexity and we need only use a simple wizard interface to benefit from its capabilities. The first step in getting good results from the ITW is to gather a representative sample of user activity by capturing a Profiler trace. There is little point running SQL Server Profiler during non-peak hours and expecting the ITW to come up with the best recommendations for queries executed during your peak periods. You need to capture activity during these peak periods, and may need to weather a bit of a performance hit from the load placed on the server by the profiling process itself during these periods. However, the benefits you may gain if any index recommendations are found can be significant.

To capture a trace for use with the ITW, open up SQL Server Profiler, connect to the server you wish to capture events from, and use the Events tab as we have done previously. The ITW only makes use of certain events and data columns and these have already been defined within a **Trace Template**. From the drop-down list of trace templates, select the SQLProfilerTuning option. By selecting this option all the events and data columns needed for the ITW have now been selected, and are ready to go. But first we should also select the option to log the trace data to a file. There is no need to enable file rollovers this time, as we will only be tracing for a short period of time.

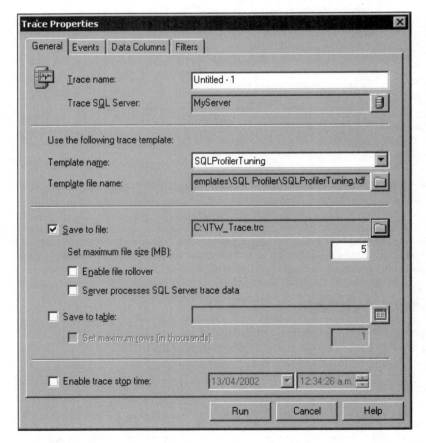

Now just let SQL Server Profiler run, collecting a reasonable representation of the queries and load that your database environment will experience under normal usage. Remember indexing is a relative configuration. While indexes improve the speed of data retrieval, they have a heavy impact on data inserts and modifications.

> **Only by having a representative sample of the types of activity that are occurring can the ITW make informed choices about the indexing that should be implemented for optimal performance overall.**

The amount of time you need to trace for will depend on how busy your application is, and how diverse the types of transactions are. If you have a busy database that is used mainly for short repetitive tasks such as data entry, then 30 minutes or an hour's worth of trace data may be all that is required. However, if you have a less busy server that is having irregular tasks performed against it, you may need to wait half a day or more to gain a true set of the operations that take place against your server.

Once you are happy you have a reasonable representation of your workload, we can begin using the ITW. First stop and close the trace file to end the capture. Next select Tools | Index Tuning Wizard. After connecting to the SQL Server on which you wish to run the analysis, you need to select a few options.

The first is if you wish to keep existing indexes. If you are happy with the current indexing scheme, and you are only looking for new indexes that may benefit some new queries, then you may wish to keep this option set. If, however, you are unsure about the benefit of existing indexes, or if the size or workload of your database has changed drastically since those indexes were implemented, then it would be best to deselect this option so the ITW can evaluate all index possibilities.

Next you need to specify if you wish the ITW to add indexed views. Unless you are running the Enterprise Edition of SQL Server 2000, there is probably no need to add indexed views, since the Query Optimizer will not automatically consider using an indexed view as a means to improve existing query performance. If you are using the Enterprise Edition though then this option should be enabled.

The third option you have on this first screen is the option to set the thoroughness of the tuning process. The more thorough the process, the longer it takes, but the better the recommendations. Unless you have to restrict the length of time the process will take, I would suggest you use the Thorough option.

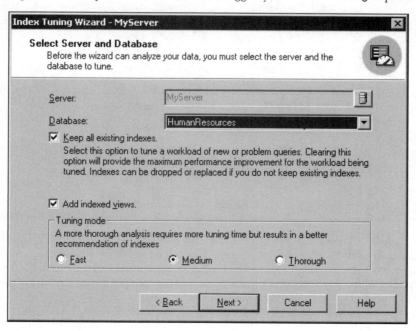

On the next screen you can point the ITW to the trace file we created previously. Also on this screen is the **Advanced** button, which gives access to the **Advanced Options** dialog box. The default options are usually OK, except for the number of queries to sample. If you have a large trace file, you may wish to increase this to more closely represent the number of rows within your trace. The records within the trace are sampled randomly by the ITW up to the number specified in this option.

> **Remember that increasing the number of rows sampled is going to increase the time taken to perform the index analysis.**

On the next screen we can select the tables that we wish to run the ITW over. Normally we would select all tables. If we know that we have unused, or very small, tables that don't require indexing we can deselect these to make the ITW slightly more efficient.

Clicking **Next** will begin the index tuning process. Depending on the size of your database, the size of your trace file, and the options you have chosen, this could be completed in seconds, minutes, or hours. However, when it does complete you will get a results screen detailing the recommended indexes that you can add to your database.

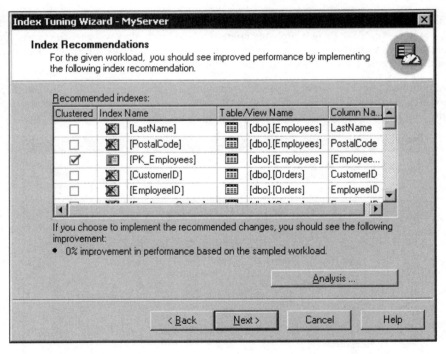

If there are recommendations then you can either choose to have the ITW apply the changes immediately, apply them at a scheduled time, or save the changes to a script file. For most production environments you would want to save these to a script file then review the recommended indexes yourself before applying them to your database. In that way you can apply the recommended changes during a period of low server activity, ensuring minimum disruption for the users connected to your server.

Moving a Database

There are many times as a developer when you may need to move or copy a database. If you are running a local copy of SQL Server on your development machine you may wish to restore a copy of a production database for development purposes, or you may wish to restore it to a development server for larger development teams. You may also be installing a copy of the database you have developed into your production environment, or on a server at a client's site.

There are several different methods you can use for copying or moving a database. These are:

❑   Using the Copy Database Wizard

❑   Detaching and re-attaching

❑   Carrying out a backup and restore

We will take a look at each of them in turn, but first we need to discuss the linkage between database users and log ins.

Log In to User Mapping

Database users are mapped to SQL Server Log ins internally using an ID (known as the SID, or security identifier) not by log in name. To keep things clear we'll review the following points:

❑   Database Users map to SQL Server Log ins, not the other way around.

❑   Database Users map to log ins using an ID, not based on the log in name.

❑   When a database is moved, copied, or restored the database users do not change the ID that they reference. However, the particular log in ID that they reference may not exist, especially if you are restoring the database to a new server.

So when you move databases around between servers you may discover that log ins and database users become unmapped. Even though two log ins on different servers may have the same name, if you are using SQL Server Authentication they will have different IDs.

To fix this problem you can either drop the existing database user that is mapped to the wrong log in, or you can use the `sp_change_users_log` in command to fix up the database user that is referencing a non-existent log in.

`sp_change_users_log` in can be used in a couple of ways; the first is in automatic mode. When using automatic mode this command will attempt to map the database user to a log in of the same name that exists within SQL Server. For example:

```
EXEC sp_change_users_log in @Action='Auto_Fix',@UserNamePattern='GlucinaL'
```

will attempt to map the GlucinaL database user to an existing log in named GlucinaL. If no match is found then the mapping will not be repaired.

The other mode of `sp_change_users_log` in is Update_One. This allows you to specifically map a database user to an existing SQL Server log in, for example:

```
EXEC sp_change_users_log in @Action='Update_One',@UserNamePattern='GlucinaL',
          @Log inName='LindaGlucina'
```

This will map the database user GlucinaL to the SQL Server log in LindaGlucina. The log in LindaGlucina is then able to access the specified database as this user.

Copy Database Wizard

The Copy Database Wizard (CDW) is a tool built into SQL Server that automates the copying or moving of databases between servers. It is particularly useful because it not only copies or moves the database, but also handles copying or moving the log ins associated with the database users. This includes all jobs, shared stored procedures, and user-defined error messages associated with each user.

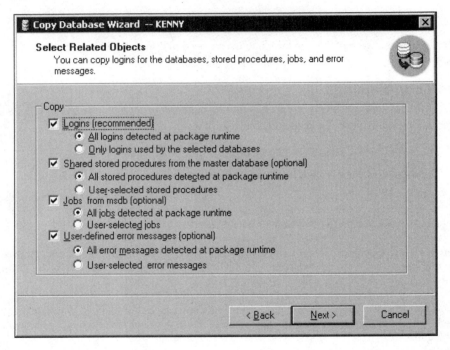

The CDW can be started from the Wizards window (opened from the Tools | Wizards menu item in SQL Server Enterprise Manager) by drilling down into the Management node.

The Wizard uses DTS to carry out the tasks involved in copying the database. From the Wizard you can either have the package run immediately, run once at a specified time, or run on a repeating schedule.

In the background the CDW actually detaches the database that you are copying, creates a network share and then copies (or moves if you are moving the database) the physical database files to the new server where it re-attaches them. For this to succeed SQL Server must be running under a domain account that has appropriate permissions on both servers, and ideally the SQL Server service would be running under the same Windows user account on both the primary and secondary server.

> **For this to happen there must be no active connections to the database. You must ensure that there aren't any when you run the CDW or else it will fail.**

Detaching / Re-attaching

As we mentioned, the CDW actually performs a detach and re-attach in the background to get the database files from one server to another. However, if you don't need to worry about transferring log ins, jobs and shared stored procedures, or if you wish to either copy the database files to a removable disk, or FTP them to a client's site, then you can perform the detach and re-attach yourself, manually.

The first thing you need to do is get the database ready for copying or moving. Make sure the schema and all the data contained within the database are how you wish them to be. Next you need to make sure all users are out of the database. You can check this by running the following query:

```
SELECT spid
FROM master.dbo.sysprocesses
WHERE dbid=DB_ID('HumanResources')
```

`master.dbo.sysprocesses` is a system table that stores the state of currently active processes. If any rows are returned then this means there are active connections to this database. If there are any connections you can either ask the users to log out (if you have the time and patience), kill their connections individually using the `KILL(spid)` T-SQL command, or kill all connections at once using the `ALTER DATABASE` command. An example of the latter is as follows:

```
ALTER DATABASE HumanResources SET RESTRICTED_USER WITH ROLLBACK IMMEDIATE
```

This will only allow the members of the `dbowner` database role, `dbcreator`, and `sysadmin` system roles to use this database after the `ALTER DATABASE` command has taken place. If you change your mind and wish the database to be available for all users again you will need to execute the following command:

```
ALTER DATABASE HumanResources SET MULTI_USER
```

Now we are ready to detach the database, but first we should make sure we know what and where all the physical files for this database are located. We can find this information from the `sysfiles` table located within our database:

```
SELECT filename
FROM humanresources.dbo.sysfiles
```

which produces a result similar to that shown here:

C:\Program Files\Microsoft SQL Server\MSSQL\data\humanresources.mdf
C:\Program Files\Microsoft SQL Server\MSSQL\data\humanresources_log.LDF

It's worth keeping a record of these file locations as we will need them soon. Our example database has only a single data file and a single log file, both located in the same place. A production database may have considerably more files forming the database, often located in different directories or on different physical disks (for performance reasons).

Next we can detach the database from SQL Server. Detaching is essentially removing the database from SQL Server, but without deleting the physical files that the database uses from disk. It sounds drastic but it isn't really, but you should **always** take a full backup of the database before detaching it just in case we make any mistakes and the database cannot be re-attached.

To detach use the `sp_detach_db` command as shown here:

```
EXEC sp_detach_db HumanResources
```

Within Windows Explorer, navigate to the path where the database files are located; in this example that is `C:\Program Files\Microsoft SQL Server\MSSQL\data\`. Once we have located these files we can decide to move or to copy the database. If we are moving the database, we move the files, and if we are copying, we copy them. Simple really! If you have another server you would like to copy the files to, do this now. For the purpose of this demonstration, I am simply going to move the files to a new directory to simulate moving to a new server. My `HumanResources` database files have now been moved to `D:\HRDB\`.

Back on SQL Server there is now no record of our `HumanResources` database. If it still shows within Enterprise Manager then you need to refresh (right-click the database's node and select **Refresh**). As I said, detaching is similar to dropping the database, so all references to it in SQL Server have been removed. To get our database back we now need to run the `sp_attach_db` command. This may be on the new server where we wish to place the database files, or on our current server after we have copied the files to another location. The `sp_attach_db` stored procedure takes the following parameters:

```
EXEC sp_attach_db DBName, FileName1, FileName2, FileName3, FileName4...
```

and will accept up to 16 database files. Interestingly enough `sp_detach_db` will quite happily detach a database with more than 16 data files but, as there isn't a command to re attach a database with more than 16 database files, I don't recommend that you do it! To re-attach our `HumanResources` database in its new location we would run:

```
EXEC sp_attach_db 'HumanResources', 'd:\hrdb\humanresources.mdf',
                  'd:\hrdb\humanresources_log.ldf'
```

Our database is available for use within SQL Server once again. The process of re-attaching also clears the single-user option from the database.

Restoring To a New Server

Backup and restore is generally used for disaster recovery purposes, but we can also use it to move databases around between servers, or for duplicating databases on a single server. Backup and restore is the only one out of the three methods I have described that doesn't require taking the database offline to carry it out (well, for the backup portion anyway) so it is the preferred method of getting copies of a production database.

I won't spend too much time covering the `BACKUP DATABASE` command, other than to say that you can use it to get a disk file containing the entire contents of a database in a single disk backup file quickly. The syntax is simply:

```
BACKUP DATABASE dbname TO DISK=BackupFilePath
```

This method is only going to be appropriate if you are dealing with databases that are maybe a few GB in size or less. Unless you have a great deal of free disk space, you probably can't just carry out this sort of backup for a database that is 150GB in size, for example. However, as our `HumanResources` database is only a few MB it is not a problem so we can back it up using:

```
BACKUP DATABASE humanresources TO DISK='C:\HR.BAK'
```

Now this backup file can be copied between servers or written to CD and taken to a client's site or e-mailed, or whatever. You can even restore to a database with another name on the same server. The `RESTORE DATABASE` command has the following syntax:

```
RESTORE DATABASE dbname FROM backupdevice
WITH MOVE logicalfile TO newfilelocation,
MOVE logicalfile TO newfilelocation,....
```

Unless we are restoring our database to a place where the database files can be recreated in the exact path where they were on the original server when the backup was taken, we must use the `WITH MOVE` option to specify the new location of the database data files. `WITH MOVE` requires you to enter the logical database file names and then specify new file paths for the physical database files to be created as part of the restore.

The logical database file names are contained within the backup file itself and we can display them just by executing the `RESTORE FILELISTONLY` command, for example:

```
RESTORE FILELISTONLY FROM DISK='C:\HR.BAK'
```

From the output of this command we can see that our logical database file names are `humanresources` and `humanresources_log`. With this information we can now restore our database from our data file. As, in this example, I am restoring to the same server that still contains the existing `HumanResources` database, I am actually going to restore to a new database with a different name thereby creating a copy of the database. The following T-SQL command accomplishes this:

```
RESTORE DATABASE HumanResourcesCopy
FROM DISK='C:\HR.BAK'
WITH MOVE 'humanresources' TO 'D:\HRDB\HumanResourcesCopy.MDF',
MOVE 'humanresources_log' TO 'D:\HRDB\HumanResourcesCopy_log.ldf'
```

This could just as easily have been another server on my network or at a completely different location.

Generating Scripts

A final DBA task that developers commonly need to carry out is scripting either part, or all, of the objects contained within a SQL Server database. This may be for creating a new data-less copy of the database, or for copying an individual stored procedure or a table out of the development database into the testing or production database. Whatever the reason, this is a common task so let's cover the ways in which this can be done.

Individual database objects can be scripted quickly and easily using the SQL Server Query Analyzer tool provided with SQL Server 2000. Simply connect to the server that contains the database you wish to script objects from and open the object browser (*F8* or the Tools | Object Browser | Show Hide) menu item, if it is not opened by default.

From within the object browser you can drill down into your tables, views, stored procedures, functions, and user-defined data type nodes. Under each of these nodes will be your specific database objects and you can right-click on each to select the following scripting options:

❑ Script Object to New Query Analyzer Window As

❑ Script Object to File As

❑ Script Object to Clipboard As

Under each of these menu items you will have the CREATE and DROP options at least. Depending on what type of object you have chosen you may also have ALTER, SELECT, INSERT, UPDATE, DELETE, and EXECUTE. However, CREATE is the option you will probably need for using the script to recreate the object within another database.

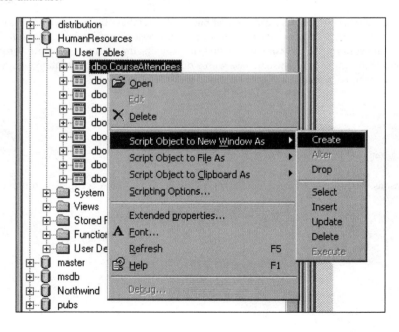

Each means of outputting the script produces the same script, so it is a case of just selecting the appropriate output method for your needs. As an example here, a **Create** script for the dbo.Employees table would produce something like this:

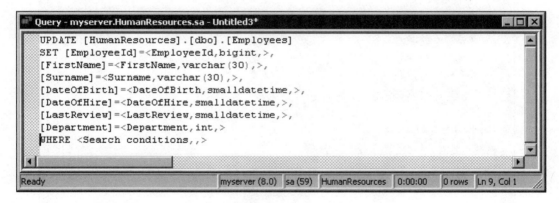

```
Query - myserver.HumanResources.sa - Untitled2*                                    _ □ ×
CREATE TABLE [Employees] (
        [EmployeeId] [bigint] IDENTITY (1, 1) NOT NULL ,
        [FirstName] [varchar] (30) COLLATE SQL_Latin1_General_CP1_CI_AS NOT NULL ,
        [Surname] [varchar] (30) COLLATE SQL_Latin1_General_CP1_CI_AS NOT NULL ,
        [DateOfBirth] [smalldatetime] NOT NULL ,
        [DateOfHire] [smalldatetime] NOT NULL ,
        [LastReview] [smalldatetime] NOT NULL ,
        [Department] [int] NOT NULL ,
        CONSTRAINT [IX_Employees] UNIQUE  CLUSTERED
        (
                [EmployeeId]
        )   ON [PRIMARY] ,
        CONSTRAINT [FK_Employees_Departments] FOREIGN KEY
        (
                [Department]
        ) REFERENCES [Departments] (
                [DepartmentId]
        )
) ON [PRIMARY] TEXTIMAGE_ON [PRIMARY]
GO
Ready                      myserver (8.0)  sa (58)  HumanResources  0:00:00  0 rows  Ln 23, Col 1
```

whereas a **Update** script for the dbo.Employees table will produce a script similar to that shown in the next screen-shot.

```
Query - myserver.HumanResources.sa - Untitled3*                                    _ □ ×
UPDATE [HumanResources].[dbo].[Employees]
SET [EmployeeId]=<EmployeeId,bigint,>,
[FirstName]=<FirstName,varchar(30),>,
[Surname]=<Surname,varchar(30),>,
[DateOfBirth]=<DateOfBirth,smalldatetime,>,
[DateOfHire]=<DateOfHire,smalldatetime,>,
[LastReview]=<LastReview,smalldatetime,>,
[Department]=<Department,int,>
WHERE <Search conditions,,>
Ready                      myserver (8.0)  sa (59)  HumanResources  0:00:00  0 rows  Ln 9, Col 1
```

Notice how the script has produced a SQL UPDATE statement containing all the columns within the dbo.Employees table. The text between the < brackets > is for you to replace with a parameter of the specified data type.

Scripting settings can be controlled from the Script tab in the Query Analyzer options dialog window (Tools | Options) and some of the useful options to be found there include:

❑   Including a descriptive header as part of the script

❑   The ability to script object-level permissions when scripting the object

❑   Prefixes the table name in the script with the database username of the table owner. For example, instead of just scripting CREATE TABLE MyTable this will script CREATE TABLE dbo.MyTable or CREATE TABLE Fred.MyTable

❑   Convert user-defined data types to their equivalent base data type during scripting

Once these settings have been selected, they will remain in force between executions of Query Analyzer.

You can also generate a script for an entire database from SQL Server Enterprise Manager. To do this, open Enterprise Manager and connect to the server that contains the database you wish to script. Like Query Analyzer, you can also script individual database objects from within Enterprise Manger but the Query Analyzer interface is much better suited for this so we will show scripting an entire database from Enterprise Manager.

Drill down into the Databases node and select the database to be scripted. Now select the Tools | Generate SQL Script menu item from within Enterprise Manager. If you select the Show All button then check the Script All Objects checkbox.

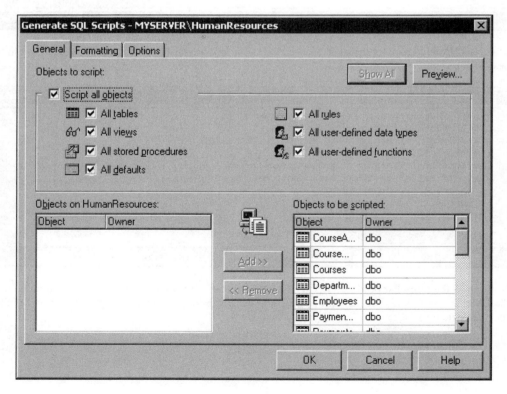

On the **Formatting** tab we can select several format options, including whether or not we want the object DROP commands to be included as part of the script. This is enabled by default, but this isn't necessary if we will be running this script against an empty database, so you can deselect this if you wish.

Finally on the **Options** tab you can select if you want to script:

❑ The command to create the database

❑ Database users and roles

❑ Server Log ins

❑ Object-level permissions

❑ Indexes

❑ Full text indexes

❑ Triggers

❑ Primary Keys, Foreign Keys, and Check constraints.

When creating a script that can be used to create the schema of the existing database you would usually choose all of these options. The final option is whether we wish to create a single file containing all of the database objects, or a script file per database object. Usually a single script will be the most suitable, but if you are using these scripts for other purposes, such as storing an out-of-database schema backup, then separate files may be more suitable.

Clicking **OK** will generate the schema file using the options you have requested; it's that easy!

Summary

There, we made it! It wasn't so painful after all. While this chapter has been by no means a complete list of DBA tasks, I hope that this insight has proved valuable, and that this knowledge will allow you to monitor and manage the databases that you are creating within SQL Server more efficiently.

The main topic we covered here was security. This is really one of the most misunderstood aspects of SQL Server when it comes to database and application design. Our key points were that log ins and database users are separate concepts, and permissions on each can be finely tuned to allow only the necessary permissions to be granted to a given database.

Next we discussed monitoring SQL Server for both performance and security. SQL Server profiler is a powerful tool for doing this on an *ad hoc* basis, and we also covered creating traces in T-SQL for more permanent logging functionality. We also saw how the Index Tuning Wizard integrates into SQL Server Profiler and how this provides invaluable advice on what indexes to create within your database.

We finished this chapter with a discussion on moving and copying databases as well as generating scripts for our database objects. Though these are some of the least glamorous topics in this book, they are part of the daily grind that all of us developing applications endure, so I hope this section has given you some useful information on how these tasks can be achieved easily and efficiently.

The wide range of our discussion here illustrates the fact that a good DBA carries out a broad range of tasks within their database environment. However, it is often the developer who is expected to not only create the application, but also deploy and provide administration support for the production environment.

12

Case Study: IBankAdventure

In this case study, we will construct a web site that ties together many of concepts discussed in this book. It is important to realize that, while we will look at the creation of the various files we need, the purpose of this case study is primarily to explore and understand the coding used to build the web site. All the necessary code for this application is available for download from the Wrox web site (www.wrox.com).

Introduction

IBankAdventure is a simulated banking application. When it's complete, we should be able to check balances, schedule payments, modify a personal profile, and simulate transactions such as deposits and withdrawals.

The following diagram depicts the logical architecture of our application:

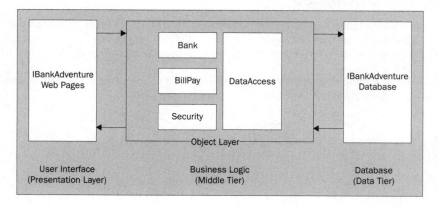

This architecture is a typical three-tier, distributed application. It provides separate components for the user interface (Presentation Layer), the business logic (Middle Tier), and the database (Data Tier).

The user interface and database are fairly straightforward in concept, however the business logic is a touch more complicated as it contains four objects. The first, DataAccess, provides database connectivity to the other objects. The Bank, BillPay, and Security objects provide the business logic for the application. This architecture provides great flexibility because of its component-based nature. For example, it is possible to change the entire user interface without ever having to modify the business logic objects or the database.

Another advantage of this architecture is that it allows for scalability. Furthermore, the manner in which the application scales is flexible so that the best cost/performance ratio can be obtained. As an example, it is rare that a web-based application uses all of a database's processing power, so adding additional machines to create a cluster for the Presentation Tier or web servers can provide a desirable performance boost.

If you are designing a web-based application to take advantage of clusters, then the distributed model also provides great reliability advantages. Let's say that each tier has a two-machine cluster dedicated to it. If one machine fails then the other machine picks up the additional workload of the failed machine.

The IBankAdventure Database

The heart of most every business application is the database, and this case study is no exception. In this section we will construct the database that will be used to drive our web site. While this case study was built using Microsoft SQL Server 2000 Enterprise Edition, any SQL Server derivative (SQL Server Developer Edition, MSDE, and so on) should work just as well, since none of the advanced features of the Enterprise Edition are being used.

Creating the Database

Before we can create any tables, the database itself must be created. This can be done by going to the SQL Server Enterprise Manager and navigating to the database server on which the database is to be created. Once the server has been selected, right-click on the server name and select New | Database.

At this point the Database Properties window will appear. Type in IBankAdventure into the Name field (as shown in the screenshot opposite):

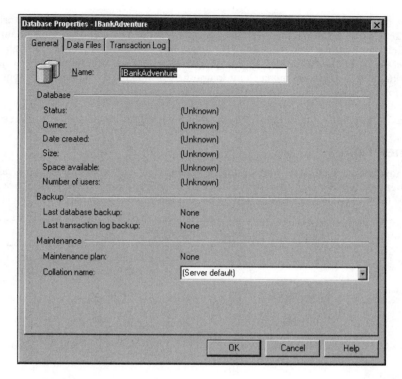

Once the name of the database has been entered, click the OK button to create the database. It should be noted that, while there are database parameters that could have been configured during this step, such as data file and log file locations, for the purposes of this case study the defaults will work just fine.

Database Tables

Now that we have a database, we need to add tables to it. The following figure shows a basic diagram of the database table structure that we will create. The SQL script used to create these tables is available at www.wrox.com. Once downloaded, you can use a tool such as Query Analyzer to run it.

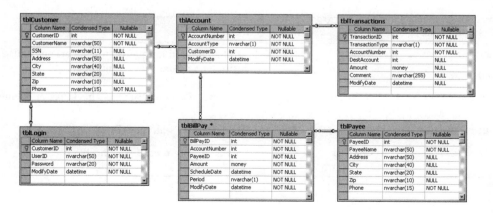

443

The columns marked with a key on the far left are primary keys. In this case study all primary keys are going to be Identity columns (the Identity property set to Yes). There are also a number of columns which do not allow NULL values, as indicated by the NOT NULL to the far right of the field names. We create columns in this way so that we get all the information required for a specific task, for example making a transfer from one account to another, or making available all the required information for a customer. This setting is a requirement on primary key fields.

We'll now take a look at the definitions of each table required for the IBankAdventure application.

The Customer Table

The Customer table is used to store all customer information such as customer name, address, and phone number. We will distinguish between bank customers and payees by creating a separate table for payees. Only the bank's own customers will be held in the Customer table.

Column Name	Type	Size	Description
CustomerID (Primary Key)	int	4	Identity column used to uniquely identify a Customer
CustomerName	nvarchar	50	Customer's full name
SSN	nvarchar	11	Social Security Number
Address	nvarchar	50	
City	nvarchar	40	
State	nvarchar	20	
Zip	nvarchar	10	
Phone	nvarchar	15	

The Account Table

The Account table is used to store all the information about the different accounts that any customer may have:

Column Name	Type	Size	Description
AccountNumber (Primary Key)	int	4	Auto-generated unique ID for the account; also the customer's actual account number
AccountType	nvarchar	1	The type of account such as checkings or savings
CustomerID	int	4	The customer's unique ID
ModifyDate	datetime	8	Last date/time record was modified

There are a two account types that could appear. They are:

AccountType Code	Description
C	Checking
S	Savings

The Transactions Table

The Transactions table is used to track all credit and debit items. Credit items will include transactions such as a customer's deposit of funds, a bank-applied credit, or payment of interest on an account. Debit items will include items such as paying out on a check written by a customer, a monthly service charge, transfer of funds, ATM withdrawals, and so on.

Column Name	Type	Size	Description
TransactionID (Primary Key)	int	4	Auto-generated unique ID for each transaction created
TransactionType	nvarchar	1	The type of transaction taking place
AccountNumber	int	4	The source account number
DestAccount	int	4	The destination account – used for transfers
Amount	money	8	The amount of credit or debit
Comment	nvarchar	255	Any comments the banker added to the transaction
ModifyDate	datetime	8	Last date/time record was modified

There are a few transaction types that could appear:

TransactionType Code	Category	Description
D	Credit	Deposit
W	Debit	Withdrawal
T	Debit	Transfer
S	Debit	Service Charge
B	Debit	BillPay

We have the TransactionType Code, which is the code that would appear in the database. Each code can be considered either a credit or a debit. For each credit we apply funds to the account and for each debit we subtract funds from the account. As we figure out the balance for each account we add up all the credits and debits to come up with a value.

The Payee Table

The Payee table is used to store all payee information such as name, address, and phone number.

Column Name	Type	Size	Description
PayeeID (Primary Key)	int	4	Auto-generated unique ID for the customer
PayeeName	nvarchar	50	Payee's full name
Address	nvarchar	50	Payee's address
City	nvarchar	40	
State	nvarchar	20	
Zip	nvarchar	10	
Phone	nvarchar	15	

The BillPay Table

The BillPay table is used to schedule automatic payments to a third party such as a telephone company, or home mortgage company. You can schedule payments to be made monthly, quarterly, annually, or on a specific date, as a one-off payment.

Column Name	Type	Size	Description
BillPayID (Primary Key)	int	4	Auto-generated unique ID for each billpay created
AccountNumber	int	4	The source account number to withdraw funds from
PayeeID	int	4	The payee to send payment to
Amount	money	8	The amount of funds to be taken from the account
ScheduleDate	datetime	8	The next scheduled date for the transaction to occur
Period	nvarchar	1	How often this will occur. This can be monthly, quarterly, annually, or as a one off.
ModifyDate	datetime	8	Last date/time record was modified

There are a few period types that could appear. The period types are:

Period Code	Description
M	Monthly
Q	Quarterly
Y	Annually
S	One-Time

The Login Table

The last table we need to create is the `Login` table. This is used to store the customer's UserID and password so they can log into the web site.

Column Name	Type	Size	Description
CustomerID (Primary Key)	int	4	Refers back to the customer
UserID	nvarchar	50	The username
Password	nvarchar	20	Customer's password
ModifyDate	datetime	8	Last date/time the UserID and Password were modified

Linking our Data Together

Now that we have our tables built, we need to link our primary keys together. For the purposes of demonstration, we will show how to relate the `tblCustomer` table to the `tblAccount` table.

The following is a list of the other relationships we require between the tables in our `IBankAdventure` database. The creation script provided for download at www.wrox.com will generate all of these automatically. However, if you want to add these relationships manually, then you can do so in exactly the same way as we will work through for the `Customer` and `Account` tables below. These relationships can also be viewed graphically in the figure in the previous section.

Primary Key Table & Field (Table.Field)	Foreign Key Table & Field (Child Table.Field)
Customer.CustomerID	Login.CustomerID
Customer.CustomerID	Account.CustomerID
Account.AccountNumber	Transactions.AccountNumber
Account.AccountNumber	BillPay.AccountNumber
Payee.PayeeID	BillPay.PayeeID

To create a relationship within Enterprise Manager we open the **Tables** folder in the `IBankAdventure` database, right-click on the **Customer** table, and select **Design | Table**. At this point the table design window is shown along with a new set of toolbar buttons along the top of the management console. Select the **Manage Relationships** button. This will show the **Properties** window for the `Customer` table with the **Relationships** tab selected.

We can now create a relationship by clicking the **New** button. At this point, the **Properties** window should look like the following:

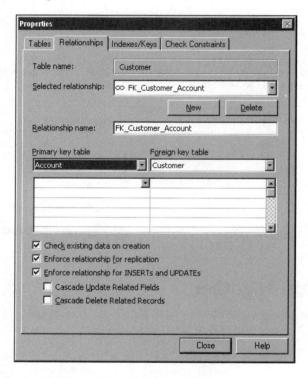

We must now select the primary key table and field, and the foreign key table and field using the drop-down lists provided. Since the `Customer` table holds the parent key in the `Account/Customer` relationship, make sure that it is selected as the primary key table. Now select the `CustomerID` field from the grid below the primary key table:

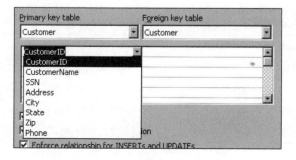

You can then perform the same steps for the foreign key table, making sure to select Account as the table and CustomerID as the field. When you are finished selecting the fields for the relationship, you may change the name of the relationship (though the default works just as well too). The window will now look like this:

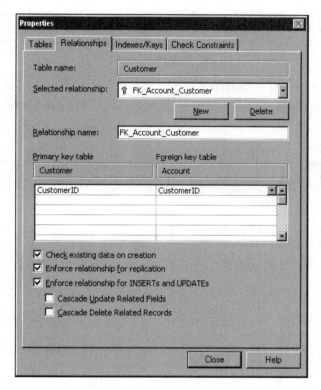

Note that when you create a relationship three checkboxes are selected by default. The first, **Check existing data on creation**, forces SQL Server to ensure that existing records in the database adhere to the relationship being created. The **Enforce relationship for replication** property ensures that if the data were to be copied to another database, it would meet the requirements for the relationship. Finally, **Enforce relationship for INSERTs and UPDATEs** ensures that records satisfy the relationship when they are added, modified, or removed.

You may now click **Close** and the **Properties** window disappears. At this point we need to save the table design in order to ensure that the changes are applied and saved. The simplest way to do this is to click on the **Save** button in the top left-hand corner of the table design window.

Stored Procedures

The IBankAdventure application uses stored procedures to gain access to the data. This method was selected over executing SQL statements directly against the database for a number of reasons:

❑ Stored procedures provide a level of data abstraction. If for some reason your database were to change (for example a field's data type changes) the alterations could be made in one location without having to recompile your application.

❑ Stored procedures improve performance. When a stored procedure is created, much of the work required to execute it (like compiling it) is done during the save, whereas with direct SQL statements all the work is done at execution time.

❑ Stored procedures allow for increased data security. Permissions can be granted to a user such that they can execute a stored procedure but are unable to access the database table directly. This means that if a user improperly gains access to the database, they can't perform mass deletes and data structure modification. At most, they would have to work within the confines of the stored procedures to corrupt data.

Managing Customer Information

We will begin with the customer data. We will need the ability to retrieve and update customer data, so let's build two stored procedures that allow us to do so.

> **Please note: you will need to ensure that the `tblCustomers` table contains some entries in order to be able to manipulate customer data later. We do not code functionality for adding customers in this application.**

To retrieve the customer's data we create a stored procedure called `sp_GetCustomerInfo`. To do so, simply type the following code into the Query Analyzer window:

```
CREATE PROCEDURE sp_GetCustomerInfo (
    @CustomerID    int
)
AS

SELECT
    CustomerID,
    CustomerName,
    SSN,
    Address,
    City,
    State,
    Zip,
    Phone
FROM tblCustomer
WHERE CustomerID = @CustomerID
```

To update the customer's data, create a stored procedure called `sp_UpdateCustomerInfo` as shown below:

```
CREATE PROCEDURE sp_UpdateCustomerInfo (
    @CustomerID    int,
    @CustomerName  nvarchar(50),
    @SSN           nvarchar(15),
    @Address       nvarchar(50),
    @City          nvarchar(40),
    @State         nvarchar(20),
    @Zip           nvarchar(10),
```

```
      @Phone          nvarchar(15)
)

AS

UPDATE tblCustomer SET
    CustomerName = @CustomerName,
    SSN          = @SSN,
    Address      = @Address,
    City         = @City,
    State        = @State,
    Zip          = @Zip,
    Phone        = @Phone
WHERE
    CustomerID = @CustomerID
```

Viewing the Customer's Account Information

At some point in the application we will need to get a list of the customer's accounts, so let's create the sp_GetAccounts procedure as shown:

```
CREATE PROCEDURE sp_GetAccounts(
    @CustomerID    int
)
AS

SELECT AccountNumber, AccountType FROM tblAccount
WHERE  CustomerID = @CustomerID
```

Next, we will need to get the balance for an account. The procedure to do so is sp_GetAccountBalance and is created as follows:

```
CREATE PROCEDURE sp_GetAccountBalance (
    @Balance         money OUT,
    @AccountNumber   int
)

AS

SELECT @Balance = SUM(Amount)
FROM tblTransactions
WHERE AccountNumber = @AccountNumber
```

Managing Customer Transactions

Some of the things that we will be required to handle are customer transactions such as deposits and withdrawals.

For adding transactions, create a stored procedure called sp_InsertTransaction as shown below:

```
CREATE PROCEDURE sp_InsertTransaction (
    @TransactionType   nvarchar(1),
    @AccountNumber     int,
    @DestAccount       int,
    @Amount            money,
```

```
    @Comment               nvarchar(255)
)

AS INSERT INTO Transactions (
    TransactionType,
    AccountNumber,
    DestAccount,
    Amount,
    Comment,
    ModifyDate )

VALUES (
    @TransactionType,
    @AccountNumber,
    @DestAccount,
    @Amount,
    @Comment,
    GetDate())
```

For viewing the list of transactions for a specific account, a stored procedure called sp_GetTransactions is created as shown below:

```
CREATE PROCEDURE sp_GetTransactions (
    @AccountNumber    int
)

AS  SELECT
    TransactionID,
    CONVERT(SMALLDATETIME, ModifyDate) AS TransactionDate,
    Comment,
    CASE WHEN TransactionType =  'D' THEN Amount ELSE NULL END AS credit,
    CASE WHEN TransactionType <> 'D' THEN Amount ELSE NULL END AS debit
FROM
    tblTransactions
WHERE
    AccountNumber = @AccountNumber
```

Note that we convert the ModifyDate column from a DATETIME type (mm/dd/yy hh:mm:ss) to a SMALLDATETIME type (mm/dd/yy) so that we pass back only the date of the transaction. Also, we create two artificial columns within the stored procedure, namely credit and debit. These artificial columns will be used by the user interface in order to display debits and credits in separate columns.

Managing Bill Payments

Next we have the data needed for making bill payments. We will need the ability to add, update, and delete our data so let's build three stored procedures that will do so.

To add a billpay create a stored procedure called sp_InsertBillPay as shown below:

```
CREATE PROCEDURE sp_InsertBillPay (
    @AccountNumber    int,
    @PayeeID          int,
    @Amount           money,
    @ScheduleDate     datetime,
    @Period           nvarchar(1)
```

```
    )

    AS

    INSERT INTO tblBillPay (
        AccountNumber,
        PayeeID,
        Amount,
        ScheduleDate,
        Period,
        ModifyDate)

    VALUES (
        @AccountNumber,
        @PayeeID,
        @Amount,
        @ScheduleDate,
        @Period,
        GetDate())
```

For deleting billpay records, we need to create a stored procedure called `sp_DeleteBillPay` as shown below:

```
CREATE PROCEDURE sp_DeleteBillPay (
    @BillPayID    int
)

AS

DELETE FROM tblBillPay
WHERE BillPayID = @BillPayID
```

To update a billpay record create a stored procedure called `sp_UpdateBillPay` as shown below:

```
CREATE PROCEDURE sp_UpdateBillPay (
    @BillPayID        int,
    @AccountNumber    int,
    @PayeeID          int,
    @Amount           money,
    @ScheduleDate     datetime,
    @Period           nvarchar(1))

AS

UPDATE tblBillPay SET
    AccountNumber    = @AccountNumber,
    PayeeID          = @PayeeID,
    Amount           = @Amount,
    ScheduleDate     = @ScheduleDate,
    Period           = @Period,
    ModifyDate       = GetDate()

WHERE
    BillPayID    = @BillPayID
```

Now that we can create, modify, and remove data, a mechanism to select all the billpays for a specific account is needed. The sp_GetBillPay procedure is used to facilitate this and is created as shown:

```
CREATE PROCEDURE sp_GetBillPay (
    @AccountNumber    int
)

AS

SELECT
    BillPayID,
    AccountNumber,
    tblBillPay.PayeeID,
    PayeeName,
    Amount,
    ScheduleDate,
    Period,
    CASE Period WHEN 'S' THEN 'One Time'
                WHEN 'M' THEN 'Monthly'
                WHEN 'Q' THEN 'Quarterly'
                WHEN 'Y' THEN 'Annually' END AS PeriodDescription

FROM tblBillPay
    INNER JOIN tblPayee ON tblBillPay.PayeeID = tblPayee.PayeeID
WHERE AccountNumber = @AccountNumber
```

The last thing we will need for billpay functionality is a list of possible payees. The first thing you will need to do is ensure that there are some records in the tblPayee table, since we will not build functionality for doing this into our application. Next we need to create the sp_GetPayee stored procedure as shown:

```
CREATE PROCEDURE sp_GetPayee
AS

SELECT
    PayeeID,
    PayeeName,
    Address,
    City,
    State,
    ZIP,
    Phone
FROM tblPayee
ORDER BY PayeeName ASC
```

Managing the Login and Password

The users will have to log in to our site. In order for them to be able to do so, we will need to be able to check for a username and password. To check a login, create a stored procedure called sp_CheckPassword as shown opposite:

```
CREATE PROCEDURE sp_CheckPassword
    (@CustomerID   int OUT,
    @UserID        nvarchar(50),
    @Password      nvarchar(20))
AS
SELECT @CustomerID = CustomerID
FROM tblLogin
WHERE UserID=@UserID AND Password=@Password
```

We also need to provide the user with a mechanism by which they can change their password. To handle this, create the sp_UpdatePassword procedure as shown:

```
CREATE PROCEDURE sp_UpdatePassword (
    @CustomerID   int,
    @Password     nvarchar(20)
)

AS

UPDATE tblLogin SET
    Password = @Password,
    ModifyDate = GetDate()
WHERE
    CustomerID = @CustomerID
```

Note the use of the GetDate() function in this stored procedure. We use this function to let us know when it was that the user last logged into the application. By doing so we provide ourselves with a rudimentary method for audit our users.

At this point we have created all the stored procedures we'll need to accomplish the major tasks within our application. As with the payees, create users for your application by adding them directly to the tblLogin table. We will build a mechanism to call these stored procedures later, in the *IBankAdventure Business Objects* section.

Database Security Strategies

This section discusses three common methods by which one could secure the IBankAdventure database. All three have advantages and disadvantages, as we shall see.

The first method by which we can secure our database is to create our own security tables and underlying authentication schemes. In typical cases tables, stored procedures, and other database objects are created to hold the users' security information such as username and password, as well as methods to check for access and permissions. In order to connect to the database, a static username/password combination is used. This is helpful when there are large numbers of users outside your network that require access (for example, if you run a large message-board site). The down side is that you must create the authentication infrastructure yourself and so are unable to take advantage of SQL Server's inherent user-based functions, such as CURRENT_USER for logging changes. This is the method used in our case study. We selected this method because of its relative simplicity to implement for demonstrations.

The second method is to use Windows integrated security. This method allows the Windows operating system to perform the necessary user authentication. The benefits of this approach include users not having to log in to an application (since their credentials are passed to SQL Server), and time saved by not writing custom authentication code. However, the drawback is that anyone who wants access to your database must be a user on your network/domain. For an application with thousands of users across multiple networks, this model becomes impractical. However, for small businesses or even divisions within a larger company, this may fulfill all the security needs and not put undue pressure on your IT staff.

The third method, SQL Server Authentication, is something of a hybrid approach. It uses SQL Server users to manage security. SQL Server users have all the benefits of the integrated security approach discussed above, but can be created within the system at run-time much like the first method discussed. Applications using this approach can take advantage of inherent SQL Server user functions (such as CURRENT_USER for logging) and security facilities (such as the use of role-based permissions). The down side is that the code to manage users can be complex, depending on your permissions scheme, and that unless handled in code, the sa user ID will have access to the application.

IBankAdventure Business Objects

Having created our database, along with the required stored procedures, we can now move on to the middle tier of our application. In this tier we will create the business objects we need for our application, as follows:

❑   DataAccess – this will provide all the functionality we need in order to connect to the database and execute our various stored procedures.

❑   Bank – this will handle all the customer and transaction information.

❑   BillPay – this will handle the scheduled payment functionality we require.

❑   Security – this will handle user authentication, and provide the user accounts with suitable capabilities.

We'll look at these in turn.

The DataAccess Business Object

The DataAccess class provides a connection to our database and executes any stored procedures we have built. This is a generic class and is not specific to this project. By creating one class to handle all our database calls we eliminate a lot of redundant code, as well as providing the ability to change our back end if we decide to switch to another type of database (such as Oracle).

Let's create this generic class now. Create a new Class Library project and call it DBHelper. Delete the Class1 file that was automatically created from the project.

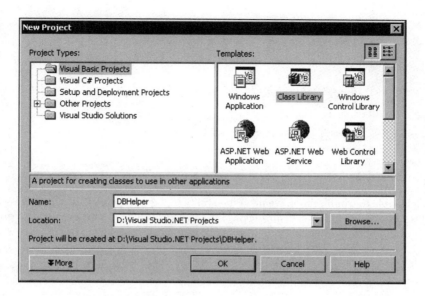

Add a new class to the project called `DataAccess.vb`.

This class provides access to the database. Add the following import statements before the class definition:

```
Imports System.Data.SqlClient
Imports System.IO
```

The `System.Data.SqlClient` namespace is used for manipulating database objects such as `SqlCommands` and `DataSets`. To begin creating our `DataAccess` class we need to declare a couple of constants so that when we add any errors to the event log, they will go to the appropriate place:

```
Public Class DataAccess
    ' Track the name of this module for error logging
    Private Const MODULE_NAME As String = "DBHelper"
    Private Const MODULE_SOURCE As String = "DataAccess"
```

We then create two private variables to hold the name of our server and database name:

```
    Private m_sServer As String
    Private m_sDataBase As String
```

Next we need to create two properties. A property is a method of an object that allows the object's characteristics to be changed. Create a property called `Server` and `Database` using the private variables we just declared:

```
Public Property Server() As String
    Get
        Return m_sServer
    End Get
```

```
            Set(ByVal Value As String)
                m_sServer = Value
            End Set
        End Property

    Public Property DataBase() As String
            Get
                Return m_sDataBase
            End Get
            Set(ByVal Value As String)
                m_sDataBase = Value
            End Set
        End Property
```

In order to be able to troubleshoot, we need the ability to log any errors that occur. We will use the WriteEntry method to enter an error message in the error log. To do this we create a procedure called LogError:

```
    Private Sub LogError(ByVal e As Exception)
            Dim LogMsg As StringWriter = New StringWriter()

            LogMsg.WriteLine("Module: " & MODULE_SOURCE)
            LogMsg.WriteLine("Source: " & e.Source)
            LogMsg.WriteLine("Message: " & e.Message)
            LogMsg.WriteLine("Connect: " & GetConnectString())

            ' Write error to event log
            System.Diagnostics.EventLog.WriteEntry (MODULE_NAME, _
            LogMsg.ToString, Diagnostics.EventLogEntryType.Error)
    End Sub
```

Next we will need to construct a private method that creates the database connection string:

```
    Private Function GetConnectString() As String

       ' Assemble the connection string
         Dim myConnectStr As String = _
           "Server = " & m_sServer & ";" & _
           "Database = " & m_sDataBase & ";" & _
           "User ID=sa;Password=;"

       ' Return the connection string
         Return myConnectStr
    End Function
```

Now that we have our connection, we need another private method that allows us to get to the data. We will need to create a SqlCommand object to facilitate data retrieval and manipulation. We will create a method, CreateCommand, to create the SqlCommand object and pass it back:

```
    Private Function CreateCommand(ByVal SQLText As String, _
                               ByVal Param() As SqlParameter, _
                               ByVal SQLCmdType As CommandType) _
                               As SqlCommand

       ' Create a new Connection object
```

```
      Dim myConnection As SqlConnection = New SqlConnection(GetConnectString())

    ' Create a new Command object
    Dim myCommand As SqlCommand = New SqlCommand(SQLText, myConnection)

    ' Set the command type
    myCommand.CommandType = SQLCmdType

    ' Add any parameters
    Dim ParamTemp As SqlParameter
       If Not Param Is Nothing Then
             For Each ParamTemp In Param
             myCommand.Parameters.Add(ParamTemp)
          Next
       End If

  ' Open the connection
       Try
             myConnection.Open()
             Return myCommand

          Catch e As Exception
             LogError(e)
             Return Nothing

          End Try
End Function
```

It is now time to create some public methods that will be used by our other objects to gain access to the database. We are going to create three new public methods named ExecuteSP, all of which will be overloaded. The purpose of overloading is to allow the caller to have a DataSet, DataReader, or nothing passed back to it, while still appearing to call the same method:

```
    Public Overloads Function ExecuteSP(ByVal SProcName As String, _
                             ByVal Param() As SqlParameter, _
                             ByVal MyDataSet As DataSet) As Boolean

    ' Create a new command object
       Dim myCommand As SqlCommand = CreateCommand(SProcName, _
                                  Param, CommandType.StoredProcedure)

    ' Create and configure SqlDataAdapter
       Dim myDataAdapter As SqlDataAdapter = New SqlDataAdapter(myCommand)

    ' Fill the DataSet object
       Try
             myDataAdapter.Fill(MyDataSet)
             Return True
          Catch e As Exception
             LogError(e)
             Return False

          End Try
End Function
```

```
    Public Overloads Function ExecuteSP(ByVal SProcName As String, _
                                        ByVal Param() As SqlParameter) As Boolean

        ' Build a new command object
        Dim myCommand As SqlCommand = CreateCommand(SProcName, _
                                        Param, CommandType.StoredProcedure)

        ' Execute the command
        Try
            myCommand.ExecuteNonQuery()
            Return True
        Catch e As Exception
            LogError(e)
            Return False
        End Try
    End Function

    Public Overloads Function ExecuteSP(ByVal SProcName As String, _
                                        ByVal Param() As SqlParameter, _
                                ByRef myDataReader As SqlDataReader) As Boolean

        ' Create a new command object
        Dim myCommand As SqlCommand = CreateCommand(SProcName, _
                                        Param, CommandType.StoredProcedure)

        ' Fill the DataReader object
        Try
            myDataReader = myCommand.ExecuteReader
            Return True
        Catch e As Exception
            LogError(e)
            Return False
        End Try
    End Function
```

Now we can compile this object and move on.

The Bank Business Object

We'll begin here by creating a new class library project called IBankAdventure that will contain the rest of our objects. Delete the Class1.vb file automatically included in the class library, and then add an empty class named Bank. This object is responsible for handling all customer and transaction information.

The first thing we need to do is add a reference to the System.EnterpriseServices namespace and to our recently compiled DBHelper namespace. The System.EnterpriseServices reference is added by selecting Project | Add Reference and selecting the references from the list of .NET namespaces.

To add the DBHelper namespace we will have to browse for the actual DBHelper.dll file we just compiled. While in the Add References window, click Browse and navigate to the DBHelper.dll file. It should be located in the bin subdirectory of the DBHelper project directory. Once you have located it, double-click on it and it will appear in the list of references to be added at the bottom of the window. Click on OK and the reference is added to the project and the dll is copied into the run directory of the IBankAdventure assembly.

Open up the `Bank` class in the code editor and add the following `Imports` statements:

```
Imports System.Data.SqlClient
Imports System.EnterpriseServices
```

We tell it that transactions will be required by prefixing the class name as shown below. The class is inherited from the `System.EnterpriseServices.ServicedComponent` object, which will provide the underlying transactional functionality. This is done as follows:

```
<Transaction(TransactionOption.Required)> Public Class Bank
    Inherits ServicedComponent
```

Next we add some private constants that will be used to differentiate transaction types and provide access to the `DBHelper.DataAccess` object we created earlier.

```
    '-----------------------------------------------------------------
    ' Private constants
    '-----------------------------------------------------------------

    ' different transaction types
    Private Const TRANS_DEPOSIT As String = "D"
    Private Const TRANS_WITHDRAW As String = "W"
    Private Const TRANS_TRANSFER As String = "T"
    Private Const TRANS_SERVICEFEE As String = "S"
    Private Const TRANS_BILLPAY As String = "B"


    '-----------------------------------------------------------------
    ' Private members
    '-----------------------------------------------------------------

    Private m_objDataLayer As DBHelper.DataAccess
```

Create the `New` method such that a new `DBHelper.DataAccess` class is created and set the `Server` and `DataBase` properties to match your database server's name and the name of your database. This will create our `DataAccess` object every time we create the `Bank` class. The code should look like the following:

```
Public Sub New()
    ' Create a new DataAccess object
    m_objDataLayer = New DBHelper.DataAccess()

    ' Set our database settings
    With m_objDataLayer
        .Server = "MyServer"
        .DataBase = "IBankAdventure"
    End With

End Sub
```

Next we create two methods that will allow us to retrieve and update the customer's information. In order to retrieve or update a customer's information, we will require the CustomerID to be passed in as a parameter to the method. For customer information retrieval we will use the Bank.GetCustomerInfo method in order to return a SqlDataReader to the caller. This will allow the caller access to the data without having the overhead of using a DataSet. The code for the Bank.GetCustomerInfo method is as follows:

```
<AutoComplete()> _
    Public Function GetCustomerInfo(ByVal CustomerID As Integer) _
                                               As SqlDataReader

    Dim myDataReader As SqlDataReader

    ' Create an array of parameters
    Dim Params() As SqlParameter = {New SqlParameter _
                                    ("@CustomerID", SqlDbType.Int)}

    ' Set the parameter values
    Params(0).Value = CustomerID

    'Get the customer information
    Try
        If m_objDataLayer.ExecuteSP("sp_GetCustomerInfo", Params, _
                                    myDataReader) = True Then
            Return myDataReader
        Else
            Return Nothing
        End If
    Catch
        Return Nothing
    End Try
End Function
```

Prefixing the method with <AutoComplete()> allows it to automatically invoke a transaction, as well as performing the SetComplete or SetAbort as appropriate.

The UpdateCustomerInfo method is created next. Since we will be modifying the user's information, we will have to provide parameters for the information that can be modified:

```
<AutoComplete()> _
    Public Function UpdateCustomerInfo(ByVal CustomerID As Integer, _
                                       ByVal CustomerName As String, _
                                       ByVal SSN As String, _
                                       ByVal Address As String, _
                                       ByVal City As String, _
                                       ByVal State As String, _
                                       ByVal Zip As String, _
                                       ByVal Phone As String) As Boolean

    ' Create an array of parameters
    Dim Params() As SqlParameter = _
            {New SqlParameter("@CustomerID", SqlDbType.Int), _
             New SqlParameter("@CustomerName", SqlDbType.NVarChar, 50), _
```

```
                New SqlParameter("@SSN", SqlDbType.NVarChar, 15), _
                New SqlParameter("@Address", SqlDbType.NVarChar, 50), _
                New SqlParameter("@City", SqlDbType.NVarChar, 40), _
                New SqlParameter("@State", SqlDbType.NVarChar, 20), _
                New SqlParameter("@Zip", SqlDbType.NVarChar, 20), _
                New SqlParameter("@Phone", SqlDbType.NVarChar, 30)}

    ' Set the parameter values
       Params(0).Value = CustomerID
       Params(1).Value = CustomerName
       Params(2).Value = SSN
       Params(3).Value = Address
       Params(4).Value = City
       Params(5).Value = State
       Params(6).Value = Zip
       Params(7).Value = Phone

    'Save customer information
       Try
          Return m_objDataLayer.ExecuteSP("UpdateCustomerInfo", Params)
       Catch
          Return False
       End Try

End Function
```

Next, the methods that will allow us access to the customer's accounts are created:

```
<AutoComplete()> _
    Public Function GetAccounts(ByVal CustomerID As Integer) _
                               As SqlDataReader
       Dim myDataReader As SqlDataReader
       ' Create an array of parameters
       Dim Params() As SqlParameter = _
            {New SqlParameter("@CustomerID", SqlDbType.Int)}

    ' Set the parameter values
    Params(0).Value = CustomerID
    Try
       If m_objDataLayer.ExecuteSP("sp_GetAccounts", Params, _
                                   myDataReader) = True Then
          Return myDataReader
       Else
          Return Nothing
       End If
       Catch
          Return Nothing
    End Try
End Function

<AutoComplete()> _
    Public Function AccountBalance(ByVal AccountNumber As Integer) As Single
```

```
        Dim myDataReader As SqlDataReader

        ' Create an array of parameters
        Dim Params() As SqlParameter = _
                {New SqlParameter("@Balance", SqlDbType.Real), _
                 New SqlParameter("@AccountNumber", SqlDbType.Int)}

        ' Set the parameter values
        Params(0).Direction = System.Data.ParameterDirection.Output
        Params(1).Value = AccountNumber

        Try
            If m_objDataLayer.ExecuteSP("sp_GetAccountBalance", Params, _
                                        myDataReader) = True Then
                Return CSng(Params(0).Value)
            Else
                Return -1
            End If
            Catch
                Return -1
        End Try
    End Function
End Function
```

We now create the `Bank.GetTransactions` method that is used to retrieve a list of all the transactions for a specified account. This method differs from what has been done so far, because it returns a `DataSet` object rather than a `SqlDataReader` object. We need to do this differently because the user interface (discussed in a later section) displays the transactions in a `DataGrid` object. A `SqlDataReader` is not a valid data source for the `DataGrid` object.

```
    <AutoComplete()> _
    Public Function GetTransactions(ByVal AccountNumber As Integer) _
                                As DataSet

    Dim myDataSet As New DataSet()

    ' Create an array of parameters
    Dim Params() As SqlParameter = _
            {New SqlParameter("@AccountNumber", SqlDbType.Int)}

    ' Set the parameter values
    Params(0).Value = AccountNumber

        Try
            If m_objDataLayer.ExecuteSP("GetTransactions", _
                                        Params, myDataSet) = True Then
                Return myDataSet
            Else
                Return Nothing
            End If
        Catch
            Return Nothing
        End Try
End Function
```

To record a transaction several methods will be created. The first, `Bank.InsertTransaction`, is a private method used to insert transaction information in the database. It looks like this:

```
<AutoComplete()> _
    Private Function InsertTransaction(ByVal TransType As String, _
                                       ByVal SourceAccount As Integer, _
                                       ByVal DestAccount As Integer, _
                                       ByVal Amount As Single, _
                                       ByVal Comment As String) As Boolean

    ' Create an array of parameters
    Dim Params() As SqlParameter = _
            {New SqlParameter("@TransactionType", SqlDbType.NVarChar, 6), _
             New SqlParameter("@AccountNumber", SqlDbType.Int), _
             New SqlParameter("@DestAccount", SqlDbType.Int), _
             New SqlParameter("@Amount", SqlDbType.Real), _
             New SqlParameter("@Comment", SqlDbType.NVarChar, 255)}

    ' Set the parameter values
    Params(0).Value = TransType
    Params(1).Value = SourceAccount
    Params(2).Value = DestAccount
    Params(3).Value = Amount
    Params(4).Value = Comment

    ' Try executing the stored procedure
        Try
            Return m_objDataLayer.ExecuteSP("InsertTransaction", Params)
        Catch
            Return False
        End Try

End Function
```

The `Bank.InsertTransaction` method will be called by one of four public methods. Remember that public methods are those that other objects can view and call. Our four methods represent the possible transactions that our system can complete, namely deposits, withdrawals, applying service fees, and transferring funds.

```
<AutoComplete()> _
    Public Function DepositFunds(ByVal AccountNumber As Integer, _
                                 ByVal Amount As Single, _
                                 ByVal Comment As String) As Boolean

        Try
            Return InsertTransaction(TRANS_DEPOSIT, AccountNumber, _
                                     AccountNumber, Amount, Comment)
        Catch
            Return False
        End Try
End Function

<AutoComplete()> _
```

```
    Public Function WithdrawFunds (ByVal AccountNumber As Integer, _
                                   ByVal Amount As Single, _
                                   ByVal Comment As String) As Boolean

        Try
            Return InsertTransaction(TRANS_WITHDRAW, AccountNumber, _
                              AccountNumber, Amount, Comment)
        Catch
            Return False
        End Try
End Function

<AutoComplete()> _
    Public Function ApplyServiceFee(ByVal AccountNumber As Integer, _
                                    ByVal Amount As Single, _
                                    ByVal Comment As String) As Boolean

        Try
            Return InsertTransaction(TRANS_SERVICEFEE, AccountNumber, _
                              AccountNumber, Amount, Comment)
        Catch
            Return False
        End Try
End Function

<AutoComplete()> _
    Public Function TransferFunds(ByVal SourceAccount As Integer, _
                                  ByVal DestAccount As Integer, _
                                  ByVal Amount As Single, _
                                  ByVal Comment As String) As Boolean

        Try
            Return InsertTransaction(TRANS_TRANSFER, SourceAccount, _
                                DestAccount, Amount, Comment)
        Catch
            Return False
        End Try
End Function
```

That completes the Bank business object.

The BillPay Business Object

The BillPay object is used to manage the scheduled payment functionality. It provides for creating, updating, and removing scheduled payments, as well as generating the information required to create a scheduled payment (such as a list of possible payees).

Create a new class file in the IBankAdventure project named BillPay.vb. Remember to add the Imports statements for the System.EnterpriseServices and System.Data.SqlClient namespaces. Because there is nothing new in the way of technology, the object code is simply listed, so here is everything you need to create the entire BillPay class:

```vb
Imports System.EnterpriseServices
Imports System.Data.SqlClient

<Transaction(TransactionOption.Required)> Public Class BillPay
    Inherits ServicedComponent

    ' different billpay periods
    Private Const SCHEDULE_ONETIME As String = "S"
    Private Const SCHEDULE_MONTHLY As String = "M"
    Private Const SCHEDULE_QUARTERLY As String = "Q"
    Private Const SCHEDULE_ANNUALLY As String = "Y"

    Public Enum Schedule
        OneTime = 0
        Monthly = 1
        Quarterly = 2
        Annually = 3
    End Enum

    '-----------------------------------------------------------------
    ' Private members
    '-----------------------------------------------------------------

    Private m_objDataLayer As DBHelper.DataAccess

    Public Sub New()
        ' Create a new DataAccess object
        m_objDataLayer = New DBHelper.DataAccess()

    ' Set our database settings
        With m_objDataLayer
            .Server = "MyServer"
            .DataBase = "IBankAdventure"
        End With

    End Sub

    Private Function GetPeriodCode(ByVal Period As Schedule) As String

        Select Case Period
            Case Schedule.OneTime
                Return SCHEDULE_ONETIME
            Case Schedule.Monthly
                Return SCHEDULE_MONTHLY
            Case Schedule.Quarterly
                Return SCHEDULE_QUARTERLY
            Case Schedule.Annually
                Return SCHEDULE_ANNUALLY
        End Select

    End Function

<AutoComplete()> _
    Public Function InsertBillPay(ByVal AccountNumber As Integer, _
```

```
                                    ByVal PayeeID As Integer, _
                                    ByVal Amount As Single, _
                                    ByVal ScheduleDate As Date, _
                                    ByVal Period As Schedule) As Boolean

        If IsDate(ScheduleDate) = False Then Return False

        ' Create an array of parameters
        Dim Params() As SqlParameter = _
            {New SqlParameter("@AccountNumber", SqlDbType.Int), _
             New SqlParameter("@PayeeID", SqlDbType.Int), _
             New SqlParameter("@Amount", SqlDbType.Real), _
             New SqlParameter("@ScheduleDate", SqlDbType.DateTime), _
             New SqlParameter("@Period", SqlDbType.NVarChar, 6)}

        ' Set the parameter values
        Params(0).Value = AccountNumber
        Params(1).Value = PayeeID
        Params(2).Value = Amount
        Params(3).Value = ScheduleDate
        Params(4).Value = GetPeriodCode(Period)

        ' Try executing the stored procedure
        Try
            Return m_objDataLayer.ExecuteSP("InsertBillPay", Params)
        Catch
            Return False
        End Try

End Function

<AutoComplete()> _
    Public Function UpdateBillPay(ByVal BillPayID As Integer, _
                                  ByVal AccountNumber As Integer, _
                                  ByVal PayeeID As Integer, _
                                  ByVal Amount As Single, _
                                  ByVal ScheduleDate As Date, _
                                  ByVal Period As Schedule) As Boolean

    ' Create an array of parameters
    Dim Params() As SqlParameter = _
            {New SqlParameter("@BillPayID", SqlDbType.Int), _
             New SqlParameter("@AccountNumber", SqlDbType.Int), _
             New SqlParameter("@PayeeID", SqlDbType.Int), _
             New SqlParameter("@Amount", SqlDbType.Real), _
             New SqlParameter("@ScheduleDate", SqlDbType.DateTime), _
             New SqlParameter("@Period", SqlDbType.NVarChar, 6)}

    ' Set the parameter values
    Params(0).Value = BillPayID
    Params(1).Value = AccountNumber
    Params(2).Value = PayeeID
    Params(3).Value = Amount
    Params(4).Value = ScheduleDate
```

```
        Params(5).Value = GetPeriodCode(Period)

    ' Try executing the stored procedure
        Try
            Return m_objDataLayer.ExecuteSP("UpdateBillPay", Params)
        Catch
            Return False
        End Try

End Function

<AutoComplete()> _
    Public Function DeleteBillPay(ByVal BillPayID As Integer) As Boolean

    'Create an array of parameters
    Dim Params() As SqlParameter = _
        {New SqlParameter("@BillPayID", SqlDbType.Int)}

    'Set the parameter values
    Params(0).Value = BillPayID

    ' Try executing the stored procedure
        Try
            Return m_objDataLayer.ExecuteSP("DeleteBillPay", Params)
        Catch
            Return False
        End Try
End Function

<AutoComplete()> _
    Public Function GetBillPay(ByVal AccountNumber As Integer) As DataSet
        Dim myDataSet As New DataSet()

        'Create the parameter values
        Dim Params() As SqlParameter = _
            {New SqlParameter("@AccountNumber", SqlDbType.Int)}

        'Set the parameter values
        Params(0).Value = AccountNumber

        ' Try executing the stored procedure
            Try
                If m_objDataLayer.ExecuteSP("GetBillPay", Params, myDataSet) _
                                      = True Then
                    Return myDataSet
                Else
                    Return Nothing
                End If
            Catch
                Return Nothing
            End Try
End Function

<AutoComplete()> _
```

```
      Public Function GetPayees() As SqlDataReader
         Dim myReader As SqlDataReader
            Try
                If m_objDataLayer.ExecuteSP("GetPayee", _
                                            Nothing, myReader) = True Then
                    Return myReader
                Else
                    Return Nothing
                End If
            Catch
                Return Nothing
            End Try
   End Function
   End Class
```

The Security Business Object

The Security object is used to provide not only authentication of any attempted login by a user, but also facilities for users to manipulate their passwords, such as updating. Add a class named Security to the IBankAdventure project, using the same steps as we have used previously for the other objects. As with the previous object, there nothing new being used here, so we just list the code. The completed class should be as follows:

```
Imports System.EnterpriseServices
Imports System.Data.SqlClient


<Transaction(TransactionOption.Required)> Public Class Security
   Inherits ServicedComponent

   '---------------------------------------------------------------
   ' Private members
   '---------------------------------------------------------------

   Private m_objDataLayer As DBHelper.DataAccess

   Public Sub New()
      ' Create a new DataAccess object
      m_objDataLayer = New DBHelper.DataAccess()

      ' Set our database settings
      With m_objDataLayer
            .Server = "MyServer"
            .DataBase = "IBankAdventure"
      End With

   End Sub

   <AutoComplete()> _
   Public Function CheckCustomerPwd(ByVal UserID As String, _
                                    ByVal Password As String) As Integer
```

```vb
    ' Create an array of parameters
    Dim Params() As SqlParameter = _
        {New SqlParameter("@CustomerID", SqlDbType.Int), _
         New SqlParameter("@UserID", SqlDbType.NVarChar, 50), _
         New SqlParameter("@Password", SqlDbType.NVarChar, 20)}

    ' Set the parameter values
    Params(0).Direction = System.Data.ParameterDirection.Output
    Params(1).Value = UserID
    Params(2).Value = Password

    ' Try executing the stored procedure
        Try
            If m_objDataLayer.ExecuteSP("CheckPassword", Params) = True Then
                Return CInt(Params(0).Value)
            End If
        Catch
            Return 0
        End Try


        Return 0
End Function

<AutoComplete()> _
Public Function UpdateCustomerPwd(ByVal CustomerID As String, _
                                  ByVal Password As String) As Boolean

    ' Create an array of parameters
    Dim Params() As SqlParameter = _
            {New SqlParameter("@CustomerID", SqlDbType.Int), _
             New SqlParameter("@Password", SqlDbType.NVarChar, 20)}

    ' Set the parameter values
        Params(0).Value = CustomerID
        Params(1).Value = Password

    ' Try to execute the stored procedure
        Try
            Return m_objDataLayer.ExecuteSP("UpdatePassword", Params)
        Catch e As Exception
            Return False
        End Try

    End Function

End Class
```

Now that we have all three classes in the IBankAdventure project completely coded, we can compile
the component so that our web site can reference it. Using the same steps as outlined in Chapter 9,
create the IBankAdventure.dll library and add it to COM+ Services.

IBankAdventure User Interface

To build the web-based user interface for our application, we will use a combination of ASP.NET and VB.NET. ASP.NET provides a rich selection of controls that can be used to create our interface. Our web site has four main areas: ATM functionality (deposit/withdrawal), Schedule Payments, User Profile, and Account Statements. All the pages within the application, except for the Login page, provide the user with a menu by which they can navigate to the other parts of the system. Finally, we'll create a (very) basic stylesheet in order to provide fundamental and consistent formatting across the application.

Securing Our Web Site

Before we start creating our pages, we must first consider what type of security we want to use in order to authenticate and authorize users. Visual Studio .NET provides four options for securing a web application, namely:

❑   None – This option means that none of the security options provided within Visual Studio .NET will be utilized.

❑   Forms – Forms Authentication provides the most flexible method of securing a web site. It allows users to have the benefits of a secured application, while providing developers with the flexibility to create their own authentication methods. This is the model we will use in the IBankAdventure application.

❑   Windows – Windows Authentication uses Windows challenge and response to determine who may gain access to the web site. This method is probably the most secure; however, it is also the most difficult to manage since every user who wishes to use the application must also be a user on the machine hosting the web-browser.

❑   Passport – Passport Authentication forces users to be registered with Microsoft's Passport. In other words, if someone wanted to use your application, they would first have to be in possession of a MS Passport account. This relieves the developer from much of the responsibility for user management functions, but sometimes users do not want to go to another site to register for an additional account just to gain entry to a web site. You can read more about Microsoft Passport at http://www.passport.com.

Create the IBank Project

The first thing we will need to do is create a web project. Open Visual Studio .NET and select File | New | Project. In the New Project window select ASP.NET Web Application. In the field labeled location change WebApplication1 to IBank:

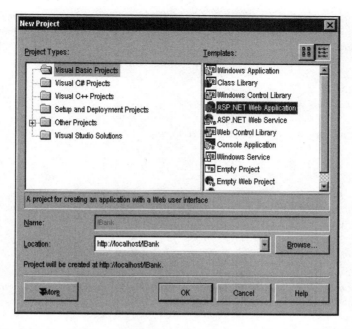

Click **OK** and Visual Studio .NET will create the web site on your local machine (denoted by the localhost in the **Location** field). When the project is created (it may take a few moments) and the project explorer is displayed, you can delete the WebForm1 file.

Now that we have a project created, we need to add a reference to the IBankAdventure.dll file we compiled earlier. While in the **Add References** window, click **Browse** and navigate to the IBankAdventure.dll file. It should be located in the bin subdirectory of the IBankAdventure project directory. Double-click on it to add it to the list of references to be added at the bottom of the window. Click on **OK** and the reference is added to the project. We also need to add a reference to the System.EnterpriseServices namespace, as we did previously.

Web.Config

To set up our user authentication mechanism we need to edit the web.config file. Remove all the default code and replace it with the following:

```
<?xml version="1.0" encoding="utf-8" ?>
<configuration>
   <system.web>
```

The next section tells the web server that Forms Authentication will be used and that the address of the login page is Login.aspx (it assumes that this file will be found in the root directory if no alternative path is specified).

```
      <authentication mode="Forms">
         <forms loginUrl="Login.aspx" />
      </authentication>
```

473

The next section provides the authorization for users. This is telling the web server to deny all non-authenticated users access to the application. A question mark, in this context, means all un-authenticated users:

```
<authorization>
    <deny users="?" />
</authorization>
```

Lastly, we shouldn't forget to close out the XML tags:

```
    </system.web>
</configuration>
```

We have now just established our site's security and we must now provide a means by which the user can log in to the site.

Login.aspx

Add a new Web Form to the project and name it Login. Click on the HTML tab, and add the following code to create a basic login page. Note that all the controls on the page are Web Form controls, but we still use HTML based tables for positioning them:

Please note: the Cascading Stylesheet for displaying our pages appropriately, Styles.css, is available to download from the Wrox web site, along with all the other code necessary for this case study.

```
<%@ Page Language="vb" AutoEventWireup="false" Codebehind="Login.aspx.vb"
Inherits="IBank.Login"%>
<!DOCTYPE HTML PUBLIC "-//W3C//DTD HTML 4.0 Transitional//EN">
<HTML>
    <HEAD>
        <TITLE>WebForm1</TITLE>
        <META CONTENT="Microsoft Visual Studio.NET 7.0" NAME="GENERATOR">
        <META CONTENT="Visual Basic 7.0" NAME="CODE_LANGUAGE">
        <META CONTENT="JavaScript" NAME="vs_defaultClientScript">
        <META CONTENT="http://schemas.microsoft.com/intellisense/ie5"
         NAME="vs_targetSchema">
        <LINK HREF="http://localhost/IBank/Styles.css" TYPE="text/css"
         REL="stylesheet">
    </HEAD>
    <BODY MS_POSITIONING="GridLayout">
        <FORM ID="frmLogin" METHOD="post" RUNAT="server">
            <H1>Welcome to IBank</H1>
            <HR>
            <TABLE CELLSPACING="0" CELLPADDING="3" BORDER="0">
                <TR>
                    <TD>Login Name:</TD>
                    <TD><ASP:TEXTBOX ID="Username"
                        RUNAT="server"></ASP:TEXTBOX></TD>
                </TR>
                <TR>
                    <TD>Password:</TD>
```

```
                <TD><ASP:TEXTBOX ID="Password" RUNAT="server"
                    TEXTMODE="Password"></ASP:TEXTBOX></TD>
        </TR>
        <TR>
          <TD> </TD>
          <TD ALIGN="right"><ASP:BUTTON ID="Login" RUNAT="server"
                            TEXT="Login"></ASP:BUTTON></TD>
        </TR>
        <TR>
          <TD COLSPAN="2"><ASP:LABEL ID="Message" RUNAT="server"
                          TEXT="" FORECOLOR="Red"></ASP:LABEL></TD>
        </TR>
      </TABLE>
    </FORM>
  </BODY>
</HTML>
```

When completed the `login.aspx` page should look as follows:

Login.aspx.vb

Now that we have Web Form completed, let's put some code behind it. This can be done by right-clicking on the `login.aspx` file in the Solution Explorer and selecting **View Code**.

First of all, we need to import some namespaces. The `System.Web.Security` namespace provides the `FormsAuthentication` object. In addition, when a page is called, it checks to see if the user has been authenticated and if they haven't, they are redirected to the login page referenced in the `web.config` file. The second namespace we import is `IBankAdventure`, so that we have access to the business objects we wrote earlier:

```
Imports System.Web.Security
Imports IBankAdventure
```

```
Public Class Login
    Inherits System.Web.UI.Page
    Protected WithEvents Username As System.Web.UI.WebControls.TextBox
    Protected WithEvents Password As System.Web.UI.WebControls.TextBox
    Protected WithEvents Message As System.Web.UI.WebControls.Label
    Protected WithEvents Login As System.Web.UI.WebControls.Button
```

This section is called when the user clicks the **Login** button.

```
Private Sub Login_Click(ByVal sender As System.Object, _
                        ByVal e As System.EventArgs) Handles Login.Click
```

Next we create an instance of the `IBankAdventure.Security` object and it calls the `CheckCustomerPwd` method. If the method succeeds we use the result, which happens to be the user's `CustomerID`, and call the `FormsAuthentication.RedirectFromLoginPage` method. This method is used to signal that the user is authenticated, holds onto the user's name (in our case, the user's `CustomerID`), and signals that the session should not be a persistent one:

```
Dim mySec As IBankAdventure.Security = New IBankAdventure.Security()
Dim iResult As Integer

iResult = mySec.CheckCustomerPwd(Username.Text, Password.Text)
    If iResult > 0 Then

        FormsAuthentication.RedirectFromLoginPage(iResult.ToString, _
                                                              False)
```

If the login fails we show an error message, remove the values from the `Username` and `Password` controls, and let the user try again:

```
    Else

        Username.Text = ""
        Password.Text = ""
        Message.Text = "Login failed. Try again."

    End If

End Sub
End Class
```

Once you have both login files created, mark `Login.aspx` as the startup page for the application.

Atm.aspx

We now add another Web Form to our `IBank` project. This page is used to mimic ATM functionality and creates `Withdrawal` and `Deposit` transactions within the database:

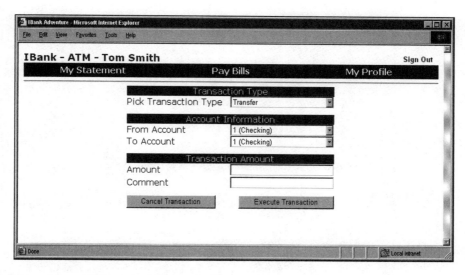

This section of the code is created automatically:

```
<%@ Page Language="vb" AutoEventWireup="false" Codebehind="Atm.aspx.vb"
Inherits="IBank.Atm"%>
<!DOCTYPE HTML PUBLIC "-//W3C//DTD HTML 4.0 Transitional//EN">
<HTML>
    <HEAD>
        <TITLE>Atm</TITLE>
        <META NAME="GENERATOR" CONTENT="Microsoft Visual Studio.NET 7.0">
        <META NAME="CODE_LANGUAGE" CONTENT="Visual Basic 7.0">
        <META NAME="vs_defaultClientScript" CONTENT="JavaScript">
        <META NAME="vs_targetSchema"
                    CONTENT="http://schemas.microsoft.com/intellisense/ie5">
```

We need to add the link to our style sheet:

```
        <LINK REL="stylesheet" TYPE="text/css"
HREF="http://localhost/IBank/Styles.css">
    </HEAD>
```

We will use `FlowLayout` positioning on all our pages rather than `GridLayout`. This allows the controls on the page to resize when the browser is resized:

```
    <BODY MS_POSITIONING="FlowLayout">
        <FORM ID="frmATM" METHOD="post" RUNAT="server">
```

The next section creates our page header. It is created by using two, single-row tables. The top table provides a title section where the page title is displayed as well as the user's name. The bottom table provides navigation to the other pages within our application. This section is on every page, unless otherwise noted:

```
<TABLE CELLSPACING="0" CELLPADDING="0" WIDTH="100%" BORDER="0">
   <TR>
      <TD ALIGN="left" WIDTH="80%"><ASP:LABEL ID="lblTitle"
      RUNAT="server" FONT-BOLD="True" FONT-SIZE="Medium" TEXT=""
      FORECOLOR="Navy"></ASP:LABEL></TD>
      <TD ALIGN="right" WIDTH="20%"><ASP:BUTTON ID="btnSignOut"
      RUNAT="server" FONT-BOLD="True" FONT-SIZE="X-Small"
      TEXT="Sign Out"  FORECOLOR="Navy" BORDERSTYLE="None"
      BACKCOLOR="White"></ASP:BUTTON></TD>
   </TR>
</TABLE>
<TABLE CELLSPACING="0" CELLPADDING="4" WIDTH="100%"  BGCOLOR="navy"
 BORDER="0">
   <TR>
      <TD ALIGN="middle" WIDTH="33%"><A STYLE="FONT-WEIGHT:  bold;
      COLOR: white" HREF="statement.aspx">My Statement</A></TD>
      <TD ALIGN="middle" WIDTH="33%"><A STYLE="FONT-WEIGHT:  bold;
      COLOR: white" HREF="billpaysummary.aspx">Pay Bills</A></TD>
      <TD ALIGN="middle" WIDTH="33%"><A STYLE="FONT-WEIGHT:  bold;
      COLOR: white" HREF="myprofile.aspx">My Profile</A></TD>
   </TR>
</TABLE>
<HR>
```

Next, we set up the user interface for the ATM page. Notice that the ddlTransactionType
DROPDOWNLIST has the AUTOPOSTBACK property set to True rather than the default value of False.
We do this so that we can hide, or show, parts of the interface that are relevant to the selected
transaction type:

```
<TABLE ALIGN="center" WIDTH="50%" CELLPADDING="0"  CELLSPACING="0"
 BORDER="0">
   <TR>
      <TD ALIGN="middle" BGCOLOR="navy" STYLE="COLOR: white"
      COLSPAN="2">Transaction Type</TD>
   </TR>
   <TR>
      <TD WIDTH="50%">Pick Transaction Type</TD>
      <TD WIDTH="50%"><ASP:DROPDOWNLIST RUNAT="server"
      ID="ddlTransactionType" WIDTH="100%"
      AUTOPOSTBACK="True"></ASP:DROPDOWNLIST></TD>
   </TR>
</TABLE>
<BR>
<TABLE ALIGN="center" WIDTH="50%" CELLPADDING="0" CELLSPACING="0"
 BORDER="0">
   <TR>
      <TD ALIGN="middle" COLSPAN="2"><ASP:LABEL RUNAT="server"
      ID="lblAccountInformation" FONT-SIZE="small" WIDTH="100%"
      FORECOLOR="white" BACKCOLOR="navy">Account
      Information</ASP:LABEL></TD>
   </TR>
   <TR>
      <TD WIDTH="50%"><ASP:LABEL RUNAT="server" ID="lblFromAccount"
```

```
          FONT-SIZE="small">From Account</ASP:LABEL></TD>
        <TD WIDTH="50%"><ASP:DROPDOWNLIST RUNAT="server"
        ID="ddlFromAccount" WIDTH="100%"></ASP:DROPDOWNLIST></TD>
      </TR>
      <TR>
        <TD WIDTH="50%"><ASP:LABEL RUNAT="server" ID="lblToAccount"
        FONT-SIZE="small">To Account</ASP:LABEL></TD>
        <TD WIDTH="50%"><ASP:DROPDOWNLIST RUNAT="server"
        ID="ddlToAccount" WIDTH="100%"></ASP:DROPDOWNLIST></TD>
      </TR>
    </TABLE>
    <BR>
    <TABLE ALIGN="center" WIDTH="50%" CELLPADDING="0" CELLSPACING="0"
     BORDER="0">
      <TR>
        <TD ALIGN="middle" COLSPAN="2"><ASP:LABEL RUNAT="server"
        ID="lblTransactionAmount" FONT-SIZE="small" WIDTH="100%"
        FORECOLOR="white" BACKCOLOR="navy">Transaction
        Amount</ASP:LABEL></TD>
      </TR>
      <TR>
        <TD WIDTH="50%"><ASP:LABEL RUNAT="server" ID="lblAmount"
        FONT-SIZE="small">Amount</ASP:LABEL></TD>
        <TD WIDTH="50%"><ASP:TEXTBOX RUNAT="server" ID="txtAmount"
        WIDTH="100%"></ASP:TEXTBOX></TD>
      </TR>
      <TR>
        <TD WIDTH="50%"><ASP:LABEL RUNAT="server" ID="lblComment"
        FONT-SIZE="small">Comment</ASP:LABEL></TD>
        <TD WIDTH="50%"><ASP:TEXTBOX RUNAT="server" ID="txtComment"
        WIDTH="100%"></ASP:TEXTBOX></TD>
      </TR>
    </TABLE>
    <BR>
    <TABLE WIDTH="50%" BORDER="0" CELLPADDING="0" CELLSPACING="0"
     ALIGN="center">
      <TR>
        <TD WIDTH="50%" ALIGN="left"><ASP:BUTTON ID="btnCancel"
        TEXT="Cancel Transaction" RUNAT="server" /></TD>
        <TD WIDTH="50%" ALIGN="right"><ASP:BUTTON ID="btnSave"
        TEXT="Execute Transaction" RUNAT="server" /></TD>
      </TR>
    </TABLE>
  </FORM>
 </BODY>
</HTML>
```

Atm.aspx.vb

This is the code that runs on the server when the page is posted back to it. The first thing that we need to do on this page, as with all the others, is include the necessary namespaces. The System.Web.Security namespace provides transparent Forms Authentication (described in detail above), System.Data.SqlClient allows us to manipulate the data return from our components, and finally the IBankAdventure namespace provides access to our business objects:

```
Imports System.Web.Security

Imports System.Data.SqlClient
Imports IBankAdventure
```

The next section of code is generated by Visual Studio .NET when you place controls on the form and set their properties:

```
Public Class Atm

    Inherits System.Web.UI.Page

    Protected WithEvents lblTitle As System.Web.UI.WebControls.Label
    Protected WithEvents ddlTransactionType As _
                                System.Web.UI.WebControls.DropDownList
    Protected WithEvents lblFromAccount As System.Web.UI.WebControls.Label
    Protected WithEvents ddlFromAccount As _
                                System.Web.UI.WebControls.DropDownList
    Protected WithEvents lblToAccount As System.Web.UI.WebControls.Label
    Protected WithEvents ddlToAccount As _
                                System.Web.UI.WebControls.DropDownList
    Protected WithEvents txtAmount As System.Web.UI.WebControls.TextBox
    Protected WithEvents lblAccountInformation As _
                                System.Web.UI.WebControls.Label
    Protected WithEvents lblTransactionAmount As _
                                System.Web.UI.WebControls.Label
    Protected WithEvents lblAmount As System.Web.UI.WebControls.Label
    Protected WithEvents btnCancel As System.Web.UI.WebControls.Button
    Protected WithEvents btnSave As System.Web.UI.WebControls.Button
    Protected WithEvents lblComment As System.Web.UI.WebControls.Label
    Protected WithEvents txtComment As System.Web.UI.WebControls.TextBox
    Protected WithEvents btnSignOut As System.Web.UI.WebControls.Button

' Web Form Designer Generated Code is here
```

The first event to fire when the page is requested is the Page_Load event. To ensure that we do not overwrite information the user has entered, we must check to see if the page is being posted back. If it isn't, we can perform our initialization routine; however, if it is, we do nothing. To achieve this add the following code:

```
    Private Sub Page_Load(ByVal sender As System.Object, ByVal e As _
                        System.EventArgs) Handles MyBase.Load
        If Not Me.IsPostBack Then
            LoadHeader()
            LoadTransactionTypes()
            LoadAccounts()

            FormatControls()
        End If
    End Sub
```

The next method is used by most of the pages to fetch the user's name from the database and show the title of the form in the header table:

```
    Private Sub LoadHeader()

        ' Get customer information
        Dim myBank As New IBankAdventure.Bank()
        Dim myCustReader As SqlDataReader = _
        myBank.GetCustomerInfo(Convert.ToInt32(Context.User.Identity.Name))

        ' Move reader to first (and only) record and personalize title
        myCustReader.Read()
        Me.lblTitle.Text = "IBank - ATM - " & _
                            myCustReader.Item("CustomerName")
        myCustReader.Close()

    End Sub
```

The following method is used to fetch the list of accounts for the specified user, and populates the
ddlToAccount and ddlFromAccount lists with the account number and account type:

```
    Private Sub LoadAccounts()

    Dim myReader As SqlDataReader = New IBankAdventure.Bank().GetAccounts _
                        (Convert.ToInt32(Context.User.Identity.Name))
        While myReader.Read()

    Dim li As New ListItem(myReader.Item("AccountNumber"), _
                        myReader.Item("AccountNumber"))
            Select Case myReader("AccountType")
                Case "C" : li.Text = li.Text & " (Checking)"
                Case "S" : li.Text = li.Text & " (Savings)"
            End Select
            Me.ddlToAccount.Items.Add(li)
            Me.ddlFromAccount.Items.Add(li)

        End While
        Me.ddlToAccount.SelectedIndex = 0
        Me.ddlFromAccount.SelectedIndex = 0

    End Sub
```

Next, we create a method to load the ddlTransactionType control with the different ATM functions
we are going to allow:

```
    Private Sub LoadTransactionTypes()

        Me.ddlTransactionType.Items.Add(New ListItem("", ""))
        Me.ddlTransactionType.Items.Add(New ListItem("Deposit", "D"))
        Me.ddlTransactionType.Items.Add(New ListItem("Transfer", "T"))
        Me.ddlTransactionType.Items.Add(New ListItem("Withdraw", "W"))
        Me.ddlTransactionType.SelectedIndex = 0

    End Sub
```

The next method is used to hide our show controls based on transaction type:

```
Private Sub FormatControls()

    'Show or hide Account Information controls based on transaction type
    Me.lblAccountInformation.Visible = _
    (Me.ddlTransactionType.SelectedItem.Value <> "")
    Me.ddlFromAccount.Visible = _
    (Me.ddlTransactionType.SelectedItem.Value = "T" Or _
    Me.ddlTransactionType.SelectedItem.Value = "W")
    Me.lblFromAccount.Visible = Me.ddlFromAccount.Visible
    Me.ddlToAccount.Visible = _
    (Me.ddlTransactionType.SelectedItem.Value = "T" Or _
    Me.ddlTransactionType.SelectedItem.Value = "D")
    Me.lblToAccount.Visible = Me.ddlToAccount.Visible


    'Show or hide Transaction Information controls based on transation type
    Me.lblTransactionAmount.Visible = _
    (Me.ddlTransactionType.SelectedItem.Value <> "")
    Me.txtAmount.Visible = (Me.ddlTransactionType.SelectedItem.Value <> _
                                                                    "")
    Me.lblAmount.Visible = Me.txtAmount.Visible
    Me.txtComment.Visible = (Me.ddlTransactionType.SelectedItem.Value <> _
                                                                    "")
    Me.lblComment.Visible = Me.txtComment.Visible

End Sub
```

If the user presses the Cancel button, we should return to the default.aspx page (we'll create this page later):

```
Private Sub btnCancel_Click(ByVal sender As Object, ByVal e As _
                            System.EventArgs) Handles btnCancel.Click
    Response.Redirect("default.aspx")
End Sub
```

The following method is fired when the user selects a type of transaction to execute. It will call the FormatControls method to show or hide the rest of the page controls as appropriate:

```
Private Sub ddlTransactionType_SelectedIndexChanged(ByVal sender As _
                            Object, ByVal e As System.EventArgs) Handles _
                            ddlTransactionType.SelectedIndexChanged
    FormatControls()
End Sub
```

The next method is used to execute the transaction requested by the user. When the transaction is completed, we will send the user back to the default.aspx page:

```
Private Sub btnSave_Click(ByVal sender As Object, ByVal e As _
                          System.EventArgs) Handles btnSave.Click
```

```
              Dim myBank As New IBankAdventure.Bank()

              Select Case Me.ddlTransactionType.SelectedItem.Value
                  Case "D" :
myBank.DepositFunds(CInt(Me.ddlToAccount.SelectedItem.Value), _
CSng(Me.txtAmount.Text), Me.txtComment.Text)
                  Case "T" :
myBank.TransferFunds(CInt(Me.ddlFromAccount.SelectedItem.Value), _
CInt(Me.ddlToAccount.SelectedItem.Value), CSng(Me.txtAmount.Text), _
Me.txtComment.Text)
                  Case "W" :
myBank.WithdrawFunds(CInt(Me.ddlFromAccount.SelectedItem.Value), _
CSng(Me.txtAmount.Text), Me.txtComment.Text)
          End Select

          Response.Redirect("default.aspx")

      End Sub
```

Our final method is executed when the user clicks on the Sign Out button in the page header. All of our pages, except for the Login.aspx page, use this functionality to allow the user to complete their session when they choose. We inform the Security object that the user wishes to log out and explicitly close the current session. At this point the user is redirected to the login page.

```
      Private Sub btnSignOut_Click(ByVal sender As System.Object, ByVal e As _
                              System.EventArgs) Handles btnSignOut.Click
          ' Force Signout and send user back to login page
          FormsAuthentication.SignOut()
          Session.Abandon()
          Response.Redirect("login.aspx")
      End Sub
```

BillPaySummary.aspx

This page is used to provide the user with a list of the scheduled payments that they have created for a given account. It will allow the user to modify or add new scheduled payments, as they desire.

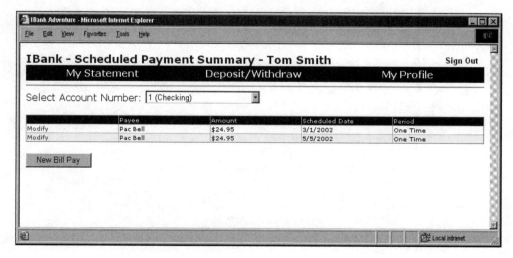

Again, the standard page header information is generated automatically:

```
<%@ Page Language="vb" AutoEventWireup="false" Codebehind="BillPaySummary.aspx.vb"
Inherits="IBank.BillPaySummary"%>
<!DOCTYPE HTML PUBLIC "-//W3C//DTD HTML 4.0 Transitional//EN">
<HTML>
    <HEAD>
        <TITLE>BillPaySummary</TITLE>
        <META CONTENT="Microsoft Visual Studio.NET 7.0" NAME="GENERATOR">
        <META CONTENT="Visual Basic 7.0" NAME="CODE_LANGUAGE">
        <META CONTENT="JavaScript" NAME="vs_defaultClientScript">
        <META CONTENT="http://schemas.microsoft.com/intellisense/ie5"
         NAME="vs_targetSchema">
        <LINK HREF="http://localhost/IBank/Styles.css" TYPE="text/css"
         REL="stylesheet">
```

In order to modify a scheduled payment, we need to pass multiple parameters to the `BillPay.aspx` page (which we create shortly) so that it finds the correct item for modification. Since we are using a `DataGrid` control to display our information, and that control allows only one database field per column, we need to find a way to capture both the `BillPayID` and `AccountNumber` and send them to `BillPay.aspx`.

The solution to this is creating a client-side script method that takes the `BillPayID` as a parameter, and retrieves the `AccountNumber` value from the `DROPDOWNLIST` control. Remember that the client-side script can access and reference our server controls because they are rendered as standard HTML controls. Further, this solution allows us a slight performance advantage in that we do not need to make a round trip to the server to call `BillPay.aspx`. Granted, this solution may be heavy-handed and not as elegant as others, but it works:

```
<SCRIPT LANGUAGE="javascript">
function ShowDetailInfo( billpayid )
{
    lst = BillPaySummary.ddlAccounts;
    url = "billpay.aspx?billpayid=" + billpayid + "&accountnumber=" +
            lst.options[lst.selectedIndex].value;
    window.navigate(url);
    return;
}
</SCRIPT>
</HEAD>
<BODY MS_POSITIONING="FLowLayout">
    <FORM ID="BillPaySummary" METHOD="post" RUNAT="server">
        <TABLE CELLSPACING="0" CELLPADDING="0" WIDTH="100%" BORDER="0">
            <TR>
                <TD ALIGN="left" WIDTH="80%"><ASP:LABEL ID="lblTitle"
                RUNAT="server" FONT-BOLD="True" FONT-SIZE="Medium" TEXT=""
                FORECOLOR="Navy"></ASP:LABEL></TD>
                <TD ALIGN="right" WIDTH="20%"><ASP:BUTTON ID="btnSignOut"
                RUNAT="server" FONT-BOLD="True" FONT-SIZE="X-Small"
                TEXT="Sign Out" FORECOLOR="Navy" BORDERSTYLE="None"
                BACKCOLOR="White"></ASP:BUTTON></TD>
            </TR>
        </TABLE>
```

```
<TABLE CELLSPACING="0" CELLPADDING="4" WIDTH="100%" BGCOLOR="navy"
 BORDER="0">
  <TR>
    <TD ALIGN="middle" WIDTH="33%"><A STYLE="FONT-WEIGHT: bold;
     COLOR: white" HREF="statement.aspx">My Statement</A></TD>
    <TD ALIGN="middle" WIDTH="33%"><A STYLE="FONT-WEIGHT: bold;
     COLOR: white" HREF="atm.aspx">Deposit/Withdraw</A></TD>
    <TD ALIGN="middle" WIDTH="33%"><A STYLE="FONT-WEIGHT: bold;
     COLOR: white" HREF="myprofile.aspx">My Profile</A></TD>
  </TR>
</TABLE>
<HR>
<ASP:LABEL ID="lblAccount" RUNAT="server" FONT-SIZE="Small"
 TEXT="Select Account Number:">Select Account Number:
 </ASP:LABEL>
<ASP:DROPDOWNLIST ID="ddlAccounts" RUNAT="server"
 AUTOPOSTBACK="True" WIDTH="50%"></ASP:DROPDOWNLIST>
<P></P>
```

Next, we create our DataGrid. After typing this code into your page, open up the Properties window for it and explore its contents, adjusting it as you feel appropriate:

```
<ASP:DATAGRID ID="dgBillPay" RUNAT="server" WIDTH="100%"
 AUTOGENERATECOLUMNS="False" FONT-SIZE="XX-Small">
  <ALTERNATINGITEMSTYLE
   BACKCOLOR="LightGoldenrodYellow"></ALTERNATINGITEMSTYLE>
  <HEADERSTYLE FORECOLOR="White" BACKCOLOR="Navy"></HEADERSTYLE>
  <COLUMNS>
```

This is the column in which we call client-side script:

```
<ASP:HYPERLINKCOLUMN TEXT="Modify"
 DATANAVIGATEURLFIELD="BillPayID"
 DATANAVIGATEURLFORMATSTRING=
 "javascript:ShowDetailInfo({0});">
   <HEADERSTYLE WIDTH="20%"></HEADERSTYLE>
 </ASP:HYPERLINKCOLUMN>
```

The rest of the columns are tied directly to fields returned from the database:

```
<ASP:BOUNDCOLUMN DATAFIELD="PayeeName" HEADERTEXT="Payee">
   <HEADERSTYLE WIDTH="20%"></HEADERSTYLE>
 </ASP:BOUNDCOLUMN>
<ASP:BOUNDCOLUMN DATAFIELD="Amount" HEADERTEXT="Amount"
 DATAFORMATSTRING="{0:C}">
   <HEADERSTYLE WIDTH="20%"></HEADERSTYLE>
 </ASP:BOUNDCOLUMN>
<ASP:BOUNDCOLUMN DATAFIELD="ScheduleDate"
 HEADERTEXT="Scheduled Date" DATAFORMATSTRING="{0:d}">
   <HEADERSTYLE WIDTH="20%"></HEADERSTYLE>
 </ASP:BOUNDCOLUMN>
```

```
                    <ASP:BOUNDCOLUMN DATAFIELD="PeriodDescription"
                     HEADERTEXT="Period">
                        <HEADERSTYLE WIDTH="20%"></HEADERSTYLE>
                    </ASP:BOUNDCOLUMN>
                </COLUMNS>
                <PAGERSTYLE FORECOLOR="White" BACKCOLOR="Navy"></PAGERSTYLE>
            </ASP:DATAGRID>
            <P></P>
            <ASP:BUTTON ID="btnNew" RUNAT="server" TEXT="New Bill
             Pay"></ASP:BUTTON></FORM>
        <P></P>
    </BODY>
</HTML>
```

BillPaySummary.aspx.vb

Now, let's create the code behind the window:

```
Imports System.Web.Security
Imports System.Data
Imports System.Data.SqlClient
Imports IBankAdventure


Public Class BillPaySummary
    Inherits System.Web.UI.Page
    Protected WithEvents lblTitle As System.Web.UI.WebControls.Label
    Protected WithEvents dgBillPay As System.Web.UI.WebControls.DataGrid
    Protected WithEvents ddlAccounts As _
                                 System.Web.UI.WebControls.DropDownList
    Protected WithEvents btnSignOut As System.Web.UI.WebControls.Button
    Protected WithEvents btnNew As System.Web.UI.WebControls.Button
    Protected WithEvents lblAccount As System.Web.UI.WebControls.Label


    Protected myDataView As DataView

' Web Form Designer Generated Code here
```

As with previous pages, we need to initialize the page control if appropriate:

```
    Private Sub Page_Load(ByVal sender As System.Object, ByVal e As _
                     System.EventArgs) Handles MyBase.Load
        If Not Me.IsPostBack Then
            LoadHeader()
            LoadAccounts()
            LoadBillPay()
            BindData()
        End If
    End Sub

    Private Sub LoadHeader()
        ' Get customer information
        Dim myBank As New IBankAdventure.Bank()
        Dim myCustReader As SqlDataReader = _
```

```
              myBank.GetCustomerInfo(Convert.ToInt32(Context.User.Identity.Name))

          ' Move reader to first (and only) record and personalize title
          myCustReader.Read()
          Me.lblTitle.Text = "IBank - Scheduled Payment Summary - " & _
                            myCustReader.Item("CustomerName")
          myCustReader.Close()
      End Sub

      Private Sub LoadAccounts()

          Dim myReader As SqlDataReader = New _
          IBankAdventure.Bank().GetAccounts _
          (Convert.ToInt32(Context.User.Identity.Name))
          While myReader.Read()

              Dim li As New ListItem(myReader.Item("AccountNumber"), _
                                  myReader.Item("AccountNumber"))
              Select Case myReader("AccountType")
                  Case "C" : li.Text = li.Text & " (Checking)"
                  Case "S" : li.Text = li.Text & " (Savings)"
              End Select
              Me.ddlAccounts.Items.Add(li)

          End While
          Me.ddlAccounts.SelectedIndex = 0

      End Sub
```

The next two methods fetch the data from the database in the form of a DataSet. It is turned into a DataView and bound to the DataGrid. The purpose of having two methods is that although this DataGrid cannot be sorted or paged through, other grids that do allow such functionality are more easily implemented in this manner:

```
      Private Sub LoadBillPay()

          Dim intAccount As Integer = _
  Convert.ToInt32(Me.ddlAccounts.SelectedItem.Value)
          Dim myBillPay As New IBankAdventure.BillPay()

          Dim myDataSet As DataSet = myBillPay.GetBillPay(intAccount)
          myDataView = New DataView(myDataSet.Tables(0))

      End Sub

      Private Sub BindData()

          Me.dgBillPay.DataSource = myDataView
          Me.dgBillPay.DataBind()

      End Sub
```

When the user selects a different account, we need to re-query the database for that account's information and display it in the DataGrid:

```
Private Sub ddlAccounts_SelectedIndexChanged(ByVal sender As _
            System.Object, ByVal e As System.EventArgs) Handles _
            ddlAccounts.SelectedIndexChanged

    LoadBillPay()
    BindData()

End Sub
```

If the user wishes to create a new scheduled payment, we will navigate to the BillPay.aspx page without any query string, thus indicating that we want to create a new item:

```
Private Sub btnNew_Click(ByVal sender As System.Object, ByVal e As _
                    System.EventArgs) Handles btnNew.Click
    Response.Redirect("BillPay.aspx")
End Sub

Private Sub btnSignOut_Click(ByVal sender As System.Object, ByVal e As _
                        System.EventArgs) Handles btnSignOut.Click
    ' Force Signout and send user back to login page
    FormsAuthentication.SignOut()
    Session.Abandon()
    Response.Redirect("login.aspx")
End Sub
```

BillPay.aspx

The BillPay.aspx page is used to add, modify, or delete a scheduled payment. Many of the concepts used in constructing this page have been used in the pages we have built so far, and should be familiar to you.

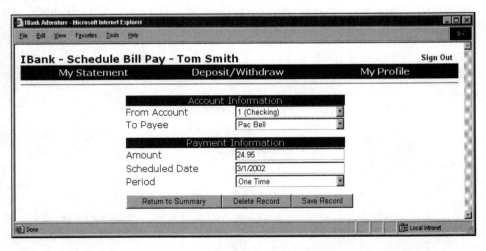

```
<%@ Page Language="vb" AutoEventWireup="false" Codebehind="BillPay.aspx.vb"
 Inherits="IBank.BillPay"%>
<!DOCTYPE HTML PUBLIC "-//W3C//DTD HTML 4.0 Transitional//EN">
<HTML>
    <HEAD>
```

```
    <TITLE>BillPay</TITLE>
    <META CONTENT="Microsoft Visual Studio.NET 7.0" NAME="GENERATOR">
    <META CONTENT="Visual Basic 7.0" NAME="CODE_LANGUAGE">
    <META CONTENT="JavaScript" NAME="vs_defaultClientScript">
    <META CONTENT="http://schemas.microsoft.com/intellisense/ie5"
    NAME="vs_targetSchema">
    <LINK HREF="http://localhost/IBank/Styles.css" TYPE="text/css"
    REL="stylesheet">
</HEAD>
<BODY MS_POSITIONING="FlowLayout">
    <FORM ID="Form1" METHOD="post" RUNAT="server">
        <TABLE CELLSPACING="0" CELLPADDING="0" WIDTH="100%" BORDER="0">
            <TR>
                <TD ALIGN="left" WIDTH="80%"><ASP:LABEL ID="lblTitle"
                RUNAT="server" FORECOLOR="Navy" TEXT="" FONT-SIZE="Medium"
                FONT-BOLD="True"></ASP:LABEL></TD>
                <TD ALIGN="right" WIDTH="20%"><ASP:BUTTON ID="btnSignOut"
                RUNAT="server" FORECOLOR="Navy" TEXT="Sign Out"
                FONT-SIZE="X-Small" FONT-BOLD="True" BACKCOLOR="White"
                BORDERSTYLE="None"></ASP:BUTTON></TD>
            </TR>
        </TABLE>
        <TABLE CELLSPACING="0" CELLPADDING="4" WIDTH="100%" BGCOLOR="navy"
        BORDER="0">
            <TR>
                <TD ALIGN="middle" WIDTH="33%"><A STYLE="FONT-WEIGHT: bold;
                COLOR: white" HREF="statement.aspx">My Statement</A></TD>
                <TD ALIGN="middle" WIDTH="33%"><A STYLE="FONT-WEIGHT: bold;
                COLOR: white" HREF="atm.aspx">Deposit/Withdraw</A></TD>
                <TD ALIGN="middle" WIDTH="33%"><A STYLE="FONT-WEIGHT: bold;
                COLOR: white" HREF="myprofile.aspx">My Profile</A></TD>
            </TR>
        </TABLE>
        <HR>
        <DIV ALIGN="center"></DIV>
        <BR>
        <DIV ALIGN="center"><ASP:PANEL ID="pnlBillPay" RUNAT="server"
        WIDTH="50%">
            <TABLE CELLSPACING="0" CELLPADDING="0" WIDTH="100%"
            ALIGN="center" BORDER="0">
                <TR>
                    <TD STYLE="COLOR: white" ALIGN="middle" BGCOLOR="navy"
                    COLSPAN="2">Account Information</TD>
                </TR>
                <TR>
                    <TD WIDTH="25%">From Account</TD>
                    <TD WIDTH="25%">
                        <ASP:DROPDOWNLIST ID="ddl_Account" RUNAT="server"
                        WIDTH="100%"></ASP:DROPDOWNLIST></TD>
                </TR>
                <TR>
                    <TD WIDTH="25%">To Payee</TD>
                    <TD WIDTH="25%">
                        <ASP:DROPDOWNLIST ID="ddl_Payee" RUNAT="server"
```

```
                                WIDTH="100%"></ASP:DROPDOWNLIST></TD>
              </TR>
          </TABLE>
          <BR>
          <TABLE CELLSPACING="0" CELLPADDING="0" WIDTH="100%"
           ALIGN="center" BORDER="0">
              <TR>
                 <TD STYLE="COLOR: white" ALIGN="middle" BGCOLOR="navy"
                  COLSPAN="2">Payment Information</TD>
              </TR>
              <TR>
                 <TD WIDTH="25%">Amount</TD>
                 <TD WIDTH="25%">
                    <ASP:TEXTBOX ID="txtAmount" RUNAT="server"
                     WIDTH="100%"></ASP:TEXTBOX></TD>
              </TR>
              <TR>
                 <TD WIDTH="25%">Scheduled Date</TD>
                 <TD WIDTH="25%">
                    <ASP:TEXTBOX ID="txtScheduleDate" RUNAT="server"
                     WIDTH="100%"></ASP:TEXTBOX></TD>
              </TR>
              <TR>
                 <TD WIDTH="25%">Period</TD>
                 <TD WIDTH="25%">
                    <ASP:DROPDOWNLIST ID="ddl_Period" RUNAT="server"
                     WIDTH="100%"></ASP:DROPDOWNLIST></TD>
              </TR>
          </TABLE>
          <BR>
          <TABLE CELLSPACING="0" CELLPADDING="0" WIDTH="100%"
           ALIGN="center" BORDER="0">
              <TR>
                 <TD ALIGN="left" WIDTH="33%">
                    <ASP:BUTTON ID="btnReturn" RUNAT="server"
                     TEXT="Return to Summary"></ASP:BUTTON></TD>
                 <TD ALIGN="middle" WIDTH="34%">
                    <ASP:BUTTON ID="btnDelete" RUNAT="server"
                     TEXT="Delete Record"></ASP:BUTTON></TD>
                 <TD ALIGN="right" WIDTH="33%">
                    <ASP:BUTTON ID="btnSave" RUNAT="server"
                     TEXT="Save Record"></ASP:BUTTON></TD>
              </TR>
          </TABLE>
       </ASP:PANEL></DIV>
    </FORM>
  </BODY>
</HTML>
```

BillPay.aspx.vb

Here is the server-side code used for the BillPay.aspx page. There are not many new concepts introduced here so our discussion will be brief:

```
Imports System.Web.Security
Imports System.Data
Imports System.Data.SqlClient
Imports IBankAdventure

Public Class BillPay

    Inherits System.Web.UI.Page
    Protected WithEvents lblTitle As System.Web.UI.WebControls.Label
    Protected WithEvents ddl_Account As _
                         System.Web.UI.WebControls.DropDownList
    Protected WithEvents ddl_Payee As System.Web.UI.WebControls.DropDownList
    Protected WithEvents txtCustomerName As _
                         System.Web.UI.WebControls.TextBox
    Protected WithEvents rfvCustomerName As _
                System.Web.UI.WebControls.RequiredFieldValidator
    Protected WithEvents rfvPhone As _
                System.Web.UI.WebControls.RequiredFieldValidator
    Protected WithEvents btnCancel As System.Web.UI.WebControls.Button
    Protected WithEvents btnSave As System.Web.UI.WebControls.Button
    Protected WithEvents ddl_Period As _
                         System.Web.UI.WebControls.DropDownList
    Protected WithEvents pnlBillPay As System.Web.UI.WebControls.Panel
    Protected WithEvents btnDelete As System.Web.UI.WebControls.Button
    Protected WithEvents txtAmount As System.Web.UI.WebControls.TextBox
    Protected WithEvents txtScheduleDate As _
                         System.Web.UI.WebControls.TextBox
    Protected WithEvents btnReturn As System.Web.UI.WebControls.Button
    Protected WithEvents btnSignOut As System.Web.UI.WebControls.Button

' Web Form Designer Generated Code here

    Private Sub Page_Load(ByVal sender As System.Object, ByVal e As _
                    System.EventArgs) Handles MyBase.Load

    If Not Me.IsPostBack Then
        LoadHeader()
        LoadPayorAccounts()
        LoadPayees()
        LoadPeriod()
```

The following section of code determines if the user is requesting to edit an existing schedule payment or create a new one. The determination is made based on the presence or absence of a `billpayid` parameter in the requesting query string. We then move on to create the other necessary methods:

```
        If Not Request("billpayid") = Nothing Then

            Session("billpay_billpayid") = Request("billpayid")
            Session("billpay_accountnumber") = Request("AccountNumber")

            LoadBillPayInfo()
        End If
    End If
```

```
    End Sub

Private Sub LoadHeader()
    '' Get customer information
    Dim myBank As New IBankAdventure.Bank()
    Dim myCustReader As SqlDataReader = _
     myBank.GetCustomerInfo(Convert.ToInt32(Context.User.Identity.Name))

    '' Move reader to first (and only) record and personalize title
    myCustReader.Read()
    Me.lblTitle.Text = "IBank - Schedule Bill Pay - " & _
                        myCustReader.Item("CustomerName")
    myCustReader.Close()

End Sub

Private Sub LoadPayorAccounts()

    Me.ddl_Account.Items.Clear()

    Dim myBank As New IBankAdventure.Bank()
    Dim myAcctReader As SqlDataReader = _
        myBank.GetAccounts(Convert.ToInt32(Context.User.Identity.Name))

    While myAcctReader.Read()
        Dim AccountType As String
        If myAcctReader.Item("AccountType") = "C" Then
            AccountType = myAcctReader.Item("AccountNumber") & _
                                            "(Checking)"
        Else
            AccountType = myAcctReader.Item("AccountNumber") & _
                                            "(Savings)"
        End If

        Me.ddl_Account.Items.Add(New ListItem(AccountType, _
                                myAcctReader.Item("AccountNumber")))
    End While
    myAcctReader.Close()

    Me.ddl_Account.SelectedIndex = 0

End Sub

Private Sub LoadPayees()

    Me.ddl_Payee.Items.Clear()
    Dim myBillPay As New IBankAdventure.BillPay()

    Dim myReader As SqlDataReader = myBillPay.GetPayees()
    While myReader.Read()
        Me.ddl_Payee.Items.Add(New ListItem(myReader.Item("PayeeName"), _
                            myReader.Item("PayeeID")))
    End While
```

```
            Me.ddl_Payee.SelectedIndex = 0

      End Sub

      Private Sub LoadPeriod()

            Me.ddl_Period.Items.Clear()

            Me.ddl_Period.Items.Add(New ListItem("One Time"))
            Me.ddl_Period.Items.Add(New ListItem("Monthly"))
            Me.ddl_Period.Items.Add(New ListItem("Quarterly"))
            Me.ddl_Period.Items.Add(New ListItem("Annually"))

            Me.ddl_Period.SelectedIndex = 0

      End Sub

      Private Sub LoadBillPayInfo()

            Dim myDataSet As DataSet = New _
      IBankAdventure.BillPay().GetBillPay(CInt(Session("billpay_accountnumber")))

            Dim dr As DataRow
            For Each dr In myDataSet.Tables(0).Rows
                If dr("BillPayID") = CInt(Session("billpay_billpayid")) Then

                    Me.ddl_Account.SelectedIndex = _
                Me.ddl_Account.Items.IndexOf(Me.ddl_Account.Items.FindByValue _
                                            (CStr(dr("AccountNumber"))))
                    Me.ddl_Payee.SelectedIndex = _
                    Me.ddl_Payee.Items.IndexOf(Me.ddl_Payee.Items.FindByValue _
                                            (CStr(dr("PayeeID"))))
                    Me.txtAmount.Text = dr("Amount")
                    Me.txtScheduleDate.Text = FormatDateTime _
                                    (dr("ScheduleDate"), DateFormat.ShortDate)
                    Me.ddl_Period.SelectedIndex = _
                    Me.ddl_Period.Items.IndexOf(Me.ddl_Period.Items.FindByText _
                                            (CStr(dr("PeriodDescription"))))

                    Exit For
                End If
            Next


      End Sub

      Private Sub btnSave_Click(ByVal sender As System.Object, ByVal e As _
                        System.EventArgs) Handles btnSave.Click

            'Perform data validations
            If Not IsNumeric(Me.txtAmount.Text) Or Me.txtAmount.Text.Length = 0 Then
                Return
            End If
            If Not IsDate(Me.txtScheduleDate.Text) Or _
```

```
                                        Me.txtScheduleDate.Text.Length = 0 Then
            Return
        End If

        'Convert data to appropriate formats for save
        Dim intAccount As Integer = _
                        Convert.ToInt32(Me.ddl_Account.SelectedItem.Value)
        Dim intPayee As Integer = _
                        Convert.ToInt32(Me.ddl_Payee.SelectedItem.Value)
        Dim sngAmount As Single = Convert.ToSingle(Me.txtAmount.Text)
        Dim dtmSchedule As Date = _
                        Convert.ToDateTime(Me.txtScheduleDate.Text)


        Dim intPeriod As Integer
        Select Case Me.ddl_Period.SelectedItem.Text
            Case "One Time" : intPeriod = _
                                IBankAdventure.BillPay.Schedule.OneTime
            Case "Monthly" : intPeriod = _
                                IBankAdventure.BillPay.Schedule.Monthly
            Case "Quarterly" : intPeriod = _
                                IBankAdventure.BillPay.Schedule.Quarterly
            Case "Annually" : intPeriod = _
                                IBankAdventure.BillPay.Schedule.Annually
        End Select

        'Create the BillPay object
        Dim myBillPay As New IBankAdventure.BillPay()

        'Save the new Schedule
        If CInt(Session("billpay_billpayid")) > 0 Then
            myBillPay.UpdateBillPay(CInt(Session("billpay_billpayid")), _
                    intAccount, intPayee, sngAmount, dtmSchedule, intPeriod)
        Else
            myBillPay.InsertBillPay(intAccount, intPayee, sngAmount, _
                            dtmSchedule, intPeriod)
        End If

    End Sub

    Private Sub btnReturn_Click(ByVal sender As System.Object, ByVal e As _
                    System.EventArgs) Handles btnReturn.Click
        Response.Redirect("BillPaySummary.aspx")
    End Sub

    Private Sub btnDelete_Click(ByVal sender As System.Object, ByVal e As _
                    System.EventArgs) Handles btnDelete.Click

        Dim myBillPay As New IBankAdventure.BillPay()
        myBillPay.DeleteBillPay(CInt(Session("billpay_billpayid")))

        Response.Redirect("BillPaySummary.aspx")
    End Sub

    Private Sub btnSignOut_Click(ByVal sender As System.Object, ByVal e As _
```

```
                        System.EventArgs) Handles btnSignOut.Click
        '' Force Signout and send user back to login page
        FormsAuthentication.SignOut()
        Session.Abandon()
        Response.Redirect("login.aspx")
    End Sub
End Class
```

default.aspx

The `default.aspx` page is required, given our security model. If the user requests a page, such as `Atm.aspx`, without having logged in, they are forced to the `Login.aspx` page and then, if the login is successful, redirected to the requested page. However, if the user navigates directly to the `Login.aspx` page and login is successful, the Forms Authentication model looks for a `default.aspx` file to send the user to.

This page is very simple and provides only navigation. Once the user navigates away from this page, they cannot navigate back to it, because it serves no real value other than as a placeholder:

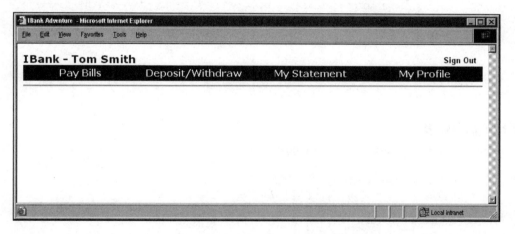

```
<%@ Page Language="vb" AutoEventWireup="false" Codebehind="default.aspx.vb"
 Inherits="IBank._default"%>
<!DOCTYPE HTML PUBLIC "-//W3C//DTD HTML 4.0 Transitional//EN">
<HTML>
    <HEAD>
        <TITLE>IBank Adventure</TITLE>
        <META NAME="GENERATOR" CONTENT="Microsoft Visual Studio.NET 7.0">
        <META NAME="CODE_LANGUAGE" CONTENT="Visual Basic 7.0">
        <META NAME="vs_defaultClientScript" CONTENT="JavaScript">
        <META NAME="vs_targetSchema"
         CONTENT="http://schemas.microsoft.com/intellisense/ie5">
        <LINK REL="stylesheet" TYPE="text/css"
         HREF="http://localhost/IBank/Styles.css">
    </HEAD>
    <BODY MS_POSITIONING="GridLayout">
        <FORM ID="Form1" METHOD="post" RUNAT="server">
            <TABLE CELLSPACING="0" CELLPADDING="0" WIDTH="100%" BORDER="0">
```

```
                    <TR>
                        <TD ALIGN="left" WIDTH="80%"><ASP:LABEL ID="lblTitle"
                        RUNAT="server" FONT-BOLD="True" FONT-SIZE="Medium" TEXT=""
                        FORECOLOR="Navy" /></TD>
                        <TD ALIGN="right" WIDTH="20%"><ASP:BUTTON ID="btnSignOut"
                        RUNAT="server" FONT-BOLD="True" FONT-SIZE="X-Small"
                        TEXT="Sign Out" FORECOLOR="Navy" BORDERSTYLE="None"
                        BACKCOLOR="White"></ASP:BUTTON></TD>
                    </TR>
                </TABLE>
                <TABLE CELLSPACING="0" CELLPADDING="4" WIDTH="100%" BGCOLOR="navy"
                BORDER="0">
                    <TR>
                        <TD ALIGN="middle" WIDTH="25%"><A STYLE="FONT-WEIGHT: bold;
                        COLOR: white" HREF="BillPaySummary.aspx">Pay Bills</A></TD>
                        <TD ALIGN="middle" WIDTH="25%"><A STYLE="FONT-WEIGHT: bold;
                        COLOR: white" HREF="Atm.aspx">Deposit/Withdraw</A></TD>
                        <TD ALIGN="middle" WIDTH="25%"><A STYLE="FONT-WEIGHT: bold;
                        COLOR: white" HREF="Statement.aspx">My Statement</A></TD>
                        <TD ALIGN="middle" WIDTH="25%"><A STYLE="FONT-WEIGHT: bold;
                        COLOR: white" HREF="MyProfile.aspx">My Profile</A></TD>
                    </TR>
                </TABLE>
                <HR>
            </FORM>
        </BODY>
</HTML>
```

default.aspx.vb

The coding for the default form is as follows:

```
Imports System.Web.Security
Imports System.Data
Imports System.Data.SqlClient
Imports IBankAdventure

Public Class _default
    Inherits System.Web.UI.Page
    Protected WithEvents lblTitle As System.Web.UI.WebControls.Label
    Protected WithEvents btnSignOut As System.Web.UI.WebControls.Button

' Web Form Designer Generated Code here

    Private Sub Page_Load(ByVal sender As System.Object, ByVal e As _
                    System.EventArgs) Handles MyBase.Load

        ' Get customer information
        Dim myBank As New IBankAdventure.Bank()
        Dim myReader As SqlDataReader = _
        myBank.GetCustomerInfo(Convert.ToInt32(Context.User.Identity.Name))

        ' Move reader to first (and only) record and personalize title
```

```
        myReader.Read()
        Me.lblTitle.Text = "IBank - " & myReader.Item("CustomerName")
        myReader.Close()

    End Sub

    Private Sub btnSignOut_Click(ByVal sender As System.Object, ByVal e As _
                          System.EventArgs) Handles btnSignOut.Click
        ' Force Signout and send user back to login page
        FormsAuthentication.SignOut()
        Session.Abandon()
        Response.Redirect("Login.aspx")
    End Sub
End Class
```

MyProfile.aspx

This page is used to modify the user's information. In addition, it will allow the user to change their password. In most production application situations, we would probably want to be more stringent with the business rules such as Social Security Number formatting. In that same vein, the password functionality should, more properly, be on its own page:

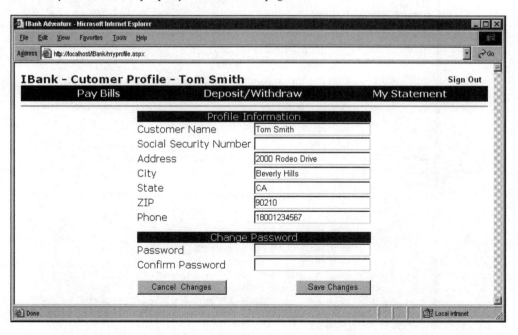

```
<%@ Page Language="vb" AutoEventWireup="false"
 Codebehind="MyProfile.aspx.vb" Inherits="IBank.MyProfile"%>
<!DOCTYPE HTML PUBLIC "-//W3C//DTD HTML 4.0 Transitional//EN">
<HTML>
    <HEAD>
       <TITLE>MyProfile</TITLE>
```

```
            <META NAME="GENERATOR" CONTENT="Microsoft Visual Studio.NET 7.0">
            <META NAME="CODE_LANGUAGE" CONTENT="Visual Basic 7.0">
            <META NAME="vs_defaultClientScript" CONTENT="JavaScript">
            <META NAME="vs_targetSchema"
             CONTENT="http://schemas.microsoft.com/intellisense/ie5">
            <LINK REL="stylesheet" TYPE="text/css"
             HREF="http://localhost/IBank/Styles.css">
    </HEAD>
    <BODY MS_POSITIONING="GridLayout">
        <FORM ID="Form1" METHOD="post" RUNAT="server">
            <TABLE CELLSPACING="0" CELLPADDING="0" WIDTH="100%" BORDER="0">
                <TR>
                    <TD ALIGN="left" WIDTH="80%"><ASP:LABEL ID="lblTitle"
                     RUNAT="server" FONT-BOLD="True" FONT-SIZE="Medium" TEXT=""
                     FORECOLOR="Navy" /></TD>
                    <TD ALIGN="right" WIDTH="20%"><ASP:BUTTON ID="btnSignOut"
                     RUNAT="server" FONT-BOLD="True" FONT-SIZE="X-Small"
                     TEXT="Sign Out" FORECOLOR="Navy" BORDERSTYLE="None"
                     BACKCOLOR="White"></ASP:BUTTON></TD>
                </TR>
            </TABLE>
            <TABLE CELLSPACING="0" CELLPADDING="4" WIDTH="100%" BGCOLOR="navy"
             BORDER="0">
                <TR>
                    <TD ALIGN="middle" WIDTH="33%"><A STYLE="FONT-WEIGHT: bold;
                     COLOR: white" HREF="BillPaySummary.aspx">Pay Bills</A></TD>
                    <TD ALIGN="middle" WIDTH="33%"><A STYLE="FONT-WEIGHT: bold;
                     COLOR: white" HREF="Atm.aspx">Deposit/Withdraw</A></TD>
                    <TD ALIGN="middle" WIDTH="33%"><A STYLE="FONT-WEIGHT: bold;
                     COLOR: white" HREF="Statement.aspx">My Statement</A></TD>
                </TR>
            </TABLE>
            <HR>
            <TABLE WIDTH="50%" BORDER="0" CELLPADDING="0" CELLSPACING="0"
             ALIGN="center">
                <TR>
                    <TD WIDTH="100%" COLSPAN="2" ALIGN="middle" BGCOLOR="navy"
                     STYLE="COLOR: white">Profile Information</TD>
                </TR>
                <TR>
                    <TD WIDTH="50%">Customer Name</TD>
                    <TD WIDTH="50%"><ASP:TEXTBOX ID="txtCustomerName"
                     RUNAT="server" WIDTH="100%" /><ASP:REQUIREDFIELDVALIDATOR
                     ID="rfvCustomerName" RUNAT="server" DISPLAY="Dynamic"
                     WIDTH="100%" ERRORMESSAGE="'Customer Name' is required."
                     CONTROLTOVALIDATE="txtCustomerName" /></TD>
                </TR>
                <TR>
                    <TD WIDTH="50%">Social Security Number</TD>
                    <TD WIDTH="50%"><ASP:TEXTBOX ID="txtSSN" RUNAT="server"
                     WIDTH="100%" /></TD>
                </TR>
                <TR>
                    <TD WIDTH="50%">Address</TD>
```

```
        <TD WIDTH="50%"><ASP:TEXTBOX ID="txtAddress" RUNAT="server"
        WIDTH="100%" /></TD>
    </TR>
    <TR>
        <TD WIDTH="50%">City</TD>
        <TD WIDTH="50%"><ASP:TEXTBOX ID="txtCity" RUNAT="server"
        WIDTH="100%" /></TD>
    </TR>
    <TR>
        <TD WIDTH="50%">State</TD>
        <TD WIDTH="50%"><ASP:TEXTBOX ID="txtState" RUNAT="server"
        WIDTH="100%" /></TD>
    </TR>
    <TR>
        <TD WIDTH="50%">ZIP</TD>
        <TD WIDTH="50%"><ASP:TEXTBOX ID="txtZIP" RUNAT="server"
        WIDTH="100%" /></TD>
    </TR>
    <TR>
        <TD WIDTH="50%">Phone</TD>
        <TD WIDTH="50%"><ASP:TEXTBOX ID="txtPhone" RUNAT="server"
        WIDTH="100%" /><ASP:REQUIREDFIELDVALIDATOR ID="rfvPhone"
        RUNAT="server" DISPLAY="Dynamic" WIDTH="100%"
        ERRORMESSAGE="'Phone Number' is required."
        CONTROLTOVALIDATE="txtPhone" /></TD>
    </TR>
</TABLE>
<BR>
<TABLE WIDTH="50%" BORDER="0" CELLPADDING="0" CELLSPACING="0"
ALIGN="center">
    <TR>
        <TD WIDTH="100%" COLSPAN="2" ALIGN="middle" BGCOLOR="navy"
        STYLE="COLOR: white">Change Password</TD>
    </TR>
    <TR>
        <TD WIDTH="50%">Password</TD>
        <TD WIDTH="50%"><ASP:TEXTBOX ID="txtPassword" RUNAT="server"
        WIDTH="100%" TEXTMODE="Password" /></TD>
    </TR>
    <TR>
        <TD WIDTH="50%">Confirm Password</TD>
        <TD WIDTH="50%"><ASP:TEXTBOX ID="txtConfirm" RUNAT="server"
        WIDTH="100%" TEXTMODE="Password" /></TD>
    </TR>
    <TR>
        <TD COLSPAN="2" ALIGN="middle"><ASP:LABEL
        ID="lblPasswordError" RUNAT="server" FORECOLOR="Red"
        VISIBLE="False">'Password' and 'Confirm Password' do not
        match.</ASP:LABEL></TD>
    </TR>
</TABLE>
<BR>
<TABLE WIDTH="50%" BORDER="0" CELLPADDING="0" CELLSPACING="0"
ALIGN="center">
```

```
                <TR>
                    <TD WIDTH="50%" ALIGN="left"><ASP:BUTTON ID="btnCancel"
                    TEXT="Cancel  Changes" RUNAT="server" /></TD>
                    <TD WIDTH="50%" ALIGN="right"><ASP:BUTTON ID="btnSave"
                    TEXT="Save Changes" RUNAT="server" /></TD>
                </TR>
            </TABLE>
        </FORM>
    </BODY>
</HTML>
```

MyProfile.aspx.vb

The code behind the MyProfile form looks as follows:

```
Imports System.Data
Imports System.Data.SqlClient
Imports System.Web.Security
Imports IBankAdventure

Public Class MyProfile
    Inherits System.Web.UI.Page
    Protected WithEvents lblGreeting As System.Web.UI.WebControls.Label
    Protected WithEvents lblTitle As System.Web.UI.WebControls.Label
    Protected WithEvents btnSignOut As System.Web.UI.WebControls.Button
    Protected WithEvents txtCustomerName As _
                                    System.Web.UI.WebControls.TextBox
    Protected WithEvents rfvCustomerName As _
                        System.Web.UI.WebControls.RequiredFieldValidator
    Protected WithEvents txtSSN As System.Web.UI.WebControls.TextBox
    Protected WithEvents txtZIP As System.Web.UI.WebControls.TextBox
    Protected WithEvents txtPhone As System.Web.UI.WebControls.TextBox
    Protected WithEvents rfvPhone As _
                        System.Web.UI.WebControls.RequiredFieldValidator
    Protected WithEvents btnCancel As System.Web.UI.WebControls.Button
    Protected WithEvents btnSave As System.Web.UI.WebControls.Button
    Protected WithEvents txtAddress As System.Web.UI.WebControls.TextBox
    Protected WithEvents txtCity As System.Web.UI.WebControls.TextBox
    Protected WithEvents txtState As System.Web.UI.WebControls.TextBox
    Protected WithEvents txtPassword As System.Web.UI.WebControls.TextBox
    Protected WithEvents txtConfirm As System.Web.UI.WebControls.TextBox
    Protected WithEvents lblPasswordError As System.Web.UI.WebControls.Label
    Protected WithEvents SignOut As System.Web.UI.WebControls.Button

' Web Form Designer Generated Code here

    Private Sub Page_Load(ByVal sender As System.Object, ByVal e As _
                    System.EventArgs) Handles MyBase.Load
        If Not Page.IsPostBack Then
            LoadCustomerProfile()
        End If
    End Sub
End Sub
```

```
    Private Sub LoadCustomerProfile()

        '' Get customer information
        Dim myBank As New IBankAdventure.Bank()
        Dim myReader As SqlDataReader = _
         myBank.GetCustomerInfo(Convert.ToInt32(Context.User.Identity.Name))

        '' Move reader to first (and only) record
        myReader.Read()

        '' Personalize title
        Me.lblTitle.Text = "IBank - Cutomer Profile - " & _
                                              myReader.Item("CustomerName")

        '' Fill in data on form
        Me.txtCustomerName.Text = myReader.Item("CustomerName")
        Me.txtAddress.Text = myReader.Item("Address")
        Me.txtCity.Text = myReader.Item("City")
        Me.txtState.Text = myReader.Item("State")
        Me.txtZIP.Text = myReader.Item("Zip")
        Me.txtPhone.Text = myReader.Item("Phone")

        'Format error text
        Me.lblPasswordError.Visible = False

        '' Close the reader
        myReader.Close()

    End Sub

    Private Sub btnSignOut_Click(ByVal sender As System.Object, ByVal e As _
                            System.EventArgs) Handles btnSignOut.Click
        '' Force Signout and send user back to login page
        FormsAuthentication.SignOut()
        Session.Abandon()
        Response.Redirect("login.aspx")
    End Sub

    Private Sub btnSave_Click(ByVal sender As System.Object, ByVal e As _
                        System.EventArgs) Handles btnSave.Click

        'If the password is changed, verify the confirmation matches
        If Me.txtPassword.Text.Length > 0 Or Me.txtConfirm.Text.Length > 0 _
Then
            If Not String.Equals(Me.txtPassword.Text, Me.txtConfirm.Text) _
Then
                Me.lblPasswordError.Visible = True
                Me.txtPassword.Text = ""
                Me.txtConfirm.Text = ""
                Exit Sub
            End If
        End If
```

```
                'save the profile information
                Dim sCustomerName As String = Me.txtCustomerName.Text
                Dim sSSN As String = Me.txtSSN.Text
                Dim sAddress As String = Me.txtAddress.Text
                Dim sCity As String = Me.txtCity.Text
                Dim sState As String = Me.txtState.Text
                Dim sZip As String = Me.txtZIP.Text
                Dim sPhone As String = Me.txtPhone.Text
                Dim sPassword As String = Me.txtPassword.Text

                'Save main profile information
                Dim myBank As New IBankAdventure.Bank()
                myBank.UpdateCustomerInfo(Convert.ToInt32(Context.User.Identity.Name), _
                        sCustomerName, sSSN, sAddress, sCity, sState, sZip, sPhone)

                'Save password information if appropriate
                If Me.txtPassword.Text.Length > 0 Then
                    Dim mySecurity As New IBankAdventure.Security()

        mySecurity.UpdateCustomerPwd(Convert.ToInt32(Context.User.Identity.Name), _
                                sPassword)
                End If

            End Sub
        End Class
```

Statement.aspx

This page allows the user to see the current balance of a specific account and get a listing of all transactions. Again, we have selected a `DataGrid` to display the information. This `DataGrid` differs from the one we created earlier, in that we have enabled paging.

By this we mean that the `DataGrid` will show only a certain number of records per page; in this case 10. If more than 10 records exist, a series of page numbers will be shown at the bottom of the grid and user can select which page to view. The code to do this is detailed below the screenshot.

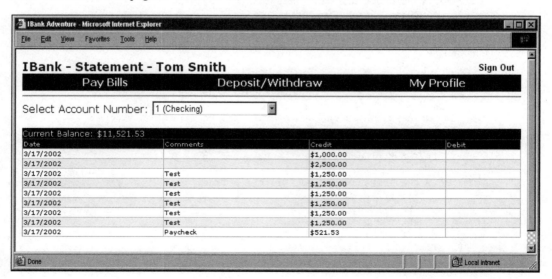

```
<%@ Page Language="vb" AutoEventWireup="false"
 Codebehind="Statement.aspx.vb" Inherits="IBank.Statement"%>
<!DOCTYPE HTML PUBLIC "-//W3C//DTD HTML 4.0 Transitional//EN">
<HTML>
    <HEAD>
        <TITLE>Statement</TITLE>
        <META CONTENT="Microsoft Visual Studio.NET 7.0" NAME="GENERATOR">
        <META CONTENT="Visual Basic 7.0" NAME="CODE_LANGUAGE">
        <META CONTENT="JavaScript" NAME="vs_defaultClientScript">
        <META CONTENT="http://schemas.microsoft.com/intellisense/ie5"
         NAME="vs_targetSchema">
        <LINK HREF="http://localhost/IBank/Styles.css" TYPE="text/css"
         REL="stylesheet">
    </HEAD>
    <BODY>
        <FORM ID="frmStatement" METHOD="post" RUNAT="server">
            <TABLE CELLSPACING="0" CELLPADDING="0" WIDTH="100%" BORDER="0">
                <TR>
                    <TD ALIGN="left" WIDTH="80%"><ASP:LABEL ID="lblTitle"
                     RUNAT="server" FORECOLOR="Navy" TEXT="" FONT-SIZE="Medium"
                     FONT-BOLD="True"></ASP:LABEL></TD>
                    <TD ALIGN="right" WIDTH="20%"><ASP:BUTTON ID="btnSignOut"
                     RUNAT="server" FORECOLOR="Navy" TEXT="Sign Out"
                     FONT-SIZE="X-Small" FONT-BOLD="True" BACKCOLOR="White"
                     BORDERSTYLE="None"></ASP:BUTTON></TD>
                </TR>
            </TABLE>
            <TABLE CELLSPACING="0" CELLPADDING="4" WIDTH="100%" BGCOLOR="navy"
             BORDER="0">
                <TR>
                    <TD ALIGN="middle" WIDTH="33%"><A STYLE="FONT-WEIGHT: bold;
                     COLOR: white" HREF="BillPaySummary.aspx">Pay Bills</A></TD>
                    <TD ALIGN="middle" WIDTH="33%"><A STYLE="FONT-WEIGHT: bold;
                     COLOR: white" HREF="Atm.aspx">Deposit/Withdraw</A></TD>
                    <TD ALIGN="middle" WIDTH="33%"><A STYLE="FONT-WEIGHT: bold;
                     COLOR: white" HREF="MyProfile.aspx">My Profile</A></TD>
                </TR>
            </TABLE>
            <HR>
            <ASP:LABEL ID="LABEL1" RUNAT="server" FONT-SIZE="Small"
            TEXT="Select Account Number:">Select Account Number:
            </ASP:LABEL>
            <ASP:DROPDOWNLIST ID="ddlAccounts" RUNAT="server"
             AUTOPOSTBACK="True" WIDTH="50%"></ASP:DROPDOWNLIST>
            <P></P>
            <ASP:LABEL ID="lblBalance" RUNAT="server" FONT-SIZE="x-small"
            TEXT="Checking Account" FORECOLOR="white" BACKCOLOR="navy"
            WIDTH="100%">Current Balance:</ASP:LABEL>
```

When creating the DataGrid, remember to set the AllowPaging property to True:

```
<ASP:DATAGRID ID="dgAccount" RUNAT="server" FONT-SIZE="XX-Small"
 BORDERSTYLE="None" WIDTH="100%" AUTOGENERATECOLUMNS="False"
 ALLOWPAGING="True">
```

```
                    <ALTERNATINGITEMSTYLE
                     BACKCOLOR="LightGoldenrodYellow"></ALTERNATINGITEMSTYLE>
                    <HEADERSTYLE FORECOLOR="White" BACKCOLOR="Navy"></HEADERSTYLE>
                    <COLUMNS>
                        <ASP:BOUNDCOLUMN DATAFIELD="TransactionDate"
                         HEADERTEXT="Date"
                         DATAFORMATSTRING="{0:d}"></ASP:BOUNDCOLUMN>
                        <ASP:BOUNDCOLUMN DATAFIELD="Comment"
                         HEADERTEXT="Comments"></ASP:BOUNDCOLUMN>
```

We will use format strings (DATAFORMATSTRING) when defining the next two columns to show their values in a currency format automatically:

```
                        <ASP:BOUNDCOLUMN DATAFIELD="credit" HEADERTEXT="Credit"
                         DATAFORMATSTRING="{0,12:C}"></ASP:BOUNDCOLUMN>
                        <ASP:BOUNDCOLUMN DATAFIELD="debit" HEADERTEXT="Debit"
                         DATAFORMATSTRING="{0,12:C}"></ASP:BOUNDCOLUMN>
                    </COLUMNS>
```

The PAGERSTYLE property determines the method used to navigate between pages. The first (default) choice is some kind of 'Next/Previous' navigation and the second is by using a listing of page numbers. We have elected to use the second method in our page:

```
                    <PAGERSTYLE MODE="NumericPages"></PAGERSTYLE>
                </ASP:DATAGRID>
                <P>
            </FORM>
             </P>
        </BODY>
    </HTML>
```

Statement.aspx.vb

The code behind the Statement form is as follows:

```
Imports System.Web.Security
Imports System.Data
Imports System.Data.SqlClient
Imports IBankAdventure

Public Class Statement
    Inherits System.Web.UI.Page

    Protected WithEvents lblTitle As System.Web.UI.WebControls.Label
    Protected WithEvents LABEL1 As System.Web.UI.WebControls.Label
    Protected WithEvents ddlAccounts As _
                                    System.Web.UI.WebControls.DropDownList
    Protected WithEvents lblBalance As System.Web.UI.WebControls.Label
    Protected WithEvents dgAccount As System.Web.UI.WebControls.DataGrid
    Protected WithEvents btnSignOut As System.Web.UI.WebControls.Button


' Web Form Designer Generated Code is here
```

```
      Private Sub Page_Load(ByVal sender As System.Object, ByVal e As _
                      System.EventArgs) Handles MyBase.Load

         If Not Me.IsPostBack Then
             LoadHeader()
             LoadAccounts()
             LoadStatements()
         End If

   End Sub


   Private Sub LoadHeader()

         '' Get customer information
         Dim myBank As New IBankAdventure.Bank()
         Dim myCustReader As SqlDataReader = _
           myBank.GetCustomerInfo(Convert.ToInt32(Context.User.Identity.Name))

         '' Move reader to first (and only) record and personalize title
         myCustReader.Read()
         Me.lblTitle.Text = "IBank - Statement - " & _
                                        myCustReader.Item("CustomerName")
         myCustReader.Close()

   End Sub
```

This following method is used to populate the `DataGrid`. Notice that we are storing the `DataSet` in a session variable because we will end up using it later, as the user navigates through the pages:

```
   Private Sub LoadStatements()

        Dim myBank As New IBankAdventure.Bank()

        Me.lblBalance.Text = "Current Balance: " & _
   FormatCurrency(myBank.AccountBalance(Me.ddlAccounts.SelectedItem.Value), _
              2, TriState.UseDefault, TriState.True, TriState.True)

        Dim myDataSet As DataSet = _
    myBank.GetTransactions(Convert.ToInt32(Me.ddlAccounts.SelectedItem.Value))

        Me.dgAccount.AllowPaging = (myDataSet.Tables(0).Rows.Count > 10)
        Me.dgAccount.DataSource = myDataSet
        Me.dgAccount.DataBind()

        Session("statement_ds") = myDataSet

   End Sub

   Private Sub LoadAccounts()

        Dim myReader As SqlDataReader = New _
                  IBankAdventure.Bank().GetAccounts _
```

```
                        (Convert.ToInt32(COntext.User.Identity.Name))
        While myReader.Read()

            Dim li As New ListItem(myReader.Item("AccountNumber"), _
                            myReader.Item("AccountNumber"))
            Select Case myReader("AccountType")
                Case "C" : li.Text = li.Text & " (Checking)"
                Case "S" : li.Text = li.Text & " (Savings)"
            End Select
            Me.ddlAccounts.Items.Add(li)

        End While
        Me.ddlAccounts.SelectedIndex = 0

    End Sub
```

The next method is called when the user elects to navigate the grid pages. First we set the page index to the one desired by the user, then reset the data source of the DataGrid to that of the DataSet that we saved earlier, and finally we perform the DataBind which shows the information in the DataGrid:

```
    Private Sub dgAccount_PageIndexChanged(ByVal source As Object, ByVal e _
    As System.Web.UI.WebControls.DataGridPageChangedEventArgs) Handles _
    dgAccount.PageIndexChanged

        Me.dgAccount.CurrentPageIndex = e.NewPageIndex
        Me.dgAccount.DataSource = Session("statement_ds")
        Me.dgAccount.DataBind()

    End Sub

    Private Sub ddlAccounts_SelectedIndexChanged(ByVal sender As _
    System.Object, ByVal e As System.EventArgs) Handles _
    ddlAccounts.SelectedIndexChanged

        LoadStatements()

    End Sub

    Private Sub btnSignOut_Click(ByVal sender As System.Object, ByVal e As _
                        System.EventArgs) Handles btnSignOut.Click
        '' Force Signout and send user back to login page
        FormsAuthentication.SignOut()
        Session.Abandon()
        Response.Redirect("login.aspx")
    End Sub
End Class
```

Where To Go From Here

We have just used VB.NET and SQL Server to build a distributed application. Though a fair representation of the technology is shown, there are areas in which improvements could be made:

❑ **Security** – One of the first things that should be done is to secure the web site using **Secure Sockets Layer** (**SSL**) technology. We are, in theory, manipulating personal financial information through the Web, and we should do so as securely as possible.

❑ **Provide Employee Functions** – One noticeable element missing from our application is the ability to add new customers and accounts. Bank employees, rather than customers, would ordinarily carry out these activities. If our site were to be a production site, we would obviously want to have this functionality available. We might even implement it on a separate site, perhaps called `IBankAdministration`, accessible only to internal resources.

Summary

In this case study we have constructed a 3-tier, web-based application using the concepts and ideas presented earlier in this book. Having worked through it, you should be able to:

❑ Describe a simple web application architecture

❑ Understand the different ways in which database security can be achieved

❑ Build simple COM+ components using VB.NET

❑ Understand the different ways in which a web site may be secured

❑ Build a web application.

ADO.NET Object Model

The .NET Class Library is massive, and the classes listed in this appendix are focused on data-related tasks. We will not be including all of the members for base classes. We will provide the hierarchy of the class and any overridden members within each class' model.

Command Classes

SqlCommand Hierarchy:	OleDbCommand Hierarchy:
Object	Object
MarshalByRefObject	MarshalByRefObject
Component	Component
SqlCommand	*OleDbCommand*

These classes represent a SQL statement or stored procedure to execute on or against a data source. There is one for Microsoft SQL Server, the SqlCommand class, and one for all other OleDb Providers, the OleDbCommand class.

Command Properties

Name	Type	Description
CommandText	string	Read-write string that will be a SQL statement or stored procedure to execute against the data source.
CommandTimeout	int	Gets or sets the timeout period for which an execution attempt of the current command will wait before quitting and returning an error. Default value: 30 (Seconds).
CommandType	CommandType Enum	Read-write property allowing us to specify the type of command that is passed to the data source in the CommandText property. Default value: Text.
Connection	Connection	Read-write property allowing you to specify which connection object this command will use.
Parameters	Collection	Returns the ParameterCollection object. Default value: empty collection.
Transaction	Transaction	Read-write property that allows the assignment or retrieval of the transaction that this command instance will execute within. Default value: NULL reference.
UpdatedRowSource	UpdateRowSource Enum	Read-write property to determine how results will be applied to the DataRow object when the DbDataAdapter.Update method is invoked.

Command Methods

Name	Returns	Description
Cancel		Cancels the executing command.
CreateParameter	Parameter	Returns a new instance of a SqlParameter or OleDbParameter object.
ExecuteNonQuery	int	Executes the command and returns the number of affected rows only.
ExecuteReader	DataReader	Executes the command and returns a new instance of the DataReader object.

Name	Returns	Description
ExecuteScalar	Object	Executes the command, and returns the value in the first column of the first row in the resultset.
ExecuteXmlReader (SqlCommand Only)	XmlReader	Executes the command and returns a new instance of the XmlReader object.
Prepare		Creates a compiled version of the command to issue to the data source.
ResetCommandTimeout		Sets the CommandTimeout property back to its default value.

Connection Classes

SqlConnection Hierarchy:	OleDbConnection Hierarchy:
Object	Object
MarshalByRefObject	MarshalByRefObject
Component	Component
SqlConnection	*OleDbConnection*

There are two connection classes – the SqlConnection class uses to connect to a Microsoft SQL Server, and the OleDbConnection class which is used to connect to a data source with an OleDb provider. Once opened these classes represent an open connection or session to the data source.

Connection Properties

Name	Type	Description
ConnectionString	String	Read-write property that contains the data source-specific information required to connect to the source.
ConnectionTimeout	Int	Read-write property that sets the amount of time, in seconds, to wait for a connection to open. The default is 15; a value of 0 will cause the connection to wait indefinitely.
Database	String	Returns the name of the database that you are connected to.

Table continued on following page

Name	Type	Description
DataSource	String	Returns the name of the server that you are connected to.
PacketSize (SqlConnection only)	Int	Returns the size, in bytes, of the network packets used to connect to a SQL Server. The default value is 8192.
Provider (OleDbConnection only)	String	Returns the name of the provider as defined in the ConnectionString property.
ServerVersion	String	Returns the version information for the server that you are connected to.
State	ConnectionState Enum	Returns the current status of the connection (Open or Closed).
WorkstationId (SqlConnection only)	String	Returns the host name of the workstation that is making the connection.

Connection Methods

Name	Returns	Description
BeginTransaction	Transaction object	Begins a database transaction.
ChangeDatabase		Changes the current database for the open connection to the one specified.
Close		Closes the connection to the database.
CreateCommand	Command object	Creates and returns a Command object.
Open		Opens a connection to the database with the information specified in the connection string.

Connection Events

Name	Description
InfoMessage	Occurs following the addition of an information message.
StateChange	Occurs following a change in connection state.

DataAdapter Classes

SqlDbDataAdapter Hierarchy:	OleDbDataAdapter Hierarchy:
Object	Object
MarshalByRefObject	MarshalByRefObject
Component	Component
DataAdapter	DataAdapter
DbDataAdapter	DbDataAdapter
SqlDbDataAdapter	*OleDbDataAdapter*

Used to populate a DataSet, these classes represent a connection and a set of data commands.

DataAdapter Properties

Name	Type	Description
AcceptChangesDuring Fill	bool	Read-write property that will determine whether or not the DataRow.AcceptChanges method is called after it has been added to the DataTable.
DeleteCommand	Command	Read-write property that will return or assign a SQL statement to delete records from a DataSet.
InsertCommand	Command	Read-write property that will return or assign a SQL statement to insert new records into the data source.
MissingMappingAction	MissingMappingAction Enumeration	Determines the action to take when incoming data does not have a matching table or column. Default is passthrough.
MissingSchemaAction	MissingSchemaAction Enum	Determines the action to take when the existing DataSet schema does not match incoming data. Default is Add.

Table continued on following page

Name	Type	Description
TableMappings	Collection	Gets a collection that provides the master mapping between a source table and a `DataTable`. Default is an empty collection.
SelectCommand	Command	Read-write property that will return or assign a SQL statement to select records from a `DataSet`.
UpdateCommand	Command	Read-write property that will return or assign a SQL statement to update records from a `DataSet`.

DataAdapter Methods

Name	Returns	Description
CloneInternals	DataAdapter	Makes a copy of the current `DataAdapter`.
CreateTableMappings	DataTableMapping Collection	Creates a new `DataTableMappingCollection`.
Fill	int	Updates the rows in the `DataSet` to match those within the data source.
FillSchema	DataTable Array	Adds a `DataTable` with a schema generated from the data source to an existing `DataSet`.
GetFillParameters	IDataParameters Array	Retrieves the parameters as set when executing a SQL SELECT statement.
ShouldSerializeTable Mappings	bool	Returns whether or not at least one `DataTableMapping` object exists and whether they should be persisted.

Name	Returns	Description
Update	int	Executes the respective Insert, Update, or Delete statements on the data source for each inserted, updated, or deleted row in the DataSet. Returns the number of rows successfully updated.

DataAdapter Events

Name	Description
RowUpdated	Occurs *after* an UPDATE command is executed on a data source.
RowUpdating	Occurs *prior* to an UPDATE command is executed on a data source.
OnRowUpdated	Raises the RowUpdated event.
OnRowUpdating	Raises the RowUpdating event.

DataColumn Class

DataColumn Hierarchy:
Object
MarshalByValueComponent
DataColumn

The DataColumn class represents the schema of a column within a DataTable.

DataColumn Properties

Name	Type	Description
AllowDBNull	bool	Read-write property that determines whether the current column will allow NULL values.
AutoIncrement	bool	Read-write property that will determine whether or not newly inserted rows will be auto-numbered.

Table continued on following page

Name	Type	Description
AutoIncrementSeed	long	Read-write property, if the AutoIncrement property is set to True, this property will determine the starting value of the auto-numbering.
AutoIncrementStep	long	Read-write property, if the AutoIncrement property is set to True, this property will determine the increment between auto-generated numbers.
Caption	string	Read-write property that will assign or return the caption of the current column.
ColumnMapping	MappingType Enum	Read-write property that will assign or return the MappingType of the column.
ColumnName	string	Read-write property that determines the name of the column in the DataColumnCollection.
DataType	Type	Read-write property that determines the type of data stored in the column.
DefaultValue	Object	Read-write property that will set or return the default value for the current column when new rows are inserted.
Expression	string	Read-write property that sets or returns the expression used to filter rows, calculate the values in a column, or create an aggregate column.
ExtendedProperties	PropertyCollection	Returns the collection of custom information.
MaxLength	int	Read-write property used to set or read the maximum length of a text column.
Namespace	string	Assigns or returns the namespace of the current DataColumn.
Ordinal	int	Returns the location of the column in the DataColumnCollection collection.

Name	Type	Description
Prefix	string	Assigns or returns the XML prefix that aliases the namespace of the DataTable.
ReadOnly	bool	Read-write property that determines whether the column allows changes once a row has been added to the table.
Table	DataTable	Returns the DataTable to which the current column belongs.
Unique	bool	Read-write property that determines whether the current column's value must be unique when compared to other rows within the same table.

DataColumn Methods

Name	Returns	Description
OnPropertyChanging		Causes the OnPropertyChanging event to fire.
RaisePropertyChanging		Sends a notification that the supplied DataColumn property is about to change.
ToString (Overridden)	string	Returns the Expression of the column, if there is one.

DataColumnMapping Class

DataColumnMapping Hierarchy:
Object
MarshalByRefObject
DataColumnMapping

This class allows us to have columns whose names within a DataSet differ from the actual column names as defined within the data source. This class maps between the two names.

DataColumnMapping Properties

Name	Type	Description
DataSetColumn	string	Read-write property that assigns or returns the name of the column from the DataSet to map to.
SourceColumn	string	Read-write property that assigns or returns the column name from a data source to map from. (This value is case-sensitive, even if the data source is not.)

DataColumnMapping Methods

Name	Returns	Description
GetDataColumnBySchemaAction	DataColumn	Returns a DataColumn from the supplied DataTable.
ToString (Overridden)	String	Returns the current SourceColumn name.

DataReader Classes

SqlDataReader Hierarchy:	OleDbDataReader Hierarchy:
Object	Object
MarshalByRefObject	MarshalByRefObject
SqlDataReader	*OleDbDataReader*

The DataReader object allows us to read a forward-only stream of data from a data source. It is similar to an ADO Recordset with a ForwardOnly cursor.

DataReader Properties

Name	Returns	Description
Depth	int	Depth of nesting for the current row (the SQL Server .NET provider will always return 0).
FieldCount	int	Returns the number of columns (fields) in the current row.
IsClosed	bool	Returns whether or not the DataReader is closed.

Name	Returns	Description
Item	Object	Returns the value of a supplied column. Also acts as the indexer of the DataReader class.
RecordsAffected	int	Returns the number of rows that were updated, inserted, or deleted as a result of the SQL statement.

DataReader Methods

Name	Returns	Description
Close		Closes the DataReader object.
GetBoolean	Bool	Returns the value of the supplied column as a Boolean.
GetByte	byte	Returns the value of the supplied column as a byte.
GetBytes	long	Returns the number of bytes read.
GetChar	char	Returns the value of the supplied column as a single character.
GetChars	long	Returns the number of characters available in the field.
GetDataTypeName	string	Returns the name of the data type as defined on the data source.
GetDateTime	DateTime	Returns the value of the supplied column as a DateTime object.
GetDecimal	Decimal	Returns the value of the supplied column as a decimal object.
GetDouble	double	Returns the value of the supplied column as a double-precision floating point number.
GetFieldType	Type	Returns the Type that matches the data type of the field.
GetFloat	float	Returns the value of the supplied column as a single-precision floating point number.
GetGuid	guid	Returns the value of the supplied column as a globally-unique identifier (GUID).
GetInt16	Short	Returns the value of the supplied column as a 16-bit signed integer.

Table continued on following page

Name	Returns	Description
GetInt32	int	Returns the value of the supplied column as a 32-bit signed integer.
GetInt64	long	Returns the value of the supplied column as a 32-bit signed integer.
GetName	string	Returns the name of the column supplied.
GetOrdinal	int	Returns the ordinal (position) of the column supplied.
GetSchemaTable	DataTable	Returns a DataTable object that describes the column meta data of the DataReader.
GetSqlBinary (SqlDataReader only)	SqlBinary	Returns the value of the supplied column as a SqlBinary.
GetSqlBoolean (SqlDataReader only)	SqlBoolean	Returns the value of the supplied column as a SqlBoolean.
GetSqlByte (SqlDataReader only)	SqlByte	Returns the value of the supplied column as a SqlByte.
GetSqlDateTime (SqlDataReader only)	SqlDateTime	Returns the value of the supplied column as a SqlDateTime.
GetSqlDouble (SqlDataReader only)	SqlDouble	Returns the value of the supplied column as a SqlDouble.
GetSqlGuid (SqlDataReader only)	SqlGuid	Returns the value of the supplied column as a SqlGuid.
GetSqlInt16 (SqlDataReader only)	SqlInt16	Returns the value of the supplied column as a SqlInt16.
GetSqlInt32 (SqlDataReader only)	SqlInt32	Returns the value of the supplied column as a SqlInt32.
GetSqlInt64 (SqlDataReader only)	SqlInt64	Returns the value of the supplied column as a SqlInt64.
GetSqlMoney (SqlDataReader only)	SqlMoney	Returns the value of the supplied column as a SqlMoney.
GetSqlSingle (SqlDataReader only)	SqlSingle	Returns the value of the supplied column as a SqlSingle.

Name	Returns	Description
GetSqlString (SqlDataReader only)	SqlString	Returns the value of the supplied column as a SqlString.
GetSqlValue (SqlDataReader only)	Object	Returns an Object that represents SQL Server's Variant data type.
GetSqlValues (SqlDataReader only)	int	Returns the attribute columns from the current row in the DataReader.
GetString	string	Returns the value of the supplied column as a String.
GetTimeSpan (OleDbDataReader only)	TimeSpan	Returns the value of the supplied column as an interval of time using the TimeSpan object.
GetValue	Object	Returns the value of the supplied column in its original format.
GetValues	int	Passes out all of the attribute columns within the current row as an array parameter.
IsDBNull	bool	Returns True if the supplied column is NULL, False otherwise.
NextResult	bool	Moves the DataReader to the next result when reading the results of a SQL batch.
Read	bool	Moves the DataReader to the next record.

DataRelation Class

DataRelation Hierarchy:
Object
DataRelation

The DataRelation class is used to maintain a parent/child relationship between two DataTable objects.

DataRelation Properties

Name	Type	Description
ChildColumns	DataColumn Array	Returns the child DataColumn of this relation.
ChildKeyConstraint	ForeignKeyConstraint	Returns the ForeignKeyConstraint for this relation.
ChildTable	DataTable	Returns the child table of this relation.
DataSet	DataSet	Returns the DataSet to which the current DataRelation belongs.
ExtendedProperties	PropertyCollection	Returns the collection that stores the extended or custom properties.
Nested	bool	Read-write property that will determine whether the current DataRelation objects are nested.
ParentColumns	DataColumn Array	Returns an array of DataColumn objects that are the parent columns of the current DataRelation.
ParentKeyConstraint	UniqueConstraint	Returns the UniqueConstraint object that guarantees the uniqueness of the parent column.
ParentTable	DataTable	Returns the parent DataTable for the current DataRelation instance.
RelationName	string	Read-write property that references the name used to get a DataRelation from the DataRelationCollection.

DataRelation Methods

Name	Returns	Description
CheckStateForProperty		Guarantees that the current DataRelation is a valid object.
ToString (Overridden)	String	Returns the RelationName as a String.

DataRow Class

DataRow Hierarchy:
Object
DataRow

This class is used to represent a row within a DataTable.

DataRow Properties

Name	Type	Description
HasErrors	bool	Returns a value indicating whether or not there are errors in the columns collection.
Item	Object	Gets or sets data stored in a supplied column. In C# Indexer for the DataRow Class.
ItemArray	Object Array	Gets or sets all of the values for this row through an array.
RowError	string	Gets or sets the custom error description for a row.
RowState	DataRowState	Gets the current state of the row in regard to its relationship to the DataRowCollection.
Table	DataTable	Gets the DataTable for which this row has a schema.

DataRow Methods

Name	Return Type	Description
AcceptChanges		Commits all the changes made to this DataRow since the last time this method was invoked.
BeginEdit		Begins an edit operation on a DataRow object.
CancelEdit		Cancels the current edit on the row.
ClearErrors		Clears the errors for the row, including the RowError and errors set with SetColumnError.
Delete		Deletes the row.

Table continued on following page

Name	Return Type	Description
EndEdit		Ends the edit currently in action on the row.
GetChildRows	DataRow Array	Gets the child rows of a DataRow.
GetColumnError	string	Gets the error description for a column.
GetColumnsInError	DataColumn Array	Gets an array of columns that have an error.
GetParentRow	DataRow	Gets the parent row of a DataRow.
GetParentRows	DataRow Array	Gets the parent rows of a DataRow.
HasVersion	bool	Gets a value indicating whether a specified version exists.
IsNull	bool	Gets a value indicating whether the supplied column contains a NULL value.
RejectChanges		Rejects all changes made to the row since AcceptChanges was last invoked.
SetColumnError		Sets the error description for a column.
SetNull		Sets the value of the supplied DataColumn to a NULL value.
SetParentRow		Sets the parent row of a DataRow.
SetUnspecified		Sets the value of a DataColumn with the supplied name to unspecified.

DataRow Events

Name	Description
ColumnChanged	Fires after a value has been changed in a specified DataColumn within a DataRow.
ColumnChanging	Fires when a value is in the process of being changed for a supplied DataColumn within a DataRow.
RowChanged	Fires following a successful change to a DataRow.
RowChanging	Fires while a DataRow is in the process of changing.
RowDeleted	Fires following a successful deletion of a row.
RowDeleting	When deleting a row this event will fire prior to the actual removal of the row.

DataSet Class

DataSet Hierarchy:
Object
MarshalByValueComponent
DataSet

This class represents the cache of data retrieved from the data source and kept in-memory. This is one of the major classes with the ADO.NET architecture and is made up of `DataTable` and `DataRelation` objects.

DataSet Properties

Name	Type	Description
CaseSensitive	bool	Read-write property determining whether or not string comparisons are case-sensitive within the `DataSet`. The default is `False`.
DataSetName	string	Read-write property either assigning or returning the name of the current `DataSet`.
DefaultViewManager	DataViewManager	Retrieves a custom view of the data within the `DataSet` that allows filtering, searching, and navigation using a custom `DataViewManager`.
EnforceConstraints	bool	Read-write property that determines whether or not constraints will be enforced when attempting update operations.
ExtendedProperties	PropertyCollection	Returns the collection of custom information
HasErrors	bool	Retrieves whether or not there are errors in any of the rows within any of the tables in this `DataSet`.

Table continued on following page

Name	Type	Description
Locale	string	Read-write property that returns or assigns the locale information used for string comparisons within the table. Defaults to a NULL reference.
Namespace	string	Read-write property that returns or assigns the namespace of the DataSet.
Prefix	string	Read-write property that will return or assign an XML prefix aliasing the namespace of the DataSet. Used in conjunction with the ReadXml method.
Relations	DataRelationCollection	Returns the DataRelationCollection that defines the relationships from parent tables to child tables. If no DataRelation objects exist, it defaults to NULL.
Site	ISite	Assigns or returns a System.ComponentModel.ISite for the current DataSet object.
Tables	DataTableCollection	Returns the DataTablecollection object consisting of the tables within the DataSet.

DataSet Methods

Name	Returns	Description
AcceptChanges		Commits all changes made to the DataSet since it was loaded or since the last time this method was invoked.
BeginInit		Starts the initialization of the current DataSet instance that is used on a form or used by some other component.
Clear		Removes all rows in all tables within the DataSet. (Erases the data, keeps the schema.)

Name	Returns	Description
Clone	DataSet	Clones the structure of the current DataSet.
Copy	DataSet	Copies the structure as well as the data of the current DataSet.
EndInit		Completes the initialization of the current DataSet instance that is used on a form or used by some other component.
GetChanges	DataSet	Returns a new DataSet that is a copy of the current DataSet with all changes that were made to it since it was loaded or the AcceptChanges method was invoked.
GetSchemaSerializeable	XmlTextReader	Retrieves an XmlTextReader object in order to implement IXmlSerializeable.
GetSerializationData	SerializationInfo & StreamingContext	Retrieves SerializationInfo and StreamingContext information in order to implement IXmlSerializeable.
GetXml	string	Retrieves the data stored in the DataSet and renders it as XML.
GetXmlSchema	string	Retrieves the XSD schema for the data in the current DataSet when the data is rendered as XML.
HasChanges	bool	Retrieves a value determining whether or not there have been changes (INSERT, UPDATE, or DELETE) to the DataSet.
HasSchemaChanged	bool	Returns whether or not the schema has been altered.
InferXmlSchema		Enacts schema on the DataSet as predefined within a file or TextReader object.
Merge		Merges the current DataSet with a supplied DataSet.
OnPropertyChanging		Causes the OnPropertyChanging event to fire.

Table continued on following page

Name	Returns	Description
OnRemoveRelation		Exists to be overridden in order to prohibit the removal of tables.
OnRemoveTable		Fires when a DataTable is removed from the current DataSet.
RaisePropertyChanging		Causes a notification to be sent that the supplied property is about to be changed.
ReadXml		Reads XML schema and data into the DataSet.
ReadXmlSchema		Reads an XML Schema into the current DataSet object from a specified source.
ReadXmlSerializeable	XmlTextReader	Reads the XML serialization information to facilitate the implementation of the IXmlSerializeable.
RejectChanges		Undoes changes that were made to the DataSet from the latter of being created or having the AcceptChanges method invoked.
Reset		Puts the DataSet back into the state which it was in upon being created.
ShouldSerializeRelations	bool	Returns whether the Relations property should persist.
ShouldSerializeTables	bool	Returns whether the Tables property should persist.
WriteXml		Sends the current DataSet object's XML schema and data to the specified destination (such as a File, String, or TextWriter).
WriteXmlSchema		Sends just the XML Schema of the current DataSet to the specified destination.

DataSet Events

Name	Description
MergeFailed	If the EnforceConstraints property is set to True, this event will occur if two rows are being merged from separate DataSet objects and have the same value for a primary key column.

DataTable Class

DataTable Hierarchy:
Object
MarshalByValueComponent
DataTable

The DataTable, which represents a typical database table, exists in memory and belongs to a DataSet.

DataTable Properties

Name	Type	Description
CaseSensitive	bool	Whether or not string comparisons will be case-sensitive within this table.
ChildRelations	DataRelationCollection	Gets the collection of child relations for the current DataTable.
Columns	DataColumnCollection	Gets the collection of columns that belong to the current DataTable.
Constraints	ConstraintCollection	Gets the collection of constraints maintained on this table.
DataSet	DataSet	Gets the DataSet that this DataTable belongs to.
DefaultView	DataView	Gets a customized view of the table, which could include a filtered view or a cursor position.

Table continued on following page

Name	Type	Description
DisplayExpression	string	Gets or sets the expression that will return a value used to display this table in a user interface.
ExtendedProperties	PropertyCollection	Gets the collection of customized information.
HasErrors	bool	Whether or not there are errors in any of the rows in any of the tables of the DataSet of which this table is a member.
Locale	CultureInfo	Gets or sets the locale information used to compare strings within the table.
MinimumCapacity	int	Gets or sets the starting size for this table.
Namespace	string	Gets or sets the namespace for the XML representation of the data stored in the DataTable.
ParentRelations	DataRelationCollection	Gets the collection of parent relations for this DataTable.
Prefix	string	Gets or set the namespace for the XML representation of the data stored in the current DataTable.
PrimaryKey	DataColumn Array	Gets or sets an array of columns that will function as primary keys for the DataTable.
Rows	DataRowCollection	Gets the collection of rows that belong to this table.
Site (Overridden)	Isite	Read-write property that returns or assigns a System.DCOmponentModel.ISite for the current DataTable.
TableName	string	Gets or sets the name of the DataTable.

DataTable Methods

Name	Return Type	Description
AcceptChanges		Commits all the changes made to this table since the last time this method was invoked.
BeginInit		
BeginLoadData		Turns off the notifications, index maintenance, and constraints while loading data.
Clear		Clears the DataTable of all data.
Clone	DataTable	Clones the structure of the DataTable.
Compute	Object	Computes the given expression on the current rows that pass the filter criteria.
Copy	DataTable	Copies both the structure as well as the data from this DataTable.
EndLoadData		Turns back on the notifications, index maintenance, and constraints after loading data.
GetChanges	DataTable	Gets a copy of the DataTable containing all changes made to it since it was last loaded, or since the last AcceptChanges method invocation.
GetErrors	DataRow Array	Gets an array of DataRow objects that contain errors.
GetRowType	Type	Returns the row type.
HasSchemaChanged	bool	Returns whether or not the amount of columns that exist in the current DataTable instance has changed.
ImportRow		Copies a DataRow, including original and current values, DataRowState values, and errors, into a DataTable.
LoadDataRow	DataRow	Finds and updates a specific row. If a matching row isn't found, a new row will be created with the given values.
NewRow	DataRow	Creates a new DataRow with the same schema as the table.
OnColumnChanged		Raises the ColumnChanged event.

Table continued on following page

Name	Return Type	Description
OnColumnChanging		Raises the ColumnChanging event.
OnPropertyChanging		Raises the PropertyChanging event.
OnRemoveColumn		Alerts the DataTable that a DataColumn is being removed from the current DataTable instance.
OnRowChanged		Raises the RowChanged event.
OnRowChanging		Raises the RowChanging event.
OnRowDeleted		Raises the RowDeleted event.
OnRowDeleting		Raises the RowDeleting event.
RejectChanges		Rolls back all changes that have been made to the table since it was loaded, or since the last AcceptChanges method was invoked.
Select	DataRow Array	Gets an array of DataRow objects.
ToString (Overridden)	string	Returns a string that is made up of the name of the table and if there is a DisplayExpression it will be concatenated after the name of the table in the string.

DataTableMapping Class

DataTableMapping Hierarchy:
Object
MarshalByRefObject
DataTableMapping

Used by the DataAdapter class when populating a DataSet, this class maintains the relationship between column names in a DataTable within a DataSet and the corresponding column names in the data source.

DataTableMapping Properties

Name	Type	Description
ColumnMappings	DataTableMappingCollection	Returns the DataColumnMappingCollection for the DataTable.
DataSetTable	string	Read-write property that will return or assign the table name from a DataSet.
SourceTable	string	Read-write property that will return or assign the source table name from a data source (case-sensitive).

DataTableMapping Methods

Name	Returns	Description
GetColumnMappingBySchemaAction	DataColumn	Returns a DataColumn from the supplied DataTable using the MissingMappingAction that was specified and the name of the DataColumn.
GetDataTableBySchemaAction	DataTable	Returns the current DataTable for the supplied DataSet using the supplied MissingSchemaAction value.
ToString (Overridden)	string	Returns the name of the current SourceTable as a string.

DataView Class

DataView Hierarchy:
Object
MarshalByValueComponent
DataView

The DataView class represents a customized view of the data to which it is bound. This view can then be sorted, filtered, edited, searched, and navigated. This class is similar to a view in a database.

DataView Properties

Name	Type	Description
AllowDelete	bool	Read-write property that determines whether deletes are allowed.
AllowEdit	bool	Read-write property that determines whether edits are allowed.
AllowNew	bool	Read-write property that determines whether new rows can be inserted using the AddNew method.
ApplyDefaultSort	bool	Read-write property that will determine whether to use the default sort.
Count	int	Returns the number of records in the DataView after both RowFilter and RowStateFilter have been applied.
DataViewManager	DataViewManager	Returns the DataViewManager associated with this view.
IsOpen	bool	Returns whether the data source is currently open and applying views of the data on the DataTable.
Item	DataRowView	This property acts as the indexer for the DataView class.
RowFilter	string	Read-write property that will act as the clause used to filter which rows are viewed through the DataView.
RowStateFilter	DataViewRowState	Read-write property that will assign or return the DataViewRowState filter used within the DataView.
Sort	string	Read-write property that will assign or return the sorted column(s) and sort order.
Table	DataTable	Read-write property that will assign or return the source DataTable.

DataView Methods

Name	Returns	Description
AddNew	DataRowView	Inserts a new row into the DataView.
BeginInit		Begins the initialization of a DataView that is used by another component.

Name	Returns	Description
Close		Closes the current DataView.
Delete		Deletes the row at the supplied index location.
EndInit		Ends the initialization started from the BeginInit method.
GetEnumerator	IEnumerator	Returns an enumerator for the current DataView.
IndexListChanged		Invoked following a successful change to the DataView.
OnListChanged		Causes the ListChanged event to fire.
Open		Opens the current DataView.

DataView Events

Name	Description
ListChanged	Fires when the list controlled by the DataView is altered.

DataViewManager Class

DataViewManager Hierarchy:
Object
MarshalByValueComponent
DataViewManager

This class maintains the default DataViewSetting collection for each DataTable that exists within a DataSet.

DataViewManager Properties

Name	Type	Description
DataSet	DataSet	Read-write property that will assign or return the DataSet to use with the current DataViewManager.

Table continued on following page

Name	Type	Description
DataViewSettings	DataViewSettingCollection	Returns the DataViewSettingCollection for each DataTable within the DataSet.

DataViewManager Methods

Name	Returns	Description
CreateDataView	DataView	Creates a DataView for the specified DataTable.
OnListChanged		Causes the ListChanged event to fire.
RelationCollectionChanged		Causes a CollectionChanged event to fire when a DataRelation object is inserted or deleted from the DataRelationCollection.
TableCollectionChanged		Causes the CollectionChanged event to fire when a DataTable is inserted or deleted from the DataTableCollection.

DataViewManager Events

Name	Description
ListChanged	Fires when a row is added to or removed from a DataView.

DataViewSetting Class

DataViewSetting Hierarchy:
Object
DataViewSetting

This class represents the default settings ApplyDefaultSort, DataViewManager, RowFilter, RowStateFilter, Sort, and Table for DataView objects that were created by the DataViewManager.

DataViewSetting Properties

Name	Type	Description
ApplyDefaultSort	bool	Read-write property that determines whether or not to use the default sort.
DataViewManager	DataViewManager	Returns the DataViewManager that contains the current DataViewSetting.
RowFilter	string	Read-write property that returns or assigns the filter to use within the DataView.
RowStateFilter	DataViewRowState	Read-write property that determines which types of rows are in the DataView.
Sort	string	Read-write property that determines the Sort to use for the DataView.
Table	DataTable	Returns the DataTable that the current DataViewSetting properties apply to.

OleDbError Class

OleDbError Hierarchy:
Object
OleDbError

When an OleDb data source returns an error or warning this is the object that collects the information.

OleDbError Properties

Name	Type	Description
Message	string	Returns a short description of the error.
NativeError	int	Returns the proprietary error message from the data source.
Source	string	Returns the name of the provider that generated the error.
SqlState	string	Returns the code following the ANSI standard for the database.

OleDbError Methods

Name	Return Type	Description
ToString (Overridden)	string	Returns the complete error message.

OleDbException Class

OleDbException Hierarchy:
Object
Exception
SystemException
ExternalException
OleDbException

When an OleDb data source returns an error or warning this is the exception that is thrown.

OleDbException Properties

Name	Type	Description
Errors	OleDbErrorCollection	Returns a collection of OleDbError objects.
Message (Overridden)	string	Returns the error message.
Source (Overridden)	string	Returns the name of the provider that generated the error.

OleDbException Methods

Name	Return Type	Description
ToString (Overridden)	string	Returns the fully qualified name of the current exception as a string.

Parameter Classes

SqlParameter Hierarchy:	OleDbParameter Hierarchy:
Object	Object
MarshalByRefObject	MarshalByRefObject
SqlParameter	*OleDbParameter*

The `Parameter` classes represent the parameters passed into, or out from a command object.

Parameter Properties

Name	Type	Description
DbType	DbType Enum	Read-write property that will return or assign the DbType of the parameter.
Direction	ParameterDirection Enum	Read-write property that will determine the type of parameter: Input, Output, Input/Output (Bi-Directional), or stored procedure return value.
IsNullable	bool	Read-write property that will return or assign whether or not this parameter accepts NULL values.
Offset	int	Read-write property that will return or assign the offset to the Value property.
OleDbType (OleDbParameter only)	OleDbType Enum	Returns or assigns the OleDbType of the current parameter.
ParameterName	string	Returns or assigns the name of the parameter.
Precision	byte	Returns or assigns the numeric precision (quantity of digits) used for the value property.
Scale	byte	Returns or assigns the numeric scale (quantity of decimal places) that the value will be representing.
Size	int	Returns or assigns the amount of bytes used to store the value within the column.

Table continued on following page

Name	Type	Description
SourceColumn	string	Returns or assigns the name of the column that was mapped to the DataSet.
SourceVersion	DataRowVersion Enum	Returns or assigns the DataRowVersion to use when loading a value.
SqlDbType (SqlParameter only)	SqlDbType Enum	Returns or assigns the SqlDbType of the parameter.
Value	Object	Returns or assigns the actual value of the parameter.

Parameter Methods

Name	Returns	Description
ToString (Overridden)	string	Returns the ParameterName as a string.

SqlError Class

SqlError Hierarchy:
Object
SqlError

When SQL Server returns an error or a warning, this class collects the information.

SqlError Properties

Name	Type	Description
Class	byte	Returns the severity level as defined from the SQL Server .NET Data Provider.
LineNumber	int	Returns the line number from the T-SQL command that caused the error.
Message	string	Returns the string describing the error.
Number	int	Returns the error number.

Table continued on following page

Name	Type	Description
Procedure	string	Returns the name of the stored procedure or remote procedure call (RPC).
Server	string	Returns the name of the SQL Server that generated the error.
Source	string	Returns the name of the provider that generated the error.
State	byte	Returns the number altering the error to provide additional information.

SqlError Methods

Name	Return Type	Description
ToString (Overridden)	String	Returns the complete error message.

SqlException Class

SqlException Hierarchy:
Object
Exception
SystemException
SqlException

The SqlException is the exception that is thrown when SQL Server raises a warning or error.

SqlException Properties

Name	Type	Description
Class	byte	Returns the severity level as defined from the SQL Server .NET Data Provider.
Errors	SqlErrorCollection	Returns a collection of SqlError objects.
LineNumber	int	Returns the line number from the T-SQL command that caused the error.
Message (Overridden)	string	Returns the description of the error.

Table continued on following page

Name	Type	Description
Number	int	Returns the error number.
Procedure	string	Returns the name of the stored procedure or remote procedure call (RPC).
Server	string	Returns the name of the SQL Server that generated the error.
Source (Overridden)	string	Returns the name of the provider that generated the error.
State	string	Returns the number altering the error to provide additional information.

SqlException Methods

Name	Return Type	Description
ToString (Overridden)	string	Returns the fully qualified name of the current exception.

Transaction Classes

SqlTransaction Hierarchy:	OleDbTransaction Hierarchy:
Object	Object
MarshalByRefObject	MarshalByRefObject
SqlTransaction	*OleDbTransaction*

The transaction class represents a SQL transaction in the data source.

Transaction Properties

Name	Type	Description
IsolationLevel	IsolationLevel Enum	Returns the selected IsolationLevel or assigns a value from the IsolationLevel enum.

Transaction Methods

Name	Returns	Description
Begin (OleDbTransaction only)		Starts a nested database transaction.
Commit		Commits the transaction
Rollback		Rolls back a transaction.
Save (SqlTransaction only)		Constructs a savepoint in the transaction. Note that OleDb provides nested transactions instead of savepoints.

Index

A Guide to the Index

The index covers the numbered Chapters and the Appendix, and is arranged in word-by-word order (so that SQL Server 2000 would appear before SqlCommand object) with symbols preceding the letter A. Unmodified headings indicate the principal treatment of a topic; the symbols ~ and * represent repeated beginnings and variant endings respectively, and acronyms have been preferred to their expansions as main entries on the grounds that they are generally easier to recall.

Profiler
auditing database security, 420
detecting unauthorized access, 423
background profiling, 424
capturing a trace, 414
filtering trace properties, 419
Index Tuning Wizard, 427
long running queries, 418
reviewing trace output, 426
SQL Server 2000 changes, 420
trace information, SqlXmlCommand object, 234
view of using SqlCommand.Prepare method, 44
Profiler events, 416
data columns, 417
Provider property, OleDbConnection class, 512
public database role, 406
warning about dangers of, 147
public key, serviced components, 318

Q

queries
concatenating queries into single resultset
ordering problems, 351
UNION ALL SQL operator, 348
generating scripts from, 400
Profiling commonly-executed, 427
Profiling long running queries, 418, 427
should avoid using cursors, 166
Query Analyzer
creating stored procedures, 450
displaying lock information, 303
generating scripts from database objects, 436
options, 438
generating scripts from queries, 400
global temporary table example, 163
loading trace files into tables, 426
restricting access to stored procedures, 147
table variables and temporary tables, 164
Query Builder
creating stored procedures with, 205
SQL statements available with, 206
Query Optimizer
scalar functions and, 189
query plans see **execution plans.**
Queued Components, 314
MSMQ, 314

R

RaisePropertyChanging method, DataColumn class, 517
RaisePropertyChanging method, DataSet class, 528
RAISERROR command, 195
Raw value, Row Formatting option, 377
RDO (Remote Data Objects), 9
READ COMMITTED isolation level, 293
default transaction isolation level, 289
example, 293
performance and, 296
unrepeatable reads and, 295
Read method, DataReader classes, 521

Read method, SqlDataReader class, 46, 126
retrieving data, 129
retrieving multiple resultsets, 135
read only restrictions
SqlDataReader, 45
READ UNCOMMITTED isolation level, 289
dirty reads and, 291
example, 290
READCOMMITTED locking hint, 302
ReadOnly property, BoundColumn class, 261
ReadOnly property, DataColumn class, 74, 77, 517
READPAST locking hint, 302
ReadToEnd method, StreamReader class, 231
READUNCOMMITTED locking hint, 301
ReadXml method, DataSet class, 58, 528
ReadXmlSchema method, DataSet class, 58, 528
ReadXmlSerializeable method, DataSet class, 528
re-attaching database files, 434
RecordsAffected property, DataReader classes, 519
RecordsAffected property, SqlDataReader class, 45, 126
updating data in database, 138
Recordset object, ADO, 10
RedirectFromLoginPage method
FormsAuthentication class, 476
REFERENCES object permission, 409
referential integrity
see also **data integrity.**
DataRelations and, 79
RegSvcs tool
registering serviced component with Component Services, 324
RejectChanges method, DataRow class, 69, 524
RejectChanges method, DataSet class, 14, 58, 59, 116, 528
RejectChanges method, DataTable class, 63, 532
RelatedColumns property, ForeignKeyConstraint class, 84
RelatedTable property, ForeignKeyConstraint class, 84
RelationCollectionChanged method, DataViewManager class, 536
RelationName property, DataRelation class, 80, 522
Relations property, DataSet class, 57, 526
relationships
ADO.NET DataReader and, 12
IBankAdventure case study, 447
Remote Debugging, 120
REPEATABLE READ isolation level, 296
example, 297
phantom reads and, 296
timeouts, 298
UPDLOCK locking hint and, 309
REPEATABLEREAD locking hint, 302
Required value, TransactionOption enumeration, 318
RequiresNew value, TransactionOption enumeration, 318
Reset method, DataSet class, 58, 60, 528
Reset method, DataTable class, 63
ResetCommandTimeout method, Command classes, 511
ResetCommandTimeout method, SqlCommand class, 40
resizing page controls, 477
resource pools, connection pooling, 35
RESTORE DATABASE command, 435

Notes

Notes

Notes

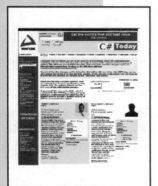

p2p.wrox.com
The programmer's resource centre

A unique free service from Wrox Press
With the aim of helping programmers to help each other

Wrox Press aims to provide timely and practical information to today's programmer. P2P is a list server offering a host of targeted mailing lists where you can share knowledge with four fellow programmers and find solutions to your problems. Whatever the level of your programming knowledge, and whatever technology you use P2P can provide you with the information you need.

ASP
Support for beginners and professionals, including a resource page with hundreds of links, and a popular ASP.NET mailing list.

DATABASES
For database programmers, offering support on SQL Server, mySQL, and Oracle.

MOBILE
Software development for the mobile market is growing rapidly. We provide lists for the several current standards, including WAP, Windows CE, and Symbian.

JAVA
A complete set of Java lists, covering beginners, professionals, and server-side programmers (including JSP, servlets and EJBs)

.NET
Microsoft's new OS platform, covering topics such as ASP.NET, C#, and general .NET discussion.

VISUAL BASIC
Covers all aspects of VB programming, from programming Office macros to creating components for the .NET platform.

WEB DESIGN
As web page requirements become more complex, programmer's are taking a more important role in creating web sites. For these programmers, we offer lists covering technologies such as Flash, Coldfusion, and JavaScript.

XML
Covering all aspects of XML, including XSLT and schemas.

OPEN SOURCE
Many Open Source topics covered including PHP, Apache, Perl, Linux, Python and more.

FOREIGN LANGUAGE
Several lists dedicated to Spanish and German speaking programmers, categories include. NET, Java, XML, PHP and XML

How to subscribe:
Simply visit the P2P site, at http://p2p.wrox.com/